Michael Leroy Oberg is Distinguished Professor of History at SUNY-Geneseo. The author of seven books on Native American history, Oberg received a SUNY Chancellor's Award for Excellence in Teaching in 2003 and a Chancellor's Award for Excellence in Scholarship in 2013.

Native America: A History, Second Edition offers a thoroughly revised and updated narrative history of American Indian peoples in what became the United States. The new edition includes expanded coverage of the period since the Second World War, including an updated discussion of the Red Power Movement, the legal status of native nations in the United States, and important developments that have transformed Indian Country over the past 75 years. Also new to this edition are sections focusing on the Pacific Northwest. Placing the experiences of native communities at the heart of the text, historian Michael Leroy Oberg focuses on twelve native communities whose histories encapsulate the principal themes and developments in Native American history and follows them from earliest times to the present.

Native America

A History

Michael Leroy Oberg
*State University of New York,
College at Geneseo*

Second Edition

WILEY Blackwell

Registered Office
John Wiley & Sons, Inc., 111 River Street, Hoboken, NJ 07030, USA

Editorial Office
350 Main Street, Malden, MA 02148-5020, USA

For details of our global editorial offices, customer services, and more information about Wiley products visit us at www.wiley.com.

Wiley also publishes its books in a variety of electronic formats and by print-on-demand. Some content that appears in standard print versions of this book may not be available in other formats.

Library of Congress Cataloging-in-Publication Data

Names: Oberg, Michael Leroy, author.
Title: Native America : a history / Michael Leroy Oberg.
Description: Second edition. | Hoboken, NJ : Wiley-Blackwell, 2017. | Includes bibliographical references and index.
Identifiers: LCCN 2017005388 (print) | LCCN 2017006550 (ebook) | ISBN 9781118937112 (paperback) | ISBN 9781118937129 (Adobe PDF) | ISBN 9781118937136 (ePub)
Subjects: LCSH: Indians of North America–History. | Indians of North America–Social life and customs. | Indians of North America–Government relations. | BISAC: HISTORY / Native American.
Classification: LCC E77 .O24 2017 (print) | LCC E77 (ebook) | DDC 970.004/97–dc23
LC record available at https://lccn.loc.gov/2017005388

Cover Image: National Anthropological Archives, Smithsonian Institute [BAE GN 03425];
Linen pattern © billnoll/iStockphoto
Cover Design: Wiley

Set in 10/12pt Warnock by SPi Global, Pondicherry, India

10   9   8   7   6   5   4   3   2   1

Contents

List of Figures

List of Maps

INTRODUCTION

In this second edition of *Native America*, I hope to convey to you something of the history of America's native peoples. As in the first edition, I will not cover everything, and I have tried to avoid what it seems to me are the pitfalls of textbook writing: an effort to be encyclopedic, to leave nothing out. I do not want my reader to feel like he or she is awash in a sea of facts and data disconnected from any coherent narrative. Textbooks too often encourage students to view the past as a collection of names and dates and places and forget that history—the study of continuity and change, measured across time and space, in peoples, institutions, and cultures—is so much more than that. History, the philosopher R. G. Collingwood aptly noted long ago, is "nothing capable of being memorized."

I hope to provide students interested in the Native American past with an understanding of how the varied parts of the story fit into a larger whole. My goal is to tell a story of native peoples, to advance an argument. To that end, I focus upon twelve native communities whose histories encapsulate what I see as the principal themes and developments in Native American history.

The Pueblos of the Rio Grande Valley in today's New Mexico and the Chumash peoples of coastal Southern California confronted Spanish soldiers and Franciscan missionaries each for the first time more than two centuries apart. Both rose up against a colonial system that brought devastation to their communities. Both lived under successive Spanish, Mexican, and American regimes. The Pueblos received enormous attention from non-Indians, some of whom sought to civilize and Christianize them and others who indulged their fantasies about the Pueblos' ways of living for a variety of purposes. Throughout, the Pueblos quietly resisted those who intended to transform them. They never fought a war against the United States, for instance, nor have they ever signed a treaty. Yet the Pueblo communities stood firmly at the center of many of the most interesting discussions of American Indian policy. The Chumash, on the other hand, slipped into relative obscurity at the end of the nineteenth century, so much so that some Californians assumed that they had gone extinct, a product of epidemic and chronic diseases introduced by Europeans, the brutality of the mission system, and intermarriage with non-Indians. Their "re-emergence" in the late 1960s and 1970s, in a sense, shows the resilience of native peoples and their ability to turn up in unexpected places, but also how a native community's assertion of Indian identity can spark ugly and acrimonious debates in societies that claim to tolerate diversity.

The Powhatans of Virginia greeted the English colonists at Jamestown in 1607 but had emerged as a regional power in the Chesapeake Bay over the course of the preceding decades. Many Americans know something of the mythical tale of Pocahontas and John Smith, but fewer understand the important role played by native peoples in the early history of this continent.

Native America: A History, Second Edition. Michael Leroy Oberg.
© 2018 John Wiley & Sons, Inc. Published 2018 by John Wiley & Sons, Inc.

By looking at the experience of the Powhatans—a collection of village communities unified under the leadership of Wahunsonacock and his heirs—from their initial attempts to welcome the English and incorporate them as subject peoples within their expanding chiefdom, to their growing disillusionment with the colonists' territorial aggressiveness, to the attacks they launched against the English in 1622 and 1644 and the wars that followed, and their subjugation and reduction to the status of tributary peoples, we gain insight into how Indians viewed those episodes that Europeans called "first contact," "colonization," and "conquest."

The Powhatans survived the English onslaught, though at great cost. They faced new struggles as native peoples living "behind the frontier" in the eighteenth and nineteenth centuries. They faced continuing assaults on their dwindling land base and way of life, but also the efforts of white Virginians to classify them along with African slaves as peoples of color. In the first half of the twentieth century, they confronted a systematic and racist campaign to eradicate all traces of their existence from the state's vital records. The Powhatans have consistently fought against those who attempted to erase them from history.

Native peoples were not simply acted upon by their would-be colonial overlords. Leaders like Uncas of the Mohegans forged alliances with the newcomers and used the threat of English violence to extend his power over neighboring native communities. He provided the English with intelligence and allies, but at the same time worked to preserve enough strength to demonstrate to the English that they needed the Mohegans, who could pose a substantial threat to the colonists should they become disaffected. This approach worked for a time—Uncas played as large a role in shaping New England's early history as did any of the region's Puritan founding fathers—but the Mohegans soon enough found themselves surrounded by English settlements, their lands and their way of life under siege. In many ways they conformed to what colonists hoped they might become: they converted to Christianity, dressed like their neighbors, farmed their lands, and served as soldiers in times of war. They were consistent friends to the English. But they also preserved in the midst of a white population that greatly outnumbered them a distinct native identity. That is a noteworthy accomplishment, one that defies the long enduring image of the "Vanishing American," and that students ought to understand. Today the Mohegans live upon what remains of their ancestral lands. Thanks to their enormously profitable casino, they have reemerged as a major power in eastern Connecticut.

The Senecas, the westernmost of the Five, and later Six, Nations of the Iroquois League, occupied a critical space in the European struggle for empire in North America, but they were never mere pawns in an outsiders' game for control of the continent. Their actions, the meaning of which are debated intensely by historians, anthropologists, and archaeologists, always were directed toward the protection of Seneca interests and the interests of the broader Iroquois League. They confronted waves of epidemic disease and numerous invasions of their homeland by enemies both native and European. Still, they were a power with whom their rivals had to reckon. They suffered the dispersal of their population following the American Revolution. They faced the efforts of state and federal authorities to "remove" them to new homes in the west, to reeducate their children, and deprive them of their lands. Yet they still reside on reservations that, if any number of people had their way, they would have left long ago. Owing to gaming and the retail sale of cigarettes and gasoline, as well as powerful assertions of their enduring sovereignty, the Senecas continue to inspire envy, admiration, and outrage amongst their neighbors in western New York.

The peoples who came to be known as the Caddos confronted three imperial powers: the Spanish, the French, and the United States. Their experience reveals the creativity with which native peoples adjusted to the new worlds created by European colonists. They held these newcomers at bay, taking from them what they wanted but rejecting much else. Increasingly, however, they found themselves less able to resist the Europeans, a process that needs to be understood in detail. No longer necessary as allies and trading partners, and with their lands coveted by growing numbers of settlers, the Caddos were driven out of their homes along the Texas–Louisiana border and relocated. The Caddos' history of movement neither began nor ended with the Indian removals of the Jacksonian period. It was not until 1867 that the United States finally established for them a reservation. Even here, security proved elusive. Much of this land they lost in the late nineteenth and early twentieth centuries.

The Caddos ended up sharing their reservation with, among others, their Kiowa enemies, a people whose historic movements covered a vast expanse of the Great Plains. The Kiowas resisted fiercely the efforts of agents, missionaries, and soldiers to confine them to their reservation. The Kiowas' experience allows us to analyze the devastating price native peoples paid for resisting the United States, but also the integrity and determination of a community that struggled to preserve the core elements of its culture in the wake of military defeat. Like many native peoples, the Kiowas transformed their reservation from a prison into a homeland.

Not all of the Plains tribes resisted the United States. The Crows, who live today on their reservation in eastern Montana, viewed their expansive and aggressive Lakota Sioux enemies as a more immediate threat than the United States, and they acted accordingly to secure an American alliance. Befriending the United States, however, provided the Crows with few benefits. Crow leaders helped their people make the difficult adjustment to reservation life, rallied opposition against the efforts of those who in the late nineteenth and early twentieth centuries hoped to break apart and appropriate their lands, and rejected the efforts of the United States to reshape their tribal government during the era of the Indian New Deal in the 1930s. Settlement on reservations could be a harrowing and demoralizing experience for native peoples, but the Crows' experience shows how they survived, how they acted to defend their way of life, and how they continue to innovate to promote and protect the interests of their community.

The Dakota, or Santee, Sioux, relatives of the Crows' Lakota enemies, attempted to incorporate the first European traders they encountered into a network of kin-based relationships. Over time, the Dakota bands learned that Europeans would not reciprocate and that they would not respect Dakota ways if they did not have to. In 1851, the Dakotas accepted a reservation in Minnesota that brought with it the worst abuses of that system. Federal forces brutally crushed their short-lived but violent uprising in 1862, an episode that demonstrated clearly the fundamental flaws in federal Indian policy in the era of the American Civil War. The Dakotas did not disappear. Today, they occupy reservations in three states and operate some of the most profitable tribal gaming enterprises in the country. Those profits, in places, have benefited individual tribal members but they have also underwritten efforts to diversify Dakota economies, improve health care and education, and preserve Dakota language and culture.

The Salish-speaking peoples of the Puget Sound region in today's Washington State, new to this volume, have histories that in many ways parallel those of the Plains tribes, even if they lived in a lush region that bore little resemblance to the harsh Great West. They confronted a host of explorers and traders before Americans began arriving to settle on their lands in the middle decades of the nineteenth century. They were compelled by American officials to sign treaties consigning them to life on reservations. And yet they did not disappear. They continued to shape the history and culture of the "Salish Sea." They stand at the center of some of the most vigorous debates over the rights of native peoples and native polities under the United States Constitution.

The Cherokees are best known for the Trail of Tears they followed to new homes in the west in 1838, a result of Andrew Jackson's policy of Indian Removal. Four thousand Cherokees died during this forced relocation. Americans are less aware of the fact that Cherokee history did not end with their removal, and the Cherokee experience offers an example of how eastern native pioneers created new homes for themselves in the American west. The Cherokees reestablished their constitutional government in the Indian Territory, only to split apart along sectional lines during the Civil War. The Cherokees survived this crisis and others as well, and continue to demand from the United States respect for their sovereignty.

Federal forces drove the Potawatomis west in 1838 as well. The Potawatomis called this ordeal the "Trail of Death." Many Potawatomis died along the way. But Potawatomi communities began moving long before Americans called for the ouster of all Indians living east of the Mississippi River, and many of them in later years returned to their homelands in the western Great Lakes. They moved for a variety of reasons: to settle near the Catholic missions established by French Jesuit priests; to improve their position in intercultural trade; to avoid the raids of native enemies; and to reconstitute communities broken apart by land loss, disease, or military defeat. The Potawatomis' history, like that of many native peoples, has been one of continual motion in an effort to preserve core values. Deciding the precise content of those core values often was a contentious process for the Potawatomis.

We will concentrate on these communities, while not neglecting the tangled and complex relationships they maintained with the colonial powers and, later, the United States. A word on terminology is in order. I use phrases like *native peoples*, *Indians*, and *Native Americans* interchangeably. Each of these terms, of course, contains flaws, but in the absence of convenient and easily comprehended alternatives, I have decided to stick with them. Careful students will remember that it was often the prerogative of the colonizer to name the colonized, of the discoverer to name those they discovered. That is how American history always has worked, and we continue to confront the problems this has caused. Alert students will question the terms employed by non-Indians to describe native peoples, and keep in mind that these labels seldom bear much relationship to what the group in question calls itself.

These native peoples lived lives of enormous diversity, and their varied experiences make clear the difficulties of generalizing about Native Americans and their history. These groups cannot be viewed as monoliths. There are Cherokees in Oklahoma, removed there during the Jacksonian period, but there are also Cherokees in North Carolina who managed with difficulty to remain on their lands. The Cherokee Freedmen, the descendants of slaves once owned by the Cherokees, contest vigorously their continuing marginalization within the Cherokee Nation. The Tonawanda Band of Senecas disagrees with the Seneca Nation of Indians on a number of issues including gaming and religion. Both assert powerfully a sovereignty they believe the United States acknowledged in the 1794 Treaty of Canandaigua. There is no one Potawatomi tribe, and it appears that there never was; indeed, there are today nine different Potawatomi communities located in Kansas, Michigan, Wisconsin, Oklahoma, and Ontario, Canada. Many of the constituent communities that made up Powhatan's chiefdom in Virginia still exist, but they no longer are unified under a single powerful leader. The Chumash of Santa Ynez, the only federally recognized Chumash community, represent only a small portion of the thousands of Californians who trace their descent to the region's native peoples. Chumash and non-Chumash alike debate, intensely at times, who ought to be considered legitimate and "real" Chumash. We will focus upon these native peoples, and others, and place them, and their varied experiences, at the center of this narrative. We will look at the local level. It was here that the conflicts and controversies emerged that shaped federal policies, came before the federal court system, and, on occasion, exploded into vicious warfare. It was at the local level where Indians confronted what one historian called the "three horsemen of the Indians' apocalypse": disease, warfare, and the encroachment of white settlers on native land, a resource that Indians and non-Indians used, and at times continue to use, in incompatible ways.

This second edition of *Native America* has been entirely updated, and coverage of the twentieth century expanded considerably. To help instructors and students make use of this text and to get the most out of their studies, I have created a supplemental website at www.michaelleroyoberg.com that includes documents, bibliographic essays, images, maps, suggestions for writing assignments, and a blog.

The point I would like students to understand as they make use of these materials is that native peoples do not exist merely as an adjunct to American history. They have stories of their own. They were not merely acted upon by Europeans. They are more than the subjects of federal Indian policies. Native history at times flowed through channels distinct from that of the United States. We will discuss these histories, and allow the experiences of these communities to rest at the center of our story. We will learn, I hope, how native peoples debated and discussed amongst themselves the courses they should follow as they confronted the newcomers who sought to remake their world, how they found native means to live within what became the United States, and to respond to or resist or ignore or shape the policies meant to control their lives.

1

Myths and Legends

The Beginning of the World

So many accounts of this continent's past begin with Europeans striding ashore, claiming this "new found land" and its human inhabitants for their respective empires. These ambitious assertions always have been challenged by native peoples, but nonetheless, over time, jurists and scholars inscribed them in American law and in the written histories from which the law springs. And with heads bowed, or with a bounteous welcome, native peoples in too many of these accounts greet their colonizers as saviors, whatever their initial misgivings. When the Algonquian-speaking peoples of Ossomocomuck first saw the English colonists sent to occupy "Virginia" in 1585, for instance, the English scientist Thomas Harriot reported that they "began to make a great and horrible crye as people which never before had seene men appareled like us." Confused and savage, "they made out cries like wild beasts or men out of their wits." Soon they calmed themselves, in Harriot's eyes, and stopped acting like beasts, and regained their wits, but only after the newcomers presented them with gifts that demonstrated and confirmed their benevolent intent. These native peoples soon would consider the great power these newcomers seemed to possess, and wonder whether they were "gods or men."

Today many Americans still believe that it is with the arrival of Europeans that their nation's history begins. We could find, if we looked, dozens of accounts of "discovery" that differed from Harriot's only in their details. These moments of encounter, depicted so often over the years in the work of American artists, historians, and myth-makers, represent the opening of a grand story—the discovery of America, the growth and development of the United States, the conquest of the American frontier. All that happened before these seminal moments, these dynamic processes, has been ignored or trivialized by earlier generations of historians, who celebrated the progress of a new nation, conceived in liberty. Yet even in Harriot's account we can see that native peoples were not merely waiting for Europeans to arrive, and American history to begin. Their beliefs, values, fears, hopes, and experiences all informed how they reacted to the arrival of these unfamiliar newcomers with whom they would create a new world. The people of Ossomocomuck incorporated these English colonists into a world where native rules prevailed.

Too often the words and phrases we use when we attempt to tell this story privilege Europeans, and their perspectives, over those of native peoples. Words like "Indian," for example, or phrases like "Native American," of course are flawed. They would have meant little to peoples whose names for themselves often translated as "people" or "the real

Native America: A History, Second Edition. Michael Leroy Oberg.
© 2018 John Wiley & Sons, Inc. Published 2018 by John Wiley & Sons, Inc.

people" or the "real human beings." But the problem with words goes even deeper than this. Too many historians, for too long, have relied upon flawed dichotomies: there was a "pre-contact" or "prehistoric" period that came before "contact" and before the arrival of Europeans ushered in the "historic" era. Native peoples obviously had long histories on this continent before Europeans arrived. They interacted and exchanged with and fought against native neighbors near and far, and these contacts bred a host of cultural practices that pertained to their "contact" with others. They did not simply drop these practices when Europeans arrived.

Words can be tricky things. Colonists *settle* but Indians do not: they are *nomads* who *wander* and *roam*. Europeans plant crops, but Indians do not, according to conventional wisdom; colonists serve as *soldiers* while native peoples fight as *warriors*. Language can emphasize difference, and an emphasis on difference can be misleading. In reality, the differences between natives and newcomers at the outset might not have been as great as our flawed language leads us to believe. Both natives and newcomers, in general, lived in towns. Both grew crops and relied upon agriculture to stay alive. Both supplemented their agricultural produce with sources of protein they acquired systematically. Native peoples in the east, for instance, managed forests, burned underbrush, and generated new growth that attracted game that could be more easily "harvested" by hunters. Newcomers, meanwhile, turned their livestock loose and allowed it to forage and fend for itself. When the "settlers" got hungry, they went out into the woods to hunt down their nearly feral cattle and hogs.

The very notion that the European "discovery of America" began the "colonial period" in American history is deeply flawed. Discovery did not reveal a new world to Europeans so much as it brought into contact two worlds, both very old. Europeans arrived on the edge of lands long inhabited by native peoples. Through the first half of the nineteenth century, native peoples controlled the vast majority of what became the United States. Their cultural traditions, and patterns of thought, and ways of comprehending the cosmos, shaped the lives of the people who called this "new world" home. While colonists clung, at times precariously, to the coast, casting their eyes eastward toward the Atlantic much more than westward, native peoples controlled the continent's interior. To understand *this* American history, a history of the peoples who were here first, we must commence our story long before the Europeans, sea-weary and frightened themselves, stumbled ashore in a world that was new only to them.

So we shall begin at the beginning, at the start of all things. The Powhatan Indians, the Algonquian-speaking peoples of Tsennacommacah, what English-speaking people later would label the Virginia coastal plain, told an English chronicler in 1610 that a "Great Hare" had decided long before Europeans arrived "how to people this world, and with what kind of Creatures." So began the Powhatans' tale of how the world came to be. The Great Hare made "divers men and women and made provision for them to be kept up yet in a great bag." The Great Hare struggled to protect the Human Beings from enormous "Caniball Spirits" who wanted to eat them. Their safety at last assured, he made the water and the fish and the land "and a great deer which should feed upon the land." But the Great Hare had enemies still. The Four Winds grew envious of his creation and killed the deer. The Great Hare, not so easily discouraged, "took all the hairs of the slain deer and spread them upon the earth with many powerful words and charms whereby every hair became a deer." The Great Hare then opened his bag of tricks and freed his people, placing "them upon the earth, a man and a woman in one country and a man and a woman in another country, and so the world took first beginning of mankind." So the Powhatans' tale of creation, their genesis, begins not with a man created in God's image but with a rabbit, a figure capable of great deeds who could harness extraordinary powers.

Figure 1.1 Emanuel Leutze's painting, *The Founding of Maryland* (1861), offers a romantic depiction of Indians welcoming the first European settlers in 1634. Courtesy of the Maryland Historical Society.

The people who came to be known as the Cherokees, who lived in a vast territory in the interior of the American southeast, told a different story. They called themselves Yunwiya, the real people, and they lived in a crowded cosmos. At first, they believed, the earth was all water. The animals lived above in a sky world, but they felt crowded. They wondered if more space might be found below. The Water Beetle went to look. He dived to the bottom of this world of water and came up with a clump of soft mud, which began to grow and grow until it became a floating island, affixed to the sky with four strong cords. Other animals followed, giving shape and texture to the earth, setting the motion of the sun across the sky. The people followed, but they shared this new world with giants, water serpents, little people, ghosts, and spirits. Animal bosses, meanwhile, took care of their own kind, and watched closely relations between the human and the other-than-human beings.

The earliest of these ancestors of the Cherokees were Kanati, a hunter, and his wife Selu. She cut up and washed in a river near their house the meat that Kanati brought home from a hunt. One day their son, who played beside this river, found another child, a stranger, who had emerged, magically, from the water. Selu and Kanati knew that the strange boy had come from the blood of the game. They decided to raise the mysterious child as their own.

The two boys grew and played together. One day, they decided to learn how their father hunted. The strange boy changed himself into a tuft of bird's down. Surely this was no ordinary child. Carried by the wind, he followed Kanati unnoticed. He watched Kanati perform a number of rituals, and then followed his father as he climbed a distant mountain. At a certain spot, and aided by the powerful rituals that he had conducted so carefully,

Kanati lifted up a large rock that covered the opening to a cave, out from which sprang a large buck. Kanati killed the deer with a single arrow and carried it home to Selu.

The strange boy told his brother what he had witnessed, and together they returned to Kanati's rock and let loose all the deer, and then the raccoons, rabbits, turkeys, partridges, and pigeons. They ignored their father's rituals and paid the animals no respect, teasing them when they entered the world. Kanati was furious. He climbed the mountain, lifted the rock, and brought out four jars that he found deep in the cave. These he opened and out came bedbugs, flies, gnats, and lice. The bugs attacked the boys. For ignoring the rituals, they would be punished.

But not chastened. They returned home, hungry and tired. Selu had no meat for them, for there could be nothing to eat when the proper rituals were ignored. Selu told the boys that she would go to the provision house to get them something. Ever curious, they followed her and watched secretly how she produced their food. They watched as Selu, the Corn Mother, leaned over her empty basket, rubbed her stomach, and filled it halfway with corn. They watched her rub her armpits, and fill the basket with beans. Convinced that their mother was a witch, the boys decided that they must kill her.

Selu, a woman of great power, a creator of life, knew her boys' intentions. She loved them still, and she instructed them on what they needed to do to feed themselves and, someday, their people. "When you have killed me," she told the boys, "clear a large piece of ground in front of the house, and drag my body seven times around the circle, and stay up all night and watch, and in the morning you will have plenty of corn." The boys murdered their mother, but they followed her instructions only in part. They cleared only a few small plots of land, and dragged Selu's body only twice around the circle. Where her blood fell, corn began to grow, and by morning it was ripe and ready. But because the boys had not done all that she had asked them to do, Cherokees learned from Selu's tale, "corn only grew in certain places."

Like the Cherokees, the people of Iroquoia, which included today's upstate New York but also a much larger region through which Haudenosaunee people regularly traveled, found their origins in a Sky World. A man and a woman lived there, on opposite sides of a hearth. Every day, the woman crossed to the other side of the fire and combed the man's hair. Soon she became pregnant and gave birth to a daughter. The Haudenosaunee called her Sky Woman. When she reached adulthood, her father's spirit told her to visit the distant village of the man who would become her husband. Like her mother before her, Sky Woman and her husband slept on opposite sides of the fire. When Sky Woman mysteriously became pregnant, her husband, filled with jealousy, uprooted a large tree and pushed her through the hole in the sky.

Sky Woman fell. The animals of the air and water below saw her falling. Ducks flew to catch her on their wings. They carried her down and placed her on Turtle's back. Muskrat succeeded in bringing mud from beneath the water which, when placed on Turtle's back, became the earth. On that world that grew on Turtle's back, Sky Woman gave birth to a daughter. There the little girl grew, and in time she became pregnant with twins by the spirit of Turtle.

The Good Twin, born first, was known by different names—Sky Grasper, or Tharonhiawagon. He was followed into this world by his evil brother, Tawiskaron, who chose to kill his mother by emerging into this world through her side. Tawiskaron convinced Sky Woman that it was Tharonhiawagon, and not he, who had slain their mother.

So Sky Woman banished the Good Twin, and cherished instead the killer of her daughter. Tharonhiawagon, a selfless exile, worked to improve Iroquoia. This he did during his years in the wilderness with the assistance of his father, the Turtle. At every step, Tawiskaron and his spiteful mother undermined his work. At last, the two twins fought and with the assistance of ritual, the Good Twin triumphed. But he could not repair all the damage his brother and Sky Woman had done. He could not make the rivers flow both ways at once, as he had intended. He could not lower the mountains raised up by his brother. With so many hardships and dangers facing his people, Tharonhiawagon taught them how to survive in this world, and showed them how to grow corn and the ceremonies and rituals necessary to keep the world in balance.

The formation of the earth on Turtle's back was the first of two founding stories recited by the Iroquois. The second involved the formation of the Iroquois League, the union of the Haudenosaunee Five Nations—Mohawks, Oneidas, Onondagas, Cayugas, and Senecas, in the metaphorical Longhouse that stretched from east to west across present-day New York State. The story of the league's formation focused upon a man named Hiawatha, left deranged by the grief caused when he lost his daughters in the endemic violence that lacerated Iroquoia. "Feuds with other nations, feuds with brother nations, feuds with sister towns and feuds of families and of clans," one telling of the "Deganawidah Epic" went, "made every warrior a stealthy man who liked to kill." Mourning and grieving, Hiawatha wandered into the woods where he encountered Deganawidah, the Peacemaker, a transcendent bearer of the Good News of Peace and Power. The Peacemaker gave to Hiawatha strings of wampum, shell beads of great ritual significance, as he spoke the words of Condolence. The first dried Hiawatha's weeping eyes. The second opened his ears to reason. The last opened his throat so that he could speak.

As with the story of the creation of this world on Turtle's back, the Deganawidah epic taught villagers the importance of maintaining balance, of alliance and exchange among the peoples of the Iroquois Longhouse. The rituals of condolence became an Iroquois gospel, a message carried by Hiawatha and the Peacemaker to all the peoples of Iroquoia and beyond. The pair traveled through the war-haunted lands of the Haudenosaunee. They faced many challenges, but none greater than that posed by the Onondaga sorcerer Thadodaho, whose misshapen body and hair made of a tangle of writhing snakes symbolized the disorder of his mind. If Hiawatha had been deranged by violence as a victim, and his grief had rendered him senseless, Thadodaho represented the opposite extreme. His own violence and wickedness had damaged him. He was a killer and a sadist. Thadodaho resisted joining the League, but over time, Hiawatha restored him to reason and to a good mind. Hiawatha combed the snakes from his hair, and straightened out his crooked and deformed body. Thadodaho became the Firekeeper of the metaphorical Iroquois Longhouse, and his home at Onondaga, near present-day Syracuse, New York, became the ceremonial center of the Haudenosaunee. It remains so today.

It is not possible to tell when the Five Nations came together. Archaeologists have offered dates ranging from 1400 to sometime around 1600 CE. The process probably occurred gradually, over generations, as the Five Nations consolidated, developing the rituals of condolence that brought peace to the Longhouse. The Senecas, the westernmost of the Five Nations and the last to join, archaeologists suspect may not have become the "Keepers of the Western Door" until sometime very early in the seventeenth century.

In the Longhouse the fifty sachems, or chiefs, of the League gathered together to discuss matters that affected the League as a whole. The league sachems, appointed by the Haudenosaunee women who played so instrumental a role in community decision-making, became men of peace. At Onondaga, a Tree of Peace grew, with its roots extending in four directions. Those who wished could follow the roots to Onondaga and join in the Great Peace. With their weapons buried beneath the Tree of Peace, Hiawatha and the Peacemaker taught, "hostilities shall not be seen or heard among you," and peace "shall be preserved" among the Five Nations.

The Grand Council of the Haudenosaunee preserved the Great Peace that ended the constant warfare and grief that had damaged both Hiawatha and Thadodaho, through the rituals of condolence and through the exchange of gifts in the form of wampum. Its function was to preserve peace, power, and righteousness, to maintain balance and order, and to preserve a good mind.

Earth divers and worlds beyond the sky—so the people who came to be known as the Iroquois and the Cherokees came to this world. Other native peoples believed that they had emerged out into the world from beneath the ground, stories of creation that rooted them firmly, and quite literally, in their homelands. The peoples of the Red, Sabine, Neches, and Angelina river valleys of today's east Texas, who by the nineteenth century were known collectively as the Caddos, lived at first in a world of darkness, beneath the surface of the earth. So said their stories of creation. Here the people found themselves short of food, so they held a council. The leaders decided that some of the people should transform themselves into animals. They would live apart from the human beings, and allow the humans to hunt them for food. The animals each had ten lives and, according to a Caddo storyteller, "when killed the first time, the second life was to arise from the blood that was spilled on the ground, and so the third life was to arise from the blood that was spilled ... and so on through their lives up to the tenth."

Yet still the Caddos lived in darkness. Led by Moon, the people and their animal relations moved westward through their never land until they emerged into the light, through the mouth of a cave near a lake somewhere on the south bank of the Red River. An old man first emerged into this landscape of myth and history. He carried in one hand fire and a pipe and in the other a drum. His wife followed, carrying corn and pumpkin seeds, symbols of the highly productive agriculture upon which the Caddos soon would rely. Others followed them, human and other-than-human beings, men and women and animals. All of them intended to come out from below but Coyote sealed the hole, enclosing the remaining people and animals under the earth. The people who had emerged out into the light grieved here, the "place of crying" in their language, for those they left behind. Their grief after a time assuaged, they spread out and split up and moved in different directions. They built mounds and ceremonial centers, cultivated their expertise as traders, artisans, and, eventually, farmers, and became members of the most socially complex communities between the Mississippi River and the Rio Grande. Caddoan peoples dominated the world into which they emerged for centuries before Europeans arrived and for more than a century and a half thereafter.

The Kiowas, who at the time they encountered Europeans lived on the Southern Plains, like the Caddos emerged from beneath the earth, and their story involves as well movement and migration before they settled upon a homeland. Saynday, an important figure in Kiowa legend, "was coming along in darkness" upon the face of a sunless earth. Saynday always was "coming along" in Kiowa stories: that is how many Kiowa stories begin. He wandered alone in a world without people and animals. Tired and lonely, he stopped to rest beside what he recognized as the rough bark of a cottonwood tree. There Saynday heard sounds—voices—coming from beneath the hollow trunk of the tree. "We are people," they told Saynday, and "we want to come out into your world." Saynday reached in and pulled the first person through a hole in the trunk, "and he watched in amazement as the people poured out as ants." As in the Caddos' story, not all who wanted to emerge into this world were able to do so. A pregnant woman, too large to pass through the opening, blocked the entrance and prevented many from entering this world. For this reason the Kiowas, whose name meant "coming out," were a small community, Saynday's people. He was their friend, he told them. He brought them the Sun and, he said, "I will teach you how to live in this world, how to find food to eat, and how to be happy."

Figure 1.2 Saynday, from Silver Horn Record Book, drawn by a Kiowa artist imprisoned at Fort Marion, in Florida, in the 1870s. Courtesy of National Anthropological Archives.

Rules for Living

These are only a few of the many stories we could tell: of emergence, of sky worlds and worlds beneath, of Great Hares and Coyotes, and of animal helpers and tricksters and other mythic beings. They are stories of creation, of origins, and of how the world came to be. They tell of movement and migration, of how the peoples of this continent came to occupy their homelands. They are histories. They have been preserved, modified, related, and recalled for generations as the peoples of the Americas sought to make sense of their past and to understand their place in the world—no different, in this important sense, than the religious traditions and creation stories of any other culture.

There are, of course, challenges in using these stories as historical evidence. Operating on the notion that to accept these stories as true is to dismiss Christian traditions as false, for many decades non-Indian scholars have condescendingly described them as "myths" and "legends." They cannot be true, these students of the native past sniffed. Rich in metaphor and straddling the line between myth and memory, these stories do not provide scholars—whether archaeologists, anthropologists, or historians—with much in the way of specifics. Tracing how the stories have changed over time is often difficult, and some clearly contain anachronisms that indicate significant revision. They cannot tell us, moreover, when native peoples emerged on this land, how many native peoples lived here, and how the enormous variety of native cultures in the Americas developed. But these are questions that critical readers will recognize exist with all religious texts.

Since the first Europeans arrived on this continent they wondered about the origins of the "Indians" they encountered. Early Anglo-Americans observed the earthworks left by native cultures, and they speculated about the people who made them. Most believed that the ancestors of the American Indians had migrated into America from Asia, but how, when, and from which parent group they originated remained a matter of debate. Some thought the Indians had descended, for instance, from one of the lost tribes of Israel. There seemed to be significant cultural similarities, these observers believed, between the cultural practices of the indigenous people of this continent and the Jews of the Old Testament. This hypothesis had a short life, and the Bible offered little additional guidance for those who wanted to understand Indian origins. Thomas Jefferson, for his part, excavated ancient burial mounds near his home in Virginia, and collected word lists from a variety of languages. Eighteenth-century Americans, like Jefferson, believed that through the study of comparative vocabularies a judicious scholar might discover the origins of the American Indians. Jefferson's studies led him to conclude that America's native peoples were the parent stock of the peoples of Asia, but few people, then as now, took him seriously.

Indeed, the evidence suggests that people first crossed into North America at Beringia, not a "land bridge" but a vast expanse of tundra and grassland in places 1000 miles wide occupied by large game animals and hunters. The movement may have taken many centuries and occurred in waves. But the earliest human arrivals in this continent need not all have arrived by crossing Beringia. They might have paddled along the coasts, from Asia to America, exploiting coastal resources for their subsistence as they moved along the Pacific Rim. Archaeological sites found on the coast of Peru, and dated to approximately 13,000 years ago, suggest that such a movement was possible. Coming to America took place over the span of centuries, but most scholars agree that all parts of the continent were peopled by the ancestors of today's "Indians" 10,000 years ago.

They did not live in isolation. By the twelfth century CE, evidence shows that the earliest native peoples practiced agriculture, growing corn, beans, squash, and sunflowers, along with other crops, and that they engaged in long-distance trade. An archaeological site in northern Colorado dated to approximately 8800 BCE, shows that the occupants traded with communities as far as 350 miles away. The commitment to agriculture produced a surplus that allowed for an increase in population, and the development of complex societies like those at Chaco Canyon near the Four Corners area in the American southwest and the Mississippian chiefdoms of the southeast. These communities developed dramatically hierarchical societies, complex networks of intercultural exchange, and an elaborate ceremonial life.

Cahokia burst onto the scene about 1000 years ago, a major American city that arose in part in response to changes in subsistence and the political organization of Mississippi valley native peoples. Cahokia had an elaborate ritual life and a complex economy supported by the labor of many thousands of ordinary people. At the height of its power, Cahokia dominated the middle of the Mississippi valley. Its population ranged from 10,000 to 40,000, depending on how one counts the many people drawn into the city's orbit through subordinate economic alliances, or who labored as slaves to support the construction of ceremonial mounds, and, on occasion, whose lives were offered up in rituals involving human sacrifice.

Cahokia depended upon the people it could control, and an environment it could not. A growing population, coupled with an extended period of drought, depleted stands of timber upon which residents relied for building and for fuel. Deforestation eliminated habitat for the game animals that supplied Cahokia's people with the necessary supplies of protein. By the end of the 1300s, the population had drifted away and settled in a number of smaller communities.

While Cahokia rose in the east, Chaco Canyon, according to one historian, "bloomed in its heyday with a cultural vitality never seen in the region before or since." Comprising sixteen "Great Houses" containing thousands of rooms, along with hundreds of ceremonial kivas great and small and a variety of other buildings, Chaco Canyon stood at the hub of a network of perhaps seventy communities spread over more than 25,000 square miles of today's American southwest. Chaco's power declined dramatically in the late twelfth century, a product in part of extended drought. But environmental change was only part of the explanation. Chaco's priesthood failed to procure the rain needed to sustain maize agriculture and their own claims to spiritual authority. The community's leaders lost support, and the people moved away. Some moved to locations more productive for agriculture where they could re-establish ties with allied peoples. The Pueblos, descendants of the Mogollan, Hohokam, and Anasazi peoples of Chaco, may have followed this route to the Rio Grande valley. Some may have forged their own autonomous communities, and others may have returned to an existence based upon hunting and gathering.

Many of them experienced warfare and violence. The post-Chaco southwest was a violent world. Slightly more than 100 of the 177 villages in the region that archaeologists have excavated show signs of conflagration, and half of these have unburied bodies indicative of a massacre. Cities rise and cities fall. Some cultures succeed in confronting the challenges they face, while others do not. Though they did not leave the written records upon which history relies, they had histories, sometimes difficult to see, that mattered to them deeply.

How many people inhabited this complicated, interconnected continent before Europeans arrived has proven a source of intense debate among historians, archaeologists, and anthropologists. James Mooney, an important early twentieth-century anthropologist, estimated that the native population of the region north of the Rio Grande totaled only 1,152,000. Much later, anthropologist Henry Dobyns estimated a population as high as 18 million for the peoples north of Mesoamerica. Mooney and Dobyns both represent extremes, and the methods they used to arrive at their figures have been vigorously challenged. Most scholars with an interest in the question today accept a figure in the lower half of that range, between 4 and 7 million people in North America prior to the arrival of Europeans.

By combining myth and history, memory and the work of legions of scholars native and non-native alike from a variety of disciplines, we can learn much about how the peoples of America lived prior to the arrival of Europeans, and how they came to occupy their homelands. Take the Crows, for example, who today live on a reservation located in southeastern Montana.

According to tribal historian Joseph Medicine Crow, the ancestors of the Crows and their Hidatsa relatives originated in the western Great Lakes, a "tree country" where they mixed hunting with horticulture. Long ago, a drought struck the region, the game disappeared, and "the green earth was parched to brown." They sent out parties to search for food, but only the hunters who had gone west returned with bison. The people moved westward and "caught up with the buffalo herds ... maybe even settling down as part-time hunters in what is now perhaps northern Minnesota and southern Manitoba."

They stayed here for a time, the Crows believed, but around 1550 they began to move to the south and west, either in flight from enemies or in search of better lands. At Devil's Lake in today's North Dakota, a Crow leader named No Vitals received a vision: a pod of seeds and instructions to travel to the west to the mountains and plant them there. No Vitals learned that his people "would someday increase in numbers, become powerful and rich, and own a large, good, and beautiful land."

No Vitals did not immediately act on this vision. His people moved to the Missouri River where they lived for a time among the Mandans, working the soil and hunting. It was not until the beginning of the seventeenth century, according to Crow tradition, that No Vitals decided to journey westward and plant his sacred seeds in the mountains. Using a dispute amongst the women over the distribution of meat as a pretext, No Vitals led some 400 of his followers away, beginning what Medicine Crow called "one of the longest and most dramatic migrations of any Indian tribe, covering thousands of miles over rough and rugged terrain, through intense winters and torrid summers, and consisting of over one hundred years of wandering." No Vitals and his people settled for a time in Alberta, but found the winters too harsh. They then moved south, slowly continuing their exodus, arriving finally at the Great Salt Lake before heading eastward again away from its undrinkable waters, crossing Wyoming and heading toward the southeast and Arkansas. Finally, they turned back to the northwest and settled in Crow Country, a stretch of land that includes today's Billings, Montana and Sheridan, Wyoming. This land, the Crow leader Arapooish said, "the Great Spirit has put in exactly the right place," for "while you are in it you fare well, but whenever you go out of it, whichever way you travel, you will fare worse."

The Kiowas, like the Crows, preserve in their oral tradition stories of a lengthy migration to their home near Rainy Mountain on the Southern Plains. Their story begins in the mountains of western Montana, a region of brutal winters and deep snows. They moved eastward, following very closely the path of today's Interstate 90. They became friends with the Crows, by now located in their homeland along the Yellowstone, and then moved into the Black Hills. They remained close to the Crows, and learned from them some of their important rituals, in particular their *tai-me*, or sun dance medicine. They remained in the Black Hills until they fell under attack by Sioux and Cheyenne raiders. They moved to the south fork of the Platte River and from there farther south to the vicinity of the Wichita Mountains and the headwaters of the Red River.

Figure 1.3 *Tai-me*, Medicine God of the Kiowas. Courtesy of National Anthropological Archives.

During this migration, which began perhaps at the dawn of the eighteenth century and lasted for 100 years, the Kiowas, according to the novelist and storyteller N. Scott Momaday, came "of age as a people." They allied themselves with the Comanches and became a major power on the southern plains, trading and raiding across what are now the states of Oklahoma, Texas, New Mexico, Colorado, and Kansas, and south into Mexico. They had found their home near Rainy Mountain.

The stories native peoples told of their origins allow us a window into how they understood their place within the cosmos and in the ordering of all creation. Europeans, many of whom themselves believed in stories of virgin birth and a talking serpent in a garden called Eden, who themselves professed to believe that the first Woman was crafted from the rib of Man, and that the Son of God came to this earth, suffered for the sins of the world, died, and was buried, and rose again on the third day, were quick to dismiss native stories as myth, legends, and utterly unbelievable superstitions. Many of their modern-day descendants continue to speak of Indian stories with similar condescension. But we should be careful here, for these stories were as meaningful and satisfying to native peoples as the Bible was to Christians. Those who would understand the Native American past must consider the archaeological, historical, and anthropological evidence, and they must be disciplined and critical as they do so. But we must, as well, accord native traditions and beliefs the same respect as any other body of myth or system of belief, Christian or otherwise. And the values and beliefs expressed in these stories—these myths and legends—are important because they reflect how native peoples understood the functioning of a universe into which Europeans soon would intrude.

We must be careful as well about generalizing. An enormous variety of native peoples lived across the continent, speaking hundreds of languages, and nourishing an immense diversity of traditional knowledge. Furthermore, we must be careful about how we choose to identify native communities. Groups like the Mohegans in today's Connecticut, for instance, emerged as a regional power in southern New England only in the seventeenth century. We do not have unambiguous evidence that they existed as an autonomous and independent group prior to the arrival of Dutch traders and English settlers in the 1620s. The communities that we label as "Pueblo" or "Caddo" or "Kiowa" or "Crow" also were dynamic, and subject to forces of historical change. We cannot and, indeed, should not assume, for instance, that the Cherokees we encounter in nineteenth-century Georgia are identical to the seventeenth-century inhabitants of the high hills in the North Carolina Piedmont. Peoples and cultures change, and careful historians and anthropologists will take that into account. We must remember that there were no "Indians" in America before Europeans arrived and imposed that and other labels upon them.

Still, there are enough beliefs, ideas, values, and views about the world that native peoples across the continent shared that we can, acting with caution and admittedly painting with a broad brush, make some general observations. Without question, native peoples saw the world in terms very different from European Christians, and these differences would become deeply important once Europeans arrived.

Native understandings of the cosmos and the place of human beings within it differed from that of Europeans. In the Christian Bible, God gave to man dominion over the earth and all that was on it. Native peoples lived in a participatory universe, one filled with sentient human and other-than-human beings. Humans interacted with an enormous variety of kin-like individuals. The other beings in this cosmos, indigenous peoples believed, could be hunted, harvested, and killed, but only if treated with the proper respect and the performance of the requisite rituals.

The indigenous peoples of this continent sought to preserve balance in their relations with each other and with the other forces that inhabited their world. To preserve this balance, they practiced ritual. Ritual allowed native peoples to acquire the power they needed to keep the world in balance. Only with ritual did the animals present themselves to Kanati and Selu's corn grow properly. This power went by different names: Algonquian-speaking peoples like the Mohegans called it *Manitou*; Iroquoians like the Seneca would have called it *Orenda*; in the west, Kiowas called it *dwdw*; and the Skokomish *shuy*. Whatever the name, the concept is common across Native America. Those who had power, and who paid attention to ritual, would experience success in warfare and in the hunt, and they would experience bountiful harvests. They would live well.

Human beings sought power. They entered trances, through privation and isolation, to receive visions. They sought meaning in dreams, as had No Vitals, or the guidance of shamans, men or women with enormous power and mastery over ritual. They danced, fasted, smoked, and prayed. They engaged in ritual to appease and to harness the powerful spiritual forces with whom they interacted, and that controlled the growth of crops, the supply of game, and the functioning of the world. With proper respect, they knew that they need not fear a bad harvest or a poor hunt or other misfortune. But should they neglect their rituals, or should their rituals fail them, native peoples believed that disaster could rain upon their communities. There could be no accidents, no random events. Bad things happened for a reason. Through ritual they hoped to keep things right. Through their rituals they mediated their relations with each other and with other beings in their cosmos.

In most communities in Native America, men hunted and fought and their role as hunters and fighters shaped their relationships with other beings in the cosmos. Native men hunted an enormous variety of animals. Men went out by themselves, in small numbers, but also organized large, communal endeavors involving hundreds of hunters. Indians on the edge of the Plains, like the Crows, organized enormous buffalo hunts overseen by spiritual leaders, in which hunters worked together to stampede herds of bison over cliffs. A Kiowa elder, as well, remembered that in the old days, before they had horses, they killed buffalo "by surrounding them and driving them over a cliff." The sight was, to the Kiowas, wonderful. "The buffalo were all piled up at the bottom, some with broken legs, others with broken backs," one remembered. The Kiowas, then, would be "full of meat." The Kiowas and their bison-hunting neighbors put the entire animal to use. Bison, Old Lady Horse recounted in 1882, "were the life of the Kiowas."

Hunting techniques such as the buffalo jump might at first glance appear wasteful, but hunting in Native America rested on a logic that would have seemed strange to Europeans. With proper respect and attention to ritual, nature could be infinitely bountiful. If hunters conducted the proper rituals, and treated the animals they hunted with proper respect, there could be no shortage of game. The line between human and other-than-human beings, they believed, was unfixed. Animals thought and reasoned. They rewarded right behavior and they could take offense if not treated properly.

Kanati, in the Cherokee legend, performed rituals before he ascended the mountain. A Cherokee hunter, in another story, wounded a black bear with an arrow. The hunter followed the wounded bear, and continued to hit it with his arrows, but the animal would not go down. Its strength puzzled the hunter. This was no ordinary bear. At last the animal stopped. He pulled the arrows from his body and gave them to the hunter. "You cannot kill me," the bear told the hunter, so "come to my house and let us live together." The hunter was fearful that the bear might kill him, or that he might go hungry, but the bear knew his thoughts and reassured him.

The bear led the hunter to a large cave, "full of bears—old bears, young bears and cubs, white bears, black bears and brown bears—and a large white bear was chief." After attending this "council," the hunter followed his new friend home. There the lines between human and other-than-human beings began to blur even further, a process repeated in dozens of stories from Native America. The hunter "had begun to grow hair all over his body and act like a bear." In time the black bear told the hunter that the villagers were coming, and that he soon would die. They could not remain together any longer. He gave to the hunter an important instruction: "When they have killed me they will drag me outside the cave and take off my clothes and cut me in pieces. You must," the bear said, "cover the blood with leaves."

The bear could see the future. As he predicted, the villagers soon came. They killed the bear "and then they dragged him outside the cave and skinned his body and cut it in quarters to carry home." They found the hunter, too, who at first they thought was another bear on account of his appearance. He had not fully returned to his human shape. The villagers wanted to take him home, to restore their lost friend to his kin and connections. Before he left with the villagers, however, the hunter followed the instructions that the bear had given him. He "piled leaves over the spot where they had cut up the bear, and when they had gone a little way he looked behind and saw the bear rise up out of the leaves, shake himself, and go back into the woods."

Successful hunters made a request, not a demand. So did fishermen. The Powhatans made offerings of tobacco smoke for their fish traps. Coast Salish people living along the waters flowing into Puget Sound performed rituals for the first salmon caught each year. They still do, aware that if they neglected their rituals the fish "would get insulted and not come anymore." The people relied upon the salmon. The line that separated human beings from salmon could blur from time to time. Stories of salmon who assumed human shape appear in the myths and legends of Coast Salish people. The salmon, thinking and reasoning, would only present itself to the people if accorded the proper respect. Animals could determine the fisherman's success or the outcome of the hunt. That is why Montagnai hunters north of the St. Lawrence River lectured incredulous Jesuit priests in the 1630s about the proper manner for treating the bones of the animals they had trapped. The Indians, according to Father Paul Le Jeune, "do not throw to the dogs the bones of beavers and female porcupines," and "they are very careful that dogs do not eat any bones of birds or other animals that are caught in nets" because, they said, "they will never be able to catch any more except with the greatest difficulty." Le Jeune thought all of this was nonsense, and he told the Montagnais so. Animals do not know, and they did not care, what humans do with their remains. The Montagnais' response reflected a great patience, and shows their genuine interest in educating their strange visitor. "Before the beaver is completely dead," they explained to Le Jeune, "its soul comes to visit the cabin of the man who kills it, and looks very carefully to see what is done with his bones. If they have been given to the dogs, the other beavers would be warned, and so they make themselves difficult to catch." Cautantouwwit, the benevolent creator to the Mohegans' Narragansett neighbors, for instance, sent a crow to carry corn and beans to the people. Southern New England Algonquians, like the Mohegans, refused to harm crows despite the damage the birds might do to their crops.

Stories like this are common across Native America. Animals must be treated well and with respect. As the Salish elder Vi Hilbert wrote, all things "had spirit and if you respected everything … it would serve us, but we had to show respect first." It is for this reason that the Dakota Sioux, according to one eighteenth-century observer, "bury the bones of the beaver and elk very carefully after eating the flesh, thinking that the spirits of these animals have influence on living ones and will inform them how they have been treated."

Animals could cause sickness and misery if mistreated. They might avenge insults. They could withdraw themselves, leaving the real human beings to suffer hunger and want. The animals had feelings, hopes, fears, and affections, and they could both help and harm their human kin. It was for this reason, Old Lady Horse remembered, that "when the white men wanted to build railroads, or when they wanted to farm or raise cattle, the buffalo" tried to protect Saynday's people. "They tore up the railroad tracks and gardens," Old Lady Horse continued, because "the buffalo loved their people as much as the Kiowas loved them." The American invasion of the Plains, she said, was at heart a "war between the buffalo and the white men." At last, Old Lady Horse sadly recalled, the buffalo recognized that they could do nothing more to protect their people. They "saw that their day was done." The buffalo gathered in council, Old Lady Horse said, decided to enter the mountains, and go back into the earth.

Like hunting, warfare involved an intense commitment to ritual. Warfare was common in early America, but native peoples fought it in a manner that led Europeans to trivialize its effects. Indians did not fight "total wars" in the European sense. Those Indian "empires" that Europeans encountered seldom aimed at the complete dispossession of their enemies when they fought, and they seldom sought to eradicate their opponents' culture and identity. They did not occupy territory and did not, in general, deny their enemies the right to exist. Rather, men fought wars for certain specific and culturally significant purposes.

If men killed, albeit in the name of sustaining life, women created. They planted and tended the crops. They bore children. Across Native America, Indian traditions reflected a widespread belief in the power of women to create life. The birth of children took place away from men, perhaps to protect them from the procreative powers of women. Menstruating women separated themselves from the community. According to the Puritan chronicler Edward Winslow, who wrote about southern New England Algonquians like the Mohegans, menstruating women lived "certain days in a house alone, after which, she washeth herself and all that she hath touched or used." Men stayed away from menstruating women and, according to the seventeenth-century Jesuit observer, Chrestien Le Clerq, the women "are accounted unclean." The women lived by themselves during this period, Le Clerq observed, and they are not permitted, "during this time, to eat any beaver, and those who eat of it are reputed bad; for the Indians are convinced, they say, that the beaver, which has sense, would no longer allow itself to be taken by the Indians if it had been eaten by their unclean daughters." And Selu, of course, from whose blood corn grew, symbolized in part the power of women to create life.

Like men, women could not succeed in their roles as growers and nurturers without power, and ritual accompanied the entire farming cycle of native peoples. The Green Corn Ceremony, common throughout the Eastern Woodlands and especially so among southeastern peoples like the Cherokees, a ritual of renewal and rebirth, strengthened the community's ties to the land and obtained for it the cooperation of the spiritual forces upon which a bountiful harvest relied.

Men as life-sustaining killers; women as creators of life: men and women lived in balance, occupying different, but equally essential places in the native cosmos. Women, in many communities, remained superior within the village—the houses and in the surrounding fields. Men held supremacy in the woods and in those matters taking place outside the village, in the realm of warriors and animals. Each complemented the other. So unlike European communities, which sanctioned and institutionalized the subordination of women to men, many native communities were matrilineal, with descent traced through the mother rather than the father. Women, in many native communities, wielded considerable power and influence.

Men and women sought to preserve balance in their relations with the variety of forces existing within their cosmos. Native peoples also sought to maintain balance in their relations with other communities. The native peoples of this continent, living themselves in thousands of communities and speaking hundreds of distinct languages, did not exist in isolation from one another. The archaeological record suggests that exchange was widespread. People exchanged ideas, rituals, and beliefs. Through exchange, communities learned from others technologies for hunting and horticulture. People—as prisoners, adoptees, spouses, and slaves—moved through these exchange networks, from one community to another, often crossing significant linguistic, cultural, and political boundaries as they did so.

As early as 900 CE, for example, the Caddoan peoples of the American interior had established far-reaching trade networks. They buried the elite members of these communities in mounds, the remains of which can still be seen in the heart of the continent. In these burials, archaeologists have found mica originally from the Atlantic seaboard, cotton and turquoise acquired from trading partners in today's "Four Corners" area, conch shells from the Gulf Coast, and copper from the Great Lakes. Trade tied the native communities that first inhabited this continent together in networks of exchange and alliance. Trade fairs, like those held annually in the sixteenth century along the Rio Grande and in the Upper Missouri River Valley, brought together an enormous variety of indigenous peoples.

Ritual governed the resulting relationships. The people who became known as the Caddos had developed an elaborate protocol for transforming strangers into friends. In every case for which evidence remains, a delegation of Caddos met the strangers some distance from the village. Led by the elite members of the community, the Caddos guided the newcomers into their village. The newcomers were bathed, and seats for the guests were prepared. Each side made speeches, stated their expectations, and then the calumet, a pipe, would be passed. The Caddos then began serving to their guests the feast they had prepared. They then exchanged gifts, an act that transformed strangers into kin and allies.

Similar rituals accompanied exchange throughout the continent. The Englishman John Smith was adopted by the Powhatan leader Wahunsonacock and appointed *weroance* of the Powhatans' band of English tributaries, even if Smith failed to pick up on the nuances of the relationship. Scores of European observers remarked upon the rituals of greeting and condolence employed by Iroquoian peoples like the Senecas, as the Haudenosaunee sought to bring their guests to a good mind, and to incorporate them through the exchange of words and wampum into the metaphorical Iroquois Longhouse. In each case exchange was more than a mere economic transaction: exchange established and preserved close social ties between the communities involved. In such a world, an inhospitable person was looked down upon; goods were shared freely. The exchange of gifts between trading partners, in the words of Iroquois orators, kept strong and bright the chain of friendship linking partners together.

Bears

A final story. In February of 1677, the Jesuit Father Claude Allouez began a journey to preach to the Anishinaabe peoples in the country the French called "Illinois." Passing near the Potawatomis, Allouez learned that a young man from the community had recently been killed by a bear. Father Claude knew the young man, a Christian convert whom he had christened Good Paulin. The unfortunate young man, Allouez learned, fired all of his arrows at the bear, but the animal—that other-than-human being—"feeling itself struck, although not by a deadly blow, rose up and sprang upon him, tore off his scalp, and disemboweled him, mangling and dismembering the entire Body." The bear had heaped upon the body of Good Paulin the type of scorn and derision that a warrior might unleash against a fallen enemy. The bear had attacked, an act of aggression that the Potawatomis felt they must avenge. So "the relatives and friends" of Good Paulin, Father Claude wrote, "went to make war on the bears." They sought vengeance, to set things right, to return the world to balance. "The war," Allouez concluded, "was so successful that, in a short time, they killed over 500 … telling us that God delivered the bears into their hands as satisfaction for the death of that Young man who had been so cruelly treated by one of their nation."

Allouez told this story because he thought it would interest his readers, and show them just how much superstition remained among those Indians to whom he and his brethren labored to bring the Gospel. Allouez knew that the bears were not a "nation," and that his God did not intervene in disputes between human beings and animals. And he knew that bears did not think and that they did not reason.

But did they? The Cherokees told the story of the hunter who lived with the bears and began to look like a bear himself. From his black bear mentor he learned how to hunt, and how to treat animals with respect. The Moravian missionary John Heckewelder, who encountered a Delaware hunter in Pennsylvania in the middle of the eighteenth century, recounted the following story: the hunter, Heckewelder said, had just shot the bear with his musket and the wounded animal cried out in pain. The hunter was disgusted. He spoke to the bear. "You are a coward," he told the wounded animal, and you "lay and whimper like an old woman." The hunters and the bears were at war, he explained, a conflict the bears had begun. Now, the hunter told the bear, "you have found the Indians too powerful for you and you have gone sneaking about in the woods, stealing their hogs." Had the tables been turned, and "had you conquered me," the hunter announced, "I would have borne it with courage and died like a brave warrior; but you, sit here and cry, and disgrace your tribe by your cowardly conduct." A wounded Potawatomi man, in another story, encountered men who transformed themselves into bears, who then stole his weapons. When he called them "Brother," they dropped what they had taken. Later, his wounds were treated by eight men, half of whom wore black paint and half of whom wore white. They promised to help him in the future. They then became wolves, and returned to the woods.

We can, like Father Claude, dismiss these stories as mere myths and legends. We might recount them, again like Father Claude, for the entertainment of our audience. But there is so much more going on here than this Catholic priest recognized. Human beings and other-than-human beings were kin. The Potawatomis visited by Father Claude, and their Ottawa and Ojibway neighbors, and scores of other native peoples as well, marked the treaties that they negotiated with Europeans with images of animals. For Potawatomis, these images represented their connection to a kinship network known as *nindoodemag*, part of a system for comprehending their world in which individuals in different communities saw themselves as bound by obligation and kinship to other humans who shared descent from the same other-than-human being. There were, for instance, otter people who looked like otters and otter people who walked upright and took the form of a human being. Shared souls, not shared blood, defined kinship and measured the ties that bound people together.

The events described by Father Claude and Heckewelder and scores of other European observers correspond in important ways with the origins stories, myths, and legends of native peoples. From them we can see that Europeans did not discover a "New World." Rather they intruded into an environment in which the native peoples of this continent had found ways to meet their material and cultural needs in emotionally, spiritually, and physically satisfying ways. They had, over the course of centuries, developed the means to maintain a critical balance, with their neighbors, amongst themselves, and with the spiritual forces that ordered their cosmos. They had developed ways of living and systems of belief that worked well for them, and allowed them to survive and comprehend their world in all its complexity. They did not live in isolation. They interacted with other communities, fighting with some and living in peace with others. They had devised culturally satisfying means for interacting and dealing with strangers, and rendering unfamiliar people familiar. When Europeans arrived they found themselves, at least at the outset, operating in a world governed by Native American rules.

2

WORLDS NEW AND WORLDS OLD

The Fundamental Violence of Discovery

In October of 1492, Christopher Columbus discovered the native peoples of the New World. He landed on the island that its people called Guanahaní, renamed it San Salvador, and then that wayward Admiral of the Ocean Sea "took possession of the island … for the King and Queen, his Sovereigns, making the declarations which are required." There was, of course, nothing new about this world, aside from Columbus's own perception, and the people he found and whose lands he claimed had for their part just discovered their first European. The native peoples of the Caribbean had lived on these islands for centuries, trading, fighting, and interacting with their neighbors and rivals. But the arrival of Columbus, and those Europeans who followed him, created a new world for the hemisphere's native peoples. So much so, that an event some Americans still see as a cause for celebration, the annual commemoration of Columbus's discovery, many native peoples view as a day for mourning the victims of an American holocaust and 500 years of genocide.

Columbus wanted the peoples of this "new world" to "feel great amity towards us," he wrote, and he knew that they were a people "to be delivered and converted to our holy faith rather by love than by force." Columbus gave to the Tainos, the people he first encountered, "some red caps and some glass beads, which they hung round their necks, and many other things of little value." The Tainos, he concluded, were simple and might easily be controlled. "They should be good servants," he wrote, and they would serve well the ends of Spanish imperialism. He sent some of them to Europe as showpieces and slaves, and promised "as many slaves as Their Majesties orders to make."

The Spanish claimed their empire by right of discovery and because the Pope "made a donation of these islands and mainland to the Ocean Sea to the Catholic Kings of Spain." So said the *Requerimiento*, a document and declaration read in Spanish to the peoples these empire-builders encountered. The Spanish demanded that the Indians "recognize the church as lord and superior of the universal world, and the most elevated Pope … in its name, and His Majesty in his place as superior and lord and king … and consent" that the priests accompanying these armed men be allowed to minister to their people. If the natives consented, "His Majesty and I in his name will receive you … and will leave your women and children free." Yet the native peoples of the New World, under the logic of the *Requerimiento*, had no alternative, and if they refused, blood would flow. The Spanish conquistadors found justification in their faith to attack, "with the help of God," and "make war everywhere and however I can and … subject you to the yoke and obedience of the Church and His Majesty." Indians

Native America: A History, Second Edition. Michael Leroy Oberg.
© 2018 John Wiley & Sons, Inc. Published 2018 by John Wiley & Sons, Inc.

who refused to listen to the words of the Lord, and who refused to accept Spanish authority, could expect so much more than coerced conversion. "I will take your wives and children," the conqueror would announce, "and I will make them slaves ... and I will take your goods, and I will do to you all the evil and damages that a lord may do to vassals who do not obey or receive them." With the zeal of crusaders and the avarice of slavers, and shaped by the blood-soaked history of their homeland, some Spanish sincerely believed that they could not be held responsible for the consequences of their acts. "I solemnly declare," the conqueror would read, "that the deaths and damages received from such will be your fault and not that of His Majesty, nor mine, nor the gentlemen who came with me."

Many deaths and much destruction followed because so many of those Spanish gentlemen behaved with mind-numbing brutality. By the middle of the sixteenth century, the great indigenous empires of South and Central America—the Incas, Aztecs, and others—had fallen to the Spanish. The conquistadors subjected "all males to the harshest and most iniquitous and brutal slavery that man has ever devised for oppressing his fellow men, treating them, in fact, worse than animals." The brutality of this conquest claimed many Indian lives. Columbus and his followers in the Caribbean, wrote the Dominican friar Bartolome de las Casas, one of the only Spanish critics of this brutality, entered "into this sheepfold, into this land of meek outcasts" and "behaved like ravening wild beasts, wolves, tigers, or lions that had been starved for many days." On the mainland, Las Casas continued, "we are sure that our Spaniards, with their cruel and abominable acts, have devastated the land and exterminated the rational people who inhabited it." Their war dogs tore native peoples to pieces. They burned Indians thirteen at a time, in memory of Jesus and the Apostles. Any resistance brought brutal reprisals. Las Casas, who described how his countrymen entertained themselves by slaughtering children, believed that after the Spanish had been in the Americas for forty years, "there have been unjustly slain more than twelve million men, women, and children," and perhaps as many as 15 million.

Old world diseases followed closely the Spanish invaders. Disease and Spanish violence cannot be separated. Millions of Indians perished as a result of exposure to common European diseases. At times, these epidemics advanced ahead of European settlement. These "virgin soil epidemics," however, were rendered more deadly by the pressures that accompanied colonization: forced labor, the exaction of tribute, and the destruction of native people's economies and subsistence systems. The very processes of colonization thus increased the susceptibility of native peoples to illness and death. A vicious cycle resulted that made it difficult for infected communities to rebound and recover. In places, disease, exacerbated by the fundamental violence of discovery, wiped out 90% of the population, robbed communities of their most vulnerable members—the elderly and the young—and damaged both the past and the future of native peoples by killing the keepers of the community's traditions and the children who would one day replenish the population.

Paths of Destruction

Over thirty distinct "pueblo" communities existed along the Rio Grande river valley as it wended its way through today's New Mexico. Speaking a number of different but related languages, and differing in some ways in their social organization, the similarities in the outward appearances and in the basic cultural orientation of the Pueblos masked some of the diversity that existed among the different communities. Near present-day Albuquerque stood a series of Southern Tiwa-speaking villages. To their north, along the Rio Grande and its tributaries, more towns could be found: Towa-speaking towns near the Jemez mountains, Keres-speaking villages along the Rio Jemez and Rio Grande, and Tewa-speaking groups to their east, not to mention towns occupied by the speakers of now-extinct languages like Tompiro and Piro.

They lived in a world of violence and change. The design of their communities suggested that safety and defense deeply concerned them. A stone wall surrounded the pueblo at Pecos, for instance, which according to the first Spanish accounts could field 500 warriors. The people who lived there, the Spanish said, prided "themselves because no one has been able to subjugate them, while they dominate the pueblos they wish." Acoma, built atop a rock in a highly defensible location, was protected by its 200 warriors who "were feared throughout the land."

The Pueblos, of course, understood the functioning of their cosmos in terms dramatically different from the Spaniards who would soon intrude into their world. Unlike the crusading Catholic Iberians, the Pueblos believed that human and other-than-human beings had entered into the world through an opening in the roof of the underworld. Powerful spiritual beings, *katsinas*, lived with them at the beginning of time and taught them the rituals necessary to survive. And with the help of these spiritual beings and with attention to ritual, the Pueblos lived well, and they succeeded in maintaining a balance with the spiritual forces in their cosmos. They planted their crops, traded and fought with their neighbors, and developed strategies and customs, like others of the continent's native peoples, for interacting with outsiders: Navajos and Apaches, for instance, began intruding into the region in the 1400s, and the first Spaniards arrived in the 1530s.

The residents of the small Zuni pueblo at Hawikuh first encountered the Spanish expedition commanded by Francisco Coronado. Two thousand people followed Coronado into what later became the American southwest, but 1300 of them were Mexican Indians from a host of communities who wore their accustomed dress and carried their accustomed weapons. The Spanish expeditionaries, too, overwhelmingly carried the *armas de la tierra*, weapons and protection indigenous to the Americas. Only forty-five of Coronado's men, for instance, wore European metal helmets. With the exception of the horses and mules that carried their baggage, and the herds of sheep and cattle they relied upon for food, and the women and children who followed them along, Coronado's party would have looked more like a force of invading Mexican warriors than Spanish knights in gleaming armor.

These men sought the wealth of the mythical Seven Cities of Cibola, and the glory and status that would earn them lives of luxury. The people of the Pueblos likely heard of the Spanish, and how they would act when they arrived. The same native networks that allowed Pueblos to travel and trade carried information as well as items for exchange. The warriors of Hawikuh perceived the threat posed by the Spanish. They poured lines of corn meal between their pueblo and the advancing Spaniards, and they ordered the invaders not to cross. The Spanish, in turn, read the *Requerimiento*. So the men of the pueblo attacked the Spaniards, protected they hoped by the power of their rituals. The Spanish and their allies drove them back and stormed the pueblo. They then put the leading men of Hawikuh to death, examples to teach the Zunis the price of resistance.

Coronado could not help but notice the small size and the lack of wealth that characterized the Zuni towns. They had nothing that he considered of value, even if by their own standards the Zunis lived lives rich in meaning. Their cities had none of the treasure that he and his avaricious men sought. Coronado sent out parties to look for evidence of wealth in other locations. Some of these parties engaged in brief but bloody conflicts like that at Hawikuh.

Some Pueblos saw in the Spanish a threat and learned of their violence first-hand. Others saw in these marauding warriors an opportunity. A young man whom the Spanish named Bigotes came from Pecos to visit the Spaniards. He brought with him impressive gifts—shields, headdresses, and well-dressed skins—and a promise to guide the Spaniards to other pueblos. Everywhere he led the Spanish, people received them well. Bigotes explained to the Spanish the importance of giving gifts. These gifts helped to make words material, less abstract, and to establish a reciprocal relationship between friends and allies. Coronado's lieutenant, Hernando de Alvarado, reported that when the Spanish erected crosses in the pueblos they visited, the residents decorated them with flowers and feathers and made to them offerings of sacred meal. The Pueblos hoped to harness that power that allowed the newcomers to do so many things that ordinary human beings could not—a perception shaped by Spanish technology, by their weapons, and the animals that carried them and their baggage.

Bigotes led a Spanish party to Taos, the northernmost of the Tiwa pueblos, and from there he led them to Pecos. Though he encouraged the Spanish in their fantasies of finding gold to the east, he told them he would not lead them there himself. After several weeks Bigotes was eager to rid himself of the Spanish. Others stepped in, none more important than an individual dubbed "El Turco," who had traveled widely through the heart of the continent. He promised to lead the Spanish to Quivira, his home, a land he described as one of enormous wealth. El Turco said that he had proof—a gold bracelet—but that it had been stolen by Bigotes. The Spanish need not worry, however, for El Turco told them there were plenty more where that one had come from.

Alvarado decided to wait, and to defer following El Turco until he received approval from Coronado. Along with El Turco, he returned to Pecos to confront Bigotes about the stolen bracelet. Bigotes knew nothing of the theft. Perhaps Alvarado should have recognized that he was caught in the midst of a struggle between two native leaders, as El Turco attempted to discredit Bigotes in the eyes of the Spanish. Perhaps he might have perceived how native peoples used the power and strength of Europeans to advance their own or their community's interests. He did not. He was frustrated. Alvarado carried both men back to Coronado for interrogation. The men of Pecos attacked when Alvarado placed Bigotes in chains, but the Spaniards drove the warriors back.

Alvarado reunited with Coronado at Tiguex. The Tiwas there would have known of earlier Spanish assaults, for that information traveled widely, and they may well have observed Bigotes and El Turco in Spanish custody. As the winter snows arrived, the Tiwas listened to Coronado's demands that they provide him with food and with shelter from the cold. They learned of the rape of a Tiwa woman by a Spanish soldier. Discontent mounted with each new Spanish demand and each new Spanish atrocity. The Tiwas could no longer accommodate the barbarous newcomers who seemed more trouble than they were worth. They consumed vital resources, and they killed people. The Tiwas knew the dangers of a head-on attack, so they struck first at the Spanish horse herds. The soldiers retaliated, burning their homes. The conquistadors drew no distinction between combatants and non-combatants. Coronado forced Bigotes and El Turco, along with others, to watch Tiwa men, women and children burn alive, a crude warning to them not to cross the Spanish.

The events of that winter changed El Turco. He had witnessed firsthand Spanish brutality. He had watched them torture Bigotes. Holding the tiger by the tail, El Turco told Coronado that he would lead the Spanish across the plains to the riches of Quivira, but his new appraisal of the viciousness of the Spaniards led him to resolve secretly upon doing something very different. He hoped to insulate his people from the irrational violence of the newcomers and lead the Spanish astray. Coronado's expedition, in the words of historian Richard Flint, "seemed like a malevolent force to be hidden from, chased away, and, if one dared, enlisted briefly for one's own cause."

So in April of 1541, El Turco led Coronado and his army out onto the southern Great Plains, a land that to the Spanish seemed featureless and desolate. Adrift in a sea of grass, the conquistadors depended upon El Turco entirely. He led them on a meandering journey into the east, going nowhere fast. The newcomers began to fear El Turco who, for a time, skillfully manipulated those fears. He convinced some of them, evidently, that he had powers approaching the supernatural—that he could foresee the future. El Turco recognized that he must be useful to the Spanish to remain alive, but that they must also fear him. He understood that the Spanish endangered his people, and he hoped to lead them to their destruction. Ultimately Coronado grew impatient with the expedition's inability to arrive at the fabled cities of gold. The Spanish began to torture El Turco. He admitted that he hoped to kill the Spanish by starvation and thirst, "so that they would not go into his country." The Spanish then put El Turco to death. They made him suffer.

Coronado later found Quivira, but he never found the wealth that he had craved. From the failure of Coronado's expedition the Spanish might have drawn a number of lessons. Coronado needed native assistance—that should have seemed clear—if he were to maneuver successfully in an environment where the Spanish found themselves playing by native rules. Conquest, for Coronado, was out of the question; alliance essential for success. But the expedition's brutality and its demands for food surpassed what the Pueblos could safely provide, and they did what they could to rid themselves of a malevolent intruder. Imperial officials in Spain and in the provincial capitals sought profit from their American enterprise, and they wanted to establish a secure foothold in the Americas and to spread what to them was the one and only true religion. They did not necessarily care about Indians in any moral sense, but they did recognize that they could achieve their goals most easily and least expensively with the assistance of native peoples. The Pueblos and their neighbors, however, encountered only the violence of the men actually engaged in colonization—the conquistadors—who destroyed any possibility for peace.

The Pueblos, and Indians farther east who encountered Coronado's party, learned that the European intruders were different from them. That the traditions of exchange and reciprocity they had nurtured over centuries, and which successfully served to mediate their relations with other native peoples, did not work seemed abundantly clear. While the Spanish possessed attractive technology, and while they might assist a native community in pursuing indigenous goals, they would only do so as long as they had something to fear or to gain from that community.

Coronado's party may have moved far enough east that those peoples who became known in the nineteenth century as the Caddos heard something of their approach, but it was the remnants of Hernando de Soto's *entrada* who became the first Europeans to intrude directly into their world. The Caddos were not a unified group—that development would occur later—but they did consist of approximately twenty-five recognizable communities organized loosely into two or three "confederacies." Eighty thousand people lived in these communities, and perhaps many more. The largest of the confederacies, the Hasinai, stood along the upper portions of the Angelina and Neches rivers. To their north, the Kadohadachos dominated the big bend region of the Red River. The Natchitoches, closely identified with the Kadohadachos, and living downstream from them, may or may not have been a separate community.

Map 2.1 The de Soto Entrada. Source: *Smithsonian Handbook of North American Indians*, Vol. 14, Southeast, pp. 14: 129. Courtesy of Smithsonian Institution.

An agricultural people, the Caddos, like other southeastern groups, cultivated corn, beans, and squash, along with sunflowers and tobacco. They hunted and fished as well, and were far less reliant upon bison for their support than were Plains peoples—Wichitas, Pawnees, and others—who lived immediately to their west. They lived in hamlets consisting of approximately a dozen houses, which their fields surrounded. These hamlets were located over a large area that at times centered upon the mounds that served as the larger community's ceremonial center.

De Soto, the governor of the Spanish outpost on Cuba, had brought his 600 men ashore near today's Tampa Bay in the spring of 1539. Over the course of the next two years, they marched through the southeastern interior, along the Appalachians, through what are today the states of Tennessee, Georgia, and North Carolina. They employed incredible violence, killing people belonging to the groups that would later coalesce into Cherokees, Choctaws, Creeks, Chickasaws and others. He encountered *micos*, or town leaders, some of whom accommodated the invaders and sought to use Soto to advance their own ends, others who defied them. Soto marched through a native south consisting of many communities, interconnected and integrated by ties of diplomacy, ceremony, and exchange. After his death, Soto's successor, Luis de Moscoso, led the survivors into the Caddo country. Though the Spaniards remarked covetously upon the turquoise and woven cloth the Caddos had acquired through trade with the peoples of the southwest, Moscoso no longer threatened as an invasion force.

Debilitated by sickness and hunger, his men were on the run. Their sojourn among the Caddos was a brief one. By the summer of 1542, the surviving Spanish had departed.

Despite its relatively short duration, the De Soto *entrada* was calamitous for the native peoples of the southeast. The invaders devastated a region stretching from Florida to Texas and well into the interior. Whatever justifications accompanied Spanish colonization—a desire to save Indian souls, a desire to enlighten and educate benighted heathen—the Caddos and other southeastern Indian peoples encountered terrifying violence, brutality, and destruction that destabilized the native south. Soto and his men gave to the Caddos and their neighbors, in anthropologist Charles Hudson's estimation, their "first taste of a people who would kidnap, enslave, and burn their villages out of pique because their sheets of copper and slabs of mica were not precious enough. They got their first taste of a people who wished to take from them everything they possessed and who would one day dig up their very graves for the value of what they contained."

The Caddos suffered a drop in population after the Spanish incursion. It was not a matter of the newcomers introducing diseases, so much as that their presence made native peoples more vulnerable to pathogens with which they already were familiar. As Soto and his men cut a swath of destruction through the region, taking Indian food, enslaving them to serve as porters, and hunting them with their war dogs, native peoples fled their towns and abandoned their fields. By the time Europeans returned to the region more than a century and a quarter later, vast expanses had been depopulated as the Mississippian chiefdoms declined. Some Caddo peoples may have moved out onto the Plains, developing a mobile lifestyle based on bison hunting. Mound-building had ceased.

The Chumash did not confront the large parties of marauders led by the likes of Coronado and Soto, but they did greet explorers like Juan Rodriguez Cabrillo, who spent five months near their settlements along the Santa Barbara Channel, both on the islands and on the coast, of today's southern California.

The Chumash had lived here for thousands of years before the Spanish arrived. They relied heavily upon fish and shellfish, but they also hunted on occasion marine and terrestrial animals. They gathered and processed acorns and a variety of wild plants and seeds, and stored these along with dried meat and fish to provide them with food throughout the year. Despite the fact that agriculture played no role in their subsistence system, the Chumash may have had the highest population density in North America at the time of contact. Perhaps as many as 20,000 people lived along the channel.

Chumash people lived in tightly organized communities. Craft specialists produced shell beads that circulated widely as currency and the chert drills used to make them. A hereditary chief, drawing upon the support of these craft specialists and religious leaders, headed each village. It is difficult to determine the precise nature of the relationships between the different Chumash communities. The name "Chumash" emerged in the early twentieth century, an anglicized corruption of an indigenous word used to describe the inhabitants of Santa Cruz Island. It is a generic label that masked considerable local autonomy. Six major Chumash languages, each related but distinct from one another, were spoken: Ventureño, Barbareño, Cruzeño, Ineseño, Purisimeño, and Obispeño, and no unified power governed all of them. Still, trade was widespread. Large plank canoes, the *tomol* boats, linked Chumash communities on the Channel Islands with those on the mainland coast and in the interior. Shell beads moved throughout these zones, with food, tools, and animal skins circulating widely over significant distances. Chiefs oversaw this exchange, ensuring that the members of their communities acquired the things they needed to stay alive.

It was this world into which Cabrillo intruded briefly in October of 1542. He came ashore for the first time somewhere near the present-day site of Ventura, California. He hoped to find cities filled with silver and gold. He wrote that "all the coast is heavily inhabited." The Chumash paddled out to the Spanish ships, inviting the newcomers to trade with them in their villages. Cabrillo gave his hosts "many gifts," he wrote, and "all along the coast" the Indians generously reciprocated. According to Cabrillo, the Chumash "dressed in skins and wore their hair very long and tangled, with very long cords intricately woven into their hair, and between these cords and the hair were many daggers of stone and of bone and wood." He did not like the way they looked, but he thought the land they inhabited "appeared to be excellent."

Chumash villagers traded with the newcomers, attempting to establish relationships based upon reciprocity and exchange. They had no reason to fear the newcomers. They treated Cabrillo using the familiar forms of conduct that governed their relations with other strangers. They attempted to incorporate the men aboard the small Spanish expedition into their world. Cabrillo brought Chumash visitors aboard his ships, and moored near their densely populated villages, the easier to facilitate intercultural exchange.

Sometime around Christmas in 1542, a group of Chumash wounded three of Cabrillo's men who had gone ashore seeking fresh water. The Chumash had become increasingly disenchanted with the Spanish visitors who relied upon them for food and hospitality. Cabrillo broke his leg jumping out of a boat to aid his men, and died from the resulting infection a bit more than a week later. Buried somewhere on the Channel Islands, his expedition might have served as a warning for what could happen to Europeans who refused to play by native peoples' rules.

Europeans may have hoped to benefit from indigenous knowledge to exploit the wealth of the new world. They may have hoped to Christianize and civilize Indians. They may have wished to cultivate native allies to secure their foothold on American shores. But the violence of the men sent to do the dirty work of colonization, time and again, doomed any prospect for peaceful coexistence, and the greed of their sponsors meant that native peoples were viewed all too often as a means to an end.

But here we must take caution. One might easily turn these stories of "first contact" into horrific morality plays that emphasize the victimization of native peoples. There were, of course, disease and violence and victimization aplenty, but to view encounter and colonization, however devastating the consequences, strictly as something done to Indians by Europeans gets at only one painful part of a complicated story. From the outset, native peoples tried to comprehend the newcomers, and to incorporate them into their conceptual universe. Indians did not anticipate, at the outset, the devastating consequences of contact with Europeans, and initially they approached them with the interests of their communities in mind, and treated the newcomers according to the norms and conventions that had informed their relations with others and that had developed on this continent over the course of centuries.

When Giovanni di Verrazzanno, the Italian mariner sailing in the service of France coasted along the North American mainland in 1524, for instance, he was greeted by native men hoisting furs on sticks, an attempt to lure his men ashore, engage them in exchange, and acquire from them the manufactured goods and material culture they possessed that seemed so strange and held such great power. This power, as we have seen, natives believed could manifest itself in people, in animals, and in things. Even items as trivial to Europeans as glass beads and copper pots were understood by native peoples to reflect great power: glass beads, for instance, served as workable metaphors for the crystals that at times and in places played a role in native curing and divining rituals.

Native peoples from the outset sought to acquire the material culture of the newcomers, and as they did so, they tried to exclude their rivals from this exchange and secure the newcomers as their exclusive allies. For example, the two young Iroquoian guides seized by Jacques Cartier during his inconclusive expedition in 1534, guided the Frenchman up the river that the newcomers would soon call the St. Lawrence to their village at Stadacona, today's Quebec. There the newcomers went ashore with their guides, and established amicable relations with Donnaconna, the sachem, or leader, of the village. When Cartier announced that he intended to continue up the river to visit the village of Hochelaga, at today's Montreal, his hosts warned him that at Hochelaga they would encounter so much snow and ice that they would surely perish. His priests, Cartier told Donnaconna, had spoken with Jesus, who assured them that he would control the weather and permit a safe journey.

The Hochelagans, perhaps unsurprisingly, were elated to see Cartier and his party when they arrived late in 1535, and they were eager to engage in exchange and gain access to the power that their rivals evidently wanted to monopolize. The headman at Hochelaga asked Cartier to rub his paralyzed limbs; he believed that the newcomer possessed the power to effect a cure beyond the powers of his shamans. Other Indians came forward as well; they desired the power of the French captain's touch. The Hochelagans gratefully appreciated the presents the French party bestowed upon their hosts.

Indians, in the St. Lawrence and elsewhere, sought to harness the powers they saw manifest in the European visitors. But they were neither incredulous nor uncritical. They helped the Europeans because they believed that doing so could benefit them. The Stadaconans, for instance, taught the French party how to counter a devastating outbreak of scurvy by showing them the curative power of white cedar bark. Twenty-five of Cartier's men died in the outbreak, demonstrating to the Stadaconans that these newcomers, however powerful they seemed, were human.

These Iroquoian peoples, however, would learn quickly that the powers of the Frenchmen could do evil as well as good. When Cartier departed in 1536, he took with him ten captives who would never see America again. Cartier would, upon his return to Stadacona in 1541, tell the natives that their countrymen were living well in France, enjoying a life of gentility, and that they had chosen not to return home. In reality, nine of the ten (including five children) had died. Cartier did more than lie, and like other prospectors, he never learned that to succeed in this old world he must adhere to native peoples' expectations of good conduct. The Iroquoian peoples in the St. Lawrence among whom he traveled seem to have grown weary of this French intruder. Late in the spring of 1542 Cartier retreated downriver, the gold and diamonds he thought he carried nothing more than worthless pyrite and quartz. A Basque sailor who visited the area later that summer learned from the Indians with whom he traded knives and axes for wolf and deerskins that they and their leader, a "chief in Canada," had "killed more than thirty-five of Jacques's men" before they departed for France.

Tsenacommacah

Native peoples made a reasoned and rational assessment of the newcomers, and of both the dangers and the opportunities that contact with them presented. Much of the time, they found the European invaders unwilling to conform to indigenous expectations of generosity and reciprocity and that they made poor neighbors and allies.

The experience of the Powhatan Chiefdom of Virginia helps to illustrate the point. Led by an extraordinary *weroance* named Wahunsonacock, better known in many accounts simply as "Powhatan," the chiefdom that his people called *Tsenacommacah* encompassed as many as 14,000 Algonquians living in some thirty communities and more than 200 settlements. Wahunsonacock had inherited the core of this chiefdom late in the sixteenth century, and from this base he extended his influence over the communities to his east, through conquest, through alliance, and through intimidation, always moving eastward toward the Chesapeake Bay.

The Powhatans understood the dangers that outsiders could pose. Spanish Jesuits established a short-lived mission on their lands in 1570. At first the Powhatans welcomed the priests, who seemed to possess great power. But the priests were generally intolerant and they were few in number. Their arrival, moreover, coincided with the beginning of a period of famine and death which it is not difficult to imagine the people of Tsenacommacah associated with the newcomers. Instead of accepting Christianity, the Indians slaughtered the starving priests, an act for which they would suffer a violent reprisal at the hands of Spanish marauders who killed twenty and took a dozen more captive. The Powhatans, a decade after this incursion, might have heard something of the English colonists at Roanoke Island. Some historians assert that Wahunsonacock had something to do with the disappearance of the "Lost Colonists" who had vanished by 1590.

These initial European visits to Tsenacommacah involved small numbers of newcomers and they were dealt with easily. More of a threat were Wahunsonacock's native enemies who pressed down upon his territories from the west. Indeed, he later would tell the English adventurer John Smith that "he had seen the death of all my people thrice, and not anyone living of those three generations but myself." He may have been referring to his advanced age and long experience, for there is no evidence that epidemic disease struck his homeland. But he might have been describing to Smith the casualties his people had suffered at the hands of his western enemies.

These factors combined led Wahunsonacock to feel no initial threat from the small group of Englishmen who settled on what he must have considered little more than a marshy wasteland along the James River in May of 1607. The colonists represented a commercial venture, the Virginia Company of London, which hoped to generate a profit from whatever its settlers might find or produce in America. They also hoped to establish a secure outpost on American shores and spread what the Company and its shareholders believed to be the one and only true religion. To achieve these goals, the Company instructed its settlers to treat Indians well, and the Company's promotional materials reveal a great confidence that not only could the Indians abandon and set aside their savagery, but that they would willingly do so when presented with the English example.

With the population of his chiefdom more than twenty-five times greater than the population of the small English outpost, Wahunsonacock had little reason to fear the colonists. He was, in his fashion, as ethnocentric as the English, convinced with equal fervor of the rectitude of his people's beliefs and their way of life. Still, he saw in the English newcomers an opportunity. The Englishmen had metal trade goods and edged weapons, and Wahunsonacock looked to monopolize trade with the newcomers. He believed that though few in number, these armed men and their weapons could be useful in his wars against his native rivals to the west. When the English colonists began dying in large numbers late in the summer of 1607, the product of a lethal combination of ecological and social factors, it was Wahunsonacock who determined to send the food that allowed the few colonists to survive. Indeed, the records from early Jamestown reveal clearly that Wahunsonacock and his followers were open to encounters with the English. They were hospitable, and they hoped for friendship and alliance with the newcomers. So open were the Powhatans to inclusion that several colonists fled from the brutal environment at Jamestown and joined the Indians. These Englishmen the Powhatans adopted and incorporated into their communities.

When a Powhatan hunting party found the bellicose Smith floundering about in an icy swamp, again Wahunsonacock showed his hospitality. Though many Americans know of this episode best for what Smith describes as its climax—his supposed rescue from certain death by Pocahontas, the beautiful daughter of Wahunsonacock—there is no reason to believe that Smith's life ever was in danger. Smith was treated well, feasted everywhere he went, and conducted about as a person of great status. The rituals of greeting and feasting that Smith participated in, and the ritual in which Pocahontas rescued Smith (if it really happened), most historians now believe were part of a process through which Smith became the *weroance*, or leader, of Wahunsonacock's new band of tributary Englishmen.

Wahunsonacock fulfilled his obligations. Smith returned to Jamestown in January of 1608. A few days later, the fort caught fire, rendering the colonists' situation desperate. In exchange for corn and other food, Wahunsonacock acquired from the colonists metal tools and bladed weapons. He may have acquired a few guns. In April, he exchanged with the English young boys to serve as cultural brokers and learn how to work as interpreters. Wahunsonacock envisioned a future of peace, with the English newcomers remaining his loyal tributaries.

He never succeeded, however, in teaching the English what he expected of them. The colonists were, indeed, close-minded students. Short of provisions, Smith in the fall of 1608 embarked on a policy of forced trade. To keep the colonists alive, he and his men took corn at gunpoint from Wahunsonacock's followers. When Smith assaulted the Nansemonds, a tributary community, Wahunsonacock at last decided to cut off all trade with the English.

Wahunsonacock's interdiction of trade, designed to chastise the English, led Smith to conclude that "it was Powhatan's policy to starve us." Accordingly, Smith hatched a plan to capture Wahunsonacock at his capital, a town called Werowocomoco, in January of 1609. Wahunsonacock, too, may have had plans to eliminate the ungrateful and, in his eyes, disloyal English leader. They met that January, both looking for an opportunity to spring their traps. The discussion between the two men, described by Smith, shows both that Wahunsonacock had failed to persuade the English to accept their role as allies and tributaries and to embrace the principles of reciprocity which he believed should undergird relations within his chiefdom, "we being all friends, and for ever Powhatans."

Wahunsonacock made one last effort to educate the man who he clearly had come to view as a rebellious lesser *weroance*. "What will it avail you to take that by force you may quickly have by love, or to destroy them that provide you food," he asked Smith. "What can you get by war, when we can hide our provisions and fly to the woods?" Wahunsonacock wanted peace, to be able to "eat good meat, lie well, and sleep quietly with my women and children, laugh and be merry with you, have copper, hatchets or what I want being your friend." Wahunsonacock wanted trade with the newcomers and a relationship but he could not bear the attacks on his people. "I never use any Weroance so kindly as your self," Wahunsonacock lectured Smith, "yet from you I receive the least kindness of any."

By the summer of 1609, the Powhatans began to avenge the insults they had suffered at the hands of the colonists. Ships carrying new arrivals to Jamestown in 1608 and 1609 helped the colony grow, providing Wahunsonacock with even more proof that the colonists intended to stay in his homeland and that their numbers would continue to increase.

Figure 2.1 Simon Van de Passe (1616), Engraving of Pocahontas. Courtesy of Virginia Historical Society, Richmond, Virginia.

Powhatan warriors began to snipe at the English. Nearly 100 colonists died between August and November of 1609, the opening months of what one historian has called the "First Anglo-Powhatan War."

The colonists suffered from poor leadership. Smith, seriously injured when a bag of gunpowder ignited in his lap, went home in October. Shortly thereafter, the Powhatans settled into a "siege" of Jamestown, surrounding the fort and opening fire on anyone who raised their head. The "Starving Time" followed, during which 110 Englishmen died, "either starved through famine or cut off by the Savages." The English fought back with a brutality that must have seemed inhuman to the Powhatans. The colonists killed women and children, and on one occasion entertained themselves by throwing captive children overboard into the James and "shooting out their brains in the water." Wahunsonacock seemed stunned by the English attacks, either unable or unwilling to take on the colonists' weapons.

The war ground to a stalemate that broke in 1613 when the English captured Wahunsonacock's daughter Pocahontas, a young woman probably of about eighteen years. Wahunsonacock would not provide the English with the ransom they demanded for her return, and she remained a captive at Jamestown. There she learned about Christianity and, in April of 1614, married the colonist John Rolfe, with whom she had a son.

The Rolfe–Pocahontas marriage, and the period of peace that followed it, heralded the arrival of what some historians have called the Virginia Company's "Golden Age." As Rolfe himself wrote, the colonists now "yearly plant and reap quietly; and travail in the woods a fowling and hunting as freely and securely from fear of danger or treachery as in England." As settlement expanded away from the bad water at Jamestown, the colony's high mortality rate began to subside. And the Company expressed during these years a renewed optimism that it could achieve its goals: a profitable and secure settlement, and the expansion of English civility and religion. Indeed, Rolfe believed that "there is no small hope by piety, clemency, courtesy, and civil demeanor, to convert and bring to the knowledge and true worship of Jesus Christ" Wahunsonacock's followers.

To prove this point, the Company sent Rolfe, his wife (now baptized a Christian and christened Rebecca), their child, and an entourage that included several Powhatans to England. Paraded before aristocrats and nobles at the English court, Rebecca Rolfe seemed living proof that the English could incorporate Virginia and its peoples into an expanding, Anglo-American, Christian, New World empire. The Indians were, as one English minister put it, "sons of Adam," in "whom there be remaining so many footsteps of God's image." But Pocahontas died in England, before she could come home, and her people along the rivers of Tsenacommacah faced new threats and new assaults.

Beginning in 1614, the colonists in Virginia devoted themselves whole-heartedly to the cultivation of tobacco, a destructive but profitable staple that quickly robbed the soil of its nutrients. After three years of planting, and with fields exhausted, planters needed new soil. This, coupled with an expanding English population composed of ill-supplied colonists, meant that the Powhatans found their lands under siege. The Powhatans always had located their towns and villages along the region's waterways, which provided them with food and a means of transportation. The English had an enormous appetite for these riverine lands for their tobacco plantations. They too wanted to be by the waterside, which provided them access to the best soil, safe drinking water, and a route for communication and transportation. An ecological conflict resulted. Indians and Englishmen sought to use identical ecological resources, which they employed in different and incompatible ways. In Virginia and elsewhere, out of that incompatibility came conflict.

George Thorpe, for instance, sent to Virginia by the Company to begin planning for Henrico College, a school for Indian children that had generous support from Christians in England, reported that the colonists despised the Powhatans. There was "scarce any man amongst us that doth so much as afford them a good thought in his heart," Thorpe wrote, "and most men with their mouths give them nothing but maledictions and bitter execrations." Thorpe observed that the colonists accused the Indians of "all the wrong and injury that the malice of the devil or man can afford." Thorpe was, it seems, a just man who was willing to punish colonists and even to kill their large mastiff dogs that frightened the Indians, but there was little that he could do to overcome the mounting racism of his countrymen. With their lands occupied by Indian-hating tobacco planters, facing the scorn and derision of a colonial population that they still outnumbered, some Powhatans concluded that the time had come to rid themselves of the English menace.

Wahunsonacock died in 1618. His successor, Opechancanough, worked to ease the English into a false sense of security. He told George Thorpe what he believed the English preacher and college planner wanted to hear. Yes, he would allow English families to settle amongst his people to teach them the doctrines of Christian religion. No, he would not object to sending Powhatan children to the English for instruction. Apparently well versed in Christianity, or an exceptionally quick study, Opechancanough convinced Thorpe that "he had more motions of Religion in him than could be imagined in so great blindness," that he believed that his own Algonquian beliefs were "not the right way," and that he wanted to learn English Christianity because "god loved us better than them."

It was a compelling and an effective act. Opechancanough fooled Thorpe. In March of 1622, Opechancanough and his followers descended upon the colonists in a devastating surprise attack. According to one English chronicler, the Powhatans "basely and barbarously murdered, not sparing either age or sex, man, woman or child; so sudden in their cruel execution, that few or none discerned the weapon or blow that brought them to destruction." In grotesque detail, the English described Powhatan violence. George Thorpe, the face of the company's philanthropic hopes, "was little regarded after by this Viperous brood ... for they not only willfully murdered him, but cruelly and felly, out of devilish malice, did so many barbarous despights and foul scorns after to his dead corpse, as are unbefitting to be heard by any civil ear." In a matter of hours, nearly a third of the 1100 colonists lay dead.

The English, of course, would retaliate with viciousness and violence of their own, burning Indian cornfields, attacking whomever they could. One colonist, calling the Powhatans to a peace parley in 1623, served them poisoned drinks, killing 150 and prolonging the war for several years. Another colonist, William Claiborne, saw opportunity in the violence. He received a patent, perhaps the first ever issued in the English American colonies, for a device that he claimed offered "an assured way and means ... to make [Indians] serviceable for many other services for the good of the whole Colony." The Company, which began its life professing a desire to Christianize and civilize the Indians, now found biblical justification for their slaughter. Virginia's governor, Francis Wyatt, declared that the goal in the English in the war that followed Opechancanough's attack was "the expulsion of the savages to gain the free range of the country for the increase of Cattle, swine, etc.," and he believed that "it is infinitely better to have no heathen among us ... than to be at peace and league with them." A poet commissioned by the Virginia Company put the same sentiments in verse. Describing the Indians who had killed the colonists, Christopher Brooke wrote that "I cannot call them men, no Character of God in them." They were, he continued, "Errors of Nature, of inhumane birth, the very dregs, garbage and spawn of the earth."

This was, simply put, one of the earliest English statements in print of harsh and violent racism towards native peoples in America. Virginia Company spokesmen, like John Rolfe and a dozen others, had viewed the Powhatans as fellow "Sons of Adam" in whom he saw "so many footsteps of God's image." Now they had been cast from the ark, denigrated in terms that called into question their very humanity.

The English created a new world for the Powhatans. According to their own pronouncements, they came to America seeking profit, a stable foothold in the Americas, and the extension of their much vaunted civility and religion. But the settlers they sent to the hellish seat they established along the James were more interested in planting tobacco than in teaching savages about the goodness of God. The Virginia Company and its colonial governors never devised a means to curb the land hunger of their colonial population. As aggressive as the newcomers proved to be, the Powhatans still sought to incorporate the English into their own communities, and into their own conceptual universe. Ceremonially appointing John Smith as tributary *weroance* in his expanding chiefdom, Wahunsonacock expected from the English

Figure 2.2 Matthaeus Merian, The Massacre of the Settlers in 1622. Courtesy of Virginia Historical Society, Richmond, Virginia.

certain things: reciprocity and respect, exchange and generosity. He and his successors, who tried to assimilate the English newcomers, expected from them too much.

The Mohegans

While Opechancanough assembled his plans and steadied his allies for an attack upon the English, a heroic assault he intended to preserve his people's way of life, the Mohegans of today's Connecticut began to come into their own as a people.

Living along the river that hopeful English settlers named the Thames, the Mohegans were closely related to other native communities in southern New England, especially the Narragansetts to their east in today's Rhode Island and the Pequots to their west. It is difficult to tell how many Mohegans lived in the region owing to the closeness of these connections. The Mohegans' largest settlement, Shantok, easily might have housed a population of several hundred people. Archaeologists estimate that the native population of New England prior to the arrival of Europeans may have been as high as 150,000.

To describe these communities as "tribes," a non-Indian construct that seldom reflected native reality, is not always helpful. For southern New England Algonquians like the Mohegans, the village was the center of their lives. These villages enjoyed a level of autonomy difficult for English observers to comprehend. Talented sachems, or leaders, could pull these village communities together into entities approximating what English and subsequent American observers called "tribes," but they remained fluid in their composition and episodic by their nature. Indeed, an examination of colonial records for early New England reveals that an Algonquian village described in one document in one year as Mohegan might later be identified as Narragansett in another and Niantic in yet another still. Villagers might shift their allegiance from one sachem to another.

The Mohegans, like Algonquians elsewhere in early America, practiced an agriculture where women planted fields with corn, beans, and squash, while men hunted and fished. Exchange amongst New England Algonquian communities was common, and these communities had developed means for incorporating and assimilating outsiders. They practiced rituals to deflect the wrath of a malevolent figure in their cosmos known by a number of different names—the English assumed that this figure was the Devil. Through ritual, they hoped to achieve order and to keep their world in balance.

And as amongst other native peoples in other parts of early America, the arrival of Europeans threatened to upset that balance. Numerous European explorers coasted the waters of the Long Island Sound, and the Dutch navigator Adriaen Block, investigating the rivers flowing through Connecticut, traded with a group he identified as "the Morhicans" in 1614. European diseases brought by explorers and fishermen preceded actual settlement. Between 1616 and 1619, an unidentified epidemic tore through the Algonquian communities along the New England coast east of Narragansett Bay. Thousands died. Thomas Morton, who settled at Plymouth Plantation on the Massachusetts coast, discovered a "new found Golgotha," with bones left littered about by the Indians who "died on heapes as they lay in their houses." The epidemic did not move west of Narragansett Bay and the Mohegans avoided at this time some of the most devastating consequences of European settlement.

While the Pilgrims, who arrived in 1620, clung to the coast, Dutch fur traders began to visit regularly the Thames and other rivers in southern New England. Dutch trade brought immediate and lasting change to the village communities lining the waters that flowed into Long Island Sound. The Dutch quickly recognized the value of wampum—small, tubular, white and purple shell beads—as a commodity in intercultural exchange. They acquired wampum primarily from the Pequots and Narragansetts in exchange for manufactured goods. Dutch traders than carried this wampum up the Connecticut and Hudson rivers to communities in the interior, exchanging it with them for furs. The Pequots and Narragansetts also involved themselves in this trade by engaging in exchange on their own, carrying surplus wampum and European trade goods into the interior to exchange for furs that they provided to the Dutch.

The resulting "wampum revolution," as one historian termed it, dramatically transformed native life in southern New England. Both the Narragansetts and Pequots moved to consolidate their control over the production of wampum, an expansionist drive that according to Plymouth's leading chronicler, William Bradford, allowed both to become "rich and powerful and also proud thereby, and fills them with pieces [guns], powder and shot." As the volume of trade increased, Algonquians spent more of their time in larger, more easily defended sites accessible to traders. Archaeological evidence shows that these settlements were likely to be surrounded by defensive palisades, a reflection of the increasing amount of warfare that resulted when different native communities tried to break into the trade.

The Pequots and Narragansetts dominated the trade, but the Mohegans were not entirely shut out. They acquired in the 1620s metal goods, including guns and bullets, in return for the foodstuffs and wampum they supplied to the Europeans. But the Mohegan sachem at Shantok, Owaneco, wanted more. He offered the Pequots an alliance, secured by the marriage of a high ranking Pequot woman to Owaneco's heir, Uncas. The alliance would secure for the Pequots the friendship of the Narragansetts' immediate neighbor, and access to the contested coast of Long Island Sound between the Thames and Narragansett Bay coveted by both but controlled by the Mohegans. The Mohegans would acquire greater access to European trade goods, they hoped, through participation in the Pequots' system of intercultural trade.

That may have been the Mohegans' intent, but clearly the Pequots understood the resulting relationship in terms very different from Owaneco. After Owaneco's death, Uncas and the Mohegans found themselves a subject people under the domination of the Pequots, forced to render them a tribute in wampum.

Uncas and other tributary peoples chafed under the Pequots' control. But because the Dutch offered the only source of highly valued European trade goods, items that held value for their utility and for the power, or *manitou*, they seemed to possess, there was little that they could do. Access to European trade goods could only be had through the Pequots, and only if one were willing to pay for the privilege.

The arrival of the Puritans in Massachusetts Bay in 1630 seemed to offer some beleaguered Algonquians an opportunity to break free from Pequot domination. Wahginnacut, the sachem of "a company of banished Indians" driven from the Connecticut River Valley, invited the newly arrived Englishmen to settle in the valley, trade with them, and protect his people from the Pequots. The Narragansetts, too, did what they could to destabilize their rival's hegemony in the valley. None of them, however, succeeded as well as Uncas in employing the English to pursue the interests of his community. Using the English, Uncas and the Mohegans emerged as a regional power.

Indeed, the Pequots' dominance over intercultural trade proved to be a remarkably short-lived phenomenon. Competition between the Pequots and the Narragansetts over access to the Dutch posts on the Connecticut River produced warfare between the Pequots on the one hand, and the Dutch and the Narragansetts on the other. The movement of English traders from Plymouth Plantation into the valley, and the migration of land-hungry colonists from the Massachusetts Bay colony intent on founding Connecticut Colony further destabilized the region. And providing a lethal context for these developments, in 1633 and 1634 smallpox struck Indians in southern New England. Indians in Connecticut, Plymouth's governor William Bradford wrote, "died most miserably" from the disease. Bradford wrote that a "sorer disease cannot befall them." Those felled by the disease, he continued, developed the sores "in abundance, and for want of bedding and linen and other helps they fall into a lamentable condition as they lie on their hard mats, the pox breaking and mattering and running one into another, their skin cleaving by reason thereof to the mats they lie on. When they turn them, a whole side will flay off at once as it were, and they will be all of a gore blood most fearful to behold. And then being what with cold and other distempers, they die like rotten sheep."

The Narragansetts, Pequots, and Mohegans all lost more than 70% of their population, a horrifying loss of life. The epidemic shattered the Algonquian world. Village communities that lost their leaders and so much of their population no longer had the numbers to survive. A significant reshuffling of peoples resulted, as survivors coalesced with others under new and ambitious leaders who rushed in to fill the void.

It was in this environment that the Pequots attacked and killed the Englishman John Stone and his eight companions along the Connecticut River. They thought Stone was Dutch, and they killed him in retaliation for an earlier Dutch assault on their people. Except that the Pequots got it wrong. They recognized their error, and tried to make peace with the English colonists. They offered wampum as compensation, and invited the English to settle on their lands in order to protect them from their enemies and to provide them with the trade goods that the war prevented them from acquiring from the Dutch. They could not hand over to the English the killers of John Stone. The Pequots explained to colonial leaders in Massachusetts that some of Stone's killers had died of smallpox, while others had been killed when Stone's ship caught fire and sank.

The Pequots were desperate. They no longer threatened the English. But Uncas, the Mohegans' leader, convinced the English colonists that they still faced a grave threat from the Pequots. He spread rumors and stories in an attempt to enlist the English in his efforts to break free from Pequot domination. Some of these stories might have been true, but it is difficult to know for sure. Uncas told a Plymouth trader that the Pequots had lied when they said Stone's killers all were dead. Five of the killers remained alive. He told the English that the Pequots had been plotting to ambush one of Plymouth's trading vessels on the river, but called off the attack at the last second. The Pequots, Uncas told the Puritans, were now planning an attack "out of desperate madness" against the English and the Mohegans.

The Puritans seem to sincerely have believed that they faced an existential threat, but all that they heard of Pequot hostility came from their many tributaries and rivals, from peoples who wanted to free themselves from the Pequots' domination. These communities saw the power of the English as a weapon they might deploy against their native enemies. The English from Massachusetts Bay, fearing the dangers of inaction, attacked. They went first to Block Island, off of the coast of Rhode Island, and roughed up Narragansett allies who had killed a settler named John Oldham. Then, under the leadership of John Endicott, they advanced on Pequot Harbor. The English burned a village, destroyed its crops, and killed a few dogs. All the residents had fled. Entirely without friends, the Pequots began to waylay careless soldiers who strayed too far from the English post at Saybrook, at the river's mouth. In April 1637, they moved upriver, and fell upon the new Connecticut settlement at Wethersfield. It was a bold stroke, and may have regained for the Pequots the confidence of some of their allies.

Uncas told the English that unless they retaliated for the Wethersfield attack, which resulted in the death of a small number of colonists and several Puritan women being taken captive, the Indians in Connecticut would view the English as cowards. Uncas demanded that they act against his enemy, or face the frightening prospect of a combined and larger native force that neither respected nor feared the Puritans. The resulting conflict is known as the Pequot War, but it can better be understood as a series of ambushes and bloody raids, a conflict between native communities into which English bystanders were dragged by skilled leaders like Uncas. In April, he guided Connecticut's forces personally to the Pequots' palisaded village along the Mystic River, and encircled it while the English attacked, so that no Pequot could escape. Few did. The English forces who first entered the fort found the fighting too fierce, so they set the village on fire. "Great and doleful was the bloody sight," wrote one English observer, "to see so many souls lie gasping on the ground, so thick in some places, that you could hardly pass along." Between 400 and 700 Pequots died in the fires of Mystic.

The English manner of warfare, the region's native peoples learned, was grotesquely violent. The Narragansetts described the English way of war, which involved the indiscriminate slaughter of men, women, and children, as "naught," or evil. They fought savagely. Uncas

Figure 2.3 Massacre of the Pequots.

learned that the Puritan desire for vengeance was great, their capacity for violence was extraordinary, and that they would not hesitate to destroy those people who stood in their way, and to enslave those left behind. He decided that he would work to remain a "friend to the English." Maintaining this friendship, he believed, could not be done from a position of weakness. The Pequots, after all, had offered the English all that they had. As Uncas worked to convince the Puritans that he and his people were allies upon whom they could rely, he also worked tirelessly to maintain the strength and power necessary to demonstrate to them that he could pose a dangerous threat should he become disaffected.

The defeat of the Pequots created a power vacuum along the Connecticut River, which the colonies of Connecticut and Massachusetts Bay competed to fill. The Narragansetts and Mohegans, as well, hoped to supplant the Pequots and dominate the region's intercultural commerce. The leaders of each community, the Narragansett leader Miantonomi and Uncas, cultivated the allegiance of the competing colonies. In this, Uncas proved far more successful. He convinced the leaders of the Massachusetts Bay Colony that he was a firm friend, that "I have no men; they are all yours," and pledged the Puritans "to command me anything, I will do it; I will not believe any Indians' word against the English; and if any man shall kill an Englishman, I will put him to death, were he never so dear to me." At the same time, he leaked information and spread rumors to the leaders of the New England colonies that the

Narragansetts were plotting against the English; that they were trying to lure the feared Mohawks and the embattled Indians who lived in the vicinity of New Netherland to join in an assault against the colonies.

Rumors of Narragansett plots continued to mount. Uncas maintained a constant drumbeat of ominous news. The point was clear. The Narragansetts threatened the English colonists. Uncas served as the eyes and ears of the English colonists on the frontier. They could have no order without him. By 1643, after a brief conflict, Uncas received the blessings of the English to put his Narragansett rival to death. That he asked the permission of the English to kill his Narragansett captive shows that he understood the provisions of a treaty negotiated between the Mohegans and Narragansetts over the disposition of Pequot survivors.

Uncas found himself walking a treacherous path between the English, his native rivals, and the growing numbers of people over whom he had exerted his influence and rendered tributary. His interests and those of the Puritan colonists had become closely intertwined. The colonists relied upon him to keep them informed about conditions on the frontier, to furnish them with military assistance, and to provide them with intelligence on the activities of native communities that might threaten English security. In return, he received certain benefits: English support as he extended his sway over other Pequot survivors and their former tributaries, and the fact that the English were more likely to believe him than any of his rivals. With English assistance, by 1643 the Mohegans had emerged as a regional power in southern New England.

New Worlds

"First contact" between natives and newcomers was a tricky thing, far more complicated than perhaps it at first seemed. Native peoples welcomed Europeans ashore, in places, but they did so for reasons that eluded their would-be colonizers. They saw in the newcomers military allies, or valuable trading partners, or people with great power who could bring benefits to their communities. Indians tried to assimilate Europeans into their world, just as much if not more than Europeans attempted to Christianize and civilize Indians.

This they did in a new world that must have horrified many native peoples. Disease and violence and enslavement tore gaping holes in the fabric of native communities. New communities formed out of the wreckage of the old in these shatter zones, a process called "ethnogenesis." De Soto utterly transformed the hierarchical chiefdoms through which he marched. New leaders, and new communities, emerged as a result of the horrors of contact. Some of them, with European assistance, became significant powers with whom the newcomers had to reckon carefully. The peoples we know of as the Cherokees, and as well the Creeks, Chickasaws, Choctaws, and Yamasees, emerged from this massive shuffling of survivors. They learned that living with the newcomers was not easy. The success of European settlement certainly was not inevitable, and in places, Indians forced Europeans to play by their rules. Europeans lacked the power to dictate unilaterally the nature of their relationships with native peoples. Still, European colonization quickly produced violence and warfare. The arrival of Europeans brought devastation to the peoples they encountered, changing their lives forever. These waves of devastation spread rapidly across the continent.

3

LIVING IN THE NEW WORLD

The arrival of Europeans, whether along the Atlantic seaboard, among the Pueblos in the southwest, or in the American southeast, sent powerful waves of change coursing across the continent. As a result, many native peoples learned about the newcomers long before they encountered them face to face. The trade goods Europeans carried moved over long established native pathways of exchange. The deadly microbes that arrived with the newcomers in places advanced rapidly as well. For those isolated from these trading networks, or spared the destruction wreaked by European pathogens, stories of the newcomers drifted into the interior of the continent. Even before their encounter with the newcomers, native people acted upon these rumors, stories, and stray pieces of information. Colonization brought significant change, but Indians did not wait passively for Europeans to act upon them. Europeans, who in the seventeenth century clung to the edge of a continent still dominated by native peoples, with its own histories, cultures, and capitals, confronted native peoples who had their own agendas, and as a result the newcomers' plans for carving out American Empires never worked out in quite the way that they had envisioned.

Mourning Wars

The Haudenosaunee Longhouse, centered at Onondaga, with the Mohawks and Senecas, respectively, as the keepers of the eastern and western doors, preserved peace among its members. Like other peoples in the Eastern Woodlands, the Iroquois lived in villages surrounded by fields planted with maize, beans, and squash, the mythical "Three Sisters." Orchards stood nearby. Iroquois women tended these crops and played a leading role in community affairs. While men served as sachems and warriors, and moved through the woods to hunt and fish and fight, within the clearings women appointed the League sachems and influenced the community's decisions about peace and war and the disposition of captives. The men and women of Iroquoia, whose gendered roles balanced and complemented one another, performed the rituals necessary to keep the world in balance and to allow them to interact effectively with the forces, human and other-than-human, that inhabited their cosmos.

They were no strangers to change, and by the time English settlers established Jamestown in 1607, the Iroquois world long had been in flux. The peoples whom Cartier encountered in the St. Lawrence valley in the first half of the sixteenth century lived in Iroquois and other communities throughout the eastern Great Lakes. The communities that adopted these villagers

Native America: A History, Second Edition. Michael Leroy Oberg.
© 2018 John Wiley & Sons, Inc. Published 2018 by John Wiley & Sons, Inc.

gained the assistance thereby of peoples with trading ties in the St. Lawrence, and some experience in dealing with Europeans—whether Cartier or the men on board the hundreds of Basque vessels that came to Canadian shores each year to dry their catch and trade for furs.

But for the most part, Haudenosaunee contact with the newcomers remained indirect. They valued the trade goods that flowed into the Longhouse both for their utilitarian function and their spiritual value. The metal tools they acquired allowed them to perform traditional tasks easily and more expeditiously, but they also manifested the great power that the newcomers seemed to possess. Iroquois men and women wanted more of these items. Even the Senecas, farthest geographically from the nascent European outposts, acquired some of these goods. Archaeologists have found European metal objects—copper and iron—in Seneca sites in the west as well as among the Onondagas and Mohawks as early as 1540, though it is unclear how these goods arrived in the Senecas' homeland. By the early seventeenth century, the quantity of these goods increased in Seneca sites, and the Senecas began to bury more of their dead with trade goods. Archaeologists believe that the Senecas joined the Iroquois League at about this time, gaining allies among the four nations to their east and the ability to carry their furs into and through the territories of their neighbors. Seneca men traveled widely to trade either with the Dutch directly or with the rest of the Haudenosaunee.

Still, other native communities limited the amount of direct contact with Europeans. The Canadian Algonquins, Montagnais, and Hurons occupied the territories between the Iroquois and the fledgling French outpost established at Quebec in 1608. The Susquehannocks, who sometime in the sixteenth century left their homes in south-central New York for the headwaters of the Potomac, occupied those lands between the Five Nations and the English settlement at Jamestown. The Mahicans, finally, occupied those Hudson valley lands that lay between the Mohawks and the Dutch.

In 1609, a significant breach in this isolation occurred. The French began to probe the margins of Iroquoia. The Dutch, meanwhile, began to explore the Hudson and other rivers flowing into Long Island Sound. By 1624, they had established Fort Orange, at the site of today's Albany and, in 1626, New Amsterdam on the southern tip of Manhattan Island. The newcomers kept their distance from the Iroquois. With a small population, the Dutch hoped to collect furs at Fort Orange and ship them to market in Holland. By 1628, aided apparently by an outbreak of European disease among their Mahican enemies, the Mohawks routed their eastern enemy and gained access to the storehouse at Fort Orange.

The Mohawks acquired from Dutch traders pipes, tobacco, and wampum, the shell beads acquired from their Algonquian trading partners on Long Island Sound and vital to the conduct of Iroquois diplomacy. Mohawk traders acquired kettles and pots that creative native artisans fashioned into metal arrowheads and ornaments. They also traded their furs for guns and ammunition. These items moved throughout the Longhouse.

The Five Nations saw commerce not simply as a business transaction—the exchange of pelts for European manufactured goods—but as part of a relationship based on reciprocity, respect, and kinship. Mohawk orators at Fort Orange lectured the Dutch on the behavior they expected from their "brothers." They provided the Dutch with etiquette lessons, rules for behaving in a relationship that had obvious economic elements but was to the members of the Five Nations also emotional and spiritual. Iroquois orators at Fort Orange spoke of drying tears, of clearing throats, of setting minds aright and removing the obstructions from the path to the Dutch post. They described to the Dutch a relationship between kin secured by the reciprocal exchange of gifts and kindness. The Dutch do not seem to have recognized the values and beliefs that shaped Five Nations economic behavior. Iroquois diplomacy, the Dutch learned, took time. Iroquois leaders sought understanding and consensus, what they called a good mind. The potential for misunderstanding always existed, and violence threatened frequently. Mohawks complained of Dutch traders, on occasion, who attempted to coerce the Iroquois into trading exclusively with them at Fort Orange. In the case of the relationship between the Five Nations and the Dutch, however, the demands of intercultural trade allowed for a working relationship. The Dutch did not intrude into Haudenosaunee territory in a sustained fashion, and they did not take their land. The principle underscoring this relationship Haudenosaunee people today call "Guswenta," which they assert is represented by the "Two-Row" wampum belt: like the two purple, parallel lines on this belt, the Dutch and the Haudenosaunee would travel the same river together in peace and cooperation, but their paths would not cross, and they would not interfere in the internal affairs of the other.

This relationship worked, but the same waves of epidemic disease that had devastated the Mohegans cut into the heart of Iroquoia, and continued to descend upon the Longhouse regularly for several decades. Measles hit in 1633, and smallpox followed the next year. The Mohawk population, which stood at 8000 at the beginning of 1634, fell to around 3000 within a matter of months. The nearby Mohawks suffered most heavily, but not even the distant Senecas were spared the devastation of epidemic disease. In the wake of these epidemics, the Senecas and their Longhouse kin lashed out at their neighbors, intensifying their decades' old raiding. The "Massawomecks," who John Smith learned had fought against the Powhatans prior to the arrival of the English in the Chesapeake, may have been Senecas. Iroquois warriors began to attack the Hurons, or Wendats, themselves members of a confederacy of Iroquoian peoples whose culture and history paralleled that of the Five Nations in important ways, in the 1630s. There were furs in the Hurons' homeland, but more than that these Iroquois warriors sought prisoners, prospective adoptees, who could take the place of Iroquois people who had died in wars and from epidemic diseases. The members of the Five Nations believed that the power of a lineage, a clan, a village, or a community suffered for each individual lost. Iroquois peoples, as well, recognized that grief unassuaged could bring destruction. This the legend of the Peacemaker made clear. The adoption of captives was one socially sanctioned way to alleviate this grief. As a result, Iroquois raids on their neighbors took on the quality of a "mourning war."

The easternmost of the Five Nations ambushed Huron parties on the St. Lawrence, as they made their way from their hunts north and west of Lake Ontario to the French post at Montreal. The western Iroquois—Onondagas, Cayugas, and Senecas—crossed the Niagara River to attack the Hurons on their own ground. These attacks increased in size and frequency over the course of the 1640s. The final assault began in 1648.

An invasion force made up mostly of Senecas attacked the Huron village at Teanaostaiae. Ravaged by the diseases brought by Jesuit missionaries, the Hurons were outmanned and outgunned. The Senecas first killed the priest, chopped up his body, and burned his remains in the church. The Senecas then pursued the Hurons who survived the initial attack, adopting hundreds of captives. The Hurons launched a number of retaliatory raids, but by the end of 1649, their villages had been destroyed, their population dispersed. The survivors took refuge near Quebec, or they fled to the west, finding respite, albeit temporarily, near present-day Sandusky, Ohio, where they became known as Wyandots. The Iroquois adopted many others and incorporated them into their towns. The Senecas absorbed more than 500 Hurons. That some of these adoptees were Catholic converts would soon color and shape Iroquois village politics. We must not assume that the adoptees surrendered their culture entirely;

they brought into their new villages systems of belief and philosophy that enriched the community and complicated its relations with outsiders.

Seneca raiders fell as well upon the Susquehannocks, who by the 1640s lived at the head of the Chesapeake Bay. In 1663, after two decades of Iroquois raids, the Susquehannocks drove back the Senecas and their Longhouse kin, inflicting heavy casualties as they did so. The defeat was the first of a number of disasters to strike the Five Nations that year. The Mohawks faced attack from Christian Indians and Mahicans armed by the New England Puritans. The Sokokis of the Connecticut River Valley repulsed a force of Onondagas, Mohawks, and Oneidas who attacked them. French-allied Algonquians, meanwhile, prepared raids against the Longhouse. Smallpox struck again, and the Dutch outposts on the Hudson fell to an English military invasion in 1664. The Susquehannocks razed Onondaga in 1666 before retiring with heavy casualties of their own, and the French launched raids against the Mohawks.

The Haudenosaunee faced a significant crisis. Disease led to more deaths, and left more Iroquois grieving. As the epidemics killed more members of the Longhouse, the Five Nations needed growing numbers of captives to fill their places. Mourning warfare, once a specific and episodic response to a specific situation, became endemic, with enormous human consequences. But that was not all. The peoples upon whom Iroquois raids fell, as the seventeenth century progressed, increasingly armed themselves with the same firearms that the warriors of the Five Nations carried. Few Iroquois war parties managed to return home without suffering casualties. A dangerous spiral resulted: disease led to more frequent mourning wars fought with firearms that made these raids more dangerous; the need for guns and ammunition to fight these wars led to an increased demand for the pelts needed to trade for them; Iroquois hunters and warriors traveled farther and farther to acquire the furs necessary for this trade, provoking new wars with native peoples farther afield. And through it all the spiral of death continued, sucking the Five Nations into a destructive cycle of warfare and violence.

Iroquois warriors in the 1660s struck native peoples to their east, Algonquians and other French-allied Indians to their north, Dakota Sioux in the Upper Mississippi River Valley, the scores of native communities huddled in the region south of the Great Lakes that the French called the *pays d'en haut*, and natives to their south like the Susquehannocks. The Iroquois absorbed an enormous number of captives. French missionaries estimated that two-thirds of the people living in Iroquoia were adoptees.

Even with these adoptees, Iroquois population continued to decline. The Iroquois suffered badly in this warfare, which could be horrifically violent. A Seneca party, for instance, in the 1660s raided a Miami village in northern Ohio. With the Miami men away hunting, the Senecas destroyed the village and took their wives and children captive. The Miami hunters, upon discovering what had happened, gave chase to the Senecas and confronted head-on the violence that could characterize indigenous warfare. Each night, according to the surviving Miami account, the Senecas ate one child. And every morning, they took another child, stuck a spear through its head, and left the child for their pursuers to find. The Senecas moved fast, but the grieving Miamis ran them down one day shy of the Senecas' village. They attacked and killed all but two of the warriors who had killed their children. They freed their remaining people. The Miamis, then, cut the hands, noses, and ears off from the two survivors, and sent the maimed men home with a grisly message: necklaces made from the heads and hands of their dead comrades. Clearly the mourning war complex no longer was fulfilling its cardinal function of restoring the Longhouse to peace and a good mind. The Mohawks had nearly 800 warriors in the 1640s; by the 1670s fewer than 300 remained in the Mohawk valley. Many had died, while others relocated to the St. Lawrence valley. The rest of the Five Nations suffered similarly, with people lost and people leaving. European observers noted the divisions in Iroquois communities between Christians and non-Christians, and those who leaned toward the French or toward the English, and between those who hoped to remain apart, and survive as an autonomous people.

Colonizing the Mohegans

The crisis that affected the Five Nations did not develop in isolation. Across the continent, the period from the 1630s through to the end of the seventeenth century was one of profound significance for native peoples, as they struggled to learn how to live with the newcomers.

In the aftermath of Miantonomi's death, Uncas's Mohegans faced the wrath of their Narragansett rivals, as well as that of the Narragansetts' numerous allies. Uncas continued to act on the lessons he had learned during the Pequot War of 1636 and 1637. Armed resistance to the English, in his view, remained a losing proposition. The Mohegans must confront the reality of the Puritans' presence in southern New England and recognize their considerable military power. The Mohegans thus must make themselves useful to the newcomers, and Uncas worked to remain always a "friend to the English." This friendship, he knew, could not be maintained from a position of weakness. The Puritans would respect only those native peoples they feared, so Uncas worked to maintain as much strength and power as possible. The Mohegans could help the newcomers, Uncas continuously told them, but his people could also pose a significant threat to the Puritan colonists should they become disaffected.

Uncas and his followers consistently informed the English when Miantonomi's successors sought to avenge his death. They peppered Connecticut, Massachusetts, and the combined United Colonies of New England with reports and rumors of sinister Narragansett conspiracies. Because the English threatened, fined, and otherwise persecuted the Narragansetts, the Mohegans learned that they could use colonial power against their native rivals; indeed, Uncas fabricated some of the stories of "conspiracy" in which the Narragansetts and a host of others stood accused of plotting against the colonists in order to bring down upon his Algonquian rivals the Puritans' wrath.

Uncas and the Mohegans maneuvered to protect their communities against a backdrop of declining Algonquian power. His great rival, Miantonomi, in 1643 warned that unless native peoples came together, "we shall all be gone shortly." Miantonomi reminded the Montauks on Long Island how "our fathers had plenty of deer and skins," and how "our plains were full of deer, as also our woods, and of turkeys, and our coves full of fish and fowl." But now, he continued, the Puritans had "gotten our land," and "they with scythes cut down the grass, and their hogs spoil our clam banks, and we shall all be starved." Miantonomi described the environmental assault native peoples faced from European colonization.

Beginning in the 1650s and accelerating rapidly thereafter, as the threats to the Puritan colonists appeared gradually to diminish, and as the English population grew and expanded rapidly, the Puritan Saints had less need for Indian allies like Uncas. Settlers in Connecticut coveted the Mohegans' lands. Some they acquired from the Mohegans' disgruntled tributaries, who willingly sold out their overlords. Uncas and his supporters transferred much of the rest to colonial friends like John Mason to ensure the goodwill and assistance of high-placed colonists. Other sales, no doubt, they undertook with more reluctance. The Mohegans, and their neighbors, often sold lands that already had been squatted upon and occupied by settlers. These lands they sold at bargain-basement prices. They hoped to acquire something

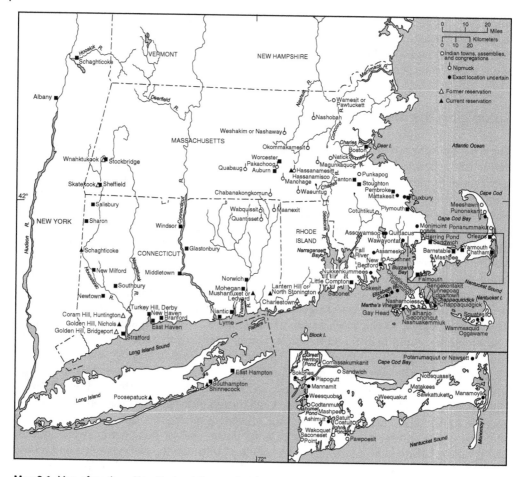

Map 3.1 Map of southern New England. Source: *Smithsonian Handbook of North American Indians*, Vol. 15, Northeast, pp. 15: 178. Courtesy of Smithsonian Institution.

for lands that, as a matter of fact, they already had lost. Mohegan land sales, like those of other native peoples, involved elements both of choice and coercion.

The loss of lands forced changes in subsistence practices, and here again the Mohegans' experience was not unique. With their dwindling supply of land increasingly encircled by colonial farms, Mohegan hunters found it more and more difficult to acquire adequate supplies of game. Mohegans and their neighbors stayed afloat by working on the margins of settler society: making wood splint baskets, catching stray hogs, hunting wolves. Some became servants in colonial households. They could exchange their labor for the few things they needed but, increasingly, all they had left that colonists wanted was land.

Settlers pressed upon the Mohegans, but so did their animals. Colonial livestock did damage in Mohegan cornfields. The voracious animals also consumed the forage upon which deer and other animals relied. And with their fields surrounded, colonized Indians like the Mohegans could no longer abandon their worn out tracts. Some Mohegans began to raise their own livestock. They also insisted on the right to gather foodstuffs of little value to the colonists on the lands they had ceded, but making ends meet became increasingly difficult.

The Mohegans and their neighbors also found themselves subject to a colonial legal system, as the English gained the power to extend their jurisdiction over their native neighbors. At the outset, colonial powers had to pay attention to native conceptions of justice: of what was right and fair, of how to adjudicate disputes, and how to bring conflicting parties to peace and balance. By the 1650s, this no longer was the case in southern New England. Colonial law defined Indians as outsiders, living within the English provinces but not as a part of the commonwealth. Colonial courts punished Indians for drunkenness, for engaging in "labor or play on the Sabbath," for not being like the colonists. They faced legal limits on their ability to purchase powder and shot, and the colonists prohibited them from purchasing horses or "any boat or boat rigging." Dispossession and the law thus worked hand in hand to bind the Mohegans and their neighbors firmly on the margins of colonial society.

They learned, as a result, to keep a low profile. They knew they would face whippings and violence for violations of colonial law in a legal system that treated them as less than second class citizens. For other offenses, sachems might be fined, a penalty that often could be paid only through the cession of land. Given the restrictions on their freedom, it is indeed remarkable how few references to the Mohegans occur in Connecticut's colonial records. Becoming invisible became a way to survive.

The Mohegans faced land-hungry English farmers and biased English judges and juries. They faced as well Puritan preachers and missionaries. In the seventeenth century, the Mohegans successfully rebuffed the efforts of the Puritans to proselytize them, and Uncas frustrated the few missionaries who tried to minister to his people. Other native communities in the northeast proved more receptive to the Christians' message, but not always for the reasons that the missionaries anticipated.

The Word of God

After a number of abortive attempts, the Jesuit fathers of New France finally succeeded in establishing missions among the Iroquois. They did so in the wake of French raids in 1665 and 1666 designed to eliminate Iroquois interference with the colony's distant native allies in the fur trade. As such the Jesuits entered communities on the defensive. Even those members of the Five Nations who had never before encountered the "Black Robes" had heard much about them, for among the large numbers of native peoples absorbed into Iroquois villages were those who had accepted the priests' Catholic faith or already had rejected it. Some told horrifying tales of the strangely dressed priests who deployed sorcery, and described how the magic they used, the Catholic sacrament of baptism, killed Indians. Many of them believed, one Jesuit priest learned, that the Black Robes carried disease and suffering everywhere they went. That the members of the Longhouse believed stories such as these is not surprising: the priests did on occasion carry disease into their missions, and because they baptized Indians only as they fell gravely ill, the Iroquois and other native peoples associated the death of their kinsmen with the actions of the priests.

But the Iroquois could not turn the French away. It was no longer that simple. Battered in warfare, they needed the trade goods that alliance with the French might bring, and that alliance required of the Five Nations a willingness to permit the Jesuits to begin preaching and building missions in their territory. Certainly the missionaries recognized, as Father Francois le Mercier observed, "that the whole country of the Iroquois was at that time greatly in fear of a renewed French invasion."

Fear of the French and a desire to acquire their trade goods certainly explains some of the Five Nations' interest in converting to Catholicism. Father Jean Pierron told the Mohawks, for instance, that unless they converted the French would not trust them. "Be assured," he said, "that we shall never believe that you wish to live on good terms with us until you serve the same Master that we serve… In order to have a firm and unshakable peace of the sort you desire, you must be like me and believe what I believe." The Mohawks, Pierron reported, soon after "devoted themselves to prayer" and he believed that "one could not ask for a greater inclination for the faith than that which appears in our Indians." At the point of a gun, some embraced a new faith.

It would be wrong, however, to dismiss the Indians' interest in Christianity as merely a means to an end. If some Catholic converts remarked upon the sinister power of the Black Robes and the destruction their arrival wrought, others welcomed the return of the Jesuits into their lives. These adoptees became, in many cases, the most fervent followers and supporters of the priests. And they could tell stories of the Jesuits' virtues, of their abilities as healers, of the power of their rituals.

Historians once interpreted Christianity and religious conversion as something done by colonists to the colonized. Religious conversion, in this sense, became an instrument of cold war in the early American contest of cultures. It was a non-violent, but no less certain, instrument of conquest. Yet the Jesuits could not have established their missions without the native peoples who listened to and considered their message, weighed that message against what they knew of the world, and concluded that the faith or the rituals of the Black Robes offered more satisfactory solutions to the problems they faced than did their traditional beliefs. Many converts combined elements of old and new, Christianity with traditional religion, in an attempt to make sense of a world that had changed rapidly before their eyes.

After the French raids of 1665, many Iroquois began moving northward to settle in mission communities linked to, but still separate from, the French colonial regime. Mohawks, Oneidas, and their adoptees moved to the village of Kanawake. Some Senecas, Cayugas, and Onondagas, meanwhile, migrated across the Niagara River into the lands that had been occupied by their Huron adoptees. In time they established themselves in mission villages as the *Iroquois du Nord*.

Protestants in southern New England attempted missions as well. Beginning in 1651, the Puritan missionary John Eliot founded the first of a dozen or so "Praying Towns" in the Massachusetts Bay Colony. Other missionaries worked among the Algonquian communities on Nantucket Island and on Martha's Vineyard. According to Eliot, "the order of proceeding with them is first to gather them together from their scattered course of life, to cohabitation and civil order and government, and then to form them (the Lord having fitted them) into visible Church-State, for the guidance whereof, I have instructed them, that they should look only into the Scriptures, and out of the word of God fetch all their Wisdom, Laws, and Government, and so shall they be the Lord's people, and the Lord above shall Reign over them, and govern them in all things by the word of his mouth." To settle in a "Praying Town," then, native peoples accepted a system of biblical control where English authorities proscribed and punished those practices that they deemed offensive and irreligious.

The rules were rigid, but a small but growing number of New England Algonquians found attractive the benefits of a close association with the English ministers. Some Indians undoubtedly converted for expedient reasons. By submitting themselves to the English, they might free themselves from their tributary obligations to sachems like Uncas. Some converts saw in cooperation with the missionaries a means to expand or increase their power in their communities. Waban, for instance, rose from a position of obscurity to become a community leader at the Praying Town of Natick in Massachusetts. Still others may have settled in the Praying Towns for the trade goods and the agricultural equipment the missionaries supplied. English goods and access to their technology provided the converts with instruments they could use to adapt to the new world created by expanding white settlements.

Still, there can be no doubting that a significant spiritual component existed in many of these conversions, and the acceptance of Christian principles and belief appears to have been tied closely to native understandings of religion, ritual, and the relative spiritual power of natives and newcomers. Waban settled with the English only after a "great sickness" killed many of his friends but left the Puritans unharmed. Totherswamp, another of Eliot's converts, settled in a Praying Town only after witnessing the horrors and loss of epidemic disease. After God sent the affliction among his family and friends, Totherswamp reported, "then my heart feared, and I thought, that now I will pray unto God."

The destruction wreaked by epidemics planted in Algonquian minds seeds of doubt. In the face of illnesses that killed Indians but did nothing to the English, some Indians feared that their rituals had lost their effectiveness. Christianity, with its own rituals, might offer a better way. Certainly Eliot believed that the destruction caused by disease would lead the Algonquians to this conclusion. "It pleased God to work wonderfully for the Indians, who call upon God," Eliot reported, "in preserving them from the small Pox, when their profane neighbors were cut off by it."

Those Indians willing to stay in the Praying Towns may as well have benefited from the Puritans' recognition of their lands as Indian space, albeit in a qualified manner. Still, the converts found that many colonists had little affection for Indians, whether Christian or not. Indians who settled in Praying Towns faced the distrust of their English neighbors, many of whom clamored for the lands Eliot set aside for the natives' use. Whether Christian or not, native peoples in New England faced the aggressions of a land hungry population, whose unwillingness to stay off of their lands by the 1670s threatened the Indians' survival.

The resulting conflict, known commonly as King Philip's War, found its origins in the colony of Plymouth Plantation. Led by their sachem Philip, known also as Metacom and Metacomet, the Pokanokets complained repeatedly to the colony's government of a long series of injuries they had suffered at the hands of English settlers. They faced a rapidly growing English population, massive pressure upon their remaining lands, and significant threats to their subsistence regime. And they had no place left to go.

As early as 1667, rumors of Philip conspiring against the English colonists began to circulate. He frequently found himself in the following years dragged before colonial courts to answer a variety of charges. The execution of three of Philip's followers for the murder of a Christian Indian who earlier had befriended and then betrayed Philip, provided the final spark. Tensions mounted. Settlers fled their exposed farmsteads after they murdered two of Philip's followers they caught rummaging around an abandoned English farm. Philip's forces retaliated for this killing in the summer of 1675.

Philip's warriors hit the English settlements at Swansea and Middleborough. Other attacks, by other native communities allied with Philip and with their own grievances against the English, led the colonists to conclude that all the natives in the region had joined in savage war against them. The Puritans in Massachusetts Bay and Plymouth attacked native peoples recklessly, alienating Indians who had hoped to stay out of the conflict, and driving them into what quickly had become a region-wide Algonquian uprising.

The inability of English troops from the Massachusetts Bay Colony and Plymouth Plantation to successfully engage their growing number of enemies produced a level of fear and frustration that manifested itself in racist violence. The Puritans sold captured Indians into slavery in the West Indies, and thus taught their Algonquian enemies that they had no reason to surrender. The Praying Indians, who one distrustful colonist dubbed "Preying Indians," the Massachusetts council dispatched to small concentration camps on the islands in Boston Harbor. Facing such treatment, many of the Christian Indians joined in the uprising. Colonial authorities executed other Indians, or fed them to colonial war dogs that tore them limb from limb.

Where colonists suspected all Indians of shedding English blood, the Mohegans recognized the importance of demonstrating their fidelity. They feared the violence of English warfare. Uncas offered his people's assistance to the English in Connecticut. Armed with English guns and freshly supplied with English powder and shot, the Mohegans seized the opportunity to prove their value to Connecticut's leaders and to settle old scores. In New England, where the Puritans had come to fear and suspect Indians of the bloodiest of murders, and where colonists could be executed for selling Indians weapons, Connecticut placed muskets in the hands of their Mohegan allies. Their participation, certainly, was limited, but they attacked their old rivals, the Narragansetts, and other native groups participating in the massive uprising.

The warfare brought short term benefits to the Mohegans in the form of adoptees and additional population. Some hostile Algonquians accepted incorporation into Mohegan village communities as an alternative to summary execution at the hands of vengeful Puritans or a short but brutal life in West Indian slavery. The Mohegans deployed the guns and ammunition they received to good effect, against the Puritans' numerous foes and for themselves. When the colony consented to pay the Mohegans for each captive they brought in, it sanctioned the types of raiding and traditional captive-taking that long had characterized native warfare. Payment in cloth, in knives and kettles and pots, and in guns and ammunition, meant that the Mohegans had access to the highly valued English trade goods that only the sale of their lands could have provided. The adoption and incorporation of captives allowed the Mohegans to engage in the practices that had, after the Pequot War, transformed them into a regional power.

It would prove to be a short-lived renascence, for after the war New England once again had little use for Indians. While the Mohegans learned to live in a postwar world in which the Puritan survivors expressed openly their hatred for all native peoples, the governor of the English colony of New York, Sir Edmund Andros, feared that the Indian warfare to his east might spill into his territory. Working with the equally talented Onondaga orator Daniel Garacontié, Andros began to forge the Covenant Chain alliance, an intercultural accord that linked together the Five Nations, the English, and other Indians into a loose union directed towards securing peace along the Anglo-American frontier.

At Albany shortly after the war began, Andros met with Iroquois ambassadors. He promised that he would protect the Five Nations from the French and from their native enemies to the north and east. In exchange, he asked the Mohawks to attack Philip's followers who had settled for the winter at Hoosick, a spot about fifty miles to the east of Albany. He provided them with arms and ammunition.

The resulting Iroquois raids made possible the defeat of King Philip. The Mohawks attacked and defeated Philip's warriors. Some of Philip's followers fled to the east. Others returned to southern New England where they ran into colonial militias that had learned how to fight Indian style and how best to employ native allies like the Mohegans. Philip's uprising came to a close where it began. Starving, reeling from defeat, and in fear of Iroquois marauders, a combined force of colonists and Christian Indians tracked down Philip on the Mount Hope Peninsula. There a Christian Indian shot and killed him. The English then cut off Philip's head, quartered his body, and hung the pieces in four trees. The Puritans sold Philip's children into West Indian slavery.

After the Mohawks' crushing blow, Andros invited the defeated Algonquians to leave southern New England where they faced the vicious prospect of postwar Puritan justice, and settle under the protection of the Crown in New York. Many accepted his offer. Some Mohegans considered relocation. The resettled Algonquian bands provided Andros with a buffer against a possible French invasion, and secured for traders at Albany more influence over the English colonists' Indian trade. He also acquired control over the conduct of much of the region's Indian policy. Many New England Algonquians had become Mohawks, and the Five Nations asserted that any meetings with the Puritans would take place in Albany with the governor of New York present. Andros, a dutiful servant to his king Charles II, shared his monarch's contempt for the small-minded Puritans, religious bigots who, among other offenses, had provoked a needless war that threatened the entire Anglo-American empire.

Colonizing the Powhatans

The Iroquois and Andros had forged the first links of what came to be known as the Covenant Chain. It benefited the English, but it also secured the northern and eastern frontiers of Iroquoia, and resulted in the adoption and incorporation of hundreds of Algonquian refugees from New England. But this was only the first step, and for Andros and the Five Nations to complete the Chain, crises facing the Powhatans of Virginia and their neighbors demanded resolution.

In the years after the uprising of 1622, the Powhatans continued to face enormous pressures upon their land. Opechancanough, reportedly close to 100 years old, led his final great uprising against the English colonists in the spring of 1644. Four hundred colonists died in the initial attacks, but the colonists recovered. By the spring of 1646, colonial troops headed by Governor-General Sir William Berkeley had captured Opechancanough and pounded the Powhatans so badly that he believed in "the almost impossibility of a further revenge upon them." After an Indian-hating frontiersman murdered Opechancanough in his jail cell, the new Powhatan leader, Necotowance, acknowledged English dominion over his people. He ceded to Berkeley all the lands between the York and the James rivers, from the falls to the Chesapeake Bay, and acknowledged the right of any Englishman to kill on sight Indians who entered the ceded territory. Governor Berkeley, in turn, promised to protect the remnants of the Powhatans from their native neighbors, and recognized their right to inhabit their remaining lands "without any interruption from the English."

The governor recognized that Opechancanough's rising, in 1644 as in 1622, had been provoked by the aggressive and unrestrained expansion of colonial settlement. Berkeley tried to relieve tension between settlers and Indians. He prohibited the enslavement of the Powhatans, for instance. He quickly called for the repeal of the provision in the 1646 agreement with Necotowance that allowed colonists to kill Indians who entered English lands. He feared that the "rashness and unadvicedness" of the colonists could lead to the indiscriminate slaughter of friendly Indians.

Yet forces of change in the colony conspired against both the Powhatans and Berkeley. The governor never found the order that he sought, nor did the Powhatans. Though the Indians lived on the margins and some by the middle of the century had begun to dress like the colonists, and speak English, competition for control of the land generated increasingly harsh assessments of native peoples. Some of the Powhatans, by 1660, served the colonists as slaves for life, despite laws prohibiting the practice. At the same time, they found themselves pinched between the English and more powerful Indians who began moving into the region. The Susquehannocks, caught between the Maryland English and the Senecas, settled by the mid-1670s along the northern bank of the Potomac River. The Susquehannocks and another Potomac group known as the Doegs had by 1676 no place else to go, and no choice but to resist colonial encroachments on their lands.

It was along the Potomac River that the events that led to Bacon's Rebellion took place. Things began in a routine enough fashion. Some Doegs and Susquehannocks took the hogs of a frontier settler who repeatedly had cheated them in trade. The Potomac settlers killed some of the Indians in a needlessly violent attempt to reclaim their livestock. The Doegs retaliated, killing several of the settlers involved. Local Virginia militiamen approached the Susquehannocks' fort along the Potomac. They met with the Susquehannock emissaries, and slaughtered them under a flag of truce. Frontier planters would pay for this treacherous and savage act with their lives. Susquehannock warriors moved along the fall lines of Virginia's rivers, taking their revenge on exposed English settlements.

Frontier settlers called upon Berkeley to commission forces to pursue the Susquehannocks. Instead of sending out troops, he ordered the construction of forts along the fall line, and ordered that mounted troops patrol between them. The settlers opposed Berkeley's plan. Not only would Indians learn to avoid the forts, but the colonists, who already faced an enormous tax burden and a weak economy, did not want to pay for their construction.

Rejecting Berkeley's authority, these colonists became rebels under the leadership of the Indian-hating Nathaniel Bacon. He led his fellow colonists out in pursuit of the Susquehannocks. Not finding them, he and his men turned on targets much closer at hand, the friendly Occaneechees and the remnants of the Powhatans, especially the Pamunkeys. Their "queen," Cockacoeske, who had led her people since 1656, had called upon her followers to reestablish the unity of Powhatan's chiefdom. Now she was a refugee, chased into a swamp by Bacon's Indian fighters. The Powhatans fled, victims of racial violence.

After the governor proclaimed him a rebel, Bacon marched on Jamestown, which he burned to the ground in September of 1676. Within a month, Bacon had died of dysentery, but he had devastated the Powhatans. At war with the Susquehannocks, and with the allied Powhatans under assault, Charles II recognized that he must find order in Virginia, his most important mainland colony.

Charles sent royal commissioners, accompanied by over 1000 English troops, to restore order. High on the commissioners' set of instructions was restoring the alliance between the Powhatans and the Virginia colonists. Peace with the Indians, the commissioners believed, meant that planters could once again grow their tobacco free from fear, ship the tobacco to market in England, and allow the king to collect customs duties on it. The commissioners Charles sent recognized that an orderly and peaceful frontier served the best interests of the empire.

In May of 1677 the Nottoways, Weyanokes, Nansemonds, and Pamunkeys, representing the remains of Wahunsonacock's chiefdom, entered into a peace treaty with the crown and his commissioners. The agreement would secure, the commissioners hoped, "the firm Grounding and sure establishment of a good and just peace with the said Indians." The Indians recognized their status as tributaries and agreed to "hold their lands and have the same confirmed to them and their Posterity by patent under the seal of his Majesties colony ... in as free and firm manner as others His Majesties subjects." So long as they maintained their obedience, they could rest secure in the possession of their lands.

The treaty of 1677 reveals clearly what imperial officials wanted to achieve in their relations with their Indian allies. They understood that frontier disorder had been "occasioned by the violent intrusions of diverse English" onto the Powhatans' lands, "forcing the Indians by way of revenge, to kill the cattle and hogs of the English, whereby offense and injuries being given and done on both sides, the peace of his Majesties colony hath been much disturbed." To remedy this problem and prevent such "evil consequences" for the future, the treaty stipulated that no colonist settle within three miles of an Indian town. From the perspective of the English, the treaty rested upon the assumption that the imperial interests of the crown would best be served when colonial Indian allies were treated well, secured in the possession of their lands, and protected from the aggression and violence of the frontier population.

Yet even with this protection, the lot of the Powhatans remained difficult. Indeed, their poverty and marginalization is inscribed in the treaty. For instance, those Indians who had secured permission, and arrived unarmed, would be allowed to gather shellfish and wild plants "or any thing else not useful to the English" on the colonists' lands. The treaty guaranteed them the scraps from their old homeland that the English did not want. The treaty required, furthermore, that no Powhatans be sold as slaves, and threatened to punish any Englishman who tried to "abuse, revile, hurt, or wrong them at any time in word or deed."

Well intentioned? Perhaps. But the Commissioners and the governors of Virginia who succeeded them were no more able to protect the Powhatans than had their predecessors. Words and laws were not enough. They could do nothing about the hatred and scorn that Virginians heaped upon their Indian neighbors. The Powhatans were too few in number to threaten the colony. They lived on the margins, objects of colonial derision. A Powhatan priest, for instance, late in the century approached the overseer on William Byrd's plantation, and offered to produce rain in exchange for two bottles of rum. The priest began powwowing, and soon the rain fell. When Byrd returned home, his overseer told him what had happened. Byrd saw an opportunity for some sport at the priest's expense. Byrd told the priest that he "was a Cheat, and had seen the Cloud a coming." Byrd teased the priest some more, but finally provided the rum. He had effectively asserted his power, and transformed a payment into a begrudging gift. When another Powhatan healer worked to charm a rattlesnake that the planter William Claiborne had captured, Claiborne mischievously struck the snake with a cane, provoking the animal and causing it to bite the healer. He recovered from the venomous bite, but to Claiborne the incident was a source of humor, a funny joke. In these two instances, the laughter says a lot. By looking at who was laughing at whom, and whose culture was mocked and derided, we can see something of the marginal position the Powhatans found themselves occupying in Virginia at the end of the seventeenth century.

When Robert Beverley wrote about the Powhatans in 1705, he noted that as a whole they were "almost wasted." Together, he wrote, "they can't raise five hundred fighting men. They live poorly, and much in fear of the Neighboring Indians." The Weyanokes were "almost wasted, and are now gone to live among other Indians." The Appomattocks had not "above seven families," and the Rappahannocks, he continued, "were reduced to a few Families, and live scattered upon the English seats." They had lost much.

Forging the Covenant Chain

In June of 1676, even before Nathaniel Bacon began his rebellion, Andros informed the Susquehannocks "that if they are afraid and not well where they are," they could resettle under the protection of the Mohawks, allowing the Mohawks to adopt even more refugees, and compensate for the losses that came from disease, warfare, and the migration to Catholic mission communities in the St. Lawrence. Andros envisioned the Mohawks and their dependents as his primary defense against a potential French invasion of Anglo-America, and a means for bringing the hated Puritan colonies to heel.

The Senecas had other plans. They had fought against the Susquehannocks for a generation. Seneca warriors, accompanied by Cayugas and Onondagas, attacked the Susquehannocks late in 1676. They did so with great effect. The Susquehannocks, according to a colonial official in Maryland, "submitted themselves" to the Senecas and settled under their protection. They provided the western Iroquois with additional population and the allegiance of a powerful trading people with ties to the south. The Senecas, too, needed allies and the surge of population the Susquehannocks could bring. This was not part of Andros's original plan, but he had little choice but to try to work with what the Senecas gave him.

Andros hoped to establish effective control over the Anglo-American frontier. From the beginning of English settlement in North America, colonial promoters sought profitable trading relationships with the Indians they encountered, and to plant productive farms and plantations on American shores. They wanted to establish an English empire in North America, and to convert the Indians to English Christianity. These colonial promoters believed that the continent's native peoples would willingly accept the gift of Christianity and civility. They believed in the capacity of the Indians for reason, and they assumed that when offered a better way that the Indians would make the only reasonable choice. The English promoters believed that Indians would cast off their cultural and religious practices, and the beliefs upon which these rested, when offered the English example. They saw Indians as potential, if subordinate, members of an Anglo-American, Christian, New World empire.

All of these plans depended, however, on the ability of colonial governors to control the frontier and its inhabitants, Native American and European. Only friendly Indians would trade with colonists; hostile Indians might set English farms and plantations on fire, as they had done in New England and Virginia, and would do shortly in South Carolina. Hostile Indians might align themselves with England's imperial rivals, and thus threaten the existence of the American empire. Philip's forces in New England obtained much of their weaponry from the French in Canada. And colonial missionaries could not hope to convert the same Indians colonial soldiers were trying to kill. Indeed, many Praying Indians, alienated by the brutal treatment they had received in New England, joined the Algonquian uprising.

Frontier settlers traded with Indians. In places they got along. Friendships developed. But a fundamental conflict existed over land. Indians and English settlers made use of identical tracts of land, but they did so in incompatible ways. It was this observation, made by Miantonomi in the early 1640s, that led to his death and to other uprisings, rebellions, and massacres by native peoples against their overlords across the continent. Conflicts developed that exploded into warfare that dramatically impacted the lives of the Mohegans, the Powhatans, and scores of other native peoples.

Andros believed that the Anglo-Iroquois alliance might resolve this conflict by removing the principal source of contention between frontiersmen and native peoples. The Algonquian losers of King Philip's War—those not enslaved or dispossessed or marginalized—settled in New York under the protection of the colony's Mohawk allies. Some of Uncas's Mohegan followers moved west at this time. The Susquehannocks found themselves under the guardianship of the Senecas. For Andros, this placed Indians out of the reach of aggressive English settlers in New England and the Chesapeake. Virginians and Marylanders received the same message from him as had the Puritans—the Indians who had fought against their colonists were now, for all intents and purposes, Iroquois, and any discussions with the Five Nations would take place in the governor's presence in Albany. Through his alliance with the Five Nations, Andros secured significant oversight of the conduct of Indian diplomacy in the colonies, but he also abandoned the belief, however elusive the ideal upon which it rested, that English colonists and native peoples might live together in peace.

Andros and New York benefited, but the Covenant Chain served Iroquois interests as well. Secure flanks set the stage for wars in the west, and Iroquois warriors and hunters looked there for new sources of captives and furs. The settlement of New England Algonquians and Susquehannocks expanded the geographic range of the Iroquois, as they moved into and through their subject people's lands. When the alliance no longer served Seneca interests, they ignored it. The Senecas always mediated between the French and the English. For them, the Covenant Chain was an alliance without allegiance. They would hold fast the Chain so long as the English fulfilled their responsibilities as allies. The Senecas would not cease pursuing their own interests because the governor of New York asserted his primacy in the English conduct of Anglo-Iroquois diplomacy.

Native Peoples and the French in a World of War

It is important to remember that in the seventeenth century few European colonists strayed far from the Atlantic. Seldom did they move beyond the fall lines of the major eastern rivers. Those who did move into the interior of the continent, like French traders and missionaries, encountered Native America, where they found themselves forced to play by native peoples' rules, and to conform themselves to the customs of this country. This is not to say that small numbers of Europeans did not effect great change, but that those Europeans who did intrude had to learn to speak the languages of the land, learn rules of personal conduct, and figure out how to persuade people—autonomous, powerful, and not subject to their control—to begin a relationship that the French hoped would lead to the incorporation of these native peoples into a colonial economic system and to their conversion to Christianity.

Take the fur trade, for example. Successful French traders learned that the exchange of peltries for European manufactured goods was more than an economic transaction. Native peoples in the western Great Lakes expected reciprocity, respect, and kinship all to precede trade. Native peoples moved freely in search of opportunities to trade. This movement, at times, brought them into deadly conflicts with their neighbors. But this trade still took place in a world ruled by Indian values: those of Anishinaabe peoples like the Potawatomis who lived in the western Great Lakes and their Dakota Sioux enemies as well. This world survived the American Revolution.

The Dakotas, or Santee Sioux, whose territory stretched in the early seventeenth century across much of today's Minnesota, the Dakotas, and to the Missouri River Valley, consisted of four distinct groups: the Mdewakanton, the Sisseton, the Wahpeton, and the Wahpekute, who remained in the eastern part of this vast domain. Here they lived by hunting, fishing, and the harvesting of wild rice and other plant foods. On occasion they moved out onto the plains to their west and south to hunt bison.

The Dakota Sioux viewed their eastern rivals—Sacs, Foxes, Ottawas, Mascoutens, Kickapoos, Miamis, Potawatomis, and Hurons, many of whom who had fled Iroquois aggression and settled in Wisconsin and western Michigan—as a threat to their security. Some of them had guns, the first that the Dakotas had seen, and other European trade goods as well. Dakota warriors struck at these refugees, seeking to protect their homelands from the intruders, but also to acquire the trade goods that the refugees had acquired from the French. One Miami chief, recognizing the precariousness of his position between Dakota and Seneca raiders, told a Jesuit father that together the Sioux and Iroquois "are eating us."

The Dakotas had a considerable history of engaging in long-distance trade. They traveled by canoe and on foot to trade fairs held in the Mandan settlements along the Missouri and at others along the James River in what is now South Dakota. Through these exchanges, the Dakotas and their Lakota kin developed rituals and cultural protocols that allowed them to conduct relations with strangers in a peaceful manner. Despite their reputation for fierceness, a reputation that the French knew well and promoted, the Dakotas eagerly sought trade with French traders and explorers.

As with native peoples in the east, the Dakotas viewed trade and exchange as more than an economic relationship. Traders who worked with the Dakotas became kin, a necessary precondition to viewing them as allies and as friends. Trust necessarily preceded trade. And for the Dakotas, kinship imposed obligations on all parties: kinsmen expected assistance from their relations when the need arose, but they also shared and exchanged what they had for the benefit of their larger community of relations.

Europeans, the Dakotas would learn, were "kinsmen of another kind." They were promiscuous and opportunistic, and would trade with anyone, even rivals of the Dakota when they felt doing so would advance their interests. The Dakotas countered these trade practices in a variety of ways. According to the French, the Dakotas took the items they felt rightfully entitled to as kin; they threatened the French and sometimes pillaged their stores. Dakota efforts to assimilate their French relations and to incorporate them into their communities increasingly ran head wise against the acquisitive and commercial demands of French traders.

The Potawatomis were one of the Anishinaabe peoples who found themselves caught between Iroquois raids from the east and the power of the Sioux to their west. Originally part of a larger alliance of "Three Fires," along with the Ottawas and Ojibwas, they appear to have lived originally in the lower peninsula of Michigan. Iroquois attacks and attacks by other nations along with growing numbers of refugees, themselves feeling the effects of war, impelled them to begin moving toward the Upper Peninsula of Michigan and into Wisconsin. Like many of the peoples of the Great Lakes region, the Potawatomis sought new homes and peace.

Movement into Wisconsin and along the western shore of Lake Michigan brought the Potawatomis into conflict with the indigenous Winnebagos. Several factors limited the Winnebagos' ability to defend their homelands from encroachment. Disease struck shortly after a Winnebago force drove back a Potawatomi war party, negating the effects of the victory. When the Winnebagos then murdered an Illinois diplomatic party that had come to visit them, they recognized that they had too many enemies at once. Retaliatory attacks by the Illinois devastated the Winnebagos. With their collapse, the Potawatomis, acting with other refugees, established a fortified village named Mechingan on the shores of Green Bay.

According to the Jesuits, by 1653 the Potawatomis had become the dominant aboriginal power on the bay, and Mechingan the most important town in Wisconsin. The Jesuits counted

400 Potawatomi warriors on the bay, along with 200 Ottawas, 100 Winnebagos, 200 Ojibwa, and 100 Mississaugas. All shared a history of having been on the receiving end of Iroquois aggression, and all found much that was attractive in Green Bay: ample, fertile soil for growing corn; waters full of fish; and forests with abundant supplies of game.

Green Bay also turned out to be a defensible location, and the Potawatomis played an important part in planning the defense of the bay against Seneca aggression. By successfully driving back an Iroquois invasion, the strength of the Potawatomis became clear. They began to assert themselves more forcefully in the region. The defeat of Iroquois forces allowed native peoples in the Great Lakes to venture out onto the St. Lawrence to trade. Though the Ottawas who served as middlemen between the French post at Montreal and the tribes in the interior largely monopolized the trade, the Potawatomis wanted to play a more direct and important role. Indeed, though the Potawatomis told Pierre Radisson in 1660 that they still feared the warriors of the Five Nations, and that "the Iroquois are every where about the river and undoubtedly will destroy us if we go down and afterwards our wives and those that stayed behind," they looked for opportunities to carry their furs to Montreal. Indeed, it was the determination of the Potawatomis and their neighbors to trade at the French post and resist those who tried to stop them that kept New France alive.

Through trade the Potawatomis obtained weapons to defend themselves and other trade goods as well. The kinship that a trading alliance expressed to the Potawatomis also secured for them the friendship of men that Indians in the region viewed as *manitou*. The Potawatomis, for instance, viewed the trader Nicolas Perrot, who arrived in 1665, as a person of great power. Their beliefs cannot be dismissed as "superstitions." They were, rather, reasonable given Potawatomi cultural premises. The Potawatomis blew tobacco smoke over Perrot, and said to him that "thou are one of the chief spirits, since thou usest iron." "Praised be the sun," the Potawatomis told Perrot, "who has instructed thee and sent thee to our country." The Potawatomis, Perrot wrote, took his knives and hatchets "and incensed them with the tobacco smoke from their own mouths." Many benefits, they hoped, would follow from alliance with the French.

In 1668 a large Potawatomi party traveled to Montreal. The governor of New France, Jean Talon, attempted to demonstrate to them the power and wealth of the French, no easy task given the small size of the outpost. He fed them bread and wine and raisins and prunes. He described the benefits of an alliance, and accepted the Potawatomis' furs and gave to them muskets, powder and shot, and other trade goods. When the warriors returned home to Wisconsin in the fall, they sent out runners, announcing to the Sacs, Foxes, Miamis, Mascoutens, Kickapoos, Illinois, and others that the Potawatomis had at their village French goods available for trade.

They hoped to monopolize the trade, but the large number of Indians gathering at Mechingan with furs drew in French traders. The Potawatomis tried to keep the growing numbers of traders from picking up furs from the Indians but they failed. They never succeeded in occupying the position of the sole middleman in the region's Indian trade. The competition did not sit well with the Potawatomis. The growing volume of trade at Green Bay caused prices to fall, and the Potawatomis argued with traders over prices for guns and gunpowder. When their warriors traveled to Montreal in 1670, they remained unhappy about the high prices the French demanded for their trade goods. The Potawatomis, the French trader Claude-Charles Le Roy Bacqueville de la Potherie wrote, maintained "so good opinion of themselves that they regard other nations as inferior to them," and had "made themselves arbiters for the tribes around the bay, and for all their neighbors; and they strive to preserve for themselves that reputation in every direction." They asserted that they were the eldest sons of Onontio, the French governor, and should be treated with respect. And of the trade goods they acquired, La Potherie wrote, the Potawatomis made "presents of all their possessions, stripping themselves of every necessary article, in their eager desire to be accounted liberal." The distribution of trade goods through exchange relationships helped the Potawatomis establish connections of mutuality and reciprocity with neighboring villages and to extend their influence and power over native villages in Wisconsin. French parsimony limited the Potawatomis' ability to realize their program, and French visitors to Green Bay learned of their growing discontent.

The French responded with a show of force, a demonstration of the power of Onontio. Perrot, acting on orders from Montreal, called a council at Sault Ste. Marie for the summer of 1671. Francis Daumont, the Sieur de Saint Lusson, traveled west to oversee the gathering. He distributed gifts to the gathered Indians—Potawatomis, Sacs, Winnebagos, and Menominees— and they acknowledged their alliance with Onontio. They received these gifts not as subjects but as the children of Onontio, a great king "more terrible than thunder," the Jesuit priest and Lusson's translator Claude Allouez told them, whose wealth filled his warehouses with "enough hatchets to cut down all your forests, kettles to cook all your moose, and glass beads to fill all your cabins." Potawatomis and French imperialists understood their alliance in very different ways.

Allouez recognized the Potawatomis' discontent, and tried to define Lusson's ceremony in terms that the Potawatomis would understand. But he was more interested in saving souls than in addressing the Indians' concerns about the nature of their alliance. He constructed his mission, St. Francis Xavier, near the mouth of the Fox River and erected a cross, thirty feet in height, near the Potawatomis' village. The members of a war party, heading out for a raid on the Dakotas, pulled down and set the cross on fire. This horrified the mission's tiny French population. When the war party suffered defeat, however, and the humiliated warriors returned home, Allouez seized the opportunity to lecture them. The Potawatomis had been defeated, he said, because they had destroyed the Christian symbol, and invited the wrath of the Christians' God.

The argument may have made sense to the Potawatomis, for they understood that bad things happened for a reason. They knew that rituals could provide their practitioners with power, but also that disrespect could call down upon a people the wrath of malevolent forces in the cosmos. Allouez had few converts in 1672 but by 1676 he had baptized more than 400, including the family of Good Paulin, the young hunter savaged by a bear.

The Potawatomis understood that the alliance they had arranged with Perrot, Lusson, and the French at Sault Ste. Marie bound them to provide the colonists with assistance when they needed it. Like other native peoples, the Potawatomis did not believe that alliance meant the acceptance of an inferior or subordinate position. They continued to exercise a considerable amount of autonomy. When an epidemic struck in the 1680s, they blamed the outbreak on Jesuit witchcraft, and killed two French colonists. Iroquois attacks continued to fall upon them into the 1680s, and the French seemed powerless to halt them. After Five Nations warriors demonstrated their power by slaughtering French colonists at Lachine in 1689, attachment to the French weakened further. In 1696, the king prohibited French subjects from traveling west to acquire furs, an attempt to soak up the glut of pelts in Montreal warehouses. The reduced supply of trade goods reaching the Potawatomis further weakened attachment to Onontio.

Despite the growing discontent, however, the alliance did not collapse, and though other Great Lakes natives discussed the possibility of turning against the French, the Potawatomis held on to their French allies. Potawatomi warriors joined the French in invasions of Iroquoia in 1684, 1687, and 1696. Maintaining this alliance was not easy, and the Potawatomis learned that not all Frenchmen could be trusted or relied upon. But the power the Potawatomis possessed came through French trade, and they had come to rely on many of the items that they could obtain most easily and least expensively from Onontio. They needed guns, obviously. As warriors spent more of their time away from the village, French cloth came to replace deerskins, and copper pots and pans replaced pots of native manufacture. The Potawatomis preserved their allegiance, despite the difficulties and challenges they had learned to overcome, because it offered the best answers to the questions they faced—about how to preserve their autonomy, and their position as a regional power. They saw themselves not as subjects of a French king but as kinsmen and allies, and they worked hard to preserve a relationship that the French understood in very different terms.

The Pueblos' Revolt

It was not until the end of the sixteenth century that Spaniards returned to the Pueblos. Juan de Oñate arrived in April 1598 with soldiers, settlers, and missionaries to claim the land in the name of the king and to promote the efforts of missionaries to convert the Pueblos to Christianity. Oñate became the first governor of the Spanish province of New Mexico. He reported that 70,000 Indians, "to make a conservative estimate," lived in the province. The Pueblos, Oñate said, "settled after our custom, house adjoining house, with square plazas." Their houses, he continued, could reach seven stories in height, and they lived in a land "abounding in flesh of buffalo, goats with hideous horns, and turkeys." The "comely" people lived in a productive and fertile land. Their religion, from his perspective, "consisted in worshipping idols, of which they have many; and in their temples, after their own manner, they worship them with fire, painted reeds, feathers, and universal offerings of almost everything they get, such as small animals, birds, vegetables, etc."

Oñate looked closely at the pueblos and the people who lived within them. The best that he saw convinced him merely that the Pueblos might, with some considerable effort, be transformed into something else, something useful to the Spanish. His American dream, premised upon the use of force, relied upon the conversion of the Indians to the Catholic faith, the expropriation of their labor, and their subordination to Spanish imperial control. For obvious reasons, few Pueblos found these prospects appealing. "Compelling" these people "to render obedience to His Majesty," Oñate wrote, "has caused me much labor, diligence and care, long journeys with arms on shoulders, and not a little watching and circumspection." At Acoma, Pueblos killed some of Oñate's men when the soldiers demanded the right to use the community's water supply. Resistance of this sort required harsh retribution. "As punishment for its crime and its treason against his Majesty," Oñate "razed and burned it completely." Oñate's men killed over 800 Acomas. The suffering did not end there, for Oñate ordered his men to cut the left foot off of every surviving adult male in the pueblo.

Brutality such as this was all too common a part of Spanish colonization, but it was not inevitable. The Spanish made choices, and they saw what they wanted to see when they looked at native peoples. When Franciscan missionaries arrived in the colony in 1605 to conduct the Pueblos to Catholicism, for instance, they might have emphasized their similarities. Like the Catholic priests, the Pueblos, whose traditions were in some ways as old as the faith that the fathers professed, practiced a system of religion that assumed an order in the world governed by supernatural laws. Powers beyond and greater than those possessed by mere mortals shaped the fate of men and women, and both Pueblos and Catholics prayed to their gods in hopes of acquiring certain benefits and influence over those powers. They both believed that humans might suffer the wrath of divine forces for failing to attend properly and sincerely to their religious rituals, and both believed in the existence of a variety of spiritual beings, some beneficent and some malevolent, who might intervene in the affairs of men and women.

In their religious practice, both Pueblos and Catholics worshipped before symbolically significant altars, listened to religious specialists set apart from society to oversee the conduct of the community's religious life, and observed the rituals and rites of passage that men and women of open minds might have seen as functionally similar, had they chosen to do so. Many Pueblos would soon observe these parallels. Catholics, if they had wanted, could as well have found ways to cross the cultural divide.

Nearly as soon as Oñate's settlers entered the region, Pueblos and Spanish settlers began to interact with each other. They learned much from one another. The settlers, it appears, taught the Pueblos techniques to improve the irrigation of their fields, and brought with them European and Mexican cultigens—fruit trees, onions, cabbages, melons, and grains, along with chilies and tomatoes—that Pueblos began to plant and grow. Some Pueblos began to convert to Christianity. Nor was cultural change a one-way street, and the small colonial population could not help but be influenced by the large numbers of native peoples amongst whom they had settled. Spanish colonists approached Pueblo healers for medicines, aphrodisiacs, and potions. Pueblo ways gained some acceptance in colonial society when the cures and remedies they offered the Spanish proved effective.

The missionaries, however, who taught both Pueblo and colonial children in their mission schools, and who encouraged these children to interact and develop friendships, chose to emphasize the differences between natives and newcomers. The Franciscans denounced the Pueblos' religion as pagan superstition, and violently assaulted the symbols of that religion. They raided the sacred *kivas*, the center of the community's spiritual life, and destroyed what they found there—the *katsinas*, the altars, powerful prayer sticks, and other sacred objects. They forbade dancing by the Pueblos, and brutally punished the practitioners of Pueblo religion with beatings, mutilation, and hanging. The Franciscans, backed by soldiers, became aggressive agents of repression.

Native peoples in the pueblos, as elsewhere, faced difficult choices. Some became Catholics, and settled in the missions where the Spanish appropriated their labor. Despite official policies that prohibited the practice, many were enslaved. Pueblo women, about whom we know little for this period, and young men of low status, seem to have been most drawn to the new religion. These "neophytes," who may have seen in the new faith a superior source of the spiritual power they needed, lived as Spanish peasants, tied to the land. Others chose to adopt the outward forms of Christian worship but continued to practice their traditional beliefs in secret. Some may have seen, in fact, no fundamental contradiction in the two faiths. They may have viewed, in Catholic ritual, analogs to indigenous belief. The cross, the most visible symbol of the priests' faith, may not have appeared significantly different from the prayer poles that Pueblos decorated as part of their ritual life. Some Pueblos, however, became increasingly likely to reach an opposite conclusion. Noting the coincidence of a catalog of misfortunes with the arrival of the newcomers, they viewed the Spanish as a menace that must be eradicated, even if that required violence.

Over the course of the seventeenth century, the Pueblo population declined significantly from 60,000 to 20,000. The number of distinct Pueblo communities fell by more than half.

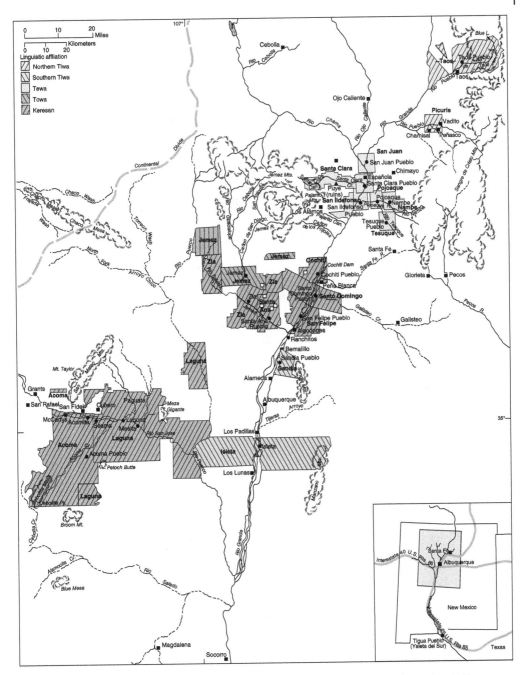

Map 3.2 Pueblos in the American southwest. Source: *Smithsonian Handbook of North American Indians*, Vol. 9, Southwest, pp. 9: 225. Courtesy of Smithsonian Institution.

Then came a fresh attack by the forces of nature. Beginning sometime around 1667, an extensive drought tightened its grip on the Rio Grande Valley. Widespread crop failures and famine resulted. An epidemic appeared in 1671, exacerbating an already grievous situation, by killing Pueblos and their dwindling supplies of livestock. Attacks by Apaches and Navajos, nomads also struggling with drought conditions, began in earnest in 1672. The hostile raiders saw in the sedentary Pueblos a subjugated population who made an easy target. In this atmosphere of acute crisis, growing numbers of converts began to question not only the power and the goodness of the Christians' god, but the value that they derived from Spanish colonial rule. Conversion and the practice of Christian rituals, in short, did not benefit Pueblo Catholics. Some contemplated returning to their traditional religion for answers.

The Spanish, of course, punished harshly those who expressed their doubts about Spanish religion or Spanish rule. The Franciscans persecuted dozens of Pueblo religious leaders, sometimes with sadistic tortures. Among the most notable of these was the shaman known as Po'pay, whom the *katsinas* had taught how to defeat the Spanish and how to organize a revolt. His message was similar to that of large numbers of native prophets who have appeared in times of trouble. The *katsinas*, Po'pay told his followers, were angry, and they would go underground until the Christians were defeated. To drive the colonizers out, the Pueblos must return to their traditional religion and rituals. Only then, he asserted, would prosperity, peace, and harmony return to the people. To those who suffered, or who had been beaten or branded or tortured, Po'pay promised relief. Not only must the Pueblos rise up and kill the Spaniards, they must destroy every vestige of Catholicism or colonization. The Pueblos should not speak Spanish, or mention Jesus or Mary. They must work together to destroy the churches, the altars, and the bells. They must abandon those crops the Spanish had brought to them and plant only maize and beans, the traditional basis of their diet. And they must do all of this in the presence of their children, so that they could learn the old ways properly. When the Christians were defeated, and the symbols of their tyranny destroyed, the ancient gods would return. For those willing to join him, Po'pay offered liberation and a vision of unity.

Sending out knotted ropes his supporters could use to count the days until the uprising, Po'pay assembled a massive movement. By no means did he have unanimous support—*caciques*, or leaders, at three pueblos informed the Spanish of the impending attack, and the Spanish captured some of Po'pay's rope-bearing couriers and tortured them until they revealed the meaning of their message. Aware that the plot had been discovered, Po'pay and his followers decided to attack a day early. They succeeded in catching most of the colonists unaware.

Po'pay's followers ran off the colonists' horses and mules, limiting the ability of the Spanish to move and share information. They then began their assaults on one colonial settlement after another. They killed over 400 of the 3000 colonists and slaughtered more than twenty of the province's thirty-three priests. The rebels destroyed the Franciscan missions.

The Spanish survivors fled. At every outpost they passed, they saw bodies and smoldering fires. They saw burning churches, altars and communion tables smeared with excrement, and mutilated statues of St. Francis. The Pueblos had learned well from the Spanish the terror and violence represented by the destruction of sacred objects. And with the surviving colonists fleeing toward Mexico, Po'pay's revival flourished, if only for a time. The Pueblos reconstructed and rededicated the kivas that the Franciscans had destroyed or filled with sand. The gods, it seemed, might now return. Po'pay denounced Catholic rites and practices. He distributed women as prizes for those who killed Spaniards. "The Indian who shall kill a

Spaniard will get an Indian woman for a wife," he said, according to one informant, "and he who kills four will get four women, and he who kills ten or more will have a like number of women."

Po'pay and his followers forged a remarkable unity, but their revolution against the spiritual and earthly domination of the Spanish would prove short-lived. They viewed women as objects of plunder. Po'pay tolerated no opposition, executed his critics, and demanded the payment of an annual tribute in wool and cotton. And he had no answer when epidemics and drought continued to ravage the Pueblos and the promises made by the spiritual leaders failed to come true. By 1696, the Spanish, with a deft combination of violence and the use of native allies, had returned and effectively reasserted their control in the colony.

Nonetheless, the Pueblo revolt of 1680 did affect subsequent Spanish colonialism in the southwest. The Franciscans, for example, upon their return to New Mexico practiced a more restrained form of missionization. They baptized children, gave communion, and oversaw marriages and burials, but they seldom interfered directly and coercively in native religious life. They accepted a compromise, a synthesis of Christian and Pueblo traditions, not because they were generous and far-sighted and gentle, but because they recognized the power of the Pueblos' commitment to their culture. The Pueblos, for their part, compromised as well. With the reconquest, the Spanish built new churches in their communities. The Pueblos could do nothing about that. They conformed to many of the outward forms of Catholic doctrine. But as they did so, they altered the Catholicism of the Franciscans to serve their own needs. The Pueblos celebrated Christmas and Easter, but with much less importance attached by them to the birth and the death and resurrection of the Christ. Christian holidays provided the Pueblos with occasions to assemble and celebrate traditional dances. They took what they wanted to take from the colonizers' religion.

Horses

The Spaniards who returned to New Mexico in the aftermath of the revolt provided the Pueblos with protection against mounted Apache warriors, and they provided the Pueblos with horses of their own. Pueblo men could now protect their communities from hostile raiders. Horses transformed the lives of those who acquired them. Horses, along with the European guns that accompanied them through indigenous trade networks, provoked a "technological revolution for the Great Plains," and the success and survival of native communities depended on the extent to which they succeeded in acquiring both. Plains Indians, who had previously hunted by foot with bows and arrows, gave up a sedentary existence reliant on agriculture for a highly mobile life on horseback following enormous herds of bison.

The rise of equestrianism, as it is called, made the world smaller. Horses allowed native peoples to carry more food, more tools, and more hides while ranging over a wider territory to wage war, raid, and trade. Mounted warriors and hunters could move farther and faster, take horses from isolated Spanish outposts, and escape their pursuers. They exchanged these horses with native peoples to their north and east. The Kiowas, as early as 1682, had obtained horses which they used in their hunting and in their raids against Utes and Navajos to their northwest and Osages and Pawnees to their northeast. They shared the southern Plains with the Comanches, probably the greatest horsemen in the region. As early as 1706, Spanish sources mention devastating Comanche raids upon the Pueblos and the Apaches.

With their Ute allies, the Comanches dominated the northern edge of Spain's fragile North American empire. The Comanches, in the words of their best historian, treated the Spanish colony "as an exploitable resource depot" where they both traded and raided, took colonial livestock and food, and engaged in an exchange network that extended out onto the Plains and that included slaves and hides for horses, corn, and metal goods. By 1716, the raiding had reached the point where colonists in New Mexico lacked the horses necessary to march out in defense of their settlements. The Spanish found themselves confronting an emerging Comanche Empire.

As among the Kiowas and Comanches, horses became central to Crow culture on the Northern Plains. Pretty Shield, a Crow woman who told her life story to anthropologist Frank Linderman early in the twentieth century, recalled learning from her grandmothers how the horse had revolutionized their lives. They could hunt more easily, so they did not worry about food. They could cover more ground, and the elderly no longer able to walk could now ride. The Crows no longer had to leave them behind. "Ahh," Pretty Shield told Linderman, "I came into a happy world."

Horses brought significant changes as well to the people who ultimately came to be known as the Caddos. For nearly a century and a half after Soto's stragglers stumbled through, they had no recorded contact with Europeans. They had, however, numerous contacts with other native communities and through them engaged in a considerable amount of trading. They lived at the nexus of the Plains and the southeast, and trade routes linking them with people as far away as the Pueblos in the west guaranteed them an important position in intercultural exchange. Beginning in the middle of the seventeenth century, Caddos faced attacks by mounted Apaches, who this early had earned a reputation among the Spanish for their martial skills. A need for military allies and trading partners, then, informed Caddo relations with Europeans when the newcomers returned in the 1680s. In this sense the Caddos treated Europeans as they treated other prospective allies, Caddo and non-Caddo alike.

Caddos encountered the wayward party led by Rene Robert Cavalier Sieur de La Salle in the mid-1680s. A diffuse group, the Caddos at this time consisted of nearly twenty-five communities, gathered into three loose confederacies: the Hasinai, the Kadohadachos, and the Natchitoches. La Salle had entered into what the Spanish later would call the Province of Tejas. Though many Texans today believe that the word "Tejas" derives from a Caddoan term for "friend," this is little more than a comforting myth masking the Lone Star State's violent past, and one that obscures the importance of the native alliances that the Spanish learned native peoples in the region called "Tejas" or "Texia." Everywhere La Salle went in the Caddo country, he saw evidence of their extensive trading connections: oil lamps and old muskets, swords, spoons, and candlesticks, as well as European clothing. The Caddos had horses, which they provided to the French in return for axes, rings, pins, and needles.

The apparent interest of the French in the Caddo country inspired the Spanish to tighten their connections to the native peoples living on the northeastern periphery of their empire. The Spanish feared that their imperial rivals might use a base in Caddo territory for military incursions into Mexico, or raids on the rich mines in Spanish territory. Indeed, the defense of these mines was for some the only reason to continue holding these unprofitable northern outposts of empire. While the French, at this time, did little to convert the Caddos to Christianity, they did provide them with guns and ammunition. The Spanish did not want the French to develop alliances with native peoples in lands that the Spanish considered their own.

Because the Caddos lived a settled existence, some Franciscan missionaries thought that the Caddos would easily be converted. In 1682, the small Spanish force that accompanied Father Damian Massanet to his mission with the Caddoan Hasinais in today's eastern Texas marched behind a standard bearing the likeness of the Virgin. For Massanet and the Spaniards, the Virgin Mary announced to all who cared to see who they were and what they stood for. The Hasinais likely knew nothing of Catholic imagery and iconography, and they interpreted the image of the Virgin according to their own cultural predispositions. The Spanish force consisted solely of men. They saw the image of the Virgin, a woman, as a symbol of peace, a proxy for the real women who did not accompany the Spanish force, and whose presence in a party normally signified that it had no hostile intent. They treated the standard of the Virgin with the respect they offered real women visitors from other communities.

Both Spaniards and Hasinais looked for something recognizable in the other. Some Franciscans, for instance, believed that years before their arrival in Texas a Spanish nun, María de Jesús de Ágreda, had traveled in spirit across the Atlantic and instructed the Indians to request a Spanish mission. When Massanet's party arrived a half-century later, they asked the Hasinais what they knew of this miraculous "Woman in Blue." A Hasinai leader told Massanet that indeed a woman fitting this description had appeared, but he likely described to the Spaniards Zacado, a figure in Hasinai myth, who taught their ancestors how to live in this world before she disappeared. The Hasinais may have viewed the Spaniards' knowledge of Zacado as miraculous in its own right.

In the early encounters between native peoples and small parties of European newcomers, conflict was not inevitable. Each of the participants tried to comprehend the other. Finding common ground, however, proved elusive, and for natives and newcomers, familiarity too often bred contempt, in *Tejas* as elsewhere.

The Spanish and the Hasinais both viewed men as warriors, and in their diplomatic encounters emphasized their strength, courage, and martial prowess. Hasinai men, one Spanish observer noted, "do not yield a point in proving themselves warlike and valiant." Similar understandings of the role of men in their communities thus provided a means for establishing alliances. With women, however, differing ideals and values caused conflict. Spanish men emphasized the importance of chastity and modesty in the women they dominated. Hasinai women secured status in their communities through their production and distribution of food. Their role as producers and givers of life balanced and complemented those of their fathers, husbands, and brothers. They were not subordinate. Women participated in the public life of the community.

The Spanish misunderstood Hasinai women. They believed that Hasinai women dressed immodestly, and they equated immodest dress with immodest behavior. "Caught up in their own personal flights of fancy," writes historian Juliana Barr, the Spaniards "read Hasinai women's expressive gestures and exposed bodies as an invitation to equate offers of food with offers of sex, conflating Indian women with Eve-like figures who enticed men to sin, if not destruction." The Spanish saw in the Hasinais' embrace of sexual mores different from their own—mores that gave to women far more power in relationships than that possessed by their European counterparts—extraordinary promiscuity. Many Spanish soldiers, apparently, believed Hasinai women were free for the taking. They raped Hasinai women with impunity.

In addition to these unbearable assaults, Hasinais faced the ridicule and scorn of arrogant missionaries who insisted that their own Catholic faith was the only way. One priest called the Hasinai *connas*, or spiritual leaders, liars, and interfered in a burial ceremony by attempting forcibly to silence the *connas*. A Father Casañas told the Hasinais' respected spiritual leader that "all he was saying was of no use and that what I was going to say to God would alone be useful to the dead man."

And while the Spanish priests acted like tyrants and religious bigots, and while soldiers preyed upon Hasinai women, an outbreak of disease in early 1691 killed one of the Spanish priests and then spread through the community. By the time the epidemic had run its course, as many as 400 Hasinais had died (the outbreak killed 3000 more Indians, in neighboring communities). The Hasinais had a simple explanation for this misfortune. Observing that those living closest to the missionaries died in the greatest numbers, the Hasinais concluded that the Spanish carried the disease. One priest reported that "the demons put it into their heads that we had brought the epidemic into the country," and told the Caddos "that we had killed them." The priests sprinkled holy water on sick Indians before they died. They had mocked Hasinai religious leaders, and interrupted their rituals. Now, the community paid the price. Some Hasinais acted on these beliefs. Father Casañas reported that some of the Hasinais "tried to kill us." As protectors and trade partners, the Spanish had failed the Caddos.

By 1693, the Hasinais had enough. They evicted the Spanish. No protests, no attempt to educate the newcomers, could prevail upon the Spanish to halt their assaults on Hasinai women. Father Massanet understood the source of the Hasinais' anger. Aware that Hasinai warriors and warriors from other Caddo communities were coming together to attack the Spaniards because of the soldiers' "beating Indians over any trifle [in order to get] their wives," the Spanish fled. Caddo warriors followed them for 400 miles until the Spanish crossed the Colorado River. Yet though the Spanish retreated, the Caddos continued to feel the consequences of European contact. They lived on the edge of a shatter zone created by disease and the English trade in Indian slaves. These forces may have combined to reduce the Hasinai population by two-thirds.

Native peoples and newcomers sought pathways across the cultural divide. In places, Indians and Europeans recognized similarities in their cultural practices that provided a tenuous base for intercultural communication and alliance. These moments, however were all too brief in early America. Father Massanet understood fully that the greatest barrier to the success of his mission was not the Indians' unwillingness to listen to his message, but the rapacity and violence of the European men who undertook the difficult work of colonization.

The Grand Settlement

From their Covenant Chain alliance with the English, Iroquoian peoples secured the southern and eastern limits of the Longhouse, obtained regular supplies of guns and ammunition, and an important role in the functioning of the Anglo-American Empire. Seneca warriors joined the bands of Haudenosaunee men who traveled west to attack Great Lakes-area tribes allied with the French, people living throughout this vast Anishinaabewaki. Indeed, the Senecas expressed considerable discontent toward the Jesuit missionaries who had begun to probe their territory some years before. One priest reported that the Senecas and Cayugas he knew had "become so insolent that they talk only of breaking the missionaries' heads." New rounds of mourning wars began after 1677.

The Iroquois expanded their attacks to the south as well. Perhaps at the urging of the Susquehannocks who earlier had settled in their midst, Senecas and other western Iroquois attacked the Conoys and Piscataways in Maryland and the Catawbas in Carolina.

Other members of the Five Nations relocated to the north, settling in mission communities in the St. Lawrence River valley. Significant numbers of these emigrants converted to Catholicism, but it is important to realize that despite the presence of Catholic churches, the emigrants continued to live as they always had lived, and they remained in communication with their Haudenosaunee brethren. Indeed, the ties binding the St. Lawrence emigrants and the Five Nations remaining in New York played an important role in shaping the subsequent history of the Iroquois and their relations with France and England. All was not well in the Longhouse. Sixty Senecas died in one month during an epidemic that struck in 1676. Two years later, smallpox swept through all of the Five Nations. Iroquois warriors suffered some significant defeats. But the captives, furs, and trade goods continued to flow in.

New France's governor, Joseph-Antoine Le Febvre de la Barre, knew that his colony's interests had come into conflict with Iroquois designs in the west. Attacks by Iroquois warriors, a significant number of whom were Senecas, limited the flow of pelts into Montreal. La Barre wanted to assert French control over the western Great Lakes, and provide French support to the native allies of New France. He led an expedition to punish the Senecas for their attacks in 1684. His 1200-man force moved slowly over the course of the summer; the 160 allied Iroquois who accompanied him showed little willingness to attack their brethren. Indeed, Iroquois orators saw through the French governor's boastfulness. Speaking for all the Five Nations, the Onondaga Otreouti said La Barre was "raving in a camp of sick men." The Iroquois would continue their attacks—on the Shawnees, the Miamis, the Illinois, and others in the Great Lakes—and this was not the concern of the French. Otreouti cautioned La Barre not to uproot the "Tree of Peace." Easily employing the language of Haudenosaunee tradition, Otreouti assured La Barre that Iroquois warriors would remain quiet unless the French threatened their territory. The Iroquois had the right to wage war against all their enemies within "the limits of our Country." The French should leave the Five Nations alone in the broad expanse of territory they claimed as their own.

The French refused to heed this warning. La Barre's successor, Jacques-Rene de Brisnay, the Marquis de Denonville, began preparations in the spring of 1687 to strike the Senecas, who the French viewed as most responsible for the destruction of the colony's trade in furs. One thousand six hundred French troops crossed the Niagara River, and headed eastward toward the Seneca homeland. More than 200 Indians from the St. Lawrence missions accompanied Denonville, but many of them deserted and warned the Senecas of his advance. On August 13, the Senecas nearly ambushed Denonville's force. The warriors mistook an advance guard for the entire French army. The Senecas then fled eastward, finding shelter with the Cayugas and Onondagas. Denonville's allies did not pursue, so the French governor spent the next week burning abandoned Seneca villages and the food stores left behind. They burned crops and caches of corn, desecrated graves, and plundered items buried with the dead. The damage was considerable, but Iroquois warriors continued to strike the Indian allies of New France and damage the colony's fur trade.

The relationship of the Iroquois to the French and the English became more complicated when the two empires formally went to war in 1689. To retaliate for Denonville's invasion of the Senecas' homeland, an Iroquois force attacked the French settlement at Lachine. Many Iroquois expected encouragement and assistance from the English to launch more raids against New France. The Five Nations, however, found the English a fickle ally, willing to employ Indians as military allies but uninterested in doing any heavy lifting themselves. French attacks on Schenectady, and an invasion of the Onondagas' homeland, met with a muted response by the English governor of New York.

Iroquois warriors fought for both the English and the French in the ensuing conflict, but avoided fighting one another. Still, considerable losses came to the Five Nations. The Iroquois had seen their homelands invaded by French armies and disease outbreaks continued to prey upon the Longhouse. Attacks by France's native allies, including the Potawatomis, took an additional toll. Perhaps as much as a quarter of the Iroquois population may have died between 1689 and 1698, when news of the peace treaty between France and England arrived.

The agreement brought no peace to the Five Nations. It did nothing to resolve the dynastic struggles that led to the imperial warfare in the first place, and did nothing to resolve the problems the Five Nations faced. Ojibwa warriors from the western Great Lakes, for instance, invaded Iroquoia and killed seven Senecas. Ottawa, Illinois, and Miami warriors killed fifty-five Senecas and Onondagas. The league could not continue fighting such costly wars.

So the Iroquois began to seek a peace agreement of their own with the French, the English, and the Indian allies of New France. Certainly a peace would benefit the French by allowing the free flow of peltries to New France. The Iroquois through peace could free themselves from a destructive cycle of warfare. Alliance with the English, moreover, would force the French to take the Five Nations' concerns seriously, while Iroquoian efforts to secure peace with the French would pressure the English to hold fast to the Covenant Chain.

The Onondaga Teganissorens traveled to Montreal to treat with the French. Hundreds of French-allied Indians from the Great Lakes attended the council as well. The Five Nations pledged to remain neutral in any future conflicts between France and England. The French promised to enforce a peace between the Iroquois and their western allies, an arrangement that allowed these allies to trade unobstructed at Montréal and allowed the Iroquois to hunt in the west. League hunters could move into the western Great Lakes without fear. In Albany, meanwhile, an Iroquois party led by Sadekanaktie signed a "deed" to the lands that the Iroquois had "won with the sword" south of the Great Lakes. In return for this cession, the Iroquois expected the king of England to protect them as they hunted in the region, in the hope "that he might be our protector and defender there." The Five Nations had deeded to the English lands over which they never exerted any significant control, and they certainly did not intend to give to the English dominion in any way over their lives. The combined treaties of 1701, it seems, which secured for the Five Nations a role as a respected and feared middleman between competing empires, and launched the Five Nations upon a challenging and difficult path of neutrality. If one empire offended the Iroquois, or attempted to limit their movement in the west, the Five Nations would aid the other. The "Grand Settlement" of 1701, as one historian called it, laid the fragile foundation for an intercultural arrangement, one in which the Five Nations worked to live in peace in the midst of competing European empires, free to trade with both, and free from the devastation that could accompany unrestrained armed conflict.

The Cherokees

For nearly a century and a half after De Soto's *entrada*, the Cherokees remained largely isolated from the direct effects of European colonization. Spanish Jesuit missionaries established outposts along the Atlantic Coast beginning late in the 1560s but achieved little success. Franciscan missionaries arrived in Spanish Florida in 1583 but they did not venture far enough into the interior to impact the Cherokees. Neither did European traders succeed in reaching the Cherokees' Blue Ridge home. Virginia traders, seeking deerskins, moved down the

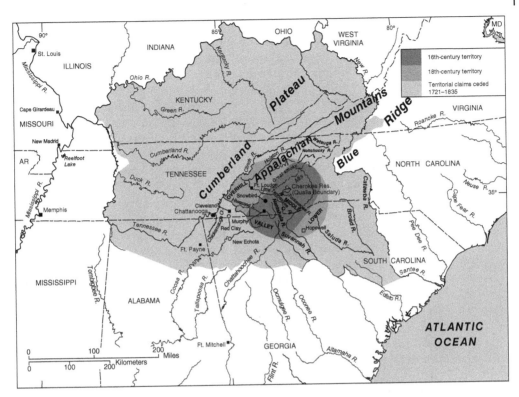

Map 3.3 The Cherokees in the east. Source: *Smithsonian Handbook of North American Indians*, Vol. 14, Southeast, pp. 14: 338. Courtesy of Smithsonian Institution.

"Occaneechee Trading Path" to swap their goods for pelts, but their travels stopped well short of the Cherokee country. They lived in towns along the rivers that flowed from the southern Appalachians. The Cherokee Lower and Middle Towns stood along the Savannah and Little Tennessee rivers. The Valley Towns stood directly west of the Middle Towns, and the Overhill Cherokees lived along the Tennessee and Tellico rivers. In each of these regions, "Beloved Towns," or capitals, developed, connected by ties of kinship and exchange with other Cherokee towns. Town and region mattered greatly to the Cherokees, but so did clan identity. Towns had members from all the clans living within them. Membership in these matrilineal clans regulated nearly all aspects of Cherokee life.

The founding of the English colony of Carolina in 1670 initiated significant change for the Cherokees and set the stage, within three decades, for sustained contact between European settlers and the Cherokees. The colony's founders hoped to achieve goals similar to those pursued by the founders of other English colonies. They wanted to derive a profit from their undertaking, plant a defensible settlement in what they well knew was territory claimed by the king of Spain, and bring Christianity and civility to the Indians. To achieve these goals, the Promoters ordered their prospective colonists to treat the native peoples they encountered with kindness and humanity. But the men who actually settled Carolina did not take the Proprietors' guidelines seriously. The Goose Creek Men, for instance, a group of immigrants from the slave colony of Barbados who settled along a tributary of the Cooper River, seized control of the colony's Indian trade and began enslaving Indians. Other traders followed.

Henry Woodward, the Proprietors' agent, in 1674 encountered the Westoes, a people who advertised their interest in intercultural trade by drawing "upon trees the effigies of a beaver, a man, on horseback, and guns." Woodward hoped to acquire from them "deare skins, furrs, and young slaves." From the Westoes, Woodward learned of their enemies, the Creeks and Cherokees, "with whom they are at continual wars." Indeed, the Westoes soon found themselves with too many enemies, for they opposed the efforts of Carolinians to enslave them, and they raided the colony on occasion. By 1680, the Carolinians had wiped out the Westoes, an event that led to an intensification of the colony's trade in Indian slaves. Moving into the middleman position occupied previously by the Westoes, a variety of Savannah River communities collected weapons from the English which they used to launch raids for deerskins and slaves. The trade grew rapidly.

In 1680 the Proprietors declared weakly from England that their appointed commissioner would "take care that no Indians that are friendly and that live within 200 miles of the territory be made slaves or sent out of the colony without special orders." The Proprietors' commissioner would "redress injuries done to the Indians," so as "not to involve the Proprietors in war." They tried to prevent settler pressure on Indian lands by prohibiting settlement within two miles of an Indian town. They ordered settlers to help Indians "fence their corn that no damages be done by the hogs and cattle of the English." The Proprietors could not, they said, "answer it to God, the King, our inhabitants, nor our own consciences that such things should continue."

Of course these things did continue. In the forty-five years after the colony's founding, the Carolinians exported Indian slaves in numbers far in excess of the number of Africans they imported. Indian slavery played a fundamental role in the growth and development of Carolina. The raids led by Governor James Moore against St. Augustine in 1702 and the nearby Spanish Catholic missions several years later produced a massive influx of native peoples as slaves. Yamasees and Creeks armed by the Carolinians killed 3000 of the mission Indians and enslaved 10,000 more. Most of them ended up in planters' fields, though the high numbers of enslaved women suggests that they performed domestic duties as well. Evidence based on the names of Indian slaves mentioned in Carolina's colonial records reveals the all-out assault on the native slaves' identity that the institution produced. Enslaved members of native communities were far less likely than African slaves to preserve traditional names, and many first-generation native slaves received from their owners African or English names.

Some enslaved native women, like their African counterparts, were freed by masters whose very limited consciences impelled them to emancipate the mothers of their enslaved children. Native slaves, as well, occasionally followed a path to freedom that simply was not open to Africans. If the enslavement of an Indian from a powerful community threatened the colony's security, officials acted to return the slave to his village, sometimes over the considerable opposition of Carolina slaveholders.

As of 1681, some Cherokees found themselves caught up in this trade. That year, an enterprising Carolinian purchased several "Seraquii" slaves from the Savannahs and sold them into West Indian slavery. Ten years later, the Proprietors expressed the sorrow they felt when they learned that James Moore, "without any war first proclaimed," had "fallen upon the Cherokee Indians in a hostile manner and murdered several of them." After this attack, the Cherokees seem to have had little contact with the aggressive Carolina traders. Cherokee communities may have had their hands full with Iroquois raiders who had traveled south to attack them.

Meanwhile, the Proprietors never developed a means to effectively govern the Anglo-American frontier. The colonial assembly in Carolina, a creation of the Proprietors, appointed nine commissioners in 1707 to oversee Anglo-Indian relations, an old technique applied to a new setting. The commissioners granted licenses to those who wished to trade with the Indians, and appointed an agent to reside for part of the year with them and prevent disputes between Indians, settlers, and traders.

Some of the agents, like Thomas Nairne, recognized clearly that the colony needed peace with Indians so that "the English American Empire may not be unreasonably crampt up." Nairne saw that alienated Indians could threaten the colony, especially if they moved into the orbit of the Spanish outpost at nearby St. Augustine or the French station on Mobile Bay. Nairne, however, never succeeded in bringing order to the colony's frontier. Indians complained of the treatment they received at the hands of colonial traders—beatings, cheating, theft, rape, and enslavement, as well as the steady encroachment of planters onto their lands. With their appeals to the Proprietors unanswered, Indians rose up. The Tuscarora War began in 1711 and spread rapidly. In the conflict, brief but bloody, Carolina troops and their Indian allies killed nearly 1400 Tuscaroras, and enslaved 1000 more. Some of the survivors found shelter in the marginal country along today's South Carolina–North Carolina border. More of them, about 2500 in all, fled northward to New York, becoming within a decade the Sixth Nation of the Iroquois League. Most of the fighting took place in the vicinity of North Carolina's Albemarle Sound. Tensions remained after the war came to a close. The Yamasee War that began in 1715 involved the Creeks, the Yamasees, the Choctaws, and dozens of other small communities who had grown tired of their suffering at the hands of Carolinians.

When the colonists began to hear rumors of an Indian assault, the Proprietors sent Thomas Nairne to assure the Yamasees that they would address all of their grievances. The Yamasees killed Nairne, roasted him, and then lashed out at the settlements. Traders were "knocked in the head," and their posts broken open and looted. Those colonists who survived the initial attacks fled to Charlestown. As with King Philip's War in New England and the conflict in Virginia that preceded Bacon's Rebellion, the English in Carolina feared that all the Indians in the region had joined in the uprising. They feared as well that the Cherokees might join with the Creeks and Yamasees.

The Cherokees sent a delegation to Charlestown in the fall of 1715. They pledged their friendship to the colonists, but would not engage in hostilities with their Yamasee relations. At Charlestown the Cherokees, according to one Anglican missionary, "made peace with us with their wild ceremonies of grave dancing wherein they stripped themselves and put their cloaths by parcels at the feet of some of the most considerable men who in return must do the like for them." These rituals of exchange, the missionary noted, were "a solemn token of reconciliation and friendship." When a Creek diplomatic party visited the Cherokees later that year, the colony's new allies put them to death, sparking years of warfare between the Creeks and Cherokees.

That warfare chastened those Cherokees who had sought an English alliance. They had thought that their gesture would ensure English assistance against the Creeks. Those who came to Charlestown expected that the English would fight beside them and act as allies. This the English did not do. After the colony destroyed the Yamasees, its leaders fomented and provoked discord between the Creeks and Cherokees. "The game" Carolina sought to play was "how to hold both as friends, for some time, and assist them in cutting one another's throats without offending either." As the Creeks pummeled them during the war and after, the Cherokees learned that the English could not be relied upon to behave as allies should.

The human costs of this business were enormous. Captive-taking had a long history among southeastern native peoples, but the Indian slave trade was something new, unprecedented, and devastating. Some native peoples joined in this trade. The Chickasaws, for example, grew from a small community to a major power player in the late seventeenth-century southeast through the wealth they acquired in the slave trade. They made war on enemy peoples with the support of Carolina because they did not yet think of themselves and their neighbors as "Indians."

But the benefits that went to those involved were short-lived. The Indian slave trade created a "shatter zone" in the southeast that emanated outwards from Carolina, carrying shockwaves of disease and violence into the interior. It was likely the violent colonial trade in Indian slaves that carried the first epidemics into the southern interior.

It is difficult to discern precisely how many native peoples lived in the native southeast in the late seventeenth century, but there may have been in 1685 just under 200,000 people. Within three decades, that figure likely had fallen to less than 100,000. The export of native slaves to the West Indies may account for half of the population loss, and death from disease and warfare the rest. So many native peoples had died that the native slave trade collapsed in the aftermath of the Yamasee War, and the region around Charleston was, by its conclusion, clear of native peoples. The spaces they once occupied were increasingly occupied by African slaves.

Native Peoples and the Nature of Empires

During the Tuscarora War, among those enslaved was a Seneca messenger sent by the governor of New York "to caution the Tuscaroras against going to war with the English." Thomas Pollock, the governor of North Carolina, the colonial government of New York, and the Iroquois all involved themselves in the effort to resolve this crisis. Freeing the captive risked alienating Carolina's Indian allies, and in particular the captain who had captured him. Keeping the Seneca diplomat in bondage, however, risked alienating the powerful Iroquois. The captive's story shows something of the complexities of managing the early Anglo-American frontier, and the importance of native peoples to the smooth functioning of English Imperialism. Indeed, the Yamasee War, in its own way, discredited the Carolina proprietors in the eyes of the English government, which viewed the war as needless and risky. South Carolina's first royal governor, Sir Francis Nicholson, who took over after the crown royalized the colony, received a commission from the king reminding him that the Carolinas had "fallen into such disorder and confusion, that the public peace and administration of justice ... is broken and violated, and the said province become wholly void of defense against any foreign enemy, or even against the incursions of the barbarous Indians, whereby the Southern frontier to our Plantations on the Continent of America, and one of the most fruitful of all our Colonies, is in great danger of being depopulated, and the trade and advantages thereof forever lost from the Crown of Great Britain." European empires in America, quite simply, needed Indian allies, a reality that colonial administrators ignored at their own peril. They could not achieve their imperial objectives—profit, security, and conversion, without peace.

Indians, for their part, pursued alliance with their new neighbors in hope of advancing the interests of their community—military, economic, spiritual, and diplomatic. In so doing, natives and newcomers at times found a middle ground, a path through the woods along which they learned to accommodate each other, to work with people who they could not compel to see things their way. Traders in places forged friendships and formed families.

Many lived for extended periods in Indian communities and felt comfortable there. Some Indians, in some places, respected the missionaries who ministered to them, and some sincerely found in the new religion solutions to the substantial problems they faced. Indians throughout North America attempted to live with the Europeans, and to incorporate them, and their technology, into their culture. They acquired from the newcomers trade goods they needed and engaged in nuanced diplomacy. But they faced an enormous challenge, and we can see Indians confronting these challenges everywhere Europeans went.

The promoters of European colonization in America, whether Dutch or French or Spanish or English, shared a number of goals in common. Though the different European powers emphasized, at different times, one or more of these goals over others, all of them hoped to profit through their enterprise, through trade or plantation. They hoped to establish secure and defensible settlements in America. And they expected that Indians would abandon their own cultural moorings and convert to Christianity. The colonists sent to America did not always share these goals, and the violent and aggressive treatment of Indians by frontier settlers was all too common. Familiarity often bred contempt, and that contempt could explode into horrific violence. Violence was a fact of life, a product of the colonists' territorial and cultural aggressiveness and native peoples' determination to preserve control over their ways of living.

4

Native Peoples and the Fall of European Empires

Penn's Woods

Towards the end of the colonial period, the provincial secretary of Pennsylvania, Richard Peters, wondered if it was "impossible for Indians and White people to live together." The history of native peoples over the course of the preceding century and more could not have left him feeling optimistic. European colonizers seldom overtly sought war with the continent's native peoples. Indeed, they recognized that they could most easily and least expensively obtain their colonial and imperial objectives with the assistance of Indians. Hostile Indians would not trade with the newcomers, nor would they allow colonists to establish stable and productive agricultural settlements. Indians at war with the colonists might seize the opportunity to play one European power off against another in order to preserve their own independence, or descend upon colonial settlements in "savage" fury. European missionaries, meanwhile, could not hope to cast their religion in an appealing light to Indians who found themselves under fire from colonial troops. Native peoples, too, sought peace, to transform strangers into kin, to establish with the newcomers relationships to benefit their communities. But conflict always arrived. The colonizers failed to achieve any sort of meaningful control over the frontier and its inhabitants, Native American and European. Settlers expanded onto Indian lands, provoking crises that too often ended in violence. Warfare became a fundamental piece of the process of colonialism.

Peters' lament shows that the history of Pennsylvania followed a trajectory similar to that of its predecessors. William Penn received his charter from Charles II in 1681, and began his "Holy Experiment" as colonial proprietor along the banks of the Delaware and the Schuykill Rivers. Peaceful relations with neighboring Indians, Penn knew, were essential for his colony's success and consistent with his Quaker beliefs. He believed that Indians and whites could live together in peace. But like other promoters of settlement, he quickly lost control of affairs in his colony. The population grew and expanded outward from the Delaware and into the Susquehanna River Valley. Penn's settlers coveted these lands but so, too, did the Six Nations. After the peace of 1701, Iroquois raiders moved through the colony and claimed the Susquehanna River valley by right of conquest. They claimed as well the power to sell the lands of other native peoples who occupied the valley—the Conestogas, a remnant of the Susquehannocks, and Delawares who moved westward as the colony's population expanded into the interior, as well as other refugee peoples—even if these groups rejected Iroquois pretensions to their lands.

Native America: A History, Second Edition. Michael Leroy Oberg.
© 2018 John Wiley & Sons, Inc. Published 2018 by John Wiley & Sons, Inc.

Penn's successors—his sons and James Logan—decided to cast their lot with the Iroquois in this multi-cultural contest for control of the region. They could claim little without Iroquois support. As Logan told the Conestogas, Conoys, Delawares, and Shawnees, the Iroquois had entered into a treaty with the colony of Pennsylvania and "have included you in it, and have obliged you to observe it as well as themselves." To the complaints of the Shawnees and others that they were nobody's subjects, Logan told them that "the Five Nations have an absolute authority over all our Indians, and may command them as they please."

Alienated by the growing alliance between Pennsylvania and the Six Nations, a pact represented to the Delawares and others most powerfully by Pennsylvania's corrupt "Walking Purchase" of 1737, native peoples moved out of the path of the expanding settlements and away from the Iroquois. They moved west and entered a region the French called the *pays d'en haut*, a middle ground occupied by scores of native peoples. Some of them fled dislocation and warfare. Others sought land, or to get away from the relentless colonists. However they came to the region, they settled in multi-ethnic villages made up of peoples with ties to many different tribal groups.

The Potawatomis in a World of Conflicting Empires

The dawn of the eighteenth century brought a new world for the Potawatomis. They had spent nearly half a century engaged in conflict with the Five Nations. They had carried warfare into Iroquoia. With the agreement of 1701, however, regular assaults by Iroquois war parties subsided. To be sure, both parties violated the peace from time to time, but the agreement of 1701 brought an important, albeit short-lived, era of relative peace to the western Great Lakes.

After 1701 the French began to develop Detroit as a center for intercultural trade. Within a few years, more than 6000 Indians, including a significant number of Potawatomis, had relocated to the lands around the newly constructed Fort Pontchartrain. Other Potawatomis left the vicinity of Green Bay and moved to Michigan's St. Joseph River Valley, where they settled around a Jesuit mission established for them in 1703.

More powerful than many of their rivals in the region, a good number of whom were refugees who had settled in the vicinity of the French in hopes of reversing their fortunes, the Potawatomis prospered during the first decade of the eighteenth century. They worked hard to maintain their alliance, and the French, in turn, took care not to offend the Potawatomis. The Potawatomis' desire for French trade goods and their need for French weaponry for their own defense balanced the needs of the French for the military and economic assistance Potawatomi villagers could provide. The parties needed each other, creating the foundation, according to anthropologist James Clifton, for a relationship based upon "mutually acceptable accommodations, mutual interdependency, and a two-way pattern of beneficial symbiosis." The Potawatomis and the French, in this sense, had constructed a "middle ground." Late in the nineteenth century, the important American historian Frederick Jackson Turner had described the American frontier as a line that moved raggedly but steadily westward, and as the "outer edge of the wave" and the "meeting point between savagery and civilization." This notion of a frontier line, with savagery on one side and civility on the other, has had a long life in the writing of American Indian history. Richard White, a historian who published *The Middle Ground* in 1991, powerfully challenged this part of the "Turner Thesis." Neither natives nor newcomers possessed the strength to impose their mores, their values, and their agendas upon the other unilaterally. With the exception of a few Jesuit priests, neither side tried to change the other. There were conversions to

Catholicism in places to be sure. But native peoples who accepted Christianity did so on their own terms, and for their own reasons.

The Fox Wars, in which the Potawatomis played a major role, shattered the short-lived peace and dominated the public affairs of the Potawatomis into the 1730s. The Foxes had many enemies who opposed the efforts of the French to include them in their growing network of alliances. These enemies, including the Potawatomis but also the Illinois, Ottawas, Ojibwes, Miamis, and Hurons, attacked the Foxes regularly beginning late in the seventeenth century. The Foxes fought against the Dakota Sioux as well.

The French encouraged peace but the problems escalated in 1711. A group of Mascoutens, close allies of the Foxes, settled on lands in southwestern Michigan that the Potawatomis considered their own. They did so at the invitation of the French. Angered by this encroachment and jealous of their trade ties to the French, Potawatomis from the St. Joseph Valley joined with a force of Ottawas and Illinois to attack the Mascouten village. They slaughtered fifty Mascoutens and destroyed the settlement. Meanwhile, a force of Foxes and Mascoutens assembled near Detroit. When they learned of the attack on their Mascouten allies, they attacked several Ottawa houses near the fort. They then began their siege, rendering the French position at Detroit dangerous. The French had few troops, and several hundred angry Fox and Mascouten warriors surrounded them.

The French sent out messengers, and by May of 1712, a force of nearly 600 allied Indians, mostly Potawatomis and Ottawas, but also including Hurons, Menominees, Sauks, Illinois, Osages, and Missouris, had arrived to relieve the fort. They surrounded the Foxes and Mascoutens, killed some and enslaved others. In a daring flight, the battered Foxes escaped through the lines of their besiegers and fled eastward. The Potawatomis gave chase. Some of the Foxes and Mascoutens made it to the Seneca country, but Potawatomis took the others prisoner. Mackisabe, a Potawatomi leader determined to extinguish "the Fire of the Fox," killed the captured warriors and spared only the women and children. Many of these the Potawatomis sold as slaves to the French. In buying these slaves, the French gave their allies further cause, and an economic incentive, for war against the Foxes.

Mackisabe traveled to Montreal in 1712. He sought guarantees of French protection against Fox and Mascouten vengeance, and an alliance with the French that excluded his enemies. He knew that the Potawatomi towns in the St. Joseph valley stood exposed to Fox attacks. Many of the Potawatomis in the western parts of Michigan thus left their homes and moved to Detroit, where they established a village on the north bank of the Detroit River under the leadership of Winamac. Other Potawatomis migrated into the region in the years that followed so that by 1718 they were the most numerous tribe at Detroit, capable of fielding 180 warriors. Just as the French sought Indian allies to help them withstand the strength of the English, the Potawatomis used their alliance with the French to resist their native enemies.

From this base the Potawatomis joined in the continuing attacks against the Foxes and Mascoutens. They captured fifty and killed over 100 more in 1715 during a raid into southern Wisconsin. They attacked the Fox position at Butte des Morts in central Wisconsin one year later. The French, during these years, hoped to reduce the fighting, and extend their alliance farther west. At Butte des Morts the French commander, Louis de Louivigny, allowed the Foxes to surrender rather than face annihilation. But the fighting continued, and both the French and the Potawatomis needed to maintain their alliance. The French needed to pay attention to the needs of the native allies upon whom they relied. The construction of Fort St. Joseph in the lower St. Joseph Valley drew French traders and Potawatomis back to the area. Military alliance was important, but so too were the ties of kinship that bound the

French and Potawatomis together. When French traders married Potawatomi women and settled amongst them, these ties became quite powerful.

The Foxes had taken heavy casualties. Their own alliance began to fall apart. In 1722, the Mascoutens began to seek out opportunities for peace. Still, Fox raids continued to damage French trade and limit the access of French traders to communities west of Detroit. The Foxes warned the Potawatomis that they owed their survival to Onontio, the French governor, and that if the Potawatomis continued to engage themselves with the French, the Foxes would "devour them." The Foxes employed creative but desperate diplomacy to sustain themselves. They made peace with the Dakotas, thus providing themselves with an escape route to the west should they face an invasion by the French or their Indian allies. They made peace with several bands of Sacs and Winnebagos as well. And the Foxes launched new assaults in Illinois, isolating the French outposts at Cahokia and at St. Joseph from Detroit. The Foxes cited the enslavement of their kin as the cause for this warfare. If the French could see to the release of these slaves, perhaps an alliance that included the Foxes might still be forged. But French colonists desired Fox slaves, providing their allies with cause to attack. The Foxes resumed their raids.

In 1729 the French decided that they needed to bring order to the chaos they had helped create. The new governor at Detroit, Charles de Beauharnois, set in motion a plan to destroy the Foxes. A large party of allied Indians, led by Potawatomis but also including Ottawas, Sauks, Miamis, and Hurons, marched on Fox territory. Recognizing that they faced a massive force without allies, the Foxes tried to flee eastward. They moved slowly across northern Illinois, slowed by their women and children. They were surrounded finally on the banks of the Illinois River. Their pursuers began a siege that lasted more than three weeks. During a thunderstorm that struck in September of 1730, the Foxes tried to break out. The hungry cries of their starving children gave them away, and their enemies wiped them out. Fewer than sixty Fox warriors survived the slaughter. A few survivors turned toward Green Bay where they settled amongst the Sauks, but the French pursued them here, too. They then fled across the Mississippi into Iowa. The French continued to pursue, determined to eradicate the Foxes, but the Potawatomis and other French-allied Indians would not abide the further slaughter of their defeated enemy. They had achieved their own objectives, apart from the French. They had wanted to push away from them a rival who made alliances with their enemies. The Potawatomis and other French-allied Indians did not seek utter annihilation. They intervened on behalf of the few remaining Foxes, explaining to Beauharnois that their long-standing enemy no longer posed a threat to anyone. The Fox Wars came to a close when France's allies, capable of limiting French power in the west, tired of the fighting. Of the Fox population, several thousand in the 1710s, only a couple of hundred remained.

There were other conflicts. Even before the defeat of the Foxes, Potawatomis joined those French-allied Indians who fell upon the Chickasaws, southern Indians whose war parties regularly attacked French traders on the Mississippi. They also had to contend with the growing influence of the English in the western Great Lakes. The English constructed Fort Oswego on the northern shore of Lake Ontario to intercept French trade moving through Lake Ontario, into the St. Lawrence, and toward Montreal. Oswego threatened the French fur trade, for the French could compete neither in terms of the quality of the goods available for trade or the prices they offered. Some of the native peoples who had settled near Detroit took the opportunity to break away from the French during King George's War in the 1740s when Britain blockaded New France. Indians interested in trade had no alternative. The Hurons and Wyandots broke away. So, too, did the Miamis. Under the leadership of Demoiselle, known to the English as Old Briton, the Miamis established Pickawillany, a village in northwestern Ohio along the upper stretch of the Great Miami River, sought alliance with the Haudenosaunee, and welcomed the arrival of English traders.

The Potawatomis faced a difficult challenge. They had maintained their alliance with the French. They had received some rewards for their assistance, but they still needed a steady supply of trade goods. British traders had superior goods, which they could provide in greater quantity for lower prices. The Potawatomis thus worked to maintain their alliance with the French, but they also tried to avoid offending the British. They managed to pull off this difficult trick only because the French viewed the Potawatomis as the sole native nation in the west upon whom they could rely completely.

Because the French could not compete economically with the British, the colonial regime decided to employ military force to drive out the British. Late in the 1740s Pierre Joseph Celoron claimed the Ohio River Valley for France. He drove the British traders from Pickiwillany but he could not convince Demoiselle to respect French claims to the region. Demoiselle traded where he wanted and with whom he wanted. In 1752, under the leadership of Charles de Langlade, the son of an Ottawa mother and a French father—a child of fur trade alliances—the French and their Indian allies attacked Pickiwillany. Most of the French allied Indians wanted to allow the Miamis to surrender. When Demoiselle emerged from the British traders' fort in which he had taken shelter, however, Langlade's warriors killed him and then ate part of his body. The attack regained for the French control of the Ohio Country, for a time, and renewed the Potawatomis' faith in the power of the French. The French constructed Fort Duquesne at the forks of the Ohio to capitalize on Langlade's raid, and the Potawatomis maintained their close relationship with them through the end of the colonial era.

Settlement and Unsettledness

The Cherokees found their world transformed after the Yamasee War. The conflict had destroyed many of the small native communities of the Carolina Piedmont, and European traders recognized that the most fruitful path for commerce led westward, towards large communities like the Cherokees. Carolina traders traveled to the Cherokee towns, but so, too, did Virginians and a few Frenchmen who wandered in from the west. The South Carolina colonial assembly, dominated by planters from the low country, believed that the aggressions and misconduct of frontier traders had provoked the Yamasee War, and it sought to regulate the conduct of Indian trade. According to a law the assembly enacted in 1717, Cherokees could trade legally with colonists only at colonial forts. They hoped to keep unruly whites from causing trouble in Indian towns, but the planters, who presided over an emerging system of African slavery, also hoped to curtail intermingling between races. The colony's population of 9580 included 2900 African and 1400 Native American slaves. The assembly feared an alliance in black and red.

Colonial elites in South Carolina proved no more capable than any of their predecessors in securing an orderly frontier. They never developed the administrative mechanisms to control traders who spread out over a large and remotely settled territory. Settlers and traders could not be controlled easily, but neither could the Cherokees. With Virginians and Frenchmen competing for their trade, they drove a hard bargain, and they wanted trade to take place in their villages. If Carolinians did not treat them properly, they would carry their trade elsewhere, and the Carolinians knew it.

There is no doubting that the Cherokees valued colonial trade goods, but they seem to have valued them initially for reasons that their trade partners failed to recognize. Most Cherokee men carried firearms by the end of the Yamasee War. Cherokees acquired alcohol as well, which certainly led to an exaggeration of typically male behavior, but not necessarily to the horror stories told by terrified English observers. At the same time they sought to acquire guns and alcohol, however, Cherokee women cut apart iron trade pots and used the pieces for making hoes. They broke apart pottery and ceramics carried west by colonial traders to make necklaces and pendants. Many of the items that Cherokees seemed to value most highly were those that traders considered trinkets and trash. To native peoples, the mirrors, amulets, crystals, glass beads, and paint reflected great spiritual power.

Cherokee men hunted for deerskins and captives, which they exchanged with traders for European goods. The warfare required to take these captives brought significant changes to Cherokee villages. Warfare and raiding became endemic, a dangerous, profit-seeking venture. Previously, Cherokee women influenced community decisions over whether to go to war and how captives ought to be treated. Now, men made these decisions, apart from women, as they took captives and exchanged them for European goods. When the Indian slave trade began to decline early in the second quarter of the eighteenth century, a product of the decimation of native peoples in South Carolina, Cherokee men devoted their time to taking deerskins. Cherokee men began to see an economic advantage in killing as many deer as possible and they may have begun to move away from a traditional view of the world that stressed the kinship of human and other-than-human beings. Men began to exercise their dominion over nature, harvesting deerskins that they saw as little more than commodities for exchange in an Atlantic marketplace. They may have ignored Kanati's rituals.

Certainly the older view continued in places, but there can be no doubting that many Cherokees had become dependent on European goods. With some exaggeration, the Cherokee Skiagunsta told South Carolina's governor James Glen in 1745 that "my people … cannot live independent of the English… The clothes we wear we cannot make ourselves. They are made for us. We use their ammunition with which to kill deer. We cannot make guns," he said, and "every necessary of life we must have from the white people."

Colonial officials in South Carolina seem to have believed that trade could lead to alliance, and that the goods English traders provided to the Cherokees could purchase their dependence. In a sense, they were right. Exchange, to the Cherokees a political act that required a reciprocal response and that established a balanced relationship between partners, Carolina officials viewed as a means to purchase an Anglo-Indian empire.

But it wasn't that simple. The colony's long-serving governor, James Glen (1743–1756), thought for instance that his colony could control the Cherokees by controlling the quantity of trade goods flowing into their villages. That alliance he viewed as necessary for the colony to expand westward, and to protect its interests from the French farther to their west. In 1751, he noted that "it is absolutely necessary for us to be in friendship with the Cherokees," for they were "reckoned to be about three thousand gunmen, the greatest nation we know of in America except for the Choctaws and while we call them friends, we may consider them a bulwark at our backs, for such numbers will secure us in that quarter from the attempts of the French." Glen, who watched the growing British movement towards war with France with tremendous concern, recognized that his colony needed the Cherokees as badly as the Cherokees needed Carolina. The colony's need for Indian allies masked for a time whatever dependence the Cherokees had on English goods.

It is important to remember that the Cherokees never viewed their history solely as an adjunct to that of the European empires. After 1701, Iroquois attacks on the Cherokees increased in frequency, as the Senecas and other Iroquois directed their men along the warriors' path to the south. This warfare, by the 1730s, certainly concerned English imperial officials. Fighting between native allies of the crown, imperial officials recognized, created an opening for the French or the Spanish to either exploit these divisions or, alternatively, to take advantage of native nations weakened by warfare and unable to serve effectively as imperial allies. Native peoples reminded imperial officials who really controlled the continent's interior every day by pursuing the interests of their communities, sometimes defiantly.

The British encouraged the Cherokees to work out a peace with the Iroquois. The Cherokees, indeed, had reasons to seek peace. The warriors who accompanied General James Edward Oglethorpe on his ill-conceived plan to strike the Spanish fort at St. Augustine had suffered terribly, and they carried smallpox home to their villages. By 1742, the Cherokees had accepted a truce offered by the Six Nations. Still, fighting continued. Cherokees continued to kill warriors from the Six Nations, and Iroquois raiders continued to fall upon the Cherokees. The lesson, perhaps, should have been clear to English imperial authorities. Despite calling upon the Six Nations and the Cherokees to cease their raids, and despite the pledges of Iroquois sachems and Cherokee leaders to work out a peace, small groups of warriors were as difficult for their leaders to control as scattered frontier settlers and isolated traders were for colonial governors. The Cherokee frontier, a land influenced by competing European empires and contested by contending native nations, was an unstable region.

Much the same could be said of the Caddo country. It had been almost two decades since the Spanish abandoned their mission outposts among the Caddos, and the chiefdoms welcomed the opportunity to trade directly with Europeans when a French expedition headed by Jean-Baptiste Le Moyne, Sieur de Bienville, visited their territory. For years the Caddos in eastern Texas had hosted large trading fairs, where they exchanged their foodstuffs, salt, and wood for turquoise and cotton blankets that came via the Pueblos. The Caddos traded horses that they had rustled or found stray with the Spanish and with Quapaws and Illinois who lived to their north. The Caddos had not integrated the horse into their culture, as Plains tribes were beginning to do, but they did view the *cavali*, their name for horses that they derived from the Spanish language, as an important commodity in intercultural exchange.

Bienville found his advance into the Caddo country slow going. He dispatched a young member of his party, Louis Juchereau de Saint-Denis, to visit the Kadohadachos and the Natchitoches. Saint-Denis exchanged guns and ammunition for salt and horses. By 1705, Saint-Denis had established a solid trading relationship with the Hasinais. Saint-Denis, indeed, was a skilled intercultural mediator. The Natchitoches, for instance, had been continually assaulted by the Chickasaws. When a flood wiped out their crops in 1702, their leader Chef Blanc asked Saint-Denis for assistance. The Frenchman suggested to Chef Blanc that his people move closer to the French post, and settle amongst the allied Acolapissas along the banks of Lake Pontchartrain. From here, Saint-Denis joined Natchitoches warriors on raids against their common enemies, and Chef Blanc allowed hungry Frenchmen to winter at his villages and live upon his stores.

The Caddos needed French guns and ammunition to hold off Chickasaw raiders armed by the English. In 1712 the French king granted to Antoine Crozat a monopoly over trade in the province of Louisiana, and Crozat urged his men on the ground to transform the colony into a money-making concern. He urged the colony to develop its trading ties with Indians in New Spain, and in this endeavor, the Caddos could play an important middleman role. By 1717, when Crozat relinquished his monopoly to an interest headed by Bienville and called the Company of the Indies, the French had come to recognize the importance of the Caddos to their imperial aspirations. Bienville placed trading with the Kadohadachos under the command of Bénard de La Harpe, a skilled and energetic trader who grounded relations with the Caddos on a firm footing. La Harpe guaranteed the Caddos that he would protect them from their enemies, and secure for them access to French goods. Caught between armed Osages and Quapaws, the trade initiated by La Harpe benefited the Caddos immensely for they now could acquire the guns and ammunition necessary to defend themselves in return for items that, to them, were easily acquired and easy to replenish—horses, pelts, and salt.

Caddos acted and Europeans reacted. French diplomatic and trading ventures among the Caddos worried the Spanish. In 1716, they tried again to establish a mission, backed by a small number of soldiers, among the Hasinais. The Hasinais welcomed the missionaries and the gifts that they brought, but they had no interest in Christianity. An epidemic that began in 1717 and that killed over 100 members of the community, carried to the Hasinais by the missionaries, strengthened the Hasinais' distaste for the priests. And while they ignored the message of the missionaries to abandon their "barbaric" ways and accept the word of the Lord, they also refused to cut their ties to the French. The priests believed that little hope existed for converting the Hasinais without force, and no possibility existed for doing that given the limited number of soldiers the missionaries had at their disposal. The Spanish withdrew their missionaries, leaving the Caddos free to develop their relationship with the French. The Caddos demonstrated clearly the limits of Spain's imperial power in the American west.

The French paid well for slaves and Caddo warriors quickly became involved in the dangerous raiding and trading that the traffic in human bondage entailed. The slave trade, in eastern Texas and Louisiana as in Carolina and the Great Lakes, commercialized the warfare of native nations, providing warriors with an economic incentive to attack neighboring peoples. In exchange for slaves, the Caddos acquired the guns and ammunition they used to defend themselves from their enemies. Some of these weapons the Caddos passed on to other native communities. They became middlemen in the regional arms trade. French weapons flowed from the Caddos to the Wichitas and Comanches, with whom they allied against the Lipan Apaches. French trade thus involved the Caddos in additional warfare but also increased their influence among neighboring peoples. The Caddos used the French as the French attempted to use them.

This interaction came with costs. Contact with the French meant continued exposure to European diseases, which continued to take their toll on the Caddos. The population continued to fall in the eighteenth century. They maintained their strength during this era of disease by consolidating. Some Caddoan communities, like the Nabitis, disappeared entirely, while others relocated and joined their neighbors. The Hasinai confederacy declined from eight chiefdoms to four in the years after the French returned. In order to maintain the strength necessary to ensure that the French recognized that they posed a significant challenge should they become disaffected, the Caddos retrenched, reorganized, and thereby preserved their communities. Traditional religious leaders, the *xinesi*, and the temples in which they conducted their rituals, the *coninsi*, disappeared after the formation of the French alliance. As they formed a smaller number of more concentrated communities, a necessary adjustment to the ravages of warfare and epidemic disease, the Caddos experienced changes at the fundamental core of their culture.

Contact with the French may, as well, have produced a degree of dependence among the Caddos upon European manufactured goods. In exchange for buffalo hides, deer skins, corn, horses, mules, and slaves, the Caddos acquired from the French guns and steel tomahawks and other bladed weapons. French observers reported that they rarely saw Caddos carrying bows and arrows. They needed European guns and steel to defend themselves from competing native communities. Caddos also acquired European clothing and blankets, tools such as scissors, awls, screws, and flints, and cosmetic items such as bracelets, beads, combs, and mirrors. They could have lived without these items but the hides from which they normally would have made their clothing were exchanged with the French and they could not produce these items themselves. That they needed the French as badly as the French needed them ensured the continuation of the alliance.

Life at the Western Door

The Senecas and their kin in the Iroquois League ultimately expected much more from their French and English allies than the two imperial powers were prepared to give, and shortly after 1701, the neutrality of the Iroquois faced significant challenges. First, though the French did little to restrain the Senecas in the west, they also did little to protect them from New France's Indian allies. A Miami raiding party killed several Senecas and Oneidas on the Great Lakes in 1704 and, one year later, a party of Ottawas took several dozen captives in the Seneca country. Some Iroquois wanted war.

The French sent Louis-Thomas Chabert de Joncaire as their emissary to live among the Senecas. Though the other Iroquois nations opposed his meddling in League politics and the favoritism he showed the Senecas, Joncaire, through deft trade and diplomacy, managed to keep the Senecas aligned with New France. In the east, Iroquois raiders aided the French in attacks on the English after war resumed between the two powers in 1702, most famously in the attack on the Massachusetts town of Deerfield in February of 1704. There, League warriors took eleven captives who they later adopted. They also demonstrated their importance to the French as allies, solidified their reputation as warriors, and in essence directed imperial warfare away from the Haudenosaunee homeland.

The British, meanwhile, hoped to enlist the Iroquois in an assault upon New France. Neither imperial power demonstrated much interest in fighting the other directly. Both employed their Indian allies to do the dirty work of extending their empires. The Iroquois quickly learned that they could rely upon neither the English nor the French as military allies. English assistance always arrived too little, too late, and too reluctantly. English military ventures during the war ended in disaster, campaigns conducted by unimpressive soldiers commanded by incompetent and pompous officers. After the Peace of Utrecht, which ended the conflict in 1713, the Iroquois emerged even more committed to neutrality.

It was not an easy neutrality to maintain. Many Tuscaroras moved north to become, by 1714, the sixth Iroquois nation. They settled in the southern parts of Iroquoia, along the Susquehanna River in New York. They may have maintained some contacts with those Tuscaroras who did not accompany them on their northern march. The immigrants left behind them warfare in the Carolinas. They settled amongst the Iroquois in opposition to the wishes of New York's governor Robert Hunter. To remain neutral, the Iroquois needed to convince their neighbors that Six Nations warriors could threaten their security should they become disaffected. The role they played in the early rounds of the European imperial struggle contributed to a perception of Iroquois strength, but the Six Nations needed additional warriors to make a convincing case. This gave the Haudenosaunee the incentive they needed to admit the Tuscaroras, a culturally related group who had followed the "White Roots of Peace" into the Iroquois Longhouse.

To sustain their neutrality, the Six Nations needed well informed and skillful diplomacy. The path their warriors took along trails south involved the Iroquois in the affairs of a growing number of colonies, including Pennsylvania, which transformed the Iroquois into overlords, granting them an empire in order to claim it for themselves. The western Iroquois could claim, with Pennsylvania's support, considerable influence.

Both the British and French, of course, intended their alliance with the Six Nations to serve the ends of empire. Both European powers wanted to control the west, and began to plan for the construction of forts in the homelands of the Iroquois. The French built Fort Niagara in 1720, an attempt to stop the diversion of furs from western Indians through Iroquoia to the better prices and more abundant goods at the British posts in New York. By the middle of the 1720s, the British began the construction of Fort Oswego, on the southern shore of Lake Ontario. The post, British imperial officials hoped, would draw in furs otherwise headed toward Montreal. Constructing Oswego may have rendered the position of the eastern Iroquois nations less important to the conduct of the fur trade, since traders could travel to a British post without passing through their territories.

These changes, however, do not appear to have affected the Senecas. The European posts were distant from the core Seneca area. The Senecas had occupied a key position in the fur trade after 1701 as geographic middlemen. Before the construction of the forts at Niagara and Oswego, western Indians traveling to Montreal or Albany had to pass through the Senecas' homeland, and doing that required the formation and maintenance of alliances, the regular exchange of gifts, and the establishment of peace. Both the English and the French made overtures to the Senecas in an attempt to persuade them to direct their western allies toward either Albany or Montreal. They also presented the Senecas with gifts to secure their assistance.

Even after the construction of Oswego western Indians traveling to the English post would have stopped along the shore of Lake Ontario in Seneca territory. Indians making this voyage still visited the Senecas, and renewed the ties of kinship and exchange that had been forged after 1701. During these years, the Senecas altered their settlement patterns. They abandoned the western "Seneca Castle" near Canandaigua Lake at some point in the 1740s and moved westward toward the Genesee River. They did not move toward Lake Ontario to intercept western Indians, but greeted these travelers at home, a sign that the alliances they forged remained strong, and that their role in the western fur trade remained viable.

As they relocated, the Senecas also abandoned life in multi-family longhouses packed tightly behind defensive palisades. Benefiting economically from the passage of western nations through their lands, and enjoying a period of unprecedented peace at home, Seneca families dispersed across the countryside in single family farmsteads that preserved an open, central hearth. Women, the performers of agricultural labor, chose to live closer to their fields and to supplies of water. They continued to plant the "Three Sisters," maize, beans, and squash, while men entered the woods to hunt. There were challenges. Alcohol acquired from traders could cause problems, and Iroquois leaders complained to the English at Albany about the effects of the rum trade on their communities. But the Senecas were far from powerless. They occupied a strategically critical territory and enjoyed an era of peace in their homeland after the settlement of 1701. They possessed abundant lands in New York, and asserted control over the lands of other nations. Because doing so made their lives easier, many colonists recognized these claims. This, coupled with the still-considerable military power of the Six

Nations, and the enormous respect with which their warriors were viewed, ensured the Senecas and the Six Nations a fundamental role in the fate of the European empires in America when imperial war returned to the continent in the 1740s. The Six Nations remained a force with which Europeans must reckon.

Behind the Frontier

There was a time when most native peoples could force Europeans to pay attention to their concerns and at least try to respect their customs. Native peoples living "behind" the frontier, among white settlers in European-American communities that had grown on lands claimed and governed by the colonists, had lost much of this ability. They could not play one European power off against another. They lived their lives as colonized peoples.

Among the remnants of the Powhatan chiefdom of Virginia, important parts of their traditional culture remained intact. Men still hunted and trapped, albeit over a much narrower expanse of territory, and with much less to show for their efforts. Women continued to plant crops, albeit on a shrinking quantity of land. From these efforts, Powhatans derived much of their subsistence, but they also directed some of this activity toward the colonial market. Pamunkeys sold the birds they hunted along Virginia's waterways to neighboring planters, directing a traditional male activity toward the colonial economy. Other Powhatans crafted pottery with flat rather than rounded bottoms, suitable for colonial tables. Engagement with the colonial market in this fashion required little in terms of cultural compromise, and allowed for a substantial measure of autonomy.

Still, native peoples in coastal Virginia, like colonized peoples elsewhere, faced significant change. The demographic decline described by Robert Beverley continued. To some degree, this decline may be a function of the surviving records—native women married English men on the margins or African Americans, leading to the disappearance of identifiably Indian names in the historical record. Some of the decline may similarly be illusory in that native peoples had learned enough over a century of contact with Europeans not to draw attention to themselves. But the decline was real. In 1786, according to reports, the Nansemonds consisted of only five people, all of them sick and impoverished. The decline in their power was easily apparent before then, for the Virginia House of Burgesses acted as if it need not worry about the negative effects of its actions upon Indians. In 1705, for instance, the Virginia assembly passed a law which defined native peoples as non-white, and placed them in the same category for discriminatory treatment as Catholics, convicts, Africans and African Americans, and other non-Christians. They could not testify in courts of law against white Virginians, the same people who sought to acquire their lands and place them in bondage.

Poverty and a lack of legal protections raised the prospect of dispossession, and the Powhatans struggled to hang on to their lands. The Pamunkeys still preserved at the beginning of the eighteenth century some of their lands but colonists pressured them into sales and seized more than the cash-strapped Pamunkeys reluctantly had agreed to sell. To counter these threats, the Pamunkey leader, Queen Anne, determined in 1715 to sell no more land to the English colonists. Her prohibition against further sales did not, and could not, hold. Her people were poor, and they needed the cash that sales of their land generated.

The Pamunkeys struggled to survive. White settlers surrounded their lands, and this made normal subsistence activities difficult. Some Pamunkeys, like an individual named Robin who appears in the colonial records beginning in 1709, had learned the shoemaking trade and lived with the English to practice his craft. Others worked on colonists' plantations as servants and slaves. Those who stayed at home must have recognized that they had little left that colonists wanted but their land. In 1748 the Pamunkeys sold over 3000 acres to the colonists. A decade later, in 1759, the Pamunkeys leased an additional tract of timber land. Because they could not testify against white people in Virginia's courts, and thus could not seek redress against lessees who did not pay, they asked the colony to appoint trustees to administer leases in their behalf. Some Pamunkeys opposed the lease and appealed to the colonial council. The council rejected the petition.

The Pamunkeys managed to hold on to a sliver of their lands throughout the eighteenth century, but not all the communities that had made up Wahunsonacock's chiefdom were able to do so. The Chickahominies, who lived on a reservation with the Mattaponis and Rappahannocks on the Upper Mattaponi River, possessed 3000 acres at the beginning of the century. By 1718, these lands were gone, sold by the white overseers the colonial governor appointed to manage them. By 1730, the Chickahominies had disappeared from a list of tributary Indians kept by the colony's governor.

Still, the Chickahominies may have persisted on the Upper Mattaponi. Records for King William County, where the reservation stood, were destroyed in 1885, but the oldest existing records, dated that year, show the existence of a settlement in the county called Adamstown. It stood not far from the old reservation, and individuals described as "Indians" in county records lived there. Adams, anthropologist Helen Rountree points out, was the name of the Chickahominies' last interpreter. If they continued to survive in the vicinity of their traditional homeland, they did so quietly, on the margins of Virginia society.

Poverty and dispossession produced additional changes in Powhatan culture. By the middle of the eighteenth century the Pamunkeys, who until 1718 had been governed by Queen Anne, now had a political system dominated by the men of the community and by the trustees appointed by the colonial governor. By the late 1760s, these trustees (non-Indians all) had acquired the power from the governor to resolve disputes among members of the community. The Pamunkeys were, to a considerable extent, a community governed by non-Indians.

These commissioners, and other non-Indians with responsibility for managing the colony's Indian affairs, felt some small obligation for the "civilization" and "Christianization" of the Powhatans. Relative to the English in other colonies, however, Virginia's Anglicans did little. The College of William and Mary founded an Indian school late in the seventeenth century. Few Powhatans were interested until 1711, when Governor Alexander Spotswood offered to exempt Powhatan communities from their tributary obligations if they sent some of their male children to the school. A couple of dozen arrived by 1715, but the Englishmen affiliated with the college felt that the native scholars failed. Students who boarded in Williamsburg were more likely to die than graduate. Those who completed their education, wrote Hugh Jones, a teacher at the college until 1721, returned home and to the ways of their people, "chiefly because they can live with less labour, and more pleasure and plenty, as Indians, then they can for us."

Jones' lament suggests that the Powhatan children educated at William and Mary found no place for themselves in colonial society and that they clung to the core of their culture. The education they received was entirely English, directed toward assimilating them into colonial communities that did not welcome them, and that by law considered them members of a subordinate class. Though the college continued to educate Indian children up to the American Revolution, and Powhatan leaders recognized the importance of literacy to native peoples confronting a colonial system, few Powhatan children attended. Of the eight Indian students at the college in the middle of the 1750s, five were Pamunkeys. A decade later, only two Pamunkeys remained.

The Powhatans learned to adapt to the new colonial reality by making themselves invisible. They learned to speak English. Most of them, by the middle of the eighteenth century, wore English clothing. They had English first names and surnames that passed from father to son. Some of them learned to hate black people. African slavery created a limit beneath which the Powhatans hoped never to fall. The English never asked, but it is clear that the Powhatans viewed many things about the English with scorn and contempt: their pushiness, their arrogant and vocal assertions of cultural superiority, their penchant for giving unwanted advice, their racism. The Powhatans could do nothing about how the English felt. But they could, as much as possible, turn away and try not to draw attention to themselves.

There are significant similarities in the stories of the Powhatans and other native peoples who found themselves living behind the frontier. Uncas's successor, his son Owaneco, recklessly sold Mohegan lands. In order to preserve what remained, the Mohegans insisted that Oweneco deed these lands "unto the Mohegan Indians for their use to plant," forever. Still the lands slipped away, as the colony began to grant Mohegan land to its own citizens without the Indians' consent.

These English settlers aggressively encroached on the Mohegans' remaining lands. Settlers in the new town of Colchester, carved out of Uncas's homeland, threatened to kill Mohegans who came too close, and they burned Mohegan wigwams. The Mohegans, Owaneco said, could "not go hunting upon our own land for fear of being killed" by the Colchester men. Connecticut settlers no longer needed to fear alienating the Mohegans. King Philip's War was a distant memory, and English men and women settled in the lower Connecticut Valley no longer lost sleep about Indian enemies carrying them away in the night. With a rapidly growing English population, the Mohegans, like the Powhatans, became a small and encircled minority.

The Mohegans did not acquiesce in their dispossession, and the resulting "Mohegan Land Controversy," a transatlantic legal dispute, would last until the eve of the American Revolution. Nobody involved the complex case ever claimed that the Mohegans' lacked land rights, or that the land belonged to Europeans by right of conquest or discovery. All acted on the assumption that the Mohegans owned their land, had the right to sell it, and the capacity as well to enter into treaties with the English crown. Samuel Mason, the Mohegans' chosen protector, told a court appointed by the Crown that Connecticut Colony had illegally seized Mohegan lands. Uncas, Mason argued, had given all of his lands to Mason's father, John, who in 1671 reconveyed the land between New London and Norwich to the Mohegans forever, "the better to secure some of their lands to them and their posterity."

The court began collecting evidence in 1705. Mohegans who testified called the court's attention to their long-standing loyalty to the English. The Mohegans always had been friends to the English. Mohegan witnesses, and their English sympathizers, testified to their dispossession at the hands of aggressive settlers. Nicholas Hallam recalled that in 1703 he had met with "about thirty or forty Mohegan Indians, men, women, and children," on a very cold and snowy day. They were crying, Hallam recalled, because the English colonists had driven "them from their planting land, which they had enjoyed ever since the English came into the country."

The court, in 1705, found for the Mohegans, but the colony appealed to the crown. No review was held and the original decision remained unexecuted. Neither the Masons nor the Mohegans complained about this inaction until 1735 when Samuel Mason's son, Captain

John Mason, reopened the proceedings. In the intervening years, Owaneco died. The sachemship passed through the hands of a number of individuals, all of them related to Uncas. Caesar, Owaneco's son, served as sachem from 1715 until 1723. Ben Uncas, Uncas's youngest son and Owaneco's brother, succeeded Caesar. He was replaced by his son, the second Ben Uncas, in 1726. Most Mohegans rejected the leadership of the second Ben Uncas, who they viewed as too close to the colonial leadership, and favored Mahomet, Owaneco's grandson. They expressed their discontent with the leadership of the second Ben Uncas, and their continued desire to fight for their lands, in written petitions and in letters to colonial authorities. The Mohegans, like other native peoples living behind the frontier, had learned the value of literacy as a tool to counter colonialism.

An appreciation of the importance of literacy—it was the only way to communicate effectively with colonial officials, to enter the world of English Christianity, and to counter the legal mechanisms of dispossession—led Samson Occom to want to learn to read. During these years, Occom remembered, the Mohegans lived a "wandering life." According to Occom, the Mohegans "depended upon Hunting, Fishing, and Fowling for their living and had no connection with the English, excepting to traffic with them in their small trifles." Perhaps to illustrate his own rise to prominence as a Christian Indian leader, Occom exaggerated the degradation of his people, who, he said, "strictly maintained their Heathenish ways, customs and religion," and did not "cultivate the land nor keep any sort of creatures except dogs which we used in hunting." They still spoke their native language, Occom said, though a few understood English. There was much else that Occom might have remembered. The Mohegans had been employed on the margins of the colonial economy for half a century by the time of his birth in the early 1720s, they had been raising small quantities of livestock, and they always had been an agricultural people. There is no doubt that they faced intense pressure to change, to become more like their Christian neighbors, something they had avoided to a greater extent than many other native peoples in southern New England during the seventeenth century.

Captain John Mason, for a time, kept a school for the Mohegans and a preacher from nearby New London named Eliphalet Adams came once every other week to preach. The Indians, Occom remembered, attended not for the religion but for the blankets "given to them every Fall of the year." Adams ran a school as well, and Occom began to learn his letters, but "all this time there was not one amongst us that made a profession of Christianity." Not all Mohegans were uninterested. The second Ben Uncas declared his acceptance of Christianity in 1736, when Occom was fourteen years old.

Other missionaries preached to the Mohegans as well. David Jewett began preaching to them in 1739 and it was during these years that the Great Awakening struck southern New England. A massive revival of enthusiastic Christian religion, inspired by dissatisfaction with the existing churches, and fueled by the preaching of a number of traveling ministers, the Great Awakening brought a religious message that many native peoples found attractive. The Mohegans were often visited by these preachers, and by lay people who "came frequently and exhorted us to the things of God." Occom, along with many others, was "impressed with the things we had heard." Occom found "a discovery of the way of salvation through Jesus Christ and was enabled to put my trust in him alone for life and Salvation. From this time the distress and burden of my mind was removed, and I found serenity and pleasure of soul in serving God."

Occom described his conversion as a sharp break with the past, but native peoples in southern New England long had engaged with Christianity. Indeed, it was only because of this exposure to Christianity that the Great Awakening held any interest for the Mohegans at all.

The Reverend M.r SAMSON OCCOM,

The first Indian Minister that ever was in Europe, & who accompanied the Rev.d Nathan.l Whitaker D.D. in an application to Great Britain for Charities to support y.e Rev.d D.r Wheelocks Indian Academy & Missionaries among y.e Native Savages of N: America

Publish'd according to Act of Parliament, Sept: 20. 1768 by Henry Parker, at N.o 82 in Cornhill, LONDON.

Figure 4.1 Samson Occom, 1768. National Portrait Gallery, Smithsonian Institution. Courtesy of National Portrait Gallery, Smithsonian Institution/Art Resource.

Involvement in the Indians' Great Awakening thus followed from earlier English efforts to proselytize New England Algonquians and the efforts of native peoples in the region to obtain education and literacy from the English.

Some took the Evangelicals' message to heart, like Occom. But others settled in at points along a line between full acceptance and outright rejection. Unlike the exclusive religion of Christians with their jealous God, native beliefs were inclusive and incorporative. Native peoples took what they wanted from Christianity. It can be misleading to look at Christianity and indigenous religions as always standing in conflict, for many Mohegans do not seem to have seen things that way. The evidence suggests, in fact, that the involvement of the Mohegans and their neighbors in "awakened" English churches was smaller in numbers and shorter in duration than some historians have suggested. Native membership in English churches dropped significantly after 1742, and the enthusiasm of the awakening for them seems to have been a short-lived phenomena.

But Occom kept at it, and it was not an easy path that he chose to follow. Occom wanted to learn more, to study, to become a minister. He knew that Eleazer Wheelock, the founder of Moor's Charity School and, later, Dartmouth College, lived nearby, and that Wheelock could provide him with a Christian education. Occom, still a teenager, asked his mother to intervene on his behalf with Wheelock, and ask him to take on a Mohegan student. According to Occom's own account, he intended initially to stay with Wheelock for several weeks to improve his literacy skills, and ended up staying for more than five years. Occom indeed learned much. He became during these years a firm Christian and a talented preacher. But he also began learning the lesson that would haunt him much of the rest of his life. There was, he learned, little room in Anglo-America for an educated Indian. No matter how much Christians claimed that they wanted to civilize the Indians and bring them to the word of God, Occom believed, they would not grant them an equal stake in the Christian society that they dominated.

A minister to Indians, Occom took a position preaching to the Montauks on the eastern end of Long Island, across the sound from Connecticut. He preached there and ran a school. He married the young and he buried the dead. He wrote and read documents for the illiterate and served as a cultural broker between native peoples and English colonists, between the weak and the strong. At times, he resolved disputes within the community.

His followers respected him, but they could not pay him well. Occom complained constantly that despite his efforts, and despite the fact that English missionary organizations like the Society for the Propagation of the Gospel promoted Occom's efforts and employed him as a symbol for what Indians might become, he was not compensated justly for his efforts. Other missionaries received much more than he. With some bitterness, Occom described his struggles. He lived in a wigwam, like his wards. He relocated twice a year to find additional firewood. He purchased his own livestock and worked his own fields. "I was obliged to contrive every way to support my family," he wrote, and "took all opportunities, to get some thing to feed my family daily." He planted his crops, which he tended before and after school, and kept a small herd of pigs. "Some mornings and evenings I would be out with my hook and line to catch fish and in the fall of the year and spring, I used my gun, and fed my family with Fowls." He sold feathers to pay for powder and shot, and at other times "bound old Books ... made wooden spoons and Ladles, stocked guns, & worked on cedar to make pails ... and Churns." Indeed, Occom was "both a school master and minister to the Indians, yea I was their ear, eye & hand, as well as mouth." To make sense of his hardships, Occom recalled the story of an Indian boy, a servant whose white master beat him ruthlessly. The boy believed, Occom said, that "he beats me for most of the time because I am an Indian." So, too, with Occom. He believed that he was paid less for his labor than other missionaries, and that his patrons ignored the considerable burdens he carried because he was a poor Indian. "I can't help that God has made me so," he wrote. Such was the life of an Indian missionary, the marginal leader of a marginal community.

The Mohegans and the Powhatans lived their lives as colonized peoples, but so too did the Pueblos. The events of 1680 showed that the Pueblos would tolerate only so much, and that a failure in the empire's management of its relations with native peoples could jeopardize all that the Spanish wanted to accomplish in North America. New Mexico itself had little to offer in terms of mineral wealth or agricultural value, but it provided an important frontier protecting the wealth of New Spain. This frontier, as the eighteenth century dawned, faced new threats.

Attacks by mounted Apaches continued. The French began to trade with Plains tribes to the east of the Pueblos. The Pawnees, Comanches, and Wichitas raided the Pueblos and the Hispanic settlers nearby, viewing the colony as a stockyard they could draw from with impunity. The horse was to these equestrian warriors what guns and ships were to Europeans. The Comanches, for example, were becoming the dominant power in those lands claimed but barely controlled by the Spanish. They traded, raided, and warred, collecting tribute and engaging in exchange with a host of partners. The Comanches attacked the Apaches, who in turn intensified their own warfare against New Mexico in search of horses, guns, and provisions. Spanish soldiers accompanied Pueblo warriors to pursue these raiders, and those the Spanish captured they enslaved. The settler population brought scores of Apaches, especially women and children, into their settlements as slaves. The Spanish enslaved many Navajos, Utes, and Comanches as well.

But this warfare limited the growth of New Mexico. Few settlers found life on the battle-scarred frontier attractive, and the colony relied for its survival on alliance with the Pueblos. These attacks forced settlers to take refuge on numerous occasions in the pueblos. Though some of the settlers benefited enormously from the warfare, Indian trade, and captive taking, most of the Hispanic population and the Pueblos suffered from the raids of the northern *barbaros*. The Spanish fortified the New Mexico frontier, but raids from the northern equestrian tribes continued. The number of troops garrisoning New Mexico was never adequate to ensure any measure of security, and the Spanish policy of enslaving native peoples guaranteed them the enmity of those they encountered.

The Pueblos thus found themselves pinched between the Spanish with whom they lived and nomadic, and increasingly well-armed warriors. The Pueblos received some protection from the Spanish, and acquired from them guns and ammunition with which to defend themselves, but they also faced significant exploitation as well. In the aftermath of the Pueblo Revolt, the Spanish had abandoned the *encomienda* system, but they continued to demand that Pueblo peoples labor for them through the *repartimiento*, a system for conscripting labor. Pueblo men reported to Santa Fe where the Spanish set them to work constructing buildings, erecting fortifications, maintaining irrigation ditches, and performing agricultural labor on Spanish lands. Pueblo women performed domestic labor, ground corn and wheat into flour, and baked bread. None were exempt, and not even pregnant women could avoid the *repartimiento*.

Indeed, there is evidence that the *repartimiento* provided an opportunity for the sexual exploitation of Pueblo women. Pueblo spokesmen complained that Spanish masters frequently raped their women. The mixed-race children who resulted from these unions, ignored by their Spanish fathers and unwelcome in the pueblos, often were abandoned at the Catholic missions. These children may have made up as much as 10% of the population of New Mexico in the eighteenth century. The women, as well, already the victims of terrible crimes, faced further disgrace. Pueblo men banished their defiled wives and daughters, leaving the unfortunate outcasts with little choice but to live on the margins of Hispanic society or to join in with another native community.

The Pueblos did not flourish under Spanish rule. The Spanish had since the 1620s struggled to govern the pueblos. In the seventeenth century, Franciscan friars and their allies closely supervised the Pueblo villages. After the *reconquista* the most powerful political figure in the towns became the caciques and religious leaders who were chosen for their knowledge of the Spanish language. The caciques, more often than not acculturated Christians, answered to the Spanish *alcaldia*, the chief constable in their area. Control over the Pueblos shifted from Catholic priests to Spanish civilians.

Some Pueblos challenged the authority of their caciques, and called upon their neighbors to resist the *repartimiento*. Many resisted the teachings of the Franciscans, who despite their desire to convert the Pueblos never considered them as candidates for the priesthood. Complete union with God was a privilege reserved for Europeans. The population remained low as well. The *repartimiento* extracted labor during the time of planting and harvest, leading to food shortages, nutritional deficiencies, and high rates of mortality. The rejection of the mixed-blood children of Pueblo women and Spanish men further depleted the population, and the loss of lands and the resulting ability to feed a growing population led Pueblo women to limit their number of pregnancies. Finally, war with the northern *barbaros* continued. The empire was not working and the New Mexico frontier was not stable.

The Great Wars for Empire

France and Great Britain went to war beginning in 1754. They had, of course, fought on a number of earlier occasions, and at the outset nobody knew that this conflict, known ultimately as the Seven Years' War, the French and Indian War, or the "Great War for Empire," would produce such decisive change in the imperial geography of North America. The earlier conflicts had produced stalemate and an uneasy borderland between France and Great Britain controlled by a large number of autonomous native peoples. But unlike previous conflicts, where the fighting in America served as a sideshow to the much larger conflict in Europe, this time France and England fought in America for control of the continent. Native peoples, who had maneuvered carefully in the presence of the French and the English for decades, found it impossible to avoid the massive conflict, one that set the stage for the American Revolution, but also fueled intense hatreds between white settlers and native peoples. That hatred would lie at the black heart of a new American empire.

The war began in the Ohio Valley. Determined to halt the expansion of rapidly growing English settlements, French forces in 1753 fortified the forks of the Ohio River, erecting Fort Duquesne on the site of present-day Pittsburgh. Both Britain and France claimed these lands. Wealthy English colonists in Virginia, who hoped to reap huge profits from the sale of western lands, decided to drive out the French. In 1754 George Washington, then a young colonel in the Virginia militia and a shareholder in these speculative ventures, failed to dislodge the French and surrendered at his hastily constructed Fort Necessity. A larger force consisting of British regulars under the command of Major-General Edward Braddock met defeat at the hands of a small number of French soldiers and a large number of allied Indians in western Pennsylvania one year later. Without the Potawatomis, Odawas, Ojibways, and many others, the defeat of Braddock's slow-moving army would not have been possible.

The large numbers of Indians from the Ohio Valley and western Great Lakes who assisted the French in the defeats of Washington and Braddock, as well as the complaints made by Six Nations spokesmen at Albany in 1754 that the Covenant Chain had grown brittle, provided alarming evidence that the British empire's relations with its native allies stood at the edge of a dangerous precipice.

British efforts to bring order to the American frontier were too little, too late. Before his death, Braddock delivered to William Johnson a commission to serve as the crown's Superintendent of Indian Affairs for the Northern Department. Johnson's close ties to the Mohawks, established through trade, gift-giving, and his marriage to the Mohawk Molly Brant, made him an ideal choice for the job. In the south, Edward Atkin received a commission to superintend the Southern Department. The superintendents quickly realized that they lacked the power to override the authority of colonial governors and British military officers, and as a result no single authority clearly exercised control over Indian affairs.

By the middle of the 1750s, any possibility of establishing order along the Anglo-American frontier had disappeared. Large numbers of native peoples allied with the French began raiding colonial settlements. They attacked English settlements in Pennsylvania, Maryland, and Virginia, and according to French accounts, killed or captured more than 120 colonists by the end of October 1755. In the fall of that year, Shawnees, accompanied by Delawares and Mingos, began to raid isolated settlements in Pennsylvania and Maryland, taking captives, burning farms, and leaving behind bloody scenes that terrified the colonists and intensified the settlers' hatred for native peoples. The Senecas joined in campaigns against English settlements to their south. Wherever the French distributed weapons and ammunition, native peoples from a variety of nations came together and recognized that they shared similar problems and a common enemy. By March of 1756, over 700 colonists had been killed or captured by warriors from dozens of native communities.

Terrified Anglo-American settlers reacted with horrific acts of violence of their own. In a gruesome act meant to send a message to provincial authorities that it was not doing enough to protect them from bloodthirsty savages, in May of 1757 Pennsylvanians parked a wagon outside the courthouse in Lancaster where the provincial government was meeting. They left the bodies of four of their neighbors in the back, including a pregnant woman, all of them scalped and "butchered in a most horrid manner."

It was, for native peoples, a massive war. Indians from the Ohio River Valley, the Great Lakes, and the southeast, came together to fight the British. Indians from many nations joined in the French campaign against the British Fort William Henry, in northern New York. Nearly 100 Potawatomis joined the thousands of French-allied Indians, and traveled more than 1000 miles to attack the large British force encircled in the massive fortification. The siege lasted several weeks, and many of the French-allied Indians fell ill. When the British surrendered, and the French decided to allow the Redcoats to leave the fort with their arms and their personal property, the natives felt betrayed. Some decided to fall upon the retreating British troops. Others attacked the wounded and the sick that the English left behind in the fort's hospital. The French allies returned home, bitter and ill. Some of the Potawatomis carried home smallpox they contracted at the fort. Many of them would be reluctant to commit their warriors to European campaigns again in the future. Some concluded that the

French were responsible for the outbreak, for "their custom in such a case is to say that the nation which called them has given them bad medicine."

But these warriors learned as well what they could accomplish through the construction of pan-Indian alliances. The French could not have taken Fort William Henry without allied warriors. Native peoples understood that their attacks, more than military actions undertaken by the French, had largely cleared the area west of the Appalachians of Anglo-American settlers. Burdened by illness, but satisfied with what they had accomplished, native nations largely sat out the rest of the conflict.

Indeed, in 1758 the tide of the war began to turn in the favor of the British. The war went badly for the French in Europe, and with a high percentage of its meager population in the field, the French colonists struggled to produce the food that they needed. With a British blockade effectively sealing off North America from Europe, New France could not supply its native allies. The British took the offensive. The French destroyed Fort Duquesne rather than allow it to fall into British hands; the British built Fort Pitt on the site. Quebec fell to British forces in 1759 and Montreal one year later. With the defeat of the French, native peoples now no longer could play one European power off against another. Those like the Senecas, who had adopted something of a wait-and-see attitude during the war, would now have to confront the British. So, too, did those nations like the Potawatomis, who long had aligned themselves with the French. What would happen now? In the absence of the French, what force would restrain the aggressiveness of Anglo-American settlers? To what extent would the English punish the Indian allies of its Catholic enemy? What place would Indians occupy in an Anglo-American empire that now reigned triumphant in North America? The initial signs provided little cause for optimism.

The Cherokees, for instance, had served as allies of the British. While warriors from many of the Cherokee towns chose to sit out the war, some recognized the benefits alliance could bring. The Cherokees found themselves at war with both the Creeks to their west and Iroquois raiders from the north. They suffered periodically from smallpox and other diseases. The Cherokees extended invitations to the Virginians and Carolinians to build forts in their country, one in each of the three clusters of settlement: the lower towns on the upper reaches of the Savannah River; the Middle Towns in the Great Smoky Mountains; and the Upper Towns, west of the mountains along the upper Tennessee River. The first of these forts was constructed at the Lower Cherokee town of Keowee in 1753. It sent a message to the Creeks and reinforced the Cherokees' understanding of what that alliance meant: military assistance against the Cherokees' native enemies.

The assistance the Cherokees provided to the English was significant. Cherokees inflicted heavy casualties on Shawnees and Delawares. A Seneca observer reported that native communities allied with the French "are much afraid of the Southern Indians, having been struck three times by them" in the spring of 1757 alone, "twice near Fort Du Quesne and once at Logs Town." They made peace with the most pro-British of the Six Nations. Militarily and diplomatically, by ensuring that the Ohio Valley nations found themselves caught between Cherokee and Haudenosaunee attackers, the Cherokees attacked the foundations of France's Indian alliance and made possible a British victory.

But the British did not live up to the Cherokees' expectations. Despite earlier promises that the British would not take their lands, the Cherokees confronted growing numbers of English settlers. The crown's superintendent for Indian affairs in the southern department, Edward Atkin, could not slow their advance. The growing numbers of settlers killed deer upon which Cherokees relied to obtain the trade goods they needed. The Cherokees feared not merely a descent into poverty but absolute dispossession at the hands of land hungry and aggressive colonists. Some Cherokees killed colonial livestock that they found grazing in their fields, and violence remained an ever-present reality along the length of white settlement.

In addition to the violence of frontier settlers close to home, Cherokee warriors returning from British campaigns to the north came under fire from frontier thugs in Virginia. The Cherokees wore yellow headbands to identify themselves as friends and allies, but such symbols meant little to settlers who believed all native peoples were enemies. The settlers lived in fear of Indian attack, and stories of "savage" atrocities, some true and some not, traveled widely through the backcountry. The Virginians murdered several Cherokees, and native peoples learned to fear as well. A missionary named William Richardson, in the Overhill towns in 1758, reported that the Cherokees spoke constantly of the murder of their comrades at the hands of savage settlers. Richardson found the Cherokees uninterested in his message of sin, redemption, and salvation, and increasingly hostile toward colonial culture. Recognizing that Cherokee discontent, a product of the all-encompassing violence they experienced, continuing encroachments upon their lands, the broken British promises to protect them, and their difficulties in acquiring the trade goods that they needed, Richardson decided to flee. He believed that the Cherokees would act shortly to avenge the many injuries they had suffered at the hands of their former allies.

They did so in the spring of 1759. Warriors from the Overhill and Lower towns attacked settlements in South Carolina, killing thirty colonists. Not all Cherokees favored retaliation for the Virginia murders. A delegation of Cherokees traveled to Charlestown to negotiate a settlement and, according to the English traveler and trader James Adair, the divisions over what to do about colonial aggressions carried the Cherokees to the brink of a "very hot civil war." But Governor William Henry Lyttleton of South Carolina did not want to talk. He demanded that the Cherokees turn over the guilty Indians for punishment under English law, ignoring the Cherokee delegation's offer to compensate the colony for its losses with French scalps and prisoners. Lyttleton held the delegation hostage until the Cherokees handed over their warriors. He thus sent the message that there could be no negotiation with the Carolinians, no peace with justice, and that Cherokees could look forward to little but slavery and subjugation.

The fighting was violent even by the bloody standards of American frontier history. Both sides killed indiscriminately. Frightened settlers and militia soldiers murdered Cherokee prisoners. Vicious colonists attacked and killed Cherokees along the Congaree River and then cut "the bodies of the savages ... to pieces" and fed them to their dogs. Colonial militiamen collected large bounties for every Cherokee scalp they took. Cherokee warriors, in turn, terrorized Carolina settlements through 1759 and into 1760, and left behind gruesome scenes of violence.

The Cherokees, however, needed powder and shot to wage their war. They could not produce it themselves. English colonists cut off their supplies once the fighting started. The Cherokees hoped to acquire additional supplies from the French but the British blockade during the Seven Years' War had eliminated shipments of ammunition to Louisiana. Hoped for assistance from the Creeks failed to materialize as well; the Creeks relied upon their Carolina partners for the trade goods they needed. A steady flow of gifts from the colony of Carolina to the Creeks kept them neutral during the conflict.

The Cherokees stood alone, and in 1761 British invasions devastated the Cherokee country. More than half of the Lower and Middle towns were destroyed by colonial fire and steel, and the soldiers burned Cherokee crops in the fields. Hunger approaching starvation resulted.

The commander of the last expedition against the Cherokees, James Grant, reported that his men burned more than 1400 acres of corn, beans and peas, and "drove into the woods and mountains to starve" perhaps as many as "5000 people, including men, women and children." The attacks, according to Carolina's Henry Laurens, reduced the survivors "to live for a considerable time upon old-Acorns, a food that we know will barely keep hogs alive & their hunger was so pinching that some of them were detected in grabbing up the grains of corn and beans after they were planted around the Fort of which several officers were witnesses." The Cherokees, Laurens wrote, also relied for food upon "the Offals of mangled horses, slaughtered for their provision upon the path, & in all their towns as we were along." Impoverished and starving, Cherokees became susceptible to disease. Leaders died, producing social and political dislocation. Frontier thugs murdered other leaders. And the destruction of Cherokee towns forced their relocation and removal. The war brought to the fore in Cherokee towns a new generation of leaders shaped by their experiences with the violent consequences of Anglo-American warfare.

The Cherokee War offered some important lessons. The pervasiveness of the violence and the indiscriminate nature of the killing testified to the existence of an extraordinary level of hatred on the American frontier. White settlers in Carolina, many of whom had moved south to avoid warfare in Virginia and Pennsylvania, became convinced that all native peoples were killers and enemies who they must strike down at the first opportunity. The Cherokees launched retaliatory attacks on the Carolina frontier for murders that took place in Virginia. All white people, to these attackers, shared in the guilt. None of them could be trusted, and all of them coveted Indian lands. The Cherokees had been forced to wage their war alone, and had suffered. Facing an English colonial regime more willing to employ violence now that the French had departed, native peoples learned from the Cherokees that they could not stand alone against aggressive colonial soldiers and settlers.

The English failed to learn the lessons raised by the Cherokee War. By the time the Seven Years' War came to a close, trade goods had been in short supply in the Great Lakes for some time. The British blockade limited the ability of the French to supply their allies, but fort commanders nonetheless shared what little ammunition they had. The French, moreover, well aware of their own weakness, treated their allies with a modicum of respect; they had little choice. Sir William Johnson understood some of this when he traveled west to inform France's former allies that they now must pay their allegiance to the British crown. He ignored orders to limit his presents to the Indians whose loyalty, his superiors believed, they should not have to purchase.

The Potawatomis and other groups in the Great Lakes had suffered during the war. They contracted smallpox at Fort William Henry and other epidemics coursed through the Great Lakes, and along the Ohio River and its tributaries. Requests by native peoples for British assistance went unanswered. Sir Jeffrey Amherst, the commander-in-chief of the crown's forces in North America after the war, reasoned from the simple but faulty premise that the British had conquered New France, and that all the land from the Atlantic to the Mississippi belonged now to Great Britain. Indians, as a result, became subjects of the crown. With the empire's treasury nearly wiped out, and with an enormous tax burden on subjects at home, Amherst looked for economy in the administration of the empire. He would curtail gifts to Indians because the loyalty of subjects should be assumed, not purchased. Amherst, moreover, hoped to bring order to the Anglo-American frontier by limiting the expansion of American settlers onto Indian lands. Amherst's policies, which included the elimination of the diplomatic presents that had served as the basis of Indian diplomacy for more than a century and the restriction of the colonists' territorial ambitions, would contribute to two significant rebellions. The second of these was the American Revolution. The first was a massive and widespread uprising of native peoples known commonly as Pontiac's Rebellion, a product of native peoples' fears that the British intended to enslave them, kill them, or take away their lands.

As early as 1761 Seneca warriors sent war belts to the Delawares and Shawnees. These wampum belts, sometimes painted red, carried a message calling native peoples to arms, and the Senecas invited their neighbors to join in a campaign against the English. They also sent messengers to the Potawatomis, Hurons, Ottawas, and the Ojibwes. Warriors, who now saw themselves as "the People of consequence for managing affairs," ignored Seneca leaders who chose still to try to work with the English. Though the Potawatomis did not join the Senecas and revealed what they knew to the British at Detroit, where they hoped to establish a trading relationship in the absence of the French, there can be no doubting that discontent in the region was widespread. With poor harvests, famine, and continued outbreaks of disease, more and more Indians in the Great Lakes region began to meet together to discuss a united opposition to the English. Many wanted to restore the French to their position as a trading partner, and to give strength to a mass movement against the British with French assistance.

Others turned to the prophets, religious leaders who awakened their communities to a sense of their own faults and the problems that had befallen them since the newcomers arrived. The most important of these was the Delaware named Neolin, but he was not alone. The prophets preached a message of redemption. Bad things, native peoples believed, happened for a reason, and drought, famine, disease, and disaster in war occurred, Neolin said, because the Master of Life was angry. Native peoples had neglected their rituals, or had performed them improperly, and now they suffered. The prophets called for a return to ritual. They were not conservatives; they willingly embraced new practices, beliefs, and traditions. One prophet, the Munsee Delaware named Papoonan, had in the 1750s combined the pacifism of Quaker religion with a call to return to ancient traditions.

Neolin was no pacifist. He placed the blame for native suffering upon native peoples. Using a diagram that depicted heaven, the earth, and all that stood between, Neolin showed his followers that the English blocked the path which they hoped to follow to heaven. Along this road, Neolin depicted the vices that the white people brought. Acceptance of these vices meant a hell on earth and in the afterlife. Indeed, Neolin argued that the disappearance of the deer resulted from the Master of Life's dissatisfaction with the Indians for so thoroughly assimilating into their ways of living many Anglo-American vices. The expansion of English settlements onto Indian lands, the English refusal to enter into reciprocal trading relationships, and the Indians' dependence on European trade, Neolin said, all angered the Master of Life.

The Master of Life visited Neolin and taught him what his people must do to avoid suffering. Because their misfortunes resulted from their own actions, they could save themselves. The words of the prophets empowered their followers. The people must return to ritual. They must cease drinking rum. Neolin called upon his followers to heed the message of the Master of Life and to "put off entirely from yourselves the customs which you have adopted since the white people came among us; you are to return to that former happy state, in which we lived in peace and plenty, before these strangers came to disturb us, and above all, you must abstain from drinking their deadly poison, which they have forced upon us, for the sake of increasing their gains and diminishing our numbers." Neolin's was, without question, a militant message that called for armed conflict with the newcomers. If native peoples heeded the Master of Life, returned to their rituals, and ignored the vices of "civilized" life, they would triumph over the English, drive them out of their country, and build the world anew.

Neolin's message spread rapidly, and those who heard it understood it in terms that made sense to them. The Potawatomis at St. Joseph, for instance, found in Neolin's message not only a demand that they resist the English, but that they abandon many traditional beliefs—in polygamy, for instance, and in the existence of guardian spirits. French observers recognized, correctly, that Neolin's message had been both shaped and tempered in its transmission by a century's worth of preaching by Catholic missionaries. What all his adherents shared, whether Ottawas like the great military leader Pontiac, or Potawatomis, Shawnees, Delawares, Senecas, Mingos, or many more, was a recognition that their people shared a common enemy and a common set of problems, and that their people suffered because of the nature of their relationships with white people.

Historians have called this movement Pontiac's Rebellion but it never had one leader. Resistance against British rule was widespread, and it had at least four centers. Near Detroit, the Potawatomis, Ottawas, Hurons, and Ojibwe gathered. At Chenussio, along the Genesee River in western New York, Seneca militants planned actions against the British at Fort Niagara. Shawnees and Delawares centered their resistance along the upper reaches of the Ohio, while the various tribes of the Illinois Confederacy gathered to their south and west at the far end of the river's valley. They never came together in a single movement.

Nonetheless warriors from these four centers of resistance attacked British posts beginning in the spring of 1763. Pontiac initially had planned to take Fort Detroit by subterfuge, bringing a diplomatic party armed with hidden weapons into the post to seize control. An informant foiled the plot but Pontiac began a siege of Detroit that he planned to maintain until French forces, he hoped, returned to assist him. The rumor of the return of the French played a large role in the thinking of native militants.

Forts Detroit, Pitt, and Niagara, the three largest British posts, held out. Built to withstand European siege warfare, the warriors simply lacked the strength to take these posts. Within weeks, however, smaller British posts came under assault, and native peoples throughout the region acted energetically to create a world without Anglo-Americans. The western Potawatomis took Fort St. Joseph through the use of stratagem. A party coming to visit the post and pay its respects to the garrison's commander, Francis Schlosser, surprised the soldiers and made off with the fort's supply of guns and ammunition. A group of Ojibwe gained access to the British post at Michilimackinac by tossing a lacrosse ball over the palisades. They entered the fort to retrieve their ball, killed sixteen soldiers, and seized the fort. Farther east, Shawnees and Delawares hit settlements on the Pennsylvania frontier with enormous fury. Many of the English settlers foolhardy enough not to flee to safer quarters in the east were found "most cruelly butchered," with one woman found "roasted," and her male neighbors left with "awls thrust in their eyes, and spears, arrows, pitchforks, etc., sticking in their bodies." In September, Seneca warriors led by Farmer's Brother attacked a British supply convoy, and then ambushed the British troops who came to relieve them, along the portage around Niagara Falls, a battle known now as the Devil's Hole Massacre. Nearly 100 English soldiers were killed on the path or pushed from the high cliffs above the river into the whirlpool below.

By fall, the warriors besieging the remaining three British posts began to move away. British forces had resupplied Fort Pitt, and native leaders learned of the Peace of Paris, the accord that officially ended the Great War for Empire and eliminated any reason to believe that the French would come to the Indians' relief. Economic concerns played a role as well. Warriors were also hunters, and they needed to prepare for the winter, something they could not do while encircling a British fort. And smallpox broke out among the Shawnees and Delawares besieging Fort Pitt. The epidemic may or may not have been spread to the Indians deliberately by the English through infected blankets, but the evidence is clear that the British tried to do this and found nothing immoral about the use of smallpox as a weapon. Henry Bouquet, the post commander, informed Amherst that he would "try to inoculate the Indians by means of Blankets that may fall in their hands." Amherst agreed entirely with the value of this plan. "You will do well," he replied to Bouquet, "to try to inoculate the Indians by means of blankets, as well as to try every other method that can serve to extirpate this execrable race." The warriors drifted away, and some carried home with them the dread disease.

War left considerable damage in its wake. Huge expanses of the Anglo-American backcountry had been depopulated. Hundreds of farms and settlements had been destroyed. Thousands of settlers fled for safer quarters in the east. Many, many native peoples died. But the war did more than leave behind sheer physical destruction. Wars always do. Pontiac's Rebellion became a race war. Neolin's message—that native peoples must return to their rituals and a proper way of life to purge their world of the corrupting and evil influence of Anglo-Americans—was both exclusive and violent. Had he had his way, nativist warriors would have eradicated Anglo-American settlers. British settlers, for their part, envisioned a world without Indians, a world they could create only with racism and violence.

The Paxton Boys, Scotch-Irish Presbyterians who believed that all Indians were enemies, and some of whom had themselves experienced the horrors and violence of an Indian attack, acted on both of these impulses. They planned to exterminate the native peoples who lived around them, and they would make no distinctions between combatants and non-combatants. Men, women, children—all were fair game. All were savages, and all were enemies. The Paxton Boys knew from experience that "the Indians that lived as independent commonwealths among us or near our borders were our most dangerous enemies, both in the last and present war, although they still pretended to be our friends." The Paxton Boys particularly distrusted the Conestogas, remnants of the Suquehannocks, many of whom had become Christians, and who lived in the vicinity of Lancaster, Pennsylvania.

Most of their suspicion fell upon an individual known as Will Sock. He lived with about nineteen others at Conestoga. Nervous Pennsylvanians reported seeing armed Indians in the settlement, and to preempt any attack, nearly fifty Paxton Boys attacked the settlement on a snowy December 14, burned the buildings, and killed the six people they found there with tomahawks. It was a savage act of violence. Provincial officials, viewed by the Paxton Boys as the coddlers of blood-stained murderers, rushed to protect the fourteen survivors, who had been away selling their wares. They rounded up the Conestogas, these vendors of baskets and brooms, and placed them in the workhouse in Lancaster, behind bars to protect them from frontier vengeance. The magistrates' efforts here were no more effective than their efforts to secure peace and order on the frontier. Two days after Christmas in 1763 the Paxton Boys broke into the workhouse. Nobody stood to offer resistance. It took no more than fifteen minutes for the Paxton Boys to slaughter everyone inside. They left the bodies in the workhouse yard.

They shot one man in the chest. They then hacked off his hands and feet, placed the barrel of a musket in his mouth, pulled the trigger, and blew his head "to atoms." The others victims lay scattered about, shot, and scalped, and cut to pieces. The bodies of two children were found near the back door of the workhouse. They may have tried to run. Will Sock and his wife lay nearby. They may have tried to shield the children from violence that they would not have been able to explain to boys and girls so young. No more than three years old, the children were innocent and harmless but the Paxton Boys spared them none of the viciousness of the attack. The Paxton Boys split their skulls with tomahawks, killing them instantly. Then, with their hatchets, they hacked once more at the children's heads, took their scalps, and rode away in base triumph.

Fourteen bodies, horribly and savagely murdered, lay in the snow late in 1763, victims of the frontier population's hatred of native peoples. Why, we might ask, did the Paxton Boys feel a level of rage so deep that they could justify the murder of children and the mutilation of their bodies? What threat did a dead man pose, whose hands and feet already had been cut away, that compelled the Paxton boys to blow his head off? This was racial and racist violence of the darkest sort and it can teach us, if we choose, the deeply troubling lessons that lie at the heart of the history of the Anglo-American frontier, stories that lie at the heart of Native America.

English imperialists hoped to achieve dominion and civility along the Anglo-American frontier. They hoped to incorporate the frontier and its inhabitants, Native American and European, into an expanding Anglo-American, Christian, New World empire. Peace with his Majesty's Indian allies, the thinking went, would allow colonists to plant stable and productive plantations, with growing populations eager to purchase consumer goods manufactured in the imperial center. Peace with Indians would allow the English empire to expand territorially along with English Christianity and civility. To achieve these goals, the English needed a peaceful and orderly frontier. In the seventeenth century, the Crown and his chosen men erected an ineffective and ramshackle system of imperial administration based of trade regulation and colonial rule through appointed governors (many of whom were military men) overseeing elected colonial assemblies. In the middle of the eighteenth century, the government introduced an important reform—the two superintendents for Indian affairs in the northern and southern departments. Yet the task these men faced was too large, and they and the individual colonial governments simply lacked the means and the willingness to preserve order along the Anglo-American frontier.

In this sense, the Paxton Boys stand as symbols of the frontier experience in America. Settlers on the frontier interacted with Indians frequently, but they also fought with them for control of scarce frontier resources. White people fought Indians in savagely violent conflicts that they viewed in racial and cultural terms. It was, of course, more complicated than that. Many native peoples did not join in the attacks on Anglo-Americans during the rebellion, but the Paxton Boys knew people who had been murdered by Indians. They had witnessed the horrible scenes that remained after warriors, themselves acting on a religious message calling for the extermination of English people, descended violently upon frontier settlements. They suspected that Will Sock, of Conestoga, knew these killers and provided them with assistance. There is no firm evidence that he did so, but the Paxton Boys' suspicions, in their own minds, justified their actions. They must attack before they were attacked; they must kill the killers. Their fears and their hatred could justify the most blood-chilling brutality. The Paxton Boys received no punishment. In response to their violent rampage, the unpopular Quaker government of Pennsylvania encouraged its population to join in the violence and "to embrace all opportunities of pursuing, taking, killing and destroying" any Shawnees and Delawares who had attacked colonists.

The Proclamation and the Indian Boundary Line

The Board of Trade in London, the administrative body in charge of American affairs within the empire, recognized that something must be done to restore order along the frontier. The costs of empire weighed heavily upon English subjects at home, with the tax burden in England during the eighteenth century nearly twice what it was in France. Great Britain needed peace, a respite from the financial burdens of war. The royal Proclamation of 1763 resulted, part of a "well digested and general plan for the regulation" of Britain's relations with the Indians. Interposing the limited authority they possessed between Indian killers and nativist prophets, imperial officials hoped to secure a peace with Indians and to "effectually reconcile their esteem and affections."

The Proclamation proposed a line running from north to south, with all "the lands and territories lying to the Westward of the sources of the rivers which fall into the sea" for the exclusive use of the Indians. The Proclamation's supporters believed it "just and reasonable, and essential to our interest, and the security of our colonies, that the several Nations of Tribes of Indians with whom we are connected, and who live under our Protection, should not be molested or disturbed in the possession of such parts of our dominions and territories as, not having been ceded to or purchased by us, are reserved to them ... as their Hunting Grounds."

Over the course of the several years following the massive uprising of 1763, the crown's appointed men held treaty councils to restore the frontier to order. As early as September of 1763, Sir William Johnson met with the Senecas to work out a peace agreement. In 1764, the British concluded peace agreements with the Shawnees and others in the Great Lakes and in the Ohio Valley and in 1765 and 1766 Johnson finalized agreements with the Six Nations. At Oswego, in the latter year, Pontiac met with Johnson and declared himself a friend to the English.

But the fundamental problems still existed. Proclaiming a frontier line was one thing. Defining it was another. Drawing the line through North Carolina, Virginia, and into Pennsylvania and New York fell to Johnson and his southern counterpart, Atkin's successor John Stuart. The Cherokees met with the Stuart to draw the precise path of the Proclamation Line through lands that they claimed.

In October of 1768, Stuart, following instructions from the Board of Trade in London, negotiated with the Cherokees the Treaty of Hard Labor. He hoped that the agreement would establish the firm boundary line that Cherokee leaders had asked for in the wake of their war against the colonists several years before. Johnson, however, ignored the Hard Labor treaty line, which left to the Cherokees lands to the west of a line running south from the intersection of the Ohio and Kanawha rivers, when he negotiated at nearly the same time the Treaty of Fort Stanwix with the Six Nations. Johnson overstepped the authority granted him by the Board of Trade. He and the Iroquois drew a "Line of Property" from the northeast to the southwest through New York and Pennsylvania to the Ohio River, and that then followed that river nearly all the way to the Mississippi.

The problem was not solely a matter of the Six Nations giving away lands occupied by other native peoples in Pennsylvania and along the Ohio (only the Mohawks lost any land in the treaty, and much of the land they ceded lay south of the Ohio River). The Iroquois had given away other peoples' lands before. The Line of Property and the Hard Labor lines overlapped, leaving much of Kentucky in dispute. The Cherokees, who lived there, had been consulted by neither Johnson nor the Iroquois, and neither had the Shawnees. Their lands now lay open to the voracious appetite of Virginia and Pennsylvania land speculators who coveted Indian lands in the west, and who would compete with them for control of Kentucky. Alexander McKee, the son of a Shawnee mother and an agent of the British government in the Ohio country, reported that the enormous number of American pioneers coming "to settle and survey the country about Fort Pitt and down [the] Ohio has set all their warriors in a rage." Backcountry settlers, described by Amherst's successor Thomas Gage as a "set of people near as wild as the country they go in, or the People they deal with, & by far more vicious and wicked," threatened the Cherokees as well. Stuart reported that unchecked settlement would soon "divest the Cherokees of every foot of hunting ground they possess beyond the mountains." Many of them had learned from the experience of the Seven Years' War and Pontiac's Rebellion to hate all Indians, and violence was widespread.

A renewal of warfare resulted. The Shawnees and other groups who participated in Pontiac's Rebellion had not been militarily defeated. Angry at the Six Nations for "giving up so much of their country to the English without asking their consent," reeling from the consequences of settler encroachment on their lands, and determined to protect what they had left, the Shawnees and their allies in the north—Delawares, Mingos, and others—invited the Cherokees and Creeks in the south to a council at Scioto. Cherokees and Shawnees both hunted in the Kentucky lands ceded by the Iroquois to the British, and they wanted to keep the settlers out. As they had done during Pontiac's Rebellion, native peoples unified to protect their lands from white people.

After the northerners met with the Cherokees and Creeks again in 1771, exchanging beads, belts, war hatchets, and scalps, Johnson began to fear that a union of northern and southern militant warriors, armed by the Spanish, could pose a significant threat to the Anglo-American frontier. Missionaries reported that Shawnees rejected their offers to preach, and chose instead to listen to the teachings of prophets who spoke in terms similar to Neolin. Traders, aware of the hostility mounting in native villages, fled to the English settlements, carrying with them horrifying tales of bellicose war parties and new rumors of native revolt.

Not all the Indians in these communities favored war upon the white intruders. This opposition had the paradoxical effect of keeping the prophetic nativism of figures like Neolin alive. So long as there were native peoples willing to trade with Anglo-Americans, to sell them land, and to counsel peace, the militants could explain defeat as the result of their native opponents' actions. Shawnee leaders like Pipe and White Eyes, who offered to meet with the English, could say little to their followers who no longer believed in white treaties and white claims to desire peace.

These claims became even harder to believe after a frontier band led by Michael Cresap, and supported by Virginia's governor John Murray, Earl of Dunmore, murdered the Shawnee wife and children of the Mingo leader Tachnedorus, also known as Logan, who was no militant. As he said in an "oration" later publicized by Thomas Jefferson, Logan stayed out of Pontiac's Rebellion. He challenged his white audience to say "if ever he entered Logan's cabin hungry, and he gave him not meat; if ever he came cold and naked and he clothed him not." He described himself as a friend of the settlers, until Cresap and his gang came "in cold blood, and unprovoked, murdered" his family, "not even sparing my women and children." Only then did he seek revenge.

Logan and his thirteen followers spread a wave of terror through the countryside. They wiped out a family—a man, his wife, and three children—at a location called Muddy Creek. Frightened settlers found another neighbor with a broadax in his chest and his wife and four children nearby, all dead, all scalped. Thousands fled to more secure locations. Logan, after the war that followed, and that bore the name of Virginia's Lord Dunmore, announced according to Jefferson that "I have killed many" and that "I have fully glutted my vengeance." But he had not done anything to help the Shawnees, and the attacks that followed failed to drive the newcomers out of Kentucky.

The Shawnees called upon other nations to join them, and some Ottawas, Delawares, Miamis, Wyandots, and Cherokees did, but most stayed away. They wanted to avoid the ravages of another war. The Shawnees stood largely alone. In the fall of 1774, Dunmore assembled a force of over 2000 Virginia soldiers to strike at the Shawnee towns along the Scioto River. He led one column from Pittsburgh down the Ohio valley while another, led by Andrew Lewis, struck out from western Virginia. An outnumbered Shawnee force attacked Lewis at Point Pleasant, near the intersection of the Kanawha and Ohio Rivers, fighting the battle to a bloody stalemate. A peace agreement negotiated at Camp Charlotte in October of 1774 followed, through which the Shawnee leader Cornstalk acknowledged Virginia's claims to Kentucky. Many Shawnees rejected the treaty, and nobody spoke to the Cherokees or other Indians in the Ohio Valley about their claims to these lands, but the British government hoped that the peace, however shallow the foundation upon which it rested, would bring some measure of order to the frontier.

Indians and Empires

The problems Great Britain faced in the wake of the Great War for Empire were not unique. In the 1770s and 1780s, the Spanish began to implement reforms in New Mexico designed to improve conditions in the province. Preferring peace to war, the "Bourbon Reformers" of New Spain cultivated alliances with friendly Indian nations and encouraged these allies with gifts to wage war against common enemies like the Apaches. Like the French, the Spanish hoped that the liberal giving of diplomatic presents could secure Indian allies in numbers great enough to bring peace to the province. Gift-giving of this order cost money, and the resulting alliances with Pueblos, Navajos, and, later, Apaches began to break down when the empire no longer could provide the funding to support the giving of gifts.

The British, too, found the costs of empire difficult to bear. White settlers encroached on Indian lands despite the Proclamation. Native peoples believed that the English would destroy them, and they noted with foreboding that "of the numerous nations which formerly inhabited the country possessed by the English not one is now existing." Parliament enacted the Revenue Act of 1764, known in the colonies as the Sugar Act, to defray "the expenses of defending, protecting, and securing" its American possessions, much of which remained firmly in the hands of native peoples. The Stamp Act, enacted by Parliament one year after the Sugar Act, would serve the same effect. Parliament and the Crown in England recognized the need for a peaceful and orderly frontier in America, not because officials in the English imperial regime loved or respected native peoples, but because they could not afford to run an empire with violence and warfare in the west. The English government, in its final attempt to bring order to the frontier, to pay for the troops who would garrison the forts in land acquired from France but still occupied by powerful native communities, ended up losing its empire. The new American empire that supplanted it would confront the same challenges. Many native peoples would find in the American Revolution the continuation of a generation of violent struggle to hold on to their homelands.

5

NATIVE PEOPLES AND THE RISE OF A
NEW AMERICAN EMPIRE

American children long have learned about the great men who led their people in the Revolution against British tyranny, who fought against long odds to win their independence, and who assembled in Philadelphia to establish a more perfect union. The "Founding Fathers," however, went by other names in native communities. Many Indians saw the Americans not as patriots fighting for freedom but as "perfidious cruel rebels" and as "white savages." They referred to them not as champions of liberty but as "Butchers" and "Killers" and "madmen." They called them "Big Knives" or "Long Knives," a name that reflected the violence they associated with the citizens of the new republic. To the Senecas, George Washington was not the father of his country, but the "Town Destroyer," for the campaign he launched against them in 1779. Indeed, when the citizens of that republic declared their independence in July of 1776, they did so not only on the grounds that all men "were endowed by their creator with certain unalienable rights" including "Life, Liberty and the Pursuit of Happiness," but because the king and his corrupt ministers had, as Thomas Jefferson put it, "endeavored to bring on the inhabitants of our frontiers the merciless Indian savages, whose known rule of warfare is an undistinguished destruction of all ages, sexes, and conditions." Many native people did fight against the Americans, and the birth of the American republic was a catastrophe for them. The new American empire rose on the ruins of Indian communities, and threatened their lives, liberties, and properties in unprecedented ways.

Change in the Far Western World

The events that Americans consider so significant in their nation's history mattered little to many native peoples. The imperial struggles between the Spanish, French, and English for control of North America did not directly impact the lives of those who lived in the west. The Kiowas, for instance, at the time American colonists banded together to protest the Stamp Tax, forged their cultural and military alliance with the neighboring Crows. A decade later, when the colonists fired the "shot heard round the world" at Lexington, the Kiowas lived in the Black Hills, at least until Lakota Sioux raiders drove them out onto the southern Plains. This migration brought them into conflict with the powerful Comanches, with whom they fought until sometime around 1790, when the Congress of the United States under the new Constitution enacted the first comprehensive law regulating Indian affairs. The Trade and Intercourse Act had little impact upon the Kiowas, but their peace with the Comanches was a critical event in their history as a people.

Native America: A History, Second Edition. Michael Leroy Oberg.
© 2018 John Wiley & Sons, Inc. Published 2018 by John Wiley & Sons, Inc.

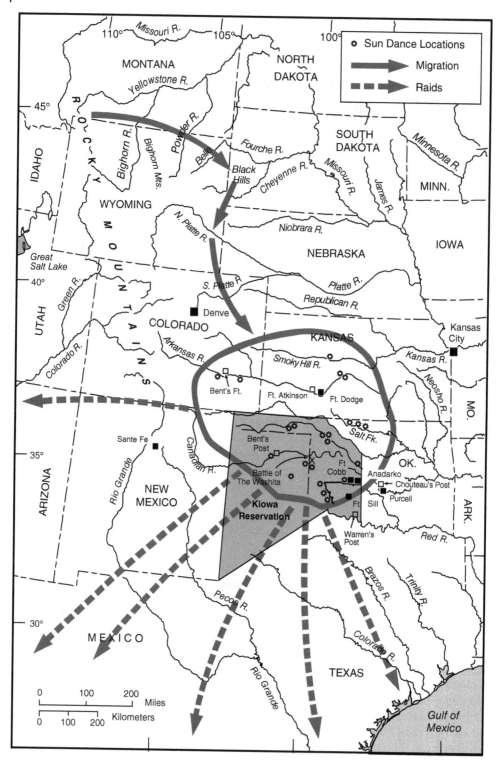

Map 5.1 The Kiowas' migration. Source: *Smithsonian Handbook of North American Indians*, Vol. 13, Part 2, Plains, p. 907 Courtesy of Smithsonian Institution.

Together the Kiowas and Comanches spent these years along the Arkansas River. Their combined war against the Osages lasted until 1834. They fought with the Caddos and with Jicarilla Apaches as well. Their mounted warriors raided Mexican settlements throughout the American southwest until their subjugation after the American civil war. The Kiowas, a small community, had allied themselves with the powerful and emerging Comanche Empire. Comanches and their allies dominated the southern Plains. They took from the Spanish tens of thousands of head of cattle. They killed many hundreds of colonists. The Spanish knew how to control sedentary communities like the Pueblos, but they found themselves powerless against well-armed equestrian raiders. The Comanches, one panicked observer wrote, "breed horses, handle firearms with the greatest skill, and obtain ample supplies of meat" from the bison they hunted. "Innumerable and rich," the Comanches and their allies avoided pitched battles, and raided constantly. The Spanish never knew where they would strike next.

Comanches raided, and exacted tribute, and forced settlers to trade with them. They expanded across the southern Plains, their horse herds growing, their population exploding. By 1780, a Comanche population of 40,000 worked to acquire corn and vegetables and fruit, guns and ammunition, and grass for their horses. It was a fragile economy in that the Comanches' reliance on guns and horses to sustain their power made them vulnerable to whomever could limit the supply of these items, but through the middle of the nineteenth century, they dominated the northern borderlands of Spanish America.

That so few Americans know the story of the Comanche Empire makes clear that the events that mattered in the lives of the Kiowas and their neighbors were not events that factor in the usual telling of American history, which for the late eighteenth century focuses mostly upon the Revolution and the birth of a new American nation. The events that took place in native communities and that mattered to native peoples have been consigned to another story, one separate, distinct and, because it is so seldom included in the larger American story, in many ways unequal.

To ignore this history is to ignore events that mattered to hundreds of thousands of people living in the interior of the American continent. The "winter counts," Plains Indians chronicles that visually depicted the major event of a year, allow us, should we choose to look, a window into their world. If we peer through it, we can see the importance of warfare in the lives of young men. Success in war helped to determine social status in Plains communities like the Kiowas and Crows. It brought prestige and honor. A warrior viewed his achievements in battle as the defining moments of his life. But there are other stories these winter counts can tell. Native peoples of the Great Plains wove their lives and their histories from a fabric different from that of Anglo-Americans: in 1765, the year of the Stamp Act, a Dakota hunting party stole twenty horses from a group of Assiniboines, a major coup and a significant victory; in 1768, while the colonists implemented their non-importation agreements to protest the Townshend Duties, the Dakotas lived in such great fear of attack that they could not leave their lodges unarmed; by 1780 the enemy who stalked them was smallpox, a deadly hunter who followed trade routes into the heart of the continent; in 1788, a winter so cold descended upon the Plains that many birds froze to death in mid-flight; only in 1790 did the Dakotas report seeing the stars and stripes of the new empire. The events the winter counts record are different to be sure, but they are no less a part of American history.

Indeed, while the American Revolutionaries struggled through their war for independence, and lived through "the times that try men's souls," the Kiowas and the Crows confronted smallpox. The epidemic originated in Mexico, where nearly 18,000 people died late in 1779. It moved north rapidly, killing over 5000 in New Mexico before slashing its way across the Plains. Nearly 16,000 of the 24,000 Arikaras died. The number of Crow lodges declined from about 2000 to 300 in the space of a few short years. As many as 14,000 Crows died. It was the first of many smallpox epidemics that would career across the Great Plains, and leave in its path many thousands of wrecked Indian lives. Forty percent of the region's population died. By bringing so much destruction to the Northern Plains, the epidemic paved the way for the emergence of the Lakota Sioux as the dominant power there. Semi-sedentary peoples like the Hidatsas, Arikaras, and Mandans suffered especially heavy losses. They could no longer effectively resist Lakota expansion out into the Missouri Valley.

During the years of the American Revolution, horses began to appear in great numbers in Crow and Kiowa communities, and began to work an additional revolutionary transformation in their ways of living. Both communities moved during these years to the homelands they would occupy when they first encountered the explorers, scouts, soldiers, and missionaries who began writing them into American history early in the nineteenth century. The Kiowas moved out onto the southern Plains. The Crows moved to their home along the Yellowstone. These movements took place against the backdrop of the epidemics. Tribes weakened by disease sought new allies, or expanded at the expense of their more heavily devastated neighbors: Lakota Sioux, the Dakotas' western kin, moved out of the western Great Lakes region, attacked the agricultural settlements of the Mandans and the Arikaras in the upper Missouri Valley, and occupied hunting grounds along the Powder and North Platte Rivers. The Crows, along with their Assiniboine and Blackfeet rivals, fought for access to the buffalo hunting lands along the Yellowstone and Missouri Rivers.

As for the Dakota, the imperial competition of the eighteenth century certainly affected their lives. France's war against the Foxes interrupted the flow of trade goods into their communities. After the conflict ended, the French looked to reestablish their connections to the westerners. Paul Marin arrived with a license to conduct the trade in 1750 and did business in the region until 1754. He, his son, and their associates visited Sioux villages along the Mississippi and Minnesota Rivers. The Marins dominated the trade for this brief period because they understood what the Dakotas wanted. Trade, to the Dakotas, was not solely an economic relationship but one based upon kinship and reciprocity. Marin and his associates developed close ties to Sioux leaders and gave gifts generously, gaining the community's trust and respect. After the Seven Years' War, scores of English traders intruded into the Dakota territory and established similar kinship ties in Sioux communities. To meet the demands of these traders, their own desire for European manufactured goods, and to honor their kinship ties, the Dakota Sioux divided their time between the bison-hunting ranges of the Plains and the woodlands of Minnesota where beaver and other fur-bearing animals were most common.

Living closer to centers of European power, meanwhile, the Caddos maneuvered carefully during these years of tremendous change. The Caddos relied upon their French allies for the firearms and ammunition that allowed them to defend themselves from a host of enemies, and they were willing to attack any party that threatened to disrupt this exchange network. In 1758, they joined with Comanches and Wichitas to attack a Spanish mission on the San Saba River. The mission had been established at the request of the Apaches, to provide them some defense from their native enemies. The Spanish retaliated by attacking a Caddo settlement along the Brazos. The fighting created a difficult situation for the Caddos. France departed Louisiana in 1763, and Spain took over. The Caddos thus faced the loss of their close ally and supplier of trade goods, and its replacement by a European power who viewed them as hostile. The new context for Caddo relations with Europeans tested the skills of their leaders.

The new Spanish governor of the province, Antonio de Ulloa, arrived in New Orleans in 1766. He recognized the importance of the Caddos' ties to the French, and that the natives could do Spain damage if not treated wisely. Ulloa wanted peace. He believed that past Spanish policies could not work with the Caddos. He would continue to act on the French model. As a result, the Caddos faced little detrimental effect immediately from their interaction with the Spanish. They did, however, face increased warfare with tribes to their west. The French had left, but many French traders stayed behind. They provided the Osages with guns and ammunition. To acquire more of these critical resources, the Osages attacked the Caddos and others to steal their horses and trade them to the French for guns. The Caddos launched a small number of retaliatory raids, but the Osages badly outnumbered them. Their best leaders could neither protect them from enemy raiders, nor shield them from smallpox. Thus the Caddos and the Spanish needed each other. In 1770, Athanases de Mézières, the lieutenant governor based at Natchitoches, began negotiations with the Caddos. Led by Tinhiouen, the Caddos accepted De Mézières' pledge of annual presents of clothing, guns, blankets, tools, beads, and alcohol. Tinhiouen promised to catch runaway slaves and to halt the movement through his lands of French and Spanish drifters in return for the bounty of a musket and cloth for each intruder. The Caddos, and especially the Kadohadachos and Hasinais, would also help moderate a peace between the Spanish and the Comanches and Wichitas.

The arrangement, for a time, secured a flow of trade goods into the Caddo villages. According to de Mézières, the 288 Caddo families located in three Caddo towns in 1770 and 1771 received 800 pounds of gunpowder, as well as weapons, ammunition, and knives. They received as well tools, beads, and decorative and ornamental items. Nacogdoches was an important center for intercultural trade, with a diverse population that rivaled that of New Orleans. Spanish traders exchanged horses and other livestock, Indian and African slaves, and arms and ammunition. At Grand Caddo, where 155 families lived, the most frequently and abundantly traded items were bullets and powder, both sold by the pound. Combs, scissors, mirrors, and beads were traded as well, but they appear less frequently in the Spanish records than supplies for guns. With these weapons the Caddos fought off their native enemies and secured the margins of Spanish Louisiana. They employed European allies to preserve their independence.

The Spanish alliance would endure for the remainder of the eighteenth century, but from the perspective of the Caddos it became increasingly dysfunctional over time. It failed to meet the Caddos' expectations for an alliance. By helping to establish a diplomatic settlement between the Spanish and the Indians they called *norteños*, moreover, the Caddos inadvertently rendered themselves less essential to the security of the empire. The friendship of the Caddos helped Spain when they confronted determined northern raiders; with a peace established, the Spanish no longer felt the need to cater to the Caddos.

The Caddos certainly noticed the growing disinterest of the Spanish in helping them. They also could not have missed the glaring weakness of the Spanish in North America. Spanish trade with the Caddos declined with their need for Caddo assistance. The crisis came to a head in 1777. Smallpox struck the Caddos. The Hasinais lost more than 300. By the early 1780s, only two families remained among the Yatasis, a Hasinai band. The Natchitoches lost much of their population as well, so that by the beginning of the nineteenth century only several dozen remained. At the same time, the Osages renewed their attacks on the Caddos and upon other communities in the region, stealing horses and hides and killing their enemies.

The Spanish lacked the power to prevent these attacks. The Osages attacked whom they wanted when they wanted. By the late 1770s, the Kadohadachos had moved closer together to defend themselves, and referred to their old homeland in the Great Bend floodplain as "the Prairie of the Enemy." The Osages could not be controlled by the Spanish, and the Caddos grew increasingly impatient with the colonial government. Antonio Gil Abamo, Mézières' successor, reported to his superiors that the Caddos vented their frustration by "destroying at every step my flags, staff of command, and medals, saying that they cannot live on the luster of these." The Caddos could not rely upon the Spanish for assistance, and retreated further downriver. The Choctaws began to attack them there in 1790, and the Caddos became so disenchanted with the powerlessness of the Spanish that they looked forward to the American takeover of Louisiana in 1803.

So many stories that might be told. The Chumash encountered few Europeans during the many decades after Cabrillo's small fleet departed. A few expeditions sailed along the coast, stopping briefly, but little evidence exists as to what they did or where, precisely, they visited. They thus had little experience with European intruders, and little reason to fear the Spanish who returned in the second half of the eighteenth century.

The Spanish in 1769 sought to secure their hold on the coast of what they called Alta California from their European rivals, and José de Gálvez, the *visitador* of New Spain, instructed Gaspar de Portolá to undertake that task. Both Gálvez and Portolá recognized that they must treat the large numbers of native people on the coast with kindness and respect. Only with the assistance of native peoples could they control California's verdant coastline. They lacked the soldiers and the funds for a military conquest, so Gálvez placed the "Sacred Expedition," in the hands of a small number of soldiers and Franciscan missionaries.

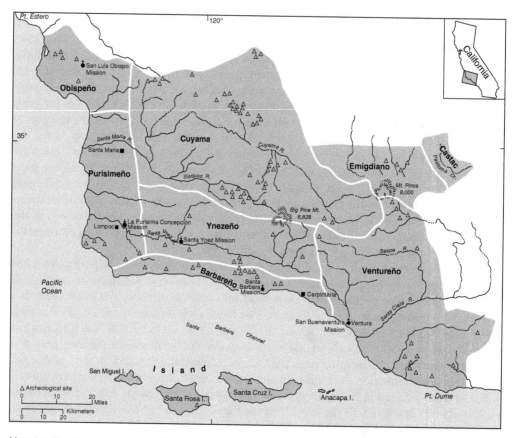

Map 5.2 The Chumash. Based on Kroeber, 1925; Grant, 1965. Source: *Smithsonian Handbook of North American Indians*, Vol. 8, California, pp. 8: 506. Courtesy of Smithsonian Institution.

More than 300,000 native peoples, speaking perhaps as many as a hundred languages, lived within the boundaries of present-day California. Sixty thousand lived along the coast between San Diego and San Francisco. A quarter of the plant species found in North America grow in California; more species of plant and animal can be found in California than in any other region of its size in North America. It was no surprise, then, that Portolá's men described the Chumash as living in thriving communities. The Chumash generously traded with Portolá's men, so much so that the Spanish leader described them as a "tractable" and "pleasant" people who felt "no fear of us." Thousands of Chumash occupied towns and villages along the Santa Barbara Channel. They lived by the waterside, harvesting an enormous variety of readily available resources. In special storage houses they kept large stockpiles of dried sardines, anchovies, bonito, and other fish, along with seeds, nuts, and grains in adequate quantities to hold numerous feasts for Portolá's men. Chiefs organized celebrations, designed perhaps to impress the Spanish newcomers with their wealth and power.

Portolá sought their alliance, but the Chumash looked to secure the friendship of these newcomers as well. The Spanish were impressed both by the abundance of food the Chumash collected, the variety of their economic pursuits, and the great reach of their trade networks. "Some of them," wrote one Spanish observer, "follow fishing" while "others engage in small carpentry jobs; some make strings of beads, others grind red, white and blue clays." The Spanish wrote that the Chumash produce "variously shaped plates from the roots of oak and alder trees, and also mortars, crocks, and plates of black stone, all of which they cut out with flint, certainly with great skill and dexterity." They made arrows to "an infinite number," and "the women go about their seed sowing, bringing the wood for the use of the house, and water, and other provisions."

Despite the obvious signs of prosperity, of regional trade and a system of currency based on the manufacture of shell beads, and despite the obvious sophistication of Chumash social organization, the Franciscan missionaries who accompanied Portolá felt that the Indians would have to change. Everywhere they looked, the Catholic priests saw signs of Chumash savagery. Though the Chumash, according to one Spanish observer, lived in "communities that have fixed domiciles," and they arranged their "well-constructed" and "spacious and fairly comfortable" houses in organized settlements, the Franciscans hoped to relocate the Chumash to missions where they could more easily control them. Junipero Serra, the Franciscan friar who led this movement, ultimately established twenty-one missions along the California coast, several of these among the Chumash. The Spanish constructed a presidio, or fort, at Santa Barbara in 1782, and a mission there, and at San Buenaventura, in 1786. La Purisima, near today's Lompoc, followed one year later and Santa Ines, near Solvang, in 1808. The Santa Barbara Channel, in Serra's view, was "full of a huge number of formal pueblos, and the most wonderful land."

In the decade and a half that followed the establishment of the mission at Santa Barbara, according to one estimate, nearly 85% of the Chumash population relocated and settled under the supervision of the Spanish priests. A number of forces, working in unison, propelled this significant and abrupt movement of native peoples.

European diseases took their deadly toll, killing as many as two-thirds of the Chumash living along the Santa Barbara Channel in the last quarter of the eighteenth century. During the same period, the enormous expansion in Spanish livestock herds compromised Chumash subsistence routines. Drought and fluctuations in sea temperature may have affected the availability of those resources upon which the Chumash relied for food. Fewer people facing significant subsistence crises, the loss of elders and ritual knowledge, and the critical numbers to maintain the integrity of their communities, the Chumash may have moved to the missions in an effort to insulate themselves from the frightening changes occurring in their world.

Once they arrived at the missions, Chumash villagers may not have seen any fundamental contradiction between their traditional beliefs and those taught by the Catholic priests. Missionaries dressed in ceremonial attire when they said mass, led their community in song, and performed sacred rituals, like their own religious leaders. Their knowledge of the sacred set them apart from the broader community. Like the Pueblos before them, Chumash villagers may have seen in the Spanish cross something analogous to the large prayer poles upon which they made their own ritual offerings. Chumash at the Santa Inés mission, for example, hung strings of dried fish and chunks of venison upon the large cross that stood outside the church. At the outset, Chumash villagers would have had little reason to view their traditional beliefs as being in any way incompatible with those of the priests.

Once a group of Chumash villagers decided to relocate to the mission, it became more difficult for those who hoped to remain behind. Village economies collapsed, making feeding those who stayed even more difficult. Those who moved to the missions began working in the Franciscans' fields, producing even more food and creating an environment where the missions seemed to offer both a source of subsistence and a community to which one might belong. But those who settled in the missions did not find relief. Death rates in the missions always surpassed birth rates. Between the years 1771 and 1820, according to one study, the average annual birthrate in the missions stood at 41 per 1000 mission Indians, while the death rate reached an average of 78 per 1000. Only two out of three children made it to their first birthday. Of these, 40% died before they reached the age of five. Few survived past their tenth birthday. Though few epidemics descended upon Alta California, chronic diseases such as dysentery took an enormous toll in Chumash lives. While the non-Indian population reproduced rapidly, Indians succumbed in large numbers to illnesses in turn made more deadly by unhealthful living conditions, a brutal work regime, and, as one archaeologist noted, "the psychological impact of mistreatment in the missions and by cultural dislocation."

Those who received baptism and survived (the Spanish called them "neophytes"), faced rigid discipline. In an attempt to impose their own sexual morality upon the Chumash, the priests confined unmarried men and women, some of whom experienced sexual abuse at the hands of Spanish soldiers, in separate crowded and unhealthful barracks. The Franciscans punished any transgression of their moral code by the neophytes with brutal beatings, the use of the lash, solitary confinement, and mutilation. Officials in the imperial center thought this brutality was not only cruel but terribly backwards. Alta California's Governor Felipe de Neve, as early as 1778 hoped to transform the Indians of Alta California into useful subjects of the Spanish Crown by guaranteeing them a rudimentary municipal government and some control over their own communities. Neve opposed the use of corporal punishment, and believed that missions, by isolating Indians from the *gente de razon*, the Spanish settlers, retarded their improvement. They should interact with colonists, learn Spanish, and assimilate into the empire. The Franciscans, led by Serra, defied these efforts with all their energy, preserving a religious institution that had fallen out of favor amongst the Bourbon Reformers who took control of the empire late in the eighteenth century.

The missionaries brutally exploited Chumash labor. The Chumash produced nearly everything consumed in or sold at the mission. They faced extraordinary limitations on their freedom. Still, Chumash men and women who settled in the missions seldom granted to the Franciscans all that the priests desired. Chumash elites continued to marry other elites, and those who led native communities outside of the missions often exercised leadership roles within. Chumash working in fields or tending Spanish livestock herds gathered traditional foods and hunted and fished as they always had done when the opportunity arose. Chumash herdsmen who worked too far from the missions to return every night established camps, like that at Saticoy near San Buenaventura, which became the basis for native communities.

Many neophytes clung to important elements of traditional belief. Some of the Chumash at Santa Inés continued to decorate prayer poles. At La Purisima, a twenty-three-year-old man raised at the mission, and "instructed in everything appertaining to religion," refused on his death bed to confess his sins and die "like a Christian." Others ran away, joining Chumash communities in the interior where they reconstructed the social and familial relationships that always had given shape to their village communities. On occasion, the Chumash challenged directly the beliefs of the Franciscans. In 1801 a Chumash woman at Santa Barbara began to preach that non-Christian Chumash would die if they received baptism. She had ingested *datura*, a hallucinogen that enabled Chumash travelers to encounter powerful spiritual forces in their cosmos. Like other prophets, she received a vision, and called upon her people to change their ways. The neophytes would suffer death as well, she said, unless they renounced Christianity, embraced their traditional beliefs, and washed their head with special water she called "tears of the sun." The movement flashed brightly and spread rapidly, and Chumash people showered the prophet with gifts and offerings. The Spanish, clearly shaken, suppressed the movement the moment they learned of it. What, one frightened priest asked, would have happened had the prophet called upon her followers to kill the priests? The priests could not control the thoughts of the native peoples who settled in their missions.

More than two decades later, a much larger uprising took place. Discontent amongst the mission Chumash had increased, and Chumash leaders at La Purisima began sending bags of beads into the interior to secure allies against the Spanish. Rumors of revolt became widespread, even if the Spanish did not take them seriously. Neophytes at Santa Inés, La Purisima, and Santa Barbara hoped to launch a coordinated attack on Sunday, February 22, 1824, during the celebration of the mass. On the Saturday before the uprising, however, an Indian from La Purisima traveled to Santa Inés to visit an imprisoned relative. The Spanish guard refused to allow the visitor to see his relative, and after an exchange of words, the guard ordered the visitor whipped for insolence. The Chumash at Santa Inés fought back. They burned most of the buildings at Santa Inés, sparing only the church. They then moved to the complex at La Purisima, which they captured after a brief firefight. The victorious Indians strengthened their defenses and prepared to hold the mission indefinitely.

The next morning, Chumash at Santa Barbara under the leadership of Andrés Sagimomatsee seized control of that mission. Well aware that they could not hold it for long, owing to the proximity of the Spanish garrison at the presidio, they looted the mission and withdrew. Some crossed the channel to their old homes on Santa Cruz Island; the majority headed toward the Tulares, a five-day march to the east in the interior. They found here shelter and a highly defensible location, establishing in effect a Native American maroon community that the Spanish could attack only with great difficulty.

The Chumash held La Purisima for nearly a month. On March 16, the Spanish attacked, exchanging musket and artillery fire with the defenders. The Spanish ultimately retook the mission, and sentenced seven of the rebels to death. Meanwhile, the Spanish marched to the Tulares. They hoped to persuade the rebels to return. At first, the Chumash refused. "We shall maintain ourselves with what God will provide us in the open country," they said. They did not turn their backs on all the changes the Spanish had brought. "We are soldiers, stonemasons, carpenters, etc.," they told the Spanish commander, "and we will provide for ourselves by our work." They saw the crafts they had learned in the missions as tools that could help them sustain themselves as free persons. The negotiations continued and finally, according to a Spanish observer, "in peace, mutual joy and satisfaction, they were convinced to take advantage of the general pardon" the Spanish had offered them to "return to the mission." When the Indians returned to Santa Barbara in June, the Franciscans felt that the rebellion had come to a close. But nearly 400 refused to return. They moved farther east, putting more distance between themselves and the Spanish. The uprising of 1824 was not simply a strike against the heavy-handedness of the mission, but part of a movement by Chumash peoples to secure their independence, to live their lives in a changed world upon their own terms.

The Salish-speaking peoples in the Puget Sound region began to encounter ships from Spain, France, Russia, and Great Britain in the second half of the eighteenth century at roughly the same time the Chumash began contending with Spanish missionaries. Manning these vessels were crewmen from Europe, of course, but also a motley collection of men from China, Japan, the Philippines, Africa, and other parts of North America. They fantasized about the potential of this lush land, one shaped by mountain, sea, and sky, as they navigated the tangled waterways and engaged in trade with the native peoples they encountered for furs. For the most part, they stayed aboard their ships, but they made their presence felt even then. When the English explorer George Vancouver arrived in 1792, after years of this shipboard trade, he described abandoned village sites, clearings now overgrown with weeds, and places where "the scull, limbs, ribs, and back bones, or some other vestiges of the human body, were found in many places promiscuously scattered about the beach, in great numbers."

Perhaps as many as 200,000 people had lived in this rich region before Europeans arrived. Some of the people Vancouver encountered—Skagits and Snohomish—possessed European weapons and others had metal goods, but Vancouver did not believe that the peoples of the Sound had encountered Europeans directly before. The Coast Salish participated in the networks of exchange that linked native peoples across the continent and over a wide region.

Dozens of distinct communities stood along the waters of this densely inhabited region, their villages located along the sheltered inlets and lining the rivers that drained into Puget Sound. Squaxin is the name often applied to those who lived at the head of Puget Sound, in a region extending from today's Olympia, Washington, to North Bay. Nisquallys and Puyallups lived in villages along the rivers bearing their names. To their north, near Lake Washington and the Duwamish River, stood Duwamish villages. The Suquamish lived across the Sound near Fort Madison Bay. Snohomish and Stillaguamish villages stood along their namesake rivers, while Lummi peoples lived around the mouth of the Nooksack River. Others—Swinomish, Skagit, and Samish, lived on islands in the sound. The Makahs, relatives of the Nootkas who lived to the north on Vancouver Island, lived near Cape Flattery. Klallam villages stood on the south shore of the Strait of Juan de Fuca and on the coast west of the Olympic Range along the Quillayute and other rivers. More Skagit villages could be found up the Skagit River, and Nooksack villages near Mt. Baker. Muckleshoots lived along the Green and White Rivers.

The relationships between these towns, the degree to which they cohered in larger polities, have proved to be a source of debate among anthropologists, archaeologists, and historians. The towns Vancouver and his men visited were most likely winter villages where semi-sedentary peoples stayed before moving to a variety of fishing, shell-fishing, and plant collection sites. Early in the nineteenth century, it appears that most people in the Puget Sound region identified themselves with their villages, which in turn were made up of collections of households who cooperated in some endeavors but who nonetheless possessed a great deal of autonomy.

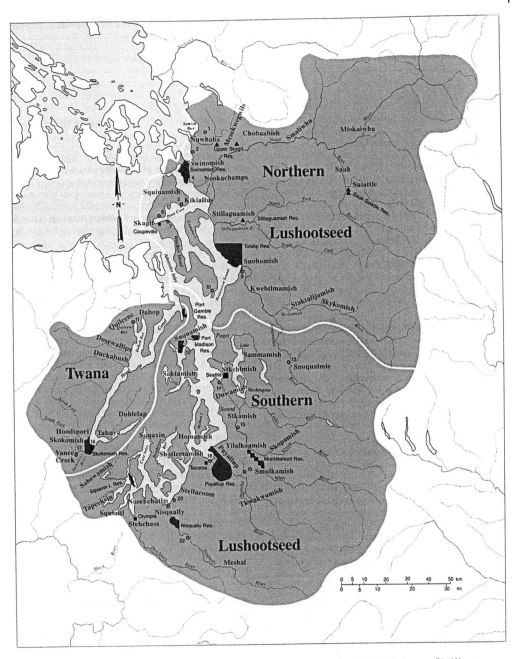

Map 5.3 Map of "Some Important Villages of Southern Coast Salish in the Early 19th Century" in Wayne Suttles, ed., *Handbook of North American Indians*, Volume 7, *NW Coast* (Washington, DC: Smithsonian Institution, 1990), p. 486.

Vancouver's men entered the sound. They interacted with these native peoples. Everywhere they went, the people the English explorers encountered made calculations and estimations of the newcomers' worth. Some of them, Vancouver wrote, feared that the food offered to them by the English was human flesh. They thus feared initially the strangeness and the savagery of the newcomers. Cautious at first, they hoped to engage the English in trade. At Eid Inlet, at the extreme southern end of the Sound, Vancouver's lieutenant Peter Puget was disturbed by the appearance of the villages he visited, "but not [by] their conduct, friendly and inoffensive, which already merited our warmest approbation."

In the years after Vancouver's departure, Europeans continued to visit the Puget Sound, exchange European manufactured goods for furs, but also for food. The sea, one observer noted in the 1820s, yielded to Coast Salish people an "abundant supply of excellent fishes of the most agreeable kind, every rivulet teeming with myriads of salmon, & the land affords an endless variety of berries & esculent roots." The traders relied upon the villagers for survival. Europeans who wanted to obtain pelts needed to accommodate the wishes of their trading partners. In 1801, for instance, the price for one sea otter pelt equaled that of one piece of cloth or two or three muskets or a case of powder. A dozen years later, the same pelt could be exchanged for four blankets, four buckets of molasses, a bucket of rice, two dozen loaves of bread, and an ax along with other trade goods.

Native peoples on the Salish Sea, then, asserted significant control over the conduct of trade. Though the arrival of Europeans could bring diseases and occasional acts of violence, it also brought economic benefits. Even with the establishment of fortified European posts in the early 1820s, the newcomers remained relatively few in number. They did not threaten the subsistence routines of native villagers. Certainly the fur trade offered new forms of wealth and new technologies. Some leaders, especially adept at managing intercultural exchange, grew wealthier and more powerful than they otherwise might have been. Some of these leaders were new men, consolidating control over aspects of a fur trade. But the arrival of Europeans did not force significant changes in their accustomed ways of living.

Declarations of Independence

The American Revolution resulted from the collapse of the British empire in the wake of the Seven Years' War and Pontiac's Rebellion. Colonists, who played an important role in the British victory over France, expected to participate fully in the new empire and to enjoy the benefits of British liberty. After the war, however, they felt that the imperial government treated them as second-class citizens, as something less than fully English, when it began to tax them without the consent of their elected colonial assemblies. When Parliament proclaimed a frontier line in 1763, they began to fear limitations on their movement and their economic aspirations enforced by native peoples allied with the Crown. The British government, overseeing what historian Edward Countryman has labeled a "composite empire," treated its American colonists as just one more group of subjects within a diverse transatlantic polity. When those colonists declared their independence in 1776 after a decade's worth of growing protest, they worked to create their own empire, one resting at least in part upon the right of citizens to dispossess native peoples and own private property, including human property, without governmental interference.

Native peoples, upon learning of the Revolution, hoped to stay out of the conflict. Guyashuta, a Seneca sachem, told British officials at Fort Pitt in 1776 that "we will not suffer either the English or Americans to march an army through our country." A few months later, he told officials of the American Continental Congress that they "must not come into our country to fight, lest you may stumble and fall on us so as to wrest the Chain of friendship out of our hands." Attempting to follow the strategy the Six Nations had employed for many decades,

Guyashuta attempted to play the competitors off against each other, and to assert the Senecas' independence from what he viewed as "an unnecessary war." Samson Occom wrote that he wished that the English and the Americans would leave "the poor Indians alone," for "what have they to do with your quarrels?"

It was a vain hope. The rebellious colonists did not leave the Indians alone. British agents pressed upon them to take up arms or to resist the calls of the Americans for assistance. French and Spanish agents, meanwhile, looking out for their own empire's sagging interests in America, also courted native peoples. While one British agent told the Senecas that the "Bigknife" should be ignored because "he had a very smooth Oily tongue" and "his heart was not good," an American officer told the Shawnees that British claims to assist them were the empty promises of Redcoats who crossed the Atlantic only "to rob and steal and fill their pockets." Native peoples had to sort out this conflicting information as they sought to make sense of a looming war that they understood would dramatically affect their lives. Native peoples would have to live with the winner.

For the Powhatans, however, the Revolution may have mattered little. Many of them spoke English, dressed and lived like their poor white neighbors, and practiced the same evangelical faith that coursed through the southern colonies prior to the Revolution. They maintained a low profile. Perhaps they tried not to bring attention to themselves. Some Pamunkeys served in Revolutionary forces, but their service did little to improve their position in a southern society based fundamentally upon an ideology of white supremacy. In its first state constitution, and in a law enacted in 1779, Virginians declared Indian lands inalienable without approval by the state's General Assembly, an attempt to guarantee not only that Virginia could oversee the sale of lands in the settled parts of the state, but to assert Virginia's claims over contested regions like Kentucky and Ohio.

The Mohegans, too, faced assaults on their lands, and continued to live their lives on the margins. The Mohegans lived close by Connecticut's white population, and they learned that many of them distrusted their Indian neighbors. Eleazar Wheelock, the Anglo-American missionary who educated Occom, learned from two men during the Seven Years' War that they thought no hope existed of converting the Indians to Christianity but with "powder and ball." No matter how civilized the Mohegans seemed, no matter how much they lived like their white Christian neighbors, some New Englanders still could not "respect an Indian, Christian or no Christian, so as to put him on a level with white people on any account, especially to eat at the same Table, no—not with Mr. Occom himself, be he ever so much a Christian or ever so Learned." Certain men, these New Englanders believed, were not created equal.

In this environment, Samson Occom continued his difficult career as a missionary. Shortly before the beginning of the Great War for Empire, he had traveled to New York, and then to the Oneida country, to try to preach to the unregenerate there. He had little success with the Oneidas, and the white New Yorkers frightened him. They were, he believed, "worse than the savage heathens of the wilderness." No Indians swore as much as New Yorkers. With war raging in the west, he appealed to the commissioners of his missionary society in Boston to find him other employment. In February of 1764 they sent him to the Niantics, close to his home and family connections at Mohegan. He traveled to England after that, preaching to audiences and demonstrating that native peoples not only could convert to Christianity, but become effective ministers of the word of God.

He returned in 1769 to Mohegan, as the Mohegan Land Controversy heated up once again. His criticism of the colony's past behavior, and his assertion that New England Indians would more likely convert to Christianity if their neighbors treated them with fairness and justice earned him enemies and a reputation for arrogance and haughtiness that is not at all reflected in his writings. Occom struggled to find work. He began drinking, and he confessed that he was an alcoholic in 1769. He preached on occasion, and despite his hardships, inspired a Christian revival at Mohegan.

It was the sermon Occom gave on the occasion of the execution of Moses Paul, a Christian Mohegan, that returned him to prominence. Paul had been drinking at a New Haven tavern in 1772. When some white patrons insulted him, Paul waited for them outside, jumped them, and killed one of his victims. In this, Paul's story conformed to New Englanders' beliefs that Indians were dangerous drunks whose lust for vengeance led them to irrational acts of violence. Paul challenged this view, and in an effort to spare himself from the hangman's noose, constructed an alternative interpretation of the events that took place at that tavern. It was not the man who he killed who suffered an act of racial violence, but Paul himself. Paul's attackers were racists, and he was no drunken reprobate, but a valued citizen of the commonwealth. His father had fought and died with New England's soldiers on the way to Louisbourg in King George's War in 1745, and Paul himself briefly served in Connecticut's forces during the Seven Years' War. He had received a Christian education and was civilized. It was the "barbaric" provocations of the man who he killed, whose "inhumane, cruel and barbarous acts" tormented him, that provoked his unfortunate outburst of violence. He did not premeditate his crime and should not, as a result, face capital punishment.

Paul's arguments failed to persuade judges in Connecticut, and after vigorously but unsuccessfully contesting his sentence of death, Paul prepared for his execution. Sympathetic ministers in town recruited Occom to deliver the sermon prior to Paul's hanging. Occom addressed a large audience that consisted of both colonized Indians and American colonists, and they likely drew very different lessons from what he said.

At one level, Occom employed the stereotypes that the white members of his audience commonly held about native peoples. Alcohol and its abuse, he said, have taken from Indians "every desirable comfort in this life; by this we are poor, miserable and wretched; by this we have no name nor credit in the world among polite nations." Not only were Indians on the path to extinction, he seemed to suggest, but Indians played a central role in their own demise. Indians were, Occom suggested, vanishing Americans, a familiar image of the continent's native peoples. But Occom did not absolve this audience from guilt for the Indians' decline. Occom identified with Paul, his "poor unhappy brother ... the bone of my bone, and flesh of my flesh." Moses Paul was, Occom said, "a despised creature." Indians were the downtrodden in Occom's view, but also humble and honorable. They were true Christians, and Moses Paul was not the only sinner. The racists and the bigots and the men who called names; those who taunted and exploited them and wished that native peoples would go away; their hatred, Occom said, rest at the heart of this crime, and for the legal system to overlook these uncomfortable facts was a gross miscarriage of justice. As the American colonists moved slowly and haltingly toward Independence, Occom and other New England Indians contemplated an independence of their own. They looked to leave New England, with its tired land, its rocky soil, and its rigid limits on what native peoples might become, for new homes in the west. Among those who settled the western frontier, were dreamers and schemers and those who sought economic opportunity. But there were also native peoples, many of them Christian and highly Anglicized, who hoped to find independence from racism, discrimination, and injustice.

The Revolution and the Longhouse

As the colonial protests against British imperial policy grew, Sir William Johnson worked to persuade the Six Nations of the Iroquois to continue to hold the Covenant Chain. The Senecas, who retained many allies in the west and felt little affection for the British, raised special concerns for Johnson. Should the Senecas choose to go their own way, or should they choose to avenge the insults and murders their people had suffered from frontier settlers in northwestern Pennsylvania, the entire western frontier of the empire might be set ablaze. Iroquois allegiance was important to the British and the allegiance of the Senecas, the largest of the Six Nations and the most firmly connected to anti-English Indians in the west, was critical.

The American rebels, gathered at the first Continental Congress in Philadelphia, recognized the strategic importance of the Six Nations as well. Members of Congress wanted to ensure that the Six Nations did not join with the British. The Americans did not ask for the Iroquois to join them as allies, for they could not afford the expenses of an Indian department on the British model, but they did want to limit the influence of imperial officials among them. The war, the American commissioners told representatives of the Six Nations at a council held at German Flats in the summer of 1775, "is a family quarrel between us and Old England. You Indians are not concerned in it." The Commissioners told the Iroquois that "we don't wish you to take up the hatchet against the King's troops. We desire you to remain at home, and not join on either side."

Thus was posed the question that divided Iroquois communities as the colonists and their mother country started fighting. Should they uphold the Covenant Chain alliance and maintain their long relationship with the English imperial government? Or should they side with the colonists. The Flying Crow, a spokesman for the Senecas, reminded a British officer of the difficulties posed by his continual requests for assistance. The Flying Crow told John Butler that the British asked the Senecas "to break the peace we live in with our American brethren." The Americans had encroached on Seneca lands to be sure, but he asked Butler, "if you are so strong, Brother, and they but as a weak boy, why ask our assistance... If you have so great plenty of warriors, powder, lead and goods, and they are so few and little of either, be strong and make good use of them." Most Haudenosaunee hoped to stay out of the conflict, for they recognized that they could lose much should they choose the wrong side.

Most of the Six Nations, the Oneidas and Tuscaroras excepted, viewed Anglo-American settlers as more of a threat to their way of life than the Crown, and after listening to the arguments of the great Mohawk leader Joseph Brant, Butler, and Sir William's successor Guy Johnson, they recognized the benefits of taking up arms against the Americans. They made this decision in an atmosphere of profound crisis. Smallpox ravaged the Onondagas over the winter of 1776 and 1777. Three Onondaga sachems, and nearly ninety others, died as a result. No political decisions could be made by the Iroquois League, nor could the League sachems condole the dead chiefs, something that they could not do easily in winter or in times of war. The Council Fire at Onondaga, the ceremonial and ritual center of the league, was extinguished in January of 1777, freeing the individual nations of the League to go their own way, to follow their own paths. Decision-making in these years of crisis was left to groups of warriors and the leaders of Iroquois villages and towns.

The fighting began in earnest in 1777. Senecas traveled east to Fort Stanwix, in present-day Rome, New York, at the invitation of British officers to "come and see them whip the rebels." At Oriskany Creek, however, they found themselves involved in an intense battle with a rebel force escorted by Oneida guides. The Seneca chief Blacksnake, one of the witnesses, recalled late in life that "there I have seen the most dead bodies of all ... that I never did see, and never will again. I thought at the time the Blood shed a stream running down on the descending ground during the afternoon." Colonel Butler told his superiors that the behavior of the Senecas during the battle "exceeded anything I could have expected from them." They fought bravely and lost much. Mary Jemison, a white woman adopted into the Seneca community, recalled the wailing and the suffering that accompanied the loss of so many warriors and leaders. "Our town," she recalled, "exhibited a scene of real sorrow and distress, when our warriors returned, recounted their misfortunes, and stated the real loss they had sustained in the engagement." The grief, she continued, "was excessive, and was expressed by the most doleful yells, shrieks, and howlings, and by inimitable gesticulations."

Iroquois raiders sought vengeance. Sometimes led by Joseph Brant, and sometimes accompanied by loyalist Rangers, they attacked frontier settlements throughout New York. At Cherry Valley in November 1778, for example, Seneca warriors killed thirty-two civilians and sixteen American soldiers. Seneca raiders destroyed settlements along the Susquehanna River in Pennsylvania. Events like the "Cherry Valley Massacre" fueled the determination of the Continental Congress to eliminate the Six Nations as a threat to the United States. The Onondagas first felt the wrath of the American patriots. Militia forces led by Goose Van Schaick destroyed the Onondaga castle in the spring of 1779. According to Onondaga refugees who fled their town, Van Schaick and his men raped women and killed their children. The Onondagas retaliated a short time later, when nearly all of their surviving warriors descended upon Cobleskill, wiping out the small settlement.

George Washington, who commanded the Continental Army, ordered a much larger operation against the western Iroquois. Major-General John Sullivan led four brigades of Continental soldiers into the Finger Lakes region of western New York in the summer of 1779. The Senecas offered minimal resistance. Most fled as Sullivan's army advanced. When the Senecas did stand and fight, Sullivan's superior numbers and firepower overwhelmed them. The Senecas suffered few casualties, but the destruction was immense, a war of terror. Sullivan's forces destroyed nearly forty Seneca and Cayuga villages. They burned over 160,000 bushels of corn, the Senecas' extensive orchards, and laid waste to their towns. It was savage warfare, an invasion designed to drive the inhabitants out of a region by destroying their ability to feed and shelter themselves.

Five thousand Senecas and Cayugas fled towards Fort Niagara after the invasion, where they joined the large numbers of refugee native peoples already drawing rations at the fort. Mohawks, Oneidas, Onondagas, Cayugas, Tuscaroras, and Senecas were there, but so too were Nanticokes, Conoys, Delawares, Shawnees, and many others. They settled in camps on the flatlands around the fort. With their crops destroyed so late in the planting season, they had no food, and the winter of 1779–80 was brutally cold. Many refugees died of starvation and exposure. They certainly became dependent upon the British for provisions. And convinced that the soldiers of the American republic sought their destruction. The Seneca Sayengeraghta told other native peoples gathered at Fort Niagara that a British defeat would mean that the Six Nations "must be miserable people ... left exposed to the Resentment of the Rebels, who, notwithstanding their fair speeches, wish for nothing more than to extirpate us from the Earth, that they may possess our Lands, the Desire of attaining which we are convinced is the Cause of the present War." Senecas equated the Americans' fight for freedom with genocide.

That is why they fought on. Sullivan had destroyed villages, not warriors. In 1780 they began to take their vengeance. Joseph Brant led renewed raids on Cherry Valley and Seneca warriors struck both to the east and south. According to British records from Fort Niagara, between February and July of 1780 400 warriors at a time were out against American settlements. Combined Iroquois and Loyalist raiding parties destroyed hundreds of bushels of corn, killed over 300 colonists, burned over 700 houses, and sacked half a dozen forts. They also made off with over 700 head of cattle. Settlers fled from the most fertile land in New York State. Sullivan's campaign had not brought security to the white settlers of the New York and Pennsylvania frontier.

The Continental Army defeated the British at Yorktown in October of 1781, ending major fighting in the Revolutionary War and securing the independence of the American colonies. The British government, in the midst of negotiating its peace treaty with the newly independent United States, sought to restrain Iroquois warriors from launching further raids. Though the warriors remained capable of striking American settlements, the wars of the Revolution devastated Seneca communities and produced a massive diaspora of Iroquois peoples. Refugees rekindled a new council fire at Buffalo Creek, and another across the Niagara at Grand River in the modern province of Ontario. Though a handful of Senecas stayed at the site of their ruined villages in the Genesee Valley, many had moved to Cattaraugus Creek near Lake Erie, and to sites farther south along the Allegany. Many other Iroquois peoples settled at Buffalo Creek, over 2000 by 1783, attempting to rebuild their lives in this refugee center. They had been battered in war, but they did not view themselves as conquered people.

Cherokees and Chickamaugas

Cherokee villagers maintained many ties of exchange and commerce with colonial traders from Savannah, Charleston, and the settlements in Virginia. They acquired from them the guns that they needed, but also a whole host of other items, including tools, pins and needles, rings, keys and bells, nails, fishhooks and combs, and alcohol. The alcohol, of course, did great damage and it could only be acquired from the traders. The Cherokees could not produce it, or the other items that they needed. They had little choice, then, but to enter into relations of exchange with traders who did not always recognize or appreciate the reciprocal expectations the Cherokees held for the conduct of trade. Certainly the traders could be useful. They brought the goods. The Cherokees granted lands to traders married to Cherokee women to serve as barriers to further white settlement. Allied traders would occupy those lands that lie between the Cherokee towns and the Virginians.

Dependence on Anglo-American trade helped pave the way to dispossession but it was not the whole story. John Stuart, the Crown's Superintendent for Indian Affairs in the Southern Department, noted that huge tracts of Cherokee land had been seized from villagers "by taking advantage of their wants and poverty, or by forgeries and frauds of different sorts in which the nation never acquiesced." They already found many of their lands handed away by the Six Nations at Fort Stanwix in 1768. A new line dividing Cherokee territory from the lands open to white settlers was drawn at Lochaber in 1770, but within a couple of months the Cherokees already complained of settlers crossing it. In 1771 colonial officials and Cherokee headmen agreed to move the line westward again, and as late as 1774 Cherokee leaders like Oconostota continued to ask the colonial governor of Virginia to restrain his colonists from crossing into Cherokee territory. At Sycamore Shoals in March of 1775, a group of land speculators from North Carolina swindled Oconostota, Attakullakulla, and other Cherokees to sign away 27,000 square miles of territory in exchange for a cabin full of trade goods.

These land sales angered many Cherokees. After Sycamore Shoals, the militant leader Dragging Canoe threatened to halt any further encroachment onto Cherokee lands. The son of Attakullakulla, Dragging Canoe opposed the policies of his father and other "old men" whose wrong-headed approach he believed brought little but suffering, poverty, and dispossession. He forged alliances with militant Indians north and south opposed to white expansion. In the spring of 1776, as the Continental Congress moved toward its declaration of independence, he accepted a gift of ammunition from Stuart and, one month later, Shawnee delegates traveled south to the Cherokee "beloved town" of Chota. There they presented Dragging Canoe with a war belt, painted red, signifying their desire to go to war against American settlers. His acceptance of the belt left the men who had signed the Sycamore Shoals agreement dejected, for they knew that they had lost control of affairs in Cherokee councils. Leaders like Attakullakulla and Oconostota would never retire completely, and the interplay between militants like Dragging Canoe and leaders more willing to accommodate the land-hungry settlers and less willing to risk the horrors of war would shape the contours of Cherokee politics through the early years of the American republic. Still, it must have seemed to the older men that their day had passed. The Cherokees would join with like-minded militants from the north in a massive movement designed to eradicate the Long Knives. Dragging Canoe and his followers, well-armed and willing, committed the Cherokees to a war against the Americans.

They struck settlements in Virginia, the Carolinas, and Georgia. They struck the settlers in the Watauga Valley of Tennessee as well, who had acquired their title at Sycamore Shoals. The intruders knew they were coming and drove them back. These were small-scale raids carried out by small numbers of warriors. Dragging Canoe planned larger assaults. Cherokees from the Overhill towns planned to attack the settlers on the Watauga once again and drive them back into Virginia. The Cherokees already suffered from shortages of ammunition, and the settlers once again defeated Dragging Canoe's men.

From July until October of 1776, American militiamen retaliated for the Cherokee raids, burning the food stores, fields, and villages from which the Cherokees had fled. With their homes close to advancing white settlements, and with whatever assistance the English might offer too distant to do any good, the Cherokees stood dangerously exposed. North Carolina troops attacked the Middle Towns and destroyed thirty-six settlements. South Carolinians hit the Lower Towns and a Virginia force hit the Overhills, destroying food supplies that could not be replaced so late in the year. Stuart wrote that the Cherokees were "distressed disarmed and flying into every nation for protection."

In the wake of the Americans' devastating counterattacks, those Cherokees who had opposed war now sought to make peace with the invaders. They had much to fear from the Americans and the British obviously could not offer them any meaningful protection. At DeWitt's Corner, Lower Town Cherokees made peace with the Georgians and South Carolinians in May of 1777, while the Overhills met with the Virginians two months later at Long Island on the Holston River in South Carolina. The agreements resulted in the appointment of agents from the states to reside at the Cherokee town of Chota and the loss of 5 million acres of lands east of the Blue Ridge in Virginia. These leaders, who parted with the lands reluctantly, hoped that the new cession and the new boundary line would form a permanent barrier. Old Tassel, however, one of the most important leaders willing to negotiate with the Americans, like many of his countrymen did not view the two agreements as a complete surrender. He asserted that the Cherokees and the settlers were different, and that native peoples could not be expected to change merely because white people wanted them to. The Americans asked, he told them at Holston, "Why do not the Indians till the ground and live as we do?" Old Tassel rejected the Americans' reasoning. "May we not, with equal propriety ask, why the white people do not hunt and live as we do? You profess to think it no injustice to warn us not to kill our deer and other game from the mere love of waste; but it is very criminal in our young men if they chance to kill a cow or a hog for their sustenance when they happen to be in our lands." Flatly rejecting the supreme arrogance of the Americans, Old Tassel told them that "*We are a separate people!*" The Creator gave to white people and Indian people "their lands, under distinct considerations and circumstances; he has stocked yours with cows, ours with buffalo; yours with hogs, ours with bear; yours with sheep, ours with deer. He has, indeed, given you an advantage in this, that your cattle are tame and domestic while ours are wild and demand not only a larger space for a range, but us to hunt and kill them; they are, nevertheless, as much our property as other animals are yours, and ought not to be taken away without our consent, or for something equivalent."

Old Tassel and other leaders understood the source of the militants' anger, but they did not believe that warfare could achieve anything but the destruction of Cherokee towns. But Dragging Canoe and other leaders rejected the treaties of 1777. His followers, who came to be known as Chickamaugas, moved westward and settled in the Little Tennessee and Hiwassee Valleys of Tennessee. They never cut ties entirely with the Cherokee, and they should not be considered dissidents who defected or seceded or discontents who formed a new tribe. But they did pursue closer communication with Shawnees and others in the Ohio Country, similarly opposed to the expansion of the Long Knives. They also acquired arms and ammunition from the British, especially after the king's forces captured Savannah late in 1778. The Chickamaugas committed themselves to attacking white settlements in what are now Kentucky and Tennessee. Perhaps as many as 1000 warriors joined with the Chickamaugas in attacks on the Anglo-American frontier.

These attacks took their toll in Anglo-American lives, and armed forces from the sovereign states launched assaults against the Chickamauga settlements scattered on both sides of the Tennessee River. Virginia forces destroyed eleven towns, 20,000 bushels of corn, and goods valued at £25,000 in April 1779. In December of 1780, the Virginians attacked the Overhill towns. They destroyed over 1000 houses and nearly 50,000 bushels of corn. Four months later, North Carolinians burned fifteen Middle Cherokee towns. The attacks drove more embittered Cherokees into Dragging Canoe's ranks. The Carolinians "destroyed their towns, stock, corn, and everything they had to support on." The Raven, a leader at Chota, told the British that the Long Knives attacked with such force that "there was no withstanding them, they dyed their hands in the Blood of many of our Woman and children, burnt 17 towns, destroyed all our provisions by which we and our families were almost destroyed by famine."

To native peoples, this seemed like genocidal warfare. Dragging Canoe believed that the rebels intended "to destroy [them] from being a people." In the wake of this destruction, some Cherokee leaders began to send peace feelers out to American military leaders. The Spanish captured the British post at Pensacola in May, leaving the Cherokees with little hope of additional aid. John Stuart's death in 1779 hurt them as well—no Crown official even approaching his level of competence was appointed in the dying days of the empire. They felt that they needed peace. The citizens of the new republic behaved aggressively toward the Chickamaugas and the Cherokees in general. Cherokees complained that they had been killed by rebels, "we hope by mistake, thinking they were from Chickamauga." Settlers pressed upon their lands, a pressure that increased after 1781. The Cherokees could not resist it easily. If Chickamauga leaders like Bloody Fellow said that they would kill every settler on lands claimed by the Cherokees, Old Tassel and The Raven at the same time sought peace. Leaders like Old Tassel would soon recognize that they had no answer to the crisis that faced the Cherokees.

England's Allies and the Confederation

As the end of the Revolutionary War approached, Americans viewed native lands as conquered territory. "A bare recollection of the facts," a committee of the Continental Congress declared, "is sufficient to manifest the obligation they are under to make atonement for the enormities which they have perpetrated." Indians, American political leaders believed, had been "aggressors in the war, without even a pretence of provocation," and now must yield their lands to the citizens of the new republic.

Land rested at the center of American concerns after the Revolution. Cash poor and deeply in debt, land provided the national government and the individual states a way to pay their soldiers and meet their obligations. States like New York, for instance, saw in the sale of Iroquois lands a way to pay for its government without resorting to a politically inexpedient program of taxation.

Title to the land—the actual ownership of the soil—the states asserted belonged to them and, in the territories that had not yet been formed into states, to the Confederation as a whole. Native peoples possessed nothing more than a right of occupancy, in American eyes. They could use the land, but they could only sell those lands to the owner of the right of preemption. The United States, or the individual states within their boundaries, claimed an exclusive right to acquire and extinguish the Indians' rights to the soil.

The results were predictable. Land was a commodity during the early years of the republic, and Americans felt that by conquest and as a result of the peace treaty with Great Britain that the Indians' lands were now theirs. Indians must yield to the land-hungry and vengeance-seeking citizens of this new empire for liberty. Most policy-makers in Congress agreed, but many of them also recognized the need for a peaceful and orderly frontier. The United States could spend its meager resources more wisely than on the costs of fighting Indian wars, and it did not take a keen observer to recognize that despite the language of the Peace of Paris, Britain still hung onto its posts at Detroit, Niagara, and Oswego, while Spain maintained its possessions in the Lower Mississippi Valley. Some British officials contemplated the creation of a neutral Indian barrier state, independent of the United States and supported by the empire, with its southern border running along the Ohio River. Men like George Washington feared that disaffected Indians might acquire weapons and ammunition from America's imperial rivals and use them to protect their lands. Indeed, Washington believed that "to suffer a wide extended Country to be over run with Land Jobbers, Speculators, and Monopolisers or even with scattered settlers is ... inconsistent with that wisdom and policy which our true interest dictates, or that an enlightened people ought to adopt and, besides, is pregnant of disputes with the Savages, and among ourselves, the evils of which are easier, to be conceived than described."

To prevent these horrors was the problem. Washington believed that "no purchase" of Indian lands should be made unless by the authority of the United States "or the Legislature of the State in which such lands may happen to be." The first constitution of the United States, the Articles of Confederation, created a decentralized national government with significant powers retained by the individual states. Article IX of the Confederation gave the United States "the sole and exclusive right and power" to oversee the trade and manage "all affairs with the Indians not members of any of the states; provided that the legislative right of any State within its own limits be not infringed or violated." What did it mean to say that Indians were or were not members of a state? How was that determination to be made? And how far did the legislative rights of a state extend? A chaotic system where states pursued their own Indian policies resulted, often with little regard for the larger interests of the union.

Take, for example, the case of the Cherokees, and their relations with the state of North Carolina and settlers in a short-lived entity called "Franklin" in the 1780s. Late in May of 1785, "the Warriors, Chiefs and Representatives of the Cherokee Nation" signed a treaty with the "State of Franklin" in which they ceded their lands in what is now eastern Tennessee. The Cherokees agreed "that the white people shall never be by us or any of Our nation, molested or interrupted, Neither in their persons or property in no Wise, or in any Manner or form whatever, in consequence of their Settling or Inhabiting the said Territory." These western settlers had long clamored for statehood. Under the leadership of their future governor, John Sevier, and in anticipation of Congress accepting the original cession, they organized themselves in December into the State of Franklin.

Congress refused to accept Franklin's appeal for admission to the Union, and considered the region still as part of North Carolina. The Carolinians, the Virginians, and the United States all viewed Franklin as a threat to peace on the southern frontier. In March 1785, for example, Virginia's agent among the Cherokees, Joseph Martin, wrote to Edmund Randolph of Virginia, informing him that at his arrival in the west he "found the Indians in greater confusion than I ever saw them." Alexander Martin, the governor of North Carolina, observed that "provocations have been, and are daily given" to the Indians, "their lands trespassed upon, and even one of their chiefs has been lately murdered with impunity." This kind of behavior posed real dangers. The Cherokees maintained considerable power. Leaders like Old Tassel continuously called upon Congress to protect their lands from encroachments that "make some of our young men in a bad way of thinking."

While Old Tassel talked, Dragging Canoe and other militant leaders renewed their attacks beginning in 1779. They continued the fight against the "Long Knives" that had been the Southern Indians' American Revolution. Bloody Fellow, an important Chickamauga leader, warned the North Carolinians that they must remove the Franklin settlers. "As soon as the leaves grow a little," he said, "if your government does not make them move off, I will come with a party and kill every man, woman and child that shall be found over the river." Rumors circulated that the Cherokees had begun to accept arms and ammunition from the Spanish in Pensacola after frontier Indian killers murdered peaceful Cherokee ambassadors. Officials charged with maintaining an orderly frontier, from North Carolina to the halls of the Confederation, worried that neutral and friendly Cherokees might join with the Chickamaugas.

Affairs in the south deeply concerned officials in Congress who, in March 1785, appointed commissioners to meet with the Indians in the Southern Department "within the limits of the United States, or who have been at war with them, for the purpose of making Peace with them, receiving them into the favor and protection of the United States, and removing as far as may be all causes of future contention and quarrels."

The Cherokee delegates who met with the Congressional commissioners at Hopewell in South Carolina in 1785 appear to have viewed the United States as the only hope for protecting their lands. Old Tassel told the commissioners that the settlers "have taken our lands for no consideration, and are now making their fortunes out of them," and "had encroached on our lands expressly against our inclination." Unsuckanail, at the same council meeting, said that "the encroachments on this side of the line have entirely deprived us of our hunting grounds; and I hope the commissioners will remove the white people to their own side."

The commissioners tried to secure some measure of justice for the Cherokees. Under the provisions of the treaty, the Cherokees agreed to an exchange of all prisoners left over from the Revolutionary War, and acknowledged themselves "to be under the protection of the United States of America, and of no other sovereign whosoever." An American citizen settling on Cherokee lands in violation of the treaty would "forfeit the protection of the United States, and the Indians may punish him or not as they please." The Cherokees and the commissioners agreed, furthermore, that "for the prevention of injuries or oppressions on the part of citizens or Indians, the United States in Congress assembled shall have the sole and exclusive right of regulating the trade with the Indians, and managing all their affairs in such manner as they think proper." In return for these grants of authority to the United States, the commissioners accepted the Cherokees' definition of their lands, thus restoring to the tribe lands taken from them by the Franklin settlers.

The commissioners recognized that the Hopewell treaty meant nothing without the cooperation of Georgia and North Carolina. They understood the weakness of the national government, and that these states would not willingly concede to Congress the right to negotiate treaties of any sort with Indians within their claimed boundaries. North Carolina, after all, still claimed the lands within Franklin, and already had tried to persuade Congress to "disavow" any treaties entered into by the commissioners. Georgia defied the commissioners as well.

While North Carolina complained of congressional usurpation of rights it believed the Articles of Confederation reserved to the states, settlers in Franklin expressed their attitude toward the Hopewell treaty by ignoring it. Settlers continued to pour onto Cherokee lands. More and more Cherokees joined with militant Chickamaugas to defend their territory, and the Franklinites would not cease their aggression. In July of 1786, Governor Sevier led the Franklin militia into the heart of Cherokee country, burning the friendly town of Cawatie, and punishing in effect the dwindling number of chiefs willing to work to maintain peace with Anglo-Americans. Sevier compelled Old Tassel to accept a humiliating treaty at Chota Ford that reaffirmed the earlier cessions. Two years later, Old Tassel was dead. A frontier settler named John Kirk, who identified himself as the "Captain of the Bloody Rangers," had lost members of his family in Chickamauga raids. Kirk marched into Tassel's village. The elderly chief walked out to meet the militia troops. He did so unarmed, and met them under a flag of truce. Kirk was in no mood to talk. He pulled out a tomahawk, bashed open Old Tassel's skull, and murdered one of the few Indians still willing to work for peace on the southern frontier. The murder of Old Tassel drove even more Cherokees into the militant ranks of the Chickamaugas.

The Six Nations and the Empire State

The provisions of the Peace of Paris that ended the war between Britain and the United States shocked the Six Nations. Britain had left its allies at the mercy of the Americans, and did nothing to protect them. Reacting to the propaganda of victorious patriots who depicted Indians as blood-stained psychopaths, the Seneca leader Sayenqueraghta noted after the war that "if we had means of publishing to the world the many acts of treachery and cruelty committed by them on our women and children, it would appear that the title of savages would with much greater justice be applied to them than to us."

Commissioners appointed by Congress would attempt to dictate a peace to the Six Nations beginning in 1783. New York State officials questioned the right of the federal commissioners to meet with Indians in the state. To the congressional commissioners, Governor George Clinton demanded "that no agreement be entered into with the Indians, residing within the Jurisdiction of this State." Not all shared Clinton's limited view of national authority, but the new United States government simply lacked the power to force aggressive states like New

York to accept an alternative interpretation. Still, at Fort Stanwix in 1784, the representatives of the Six Nations, led by the Mohawk Aaron Hill, chose to negotiate with the commissioners sent by the Congress rather than the rival state commissioners appointed by Clinton. The resulting treaty must have disappointed Hill, for the United States Commissioners dispensed with the long-established and familiar practice of Iroquois treaty protocol, acted the part of haughty conquerors, and demanded of them a cession of their lands *west* of a line drawn four miles *east* of the Niagara River. As Philip Schuyler told the gathered Iroquois, "we are now masters, and can dispose of the lands as we think proper or most convenient to ourselves." And, "as we are conquerors, we claim the lands and property of all the white people as well as the Indians who have left and fought against us." The United States made no offer to pay for the cession it dictated, and agreed to "give peace to the Senecas, Mohawks, Onondagas, and Cayugas, and receive them into their protection" only in return for a huge cession of land.

The border defined at Fort Stanwix became an international boundary, one that prevented the Iroquois from playing the British off against the Americans. Their lands, no longer located on the frontier or as part of a permeable borderland, lay now entirely within the boundaries of the United States, a new nation committed to the dispossession of the Six Nations and the transformation of Indian land into agricultural settlements. By separating the Iroquois from the British, the Senecas and their Longhouse kin would no longer be able to threaten frontier settlements and British posts in the Niagara River Valley would become more vulnerable without an Indian buffer.

Other assaults on Seneca lands commenced shortly after Fort Stanwix. While their neighbors had to contend with state interests who acquired Iroquois lands through fraudulent treaties, the Senecas contended with forces from outside the state. Massachusetts, the colonial charter of which had specified no western limit, claimed much of the land in New York State. In December of 1786, representatives from New York and Massachusetts met in Hartford to hammer out their differences. The "Articles" to which the two states agreed gave New York "all the claim, right and title which the Commonwealth of Massachusetts hath to the Government, Sovereignty, and Jurisdiction of the Lands and Territories so claimed by the State of New York." Massachusetts received, for its part, "the right of pre-emption of the soil from the native Indians," which it promptly sold to a group of speculators headed by Oliver Phelps and Nathaniel Gorham.

The speculators met with the Senecas and others of the Six Nations at Buffalo Creek, in the summer of 1788. The Senecas were struggling: there is no doubt that the population of the Six Nations dropped during the war years, and the Senecas shared wholly in those losses. Invasion, disease, hunger, cold, and alcohol killed many. Though some small pockets of Senecas remained in the Genesee Valley, most of them had gathered with other Iroquois refugees at three locations. The largest of these, Buffalo Creek, housed over 2000 Iroquois. A quarter of that number lived farther south along the shores of Lake Erie at Cattaraugus, while 900 more lived at a site called the Loyal Village, less than ten miles from Fort Niagara. The trade goods they received from the British helped them survive, and at least one observer believed that "the immediate intercourse they have with the British" allowed them to be "far better clothed than those Indians were in towns at a greater distance." Other Senecas lived with members of the Six Nations at Grand River, across the Niagara in Ontario. Though the Senecas faced fewer problems than did their eastern neighbors, they had to contend with all the problems that settlement could bring: the encroachment on their lands by white farmers who viewed their lands as open range, and who loosed their livestock on Indian corn fields and who deforested woods reducing the supply of game; the violence of frontier thugs who destroyed Indian property, cut timber on their lands, and threatened Iroquois peoples with vengeance for their acts during the war. New York became a frightening new world for the Senecas and their neighbors.

Phelps and Gorham persuaded the sachems present to sell them a huge tract of land in return for the equivalent of roughly $5000. Furthermore, Oliver Phelps signed a bond in which he promised to pay to the "Sachems, chiefs, and warriors of the Five Nations" an annuity amounting to "two hundred pounds lawful money of the state of New York" with the payment to be made on July 4 "annually forever." Many Senecas objected to this sale and Cornplanter, who signed the deed to Phelps and Gorham, received death threats. Some Senecas spoke of fighting to preserve these lands, others of ending their own lives rather than living with the pain of a lost homeland. Cornplanter complained that he had been deceived by Phelps, who he said had promised the Senecas twice the amount stated in the deed, and that he had signed the treaty on the advice of the missionary turned real estate agent Samuel Kirkland. Red Jacket later complained that it cost the Senecas more than the annuity was worth to travel each July to collect it. It was a small sum of money, and within a couple of decades, the annuity no longer was paid to the Senecas. Phelps and Gorham's project, by that time, had long since gone out of business.

Confederations

In the fall of 1783, officials from the American congress informed native peoples in the Ohio Country and western Great Lakes that they had forfeited their lands to the United States because they supported Great Britain during the war. The new nation, its emissaries pointed out, was "disposed to be kind" to its Indian enemies, and they would allow them to occupy small tracts for their exclusive use within their old homelands. All the rest they must yield as the price for peace.

To the Potawatomis, this language seemed like bluster. In their last military engagement of the war, they had joined with warriors of other nations and a small number of British troops to kill seventy Kentuckians at the Battle of Blue Licks in August 1782. They had never ceded their lands to the British or the French, and thus rejected the claim that somehow they could lose those lands through the actions of their former ally. Still, along with other native peoples in the region, they saw the threat inherent in American rhetoric. The Americans' demand for their lands strengthened those who called for a unified resistance against the Long Knives, and generated an awareness of the shared threats that they and their neighbors faced. The Peace of Paris, which would legitimize an American invasion of native lands in the Ohio River Valley and the Great Lakes, brought no peace to the Potawatomis.

Native people met at Detroit. Encouraged by British agents, they began to talk of a unified resistance. The dangers they faced were enormous. In January of 1785, American commissioners coerced representatives from the Wyandots, Delawares, Chippewas, and Ottawas at Fort McIntosh to cede their lands north of the Ohio. The Americans required that they deliver to the United States hostages until "all prisoners, white and black, taken by the said nations" had been returned. Other native peoples rejected the calls of the American commissioners to negotiate, diplomacy by coercion. Shawnee warriors crossed the Ohio River and began to attack settlements in Kentucky. Potawatomis from St. Joseph teamed up with Miamis to kill settlers in Illinois.

By early 1786, officials in the American congress recognized that "the uniform tenor of the intelligence from the Western country, plainly indicates the hostile disposition of a number of Indian nations, particularly the *Shawanese, Puteotamies, Chippewas, Tawaas and Twightees.*" Joined by Mingos and militant Chickamaugas from the south, together they drew in "other nations to unite ... in a war with the Americans." Some members of Congress understood that American demands for land had provoked this Indian resistance, and some of them began to fear the prospect of a massive Indian war that the new nation simply could not afford.

In December, Potawatomis, Shawnees, and many others, including a few Chickamauga Cherokees, gathered to deliver to the United States a "Speech of the United Indian Nations." They said that "all treaties carried on with the United States, on our parts, should be with the general voice of the whole confederacy." The members of this new confederation further informed the United States that they would hold "all partial treaties as void and of no effect." They would meet with the United States, as a united confederacy, in the spring of 1787. Until then, they requested of the Americans, "in the most earnest manner, to order your surveyors and others, that mark our lands, to cease from crossing the Ohio, until we have spoken to you." They did not want war, but they did insist that the United States negotiate with all the confederated nations together. "It shall not be our faults if the plans which we have suggested to you should not be carried into execution." If "fresh ruptures ensue," and warfare and invasions of their territory continued, the confederated nations declared to the Americans that they would "most assuredly ... defend those rights and privileges which have been transmitted to us by our ancestors; and if we should be thereby reduced to misfortunes, the world will pity us when they think of the amicable proposals we now make to prevent the unnecessary effusion of blood."

A New Order for the Ages

Some members of the Continental Congress understood the importance of a peaceful and orderly frontier, and on a number of instances they sought to assert more authority over the conduct of Indian affairs. They did so unsuccessfully. In 1786, for instance, Congress approved an ordinance that failed to clarify the ambiguous language of Article IX. States like New York, North Carolina, and Georgia, all with powerful Indian communities living within their claimed boundaries, continued to conduct Indian relations on their own without regard to national interest.

There can be no doubt that the failure of the Continental Congress to control the states in the realm of Indian affairs led in part to the collapse of the Confederation and its replacement with a more powerful federal government under the Constitution of 1787. The new Constitution replaced the vague language of the Articles of Confederation with an assertive statement of federal authority over the conduct of Indian affairs: once the Constitution became the "supreme law of the land," Congress would possess the exclusive authority "to regulate Commerce with foreign Nations, and among the several States, and with the Indian Tribes." That little debate or discussion of Indian policy took place at the Philadelphia Constitutional Convention suggests that the vast majority of the delegates believed that the administration of Indian affairs and the conduct of Indian policy should be placed firmly in the hands of the new national government. Certainly to James Madison one of the most pressing inadequacies of the Confederation had been the weakness of the national government in the realm of Indian affairs. Madison had been disturbed, for example, by the conduct of the state of New York when it purchased huge tracts of land from the Oneidas, Onondagas, and Cayugas, but he feared the consequences of a clash with defiant state authorities. He listed the behavior of the states in the realm of Indian affairs as one of the principal "vices of the political system of the United States" under the Articles of Confederation.

President George Washington and his first Secretary of War, Henry Knox, who together designed and implemented the Indian policy of the new nation, believed that they must preserve order along the new nation's frontiers by controlling the several states. The sparse language of the Constitution gave Congress no control over native communities or the individual native peoples living in them. The Indian affairs clause of the Constitution was intended to exclude the states only, and the founding fathers did not pretend that they controlled the internal workings of native nations. Nothing in the Constitution affected the sovereignty of native peoples. Indeed, the immediate post-Revolutionary claims that the Indian allies of Great Britain had been conquered during the war went unheeded by powerful and autonomous Indian confederacies. Washington and Knox recognized that the pretense of conquest, coupled with the government's inability to control its land-hungry settlers, could only involve the young republic in a continuous cycle of expensive warfare, something that the new nation simply could not afford. Indeed, Washington told his Secretary of the Treasury, Alexander Hamilton, that peace with Indians was impossible "while land-jobbing and the disorderly conduct of our borderers is suffered with impunity, and whilst the States individually are omitting no occasion to interfere in matters which belong to the general Government." The President believed that "the interferences of the States, and the speculations of individuals, will be the bane of all our public measures."

It thus followed that Congress would enact in July of 1790 the first of several Indian Trade and Intercourse Acts. The law established licensing procedures for Americans who wished to engage in trade with native peoples, and penalties for unlicensed traders. With regard to the purchase of Indian lands, the law read that no sale "shall be valid to any person or persons, or to any state, whether having the right of pre-emption to such lands or not, unless the same shall be made and duly executed at some public treaty, held under the authority of the United States." The law also held that American citizens committing crimes against Indians would be prosecuted as if they had committed the same crime against a white person, under the laws of the state or territorial district in which they resided.

Congress enacted the Trade and Intercourse Act to provide the president with the power to oversee the orderly expansion of American settlement, something that Washington and Knox believed could best be achieved if peace were maintained with the Indian nations. Washington hoped to exert federal control over the direction of Indian affairs, and to limit the ability of frontier whites and land-hungry states to poison the nation's relations with its Indian neighbors. By establishing licensing procedures for traders entering Indian country and requiring that Indian lands be acquired only under the authority of the federal government, Washington secured in theory at least one means to prevent an expensive Indian war. By requiring that whites guilty of crimes against Indians be treated as if they had committed the crime against another white person, the Indian Trade and Intercourse Act at least on paper committed the United States to a principle of justice defined by Americans for Indians.

Washington's policies were firmly grounded in historical precedent. During the colonial period, governors worked to prevent colonists from encroaching on Indian lands. They prohibited the purchase of land from Indians without the consent of the governor and his council. In places, they forcibly removed settlers who illegally had moved on to Indian lands. Colonial governors wanted to establish secure colonies in the Americas producing the staple crops upon which the Crown collected customs revenue. At times, and in places, they promoted efforts to extend their version of Christianity. None of these goals could be achieved while warfare raged in the colonies, so governors worked to maintain peace with their Indian neighbors. If native enemies set colonial farms and plantations ablaze, the colonies of course could not prosper. Trouble with Indians, moreover, provided opportunities for England's imperial rivals to lure offended natives into alliances with potentially devastating consequences. Finally, colonial governors recognized that they could not hope to civilize and Christianize the same Indians they were trying to kill. Peaceful relations with the Indians were the easiest and least expensive way for the colonies to prosper.

Washington, as the president of the fragile young republic, faced similar problems. The British still held posts to the west of and within the newly independent American states and the Spanish and French posed diplomatic challenges in the south. Disaffected Indians might enlist America's imperial rivals. Warfare with Indians would sap the fragile economy of the new nation. Finally, the United States could not hope successfully to "civilize" Indians if natives only encountered a lawless and unsavory population of aggressive frontier whites, intent on cheating them in trade and encroaching upon their lands. From Washington's perspective, peace with the Indians was in the best interests of the United States, and that could most easily be achieved if the United States, through enactments like the Indian Trade and Intercourse Act, honored its treaties with the Indians and protected Indian lands from the unauthorized and unwarranted encroachment by white settlers.

The New Nation faced significant challenges, and considerable disaffection remained in Iroquoia, especially amongst the Senecas. Timothy Pickering, sent by President Washington to meet with the Senecas in 1790, found that the gathered Iroquois did not trust him, and that "*white man* is, among many of them, but another name for *Liar*." Pickering knew that the Senecas did not trust Washington, either. They considered me, he wrote to the President, "as your representative, and my promises as the promises of *Town Destroyer*." Pickering nonetheless followed Washington's instructions and informed the gathered Indians "that all business between them and any part of the United States is hereafter to be transacted by the general government" and not the states.

Shortly thereafter, the president met at Philadelphia with Cornplanter, the great Seneca leader, and informed him that "the General Government only, has the power to treat with the Indian nations, and any treaty formed, and held, without its authority will not be binding." Washington hoped that the hostilities of the Revolutionary War could be forgotten, and that in the future, "the United States and the Six Nations should be truly brothers, promoting each other's prosperity by acts of mutual friendship and justice." President Washington knew that the Senecas were unhappy about the terms dictated to them immediately after the war at Fort Stanwix and he understood that it was mostly lands used by the Senecas that had been relinquished. Washington understood the proximity of the British at Niagara to the Senecas. He knew as well of the anger of the Six Nations about the terms of agreements some of their members had entered into with New York to cede lands within the state. He explained, however, that "these evils arose before the present Government of the United States was established, when the separate States, and individuals under their authority, undertook to treat with the Indian tribes respecting the sale of their lands." Now, however, the situation was "entirely altered; the General Government, only, has the power to treat with the Indian nations, and any treaty formed, and held without its authority will not be binding." Washington wanted the Senecas to understand the significance of the replacement of the weak Confederation with a strong central government under the Constitution. "Here," he said, "is the security for the remainder of your lands. No State, nor person, can purchase your lands unless at some public treaty, held under the authority of the United States. The General Government will never consent to your being defrauded, but it will protect you in all your just rights." Should anyone defraud the Indians of their lands, Washington told the Senecas, "and you can make satisfactory proof thereof, the federal courts will be open to you for redress, as to all other persons."

In 1791 Pickering again met with Iroquois delegates, mostly Senecas. Pickering once again tried to conciliate the Six Nations, who he feared might join with the powerful western confederacies, including the Potawatomis, the Chickamaugas, and others, who remained thoroughly capable of defending their homelands from invasion. It was the effectiveness of these native forces that made the Senecas' disaffection so critical. Should the Senecas join with those committed to resisting the Americans in the west, the frontier from New York to Georgia stood open to assault.

Congress was aware of the problem. While the delegates to the Constitutional Convention debated the provisions of the new Constitution in Philadelphia in the summer of 1787, Congress enacted the Northwest Ordinance in which it declared that "the utmost good faith shall always be observed toward the Indians, their lands and property shall never be taken from them without their consent; and in their property, rights and liberty, they never shall be invaded or disturbed, unless in just and lawful wars authorized by Congress." But squatters encroached upon their lands, invaded their property, rights, and liberties, and drove them to negotiate unjust treaties. Early in 1789, the governor of the Northwest Territory, Arthur St. Clair, negotiated a treaty with the Potawatomis, Sacs, Chippewas, Delawares, Ottawas, and Wyandots in which they reaffirmed the earlier cessions and agreed to further restrictions on their freedom. St. Clair believed that he had broken the opposition by the terms of the treaty. He was wrong. By the summer, native peoples were raiding frontier settlements north of the Ohio.

With native peoples unwilling to give away their homelands through negotiation, St. Clair decided on a military solution. The Indians would fight for their lands and their way of life. In September of 1790, General Josiah Harmar led a force of 1450 regular soldiers and Kentucky militiamen out against the native towns along the Wabash and Maumee rivers in what today is the state of Indiana. Native peoples from many nations—Shawnees, Miamis, Ottawas, Potawatomis, Weas, and Kickapoos—ambushed Harmar's force along the Maumee and killed 180 of his men. The defeated American force returned home by the end of October.

The defeat of Harmar's invasion emboldened those native peoples willing to resist American forces, and swelled their ranks. Potawatomis and Shawnees, along with Delawares and Miamis, attacked a settlement called Dunlap's Station just north of Cincinnati in January of 1791, while Potawatomis joined with Ottawas and Chippewas to attack targets elsewhere along the Ohio. By the spring, land speculators in the Ohio country complained that they found it difficult to recruit prospective settlers. "The Indians kill people so frequently," they wrote, "that none dare stir into the woods to view the country."

Native peoples had their own fears, of course. When Kentucky militiamen attacked a cluster of villages in northern Indiana where Potawatomis and many other native peoples lived, they threatened them with extermination. If native peoples refused to make peace, Brigadier General Charles Scott said, "your warriors will be slaughtered, your towns and villages ransacked and destroyed, your wives and children carried into captivity." Many of those who lived in the Ohio country saw in the United States, whatever its claims to desire peace, an existential threat to their existence. All they needed to do was remember events like the massacre at Gnadenhutten in 1782, when soldiers from Pennsylvania held a vote on whether or not to kill the 100 Christian Indians they had taken captive. This was, for native peoples, American democracy at work. As the Christians sang the last hymns they would sing, savage militiamen began to murder them, thirty men, three dozen women, and thirty-two children in all.

Meanwhile, Congress had already laid plans for another military invasion to take place in 1791. St. Clair led American forces into the Miami River Valley in September. Most of his soldiers were militiamen, poorly trained and poorly supplied. Before dawn on November 4, a force that consisted of Potawatomis, Shawnees, and large numbers of others—Ottawas, Chippewas, Wyandots, Mingos, Delawares, Miamis, and a few Chickamauga Cherokees—attacked St. Clair's much larger force. The soldiers panicked and ran. Over 640 soldiers were killed or captured or unaccounted for. Another 250 were wounded. Fewer than 500 men made it to safety unharmed. They killed only a small number of Indians in the largest defeat ever suffered by American military forces at the hands of native warriors. Twenty percent of the American military had been wiped out in one day.

By 1792, native peoples from many nations had gathered at a site called the Glaize, near today's Defiance, Ohio. There they reflected upon the meaning of their victories over the American forces. Native peoples with grievances against the Americans settled there, and their numbers included Potawatomis, Shawnees, Delawares, Miamis, Sacs, Foxes, Ottawas, Hurons, Munsees, Conoys, Mingos, and Cherokees and Creeks. The presence of the southern nations showed that the diplomatic connections between militants north and south remained strong. American agents feared that the powerful and well-armed Creeks and Chickamaugas would join with the Shawnees and other northerners to attack American settlements. The Indians gathered at the Glaize, according to the Shawnee leader Painted Pole, would unite to resist further invasions. The inability of the American government to control its vicious back-country settlers, and its own rapacious desire for Indian land, had unified its many enemies into a powerful native force.

1794, A Year of Consequence

Late in the summer of 1794, American general Anthony Wayne led his force of 3000 soldiers toward the Maumee Valley. There, on August 20, he defeated the confederated tribes at the Battle of Fallen Timbers. Although casualties were roughly the same on each side, the Americans took the field, and razed the Indian towns. The fleeing warriors headed toward the British post at Fort Miami. British agents had remained active in the Northwest since the close of the Revolution, and they had armed and encouraged the natives' resistance to American expansion. Now, however, they kept closed the gates to their forts and refused to fire upon the pursuing Americans. Once again, the British abandoned their native allies and demonstrated, if the point still required demonstration, that native peoples in the Old Northwest needed the British more than the British needed them.

They now had no choice but to make peace with the United States. A year after the battle, at Greenville, the Potawatomis, Shawnees, Delawares, Ottawas, Chippewas, Miamis, Weas, Kickapoos, Piankashaws, and Kaskaskias agreed to a peace that "shall be perpetual ... between the United States and Indian tribes." They paid as the price of that peace a massive cession of lands to the United States. The confederated tribes gave up tracts of land in Indiana and Illinois, and, more significantly, all of southern and eastern Ohio.

The Treaty of Greenville revealed the sort of changes that the United States hoped to bring to its defeated enemies. Each of the nations signing the treaty would receive an annuity, a yearly payment of money and other items the tribe could use to supply its wants. If the tribes should "desire that a part of their annuity should be furnished in domestic animals, implements of husbandry, and other utensils convenient for them, and in compensation to useful artificers who may reside with or near them, and be employed for their benefit," they need only to inform the federal agent stationed nearby and "the same shall at the subsequent annual deliveries be furnished accordingly." The United States would thus see to the civilization of the Indians, by transforming them from wandering hunters into settled farmers on the American model. Because farming required less land than the hunt, the thinking went, more land soon would be opened for settlement and expansion. To make this argument, of course, required the Americans who wrote the treaties, like Wayne, and those who ratified and proclaimed them, like the members of Senate and the president, to ignore the vast Indian cornfields that American forces destroyed, or the herds of cattle and swine that even now native peoples relied upon for food. To save the Indians, Americans would civilize them, and civilization required that they live upon less land. Americans took native land in the name of helping native peoples become civilized. Taking, as one historian put it, became giving.

As Anthony Wayne invaded the Maumee valley, the American commissioner Timothy Pickering met with the Six Nations at Canandaigua in western New York. He hoped to resolve long-standing difficulties with the Senecas. Their lands formed the central issue at the council. Through the Treaty of Canandaigua, signed on November 11, 1794, Pickering and the Senecas redefined the boundaries of the Seneca estate. The new western boundary of their lands ran "along the river Niagara to Lake Erie." This gave to the Senecas access to the river and the islands and access to British Canada to their west, a freedom, they hoped, that gave them an outlet and the opportunity to avoid the fate of other encircled Indian tribes. The Senecas did not wish to become "mere makers of baskets and brooms." This was an important concession. The ability to move through space, to interact with Haudenosaunee communities distant from them, was of immense importance to Iroquois peoples. Pickering also agreed to pay to the Senecas "a quantity of goods to the value of ten thousand dollars," and, further, that "with a view to promote the future welfare of the Six Nations," an annuity of $4500.

As with the treaty negotiated eight months later at Greenville, the United States sought to civilize the Six Nations and transform them into farmers on an American model. To the Senecas, however, the 1794 Treaty of Canandaigua recognized their sovereignty. Pickering pledged that the United States would never claim the Senecas' lands, "nor disturb the Seneka nation, or any of the Six Nations, or their Indian friends residing thereon and united with them, in the free use and enjoyment thereof." They could, they hoped, live upon their lands without the interference of outside authorities, and with the protection of the United States against unlawful intrusion. The treaty, the Senecas believed, recognized their right to exist upon their ancestral lands as a nation free from outside interference.

The Cherokees also negotiated a treaty with the United States in 1794. Earlier cessions had failed to satisfy the Americans' insatiable hunger for Cherokee land, and the Chickamaugas continued to resist white encroachment. In 1792, the Chickamaugas, aided by Creeks and Shawnees, attacked Buchanan's Station in today's Tennessee, an assault that showed that native peoples in the north and the south remained committed to working together to defeat the Americans. But divisions remained in these communities as well. Some Cherokees, who rejected armed resistance and feared the consequences of more torched villages and burned cornfields, of the terrors of warfare and frontier retribution, tipped off territorial governor

William Blount about the impending assault. Blount's forces were ready when the combined force arrived, inflicted heavy casualties, and drove them off.

Chickamauga resistance came to a close two years later. The Spanish decision to cease trading guns and ammunition to their native allies, a product of diplomatic and military changes in Europe, left Indians in the region dangerously exposed. In the fall, American militias destroyed the Chickamauga towns and the surrounding fields, killing seventy men. There seemed little hope for continuing the resistance movement, and the Cherokees signed the Tellico Blockhouse Treaty in 1794. The agreement reaffirmed an earlier treaty negotiated at Holston in 1791 through which the Cherokees ceded lands to the United States and agreed to a lasting peace. The Cherokees would not take up arms against the United States again until they decided, with enormous trepidation, to side with the Confederacy during the American Civil War.

The White Man's Republic

George Washington had hoped, he said in 1794, to oversee the orderly expansion of American settlement while pursuing a policy "calculated to advance the happiness of the Indians and to attach them firmly to the United States." He wanted peace, and to see to the "civilization" of native peoples. To this end, congress enacted and he signed the Trade and Intercourse Acts, designed to ensure order along the frontier and peace in relations between native peoples and the citizens of the young republic. He abandoned the conquest theory advanced by the Continental Congress in the immediate aftermath of the Revolution for a system based on treaties that, he hoped, would regulate American expansion while guaranteeing native nations the lands that they did not cede.

Yet Washington that same year lamented "the insufficiency of the existing provisions of the laws toward the effectual cultivation of peace with our Indian neighbors." By 1796, the final year of his presidency, Washington still hoped to restrain "the commission of outrages upon the Indians," but he feared that "scarcely anything short of a Chinese wall, or a line of troops, will restrain Land jobbers, and the encroachment of settlers upon the Indian territory."

The policies advanced by Henry Knox and he failed to achieve their cardinal goals for a number of reasons. Many native peoples, of course, already considered themselves civilized, and saw little attractive in the arrogant assumption that they must abandon their culture in order to survive. Others dressed like their white neighbors, bore Anglo-American style names, and lived in American-style housing. Many of them spoke English. They may have listened to missionaries who worked to save their souls. But they borrowed selectively, took what they wanted, and they lived on the margins of American society in communities of their own making. Though they incorporated substantial amounts of Anglo-American material culture into their lives, they remained quietly indifferent to what many Americans felt they had to offer native peoples.

Those native peoples who did work with the Americans—the leaders who, hoping to avoid the horrors of wars they feared they could not win, or the continuing loss of their lands—signed treaties guaranteeing them all that remained until they were ready to sell. They may have attended to the missionaries, accepted agricultural implements and livestock, and tried to make changes in their ways of living because they believed that doing so offered the best chance for their people to survive. But making these changes raised all sorts of challenges.

The frontier, we must remember was a violent and at times a frightening place. Many settlers living on war-ravaged frontiers simply could not trust their Indian neighbors. Settlers in the Ohio country, for example, experienced the horrors of warfare just as did Indians. Some of them witnessed the death of friends and neighbors in Indian attacks. More of them heard horrifying stories of Indian attack. These settlers had occasion to fear Indians. They acted, with violence and decision, to save themselves. Settlers found in their fears justification for horrible acts of terror. They could, as did Ohio country settlers in 1782, conclude that the singing of psalms by Christian Indians at the Moravian mission at Gnadenhutten was not the expression of praise but the ranting and boasts of savages who had wet their hands in the settlers' blood.

These acts of violence, along with the failure of the young republic to control its land-hungry settlers, and the continued suffering in many native communities, gave encouragement to those leaders who called for an armed resistance against the Americans. By 1794, much of this resistance had collapsed, and native peoples paid an enormous price for it. Warfare, and the resulting dislocation, devastated native communities. The Cherokees surrendered over 20,000 square miles of their territory. The Six Nations, combined, lost much more, and the population of both nations declined significantly between 1776 and 1794. The birth of the new republic, an "empire for liberty" in Jefferson's view, proved catastrophic for many native peoples.

6

Relocations and Removes

Native peoples confronted a new national government led by men who hoped to bring to them the benefits of American civilization and Christianity. The Americans believed that in so doing, they offered native peoples an opportunity for progress, to be like them, and to become fully human. The harsh realities of governing the Anglo-American frontier, however, always tempered and warped that benevolence. The new United States government, after all, remained a fragile thing in the 1790s and beyond, and it could never control its frontier population. While George Washington lamented frontier disorder, American settlers relentlessly pressed upon Indian lands. They provoked conflict and, in all too many instances, extraordinarily violent warfare. In the wake of these conflicts, native peoples and the United States entered into treaties, traditionally viewed by Europeans and Americans as legal agreements between sovereign powers, and defined by the Constitution with congressional statutes as the "supreme law of the land." Through these treaties the United States attempted to secure peace but also to acquire native land. American officials, regardless of the depth of their benevolence, always assumed that their settlements would advance as native peoples retired. Whether Indians accepted the civility offered by the agents of the new American empire, or fell victim to its Long Knives, the rise of the United States meant the dispossession of native peoples and aggressions upon their culture. Little wonder that so many native peoples saw the expanding United States as a threat to their existence. And with every defeat and every cession, every relocation and every remove, native peoples faced the prospect of carving out new homes and living their lives within an ever-tightening circle.

The Mohegans' Struggle for Independence

Many Mohegans, along with other native New Englanders, had migrated to the Oneida homeland in central New York in the early 1770s. There they established a settlement called Brothertown. Their residence there was short-lived, for they fled the ravages of frontier violence during the Revolutionary War and returned to the relative safety of Stockbridge in Massachusetts. But even there the American patriots' struggle against the forces of the king would not leave them alone. Many fought in the war, taking up arms in the fight for the colonists' independence. They enlisted and volunteered and served as substitutes for wealthier men. Some of them, undoubtedly, found inspiration in the new nation's ideals. Others fought in order to prove their loyalty to distrustful neighbors, or to collect some meager payment. American freedom was like that, secured largely, but not exclusively, by people on the bottom

Native America: A History, Second Edition. Michael Leroy Oberg.
© 2018 John Wiley & Sons, Inc. Published 2018 by John Wiley & Sons, Inc.

of the social pyramid. The emigrants returned to Brothertown in 1783, after the war. Mahicans from Stockbridge accompanied them. They struggled during their early years in New York. "The late unhappy wars," they wrote in a petition intended to gain for them the financial support of "all benevolent gentlemen," had cost them everything. In a desperate declaration, the Brothertown Indians sought "help from the People of God, for the present; for we have determined to be independent as fast as we can, that we may be no longer troublesome to our good friends."

Their experience as refugees colored their views of Christianity and the Christian God. The Brothertown Indians had done, it seemed, all that had been asked of them. They farmed. They sincerely accepted the missionaries' religion and they made it their own. But they continued to suffer. Some came to believe that the problems they faced were a reflection of God's will, a belief that God had cursed them in the present for the sins of their non-Christian ancestors. What a burden these beliefs must have been. They were Christians who believed that they were doomed to be punished by the Christian God. And while they confronted what they saw as God's curse, they also dealt with white Christians, who added insult to injury. Many of them, the Brothertowns learned, were racists, thugs, and liars who benefited directly from their dispossession and their misfortunes.

The Brothertowns continued to appeal to American Christians for funds. They received fewer donations than they had hoped, but the Brothertown community grew. It approached slowly the independence its founding fathers desired. Samson Occom, who helped found Brothertown, arrived in 1789. Leaving Connecticut behind forever, he served as the spiritual leader of the Christian community for the rest of his life. By 1800, 240 people lived at Brothertown in sixty households. By 1813, they had cleared 2000 acres and were "considerably advanced in agricultural knowledge." The Brothertowns maintained large herds of livestock, and had a pair of saw mills, a grist mill, three dozen framed houses and barns, and an assortment of ploughs, sleds, carts and wagons. Their lives as pioneers on the New York frontier in important ways resembled those of their white neighbors.

Those Mohegans who participated in the remove to Brothertown were, according to Samson Occom's biographer W. DeLoss Love, "the most intelligent and religious portion of the tribe." They were suited, Love seemed to suggest, for life as farmers on an American model. This readiness for success made them, in his view, something different from those Mohegans who remained behind in Connecticut, who continued to practice a mixed-subsistence style of farming. There is little doubt that significant numbers of Mohegans left New England and that this population loss hurt the community. A census of the state of Connecticut taken in the summer of 1782 showed that only 135 people remained behind at Mohegan living in twenty-eight households. Of those households with children, thirteen had both parents present while eleven had only one. The widows of Mohegans who had fought for the independence of the American nation headed eight of these one-parent families. The wealthiest Mohegan, a preacher named John Cooper, owned only two cows and a yoke of oxen for work on his farm.

In many ways the Mohegans lived like their non-native neighbors, but they still preserved important parts of their traditional culture, enough for well-meaning whites to continue to rationalize the marginalization of the community. The Mohegans' remaining lands along the Thames in Connecticut were well situated for a variety of subsistence activities. They could fish both in the river and on Long Island Sound, and harvest shellfish and reeds at the river's mouth. The nearby woods still supported some hunting, and they grew corn, beans, and squash in fields that, to Anglo-American observers, still appeared unkempt and untidy. Yet while they pursued these activities in a traditional fashion, the Mohegans adopted certain elements of the broader rural culture: they began to fence their fields, to raise livestock, to take Anglo-American surnames, and to dress like Anglo-Americans. They owned particular tracts of land, and passed those lots down to their heirs. A small number could read and write and all spoke at least some English.

But the mixed-subsistence economy employed by many Connecticut Mohegans no longer could meet all of their needs. Anglo-American farmers had entirely surrounded the Mohegans' shrinking settlements. To purchase the items they needed, whether clothing or medicine or consumer goods, they needed cash. Acquiring that cash required a more extensive engagement with the American economy. Mohegans leased portions of their land, or sold off small parcels to generate income. Others sold timber. But most Mohegan men, at one time or another, and many Mohegan women, left their homes in search of work. This was another type of Indian removal.

Mohegan women manufactured baskets and brooms, made from raw materials harvested on Mohegan lands. They found a small market for their traditional skills. Mohegan men, like other New England Indians, traveled to port towns and shipped out on whaling voyages. Borrowing on credit what they needed between expeditions, some Mohegan whalers found themselves obligated to venture out on further voyages, becoming in effect bond laborers beholden to the ships' masters. But some succeeded in this dangerous work. On board the whaling ships lived a community of a couple of dozen men who left their homes for years at a time. Skill on these voyages mattered more than race. Whaling allowed skilled native men to achieve a status higher than in any other line of work open to them.

On land, however, the Mohegans struggled to preserve their independence. Their white neighbors, if the experience of Uncas's heirs was like that of other native villagers in New England, could manipulate Mohegan debt to extract Indian labor. Creditors forced Mohegan parents to sell their children's labor to fend off litigation or the poorhouse. Many native children in southern New England, as a result, labored in white households under indentures that carried them into their late teens and twenties. "Many" of Connecticut's Indians, one reporter observed on the eve of the American Revolution, "dwell in English families." Indentured servitude impacted the Mohegans deeply. Removed from the care and protection and the love of their parents, and isolated from one another in English households, these Mohegan children found themselves in a poor position to carry on and sustain a culture.

But those Mohegans who could returned home in spring for the annual spawning runs of fish, and to prepare the fields for planting. They returned to an embattled community. Living in the United States forced them to make painful compromises and adjustments against extraordinary odds to preserve community land and resources. They faced a painful irony. As their material lives in many ways came to resemble ever more closely those of their white neighbors, the Mohegans faced a rising tide of racism that seemed for many outsiders to justify the Mohegans' position near the bottom of the social pyramid. The Indians no longer dressed differently or farmed differently or even spoke differently; something other than culture, then, must account for their inferiority. Race provided an intellectually lazy but incredibly powerful justification for discrimination and exploitation.

A few reformers tried to help the Mohegans, to do them some justice. Sarah Huntington, a white woman from Norwich with an "enormous missionary zeal," worked with Samson Occom's sister and her daughters in the Tantaquidgeon family to establish a Sunday school and to build a Christian church at Fort Hill at the center of the Mohegans' historic homeland. By 1831, Huntington had secured funding from the federal government for hiring a full-time teacher. But many of their neighbors had little interest in these activities. Despite the fact that the Mohegans remained on their ancestral lands, and fought attempts by Connecticut politicians to open what remained to white speculators, even those who did not see the Mohegans as the dregs of a savage race sullied by intermarriage with African Americans expected that they soon would disappear. Indeed, when in 1842 the Mohegans buried John Uncas, the last male descendant of Uncas, a New Jersey newspaper lamented the "passing away of a whole tribe of men, once the free, dauntless lords of the soil." The paper failed to note that Uncas was buried in the tribe's ancestral burial ground, presumably by the same "extinct" Mohegans who came to mourn his passing.

The vanishing of the Indians, the editor of that New Jersey paper wrote, was "the natural, inevitable result of the progress of society," and the United States based the various Indian policies it pursued on the assumption that native peoples ultimately would disappear. Americans interested in the development and implementation of the new nation's Indian policy always hoped to assimilate native peoples and to effect massive culture change. Speaking to his "Friends and Children" in the Cherokee Nation, for instance, Thomas Jefferson explained the virtues of massive culture change. "When a man has enclosed and improved his farm, builds a good house on it and raised plentiful stocks of animals, he will wish when he dies that these things shall go to his wife and children, whom he loves more than he does his other relations, and for whom he will work with pleasure during his life." Farming would bring further changes. "When a man has property," Jefferson continued, "earned by his own labor, he will not like to see another come and take it from him because he happens to be stronger, or else to defend it by spilling blood." The Cherokees would develop efficient systems of law, and "find it necessary then to appoint good men, as judges, to decide contests between man and man, according to reason and to the rules you shall establish."

It was quite a program. Jefferson and his contemporaries believed that the government must encourage native peoples "to abandon hunting, to apply to the raising of stock, to agriculture, to domestic manufacture, and thereby to prove to themselves that less land and labor will maintain them in this better than in their former mode of living." He hoped that Indians then would recognize that "the extensive forests necessary in the hunting life" had become "useless" as the neighboring white population increased and as they became farmers, and that "they will see the advantage in exchanging them for the means of improving their farms and of increasing their domestic comforts." Jefferson also encouraged the establishment of government trading houses amongst the Indians, to teach them "the wisdom of exchanging what they can spare and we want for what we can spare and they want." By leading native peoples "to agriculture, to manufactures, and civilization … and in preparing them ultimately to participate in the benefits of our Government," he told Indiana governor William Henry Harrison, "I trust and believe we are acting for the greatest good."

Jefferson, like earlier Europeans and European-Americans who looked out at native peoples, believed that Indians existed at an earlier point in time. They were "primitive," but they could be helped. He saw in them great potential, but only the potential to become something else. Ignoring the obvious and clear importance of agriculture in native societies, and the abundant evidence that native peoples were far from wandering nomads, Jefferson embraced a "four-stages theory" of human development. All societies, Jefferson believed, necessarily advanced through a series of stages as they progressed upward. Writing late in life, Jefferson saw this developmental program writ large on the American continent. "Let a philosophic observer commence a journey from the savages of the Rocky Mountains, eastwardly towards our seacoast," he wrote. "These he would observe in the earliest stage of association living under no law but that of nature, subsisting and covering themselves with the flesh and skins of wild beasts." The observer, Jefferson continued, would "next find those on our frontiers in the pastoral state, raising domestic animals to supply the defects of hunting. Then succeed our own semi-barbarous citizens, the pioneers of the advance of civilization, and so on in his progress he would meet the gradual shades of improving man until he would reach his, as yet, most improved state in our seaport towns." The observer would thus see the equivalent "to a survey, in time, of the progress of man from the infancy of creation to the present day." Europeans had advanced from their own savage origins, Jefferson believed. So, too, would native peoples. Teach them to farm, teach them to become civilized, and the Indians would blend into American society. They must. Jefferson believed that "the ultimate point of rest and happiness for them is to let our settlements and theirs meet and blend together, to inter-mix, and become one people."

Jefferson never realized how unappealing his understanding of history and the development of human societies seemed to many native peoples, and he had no patience for those who did not appreciate the wisdom of his policies. As native peoples gave up their lands, they would receive in return the benefits of American civilization. And "to promote this disposition to exchange lands, which they have to spare and we want, for necessaries, which we have to spare and they want," Jefferson wrote in a private letter to Governor Harrison, "we shall push our trading houses, and be glad to see the good and influential among them run in debt, because we observe that when these debts get beyond what the individuals can pay, they become willing to lop them off by a cession of lands." Through these means, he continued, "our settlements will gradually circumscribe and approach the Indians, and they will in time either incorporate with us as citizens of the United States, or remove beyond the Mississippi." Jefferson could see no place for Indians to remain Indians within the "empire for liberty" that he hoped to create.

Many native leaders recognized that they had little choice but to work with the leaders of the United States, and that they would have to accommodate themselves to certain cultural changes. Cornplanter, the Seneca leader who lived along the Allegheny River in the south-western corner of New York State, invited missionaries from the Society of Friends to the Allegany Reservation, and his followers accepted many of the technological changes that they brought. Arriving in 1798, the Quakers saw as their mission "to instruct the Indians in husbandry & the plain mechanical arts & manufactures directly connected with it." Cornplanter's people farmed and raised livestock, and floated timber to markets in Pennsylvania.

The Mohican-Stockbridge leader Hendrick Aupuamut conducted diplomacy on behalf of the United States and native communities, attempting to broker peace between militants in the western Great Lakes and American forces. And Black Hoof, the Shawnee leader who led his people's warriors against the forces of the United States in 1790 and 1791, visited Washington late in 1802 to ask the government to supply his followers with agricultural implements and livestock. If the Shawnees began to farm and model their material existence on that of their white neighbors, Black Hoof hoped, the United States might allow them to hold on to their lands. With the help of Quaker missionaries, Black Hoof's followers at the Shawnee town of Wapakoneta began to erect fences, plant and harvest corn, and begin construction of saw and grist mills. They were, in the eyes of their American patrons, showing signs of progress. In nearly every Indian community, one or more leaders urged their people to choose a new path, to make certain changes in their culture in order to hold on to their homelands. They pursued strategies designed to protect and preserve their people. Aupumaut hoped to employ strong relations with the United States as a barrier both against the Iroquois among whom his people lived and the territorially aggressive state of New York. Black Hoof wanted to remain on his ancestral lands and was willing to accommodate himself to new realities. The changes they proposed were significant, and native communities divided over whether the path these leaders chose to follow served their communities' interests.

The Rise of the Prophet

Potawatomis living along the upper Wabash, Elkhart, and Huron rivers in Indiana after 1795 worked hard to preserve peaceful relations with the Americans. They returned prisoners who came into their hands, and warned government officials of plots and rumors of hostile intent. Those Potawatomis living along the St. Joseph also worked to maintain friendly relations with the United States, meeting with American leaders frequently and apologizing for occasional violent acts by their young men. The Potawatomi leaders Five Medals and Topnebi met with President Jefferson and a convention of Quakers in Baltimore in 1801, after which the Quakers established a short-lived model farm along the Wabash to teach the Potawatomis and their neighbors how to work the soil. Though the farm failed owing to lack of interest on the part of almost all Potawatomi men, the diplomacy that led to its establishment reveals the extent to which some Potawatomi leaders recognized a need to learn to live with the Long Knives.

Those Potawatomis who lived closest to the expanding American settlements found themselves with little choice but to learn to dance with the devil. President Jefferson had urged Governor Harrison to do what he could to acquire title to native lands in the Northwest. Between 1803 and 1809, Potawatomi leaders entered into six treaties that ceded large tracts of land to the United States. In 1805, for instance, Potawatomis led by Topnebi and Winamek, along with representatives from the Ottawas and Chippewas, gave up a large portion of northern Ohio to which the Potawatomis had a weak claim. With the fur trade in decline, and with the supply of game dwindling with the advance of white settlement, the Potawatomis became increasingly reliant upon the provisions and the annuities that treaties could bring. Signing away rights to lands that they could not claim as exclusively their own, that they seldom used, or that remained marginal to those they actually occupied, seemed to some Potawatomi leaders a viable if risky strategy for securing the supplies they needed to stay alive.

Yet these annuities did not provide a long-term answer to the problems plaguing the Potawatomis—the gradual breakdown of an economy based on trapping furs, hunting game, and growing corn, beans, and squash in their fields. Although many of the older leaders continued to profess their desire to preserve peace with the United States, they had no ability to prevent younger warriors from acting out. And after 1805, discontent mounted among the Potawatomis, especially in the west. Cessions of land meant that more and more white farmers moved closer to the Potawatomis. As they cleared the land and planted their fields, they altered the game potential of the region, further threatening Potawatomi subsistence. The fur trade continued its decline in significance. Furthermore, the annuities that village leaders hoped would bring some relief were distributed badly by the United States. The western Potawatomi believed that they received less than their fair share of the annuities, while those who lived along the Huron River, and could come closest to claiming any lands in Ohio, resented sharing their annuities with Potawatomis who lived farther to the west. And despite the construction of American forts, the presence of federal troops, and continued revisions to the federal Indian Trade and Intercourse Act, alcohol continued to flow into Potawatomi communities from lawless white traders. The attempt to get along with the Americans, it seemed, brought them nothing but trouble. Many western Potawatomis, led by men like Main Poc, already led assaults on their native enemies in the lower Wabash valley. Their discontent—fed by a reduced supply of game, frustration over land sales and the distribution of annuities, and the devastation wreaked by alcohol—left the Potawatomis, in the words of anthropologist James Clifton, open to the "appearance of someone with a large, appealing, and culturally appropriate solution to the many disturbing problems that plagued the tribes of the region."

Figure 6.1 Tenskwatawa, c.1775–1837. National Portrait Gallery, Smithsonian Institution. Courtesy of National Portrait Gallery, Smithsonian Institution/Art Resource.

That individual was the Shawnee prophet, Tenskwatawa, whose people suffered from many of the same problems that plagued the Potawatomis. With his better-known brother Tecumseh, Tenskwatawa led a spiritual movement that responded both to white land hunger, American racism, and the Jeffersonian notion that native peoples should transform themselves into yeoman farmers.

Known originally by the name Lalawethika, Tenskwatawa by any standard had failed in life. An incompetent hunter who had managed to maim himself with an arrow, and an alcoholic, one day in 1805 he fell into a coma. While his body lay still, and while his neighbors feared that he had died, his soul traveled. When he recovered, Tenskwatawa, the "Open Door," shared with his neighbors what he had seen. He had left his body, he said, and found himself "traveling along a road" through the spirit world, until he came "to where it forked." The path to the right, he learned, "led to happiness and the left to misery." He could not enter the paradise to his right, but he glanced in and saw "a rich, fertile country, abounding in game, fish, pleasant hunting grounds and fine corn fields." Heaven was the Shawnees' homeland before the Long Knives arrived. Tenskwatawa followed the path of unhappiness, and he saw large numbers of his countrymen moving into a world of eternal fire and hellish torture.

This vision of hell, undoubtedly inspired by Christian missionaries (there is little evidence that native peoples had previously believed in an afterlife of eternal torture in a fiery furnace), changed Tenskwatawa. He renounced alcohol, and vowed to reform his life. He called upon his neighbors to do the same. Further visions helped him to clarify his teaching, and to provide the foundation for a religious movement that appealed to native peoples across the Old Northwest.

At Wapakeneta, Black Hoof's village, Tenswatawa preached his social gospel to Senecas, Ottawas, Wyandots, and Shawnees. He did not call for a simple return to the past. A product of a Great Lakes region where native peoples interacted frequently with each other and had, for a century and a half, learned bits of Christian theology from missionaries, Tenskwatawa's religion fused the influences that shaped Indian life in the Great Lakes. He urged his followers towards moral regeneration. He required that they abandon the "poison and accursed" alcohol traded to them by American settlers. He called upon his growing number of followers to cease fighting amongst themselves. They must love one another or die. He called upon men and women to honor their marriages and he discouraged polygamy.

He asked his followers, as well, to abandon their desire to accumulate property. Native peoples, he said, should neither keep nor eat cattle, sheep, and hogs, and must use instead those animals provided by the Master of Life: deer, bears, and fish. His followers could keep their guns, but they must hunt with bows and arrows and discard their American clothing. Their material culture should approach as closely as possible that which existed prior to the arrival of Europeans.

The Americans, Tenskwatawa preached, were "children of the Evil Spirit," and native peoples should have no contact with them. Shawnee women living with white men should return to their community. Preaching a message of racial purity, he told these women to leave their children with their white fathers. He wanted communities to be "all Indian" again, and Tenskwatawa called upon his followers to confess their sins. He borrowed selectively from both Christianity and a long tradition of prophetic resistance to the expansion of Anglo-American settlement. This renewal of ritual, Tenskwatawa urged, would cure the sick and restore game to the forests. The world would return to balance.

Not all native peoples found Tenskwatawa's message appealing. Traditional Potawatomi religious leaders rejected his teachings and saw in the new religion a threat to their position in their communities. Tenskwatawa denounced many traditional religious practices as corrupt and believed that his community's sufferings proved their ineffectiveness. Other Potawatomis continued to raid traditional enemies like the Osages, entirely ignoring Tenskwatawa's calls for intertribal peace and unity. What Tenskwatawa had to say did not address their concerns.

Shawnee leaders like Black Hoof, who had led war parties against the forces of the United States, did not believe that the program of resistance called for by Tenskwatawa would help Shawnee peoples, and he urged accommodation. But the forces with whom accommodationist leaders like Black Hoof worked—the missionaries, the federal agents, and other chiefs who competed with each other for their share of revenue from annuities—were divided among themselves. And those divisions limited their ability to confront effectively charismatic and compelling religious leaders like Tenskwatawa. Indeed, other prophets, like the Ottawa leader named Trout, preached a message similar to that of Tenskwatawa, and the appeal of these messages seemed to be growing. The policies of the divided annuity chiefs did nothing to address the problems they faced. As historian Gregory Evans Dowd put it, they became "the anvil upon which the prophets forged this early nineteenth-century phase of the struggle for Indian unity."

Tenskwatawa's following grew. Potawatomis from Michigan, Illinois, and Wisconsin traveled to Greenville to learn from him, and they carried his message to the Sacs, Winnebagos, and Menominees. In 1808, the Shawnee prophet led his followers away from Greenville and the growing number of American settlers in the area. They established Prophetstown, Tippecanoe, in northern Indiana. Warriors from throughout the region and from many nations relocated there to learn from the prophet.

Prophetstown was established near the village of Main Poc, the Potawatomi leader. Main Poc did not share all of Tenskwatawa's views. He traded alcohol at Prophetstown, something specifically prohibited by the Prophet. Ignoring Tenskwatawa's calls for unity, Main Poc continued to launch raids against the Osages. He launched raids against Indian and white enemies to acquire horses and other items that he and his followers could exchange for the goods and services of Anglo-American traders and blacksmiths. What he shared with Tenskwatawa was an aversion to the sorts of cultural change promoted by American officials: farming on the white model, which threatened to transform Indian men into women, for agriculture was women's work in many native communities.

Officials from the United States knew they had a problem, and they tried to keep the Indians quiet. At times it seemed like American officials had nothing but threats. Michigan's territorial governor William Hull, for instance, was ordered by Jefferson in 1807 to tell the Potawatomis that "if ever we are constrained to lift the hatchet against any tribe, we will never lay it down till that tribe is exterminated." They must remain at peace, or else. Jefferson conceded that in an Indian war, some American settlers and soldiers might die. But "we shall destroy all of them." This language of obliteration was no way to win hearts and minds.

Growing numbers of militants had gathered at Prophetstown. The land hunger of American officials gave more native peoples cause to join them. The constant pressure on Indians to sell land served as evidence that the United States wanted nothing less than to root them out as a people and dispossess them. In the summer of 1809, the United States acquired 3 million acres more of land through the notorious Fort Wayne treaty. Representatives from the Delawares, Miamis, Weas, Kickapoos, and Eel River Indians signed the agreement, but the Potawatomis led by Winamec and Five Medals comprised the largest delegation. Winamec coerced reluctant Miami leaders, who wanted to avoid war but also to hold on to their lands, into signing. Potawatomis helped the United States obtain what it wanted at Fort Wayne. They expected, in return, to receive the lion's share of the trade goods the government would distribute as payment. Winamec and Five Medals resented Tenskwatawa's influence, which seemed to grow at the expense of older men like themselves. The favor of the United States, these Potawatomi leaders hoped, would strengthen their leadership position within their divided communities by providing them with a large quantity of supplies that they could distribute to their hard-pressed followers.

Instead of winning for them the support of their people, the Treaty of Fort Wayne launched natives in the region on a path towards armed resistance. More and more warriors flocked toward Prophetstown to join in the intertribal alliance against the Long Knives called for by Tecumseh, the prophet's immensely talented brother. Their hostility was directed primarily toward the government chiefs who signed the Treaty of Fort Wayne. These chiefs, Tecumseh said, had no right to sell land and he told Harrison, in August 1810, that he intended "to kill all the chiefs who sold you this land." Winamac fled, fearing for his life. Tecumseh would not allow the survey or settlement of the lands ceded at Fort Wayne. A firm believer in his brother's religious message, and aware that Harrison intended to enforce the treaty, Tecumseh rallied support for an alliance against the Americans. He believed there could be no compromise with the Long Knives, and he began to travel to secure the allegiance of neighboring peoples. The land, Tecumseh argued, belonged to all the tribes, and "no sale was good," he told Harrison, "unless made by all the tribes." In the fall of 1810, Tecumseh traveled through Illinois and Wisconsin, visiting the Potawatomis and others. He called for intertribal unity, a movement of all native peoples against the Americans. Harrison believed that the forts and settlements in the west faced the prospect of a large and orchestrated assault by disaffected native peoples. Eastern Potawatomi would attack Fort Wayne. Kickapoos, Piankashaws, and Shawnees would strike Vincennes, while Ottawas and Ojibwe would attack Detroit. The Sacs would attack American forces on Mackinac Island and Main Poc would lead his forces against Fort Dearborn. Large numbers of warriors gathered at Prophetstown, led by Shawnees and Potawatomis but also including Kickapoos, Ojibway, Ottawa, Sauks, and Winnebagos.

Tecumseh departed for the south in 1811, hoping to pick up allies among the Creeks, Cherokees, Chickasaws, and Choctaws. During his absence, Harrison decided to act. He marched his forces toward Prophetstown. He built a fort on the site of modern Terre Haute, the first American post inside the bounds ceded in 1809. In early November, his forces arrived outside Prophetstown. Tenskwatawa urged his warriors to attack Harrison's forces on the morning of November 8, two hours before dawn, assuring them that the Master of Life would protect them. Harrison's forces held their ground, however, and after a hard fight drove off Tenswkatawa's warriors.

The Battle of Tippecanoe, historian R. David Edmunds wrote, "was less an American victory than a personal defeat for Tenskwatawa." His rituals and incantations had proven ineffective. Though Harrison had succeeded in breaking up the large gathering of warriors at Prophetstown, and the warriors scattered in the battle's aftermath, they retained their ability to attack. Hostile Potawatomis, who had concentrated at Prophetstown in November, now hit targets from Illinois into Ontario. Forces led by Main Poc attacked numerous frontier settlements. Tecumseh returned from the south in February of 1812 and reestablished himself at Prophetstown. His men outnumbered easily the small number of American soldiers in the west.

Their anger fused with the British war against the United States that began in 1812. Potawatomi and other warriors led by Tecumseh drove back an American invasion of Ontario and, in August, Potawatomis led by Main Poc, and well supplied with British arms and ammunition, attacked American soldiers and settlers retreating from Fort Dearborn. After fasting and smoking and honoring the appropriate rituals, Main Poc's men fell upon the American forces. Fifty soldiers died in the initial attack. Two women and twelve children also died. Main Poc's warriors took thirteen prisoners whom they tortured to death over the course of the next several days. By August, the British and their Indian allies controlled the upper Great Lakes. The Potawatomis planned on besieging Fort Wayne.

But Harrison held Fort Wayne and in September he sent forces to punish the Potawatomis and their neighbors. They attacked villages whether hostile or not. Major Samuel Wells burned Five Medals's Town and Little Turtle's town as well. These were the Americans' friends. The Americans took the offensive. They advanced on Detroit. Potawatomi and Shawnee raids on frontier settlements failed to halt their advance. By September of 1813, American forces controlled Lake Erie, and threatened to isolate the British at Detroit. Shawnee and Potawatomi warriors supported the British retreat across the river into Canada. But because the peoples who followed him lived in Michigan, Illinois, and Indiana, Tecumseh called upon the British to make a stand at Moraviantown. Here, on October 5, 1813, American forces killed Tecumseh as he tried to rally his forces.

The British could no longer supply their Indian allies, and the resistance movement lost momentum after the death of Tecumseh. The Shawnees and Potawatomis and others faced severe shortages of food. They were weak, and would have to work out in detail their relations with a victorious young republic that finally had secured its independence from Great Britain. They would face the United States without European allies.

Handsome Lake

The 1794 Treaty of Canandaigua stated that the lands belonging to the Six Nations should "remain theirs until they should choose to sell the same to the people of the United States who have the right to purchase." It also stated that the western border of the Seneca homeland ran "along the river Niagara." The Six Nations, according to the Seneca orator Red Jacket, long had considered themselves the occupants of a borderland between the British and the United States. Now, at the end of the eighteenth century, Red Jacket and the Senecas found themselves under assault by "a cunning People without Sincerity," Americans who asserted that the Senecas lived *within* the United States. As the international boundary restricted Seneca options to the west, American settlers advanced on their homeland from the east. The Senecas found themselves under siege. Phelps and Gorham were only the beginning.

In 1790, the two would-be land barons defaulted on their payments to Massachusetts, and the commonwealth in March of 1791 sold the right of pre-emption, or the right of first purchase, to the remaining Seneca lands (approximately 3.75 million acres) to Robert Morris, one of the wealthiest men in America, who in turn sold his rights to the Holland Land Company in December of 1792. Before they would pay, the Holland investors insisted that Morris extinguish the Senecas' title to the lands in question.

The warfare that had raged in the northwest delayed Morris's plans for several years. Finally, in 1797, his son Thomas traveled to Big Tree on the Genesee River to conduct a treaty. Morris encouraged his son to employ all means to acquire the Senecas' lands, including bribery, the use of alcohol, and the encouragement of factionalism. He did so. At Big Tree, the Senecas parted with all of their land, save for 200,000 acres distributed across eleven reservations. In exchange for this massive cession of lands, Morris agreed to pay "the sum of one hundred thousand dollars, to be by the said Robert Morris vested in the stock of the bank of the United States, and held in the name of the President of the United States, for the use and behoof of the said nation of Indians." The Senecas would receive as a payment, each year, the interest earned on this investment. Why did they sell? Certainly Morris behaved badly, using alcohol and bribes to achieve his ends. But resisting the pressure to sell land was difficult. There was, after all, no person other than Morris with the legal right to purchase their lands, and white trespassers steadily encroached on the Seneca domain. Facing the loss of all their lands, they preserved ownership of eleven critical tracts and, in a sense, transformed the rest of their vast domain into an annual cash payment designed to help them live in the presence of rapidly increasing numbers of non-Indians.

Doing so was not without cost. Annuities were never adequate to offset what had been lost. The crises of the Revolution—Sullivan's invasion; homelessness after their villages had been burned; the painful life of refugees; and, finally, pestilence in the form of dysentery, smallpox, and measles—further combined to reduce dramatically Seneca population and damage Seneca morale. Drunkenness became a serious social problem after the war. Some Senecas committed suicide. And with the Treaty of Big Tree, the Senecas lost much of their homeland.

The Quaker missionaries who arrived at the isolated Allegany reservation at the invitation of Cornplanter attempted to offer one solution to these problems. They hoped to teach the Senecas to farm and to raise livestock and there were some takers. Cornplanter's followers drew selectively from what the missionaries offered. Elsewhere, leaders like Red Jacket resisted the establishment of missions and schools. Many Senecas distrusted white Americans, whatever the intentions of the missionaries, and hoped to keep the growing numbers of settlers off of their remaining lands.

An alternative to the Quakers' message existed at Allegany. Born in 1735 in a Seneca village along the Genesee, Cornplanter's half-brother Handsome Lake had, like Tenskwatawa, lived a life of dissipation. Late in 1799, as he lay ill, "three spiritual beings, in the forms of men, sent by the Great Spirit, appeared before him." They carried him to the spirit world, and taught Handsome Lake the "will of the Great Spirit, upon a great variety of subjects, and particularly in relation to the prevailing intemperance." Handsome Lake visited "the realm of the evil-minded," where he beheld "the punishments inflicted upon the wicked, that he might warn his brethren of their impending destiny."

We have seen this before. Spirit travelers, departing this world for a time to learn lessons to save their people from destruction, called upon their people to reform their ways, to pay attention to their rituals. Tenskwatawa had made such a journey. So had the Cherokee hunter who lived for a time with the bears. And the Chumash visionary from Santa Barbara in 1801. To the crises facing native peoples, these prophets offered a response.

Handsome Lake began to preach to the Senecas and their Longhouse kin. His followers codified his teachings into the *Gaiwiio*, the code of Handsome Lake. He did not call for armed resistance: enveloped by white settlements, Handsome Lake and other Senecas knew that armed resistance to the expansion of white America was suicide. He and his followers did, however, assemble a rich gospel that defined sin, and what one must do to achieve salvation. He defined heaven and hell, and gave guidance to the Senecas and their neighbors on how to live well in a world dominated by white people who were different, and who threatened fundamentally native ways of living.

Like Tenskwatawa, Handsome Lake looked past tribal and geographic boundaries. He described his followers as Indians, people who had something in common that distinguished them from "the white-skinned race," one of the "different classes" of humanity, "which were

RED JACKET.
Seneca War Chief.

Philadelphia, Published by E. C. Biddle.

Figure 6.2 Red Jacket by Albert Newsam, after a painting by Charles Bird King. National Portrait Gallery, Smithsonian Institution. Courtesy of National Portrait Gallery, Smithsonian Institution/Art Resource.

placed separate from each other, having different customs, manners, laws and religions." The Indians, Handsome Lake believed, "were entitled to a different religion, a religion adapted to their customs, manners and way of thinking."

That way of thinking would have been familiar to many native peoples who found their communities in crisis. Bad things happened; disasters struck. But there could be no accidents; no random events. Disaster struck because of the displeasure of forces in the native cosmos; because of sin. Native peoples, Handsome Lake preached, must sin no more, reform their ways, and restore their rituals. Handsome Lake's creator bore important similarities to the good twin, and Tawiskaron, the evil twin, presided over Handsome Lake's hell. Instead of fighting in the distant past to give shape to the cosmos, however, in Handsome Lake's cosmology they fought for the allegiance of Iroquois men and women, both on earth and in the hereafter. In this sense, the *Gaiwiio* relied upon older religious traditions. But there were innovations. Handsome Lake's belief in the very existence of a heaven and hell was one. His calls for self-control and temperance, and his denunciation of sin and belief in the importance of confession show that his religious vision was not entirely isolated from that of neighboring Christians. Like Tenskwatawa, Handsome Lake's visions fused a variety of elements into a consistent religious system designed to save the Senecas and their native neighbors from destruction. His teaching empowered his believers to take steps to address the problems they faced.

Handsome Lake denounced the sin of drunkenness. "How many of our people have been frozen to death," Handsome Lake asked, and "how many have been drowned while under the influence of the strong waters?" Those who drank suffered on earth. They destroyed their communities, or their own lives, or were "thrown into houses of confinement by the pale faces." The Great Spirit commanded followers of the *Gaiwiio* to abandon the drinking of alcohol, a great sin.

Drunkenness brought great destruction to the Senecas but so, too, did the sale of land. Handsome Lake told his followers that "your chiefs have violated and betrayed your trust by selling lands." All should enjoy the land equally; nobody had the right to sell it. After Big Tree, nothing "is now left of our once large possessions, save a few small reservations." Any sale of land, Handsome Lake said, was a sin that offends the Great Spirit. The Senecas in his audience, Handsome Lake said, should remember that "you occupy and possess a tract in trust for your children," and that "you should hold that trust sacred, lest your children are driven from their homes by your unsafe conduct."

The Senecas must preserve their lands, but Handsome Lake recognized that his followers lived in the midst of white people. Compromises had to be made. The Creator intended for the Senecas to live off animals they hunted but because of the presence of the Americans, soon "there will be no more game for the Indian to use in his feasts." The Senecas, Handsome Lake taught, could thus raise domestic animals. "The pale-faces are pressing you upon every side." Senecas could tend cattle, and build comfortable houses. This was, he told his listeners, "all you can safely adopt of the customs of the pale-faces."

Those other customs were the source of so much pain for the Senecas, and Handsome Lake's religion taught his followers what to do about them. Handsome Lake journeyed in one of his visions along a road until he reached a fork. One path led to the House of the Great Spirit. The other led to the House of Torment, a hell reserved for Seneca sinners. Handsome Lake visited this hell. He looked down on the many rooms in a dark, soot-stained mansion in the land of Torment. In one chamber, he saw a drunkard, forced by the Punisher to drink molten metal, which he spewed from his mouth in a blaze of fire. Handsome Lake saw a husband and a wife. They began to argue and their tongues and eyes became so distorted that they could neither see nor speak. It was a frightening place: card players burning, wife-beaters striking women as their arms exploded; alcohol venders with their flesh rotting away; fiddlers, sawing off their arms for all of eternity. These were the sins of white men and women, and through the *Gaiwiio*, Handsome Lake's followers learned to avoid them.

Dispossessing the Senecas

Handsome Lake's message spread, and without question sparked something of a reformation in the morals and conduct of his adherents. But he could do nothing to stop the relentless pressure exerted by outsiders to acquire the Senecas' lands in western New York.

The land speculator David A. Ogden acquired from the Holland Land Company in 1810 the pre-emptive rights to purchase the eleven Seneca reservations remaining to the tribe after the 1797 Treaty of Big Tree. Ogden and his associates wanted to remove the Senecas to some location in the west, whether Mississippi or Arkansas or someplace "in the neighborhood of Green Bay." The well-connected Company called upon its allies for help. With Company support, Jasper Parrish, the federal agent charged with protecting Seneca lands, traveled to Washington in 1817 to persuade Secretary of War John C. Calhoun that removal was in the Indians' best interest. The agents lacked the power to preserve order, and frontier pressure on Seneca lands "causes the agents considerable time and trouble to settle with and satisfy the injured person, so as to preserve our peace and friendship unbroken." Parrish, like a growing number of Americans, believed that "under these circumstances I think it would be for the interest of the United States, and also for the welfare and the happiness of the Six Nations could they be persuaded to concentrate themselves." Removal he saw as a means to protect the Indians from the citizens of the state of New York, who encroached upon their lands, stole their possessions, and threatened the safety of all concerned.

Ogden, meanwhile, painted a bleak picture of the Senecas' future if they remained in New York State. "The History of every Indian tribe on the Atlantic Coast," Ogden wrote, "proves that they cannot long exist in their savage character in the Neighborhood of civilized Society, that becoming partly Christian, partly Pagan, partly civilized, and partly savage, they are rendered more and more debased and degenerate and finally become extinct, without having rendered themselves capable of any national enjoyment, or having contributed in any degree, to the stock of the public good." Ogden hoped that the president would get his point: "The Savage," he said, "must and ought to yield to the civilized state, and that this change cannot be effected otherwise than by the Agency of the Government."

Ogden found allies in the New York State Legislature. Regarding the Indians, a legislative committee asserted in 1819 that "their independence as a nation ought to cease," and "they ought to yield to the public interest, and by a proper application of power they ought to be brought within the pale of civilization and law and if left to themselves will never reach that condition; that such bodies retaining such savage traits ought not to be in an independent condition and that our laws and manners ought to succeed theirs; suitable quantities of lands to be reserved for them." The State Senate, shortly afterwards, requested that the governor "cooperate with the Government of the United States in such measures … to induce the several Indian tribes within this State to concentrate themselves in some suitable situation." The Senate, however, in a statement that aptly characterized the state's approach to dealing with its Indians, insisted that the governor take these actions "either with or without the cooperation of the government of the United States."

Rhetoric such as this from New York State mirrored the arguments occurring at the same time in the southern states, where a states' rights ideology nourished disputes over federal Indian policy. As the federal government and its agents among the Creeks and Cherokees sought, half-heartedly and ineffectively, to protect Indians from their neighbors, and as missionaries and philanthropists promoted their "civilization" and "improvement," southern state legislatures and courts argued that all who resided within a state, including Indians, must conform to its laws. The United States Supreme Court, later, would reject this limited federalism, but southerners had the power to blithely ignore officials of the national government. The resolution of 1819 shows that New Yorkers shared a similar states' rights ideology when it came to native peoples. The Senecas, and the rest of the Six Nations of the Iroquois, faced a relentless and grasping foe determined to drive them from their homelands. Many forces conspired for their removal.

Secretary of War Calhoun believed that Indians depended on the United States like a child relied upon its parents. Removal seemed to Calhoun a logical solution to the "Indian Problem." If they relocated to the western side of the Mississippi River, they would distance themselves from the unsavory influence of frontier whites, and gain additional time to become "civilized." Taking once again became giving. He believed that the United States, rather than the tribes themselves, must decide what was in the Indians' best interest.

Morris Miller, the United States agent appointed by Calhoun to negotiate on the Ogden Company's behalf, told the Senecas that the president sees "you scattered here and there, in small parcels everywhere, surrounded by white people. He sees," Miller continued, that "you are fast losing your national character, and are daily more and more exposed to the bad examples of your white Brothers, without the restraint of their laws and religion. He sees that this frequent and uncontrolled intercourse, instead of doing good is doing injury to you and to them. Your great Father sees all these things, with grief and concern. He lays them much to heart; and thinks it impossible for you, under such circumstances, to retain the character of an independent nation." Removal was in your best interest, Morris argued. But the Great Father must look after his white children as well, Miller continued, and from them he heard their discontent "at seeing the lands in your occupation remain wild and uncultivated; neither paying taxes, nor assisting to make roads and other improvements; nor in any way contributing to the public burthens, as white peoples' lands do." The president knew "that you occupy more land than you can advantageously till, or use for any valuable purpose; whilst at this same time the scarcity of game prevents your engaging in those pursuits, to which your fathers were accustomed." The solution was simple. The president, Miller told the Senecas, desires "that you should live at a greater distance from white people, so that you may be more secure in the enjoyment of your property. And that he can with greater convenience, and less expense cause you to be instructed in agriculture, and the useful arts; and your children to be taught to read and write, and that your nation may thus be rendered an industrious and happy people."

The Senecas rallied to oppose land cessions. Quaker missionaries, too, supported the Senecas. Led by Red Jacket, the Senecas refused to sell to the Ogden Company in 1819, and successfully resisted the Ogden Company's efforts to acquire their largest reservations.

It was not "savage" Senecas that the land barons worried about, but those who had adopted selectively elements of the Quakers' civilization program to strengthen their hold on a homeland increasingly surrounded by white New Yorkers. If the Friends hoped to preserve the Senecas by insulating them from corrupting outside forces and transform them into a nation of self-sufficient subsistence farmers, the Senecas made choices designed to protect their independence. To make a living and to acquire cash, some Senecas sold alcohol in western New York that they acquired downstream in Pittsburgh. Others continued to hunt. Even as the white population in western New York increased, Seneca hunters still found deer plentiful, as well as raccoon, mink, and muskrats, all of which seemed to thrive as the white population increased. According to the Mohawk John Norton, who visited the Senecas in 1809, they could "conveniently take skins, meat and timber to Pittsburgh, where they generally get a good price for these articles." The trip downriver took only two or three days.

Seneca farmers found markets for their crops. The flax Seneca farmers planted they sold to whites rather than use it for themselves or their families. Non-Indian observers writing during the war of 1812, a time of scarcity in western New York, reported buying corn from Indian women. The Senecas used their land, one observer noted, "not only for their own subsistence but sell considerable to white people." At Allegany, eighty Seneca families consisting of 439 individuals possessed 479 cattle, 58 horses, 350 hogs, and "699 acres of improved land in which 70 acres of meadow is included."

Some of the swine kept by Senecas they butchered and salted for family consumption but much of the rest they sold for cash. The Quakers encouraged the Senecas to acquire livestock, for food and as draft animals. But the Senecas, much to the concern of at least some members of the Society of Friends, seemed more interested in acquiring horses than oxen. The Senecas' white neighbors used horses for labor and transport in their lumbering activities; Quakers, who were concerned about the Senecas' participation in the timber economy, thus viewed the growth of the Senecas' horse herds as a potential problem.

Senecas frequently asked the Quakers to assist them in erecting saw mills. Cornplanter operated the first saw mill in Cattaraugus County beginning as early as 1795. Friends helped the Senecas operate their own mills, too, where they cut their timber, formed them into rafts, "and float them down to Pittsburgh, at the time of high water." The Senecas carried with them "their Peltry, furrs, and good canoes, to push up their return cargoes." The Senecas' desire for clearing land, which the Quakers mentioned frequently, was less about readying fields for the plow than it was about selling lumber for a profit. The Quakers could only appeal to them and ask them to consider "whether you would not have been in a better situation generally if you had employed the same time which you have spent in cutting and rafting timber in cultivating your good land."

By the 1820s, Senecas interested in participating in the timber trade cut trees, hauled the logs to the Allegany River, and rafted the unmilled logs downstream to Warren, Franklin, and Pittsburgh, in Pennsylvania. Some Senecas earned reputations as especially skilled pilots, a talent for which they were well paid. As with the sale of their agricultural produce, Seneca timbermen, floating downriver with their logs and other items, participated in a complex regional economy. Senecas traveled widely to exchange raw materials in the form of unmilled logs, processed items like furs and salted pork, and finished goods like moccasins, shingles, and finished lumber, for cash and goods unavailable to them locally.

It is difficult to overestimate the importance of the Quakers' contributions to Seneca economic life. But the Senecas always engaged with the missionaries on their own terms. They accepted elements of the Friends' technology and advice and much of the economic change that they advocated, but they did not become Quakers. They did not alter their religion. They engaged selectively with the market economy, preserving much of their freedom of movement, a significant degree of their autonomy, and their connections to Iroquois people living on their reservations and elsewhere.

Seneca resistance to the Ogden Company was strongest on these western reserves, but along the Genesee River the Ogden Company enjoyed more success. In August of 1826, Senecas along the river ceded their land to the Ogdens and agreed to reductions in the size of the Buffalo Creek, Tonawanda, and Cattaraugus reservations. They sold more than one-third of their remaining lands. But the sale, it turned out, did not represent the wishes of the majority of the Senecas, and they and their supporters immediately contested the legality and the morality of the treaty. Many of those who signed it, the Senecas argued, feared that if they did not sell they would lose their lands outright to squatters that nobody seemed able to control. Others believed that by signing the treaty they would satisfy the Ogden Company's voracious appetite for Seneca lands. Some of them hoped that after this cession, which they agreed to reluctantly, the Ogden Company would leave the Senecas in peace upon their remaining lands.

Other Senecas, however, painted a much more sinister portrait, and their numerous protests finally caught the attention of President John Quincy Adams. According to Seneca informants, the interpreters at the council threatened the gathered Indians with removal if they refused to sell. Jasper Parrish, the federal agent, offered bribes to certain Senecas in return for their signatures. This disturbing evidence delayed the treaty's consideration by the Senate, and the agreement never received proper ratification. But the government did nothing more, and in effect acquiesced in a fraudulent, unethical, and illegal treaty that carved a huge gash of territory out of the Seneca estate. Acquiring Indian land was the goal, and too often the corrupt means used to obtain it were ignored entirely.

The Senecas worked within a system of rules they had not chosen. Indian land sales involved elements both of choice and coercion. Indians simply could not afford to ignore the efforts of their white neighbors to purchase their lands. It is in this light that we ought to view the several treaties and deeds which representatives of the Seneca nation signed in the late eighteenth and early nineteenth centuries. If the Senecas, and native peoples similarly situated, refused to sell their lands, they faced losing them outright to the squatters, outlaws, and speculators who regularly exploited the weakness of government on the frontier.

And whether or not the preemption-holders paid a fair price, the Senecas did receive payments for "the use and benefit of the nation" in exchange for their lands. The funds held in trust by the president of the United States as part of the 1797 treaty at Big Tree, the Senecas argued were so held because "our Father," the president, "loved his red children, and would take care of our money, and plant it in a field, where it would bear seed forever, as long as trees grew, or water run." Federal Indian agent Erastus Granger believed that an efficiently expended and applied annuity would help the Senecas live better on less land, and "might be used to great advantage in furthering agriculture and in generally ameliorating the condition of the Indians."

When Congress or the state of New York failed to appropriate the necessary funds, or other factors delayed or prevented the timely payment of annuities, the Senecas suffered. "Our money," a group of Seneca chiefs wrote in a petition to the president, had been of great service to the nation. "It has helpt us to support our old people, and our Women and children," they wrote. The Senecas' agent in 1838 asserted that "the annuities paid to them by the United States and the state of New York constitute a considerable portion of their means of living."

It was a struggle to remain where they were. In an 1810 address urging the secretary of war to honor Seneca treaties, Red Jacket said that "For three years past we have received injuries from the white people. Our cattle and horses," he continued, "have been stolen and carried off; and although we have made complaint to your agent yet we have not received any compensation for our losses." New Yorkers who sat on juries seldom convicted their peers of these crimes. Indeed, the Senecas' reservations, Jasper Parrish observed later, "are surrounded by settlements of whites." The result, he said, is "frequent depredations, petty thefts, and trespasses committed on each other by whites and Indians; most frequently commencing on the part of the former."

Parrish, and others, saw in the inability of frontier agents to protect the Iroquois from the worst abuses of the white frontier population an important rationale for the removal of the New York Indians. But the Senecas did not want to relocate, and despite bitter factionalism at times, and the pressure placed upon them by land speculators, settlers, missionaries, and government agents, they found a way to resist their complete dispossession and wholesale removal to the west.

Pioneers and Exiles

When people speak of "Indian Removal," the image of the Cherokees' "Trail of Tears" most often seems to come to mind. But Indian removals began long before Andrew Jackson's election, as the story of the Senecas makes clear. These removals resulted from the harrowing work of epidemic disease, warfare, and the relentless pressure of white settlement on Indian lands. Many Senecas, for instance, left their homes in New York for new lives in Ohio in the first half of the eighteenth century. The reasons for this movement cannot be identified with certainty, but the migrants may have fled after a period of unusually poor harvests. The Sullivan campaign of 1779 provoked a massive relocation of Iroquoian peoples, producing 5000 refugees outside of the British post at Fort Niagara. After that peace that brought no peace, the 1783 Treaty of Paris ending the Revolutionary War, many Iroquois fled across the Niagara River to re-establish a new Iroquois council fire at Grand River in Ontario. Removal was a fact of life for native peoples.

As a federal policy, removal found its earliest advocate in Thomas Jefferson. He saw the possibility of moving eastern Indians west of the Mississippi as a justification for the Louisiana Purchase, an act that Jefferson felt may have been unconstitutional. Jefferson pursued removal in negotiations with several tribes, as did his successor, James Madison. Like all the Indian policies embarked upon by the United States, removal grew out of the failure of its predecessor. White frontier settlers pressed relentlessly upon Indian lands. The settlers' livestock destroyed Indian cornfields. The frontier population cut timber on Indian lands, cheated them in trade, and provided them with alcohol. All this occurred despite federal laws and treaties that guaranteed Indians the undisturbed possession of their remaining lands. Native peoples suffered as a result of their contact with American settlers, and the national government claimed that it was powerless to halt the onslaught.

Removal was thus the latest proposal to "save" the Indians and bring order to the frontier. As the Indians dwindled in numbers in the face of the rising tide of white settlement, policymakers felt a need to act. Indians faced extinction unless the "Great White Father" preserved his "Red Children." In the west, Indians would be free from the problems caused by non-Indians pressing upon their lands. Removal would buy them time to become civilized before once again they contended with a surging white population.

Many Indians, in fact, left the eastern United States before Congress officially implemented the policy of removal in 1830. Their lands and their way of life under assault, they left for new homes on the other side of the Mississippi because they wanted to free themselves from interference by white Americans. They did not relocate to a howling wilderness, and they did not move in order to become civilized. They hoped to isolate themselves from further insult and injury at the hands of aggressive white settlers.

A small number of Brothertowns, for instance, joined the New York Indians who scouted out new homes amongst the Menominees and Winnebagos in Wisconsin, an effort on their part to avoid the growing numbers of white settlers in the Oneida country in central New York. They settled with other native pioneers in a region they shared with the descendants of French fur traders and with American military officials. Potawatomis crossed the Mississippi, settling in the region of Cape Girardeau, likewise seeking to put distance between themselves and growing numbers of white settlers.

With the election of Andrew Jackson in 1828, the westerner, war hero, and Indian fighter, the pace of this relocation increased. Frontier interests triumphed in the direction of federal Indian policy. The men who formulated Jacksonian Indian policy expressed repeatedly that a new era had dawned, but many national political leaders and reformers worried about the effects of the president's policies. Much of the national debate over Jackson's plans revolved around the troubled relationship between the state of Georgia and the Cherokee Nation. In 1802, Georgia had ceded its western lands, comprising the present-day states of Alabama and Mississippi, to the United States. In return, the national government agreed to extinguish the Indian title to these lands as soon as that could be done "peaceably and upon reasonable terms."

The federal government attempted to fulfill its obligation to Georgia. During the final year of his presidency, Thomas Jefferson persuaded more than 1000 Cherokees to move to new homes across the Mississippi in Arkansas. In 1817 the Cherokees parted with another large quantity of their lands. More Cherokees moved to Arkansas. By 1819, 3000 Cherokees had relocated to the western side of the Mississippi.

In the meantime they had learned that resistance of the sort engaged in by the Creek "Red Stick" nativists was doomed to failure. Cherokees served with American forces in the war to put down the Red Sticks. They fought at Horseshoe Bend, the battle in 1814 that made Andrew Jackson a hero in much of the American south. Jackson, bestowing upon his Cherokee officers medals he had received from President James Madison, told them that "you have shown yourself worthy of the friendship of your Father, the President."

The 12,000 Cherokees who remained behind were growing increasingly committed to holding on to their lands. In 1819 the Cherokees ceded 3.8 million acres more of their lands to the United States. Over the course of half a century, they had given up more than 58 million acres in five states. They did so this time with the assumption that they would be able to retain the 10 million acres remaining in their possession. The Cherokees' increasingly assertive national council voted to deny citizenship in the Cherokee Nation to any person who chose to emigrate from the tribe's land in the east. In 1822 the Cherokees informed federal officials that they had determined "to cede not one foot more of land." Though President James Monroe continued to try to persuade the Cherokees to leave, and asserted that removal "would not only shield them from impending ruin, but promote their welfare and happiness," it was clear that the United States had acquired all the lands that the Cherokees willingly would sell upon reasonable terms.

Many Cherokees had learned to play politics American-style. They had made changes to the way they lived upon the land, and they planned on staying where they were. Moravian missionaries entered Cherokee territory in 1800, and representatives from the American Board of Commissioners for Foreign Missions followed in 1817. They operated schools attended mainly by children of mixed heritage, and produced a talented group of leaders literate in both English and in Cherokee, which acquired a written language thanks to the work of George Guess, better known as Sequoyah. The children who emerged from this educational system came to oversee the Cherokee Nation's relations with the United States in the 1820s. This "mixed-blood elite" farmed on an American model, and grew cotton worked by African American slaves for sale at market. They owned more wealth than their more traditional neighbors, and publicized their progress to a growing population of sympathetic reformers in the northeast, who read avidly of the number of spinning wheels, plows, hoes, and acres cultivated amongst the Cherokees. The federal "civilization" programs helped equip the leaders with the talents they needed; the pressure exerted by those clamoring for their lands made clear the need for a movement geared toward Cherokee nationhood. Talented leaders, literate in English and fluent in the conduct of American politics, fought to preserve their homeland.

These leaders began to act as a national government. They corresponded with supporters, published a newspaper called the *Cherokee Phoenix*, wrote their own legal code, and, in 1827, ratified a national constitution. This Cherokee elite thus used the federal government's civilization program as a weapon against those who sought to dispossess them. The Cherokee constitution reflected the widespread change in the nation, as their leaders decided to abandon older forms of tribal government and social organization in favor of a national framework that they felt was better suited to resist efforts to drive them from their land. The constitution, written in order to "establish justice, ensure tranquility, promote our common welfare, and secure to ourselves and our posterity the blessings of liberty," confined political rights to Cherokee males, denied political rights to women and African slaves and, like several state constitutions, required that all office-holders believe in God, in heaven, and in hell.

Not all Cherokees approved of these far-reaching changes. Being Cherokee could mean different things to different people. Some accommodated change more selectively, or not at all. A leader named White Path opposed the Cherokee constitution and called for the Cherokees to abandon Christianity. Many other Cherokees failed to share in the prosperity of the elite, and many Cherokee women opposed political changes that reduced their considerable influence in a matrilineal society. The Cherokee Nation, as it referred to itself in the 1820s, in important ways mirrored the values of the American nation.

The Cherokee constitution incensed land-hungry Georgians who wanted Indians out of the state, whether civilized or not. The Georgians argued that the Cherokee Constitution established an *imperium in imperio*, the creation of one state within the borders of another, without the consent of the latter, and, as such, that it violated the new states clause of the federal Constitution.

These Georgians saw in Andrew Jackson an ally, and believed that the first frontiersman elected to the presidency would aid them in dispossessing the Cherokees. In advance of his inauguration, the state enacted a series of laws extending its civil and criminal jurisdiction over the Cherokees. Jackson's Secretary of War, John H. Eaton, told a Cherokee delegation in the Capitol that they could not expect any protection or assistance from the executive. The Cherokees, Eaton said, faced "but a single alternative, to yield to the operation of those laws, which Georgia claims, and has a right to extend throughout her limits, or to remove, and by association with your brothers beyond the Mississippi to become united as one Nation."

Jackson mirrored these sentiments in his first annual message to Congress in December of 1829. The Indians, Jackson said, should leave their homes in the east. This immigration "should be voluntary," he continued, "for it would be as cruel as unjust to compel the aborigines to abandon the graves of their fathers, and seek a home in a distant land." Nonetheless, Jackson said that the Indians "should be distinctly informed that if they remain within the limits of the States, they must be subject to their laws." In February of 1830 the president's supporters introduced the Indian Removal Bill in Congress. Opponents of the legislation understood that Jackson and his supporters would leave native peoples defenseless before state authorities. Driving the Indians across the Mississippi, they argued, violated treaties. Jackson's critics did not believe that removal would be voluntary: in Georgia, the state's imposition of its jurisdiction over the Cherokees deprived them of access to the courts. People of color could not testify against white people in Georgia. With no protection of their rights to person or property, the state would compel the Cherokees to remove. The policy of removal, in the eyes of Jackson's opponents, was unjust, immoral, and a violation of the nation's principles.

Morality and justice did not carry the day. It seldom has in the history of American Indian policy. The Cherokees had appealed to Jackson, seeking protection from the operation of the state of Georgia's laws; that got them nowhere. With the passage of the Indian Removal Bill in the summer, after a long and emotional debate that inspired pro-Indian reformers throughout the northeast, the Cherokees knew they could expect no relief from the legislative branch of the national government either. That left only the judicial branch.

The Cherokees appealed to the United States Supreme Court. They argued that as a sovereign and independent nation, they were not subject to Georgia's laws. While Chief Justice John Marshall, in the case of *Cherokee Nation v. Georgia* (1831), clearly sympathized with elements of the Nation's argument, he asserted that they were not sovereign nations but rather "domestic dependent nations," whose relationship to the United States resembled that of a ward to its guardian, and that he did not have the necessary jurisdiction to hear a direct appeal from them to the court. But what did it mean to describe native communities as "domestic" and "dependent"? The United States Constitution, after all, allowed the national government nothing more than the right to "regulate commerce" with the Indian nations, and the federal government had thus far claimed no direct authority over the internal workings of native communities. In 1832, in *Worcester v. Georgia*, Marshall held unconstitutional a Georgia statute that prohibited the residence of whites upon Cherokee land without first swearing an oath of loyalty to the state. Georgia convicted two missionaries for violating this law; Marshall ordered the prisoners released on the grounds that Georgia's laws violated the United States Constitution. The Cherokee Nation, he wrote, "is a distinct community, occupying its own territory, with boundaries accurately described, in which the laws of Georgia can have no force, and which the citizens of Georgia have no right to enter, but with the assent of the Cherokees themselves, or in conformity with treaties, and with the acts of Congress. The whole intercourse between the United States and this nation, is, by our Constitution and laws, vested in the government of the United States." Marshall ruled that Georgia's laws "are in equal hostility with the acts of Congress for regulating this intercourse, and giving effect to the treaties," which were the supreme law of the land.

President Jackson never enforced the *Worcester* decision, arguably the most important case ever decided in the field of American Indian law. Though the complexities of the law in the 1830s did not legally require him to act, Jackson strongly sympathized with the state's position, and he did nothing to uphold the authority of the Supreme Court. Under the leadership of Principal Chief John Ross, who continued to try to persuade the United States to live up to its claimed ideals, the Cherokees struggled to hold on to their homeland. They fought until 1835. That year, a tiny fragment of the Nation, led by Elias Boudinot and John Ridge, signed the Treaty of New Echota, exchanging the Cherokees' lands in Georgia for new homes in the Indian Territory.

Figure 6.3 Cherokee Chief John Ross (1841). National Portrait Gallery, Smithsonian Institution. Courtesy of National Portrait Gallery, Smithsonian Institution/Art Resource.

Not all the southern Indians left. Significant numbers of Indians, like Cherokees who stayed in North Carolina, managed to avoid "removal." Ridge and Boudinot, for their part, did not believe that their people could ever find justice in their homelands, or protect their property from land-hungry frontiersmen who already were overrunning and dispossessing them. They knew about racism. Both had married white women when they attended a boarding school in Connecticut as young men. Their white neighbors threatened to destroy the school and burned effigies of Boudinot and Ridge on the town green. Having lost their faith in the republic, they did what they felt was best.

The 1838 forced migration of the Cherokees killed thousands of men, women, and children. Four thousand died on the journey west, perhaps more, perhaps less. The conditions were brutal, but so were the soldiers who herded them into stockades and then forced them westward at gunpoint. Those who signed the Treaty of New Echota were not spared the suffering. John Ridge, Elias Boudinot, and a handful of others had betrayed their nation, their enemies claimed, and violated Cherokee laws that made it a capital crime to cede the nation's lands. They truly believed that they had no alternative, and that to remain in Georgia meant subjection to a racial order that offered them no rights and no protections. Still, they had broken the nation's laws, and they paid for their crimes with their lives.

The Cherokees, of course, were not the only nation to suffer Indian removal. Indeed, reducing the story of removal to the "tragedy" of the Cherokees does a disservice to history and an injustice to the many tens of thousands of native peoples who suffered as a result of this horrible instance of ethnic cleansing, American style. After the War of 1812 and the destruction of the Shawnee prophet's resistance campaign, the Potawatomis recognized that they no longer could militarily resist American expansion. With the British eliminated as a threat in the Great Lakes region, Americans no longer felt the need to placate the peoples of the Great Lakes, and in the eight years after the end of the war the Americans built a number of new fortified posts near the Potawatomis. The agents at these forts worked with the chiefs closest by, conveniently assuming them to be the principal political figures in their communities. The growing white presence, then, led not only to the increased fragmentation of Potawatomi communities already reliant upon American annuity payments to acquire the things they needed to stay alive, but growing shortages of game. The Potawatomis sold lands to acquire the annuities they needed to remain alive.

White observers noted that the Potawatomis seemed to be suffering. Thomas L. McKenney, an early supporter of Jackson who later broke with him when he recognized the coerciveness of the "removal" policy, wrote that the Potawatomis "catch fish, and plant patches of corn; dance, hunt, get drunk, when they can get liquor, fight, and often starve." The Potawatomis must be removed, reformers like McKenney argued, to save them from the scourge of American civilization. This depiction of Potawatomi life was completely misleading. They lived in permanent agricultural settlements. They had acquired horses and livestock. But the widespread belief that native peoples were struggling nomads suffering within their current bounds made their removal seem at the same time inevitable and, for some, merciful. That the belief was false did not seem to matter.

After Jackson's election, no doubt remained that the Potawatomis would relocate. The Potawatomis wanted to control the process as much as possible. Some 2500 Potawatomis, perhaps a third of the population, left for Canada between 1833 and 1845. Removal for them represented a rejection of all that the American republic stood for. Those who remained faced relentless pressure to sell their lands. A series of treaties negotiated in the mid-1830s between representatives of the national government and small groups of Potawatomis scattered across Indiana and Michigan required that they remove to lands the government set aside for them in Kansas. Not all of them went; some remained in Wisconsin and Michigan, but their numbers were few. Two major streams of migrants moved west.

The largest group marched to the Osage River Reservation in eastern Kansas along the Potawatomi "Trail of Death." They traveled, a Catholic priest who accompanied them wrote, "with bayonets prodding their backs." Many walked, but the sick rode in wagons carrying the baggage, "rudely jolted, under a canvas which, far from protecting them from the dust and heat, only deprived them of air." Many died, including twenty-eight children, a devastating loss. Once at the Osage River reserve, life was difficult. Factionalism gripped the migrants. The most traditional Potawatomis found themselves forced to live under rules set by an Americanized tribal elite, whose power depended in turn on the good will of the federal agent who oversaw the reservation. They found themselves demoralized, and their traditional culture denigrated.

The measure of this despair can be seen in the abuse of alcohol by the Potawatomis at Osage River. Located close to white settlements in western Missouri, liquor peddlers overran the reservation. According to one observer, on the day the agent distributed annuities to the Potawatomis, "liquor is rolled out to the Indians by whole barrels," and illegally sold in the presence of the agent. "Wagon loads of the abominable stuff arrive daily from the settlements, and along with it the very dregs of our white neighbors."

Other Potawatomis left their homes in Wisconsin, Illinois, and Missouri to settle in Iowa, near Council Bluffs. Known as the "Prairie Band" of Potawatomis, they occupied what the United States Commissioner of Indian Affairs considered "some of the best and most desirable lands" in Iowa. As a group, they rejected the leadership of the more acculturated leaders who had immigrated to Kansas. Relatively isolated from American settlements, the nearest of which stood more than 200 miles away, and unwilling to welcome missionaries into their community, the Prairie Band sought to preserve Potawatomi culture and their identity as a distinct people.

That determination was a problem for the United States. Federal officials hoped to move Indians westward so that white settlers could occupy their lands. They wanted simplicity, and not the hassles that came with trying to figure out which Potawatomis should be paid what share of the annuities the United States owed to the tribe. The Prairie Band did not want to join with those at Osage River. They saw themselves as a separate people. After a decade of trying, the United States in 1846 entered into a treaty with "the various bands of the Pottowautomie Indians" to unite them in the Indian Territory so that they could "again become one people, and receive their annuities and other benefits in common." The Prairie Band relinquished their lands in Iowa, but told the United States agent not to expect a single council fire. The Kansas Potawatomis agreed to leave the Osage River Reservation. In return, the United States granted them 576,000 acres on the Kansas River, and the interest on a sum of money held in trust by the United States for the benefit of the Potawatomis.

The Potawatomis' odyssey carried them across the American Midwest, and the occupation of the continent's heartland and the American south by white settlers could not have taken place without the "removal" of native peoples like the Potawatomis and Cherokees, and many others. Federal officials devoted an enormous amount of attention to clearing native peoples from the vast expanse of territory between the Appalachians and the Mississippi. But they also wanted to clear native communities out of the increasingly settled east. In New York, the Senecas continued to contend with their "steady enemy," the Ogden Land Company. Aided by Quakers who opposed Jacksonian Indian policy, the Six Nations put up a courageous fight. The chiefs and warriors of the Senecas, Oneidas, and Onondagas at Buffalo Creek asked the Commissioner of Indian Affairs to inform President Jackson that they "were fully satisfied with our present location, and prefer to remain on these lands which the Great Spirit gave to our fathers." Owing to their efforts no one in Washington with even a passing familiarity with Indian affairs could doubt that the majority of Iroquois did not want to leave western New York.

But Indian removal was not about what Indians wanted. The Ogden Company appealed to the interests of land-hungry frontier settlers. They appealed to the benevolence of reformers as well, arguing with no apparent sense of contradiction that removal would benefit the Indians by isolating them from the unsavory influence of those land-hungry settlers. This was an old argument indeed: we must remove the Indians to save them. If we do nothing, they will become extinct and pass into history.

The Ogden Company had too much invested to rely solely on arguments. Prior to the 1838 Buffalo Creek Treaty and after its revision by the Senate in 1839, the Company's agents bribed Indians to persuade their brethren to accept relocation in the west. They met in a tavern, the better to "facilitate" negotiations with gifts of alcohol. They used threats of violence. Seneca chiefs learned that "if we do not consent to emigrate to the West, that measures will be taken by the General and State Governments by which we shall be made to remove." A number of Seneca chiefs who had opposed any removal were alarmed to find that they had signed statements indicating that they understood and approved of the Buffalo Creek Treaty. How did this happen? According to the Seneca chiefs in question, "the agents of the Ogden Land Company," they said, "have taken private Indians to the Commissioners pretending to him that they were chiefs & have hired them to misname themselves by adopting the names of chiefs in the opposition & have so obtained many names now affixed" to the treaty. They found imposters. The American commissioner, the chiefs added, was "as ready to deceive as any agents of the Company."

Through the fraudulent Buffalo Creek Treaty, the Senecas relinquished all their remaining lands. All the Indians living at Buffalo Creek, Tonawanda, Cattaraugus, and Allegheny would remove to new homes in the Indian Territory within five years. After a long debate, President Van Buren proclaimed the accord in 1839, but he did so reluctantly, and a powerful protest campaign led by the Senecas and their Quaker allies prevented the implementation of the treaty. Senecas sent delegations to Washington, and they confiscated the timber cut by trespassers on what they still considered their lands. They lobbied, and acted with determination to defend their nation's interests. In 1842, the Quakers and officials from the Ogden Land Company broke the impasse and negotiated a supplement to the Buffalo Creek Treaty. Both parties understood that the Senecas disliked the 1838 treaty. The Indians would reluctantly have given up a portion of the lands on each of their remaining reservations, but they never would have consented to relinquishing any of them in their entirety. Under the 1842 Supplemental Treaty, however, that is precisely what happened. The Cattaraugus and Allegany reservations, where Quaker missionary activities were strongest, would be returned to the Senecas; Tonawanda and Buffalo Creek would remain in the hands of the Ogden Company. After a long hard fight the Tonawanda Senecas would in 1857 "win" the right to purchase back a portion of their original reservation, even after they had opposed all attempts to acquire their lands. Buffalo Creek, already overrun by white settlers, and close to the growing city of Buffalo, was gone. Most of the Indians there removed to Cattaraugus.

In 1846, a man named Abram Hogeboom traveled to the remaining reservations in New York State. He had authorization from the United States government to recruit Indians to relocate to the Indian Territory. Hogeboom, with some difficulty, gathered 192 prospective immigrants, among them sixty-six Senecas. They appear to have desired, not to assimilate, but to continue to live their lives as Haudenosaunee away from the aggressive New Yorkers. All but one of the immigrants survived the arduous process of moving across the country, an incredible stroke of good fortune, but they found life once they arrived at the Osage Agency in Kansas tough. The new arrivals began to die rapidly. They buried eighty-two of their fellow emigrants between 1846 and 1847. After this they wanted to go home. Ninety-four of the original 192 emigrants arrived back in New York in 1847. Only a handful chose to stay behind.

Removal did not affect solely those tribes who lived on the eastern side of the Mississippi River. It impacted the lives of native peoples in the west as well. Shortly after the Louisiana Purchase, for instance, the Caddos found their lands in Louisiana overrun by thousands of American settlers. They welcomed the opportunity to trade that an American trading factory provided. At these sites, government officials attempted to oversee intercultural exchange, guarantee an adequate supply of goods, and keep peace on the frontier. Despite the Caddos' misgivings about the growing numbers of immigrants, they maintained their alliance with the United States, refused to join the Creek Red Stick uprising in 1813, and would have aided the Americans against the British had not Andrew Jackson defeated them so quickly at New Orleans early in 1815.

It was after the war that the relationship between the Americans and the Caddos began to deteriorate. The number of settlers encroaching on the Caddos' lands in the Red River valley and moving to new homes in Mexican Texas brought significant disruption in terms of land loss and the destruction of game upon which the Caddos relied. These new arrivals embraced and nourished a style of thought that one historian has called "the Texas creed": a belief that the Anglo-Americans who settled in Mexican Territory and who squatted on native peoples' lands were culturally, politically, and racially superior to all others and, that they were justified to employ violence to uphold white superiority. After the United States government disestablished its factory system, independent traders overran Caddo country. The Caddos told Thomas McKenney that the traders tailed them "like wolves," selling illegal alcohol and cheating them in trade. The arrival of emigrant Indians, driven out of the east into the Caddo country, intensified these problems: 500 Choctaws, some Kickapoos from the Midwest, a handful of Delawares, and a few Shawnees. Initially the Caddos welcomed the newcomers as allies against their Osage enemies, but as their numbers grew, augmented by a rising number of Cherokees, the Caddos felt themselves pinched.

The presence of Europeans certainly had affected Caddo culture. Many of them spoke French or Spanish or English, and they had incorporated elements of American-style clothing into their dress. They raised chickens and hogs. They did not want to abandon their homelands. They held out until 1835. That summer, they met with Jehiel Brooks, the agent appointed for them by Andrew Jackson. They needed food, and relief from the settlers encroaching on their lands. Brooks informed them that the United States could do little to protect them from settlers, and that the president would tolerate no resistance. With Mexico attempting to lure friendly Indians to settle in Texas, an attempt to stop the hordes of Americans illegally crossing the border into what was still Mexican territory, the Caddos made the "sorrowful resolution" to sell their lands. In exchange for payments which they received only in part, the Caddos entered into a treaty in which they ceded their lands and promised "to remove at their own expense out of the boundaries of the United States within one year."

The Texas Revolution, which began shortly after the signing of this treaty, complicated the Caddos' removal. The Texans quickly won their independence from Mexico, a newly independent nation itself weakened in large part because of endemic Indian raiding. Large numbers of heavily armed Anglo-American settlers in Texas led Comanches and their allies— Kiowas and others—to direct their attacks to other parts of northern Mexico. These raiders transformed the northern borders of Mexico into a zone of exploitation, from which they harvested tribute, acquired livestock, and raided for plunder. When Mexico's economy collapsed under the weight of this raiding, the Comanches and their allies turned their attention eastwards toward Texas. The Lone Star Republic's first president, Sam Houston, hoped to

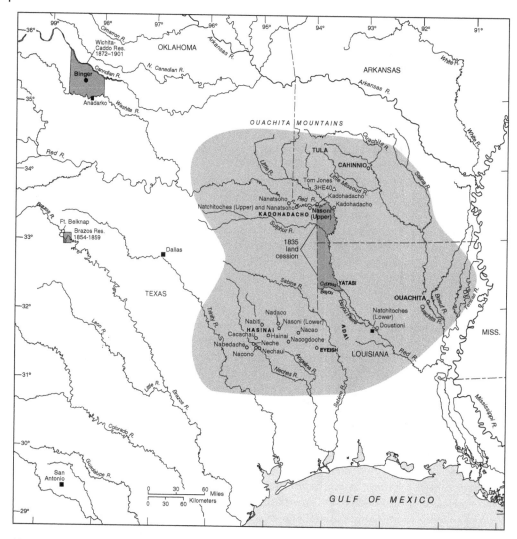

Map 6.1 Caddo Country. Source: *Smithsonian Handbook of North American Indians*, Vol. 14, Southeast, pp. 14: 617. Courtesy of Smithsonian Institution.

secure a peace with the neighboring native peoples. The Kiowas, Comanches, and Lipan Apaches, however, facing the viciousness of Texas Rangers who Houston could not control and who attacked and killed without remorse, had the ability to fight back with devastating effectiveness. To many Texans, Houston seemed weak and unable to protect them. In 1838, the Texans elected the Indian-hating Mirabeau Lamar to replace Houston. Lamar promptly called for a war of extermination against native peoples in the republic. He wanted ethnic cleansing in Texas, and his soldiers slaughtered men, women, and children. The Caddos, wrote one of Lamar's allies, "ought to be exterminated," the others as well. By the summer of 1839, Texan forces had burned villages belonging not only to the Caddos but to Cherokees, Shawnees, Delawares, Creeks, and Seminoles as well. Most fled into the Indian Territory, as white settlers took over their lands.

It was Lamar's desire, he wrote, "to have the entire western country cleared of the enemy." Lamar reaped the whirlwind he had sown, as displaced native peoples raided Texas settlements. Kiowas and Comanches launched dozens of attacks. Some Caddo bands participated in these raids. But Kiowa, Comanche, and Caddo leaders learned as well that fighting the Texans could only result in death, destruction, and dispossession. Recognizing the need for unity and for peace, the Caddos welcomed the chance to return to Texas when Sam Houston once again became president. The Caddos agreed to assist Houston by serving as mediators between the Texans and hostile Indians, and in return were permitted to settle on lands along the Brazos River. There they would serve as a buffer, protecting Texans from Comanches and Kiowas. When Texas became part of the United States, the federal commissioners negotiated a treaty with the Texas tribes, including the Caddos, in which the Caddos agreed to place themselves "under the protection of the United States." Indians were a federal problem now. The Texans did little to assist the Caddos' agent, Robert Neighbors, and began to push hard for the dispossession of the Texas Indians and their expulsion from the state. Many state residents found appealing once again the policies of extermination pursued by Mirabeau Lamar, and they accepted that chronic racial violence as the price of civilization was a vital component of the Texas creed.

Removing from the Missions

Mexico won its independence from Spain in 1821. Under the supervision of Jose Figueroa, the Mexican government of Alta California began the process of secularizing the missions and liberating the neophytes from what reformers viewed as a primitive and retrograde institution. The Franciscans had baptized 65,000 Indians but in 1821 only 22,000 lived in the twenty missions they had founded. Of the 60,000 Indians the fathers buried, nearly 25,000 of them were children under the age of ten. By 1834, less than 2000 Indians remained in the missions. Secularization, in essence, phased out an institution that had fallen out of favor and that had entered a long decline even before the Chumash revolt of 1824. Under Figueroa's plan, commissioners appointed by the governor would distribute parcels of mission land to the Indian residents, as well as half of the mission's livestock, tools, and seed. The Indians who received lands faced some limitations on their freedom. They could sell neither the land they received nor the livestock, and Figueroa required them to assist in the maintenance and cultivation of the undistributed lands on the former mission grounds. Priests would live nearby. If they chose, the Chumash could apply for emancipation from the mission and from their condition as neophytes.

Although the mission Indians enjoyed something less than full freedom, they certainly possessed more control over their lives than they had under the Franciscans. Figueroa abolished the dormitories designed to keep unmarried men and women apart. Those who had been emancipated could come and go without asking, and they could worship as they chose. Understandably, some of them sought to distance themselves from the missions. Some returned to their homelands where they practiced once again rituals and traditions that the priests had attempted to stamp out. Chumash from Mission San Buenaventura established Kamexmey and those from Santa Barbara established Qwa' near today's Goleta Estero. These communities, in some ways, looked similar to those described by Portola seven decades before: tule houses; granaries and storage houses for dried foods; sweat lodges and shrines. The residents built canoes and manufactured shell beads, revitalizing ancient crafts.

They refused to work for the Mexicans, and they attempted to remain independent. Removal away from the missions secured, for a time, their freedom.

Others moved into the Mexican settlements, taking jobs as domestics in non-Indian households. Some worked crafts and trades they had learned in the missions. They worked as servants, laborers, shoemakers, blacksmiths, saddlers, bakers, and cooks. One made his living by playing violin. Many of them faced brutal exploitation and lives of poverty. Some employers paid them only in alcohol, a practice that did grave damage in already weakened native communities. Those Chumash who had learned how to ranch and farm found work on the large *ranchos* carved from the missions. They worked the fields and tended the herds of wealthy land barons on vast tracts that decades before had belonged to their people. Few Chumash obtained the lands that Governor Figueroa had promised, and those who did faced harassment by Mexican settlers. Most of the settlers saw the Chumash and other native peoples as the foundation for a dependent laboring class, and they acted to tie them to the land.

In 1845, Governor Pio Pico began to sell what remained of the missions. He sold La Purisima after a smallpox epidemic in 1844 caused the few Chumash in the vicinity to flee. In June of 1846, a month shy of the raising of the American flag in California, Pico sold the missions at San Buenaventura, Santa Barbara, and Santa Inés. The epidemic, and the vast increase in settlement that accompanied the American takeover, caused further fragmentation in Chumash communities, and created, once again, a new world for the peoples of Alta California.

The Optimism of the Imperialist

In the same year that Governor Pico completed the sale of the Chumash missions, and in which the United States launched its aggressive and expansionist war against Mexico, Commissioner of Indian Affairs William Medill stated that "apathy, barbarism and heathenism must give way to energy, civilization, and Christianity." Given American racial beliefs, he could have been speaking of Mexicans as well as Indians. In America, Medill continued, this expansion "has been attended with much less oppression and injustice than has generally been represented and believed." Certainly there had been some damage done. But Medill felt these injuries could easily be justified, and many of his contemporaries would have agreed. "If, in the rapid spread of our population and sway, with all their advantages and blessings to ourselves and to others, injury has been inflicted upon the barbarous and heathen people we have displaced, are we as a nation alone to be held up to reproach for such a result?" Medill thought not. "Where," Medill continued, "in the contest of civilization with barbarism, since the commencement of time, has it been less the case than with us; and where have there been more general and persevering efforts, according to our means and opportunities, than those made by us, to extend to the conquered all the superior resources and advantages enjoyed by the conquerors?" If native peoples had suffered (and Medill conceded that a "rapid decline and disappearance of our Indian population" had occurred), the cause was not "willful neglect or ... deliberate oppression and wrong," but rather problems that might easily be fixed now that native peoples had been relocated to new homes in the west. Christianization and civilization, dominion and civility, were the key. Medill never seemed to doubt that these reforms would easily, and completely, solve the nation's Indian problem.

7

THE INVASION OF THE GREAT WEST

As the citizens of the republic began the difficult work of colonizing the west, the United States confronted the age-old challenge of governing the frontier and incorporating the people who lived there, native and newcomer, into an expanding American state. As in the past, natives and newcomers competed for control of the land in ways that ultimately were incompatible. And as in the past, that fundamental incompatibility bred aggression, violence, and warfare. The American invasion of the Great West brought devastating change to native peoples.

The people of the Great West had learned through the course of their long history much about encounter and exchange, and the Americans were not the first outsiders they had seen. Lewis and Clark, for instance, leading their "Corps of Discovery" into the Great West found native peoples wearing woolen blankets acquired from British and French traders, carrying guns, and speaking bits of English and French. In this sense, at least, Lewis and Clark discovered less than they thought. All that they saw had been seen before by native peoples. The peoples of the American interior were not idly waiting for the Americans to arrive and for their history to begin. But the nineteenth-century American invasion intensified the pace of change, a process the historian Elliot West called the "unsettling of mid-America." Native peoples encountered the pioneers, those farming families who moved out onto and across the Plains, relentless and unceasing, who displaced them, appropriated their lands, and destroyed the material basis upon which their way of life depended.

Pledges and Promises

At the time Lewis and Clark set out from St. Louis in 1804, the Dakota or Santee Sioux lived on lands along the Minnesota and Mississippi from the meeting point of those two rivers south into northern Iowa. They still traveled north on occasion to harvest wild rice in their ancestral homeland near Mille Lacs, but this became increasingly difficult as they found themselves pressed by the Ojibwe to their north and the Sauks and Foxes from the south and east. In the Mdewakanton, Wahpekute, Wahpeton, and Sisseton villages along the rivers, somewhere between 4000 and 5000 people lived.

The Santees hoped to preserve their trading connections with the British, and the access to European manufactured goods that came with them. But because their trading relationships were based more on kin connections than allegiance to a European empire, the Americans, who occupied Mackinac Island in 1797, had an opportunity to break into this

Native America: A History, Second Edition. Michael Leroy Oberg.
© 2018 John Wiley & Sons, Inc. Published 2018 by John Wiley & Sons, Inc.

trade if they could provide the Santees with the trade goods they desired and fulfill the reciprocal obligations that the Sioux expected from their kin.

The Dakotas welcomed the new nation's emissaries, and eagerly sought from the United States an alliance. The Mdewakantons provided the American explorer Zebulon Pike with 100,000 acres in exchange for a couple of hundred dollars' worth of gifts, a deal which may well have appeared advantageous to the Santees. Pike, after all, promised to establish a fort in their territory and to defend them from the attacks of their native enemies. "These posts," he said, "are intended as a benefit to you." He offered them military protection and a "to establish factories at those posts, in which the Indians may procure all their things at a cheaper and better rate than they do now, or that your traders can afford to sell them to you, as they are single men who come far in small boats." The Americans could supply a greater quantity of trade goods for a lower price than could the British.

The Santees never played the role of pawn in the Anglo-American contest for control of the Great Lakes. They welcomed the Americans as trading partners and kin, and expected their new allies to live up to the promises made by Pike in 1805. When the Americans failed to provide the Santees with the goods they needed, some warriors joined with the British against the United States. They pursued a distinctly Sioux diplomacy, using the opportunities presented by the Anglo-American struggle in the early nineteenth century to pursue the interests of their communities. Though they freely shifted their allegiance from one power to another, the experience of these unsettling years made it abundantly clear that the Santees could survive only with great difficulty. They needed the weaponry that only Europeans could provide. They knew that regardless of the outcome of the war, they would have to live with the winners. As it became obvious to the Santees that the British would not prevail, they began to withdraw their support and make additional overtures toward the Americans.

The Dakotas welcomed Benjamin O'Fallon at the head of fifty American infantrymen because he promised American trade, his assistance in preventing intertribal warfare, and protection from the threat of starvation. Thus, the establishment of Fort Snelling at the confluence of the Minnesota and Mississippi rivers in 1819, seen by the United States as a critical strategic move directed toward ousting the remaining British traders from American territory, preserving peace on the frontier by policing white settlers, and fostering the fur trade, the Dakotas viewed as a promise of assistance from the Americans. The United States would provide the Sioux with trade goods, and with the presents necessary to maintain and preserve kin connections. The Dakotas acquired supplies, food and trade goods from the fort, had their guns and tools repaired by the fort's blacksmith, and received from the garrison at least some protection from the growing numbers of traders who entered their homeland. The establishment of Fort Snelling served both American and Santee interests.

Still, the Santees found themselves living in an ever-tightening circle. The establishment of the American posts meant that traders occupied Dakota territory year round, and they sought to transform the fur trade into an economic rather than a kinship relationship. They placed pressure on hunters to bring them their best pelts, rewarding the hunters' efforts through gifts and presents. Traders began to influence village politics, as hunters looked to the traders who controlled the supply of goods more directly than they did to village chiefs. Though much of their culture remained unchanged, and they still lived most of the year on buffalo, there was no masking the growing influence of outsiders on the conduct of Santee public life.

By the 1820s, the surviving evidence suggests that the Dakotas found it increasingly difficult to find adequate supplies of game. To feed their families, Dakota hunters entered into those borderlands that lay between their homeland and those of their enemies.

Increased intertribal warfare resulted, as market forces pushed the Dakotas, in the words of Wanmdisapa, "into the jaws of our enemies." Traders' account books show that the hunters returned each year with less deer, muskrat, and beaver. Unable to pay for the supplies they purchased on credit, Dakota hunters found themselves indebted to the traders.

Federal officials recognized that they needed peace in the west, and they undertook efforts to persuade the Dakotas to live on less land and to begin farming more intensively on a European-American model. But none of this could be accomplished while the Dakotas remained at war. In 1825 300 Dakotas attended the intertribal council sponsored by the United States at Prairie du Chien, yet another gathering that from the Dakotas' perspective promised to benefit them and the Americans. In order to promote peace between the Sioux and their neighbors—the Ojibwe, Sacs and Foxes, Menominees, Iowas, Winnebagos, Ottawas, and Potawatomis—and "to establish boundaries among them and the other tribes ... and thereby to remove all causes of future difficulty," the assembled tribal delegates agreed to "a firm and perpetual peace."

The peace was neither firm nor lasting, and the Dakotas faced repeated calls to cede their lands. As the number of settlers encroaching upon their homeland steadily increased, the amount of game correspondingly declined. The Dakotas' federal agent, Lawrence Taliaferro, called upon them to sell their remaining village on the east side of the Mississippi, and told them that the annuities the tribe received for the sale would ensure their survival.

The Dakotas trusted Taliaferro. He had used his own resources to purchase food and clothing for them in the past, and they believed his promises to care for them. He had acted as an ally, as kin. They understood that a much larger annuity could provide them with the means to acquire the material goods and support that they needed. Dakota leaders thus willingly accompanied Taliaferro to Washington to negotiate a treaty. There they ceded all of their lands east of the Mississippi, receiving in return an annuity in goods worth $25,000 for twenty years, and an annuity in cash based on the interest accruing from a permanent trust fund of $300,000. The government allocated an additional sum of money to erase the debts Santees owed to individual American traders.

The annuities helped in the short term. The payments reinforced the bonds of kinship between them and the government, and the agents who distributed thousands of dollars' worth of supplies the Santees viewed as friends and allies. The population of the villages increased slightly, a fact that can be explained in part by the increased quantity of food available. The kin-based relationship the Santees sought with their ally seemed to be working. But the relief provided by the annuities only masked for a time the Santees' dependence. As the supply of game continued to decline, the price for trade goods increased. The Dakotas found it increasingly difficult to remain free from indebtedness. Each year, more of their annuity funds went directly to the traders. By the end of the 1840s, most Santees were destitute. The number of white settlers in Minnesota, which became a territory in 1849, continued to increase. Hard-pressed and impoverished, the Dakotas, under the leadership of Little Crow, signed treaties in 1851 at Mendota and Traverse des Sioux in which they gave up their claims to all their lands in Minnesota save for reservations along both sides of the Minnesota River north of New Ulm, and extending upriver for 140 miles.

While the Dakotas confronted the land hunger and territorial aggressiveness of the American republic, the Kiowas' history remained still one of movement and migration when Lewis and Clark set out to cross the continent. The Kiowas encountered the occasional trader as they moved across the Plains, frequenting the valleys of the South Platte, the Arkansas, and Red Rivers. Their history still very much followed its own trajectory. They suffered from the

Figure 7.1 Little Crow. Courtesy of National Anthropological Archives.

effects of European diseases before they had established any sustained contact with the newcomers. Smallpox hit the Comanches and Kiowas in 1816. "I bring death," the dread disease told Saynday in one Kiowa legend, and "I am one with the white men—they are my people as the Kiowas are yours." By the 1820s, the Kiowas and Comanches fought regularly with the Cheyennes and Arapahos, migrants themselves who had followed the bison herds and hoped to avoid the growing power of the Lakota Sioux on the northern plains. Kiowa warriors undertook frequent raids against the Osages and Utes as well. 1833, the same year in which Dohasan became the principal leader of the Kiowas, was "the summer that they cut off their heads," according to a Kiowa winter count. An Osage party attacked an undefended Kiowa village while the warriors there were away pursuing Utes. The Osages slaughtered the old men, women, and children they found there, and took the Kiowas' *Tai-me* medicine. The Kiowas, still grieving, held no sun dance for the next two years.

In 1834, the Kiowas experienced their first extensive contact with the forces of the United States. Dohasan, several other Kiowas, and representatives from other tribes on the southern Plains met with American military officers at Fort Gibson. The Kiowas did not join in the peace treaty the United States negotiated in 1835 between the Comanches and Wichitas and the immigrant tribes in the Indian Territory, but they did negotiate an agreement at Fort Gibson in 1837 in which they pledged to join in the pact negotiated two years before and leave off their attacks on the immigrant tribes. They also promised "that the citizens of the United States are freely permitted to pass and repass through their settlements or hunting ground without molestation or injury" and that the Kiowas would compensate just claimants for damages caused by Kiowa warriors. In return, they received presents from the federal authorities, "nothing being asked from the said nations or tribes in return except to remain at peace ... which their own good and that of their posterity require."

Kiowa history still flowed through its own channels, a fact made clear in the Kiowa winter counts. They fought frequently. In the winter of 1836–7, an important war leader died while on an expedition against the Mexicans, the notable event of the year, while another Kiowa party raided along the upper Missouri. They raided across an immense range of the American west. Smallpox struck the Kiowas in 1839, the same epidemic outbreak that nearly exterminated the Mandans before it moved south out onto the Plains. Cholera followed nine years later, killing many more than had the smallpox. Warfare remained common as the Kiowas and their neighbors competed for access to the herds of bison that roamed the southern Plains.

In an effort to eliminate the destructive intertribal warfare that resulted from this competition, the Comanches and Kiowas made peace with the Cheyennes, Arapahos, and Kiowa-Apaches in 1840. They could agree that they should share the plains, and that outsiders should be excluded. But in allowing the extensive hunting of bison along the Arkansas River, the Kiowas and their neighbors began to face dangerous shortages of food. The Kiowa winter count for 1841 indicated "many bison," but years like these became increasingly rare. The Plains tribes' own horse herds already placed some stress on bison, for horses relied on the same food and drank from the same watering sources. Commercial hunting of bison, and the white demand for buffalo hides, already had impacted bison numbers. A period of reduced rainfall beginning in the 1840s reduced bison numbers further, as did the growing white population on the Plains.

Bison rested at the center of the Plains horse cultures, and the Kiowas relied on bison for food, shelter, and clothing. They traded buffalo robes to non-Indians in exchange for items that they could not craft themselves. The bison was as central to the survival of the Plains tribes as corn was to native peoples in the east. But by the 1850s, the animal simply no longer could be relied upon to provide for all of the people's needs. The Comanches, for instance, were at the peak of their power in the middle of the nineteenth century when the United States began to assert its own influence on the southern Plains. The Comanches dominated the region, but their power rested upon a shaky foundation. A growing population demanded growing horse herds, and growing horse herds placed intense pressure on the southern Plains ecosystem, which included bison habitat. A camp consisting of 1000 horses could consume seven acres of grass each day during periods of abundant rain. Witnesses reported that hunger forced the Comanches to begin slaughtering horses in 1850, while other federal agents reported tribes on the southern Plains starving for much of the year. As the United States emerged as a power in the west, native peoples confronted not only a territorially aggressive nation determined to incorporate the southern Plains into the national domain, but environmental changes that threatened their ways of life as a people.

The Crows, too, began to face changes brought by the intrusion of the Americans into the west. They had completed their migrations sometime late in the eighteenth century, settling in Crow country on the Yellowstone River. They rarely encountered outsiders, save for an occasional trader. By the time Lewis and Clark began their expedition in 1804, however, the Crows began to expand outward in an effort to control the regional trade in furs. Through trade, the Crows could acquire not only wealth but the power that European weapons, tools, and horses reflected. With European guns and the horses they increased the amount of territory under their control and they could kill additional game, acquire additional pelts, and control an ever larger piece of intercultural trade.

This expansion, then, increased the wealth of the Crows, but it carried with it conflict with rival communities. They fought with Lakota Sioux, Cheyennes, and Shoshones to their south, and with the Blackfeet to their north. The warfare could be devastatingly violent. In the early 1820s, according to one account, a large force of Lakota warriors attacked a Crow village, killing half of the people who lived there. In this context, the arrival of the Americans in force on the northern plains presented the Crows with an opportunity. Increased competition for furs produced increasing amounts of warfare. With Lakotas, Cheyennes, Blackfeet, and Arapahos all willing to fall upon the Crows, and with a regular and dependable supply of weapons and ammunition essential, a Crow delegation led by Red Plume visited the American expedition under the command of General Henry Atkinson and Benjamin O'Fallon on the upper Missouri in August of 1825. A treaty of friendship resulted. The Crows acknowledged that "they reside within the territorial limits of the United States," a claim that likely meant little in the far west, and the United States pledged "to receive the Crow tribe of Indians into their friendship ... and to extend to them, from time to time, such benefits and acts of kindness as may be convenient, and seem just and proper to the President of the United States." The Crows had sought out new allies and, in their view, had successfully enlisted their aid against a wide range of native enemies.

Atkinson wanted more than the Crows' words. He demanded that they surrender several "Iroquois" captives that they had amongst them. Red Plume denied having the captives and, despite what he perceived as a grave insult, intended to overlook Atkinson's terrible breach of etiquette. Several Crow warriors, however, angered by the treatment they had received at the hands of Atkinson's men, spiked the cannons that the Americans carried with them. Atkinson recognized that he had gone too far, and tried to smooth over the difficulties by delivering to Red Plume the next day additional presents.

Red Plume might easily have followed the advice of his supporters that he abandon his alliance with the United States. The River Crow leader Sore Belly refused to ally himself with the Americans. But Red Plume recognized that the Americans could be formidable enemies or valuable allies. They might be taught how to behave. Red Plume did not expect that they would disappear and he knew his people needed the supplies only American traders could provide. It was a difficult decision, but Crow leaders hoped that an alliance with the United States might protect them from the expanding Lakota and their aggressive allies.

The warfare continued. Known for the quality of their horses, the large numbers of bison and other game animals in their homeland, and the ample supply of trade goods they acquired from American traders, the Crows' homeland attracted large numbers of native people. Embattled Hidatsas, Mandans, and Shoshones sought protection and ammunition from the Crows. Enemy raiders—Blackfeet, Cheyennes, Arapahos, and, especially, Lakotas—came too. Crow warfare with the Blackfeet, wrote the American explorer Benjamin Bonneville in 1832, was "gradually wearing them out." And whether friendly to the United States or not, hostile raids continued to rain upon the Crows. Sore Belly, the opponent of the 1825 Atkinson–O'Fallon treaty, died in a hail of gunfire as he charged a large group of Blackfeet who had come to lift his siege of the American Fur Company's Fort Mackenzie at the falls of the Missouri.

By the late 1840s, Lakota warriors regularly invaded the Bighorn valley and Blackfeet raiders attacked the Crows from the north and west. The Crows lived on a battleground, surrounded by hostile and expansive native powers. Tightening their alliance with the Americans seemed a reasonable course of action. Only with American guns and ammunition could the Crows hope to hold off their invaders. The United States, however, was less interested in helping the Crows than in bringing order in advance of settlement to the frontier. In 1851 at Fort Laramie, American officials oversaw a council attended by Lakotas, Cheyennes, Arapahos, Assiniboines, Gros-Ventre, Mandans, and Arikaras in which the assembled delegates agreed "to abstain in the future from all hostilities whatever against each other, to maintain good faith and friendship in all their mutual intercourse, and to make an effective and lasting peace." The treaty defined the territories belonging to each of the participants, and promised an annuity of $50,000 to be divided among them all on the basis of population. There was no meaningful enforcement mechanism, short of a weak federal warning that violators of the agreement might forfeit their share of the annuity. Like the Dakota Sioux and the Kiowas, the Crows found themselves with little choice but to negotiate with a federal government that seemed uninterested in fulfilling its pledges and promises to its native allies.

Far to the south and west, the Pueblos also learned of the challenges that came with the Americans. After Mexico won its independence from Spain in 1821, the new government established cordial relations with the 10,000 Pueblos who comprised approximately one-quarter of the population of New Mexico. Under the Plan of Iguala, adopted in February of 1821, the new Mexican state declared native peoples citizens with equal rights. This was a promise that it could not uphold. At Pecos, for instance, Mexican settlers in 1829 claimed the Pueblos' lands. The native population of Pecos Pueblo had fallen significantly, and the squatters wanted their title recognized by the Mexican government. "Nothing can be worse," they said, "than to see ourselves despoiled of our land in which the oldest down to the youngest … have shed the sweat of their brow in order to make it provide our subsistence." The authorities decided against the settlers, but the Pecos Pueblos were too few to keep them off their lands. By the 1830s, much of the community's land was in the hands of the settlers. The Mexican government had problems larger than protecting Indians. With its trade open to outsiders, American opportunists came to Mexico to exchange their wares. They described the inhabitants of New Mexico, both Pueblo and Mexican, as backwards and barbaric, as people "peculiarly blessed with ugliness," a "lazy and gossiping people," who lived "in darkness and ignorance."

This racist rhetoric provided a justification for empire. American imperialists would occupy the land, but as they did so they would uplift and enlighten Mexicans and Indians who they viewed as backwards, barbaric, and savage. After the Pueblos' homeland became part of the United States as a result of the Treaty of Guadalupe Hidalgo, the agreement that ended America's war against Mexico, federal officials had to decide what to do with the Pueblos. The United States recognized Pueblo land rights and acknowledged that they possessed title to their 700,000 acres of land. But how to protect them from the squatters, the traders, and the trespassers? Were the Pueblos citizens, with rights that other American citizens must recognize? Or were they something else? In 1851, Congress extended congressional oversight to the Pueblos, applying the provisions of the 1834 (and final) Indian Trade and Intercourse Act to the New Mexico territory. This action conformed to the wishes of many Pueblos who saw the assistance of the United States government as essential to protecting their lands from further trespass. Yet the extension of federal law did not seem to matter. The Pueblos enjoyed more numerous opportunities for trade with the establishment of American posts, but they also fell victim to smallpox and the machinations of alcohol venders and land speculators whose profit was dependent on evading federal law. Because the Pueblos were largely peaceful, federal authorities paid them little attention. Their agents seldom visited. As late as 1870, a Pueblo spokesman told an American official that because his people did not steal they received no protection from the government, "but if they stole like the Navajo they would get something." The territorial government and the United States Congress seemingly lacked both the power and the willingness to keep trespassers off of Pueblo land and to enforce in any meaningful way laws designed to protect them.

Like the Pueblos, the Chumash remained exposed after the secularization of the missions and the American takeover of California. In 1850, the new state legislature enacted a law allowing for "the Government and Protection of the Indian" that permitted the virtual enslavement of California natives. Any Chumash or other California Indian, on the testimony of a white man, could be declared a vagrant, jailed, and sold for a term of not more than four months. Furthermore, Californians could "indenture" Indian youth in the state, and hold the children in servitude until they reached the age of eighteen if male, or fifteen if female. In 1860, the state legislature expanded the rights of the settlers to hold Indians in bondage until they reached the ages of twenty-five for men and twenty-one for women. Some children as young as two years of age were thus indentured. The law remained in effect until 1863, the year of Lincoln's Emancipation Proclamation. Neither could California Indians vote, own firearms, or testify against white people in courts of law.

The political, legal, and economic marginalization of the Chumash was coupled with their continuing demographic decline. Smallpox hit in 1844. Waves of immigrants poured into California, especially after the discovery of gold, and pressed upon their lands. As native peoples found themselves outnumbered by the enormous numbers of newcomers, they continued to succumb to disease. According to one estimate, the Indian population of the state declined by one-third between 1845 and 1850, as the Chumash and their native neighbors fell victim to the new diseases brought by new immigrants.

But there was more to it than disease. Californians enslaved and murdered Indians. The seizure of native peoples' lands, their confinement on reservations, and outright slaughter reduced the state's indigenous population by as much as 80% between 1850 and 1860. A newspaper editorial in 1866 suggested that "it is a mercy to the red devils to exterminate them," and that diplomacy was a waste of time. "There is one kind of treaty that is effective—cold lead."

The destruction of California's native peoples was popular, democratic, and supported by the state's elected government. Californians called out their militias and deployed their forces on behalf of land-hungry settlers. Thousands of white Californians took part in the slaughter of Native American men, women, and children.

Still, small Chumash communities continued to exist, despite the great odds they faced. An 1855 map showed that Kamexmey and two other small communities stood near the mouth of the Ventura River, and the community at La Cieneguita still stood near the old Santa Barbara mission. The populations of these small settlements declined in the decades after the American takeover, and their lands continued to slip away. Still, signs remained of some Chumash clinging to their traditional culture in the face of enormous obstacles.

In 1853, a party of hunters led by a Californian named George Nidever encountered an elderly Chumash woman on San Nicolas Island. Nidever's party found her "busily employed in stripping the blubber from a piece of seal skin which she held across the knee, using in the operation a rude knife made from a piece of iron hoop stuck into a piece of rough wood for a handle." She welcomed the white men, who could see that she lived in a camp comprising "several huts made of whale's ribs and covered with brush, although it was long since they had been occupied that they were open on all sides and grass was quite high within." She had lived there for a long time, perhaps since the uprising of 1824. The white men saw that "there were several stakes with blubber on them," and that there "was blubber also hanging on a sinew rope." She had baskets, and "fishhooks made of bone, and needles of the same material, lines or cords of sinews for fishing and the larger rope of sinews [which] she no doubt used for snaring seals on the rocks where they came to sleep."

At the invitation of the hunters, she accompanied the men as they hunted otter and seals on the islands. She traveled with them for several days. When the wind began to blow too strongly, "the old woman conveyed to us by signs her intention to stop the wind." Nidever observed that "she then knelt and prayed, facing the quarter from which the wind blew, and continued to pray at intervals during the day until the gale was over." Nidever described a Chumash woman living her life in time with a very old rhythm.

The arrival of the woman in Santa Barbara, however, made clear how much the Chumash world had changed. Less than a century after the Portolá expedition, few Californians had seen Chumash people. The old woman became a curiosity, an exhibit for the amusement of non-Indians interested in an "extinct" people. According to Nidever, "for months after, she and her things, as her dress, baskets, needle, &c. were visited by everybody in the town and for miles around outside of it." Chumash people were exotic enough, one enterprising ship's captain thought, that he offered Nidever $1000 for the woman. He wanted to place her on display in San Francisco, and he was willing to split the take with Nidever. Nidever refused. He learned bits of her story. She had lost a daughter, and she had grieved for many years. It was the defining event in her life. She did not have long to live. At Santa Barbara, she fell sick five weeks after her arrival and died, Nidever curiously noted, because of "eating too much fruit." The priests at the mission church baptized her after her death and christened her Juana Maria.

The United States wanted to allow Americans to move across the continent, to harvest the vast wealth of the great west, but to do so in a fashion that did not force the government to fight expensive and, many believed, unnecessary wars. The United States entered into scores of agreements similar to those it negotiated with the Kiowas, Crows, Santee Sioux, and many others, but in every instance it simply lacked the power and the willingness to uphold its pledges and its promises.

Settling In and Settling Down

Many Indians never left the eastern United States. They stayed on their ancestral lands, living close by their white neighbors, doing what they could to retain their identity as native peoples. The descendants of Wahunsonacock's chiefdom continued to reside, for instance, on small parcels of land in the Virginia Tidewater. They were poor, and lived on the margins of the commonwealth, but their lives resembled in important ways that of their impoverished white neighbors. By the nineteenth century, many Powhatans had Anglo-American first and last names. They had spoken English fluently for a century, and their aboriginal languages had died off; an Episcopal minister in 1844, interested in Indian languages, could collect only a dozen words from the oldest Pamunkeys. Most of the Powhatan remnants became Baptists, still an egalitarian faith in the early nineteenth century. The threats they faced to their identity as native peoples were real. They did not seem like "Real Indians." Owing to intermarriage, some of them looked black and some of them looked white. So said white Virginians, anyways, who became increasingly concerned about racial distinctions as northern abolitionists began to launch fusillades against the institution of slavery. As white southerners emphasized the purity of their whiteness, and southern state legislatures passed laws designed to lower the status of non-white people, the Powhatans emphasized their Indian identity. Only by showing that they were not black, could they escape the fear, the distrust, and the hatred white Virginians felt toward those they enslaved. They emphasized how they had assimilated, and indeed they had. At times they mouthed the same anti-black rhetoric as their neighbors. But trying to fit in did them little good. Virginians wanted their land. The state attempted, unsuccessfully, to divide up the Pamunkey reserve in the 1830s. The Pamunkeys hung on, but others had no such luck. The Gingaskins, after two members of the community were implicated in a rumored slave uprising, saw their lands broken up and distributed to the heads of families. Gradually the recipients of these parcels sold out, becoming, for all intents and purposes, entirely landless.

Only a small number of Senecas moved west, and most of the survivors of that horrible year returned home where "with scarcely an exception" they "lived in a destitute condition, and many of them are yet suffering from disease." As these emigrants conducted their odyssey into the west, political ferment manifested itself on the Seneca reservations in New York State. Fearful, according to their Quaker supporters, "lest *again*, these remnants of their land might be wrongfully wrested from them," a group of Senecas petitioned the New York State legislature for a law to protect them "from their own chiefs." The petition, according to the Quakers, presented "to the world, the curious spectacle of a nation seeking from a foreign state, a security against the officers of their own government."

The Senecas had made considerable adjustments to their way of life in order to survive in western New York. They grew corn, oats, wheat, potatoes, and a variety of garden crops. Thousands of fruit trees stood in Seneca orchards. They raised cattle and kept hogs, horses, and sheep. According to Henry Schoolcraft, who visited them in 1846, "the style of their buildings, fences and household furnishings," he wrote, "as well as the dress of the males, is not essentially different, and little, often nothing at all, inferior to that of their white neighbors."

In addition to their agricultural pursuits, the Senecas lived by renting land to their white neighbors, selling timber and finished lumber, fishing and hunting, and working as agricultural laborers. And they looked to the future as well. A small number of Senecas had acquired "a collegiate or academic education," and 350 children attended various "private or missionary schools" near the reservation. They hoped to stay on their lands.

Yet to many Senecas, their traditional chiefs had failed them during the removal crisis. Some had taken bribes. Some misused the Senecas' annuity funds, the moneys the Senecas had received for the sale of their lands. The New York State Legislature in May 1845 enacted a law "for the protection and improvement of the Seneca Indians." Through the enactment, the state of New York determined a framework of government for the Seneca reservations that bore little resemblance to Seneca tradition. The state certainly had no legitimate right to do this, for the law interfered with Seneca internal affairs and seemed to violate the 1794 Treaty of Canandaigua. But, very quickly, the Senecas began to organize into "Law" and "Anti-Law" factions, based on whether or not they approved of the state's handiwork. The conflict lasted until 1847, when the state amended its original law to allow for the popular election of the officers it identified initially in 1845. In the meantime, the United States allowed for the payment of all annuities "to the heads of families and other individuals entitled to participate therein."

These legislative enactments provided the backdrop against which the Senecas acted out their Revolution in 1848. The chiefs traditionally had received and distributed annuities, and they resisted any change in that arrangement. As Quaker observers reported, "to be deprived of the power to handle the people's money was more than they could bear." The majority of the Senecas, however, "became convinced, that neither peace nor security could be enjoyed by the people, until the chiefs should be shorn or every vestige of their official power." Thus, a national council late in 1848 declared itself a constitutional convention and announced the creation and founding of the Seneca Nation of Indians. The constitution that this convention produced described the failure of the chiefs, and the delegates present declared that "we cannot enumerate the evils growing out of a system so defective, nor calculate its overpowering weight on the progress of improvement." In particular, the chiefs had withheld portions of the annuity for the purposes of government, calling the withholding of the annuity a "tax." The manipulation and improper use of the annuity funds led to the overthrow of government by the chiefs.

The Senecas had suffered much. All native peoples had. Here, however, was evidence of a native nation organizing and acting to protect its interests within the American republic. The new Seneca constitution, which both the state of New York and the United States recognized, established a government consisting of an elected council presided over by an executive department consisting of a president, a clerk, and a treasurer. It marked the transformation of the Senecas from a kinship-based community to a territorial government based on residence at the two remaining Seneca reservations (the Tonawanda Senecas remained apart from the Seneca Nation of Indians and a member of the Iroquois League). By the mid-1850s, the Seneca Constitution had achieved legitimacy. Though political contests could be as partisan and competitive as those in the surrounding non-Indian communities, and though the Senecas might disagree deeply over the course the Seneca Nation should follow, all grew to accept a constitution that emerged from a conflict over how the nation's lands ought best to contribute to the survival of the nation.

If the Senecas took steps to ensure that they would remain upon their lands, so, too, did the Mohegans. Many white New Englanders opposed Jackson's policy of Indian Removal, and viewed the program as coercive, violent, and inconsistent with the principles of Christianity and American justice. As they protested the policy, they depicted native peoples as "noble savages," as virtuous people who already had endured enormous persecution. This did provide some benefits, in that it generated a certain amount of sympathy among white New Englanders, but it also had a significant drawback. The Mohegans, like other New England native peoples, had intermarried with those on the margins—both white and African American. As a result, they did not look like the "noble savages" of myth and memory. The Mohegans, to many New Englanders, did not look like real Indians.

But still they remained on their lands. Observers pointed out that though alcohol and disease took a heavy toll in New England Indian lives, improvements had occurred over the course of the nineteenth century. Life expectancy and other measures of wellbeing increased. Fewer Mohegan men worked in whaling, choosing instead less dangerous work as farmers. The Mohegans preserved important elements of their culture, as elders taught Mohegan children the songs, stories, and histories of their people. They sold traditional wares—baskets and brooms—to their white neighbors but they also became more integrated into the regional economy. They began holding a "Wigwam Festival" early in the 1840s, a gathering of Mohegans in Montville where they danced, bought and sold traditional food and handicrafts, and celebrated the community's continued survival. They participated in historical pageants and commemorations, asserted their important role in New England history, and reminded their white neighbors that the Mohegans endured. The Mohegan Church, founded along with a school for Mohegan children in 1831, became the center of the Mohegan community.

The point is that native peoples survived the "Indian Removal." Many communities preserved their hold on their lands on the eastern side of the Mississippi River. Even native peoples whose leaders signed removal treaties remained in the east. The Eastern Band of Cherokees evaded the forced march west along the Trail of Tears, and stayed in the mountains of western North Carolina. Several Christian Potawatomi bands remained along the shore of Lake Michigan. Many of them were poor, and they lived their lives on the margins of American society, often intermingling with poor whites in remote communities. But they did survive.

Homesteaders

In the Great West the tribes relocated as a result of the removal policy faced considerable difficulties, but they reconstituted and reformed their societies. They too were pioneers, immigrants into the west. Potawatomi pioneers, like other western settlers, faced the attacks of native peoples determined to preserve their homelands from intruders. Pawnee warriors began to attack shortly after the treaty of 1846. The Potawatomis, however, had learned from their neighbors in the east how to fight in ranks, alternately firing and reloading. After several years of raids, the Pawnees and Potawatomis agreed to a peace and a defensive alliance against the Cheyennes, the Lakotas, and the Osage. In these conflicts the Potawatomis also fought effectively, but they could not achieve through military means what they wanted. The Cheyennes, after all, adjusted their tactics as well, and effectively prevented the Potawatomis from hunting bison on the high plains. They remained confined to their Kansas reservation.

Here they faced missionaries, federal agents, and others who hoped to Americanize them. Some of these innovations the Potawatomis welcomed. They had little choice but to alter their subsistence routines and they incorporated many of the suggestions made by American authorities over how best to live upon their lands. But many Potawatomis responded with little enthusiasm to suggestions that they abandon traditional religion. Some left the reservation, moving back into Iowa, or migrating with Seminoles and Kickapoos from Kansas to Mexico. Others quietly resisted American advice that they abandon so fundamental a part of their identity as native peoples. They continued to "remove," but they did so for their own complicated reasons.

The Potawatomis also tried to curb the influence of American traders in their communities. According to policies set by Commissioner of Indian Affairs William Medill in 1846, annuities would be distributed on a per capita basis to individual members of the tribe. Traders in Kansas opposed this change in policy. Under the older system, agents paid a portion of the annuities directly to traders in order to erase "national debts," or money owed by Potawatomis to individual traders. A subsequent innovation introduced in 1834 required that annuities be delivered to chiefs, who would pay the personal debts of their followers out of the funds that they received. The system was rife with corruption, as scheming traders could use gifts and bribes to encourage the avarice of unethical chiefs.

The Potawatomis, like other reservation Indians, relied upon their annuities, and they watched closely their distribution. Prairie Potawatomis, for instance, frequently protested how the "Mission band," the original Kansas immigrants, handled their money. They called for their fair share, and they wanted to preserve their own separate institutions on the reservation. The Prairie Band, more culturally conservative than those Potawatomis who earlier had migrated to the Indian Territory, distrusted the Metis (or mixed blood) leadership of the Mission band. These leaders had their virtues: their literacy and knowledge of American institutions enabled them to advocate for the Potawatomis. Their commitment to an American way of life, however, alienated many of the Prairie Band.

Many of these Metis leaders worked closely with federal officials and the traders. They profited from the relationship, operating ferries and other businesses, overseeing much of the Potawatomis' trade, and serving as official government interpreters. They were influential, and willing to embrace much of what the American republic had to offer. Indeed, as the United States lurched towards its Civil War, and as the opening acts played themselves out in "Bleeding Kansas," a new state with a rapidly growing white population, the Potawatomis entered into a treaty with the United States that opened much of their land for settlement and exploitation. Proclaimed in November of 1861, the treaty reflects the divisions that gripped the Potawatomis. Of the 576,000-acre reservation established in 1846, the Prairie Band, "those members of the said tribe who desire to hold their lands in common," retained 77,358 acres. The United States pledged to "allot land in severalty to those" Potawatomis "who have adopted the customs of the whites and desire to have separate tracts assigned to them." The agent set aside 152,158 acres for this purpose, land that was distributed to the "Citizen Band of Potawatomis." Should the allottees prove to federal authorities and a tribal "Business Committee" of mixed-blood leaders "that they are sufficiently intelligent and prudent to control their affairs and interests, that they have adopted the habits of civilized life, and have been able to support, for at least five years, themselves and their families," they would receive legal, fee simple title to their lands, and become citizens of the United States with rights equal to those of other citizens. The remainder of the reservation, nearly 350,000 acres, the government turned over to settlers and to railroad interests.

Those Potawatomis who took allotments confronted the challenges of citizenship in the American nation. Citizen Potawatomis did not receive their share of the tribe's annuity on time, a product of the inefficiency of Congress, so the state of Kansas seized much of their land and sold it for back taxes. A new treaty in 1867 secured a home for the allottees in the Indian Territory. Most of the members of the Prairie Band remained in Kansas, though some of them began to trickle back to remote areas in the east, in Michigan and Wisconsin. They worked their lands, or found employment in local timber enterprises. They had no intention of going anywhere.

If the Cherokees hoped to free themselves from the oversight of the federal government, they too must have been disappointed by the effects of their removal. Shortly before departing on the Trail of Tears, John Ross and the Cherokee council formally transferred the government of the Cherokee Nation to the Indian Territory. Though other Cherokees had migrated earlier, Ross and his followers hoped to re-establish themselves as the only legitimate government of the Cherokee Nation.

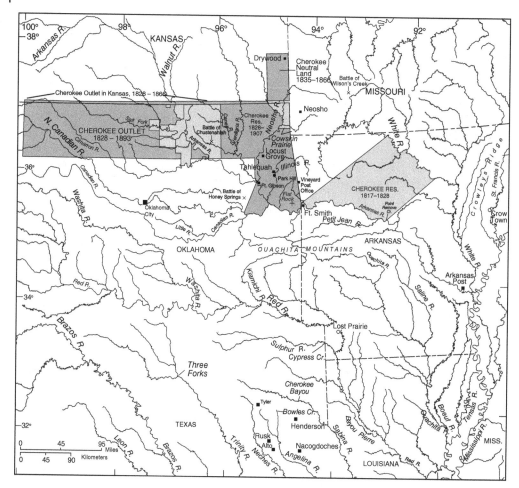

Map 7.1 The Cherokee Nation in the Indian Territory. Source: *Smithsonian Handbook of North American Indians*, Vol. 14, Southeast, pp. 14: 355. Courtesy of Smithsonian Institution.

Making such a claim was easier than acting upon it. The emigrants were forced to leave much behind when the American soldiers rounded them up, and they struggled during their first few years in the west to clear land, build housing, and to acquire the tools and livestock they needed to reestablish themselves. Ross's claim, moreover, roused opposition from both the so-called Old Settlers—Cherokees who had migrated to the Indian Territory earlier—and the members of the "Treaty Party" who had signed the Treaty of New Echota. Both parties objected to the notion that the political institutions they had crafted in the west should be shunted aside by Ross and his followers.

Ross worked to win over this opposition. With the support of a number of Old Settlers, Ross assembled a governing coalition under a new constitution based upon that of the Cherokee Nation. Ross served as president. His efforts to win support, however, fell apart when the three leading members of the Treaty Party—Major Ridge, John Ridge, and Elias Boudinot— were hacked to death in front of their horrified families in retaliation for signing the New Echota treaty. Whether viewed as the assassination by Ross's supporters of their opponents, or the legitimate execution of Cherokee law for illegally selling land, the killings tore the Nation apart, sparking guerrilla warfare and revenge killings. Murder became a normal part of life in the Cherokee Nation.

The violence threatened the Cherokee Nation, for the United States considered intervening in the nation's politics to restore order. Some federal officials called for the dissolution of the Cherokee government, or the partition of the nation's territory along partisan lines. In each of these instances, the Nation no longer would exist. Ross and his supporters thus argued passionately against American involvement. They suggested that the Cherokees, a "Civilized Tribe," might have a beneficial influence on their more savage neighbors, and thus promote the objectives of American Indian policy. They argued, as well, that the Cherokees had already suffered enough through their forced relocation. By leaving the Cherokees alone and staying out of the tribe's business, Ross suggested that the United States might atone for its sins.

These arguments could not carry much weight, especially with the continued violence in the Cherokee Nation. In 1846, at the urging of the United States, and under the threat of American intervention, the Cherokee factions negotiated a settlement at Washington in which they agreed that the "difficulties and differences ... existing between the several parties of the Cherokee Nation ... shall, as far as possible, be forgotten and forever buried in oblivion." Furthermore, "a general amnesty" was declared, and "all offenses and crimes committed by a citizen or citizens of the Cherokee Nation against the nation, or against an individual or individuals, are hereby pardoned." Ross conceded to the Old Settlers a share of the Nation's annuity funds and agreed that the Nation's money ought to be used to compensate the members of the Treaty Party for their losses.

The treaty, signed by Ross's "Government Party," the "Treaty Party," and the "Old Settlers," brought eight years of violence and turmoil to a close, and allowed the Cherokees to recover from the horrors of the removal period. Cherokees could look on the 1846 settlement with some pride. The Nation had survived, and the competing factions had resolved the issues that had torn them apart. Still, the treaty makes clear that the Cherokees, despite all their talk of sovereignty, their assertions of national pride and confidence, were, in fact, a colonized people. The Cherokees negotiated the treaty at the urging of a federal government that never questioned its right to intervene in Cherokee affairs should the need arise, and to dismantle their government and impose new institutions upon them. The Cherokee Nation had survived its period of bloodshed and turmoil, but in a sense it had done so only because the United States allowed it to do so. But in the process, the Cherokee Nation in the west became something federal officials did not anticipate. There existed substantial evidence of prosperity in this homeland by 1846. A group of about 300 families constituted an elite class. They grew cotton, hemp, corn, and tobacco on plantations of several hundred acres. Many of them owned African slaves, and they used the latest agricultural technology, including the McCormick reaper. They sent their sons to educational institutions in the east. They purchased the finest manufactured goods from vendors in New Orleans and St. Louis, and lived a life that would have seemed familiar to the southern plantation elite. The Cherokee Nation's leaders had transformed their space in the Indian Territory into a homeland for a people whose history would become ever more diasporic.

And that was something federal officials could not easily abide. Having isolated the emigrant tribes in the Indian Territory, and insulated them at long last from the unsavory influence of the neighboring white population, Americans eagerly hoped to transform and uplift the Indians, fulfilling the age-old desire to Christianize and civilize native peoples. Those who advocated these changes felt a definite urgency. Indians seemed to be fading away.

Savages could not exist in competition with civilized people, the reformers argued. Commissioner of Indian Affairs T. Hartley Crawford, for instance, in his annual report for 1838, believed that only education could lift native peoples "out of the mire of folly and vice in which they are sunk." Yet "the learning of the already civilized and cultivated man," Crawford said, "could not be advantageously ingrafted on so rude a stock." Teaching native peoples to read and write, he believed, was "to throw seed on a rock." No, to "win an Indian from the waywardness and idleness and vice of his life," Crawford said, "you must improve his morals, as well as his mind, and that not merely by precept, but by teaching him how to farm, how to work in the mechanic arts, and how to labor profitablye... Manual labor schools," Crawford concluded, "are what the Indian condition calls for."

Indeed, reformers throughout the United States employed this model of education for their Indian students. Seneca boys enrolled at the manual labor school founded by the Quakers at Cattaraugus learned the latest farming techniques and skills such as blacksmithing and leatherwork, while girls learned how to "wash and iron clothes ... make bread, do plain cooking, and every other branch of good housewifery, pertaining to a country life."

Education was essential, American officials believed, but native peoples needed something more. "Common property and civilization," Crawford believed, "cannot co-exist." Fifty years before Congress enacted the General Allotment Act, he looked forward to breaking up Indian lands and distributing parcels to individuals. The "individuality of property," Crawford said, "produced the energy, industry and enterprise that distinguish the civilized world, and contributes more largely to the good morals of men than those are willing to acknowledge who have not looked somewhat closely at their fellow beings." Holding land in common promoted laziness, and a lack of initiative. With private property, however, Crawford believed "comes all the delights that the word home expresses; the comforts that follow fixed settlements are in its train, and to them belongs not only an anxiety to do right that those gratifications may not be forfeited, but industry that they may be increased." The Indians must be given the incentive to work that private property entailed. Only then, Crawford believed, could "their habits ... be materially changed."

Concentration

Advocates of Indian removal assumed that the amount of land in the west was so vast that they could easily isolate the emigrant tribes from the dangerous consequences of contact with frontier whites. Experience soon taught them the error of this assumption. After the discovery of gold in California in 1849, ever more Anglo-Americans intruded upon the lands of native peoples as they crossed the continent. This movement brought massive disruption—disease, alcohol, and violence. But white Americans viewed this expansion as part of their Manifest Destiny and as part of God's plan: native peoples could not be allowed to stand in the way.

The situation called for new solutions. Commissioner of Indian Affairs Medill in 1848 first discussed the plan of concentrating native peoples on the northern and southern Plains, allowing the tide of white emigration to flow across the prairies without the interference of Indians. Luke Lea, Medill's successor, stated the new policy with more force. "There should be assigned to each tribe, for a permanent home, a country adapted to agriculture, of limited extent and well-defined boundaries; within which all, with occasional exceptions, should be compelled constantly to remain until such time as their general improvement and good conduct may supersede the necessity of such restrictions." Lea believed that it was absolutely essential that the size of the reserves in the west be reduced, and that the other western tribes "be placed in positions where they can be controlled, and finally compelled by stern necessity to resort to agricultural labor or starve." Lea never doubted the ability of the Indians to improve themselves, but he did not believe that they would make this choice unless forced to do so.

Indeed, for many American policy-makers, only the concentration of native peoples on reservations could save them from extinction. "So sure will these poor denizens of the forest be blotted out from existence," wrote Commissioner George Manypennny in 1856, "unless our great nation shall generously determine that the necessary provision shall at once be made, and appropriate steps be taken to designate suitable tracts or reservations of land, in proper localities, for permanent homes for, and provide the means to colonize, them there-upon." Manypenny oversaw the negotiation of many of the early concentration treaties that significantly reduced the amount of land held by native peoples, and established for them reservations secure, he hoped, from the encroachments of outsiders. Here, on these reduced tracts, missionaries, agents, and educators, could undertake the urgent work of saving the Indians. Once again, the men who shaped and executed American Indian policy found ways to view taking as giving.

The United States pursued the new policy of concentration despite abundant evidence that it could not work. Take, for instance, the case of Coast Salish people who lived along the waters pouring into Puget Sound. In 1846, the region that became the Oregon Territory became part of the United States, the result of a treaty negotiated with Great Britain. Settlers moving westward began to pour in, encouraged by the 1850 Oregon Land Donation Act. The act offered free land to newcomers, even though native communities still lived in the region. The encroachment of Anglo-American newcomers on native peoples' lands, here as else-where, generated tensions. In 1848, Patkanim, a Snoqualamie leader, attacked the American post at Fort Nisqually. Between 1850 and 1852, Americans established settlements on lands belonging to the Nisquallys, Puyallups, Duwamish, and their neighbors. In March 1853, the population north of the Columbia River had grown large enough to justify, in the eyes of Congress, the creation of Washington Territory under the leadership of its first Governor and federal Indian agent Isaac Stevens.

Native peoples interacted frequently with the newcomers. Native leaders like Snatlum of the Skagits, Chowitsut of the Lummis, and Leschi of the Nisquallies grew in wealth and power through the important role each played in intercultural trade. The pioneer Ezra Meeker, reflecting upon the history of Washington Territory, wrote that "it was impossible to write of the white race inhabiting the region around the headwaters of Puget Sound ... without refer-ence to the Indians, who constituted a large majority of the population, and whose everyday life was so intimately connected that the one could not be written without the other."

But as white settlement increased, so, too, did the likelihood of violence. Several settlers, for instance, in 1853 lynched an Indian named Mesatchie for the murder of his wife. The lynch-ing precipitated a series of retaliations: a white man named McCormack was killed near Lake Union, and two more native people hanged in Seattle. Few of the settlers thought highly of the native peoples whose lands they were appropriating. Fueled with the ideology of Manifest Destiny, and reflecting upon this early period in Washington's history, one of them argued that "our race, following their destiny in obedience to God's great law that the earth shall be made to contribute to the benefit of His creations," made better use of the land than native peoples who, he wrote, "make no fixed habitation, really occupies no land, and surely reduces none to possession."

Ancient racist views like these fueled the effort of the territorial government to etch a deep divide between interconnected native and newcomer communities. White people would supplant native peoples on the Salish Sea, and Americans could consider this God's will. Discrimination came easily, and with religious sanction. "Persons having more than one-half Indian blood," for instance, were deemed incompetent to testify in the territorial courts of law. Settlers, who on occasion still had to play by native rules when they lacked the power to beat, cheat, or coerce compliance, believed that American laws should prevail in the Washington territory.

Governor Stevens believed that the solution to the mounting tensions in his territory lay in the policy of concentration. American settlers were coming to Washington, and their numbers would increase. Unless steps were taken, the amount of conflict in the territory would also continue to grow. He did not doubt the inferiority of Indians relative to whites, but he believed that they might be educated and assimilated, becoming in the process productive, if subordinate, members of Anglo-American society.

In August of 1854, the commissioner of Indian affairs instructed Governor Stevens to negotiate "articles of agreement and convention with the Indian tribes in Washington Territory," and "to unite the numerous bands and fragments of tribes into tribes." It is an arresting statement. There were too many polities, and Stevens must impose order, and make sense of the situation. These new entities, the "tribes" which Stevens would construct from the dozens of village communities lining the Puget Sound, he would concentrate "upon the reservations which may be set apart for their future homes." Here, the United States would provide for their future welfare while it readied them for self-sufficiency, taught them to become farmers on lands suited best for their traditional mixed economy of fishing, hunting, and gathering, and regulate and control their movements. Indians would be concentrated, Stevens believed, and the policy was in their best interest.

Stevens called councils and began to meet with the native peoples of the Salish Sea. He moved quickly. Negotiations were conducted in the Chinook language, a trade jargon with a limited vocabulary poorly suited to the demands of intercultural diplomacy. When Indians balked, Stevens reminded them of the bad white men who might prey upon them and their lands. With their settlements scattered over a large area, there was little that he could do to protect them. Best to concentrate on reservations, with their right to their lands guaranteed by the United States. Over the next several months, he negotiated agreements at Medicine Creek with the "chiefs, head-men, and delegates of the Nisqually, Puyallup, Steilacoom, Squawskin, S'Homamish, Stehchass, T'Peek-sin, Squi-aitl, and Sa-heh-wamish tribes and bans of Indians"; at Point Elliott with the representatives of the "Dwamish, Suquamish, Sktahlmish, Sam-ahmish, Smalh-kamish, Skope-ahmish, St-kah-mish, Snoqualmoo, Skai-wha-mish, N'Quentl-ma-mish, Sk-tah-le-jum, Stoluck-wha-mish, Sha-ho-mish, Skagit, Kik-i-allus, Swin-a-mish, Squin-ah-mish, Sah-ku-mehu, Noo-wha-ha, Nook-wa-chah-mish, Mee-see-qua-quilch, Cho-bah-ah-bish, and other allied and subordinate tribes and bands of Indians"; Point No Point with the "chiefs, headmen, and delegates of the different villages of the S'Klallams"; Neah Bay with the Makahs; and Quinault River with the "different tribes and bands of the Qui-nai-elt and Quil-leh-ute Indians." He extinguished the Indian title to more than 64 million acres of Indian land in Washington Territory.

Stevens obtained a lot for very little. Each of the treaties he negotiated required massive cessions of land and relocation to and concentration on a number of small reservations. In return, each of the "tribes" that Stevens, in effect, created, received annual payments in goods and "the right of taking fish, at all usual and accustomed grounds and stations," which Stevens said was "secured to said Indians in common with all the citizens of the Territory."

But the terms of these agreements left the native peoples of the Salish Sea deeply dissatisfied. The treaties, Meeker recalled, "were urged upon reluctant people in great haste," while "time was not given to properly mature plans to consult the wishes and quiet the jealousies of the Indians." Different native communities, "whose interests ran upon different lines," were concentrated together "upon reservations not of their choosing." Although he initially worked to establish two or three reservations, Stevens reluctantly accepted eight precisely to address this problem. But the measures he pursued did not go far enough. The Duwamish, for instance, according to Meeker were required by the terms of the Treaty of Point Elliott "to remove from their place of abode from time out of memory to a new district, among strangers whom they feared, give up all their associations, their hunting grounds, their fisheries, to go where they were to be herded, as they thought, until some disposition could be made of them."

Concentration was supposed to open land to settlement by white Americans, and place native peoples upon reservations where they could be insulated from the most destructive elements in white society while they assimilated into American society. It did not work out that way. A Tulalip shaman named Chaoosh, or Dr. Chouse, was so upset about the provisions of the treaty that he warned that the relatively small number of settlers might easily be wiped out by unified native peoples. Leschi, the Nisqually chief, and leaders among the Puyallups as well, were angry about the reservations they had been assigned.

Fighting began on the eastern side of the Cascades, but soon it flared up on the western side as well. While many settlers leapt to the conclusion that they faced a massive anti-white resistance movement involving Indians throughout the Territory and beyond, Governor Stevens told a cheering audience that there would be no accommodation with the enemy, and "that the war shall be prosecuted until the last hostile Indian is exterminated." He stoked the settlers' fears, stirred up their bloodlust, but the number of native peoples in arms in the west remained small, not more than a few hundred.

Indeed, the war revealed the many connections that continued to link natives and newcomers along the Salish Sea. These Indians who took up arms against the settlers did not fight against all things white, but rather, in response to the new, unfamiliar, and unfair world created by the Stevens treaties and increasing white settlement. The soldiers who pursued Leschi, for instance, took his horse herds and "put them into service against him." Leschi opposed moving to the reservation, in part, because doing so would have compelled him "to either sell or abandon" his large horse herds, and "his accumulation of years would be of no value to him." Friendly Indians warned settlers of impending attacks. Friendly Indians saved the young town of Seattle. Though Stevens executed native leaders who took part in the attacks, including Leschi, and though many settlers viewed all Indians as enemies, the reality was so much more complex.

Despite the treaties and war, many native peoples remained in and around Seattle after the conflict and the executions of those accused of leading the uprising. The growth of the town relied upon Indian labor. Native people cut and moved timber, fed settlers, washed laundry, and even delivered mail. They worked as domestics, hunters, and haulers. As its best historian has written, "let there be no mistake: without the labor of Indians, Seattle would have been still born." With their labor in demand, many native peoples avoided life on reservations, and carved a narrow space for themselves in an Anglo-American territory. There have been Indians in American cities as long as there have been American cities.

The example offered by the Puget Sound shows the complexities that came with attempting to disentangle connected native and newcomer communities and placing Indians on reservations. And there were numerous other examples that would have revealed to federal officials, had they chosen to look, the difficulties involved in achieving the federal policy of concentration.

Federal officials might have looked to the experience of the Caddos, after all, who faced frequent raids both from enemy Indians and from white Texans who coveted their lands. The Caddos respected their federal agent, Robert Neighbors, but they learned quickly that he lacked the power to protect them from alcohol vendors and white squatters. Neighbors complained to Commissioner Medill in 1848 that trespasses on native land "regardless of the consequences ... must necessarily and inevitably lead to serious difficulty." Neighbors called upon the Texas government, which retained control of lands in the state, to cede a tract for the establishment of a reservation. Neighbors wanted to protect the Caddos from hostile Indians and from the Texans themselves. They had murdered dozens of Caddos, and these Indian killers hated Neighbors and all that he stood for. Only after five years of bloodshed did the Texas legislature finally heed Neighbors' call and grant to the United States a tract "for the use and benefit of the several tribes of Indians residing within the limits of Texas."

The Caddos recognized that life on this Brazos Reservation would require of them certain changes. They began to send their children to the schools opened and operated by Neighbors, and they continued to adopt white husbandry and agriculture. Visitors to the reservation, Neighbors noted, "are astonished at the progress made by the Indians in the arts of civilized life." In 1856, he reported that the Caddos and other native communities settled on the Brazos reserve "have neat cottages, with good gardens and fields adjacent, and the many conveniences to be seen on every hand give me abundant evidence of the progress made by the Indians since their settlement." In this, the Caddos followed in the footsteps of the Potawatomis, Cherokees, and Senecas in making important adjustments to life on the reservation. By 1857, the Caddos had accumulated a "fair stock of horses, cattles, and hogs, and are paying particular attention to stock raising." Neighbors believed that "in a few years their condition will bear comparison with our frontier citizens." All seemed to be going well.

These changes, however, rested upon a fragile foundation. The Caddos tried to be good neighbors to the settlers living near them. According to their agent, they "held themselves ready and willing to assist in rescuing any property stolen from the citizens on this frontier by the roving bands of hostile Indians." Caddo men accompanied Texas Rangers and federal troops in raids against the Comanches, for instance, whose attacks terrified Texas settlers. The most perceptive Texas authorities recognized the importance of the Caddos' assistance, but settlers in the vicinity of the Brazos reserve inclined to place the blame for the attacks upon all Indians, whether friendly or not.

In late December of 1858, a group of Texas frontiersmen fired on a group of Caddos. Three women and four men died. Ten more received serious wounds. After telling their story, some of the survivors fled from the reservation. Authorities in Texas did little to bring the killers to justice. Despite the efforts of federal authorities who, in Neighbors' case especially, energetically advocated for the Caddos, there seemed nothing that the United States could do to protect them. Neighbors received orders to remove the Caddos to "where they can be protected from lawless violence, and effective measures adopted for their domestication and improvement." That meant leaving Texas. Neighbors guided the Caddos to new homes north of the Red River, and advertised the abandonment of the Brazos reserve in local newspapers—white settlers need not do anything rash, he suggested, for the Indians were leaving. The settlers could have the land. In August of 1859 Neighbors wrote to his wife, informing her that "I have this day crossed all the Indians out of the heathen land of Texas, and am now out of the land of the Philistines."

This removal, like all removals, presented the Caddos with a variety of difficulties. Kiowa and Comanche raiders haunted the removing party, stealing their horses and cattle.

The degree to which the Caddos had incorporated elements of American culture made them an inviting target. Extreme heat and inadequate supplies of water created great discomfort and concern. Still, Neighbors was careful; only six Indians died. He managed to guide them safely to their new homes at the Wichita Agency in the Indian Territory. The reservation experiment in Texas had failed. Local whites would not tolerate an Indian presence close to home, whether friendly or not. After the Caddos departed, Neighbors became the last casualty of the removal. As he returned home to Texas in September of 1859 to settle his affairs, an angry frontiersman who had suffered in Comanche raids stepped out from behind a building and shot Neighbors in the back.

The Dakotas' experiences on their Minnesota reservations also showed early on that significant problems existed with the concentration policy. The Santees signed a treaty in 1851 after accepting federal assurances that the cession would benefit them. They trusted their white father. The sale would provide them with the annuities they needed to purchase the necessities for survival.

Federal officials viewed the treaty differently. They hoped to civilize and Christianize the Santees, to teach them the value of private property, and transform them into farmers on the white model. By reducing the amount of land they owned, and opening the ceded lands to white settlement, Commissioner of Indian Affairs Luke Lea noted that the Dakotas would now "be surrounded by a cordon of auspicious influences to render labor respectable, to enlighten their ignorance, to conquer their prejudices." Reservation life would bring preservation to the Dakotas.

The government established two federal agencies to oversee the civilization program, the Lower Sioux Agency at Redwood, and the Upper Sioux or Yellow River Agency. Some Dakotas accepted the changes proposed by their agents. Leaders like Wabasha, Wakute, and Mankato cut their hair. Others encouraged their followers to begin farming and living and dressing like their growing numbers of white neighbors. Yet these changes generated divisions. According to Big Eagle, those who "took a sensible course and began to live like white men" received special treatment from the agents. "The government built them houses, furnished them tools ... and taught them to farm." The "Blanket Indians," or the "Long-Hairs" who rejected the benefits of American civilization, resented this special treatment. They objected to the pushiness and cultural arrogance of the agents and missionaries. As Big Eagle observed, "the whites were always trying to make the Indians give up their life and live like white men ... and the Indians did not know how to do that, and did not want to anyway." Too much change, Big Eagle said, called for in too short a period of time. Big Eagle and many other Dakotas resented the racism of white men who "always seemed to say by their manner when they saw an Indian, 'I am much better than you,'" and he did not like that "some of the white men abused the Indian women in a certain way and disgraced them."

Some warriors assaulted the farming Indians. Some may have shot at and poisoned Christian converts. Those who accepted the government program seemed to ignore many of their obligations to their neighbors. The houses built for farmer Indians had their own cellars that encouraged the hoarding, rather than the sharing, of food. The acceptance of Christianity signaled in part the abandonment of the teaching of Dakota shamans. The refusal to join warriors at the agent's request signaled the declining authority of traditional leaders. The civilization program threatened in fundamental ways Dakota culture and community, and their world was out of balance.

Other sources of tension gripped the Dakotas. The white population of Minnesota continued to grow as large numbers of Germans and Scandinavians settled near the two agencies.

Many Dakotas learned to hate the emigrants, who not only took their land and ran off their game, but refused to share what they had with hungry Indians. The Dakotas viewed them as intruders.

The settlers did not want Dakota hunters trooping across land that they felt was theirs, but the conduct of federal authorities at the agencies left them with little choice. Agents and other employees used their positions all too often for personal enrichment. They overcharged the government for goods and services that they provided to the Dakotas, and they claimed for themselves a share of the Dakotas' annuities. They held much of the rest of the annuity money for payment of debts to traders. What's more, in an effort to encourage Dakotas to embrace the civilization program, the agents withheld annuity payments to traditional Dakotas. Without food and money, the discontented left to search for game. They viewed the farmers and traders and agents as fundamental threats to their existence. They were very hungry. When Little Crow complained about the behavior of the traders, Andrew Myrick, one of their number, announced that "so far as I am concerned, if they are hungry let them eat grass or their own dung." Astute observers recognized how dangerous the situation had become. The Episcopal Bishop for Minnesota, Henry B. Whipple, solemnly warned that "a nation which sowed robbery would reap a harvest of blood." Nobody paid him much heed.

By the summer of 1862, the annuities still had not been paid. Four Dakotas rummaging for food killed several white settlers who confronted them near Acton, Minnesota. Rather than surrender the four warriors, the traditional Indians at the Redwood Agency resolved upon war. Before they struck, however, they sought the advice of Little Crow. He had participated in the government's civilization program. He told the warriors that "the white men are like the locusts when they fly so thick that the whole sky is a snowstorm. You may kill one—two—ten," he said, "as many as the leaves in the forest yonder, and their brothers will not miss them." However many you kill, ten times more will come to kill you. "Count your fingers all day long and white men with guns in their hands will come faster than you can count."

He doubted that the Dakotas could prevail, but he reluctantly joined in the assaults. He feared the consequences of the earlier attack on the settlers, and he knew the demands for vengeance would be great. Best to take a stand now. On August 18, 1862, the Dakotas fell upon the Redwood Agency, killing two dozen agents and traders. The attacks thereafter became more general. Nearly 400 settlers died in the first few days of fighting. The Dakotas then attacked Fort Ridgely and New Ulm. The settlers drove back both attacks and from late August the Dakotas went on defense. Some called for opening negotiations with the federal authorities for peace. Light Face, a Sisseton, said that "he lived only by the white man and, for that reason, did not want to be an enemy of the white man; that he did not want the treaties that had been made to be destroyed." Meanwhile, the federal forces converged on the Dakotas. Led by Colonel Henry Sibley, the American troops defeated a Dakota attack at Wood Lake in September.

Many of the Dakotas fled. Sibley convened a military tribunal to collect evidence against those who participated in the uprising. By November, he had condemned over 300 to death. As the condemned marched downriver, they faced the insults and anger of the frontier population. White settlers pelted the prisoners as they moved toward the place of execution. A white woman, one observer noted, rushed "up to one of the wagons and snatched a nursing babe from its mother's breast and dashed it violently upon the ground." The child died several hours later. President Lincoln pardoned most of the condemned, many of whom, along with their families, had converted to Christianity while imprisoned. They had found some hope in the new religion. The President ordered them incarcerated at Davenport, Iowa.

Thirty-eight others, Lincoln concluded, did deserve to die. On the day after Christmas, they went to the gallows. As they waited for the trap to open, they sang their war songs and said their farewells to their families. It was the largest mass execution in American history. Little Crow escaped, but only for a time. He fled west, but returned later to the Minnesota valley. On July 3, 1863, a settler gunned him down as he picked berries near Hutchinson, Minnesota. His scalp was placed on display.

The rest of the Santees faced the wrath of Minnesotans who no longer would tolerate an Indian presence within the state. In response to calls for the removal of the Santees, Congress appropriated funds for their relocation. No treaty, no opportunity for the Indians to offer their consent. From Fort Snelling, they boarded steamboats and barges. Thirteen hundred in all, they headed toward Crow Creek, a location along the Missouri in South Dakota. Dry and desolate, lacking in timber and quality soil, the federal agent at Crow Creek said the entire region was "one wilderness of dry prairie for hundreds of miles around." Food was in short supply and of poor quality, a product of federal corruption and incompetence. A congressional investigator, examining conditions at Crow Creek in 1865, found that "for six weeks after they arrived ... they died at the average of three or four a day." Over 80% of the Dakotas who moved to Crow Creek were women and children. The men had died in the uprising or sat in prison. The commander of Nebraska's Second Volunteer Cavalry, Robert W. Fornas, described the Dakota women as "filthy hags whose ugliness was only equaled by their want of anything like modesty or virtue," but his men raped those women and the trauma of the experience continues to haunt their ancestors. More than 250 had died by the end of 1864 when federal officials began moving the Dakotas to a new reservation, Santee, along the Niobrara River in Nebraska. On the newly established Santee Reservation, the exiles suffered continuing population decline as infant mortality remained high and diseases periodically swept the reservation.

Still, they attempted to adjust. They grew wheat, built houses, made use of wagons and plows, and tended livestock. A class of Santee craftsmen trained on the reservation emerged at the Agency. By 1880, the residents of the Santee reservation had purchased ten reapers and ten fanning mills, and began to produce more crops each year.

Like other reservation communities, the Santees made changes to their political system to help them adjust to their new reality. In 1876, the Indians submitted a petition asking that the reservation be divided into four districts represented by two councilors serving for terms of two years. Leaders chosen for their ability to interact with white society came to the fore. They also accepted changes in how they held their lands. Some Indians supported allotment so strongly that they left the reservation, establishing homesteads in the vicinity of Flandreau, South Dakota. To prevent others from leaving, their agents, the Quakers Samuel and Asa Janney, called for the allotment of the Santee Reservation. By 1871, the Santees had constructed nearly eighty houses, with the allotted lands held in trust for the tribe by the federal government. In 1885, President Chester A. Arthur opened the unallotted lands, those not distributed to Santee heads of households, to white settlement, a move popular in Nebraska. The Santees controlled more than 71,000 acres, along with 1300 reserved for the agency. Arthur's order opened up more than 42,000 acres to white settlement, a large chunk of the reservation.

While some of the Dakotas ended up at the Santee Reservation, others avoided the initial relocation to Crow Creek. They had lived a nomadic existence in the aftermath of the uprising, ultimately returning to Minnesota and settling at the Coteau des Prairies. Delegates from the Sisseton and Wahpeton bands traveled to Washington in 1867 and signed a treaty

Figure 7.2 Portrait of Group of Dakota Boys, Two With Infants, and Non-Native Woman and Non-Native Man, 1880. Courtesy of National Anthropolgical Archives.

establishing two reservations. Government officials recognized Gabriel Renville, a committed farmer but also a traditionalist who opposed conversion to Christianity, as the leader of the Sisseton Reservation.

The history of the Sisseton Reservation parallels that of Santee in important ways. Government agents instructed the Indians on how to become economically self-sufficient, an effort hampered by the sorts of natural disasters with which Midwestern farmers contended in the late nineteenth century—drought and grasshoppers. Allotment came to Sisseton as a result of the 1867 treaty. By 1889, 1971 allotments had been made. Of the original 900,000 acres on the Sisseton Reservation, allottees received a third, while a much smaller parcel was reserved for the agency buildings. The remaining two-thirds of the reservation were made available to white settlers, at the bargain basement price of $2.50 per acre. The settlers did not want Indian neighbors, but they sure wanted their lands, and the reservation, like Santee, took on a checkerboard appearance with white homesteads interspersed in a crazy-quilt pattern with Indian allotments.

The 1867 Washington Treaty also led to the creation of the Devil's Lake Reservation in North Dakota (it was subsequently renamed Spirit Lake). The Sisseton and Wahpetons settled there made, one observer wrote, "comparatively rapid progress, evincing considerable capacity in taking on the habits and customs of civilized man." Catholic missionaries ministered to those Dakotas who settled there. But allotment at Devil's Lake resulted in the same degree of dispossession that occurred at Santee and Sisseton. By the late 1890s they were impoverished, and they had "nothing from which they can obtain any revenue, and they cannot depend upon the bounty of the government."

The Indians' Civil War

For native peoples the American Civil War had little to do with whether or not the institution of slavery survived, or whether the states' rights constitutionalism of the south would prevail. The Santee Sioux, of course, decided that the transfer of federal troops from Minnesota to the east offered their war for survival a chance of success. They figured wrong. It was during the war years, as well, that Colorado militia troops under Bible-toting commander J.M. Chivington barbarously massacred Cheyennes and Arapahos at Sand Creek, in the southeastern corner of the territory. While a small number of soldiers refused to take part in this slaughter of innocents, clergymen in Colorado praised Chivington's actions. "We believe our only hope for safety as a Territory," they wrote, "lies in the repetition of like battles with the same results." Bodies mutilated, children murdered: the *Rocky Mountain News* observed that "Cheyenne scalps are getting as thick here as toads in Egypt. Everybody has got one and is anxious to get another to send east." Outside of Colorado, and especially in Washington, DC, Sand Creek provided stunning proof that all was not well in the conduct of the American nation's Indian policy, and that native peoples would continue to suffer as a result.

The Civil War meant different things to different native communities. Pamunkeys and Mattaponis in Virginia attempted to remain neutral during the war. Some reportedly fled to Canada to avoid conscription into the Confederate Army. Mohegans in Connecticut found themselves subject to the draft. They protested, offering in the process a defiant statement on their sovereignty and nationhood. They had never been granted nor had they asked for the rights of citizens of the United States or Connecticut, and they had lived, according to one tribal spokesman, "in a tribal form from time immemorial." They asserted that the United States Constitution exempted them from military service because, as a community, they were "already reduced by war and other pestilence." The state seems to have ignored the Mohegans' complaints, and their men served in "colored" units.

The war threatened the Mohegans' existence as a people. Republican leaders in the northern states, eager to grant full political rights to African Americans, wondered why native peoples should be treated differently. Indians, these reformers observed, lived lives very similar to those of their white and black neighbors. Why should they not have at least some of the same rights and responsibilities? Massachusetts led the way, "terminating" several of the tribes in the state. By the 1870s, Connecticut was following suit.

If the Mohegans reluctantly participated in the war, Senecas in western New York eagerly sought opportunities to participate in the Union effort. Very clearly they objected to the actions of the southern states—the secession movement, the attack on Fort Sumter, and the virulent white supremacy that fueled the southern rebellion. The Senecas respected warriors, and saw participation in the war as consistent with that tradition. From the outset, they sought to enlist. Early in the war Tonawanda Senecas traveled to the town of Geneseo to join the unit assembling there under General Samuel Wadsworth, but he turned them away.

They did not give up. Led by Ely Parker, the Tonawandas by May of 1862 had at last persuaded the Bureau of Indian Affairs to permit Seneca soldiers to enlist in the Union cause. Seneca soldiers fought in integrated units, side by side with white soldiers from New York. They received the same pay as white soldiers. The objections of New York's leaders to their enlistment reinforced the Senecas' long-standing distrust of state officials while interaction with their white comrades provided Seneca soldiers with an unparalleled opportunity for interacting with white society. The Senecas emerged from the Civil War determined to protect their culture and the autonomy of their communities, but also with new skills and tactics for doing so.

Senecas fought for the Union. Other native peoples found themselves caught between Confederate and Union forces. The Caddos, for instance, who continued to suffer from the distrust of the Texans and raids from Kiowas and Comanches after settling in the Indian Territory, viewed the Civil War as one more crisis they had to face in the aftermath of their relocation. Union troops who had occupied the forts near the Wichita agency relocated, and the Caddos had little choice but to enter into an agreement with the Confederacy in August of 1861 that essentially restated their treaties with the United States. Caddos, however, did not trust the Confederate government to protect them from the Texans. Some left the Indian Territory and sought refuge in southeastern Kansas, near the Neosho Agency.

Some of these refugees joined a band armed by the Union and, in October of 1861, attacked posts occupied by Confederate forces in the Indian Territory. There they heard that a group of Tonkawas, a tribe from the Wichita Agency that had remained loyal to the Confederates and had historically been friendly with the Texans, had killed a Kadohadacho boy. The Union-backed band attacked the Tonkawas, and killed over half of their number. Only 140 Tonkawas survived the day-long battle.

Fighting for the Union brought few benefits to the Caddos. They had relocated, out of the Indian Territory, and were living near the mouth of the Little Arkansas River. There they suffered from hunger. Their population declined as their migrations continued. Perhaps as many as one-quarter of the Caddos died during the war years. It was not until 1867 that they finally returned to their home at the Wichita Agency. The war only intensified the suffering and forced relocation that had characterized the Caddos' history during the nineteenth century.

The Civil War brought suffering to the Cherokees as well, upsetting the fragile prosperity the nation had established after the settlement of 1846. John Ross succeeded in obtaining from the Congress appropriations to compensate the tribe for the money it had expended to pay for its own removal, something the government had obligated itself to pay. The infusion of cash that resulted helped the Cherokees build a public education system and a national orphanage, and to defray the costs of tribal police and courts, the tribal newspaper, and the salaries of tribal employees.

Yet this prosperity rested upon a fragile foundation. Most Cherokees farmed small plots, raised a few head of livestock, and tended gardens and orchards, raising and making much of what they needed. Many of these small farmers retained the Cherokee language and preserved important parts of the traditional culture. They participated in the public life of the nation, for the written language meant that one did not need to speak English to be politically active, but increasingly a mixed-blood, slave-owning elite dominated the Nation's affairs. As many as 4000 African slaves belonged to the Cherokees, with ownership concentrated among this small elite.

Many of the slaveholding Cherokees naturally inclined toward the southern position as the sectional debate over slavery intensified in the second half of the 1850s. Ross, a slaveholder himself, feared that taking a stand on the issue could threaten the unity that had been forged at so great a cost after removal to the Indian Territory. Despite his efforts, however, the issue would not go away.

In 1855, the Keetoowah society formed amongst those Cherokees who worried that attachment to the south could threaten Cherokee culture and tribal autonomy. The Keetoowahs, ostensibly an organization of "full-bloods," but in reality consisting of many mixed-blood and Christian Cherokees, opposed the dominance of the pro-slavery Cherokees who had organized themselves into the Knights of the Golden Circle. The Keetowahs recruited candidates to run for office, but also served as something of a mutual assistance organization, aiding their members through tough times. The Keetoowahs defined a Cherokee patriot as one who stayed true to traditional values, spoke the Cherokee language, and supported the tribe's sovereignty.

These tensions threatened to tear the nation apart when the Civil War began. Ross hoped to remain neutral. "Our political relations are with the Government of the United States," he said in October of 1860. But "our duty is to stand by our rights, allow no interference in our tribal affairs from any source, comply with all our engagements, and rely upon the Union for Justice and protection." That was easier said than done. Stand Watie, Ross's Treaty Party rival and a powerful advocate for secession, received a commission from the rebel government to lead 300 Cherokee fighters against Union forces in Kansas and the Indian Territory. Seeing neutrality collapse in front of him, and painfully aware that the demands of the war had prevented the federal government from paying its annuities to the Cherokees, Ross in August suggested to the Cherokee council that the Nation negotiate a treaty with the Confederacy. The war had gone poorly for the northern states in 1861, and Ross recognized that he would have to live with the winners.

Ross and the Cherokees finalized their treaty with the south in October of 1861, linking their national sovereignty with slavery, asserting their right to hold black people in bondage. The Confederates, however, failed to offer the Cherokees any meaningful assistance. In March of 1862, Union forces defeated a Confederate force at Pea Ridge, in Arkansas, and began to march into the Indian Territory. Ross saw an opportunity to change course. Arrested by federal troops, he traveled east hoping to reestablish the Cherokee Nation's relations with the United States. But by this point, many Cherokees remained committed still to the Confederate cause.

During his absence, civil war ravaged the Cherokee Nation, a reprise of the violence of the 1840s. Raids, assassinations, and the pillaging of farms and plantations destroyed the prosperity of the nation. By 1863, one-third of the adult women in the Cherokee Nation were widows, and a quarter of the children were orphans. A population of 21,000 at the beginning of the war had fallen to less than 14,000 in 1867. Twelve hundred children had been orphaned. Much of what Ross had hoped to avoid had occurred. The United States dictated a treaty to the Cherokees in 1866 that forced the nation to cede much of its territory and to recognize their former slaves as citizens. Cherokee racism and Cherokee sovereignty had marched hand in hand, and both forces suffered a significant blow after the Civil War. The Cherokees had adopted African slavery as part of the American civilization program. Their use of African American bond labor, in a sense, served as an assurance of the Cherokees' civility and improvement in the American south. The institution, however, produced deep fissures in Cherokee society that the crisis of the Civil War exacerbated, and that continue to vex the Cherokee Nation.

Peace and War

Concentration, and the development of the reservation system, advanced despite the turmoil of the sectional crisis. A number of tribes accepted reservations in return for the cession of their lands. The treaties obligated the United States to pay the tribe for these cessions and, in general, to help them adjust to reservation life by constructing and staffing schools, employing tradesmen to aid the Indians, and preventing the encroachment of outsiders onto the reservations. Other articles commonly included in the concentration treaties prohibited the introduction of alcohol onto the reservation and allowed the president, as in the case of the treaty negotiated with the Nez Perce in 1855, to survey the reservation "into lots, and assign the same to such individuals or families of the said tribe as are willing to avail themselves of the privilege, and will locate on the same as a permanent home." The Coast Salish in Washington, and the Poncas, Snakes, Osages, Utes, Navajos, Kansas, Shoshones, Bannocks, Arikara, Gros Ventre, Quapaw, Mandan, Hidatsa, Crows, Omahas, and many others in the Great West accepted reservations, ceding millions of acres of land to the United States in exchange for reservations.

Others accepted much reduced reservations as a result of their involvement in the American Civil War. Each of the so-called "Civilized Tribes" of the Indian Territory who had aided the Confederacy signed Reconstruction treaties that punished them for their involvement. The Cherokees, for instance, agreed to abolish slavery, grant some political rights to their former slaves, cede the western portion of their reservation, and grant a right-of-way for an antici-pated transcontinental railway. These Reconstruction treaties, as well, looked towards the policy of allotment. "Whenever the Cherokee national council shall request it," the Nation's 1866 treaty reads, "the Secretary of the Interior shall cause the country reserved for the Cherokees to be surveyed and allotted among them, at the expense of the United States."

While so many tribes made the decision to give up their land, others resisted entirely the notion that they should accept reservations. Violence engulfed the Great Plains. The Kiowas, along with their Comanche allies, raided the Caddos and settlers on the southern Plains from Texas and into Mexico. They raided wagon trains crossing the continent along the Santa Fe Trail as well, threatening supply lines to American military outposts in the southwest. Late in November 1864, Colonel Kit Carson's force of over 300 cavalrymen and some 75 Apache and Ute scouts attacked an encampment of over 150 Kiowa lodges at Adobe Walls in the Texas Panhandle. Several thousand Kiowa, Comanche, and Kiowa-Apache warriors, led by Dohasan, Satank, and Satanta, emerged to defend their settlement. Carson's scouts succeeded in burn-ing the village, but the Kiowas and Comanches fought with determination. The battle lasted all day until Carson successfully retreated.

Nearly a year after the battle, in October 1865, the Kiowas and Comanches met with the United States at the Little Arkansas River. They promised that they would not molest travelers on the Santa Fe Trail, and that they would remain at peace with the United States. But they did not want to give up their country. The United States, however, would not grant peace without a cession of lands and the acceptance of a reservation in Oklahoma and Texas. Texans, the Kiowas knew, would respect these boundaries no better than they had the provisions of earlier agreements, and the federal government did not provide the annuities and treaty goods it had promised in a timely manner. The Kiowas' anger grew. They did not like the threats they received from American authorities. Dohasan said that the Americans are "like a child, and like a child gets mad quick." When Kiowa warriors, he explained, "to keep their women and children from starving, take from the white man passing through our country, killing and driving away our buffalo, a cup of sugar or coffee, the white chief is angry and threatens to send his soldiers." In 1866 a party led by either Kicking Bird or Satanta raided Montague County, Texas, killing a settler named James Box and abducting his wife and daughters. They stood accused, as well, according to their agent, C.H. Leavenworth, of taking the scalps of seventeen American soldiers, "threatening our posts on the Arkansas," and pre-paring to enter "into a compact with the Sioux for hostilities against us."

While the Kiowas struck on the southern Plains, Lakota Sioux warriors led by Red Cloud and Crazy Horse fought American forces in retaliation for the opening of the Bozeman Trail, a wagon road that led from Wyoming to the goldfields in western Montana. The trail crossed through land that the United States had guaranteed to the Crows at Fort Laramie in 1851. Despite receiving invitations to fight, the Crows stayed out of the conflict. They had no interest in aiding the Lakota who had expanded into the Yellowstone and Bighorn valleys.

Red Cloud's warriors managed to cut off much of the traffic along the Bozeman Trail. When the United States decided to use force to open the road late in 1866, its campaigns went badly. Captain William Fetterman rode out of Fort Phil Kearny in pursuit of a group of Lakota and Cheyenne warriors. A short distance from the fort, Crazy Horse's warriors wiped out Fetterman and his men. The decisive Lakota victory provoked some American policy-makers, like General William Tecumseh Sherman, to call for a war of extermination against the Plains tribes to enforce the policy of concentration. Others were not so sure. Some thought that order might be achieved on the Plains if Congress transferred oversight of the Bureau of Indian Affairs from the Interior Department (created in 1849) to the War Department (which had been in charge of Indian policy prior to that date). Most thought that the warfare on the Plains, occurring as the United States tried to demobilize from the Civil War and restore order to a country that had lost over 600,000 men in five years of bloody fighting, demonstrated the limitations of any purely military solution to the nation's Indian problems. Many Americans in the east hoped to avoid more Sand Creeks.

A commission appointed by President Andrew Johnson, charged with investigating the condition of Indians in the United States, and headed by Wisconsin Senator James Doolittle, found that that nation's Indian population was "rapidly decreasing in numbers." Diseases still took a toll, as did their own "intemperance" and "wars, among themselves and with the whites." The majority of these Indian wars, the Doolittle Commission found, "are to be traced to the aggressions of lawless white men, always to be found upon the frontier." Nearly any Indian could have told Congress that. An additional "potent cause of their decay," Doolittle concluded, stemmed from "the loss of their hunting grounds and the destruction of the game upon which the Indian subsists." This problem had only intensified in recent years. "In their eager search for gold or fertile tracts of land, the boundaries of the Indian reservations are wholly disregarded" by white settlers. "Conflicts ensue," Doolittle reported, and "exterminating wars follow, in which the Indian is, of course, at the last overwhelmed if not destroyed." Unless the government undertook dramatic action, "the irrepressible conflict between a superior and an inferior race" would result in the extinction of the Indians.

Doolittle and his colleagues described problems that had plagued those charged with administering and overseeing Indian affairs for more than two centuries. Indians still possessed tracts that white people wanted. Doolittle wanted peace. It was the humane course, and it was less expensive. As Doolittle and his associates compiled their report, however, raids continued on the southern Plains. Kiowa and Comanche warriors drew their annuities at the agency established for them on the Little Arkansas, but then departed on raids against Texans and Mexicans. Fighting continued in the Powder River country as well, as Red Cloud, Crazy Horse, and the other Lakota leaders kept closed the Bozeman Trail and kept out the invaders. Among the Lakotas and others on the northern Plains, however, as among the Kiowas and Comanches, a growing number of leaders began to call for peace. In response to these developments and the recommendations of the Doolittle committee, President Johnson appointed the Peace Commission in 1867 to persuade the Plains tribes to accept reservations and to encourage them to become farmers and stock-raisers on less land. Headed by a Methodist minister named Nathaniel Taylor, who believed that "the Indians can only be saved from extinction by consolidating them as rapidly as it can peacefully be done on larger reservations, from which all whites except Government employees shall be excluded," the peace commissioners hoped to establish two large reserves, one west of the Missouri River and north of Nebraska, and another west of the Arkansas River and south of Kansas, thus opening a corridor for the flood tide of American immigration to pass through the heart of the continent.

Taylor and his fellow commissioners first met with the Kiowas, Comanches, and others on the southern Plains. Taylor reiterated what had come to be the position of American policy-makers: native peoples faced extinction and destruction, unless they ceded their lands and moved to reservations. Only on reservations could the government protect them from immoral and violent frontiersmen as the Indians learned how to live life as civilized peoples. The bison herds dwindled as the number of white settlers increased. Nothing could change these facts. If the Indians wished to live, American officials promised to show them the way. The Peace Commission proposed solutions to very old problems but they offered few innovations: give up your lands, and we will protect you from the white people whose land hunger cannot be abated; abandon your culture, become like us, and you shall live. Accept the gift of American civility, or die.

The Kiowa leaders who spoke at the council at Medicine Lodge Creek made clear that they understood what the United States wanted them to relinquish. Satanta, the great Kiowa leader, did not want surrender the lands along the Arkansas. "I love the land and the buffalo," he told the commissioners, "and will not part with any." He told the commissioners that he loved "to roam over the wide prairie, and when I do it I feel free and happy, but when we settle down, we grow pale and die." He reversed Taylor's argument, in a way. The reservation would kill the Kiowas, Satanta said. It posed a far greater danger than continuing to live their traditional life.

Satanta joined Kicking Bird, Satank, and other Kiowa leaders in reluctantly signing the Treaty of Medicine Lodge Creek. The Kiowas, Comanches, and Kiowa-Apaches received together a reservation in the Indian Territory carved from lands ceded to the United States by the "Civilized Tribes." Both the United States and the tribes expressed their desire for peace and pledged to preserve it. The Kiowas sought a new way, a way free from war. The government agreed to construct an agency with saw and grist mills, and agreed to provide the Indians with a "physician, teachers, carpenter, miller, engineer, farmer and blacksmiths," while the Kiowas and Comanches promised "to compel their children, male and female, between the ages of six and sixteen years, to attend school" where they would receive "the elementary branches of an English education." The Kiowas and Comanches promised not to oppose the construction of a railroad through their lands, and that "they will never capture or carry off from the settlements white women or children" and "never kill nor scalp white men nor attempt to do them harm." They could continue to hunt on any lands south of the Arkansas River, "so long as the buffalo may range thereon in such numbers as to justify the chase." Nobody in the government expected that to last for very long.

With the negotiation of the Treaty of Medicine Lodge Creek, the federal government had nearly completed its work of concentrating the Plains tribes. Much, however, remained to be done. In the summer of 1868, the commissioners met with the Lakotas and others at Fort Laramie on the northern plains. The treaty the commissioners negotiated with the Lakota Sioux and the Arapahos followed the basic outline of the Medicine Lodge agreement. Some Santee Sioux, who had relocated with their Lakota kin, signed the agreement as well. The Indians and the United States agreed to end their hostilities, and the government created a Sioux reservation that consisted of the entire present-day state of South Dakota west of the Missouri River. The treaty included plans to civilize and educate the Lakota.

Figure 7.3 Satanta, Kiowa Leader. Courtesy of National Anthropological Archives.

The Commissioners met with other nations as well at Fort Laramie. They negotiated, for instance, an important treaty with the Crows, who had found the lands guaranteed to them in 1851 increasingly overrun both by white trespassers and Lakota hunters. The Crows saw in alliance with the United States the only effective means to protect their lands from these outside forces. To win this support, the Crows agreed to a massive cession: they held on to 8 million acres out of the nearly 38 million they had claimed as their own. The commissioners marked out a reservation for the Crows south of the Yellowstone River that included the Bighorn and Little Bighorn Rivers.

In both sets of treaties the commissioners promised to provide the Indians who signed with supplies to ease their transition to reservation life. Congress failed to appropriate the funds to fulfill its obligations until nine months after the signing of the Medicine Lodge Creek Treaty. Native peoples, meanwhile, needed to eat. Many left the reservation to hunt or to pillage food from white settlers who had moved on to their former lands.

To William Tecumseh Sherman, who had served on the Peace Commission, this behavior seemed outrageous, and he believed that only force could achieve the ends of federal policy. One could not negotiate with savages. "These Indians," he sputtered, "require to be soundly whipped and the ringleaders in the present trouble hung, their ponies killed, and such destruction of their property as will make them very poor." Sherman placed Philip Sheridan in charge of the campaign, intended to strike the Indians over the course of the winter of 1868–9, when the harsh weather reduced their mobility. The responsibility for any bloodshed,

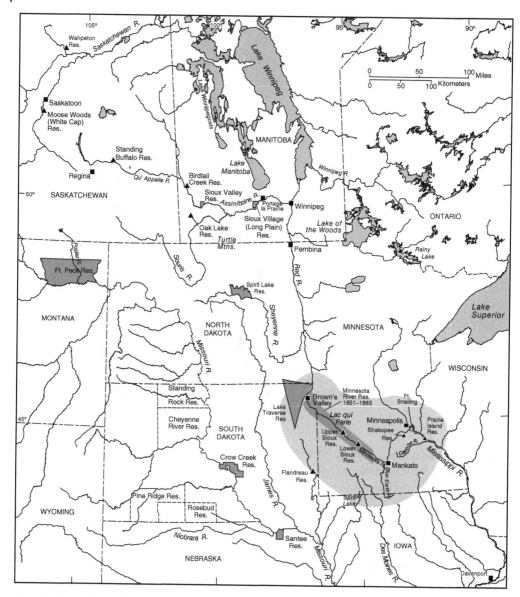

Map 7.2 Santee Sioux Territory. Source: *Smithsonian Handbook of North American Indians*, Vol. 13 (2), Plains, pp. 13: 762. Courtesy of Smithsonian Institution.

Sherman told Sheridan, rested with those Indians who refused to honor the terms of the treaties that they had signed.

Brutal but effective, the Winter Campaign shattered Indian resistance and Indian lives. The defeated natives, more refugees than warriors, returned to their reservations. The campaign was a great tactical success. But it did nothing about the underlying problems that had compelled the Indians to leave the reservation in the first place.

To address these problems became the concern of those supporters of President Ulysses S. Grant who called for a new "peace policy." The president at first placed Quakers in charge of a number of agencies, but soon allowed the participation of other Christian denominations. By 1872, Baptists, Presbyterians, Methodists, Catholics, Reformed Dutch, Unitarian, Episcopalians, Lutherans, and Congregationalists all had taken charge of Indian agencies across the American west.

Religious men, Grant's supporters believed, were less inclined toward the corruption that had plagued the reservations and contributed to the sorts of violence that broke out in Minnesota. To improve efficiency and honesty in the administration of Indian affairs, Grant appointed a Board of Indian Commissioners, unpaid volunteers to "exercise joint control with the Secretary of the Interior over the disbursement of the appropriations made by this act or any part thereof that the President may designate." With instructions drawn up by the Tonawanda Seneca Ely S. Parker, the first Native American to serve as the Commissioner of Indian Affairs, the commissioners worked to determine the proper "legal status of the Indians," to define "their rights and obligations under the laws of the United States, of the States and Territories and treaty stipulations," and whether additional treaties should be negotiated with Indian tribes. Parker's instructions to the commissioners show the concerns of "Peace Policy" advocates: the concentration of native peoples on reservations, their "humanization, civilization, and Christianization," and the settling of the legal status of native peoples under American law and the Constitution.

The commissioners issued their report in November of 1869. Though they believed that the federal government historically had "evinced a desire to deal generously with the Indians," the actual treatment native peoples had received was "unjust and iniquitous beyond the power of words to express." The rights affirmed in treaties, the commissioners reported, "have been assailed by the rapacity of the white man," and "the arm which should have been raised to protect them has been ever ready to sustain the aggressor." In addition to this "shameful record of broken treaties and unfulfilled promises," the commissioners noted that despite all laws and regulations, "the history of the border white man's connection with the Indians is a sickening record of murder, outrage, robbery, and wrongs committed by the former as the rule, and occasional savage outbreaks and unspeakably barbarous deeds of retaliation by the latter as the exception."

The commissioners understood the problem, they felt, and they proposed solutions. They supported concentration, and favored the creation of large reservations with large numbers of native peoples, the better to prevent the encroachments of frontier whites. Once there, government agents should teach the Indians about "the advantage of individual ownership of property," and should give them "land in severalty as soon as it is desired by any of them, and the tribal relations should be discouraged." The members of Indian tribes, the commissioners urged, must be transformed into the citizens of a republic who embraced American ideals of private property. "To facilitate the future allotment of the land the agricultural portions of the reservations should be surveyed as soon as it can be done without too much exciting their apprehensions" and the "titles should be inalienable from the family of the holder for at least two or three generations."

In addition to moving toward allotment, the commissioners called for the abolition of treaty-making, a belief shared by Ely Parker. "The Indian tribes of the United States," he wrote, "are not sovereign nations ... as none of them have an organized government of such inherent strength as would secure a faithful obedience of its people in the observance of compacts of this character. They are held to be wards of the government, and the only title the law concedes to them to the lands they occupy or claim is a mere possessory one." A number of Supreme Court decisions supported Parker's reasoning, even if the Constitution said little to this effect. It was time, Parker argued, that notions of tribal sovereignty "should be dispelled, and the government cease the cruel farce of thus dealing with its helpless and ignorant wards."

Congress acted on Parker's suggestions, declaring in March of 1871 that "hereafter no Indian nation or tribe within the territory of the United States shall be acknowledged as an independent nation, tribe, or power with whom the United States may contract a treaty." All earlier treaties would remain in force, part of the Supreme Law of the land, but no more would be made. Indians could not be both wards of the government and nations capable of negotiating treaties, Parker and those who shared his views asserted.

Parker's views, and those expressed by the Board of Indian Commissioners, reveal that little about the Peace Policy could be called new. Secretary of the Interior Jacob D. Cox, Parker's superior, acknowledged that theirs was not so much a new policy as it was "an enlarged and more enlightened application of the general principles of the old one." Francis Walker, Parker's successor, pointed out in 1872 that "when the expansion and development of a civilized race involve the rapid destruction of the only means of subsistence possessed by the members of a less fortunate race, the higher is bound as a simple right to provide for the lower some substitute for the means of subsistence which it has destroyed." This could not be done with handouts, "but by directing these people to new pursuits which shall be consistent with the progress of civilization upon the continent; helping them over the first rough places on 'the white man's road,' and, meanwhile, supplying such subsistence as is absolutely necessary during the period of initiation and experiment."

The Kiowas offered one of the most significant challenges to the Peace Policy. President Grant placed the Kiowa-Comanche-Apache (KCA) Reservation, established as a result of the Medicine Lodge Creek treaty, under the administrative control of the Society of Friends. Native peoples from ten tribes, with a combined population of over 5000, resided on a tract roughly the size of the state of Connecticut. Approximately 1900 Kiowas lived there. The Quakers found no more success than any of their predecessors in preserving peace along the frontier and in persuading the Kiowas to abandon their traditional way of life for a settled agricultural existence.

Kiowa winter counts reveal a people still tenaciously committed to their culture. In 1868, the Kiowas mentioned neither the Medicine Lodge Creek Treaty nor the warfare that preceded it, but rather a disastrous battle with the Utes, in which the Kiowas lost three of their sacred *Tai-mes*. They had not suffered so serious a defeat in battle since their traumatic loss to the Osages in 1833.

The Kiowas certainly suffered other adversities in 1868. They had signed the Medicine Lodge Treaty, Satank said, in hope that "a better time has come," but Congress never appropriated the funds necessary to fulfill its obligations, or to build the agency headquarters it had promised to build. The Kiowas and Comanches left the ill-equipped reservation. In search of food and horses, they struck the Caddos and Wichitas. They also hit white settlements along the Saline and Solomon rivers in Kansas, killing more than a dozen settlers. Fearing the consequence if native peoples left their reservations and defied the federal government, American forces rode out against the Kiowas. Along the Washita River in November of 1868, cavalrymen under the command of George Armstrong Custer attacked a large village housing Kiowas, Comanches, Arapahos, and Cheyennes. The brunt of Custer's assault fell upon Black Kettle's band of Cheyennes. Black Kettle survived the massacre of his followers at Sand Creek in 1864, but he died fleeing from the Washita. By December, the Kiowas had returned to their reservation, hoping to avoid the violence and savagery of the American cavalry.

Although they returned to the reservation, the Kiowas stayed away from the new agency that the federal government constructed near Fort Sill. Lawrie Tatum, the Quaker missionary and farmer placed in charge of the agency, arrived in the summer of 1869 to find the Indians uninterested in his plans for their refinement and improvement. They visited Tatum every week or so to collect the rations promised them at Medicine Lodge Creek, but they looked with disdain upon the agency employees who operated the model farm. By early 1870, Tatum concluded that the Kiowas could not be trusted. They stole eighty mules from the agency corral, scalped and cut the ears off an agency employee, shot another white man on Tatum's front porch. They sharpened their knives and rammed cartridges into their rifles as they listened to Tatum speak. The Kiowas did not fear their agent. They continued their raids into Texas as well, killing settlers and taking captives.

The Kiowas tested their Quaker agent's commitment to pacifism. Most of the agency employees left after the attacks of 1870, and Tatum called upon federal troops for protection. The Kiowas, he said, "have undoubtedly ... carried on their depredations this year without cause; everything reasonable has been done for them by the officers and others in this vicinity that could be done; they have received no injustice, indignities, or insults from citizens or soldiers." Only force could compel the Kiowas to adhere to the terms of the Medicine Lodge Treaty.

The Kiowas fought to protect a way of life. They asserted, correctly, that the United States had failed to fulfill its promises and especially that the Great Father in Washington had failed to prevent white hunters from slaughtering thousands of bison on lands that the Kiowas believed were reserved for their hunting. Tatum complained of his inability to control the Kiowas; he had an equally small ability to restrain white settlers.

The Kiowas' grievances did not matter any longer to federal authorities. In May of 1871, a Kiowa party led by Big Tree, Satanta, Satank, and others moved out to the Salt Creek Prairie, intent on ambushing the wagon convoys that occasionally passed by on the way to Fort Sill. They allowed a small train to pass by unmolested, not knowing that General Sherman rode aboard one of the wagons. They fell on a larger wagon train, killing many of the teamsters before they burned the wagons, and carrying away the fort's grain supply and over forty mules.

Tatum summoned the Kiowa leaders to the agency. With Sherman present, Tatum asked them if they knew who had led the Salt Creek attack. Satanta boldly took credit. The agent had not listened to the Kiowas' complaints about violations of the treaty, so they had raided in Texas. Tatum ordered the arrest of Satanta, Big Tree, and Satank. With some difficulty, and over the objections of other Kiowas at Fort Sill that day to collect their rations, Tatum manacled the three leaders and placed them in a wagon bound for Texas and trial. On the way there, Satank worked his hands free. The old man had suffered much. His son died during a raid on Texas in 1870. Satank went south then and found his son's bones. He placed them in a blanket and carried them with him wherever he went, speaking always of his son as if he were present. He had lost much, and now he would fight one last time for his freedom. He grabbed a soldier's rifle but before he could take aim he died as the soldiers opened fire. A Texas jury, a short time later, found Satanta and Big Tree guilty of murder and sentenced them to hang.

A delegation of Cherokees tried to restore order. The Cherokees feared that continued violence at Fort Sill might provide federal policy-makers with the excuse they needed to dismantle the Indian Territory and the tribal governments that had developed there and incorporate the native peoples there within the bounds of an American state. The Cherokees did manage to secure the release of some of the Kiowas' captives, but not enough to quiet those who called

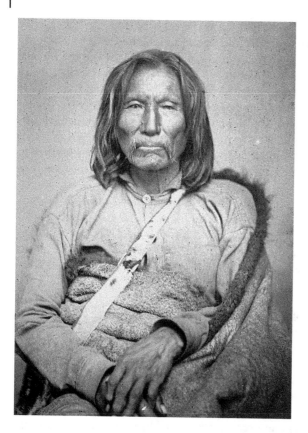

Figure 7.4 Satank, Kiowa Leader. Courtesy of National Anthropological Archives.

for a punitive war against them. Ely Parker concluded that "lenient measures and forbearance toward these restless and war-loving spirits appear to have no effect in restraining their passions, plunder and war, and a severe treatment would seem to be the only wise and proper course to pursue."

Seneca, Kiowa, and Cherokee stories intersected here in the Indian Territory. The Kiowas resisted the changes the government attempted to impose upon them. They would not quietly remain on their reservation. Cherokee leaders, who themselves knew much about the struggles of native peoples to live their lives in their own way, attempted to relieve the tensions the Kiowas' resistance produced, mediating between native warriors and the American state. And Parker, the Tonawanda Seneca responsible for implementing federal Indian policy, and the President's trusted friend, saw in the Kiowas' attempt to hang on to their way of life and unwillingness to conform to what the United States expected of them cause for war. The Kiowas, he believed, were not learning the lessons taught by the Quakers. The armed might of the military must act as a stern teacher, and force them to confront the reality of reservation life.

The events in the Indian Territory make clear the difficulties of generalizing about the experiences of native peoples. There was no single response to federal policies. Rather, native peoples debated and discussed among themselves the course they should follow. The Kiowas struggled to imagine living a life imprisoned on reservations. Many of them resisted, lashing out in attacks that in the end cost them dearly. The Cherokees, struggling to preserve their hard-won political stability and prevent outside interference in the Indian Territory, engaged in careful diplomacy to eliminate potential threats to their autonomy. Parker, of course, had lived away from New York for many years, in the army and in the presence of men who believed that, like delinquent children, native peoples must be placed on reservations whether they liked it or not. Concentration was for their own good.

Even Lawrie Tatum had abandoned pacifism, a decision that caused him to run afoul of Quaker authorities in the east. He supported the life sentences given to the Kiowa leaders. Under pressure from his superiors, and exhausted from a job that he simply lacked the power to do, Tatum resigned in March of 1873. His replacement, James Haworth, hoped once again to employ leniency to win over the Kiowas and Comanches. He called upon Texas authorities to release Satanta and Big Tree, and he believed that if treated respectfully, courteously, and peacefully, the Kiowas would abandon their warlike ways and embrace at long last a farming way of life.

In October, the Texas authorities released the Kiowa leaders. According to the agency teacher, Thomas Battey, the return of Satanta brought enormous relief to the Kiowas. "Joy beamed upon every countenance and their happiness was exhibited," Battey wrote, "as might be expected, in the most wild and natural manner." But any hope that Satanta's release would bring peace to the KCA Reservation quickly dissipated. Satanta no longer retained much influence; leadership had passed to younger men, who recognized that the release of their leaders addressed only one of a number of significant grievances. Life on the reservation remained miserable. Food remained in scarce supply and the number of bison continued to decline. The trespasses of hunters and swindlers and horse thieves and "dissolute white men" continued. Some Comanches, at least, began to follow a prophet named I'sätaí who had received from powerful spirit forces the ability to heal the sick and bring the dead back to life. He promised to produce cartridges from his stomach, and to make his followers bullet-proof. The Kiowas and their neighbors lived in communities in crisis, and felt they had little choice but to fight.

Comanche raiders hit Texas. So, too, did the Kiowas, who admitted to Haworth that they had stolen livestock from white farmers. Haworth refused to punish his wards, and instead reminded them of their obligations under the Medicine Lodge Creek Treaty. Comanche raiders then struck a white homesteader family, killing them all, and leaving the body of a seven-year-old girl scalped and hanging from a tree. Local newspapers began to blame the Quakers for the violence. When a group of outlaws established a hunting camp at Adobe Walls and slaughtered bison by the thousands in the Indians' hunting grounds, and when they sold alcohol and firearms to the Indians in return for stolen livestock, it became clear that the problem had grown to enormous proportions. Kiowas, Comanches, and Cheyennes all participated in resulting warfare.

By the summer of 1874, the Red River War had begun. Comanche, Cheyenne, and Kiowas under the leadership of the Comanche Quanah Parker attacked the illegal traders and buffalo hunters entrenched at Adobe Walls in June. Seven hundred warriors joined in the assault. The hunters, though badly outnumbered, managed to repel the attackers after two days of fighting. Federal authorities knew that "the tribes would have remained peaceful had it not been for hide-hunters and horse thieves," but they also believed that the native peoples of the southern Plains must be crushed militarily, once and for all.

Five American army columns converged on the Texas Panhandle, where the Kiowas, Comanches, and Cheyennes remained after the Adobe Walls fight. Federal troops relentlessly pursued them, slaughtering bison and horses as they advanced. Hunger, harsh weather, and the fear of being caught by federal troops led to their surrender. They had fought to protect their way of life, but they could not win on the battlefield. As early as October of 1874 some had returned to the reservation. By the spring of 1875, all of the "hostiles" had come in.

They were not treated gently. Army officers at the agency incarcerated the "ringleaders" guilty of "crimes" against the Americans. The officers returned Satanta to the Texas State Penitentiary. After three years, he committed suicide by leaping from a window to his death. The soldiers herded others—several dozen in all—aboard eight wagons and carried them to the nearest railroad station. From there, the Americans sent them to Fort Marion, on the Atlantic Coast of Florida. Placed under the charge of Lieutenant Richard Pratt, the Kiowa captives received education in English and instruction in Christianity.

In 1846, federal officials had estimated that 12,000 Comanches lived on the southern Plains, along with 2000 Kiowas. At the end of the Red River War, the Comanches had lost more than 85% of their population. Only 1721 remained in 1875, along with 1070 Kiowas. The Kiowas would never again take up arms against the United States. The Comanche empire had fallen. The Red River War ended military conflict on the southern Plains, but wars took place elsewhere. The Modocs of California fought federal forces beginning in 1873 who sought to drive them back to their reservation. The Great Sioux War of 1876 brought conflict to the northern Plains.

Many Lakota Sioux spent part of the year on the Great Sioux Reservation but moved out onto the Plains of eastern Montana to hunt in the spring and summer. They resented the American failure to adhere to the terms of the Fort Laramie Treaty, and especially the hordes of prospectors who began to intrude into the Black Hills following gold strikes there in 1874. The Lakotas ignored demands that they return to their reservation—why should they honor a treaty that the white people had ignored—and by the spring of 1876, four army columns began marching toward the Powder River Country to force the Sioux to return.

Much of the fighting that followed took place on lands the Crows considered their own. With the removal of the forts along the Bozeman Trail, no American military presence remained to prevent Sioux encroachment on lands to their west. Conflict between the Sioux and the Crows increased, and the size and scope of this warfare intensified. Plenty Coups, the great Crow leader who oversaw his people's adjustment to reservation life, remembered that he and his followers "knew the white men were strong, without number in their own country, and that there was no good in fighting them." The Crows calculated their best interest, and that meant assisting the American forces. "Our leading chiefs," Plenty Coups said, "saw that to help the white men fight their enemies and ours would make them our friends." Already at war with the Sioux and their allies, they might as well fight them now with the assistance of the Americans. "Our decision was reached," Plenty Coups concluded, "not because we loved the white man who was already crowding the other tribes into our country, or because we hated the Sioux, Cheyenne and Arapaho, but because we plainly saw that this course was the only one which might save our beautiful country for us."

The Crow leaders recognized that the Americans faced a formidable enemy. Large numbers of Sioux and Cheyenne warriors gathered in the Little Bighorn Basin, led by such stalwart leaders as Crazy Horse, Sitting Bull, Gall, Hump, and Lame Deer. On June 17, 1876, warriors led by Crazy Horse forced the American column led by General George Crook to withdraw at the Battle of the Rosebud. Crow horsemen formed a screen that shielded Crook's men from Crazy Horse's warriors and bought them the time they needed to withdraw. Eight days later, an American force led by Lt. Col. George Armstrong Custer foolishly attacked the village along the Little Bighorn. Two thousand warriors camped there. They determined to defend themselves and their families. Custer had no idea what he had stumbled into. Depicted so often in American myth as a famous "Last Stand," Custer's defeat was a rout. The Sioux and their Cheyenne allies mowed them down as they fled from a village so much larger than they had anticipated. The Sioux wiped out Custer's command in the time, one Sioux observer later noted, that it took a hungry man to eat his dinner. Only Custer's Crow and Arikara scouts, who recognized the power of the Sioux, survived.

The Lakotas won the battle, of course, but they lost the war. Once again, winter campaigns drove the Sioux and their allies back the reservation. By the spring of 1877, most had returned. Crazy Horse surrendered at the Red Cloud Agency in May. He died four months later, stabbed to death during a guardhouse scuffle. Sitting Bull, who had fled across the border into Canada, held out until 1881, before he returned.

The advocates of the Peace Policy recognized that they needed to alter their approach. They recognized the extent to which they relied upon violence, coercion, and conquest to place native peoples upon reservations and to keep them there. Reservations had once seemed an attractive solution to the Indian Problem. By isolating native peoples from the vices of the surrounding white population, the reservation, its advocates hoped, bought them time to become civilized and Americanized. But neighboring whites seldom respected reservation boundaries, and corrupt government agents undermined the paternalistic concern of the federal government to care for its Indian wards. Congress failed to provide reservation Indians with the supplies they needed to undertake the great transition their White Father envisioned. Native peoples found themselves under siege. They no longer could live their accustomed way of life in their homelands. Neither could they live well on the reservation. Whether they moved to the reservations voluntarily or as the result of military conquest, they suffered. But they did not disappear. Despite the efforts of federal agents, missionaries, and teachers to eliminate their culture, and despite their own decisions to make use of some of what the Americans offered them, these communities survived.

8

THE AGE OF DISPOSSESSION

"Conform To It or Be Crushed By It"

In 1881 the editors of the *Journal of the Military Service Institution* published a number of essays, written by experienced army officers, attempting to answer "Our Indian Question." All the contributors agreed that native peoples who did not change faced certain extinction. All rued the tragedy of Native America's encounter with the United States. "If the graves of the thousands of victims who have fallen in the terrible wars of race had been placed in a line," thought Colonel Nelson Miles, "the philanthropist might journey from the Atlantic to the Pacific, and from the Lakes to the Gulf, and be constantly within sight of green mounds." All agreed that the government must act urgently to save the remnants of "this doomed race."

But what to do? All of them believed that the federal government had a role to play. None of the contributors thought for a second about asking native peoples for their thoughts. They all agreed that the president should place the Bureau of Indian Affairs under the control of the War Department, because military men could administer Indian affairs more effectively than the civilians at the Interior Department. Agents too often carried with them to their posts naïve notions about Indians, "derived from legends and stories, fictions and extracts from the newspapers," and knew nothing about the effect that "force, discipline, courage, coolness, and self-possession produce upon the savage mind." All agreed, as well, that little hope existed for educating Indian adults, though the children, with proper support, might be transformed into productive citizens of the republic. They believed that native peoples should not be transformed immediately into farmers, but rather that agents should teach them how to herd and raise livestock. Finally, all called for a reconsideration of the reservation policy. No line drawn on a map had ever succeeded in halting the "tidal wave of immigration that is sweeping over every obstacle." Meanwhile, the government incarcerated native peoples on reservations, where the Indians held their land in common, "under their own tribal superstitions." This antiquated and barbaric practice, Captain Thomas Woodruff of the 5th Infantry wrote, prevented Indians from nurturing "the idea of home, of individuality, of personal responsibility," and so conspired to keep "them savage and nomadic forever." The officers agreed that the allotment of lands to individual Indians offered the best chance for saving the Indians.

The officers shared a belief that the hunger of the frontier population for native land produced unspeakable acts of cruelty. Changes, all agreed, needed to be made. Many government officials by the last quarter of the nineteenth century shared this belief. Commissioner of Indian Affairs John Q. Smith in 1876 doubted that "any high degree of civilization is possible without individual ownership of land." The "allotment to them of lands in severalty" and the

Native America: A History, Second Edition. Michael Leroy Oberg.

"extension over them of United States law and the jurisdiction of United States Courts" would protect native peoples on reservations that had become "a refuge to the most lawless and desperate whites in America." Private property, Interior Secretary Carl Schurz argued in his annual report for 1880, "will inspire the Indians with a feeling of assurance as to the permanency of their ownership of the lands they occupy and cultivate; it will give them a clear and legal standing as landed proprietors in the courts of law; it will secure to them for the first time fixed homes under the protection of the same law under which white men own theirs," and "it will eventually open to settlement by white men the large tracts of land now belonging to the reservations, but not used by the Indians." Everyone would benefit. Indeed, Smith's successor as head of the Bureau of Indian Affairs, Hiram Price, argued that allotment would lead Indians finally to learn English and the American way of life. And the government did not need to ask the Indians' permission: "We are fifty millions, and they are only one-fourth of one million," Price said. "The few must yield to the many."

Indeed, many reformers called for allotment: the Indian Rights Association, a group led by wealthy easterners and founded in 1882, thought allotment offered a solution to the nation's Indian question. By 1883, the Board of Indian Commissioners, the Boston Indian Citizenship Association, the Women's National Indian Association, the Ladies National Indian League, and the Lake Mohonk Conference of the Friends of the Indian all studied the nation's Indian affairs, discussed various proposals to solve the "Indian problem," and called upon their members to agitate for reform.

Reformers wanted to Christianize the Indians, teach them to speak English, learn how to farm and function in the American economic system, and allot their lands. For years, in fact, reformers contemplated allotment on the grounds that only by bestowing upon native peoples private property with a fee simple title recognizable under American law would they have the incentive and means to work like Americans did. Allotment, as an idea, had been around for many decades, but by the 1880s, it had come to occupy a position of prominence in the reformers' concerns that it had not held previously.

The General Allotment Act, introduced by Senator Henry Dawes of Massachusetts in 1887, authorized the president, "whenever in his opinion any reservation or any part thereof of such Indians is advantageous for agricultural and grazing purposes," to survey and divide up the lands with each head of household receiving sixty-four acres and an additional amount depending on the number of dependents he had. The government would act as a trustee and ensure that the allotted lands could not be sold by the individual allottee for twenty-five years, a period intended to provide the Indians with time to learn how to farm, to manage their lands, and become "civilized." After the Indians received their allotments, Congress empowered the government to sell the excess lands, creating a fund to pay for the Indians' improvement. Government leaders hoped, moreover, that by opening land to white settlement they would relieve the pressure upon native land.

Spelatch

Spelatch, wrote the Skokomish artist Bruce-subiyay Miller, that period when his ancestors faced enormous pressure to settle themselves on reservations and make fundamental changes to their ways of living, "turned everything as we knew it upside down." His people "fell into disarray" and lost their *shuy.* Miller likened his ancestors' experience to that of "a shipwreck where everyone was trying to find something to cling to, to save their lives." Some turned to alcohol. Some tried to assimilate, or turned to Christianity in order to find "a firm place to stand in the midst of that capsized world." It was difficult, and many of them struggled, for they found that "the things that they venerated, that gave them their vital life force and their strength for survival, suddenly were condemned as evil."

Certainly the decades following the Stevens treaties brought great change to the native peoples who lived along the Salish Sea. As elsewhere, a boom in the non-Indian population and the resulting land hunger motivated much of this change. In 1870, Seattle was a village occupied by 1100 people. By 1890, more than 42,000 lived there. If in 1860 native peoples made up half the population of the Puget Sound area, by 1890 the newcomers outnumbered them by twenty to one. They wanted the Indians to remain on their reservations, and for the boundaries of those reservations to be defined precisely. Many non-Indians encroached upon native peoples' lands. Governor Stevens had included in the treaties provisions for allotment, and this offered both federal and territorial authorities room to argue that dividing up the reservations would give individual Salish people their own tracts of land and open the excess to development.

American officials policed the cultural life of the Indians who agreed to remove to their reservations. Agents banned healing rituals, gambling games, *potlatch* ceremonies, and cohabitation before marriage. At Tulalip, a federal agent punished a young man for "extremely vulgar language." Others found themselves in irons for a host of insults real and imagined. This coercive enforcement of morals was too often for native peoples a one-way street. Native peoples faced punishment for consuming alcohol provided them by white traders in violation of American law. The missionary Myron Eells, who served at Skokomish, learned of the agent's half-hearted efforts to prosecute liquor dealers, "sometimes before a packed jury, who, when proof was positive, declared the prisoner not guilty; of having Indian witnesses tampered with, and bought either by money or threats."

While limitations on their freedom and attacks on their cultural practices were significant, their creative adaptations to this new world should not be overlooked. Skagits found opportunities for trade and employment in logging camps that popped up in their territory. They frustrated those federal authorities charged with conducting the nation's Indian policy. While the Makah's federal agent in 1865 suggested that "one of the most practical methods of directly benefiting these Indians is by aiding them in their fisheries," most continued to push for them to take up agriculture on the white model. In 1895, the Commissioner of Indian Affairs noted in his annual report that native peoples on Puget Sound "are not systematic farmers." Most of them, he wrote, spent as much time as they could "in their canoes, fishing, especially during the salmon season."

During the formative years of the commercial salmon canning industry, the labor of native peoples like the Lummi was essential. Their traditional subsistence activities allowed them entry into the market economy, and a means to acquire cash and consumer goods. The earliest canneries obtained most of the fish they processed from native peoples who, as the Lummis' agent lamented, in 1891 were now "more independent" and showed "less inclination to cultivate their land than do the Indians of most of the reserves."

There was a lot of money to be made in the salmon industry, and the canneries gradually worked to consolidate their control over every step in the production process, including fishing. Canneries, for instance, constructed large fish traps below the Lummis' fishing locations, limiting their catch. In 1894, the Lummis complained to the Commissioner of Indian Affairs. They were fighting, in a sense, for their independence. "Several years ago white men began to encroach on our ground," they wrote. Initially, "we were willing to have them share with us the right to fish." But the canneries, and the white fishermen they increasingly employed, did not want to share. They obstructed Lummi fishing. "They have driven us from our old camping ground on the beach" where they processed their catch, and "made additional obstructions to prevent our catching fish." The Lummis called upon the commissioner to protect their rights to fish under the terms of the treaty they negotiated with Governor Stevens. And when the commissioner refused to act, the Lummis filed suit to enforce their treaty rights. That they lost their case in 1897 should not cause us to miss the gravity of the issue to them.

Native peoples continued to make adjustments. Some became wage laborers in the canneries, processing the fish caught now largely by non-Indians. They continued to find ways to get by, to adapt to the new world created by the growing white population. The adjustments they made took many forms. The Indian Shaker Church, for example, an indigenous religious movement founded by a Squaxin named John Slocum in the early 1880s, spread rapidly from its birthplace in the southern Puget Sound to communities in British Columbia, Idaho, Oregon, and northern California. John Slocum returned from the land of the dead with a prophetic message from God, that his followers should reform their ways and abandon their vices. Despite the opposition of the established churches, the Indian Shaker Church in 1910 organized and became a legally incorporated religion under Washington State law that met the needs of native peoples living on and off reservations in the Pacific Northwest.

Native peoples in Washington State refused to disappear. They found their traditional ways of living under attack, their cultural values denigrated, and their lands encroached upon.

Figure 8.1 Portrait of Messiah Squ-Sacht-Un, Called John Slocum, and with Chief High Priest Ai-Yal or Louis Yowaluch, Both Shakers of Puget Sound, 1892, BAE GN 03021 06487500, NAA, SI.

Changes to the urban landscape of Seattle and elsewhere on Puget Sound transformed the region in ways that made it seem strange and unfamiliar. Some found themselves *spelatched*, with "everything they had known that gave them security … pulled out from under them." But, still, in this world "turned upside down," they remained, peoples on the margins to be sure, but survivors still.

Ghost Dancers

Meanwhile, native peoples across the Great West tried to recover from the series of devastations that had accompanied their concentration on reservations. They did not discuss theoretical issues of Indian policy or promote the virtues of allotment. They learned by necessity to live under a new reality at times very different from all that they had known before. After concentration, Pretty Shield recalled, the Crows "began to stay in one place, and to grow lazy and sicker all the time." Men, who had been brave warriors and hunters, now "began to drink the white man's whiskey, letting it do their thinking." Bison had grown scarce, and when they went away, Plenty Coups said, "the hearts of my people fell to the ground, and they could not lift them up again." Mourning the loss of the bison, Pretty Shield recalled that "my heart fell down when I began to see dead buffalo scattered all over our beautiful country, killed and skinned, and left to rot by white men." Diseases continued to prey upon native peoples, carrying them away as they struggled with the loss of lands, the disappearance of game, and continuing assaults on their culture and identity.

Far in the west, a Paiute shaman named Wovoka began to preach a message that combined Christian themes with nativist principles to answer these concerns. Wovoka, the messiah, had received visions, and he promised his followers peace and prosperity if they lived honest lives and performed the Ghost Dance. The new ritual, Wovoka taught, offered his followers a way to restore their world to balance.

Word of the new religion spread rapidly. Native peoples sent emissaries to learn from Wovoka. As they did so, they transformed and altered elements of the original message. Lakotas, for instance, who returned from visiting Wovoka in March of 1890, taught that performing the Ghost Dance would bring back the buffalo and cause white people to disappear. The Lakotas had many grievances. Hunger constantly hounded reservation Indians. The government broke up the Great Sioux Reservation in 1889, reducing the lands held by the Lakota and severing the binds connecting communities together. Sensing discontent, federal troops remained a heavy presence in Lakota country. The Lakota believers wore "Ghost Shirts" that some believed would stop bullets, and this made the federal authorities nervous. They worried that Sitting Bull, the great Lakota leader, would join the movement. When American authorities and the newly constituted tribal police tried to prevent this, Sitting Bull resisted arrest. He and seven others died in a gunfight on December 15, 1890.

Another group of Ghost Dancers, led by Bigfoot, and consisting of many women and children, fled out onto South Dakota's badlands. The government sent 9000 troops to South Dakota, and 5000 of these to Pine Ridge. Fully a third of the United States Army, in its largest mobilization since the end of the Civil War, took up positions to suppress this peaceful protest. Federal troops surrounded them at Wounded Knee Creek in advance of moving them back to the Pine Ridge Agency. When the cavalrymen went to disarm Bigfoot's followers, a shot was fired, perhaps accidentally, when a deaf young man refused to surrender his weapon. The federal troops opened up with rifles and artillery. One hundred and forty-six Indians died, including forty-four women and eighteen children. It was the last military engagement between native peoples and American soldiers on the Plains, and the Wounded Knee massacre wiped out a religious movement among the Lakota Sioux that offered them hope for the future and a means for making sense of their life on reservations.

Most accounts of the Ghost Dance Movement end with the Sioux at Wounded Knee, and the movement is too often cast as the tragic and desperate conclusion to the Plains Wars. But other native peoples found these prophetic messages appealing. The Caddos, for instance, embraced the Ghost Dance early and continued to practice it longer than many of the other tribes on the plains. They had tried to work with government agents after the re-establishment of their reservation. They began raising stock, and erected fences and log homes. Many of them tended orchards, and some had substantial agricultural operations. Their success led the government to consolidate the Wichita Agency with the Kiowa Comanche Agency along the Washita River in 1878. The Caddos might serve as an example for their less "civilized" neighbors. As the Kiowas and Comanches arrived, however, they stole Caddo horses and destroyed their fields.

Meanwhile the Caddos suffered a continuing decline in population. Over the final two decades of the nineteenth century, Caddo population declined 27%. In 1891 and 1892 alone, during a particularly brutal year, whooping cough, measles, and pneumonia swept through the reservation, and killed nearly 400 Indians. In an atmosphere of such crisis and despair, the Caddos found much that appealed to them in the Ghost Dance.

An Arapaho named Sitting Bull carried Wovoka's message to a Ghost Dance celebration held along the South Canadian River in the fall of 1890. There the Caddos learned the songs and rituals of the Ghost Dance. John Wilson, or Moon Head, a Caddo who had French and Delaware ancestors, translated Wovoka's message and preached it for several years. In the fall of 1891, the Caddos sent their own delegation to visit Wovoka, and to learn more.

Caddo Ghost Dancers, the anthropologist John Swanton learned early in the twentieth century, danced "for days and nights together from the middle of the afternoon until the sun was well up in the morning." They danced regardless of the weather. "Cold weather had no deterrent effect," Swanton learned, and the Caddos "kept up the dance in the snow," with some of the dancers falling into a trance and "lying unconscious in the snow for half an hour at a time." Caddo women participated along with the men. Unlike the Lakotas, they did not anticipate the return of the bison, but they did sing of reunions with lost relatives. The Ghost Dance would eliminate disease and restore their dead friends and family members. The Ghost Dance helped the Caddos make sense of the significant losses of population they had experienced in the nineteenth century and to look forward to a better day.

According to James Mooney, a contemporary of Swanton's who also studied the Ghost Dance movement among the Caddos, "they were the first ... to take up the dance, and have manifested the greatest interest in it from the time it was introduced among them." Though the Ghost Dance gradually declined among the Caddos, the songs remained a part of their culture. By the 1890s, most Caddos had joined one of a number of Christian denominations at work on the reservation, but they embraced the Ghost Dance as well. Both ritual traditions helped Caddos deal spiritually with the dramatic transformations demanded by reservation life.

The Kiowas received word of the Ghost Dance at the same gathering as did the Caddos. The movement resonated with the Kiowas. They too had struggled on the reservation, and suffered from hunger, poverty, and the loss of their leaders after the Red River War. The Kiowas, like other native peoples, believed in the importance of preserving spiritual power, and the troubles they experienced convinced many that they needed to return to ritual. A prophet named Pá-iñgya began preaching in 1887 and claimed, through ritual, the ability "to resurrect the dead and destroy his enemies with a glance as by a lightening stroke." Pá-iñgya kindled a sacred fire from which his followers warmed their houses. He called upon them to return to ritual, to abandon all the elements of white culture that had brought so much destruction to Kiowa lives. Other shamans emerged to call, through ritual, for the bison to return. Like Sayday, the Kiowas believed that through ritual they could persuade the bison to return to them from underneath the world.

In October of 1890 a large number of Kiowas gathered at the mouth of Rainy Mountain Creek to celebrate the Ghost Dance. Kiowas believed that the new religion could give them the power they needed to survive, to live in a new world created by warfare and disease and dispossession. Not all Kiowas were persuaded. A'piaton, a skeptic who had watched other prophets fail, traveled to Nevada to learn more about Wovoka. A'piaton returned in February of 1891, and told a large gathering at the Anadarko Agency that the Ghost Dance possessed no power. A'piaton told the Indians that Wovoka's message offered no solutions to the problems facing the Kiowas. It was, Mooney learned from several Kiowas who attended A'piaton's talk, one of the saddest days in the history of the tribe.

Native peoples continued to embrace prophetic and revivalistic movements after the disaster at Wounded Knee. Agents and missionaries frequently denounced and proscribed the practices that accompanied them. Surely these movements indicated that all was not well on the reservations, and the regeneration that reformers had hoped would occur had not taken place in the ways they anticipated. As a result, reformers called upon Congress to accelerate the process of allotment, confident that the granting of lands in severalty to individual Indians would bring them finally and forcefully into the modern world.

The Assault on Indian Identity

With native peoples working their individual allotments and the government serving as their trustee for a twenty-five-year period, reformers expected a new generation of Indians to emerge, educated, Christianized, and ready to take their place as citizens of the republic. This frenzied enthusiasm drowned out the few critics of the new law. That Congress felt compelled to quickly begin revising the Dawes Act, however, might have suggested that the legislation possessed significant shortcomings. In 1891, Congress authorized the Secretary of the Interior in cases where "any allottee ... can not personally and with benefit to himself occupy and improve his allotment" because of "age or other disability," to lease his lands. Easterners promoted the legislation to aid those persons who physically could not work their allotments, allowing aged or infirm allottees a way to derive a living from their lands. Westerners, however, strongly supported the legislation as well. By exploiting inexperienced native landholders, real estate swindlers could acquire control of Indian lands through the leasing of tracts for farming and grazing. The legislation violated the spirit of the Dawes Act, where the government pledged to hold lands in trust for twenty-five years to protect native peoples while they learned to work their allotments. Leasing was only the first of a number of revisions to the Dawes Act that hastened the rate of Indian dispossession.

The number of allotments made by the Interior Department and the Bureau of Indian Affairs increased rapidly. In 1888, the first year the legislation was in effect, the Bureau of Indian Affairs made 3349 allotments; four years later, the Bureau of Indian Affairs authorized

8704. This rapid pace was apparently not fast enough, and many Indian reformers called for changes to the Dawes Act that would subject new lands to allotment and accelerate the opening of Indian lands to white Americans.

With the Burke Act of 1906, Congress amended the original requirement that the Secretary of the Interior hold the allottees' lands in trust for a period of twenty-five years and granted him the discretion, "whenever he shall be satisfied that any Indian allottee is competent and capable of managing his or her affairs … to cause to be issued to such allottee a patent in fee simple." Qualified Indians need not wait twenty-five years to receive title to their allotments and assume the burdens of citizenship in the American republic.

Yet by establishing procedures where, according to Commissioner of Indian Affairs Francis Leupp, "any Indian who is earning a livelihood at any honorable occupation, if he wishes to own his lands in fee, should have the privilege at once," the Burke Act led to "forced patenting," the practice of granting fee simple title to Indians whose lands white settlers and speculators desired but who may not yet have mastered the knowledge necessary to preserve their lands. First unleashed upon the Omahas in Nebraska, the policy of forced patenting compelled 20,000 Indians to accept fee patents for their land, and with this citizenship and the obligation to pay state and local taxes. The policy was disastrous for Indians. Ninety-five percent of the Omahas lost their lands. Ninety percent of the Crows sold their allotments or mortgaged them at ruinous rates. Many Indian allottees, freed from the protections offered by a federal guardian, lost their lands because of an imperfect understanding of the requirements of land-ownership under American law.

The increased granting of fee simple title to allottees, however, and the removal of federal trusteeship, did result in an increase in the number of Native American citizens of the United States. Perhaps as many as 12,000 native persons served in the United States armed forces during the First World War, including Potawatomis, Cherokees, Dakotas, Crows, Kiowas, Caddos, Pueblos, and Senecas. Most volunteered. Seventeen thousand native peoples registered for the draft. Ninety percent of the students of military age in the government's off-reservation boarding schools volunteered, as did between 20 and 40% of the men of fighting age on the nation's reservations. Native soldiers died at twice the rate of non-Indian servicemen. A high percentage of them, relative to other populations of soldiers, served as scouts, runners, and snipers, risky jobs for which American officers thought them uniquely suited. Fully a quarter of the adult male Native American population took up arms.

There were pockets of apathy in some places, opposition in others. Pueblos resisted conscription, as did the Senecas. This resistance drew little comment from the general public, and government officials emphasized the patriotism of native peoples. Indians did suffer for their participation. The Seneca Jesse Cornplanter came home from the war to learn that his parents, sister, brother-in-law, and two children had died from the influenza epidemic in 1918. More than 6200 native peoples died of influenza in 1918, 2% of the total Indian population. Advocates for Indian assimilation, however, paid little attention to these hardships, and for them, the readiness with which native peoples participated in the war suggested that they were more than ready to assume their just rights and responsibilities as citizens.

Indeed, many reformers viewed Indian reservations as "a prison pen where human beings are doomed to live amid sad memories of their ancestors and among ghosts of the dead." During the war Cato Sells, the Commissioner of Indian Affairs, announced in his "Declaration of Policy" that "the time has come for discontinuing guardianship of all competent Indians and giving even closer attention to the incompetent that they may more speedily achieve competency." He accelerated the pace of forced patenting, despite its disastrous consequences.

Federal superintendents at the Santee, Sisseton, and Potawatomi reservations, among others, all informed Sells that the issuing of patents had resulted in widespread and rapid Indian dispossession. One report suggested that only 13% of the native peoples who received fee patents used their land wisely. Eighty percent, meanwhile, had been entirely dispossessed. Still, Sells moved forward. All able-bodied Indians, he said, "of less than one-half Indian blood," would receive "full and complete control of all their property." Native peoples of more than one-half Indian blood would receive title if they could demonstrate their competence to reservation agents. Graduates of Indian Schools, Sells believed, demonstrated their competence by completing their course of study. Sells looked forward to the "dawn of a new era in Indian administration," which he hoped would lead to "the ultimate absorption of the Indian race into the body politic of the Nation" and "the beginning of the end of the Indian problem." All Indians who served in the military during the war, regardless of their blood-quantum, received citizenship as a result of a law enacted by Congress in November of 1919.

Allotment, as defined in the original Dawes Act, was conceived as a gradual process. The federal government would protect Indian allottees for twenty-five years as they learned how to function as farmers on lands carefully selected for that purpose. Only at the end of this period of guardianship would allottees become citizens of the United States. Like many earlier Indian policies, the promoters of allotment believed that their legislation would save native peoples who otherwise faced extinction. The subsequent amendments and revisions to the Dawes Act, however, made clear the extent to which western interests drove the conduct of American Indian policy. Westerners wanted Indian lands. Ten western states joined the union in the quarter-century after the passage of the Dawes Act, and their representatives in Congress effectively pushed for the acceleration of the allotment process.

Government officials acted as if they did not need the consent of the Indians to pursue a policy they believed was in the best interest of native peoples. Indians, after all, could not possibly look after themselves, and they needed the strong hand of the federal government to save them. Designed to lead their dependent wards toward independence and full citizenship, however, the internally inconsistent policy of allotment left them impoverished and more dependent than before. The Santees at the Devil's Lake Reservation, for example, struggled to survive after their lands had been allotted. They suffered from bad harvests and poor conditions, despite a willingness to make a go of it as farmers. They lived on boiled corn and turnips. Hunger compelled them to eat their horses, and they lacked the land necessary to raise enough money to replace them. The number of deaths on the reservation exceeded the number of births, a product of the poverty allotment and dispossession produced. Their experience was typical. By 1900, the Indian estate in America had been cut in half, from 155.6 million to 77.9 million acres.

The authoritarian streak that characterized allotment manifested itself in other areas as well. In 1883, Secretary of the Interior Henry Teller called for the prohibition of dancing on Indian reservations. Commissioner Thomas Jefferson Morgan, in a set of rules for Indian courts on reservations drawn up in 1892, declared that "any Indian who shall engage in the sun dance, scalp dance, or war dance, or any other similar feast, so called, shall be deemed guilty of an offense" punishable by the withholding of rations or imprisonment. Native peoples clung to their dances despite these rules, and by the early twentieth century some agents, like those among the Kiowas, realized that prohibiting dancing was not worth the trouble it caused. Native peoples clung to dancing as part of the vibrant core of their identity as Indians. The new rules were meant not only to promote assimilation, but to proscribe religious rituals that had met the needs of native peoples for many generations and to eliminate social gatherings that gave meaning to what seemed at times a bleak reservation existence. They would not give up dancing easily.

The Bureau of Indian Affairs expected its agents to enforce policies like those banning dances and regulating the conduct of religious ceremonies on reservations. Federal Indian agents, however, did not act alone. Missionaries and educators worked together with federal officials to effect the assimilation and incorporation of native peoples into the American body politic. The best known of these educators, that great self-promoter Lt. Col. Richard Henry Pratt, in the aftermath of the Red River War carried seventy-two prisoners, including twenty-seven Kiowas and one Caddo, across the continent to Fort Marion on the Atlantic coast of Florida. Pratt believed strongly that these warriors, most of whom were in their twenties and thirties, might be educated and become productive members of society. One attempted suicide, and another was gunned down when he jumped from the train carrying him east, but the rest settled into a life in prison. A number of the men learned to read and write English.

Rapid assimilation, in Pratt's view, offered the best solution to America's "Indian problem." The Fort Marion experiment convinced Pratt that native peoples could be educated if they were removed from the influence of their elders and a reservation environment that, in his opinion, encouraged the retention of uncivilized manners. The older generation of Indians, Pratt suggested, hide-bound by the past, could not be helped, but hope still remained for their children. The last Indian war, in a sense, would be waged against them. Pratt never doubted the capacity of Indians for improvement, but he believed firmly that civilization must triumph over savagery, and he opposed any distraction or force that threatened to keep "the nation's attention and the Indian's energies fixed upon his valueless past." So he founded the Carlisle Indian Industrial School in Carlisle, Pennsylvania, in 1879, the first of several off-reservation boarding schools built in the final decades of the nineteenth century.

At Carlisle, Pratt intended to kill the Indian and save the man, he said, and to eradicate the Indian past in order to give them a chance for the future. Pratt and his instructors undertook a systematic assault on the identity of the Indian children placed in their care. First, the Carlisle staff attempted to shatter the child's ties to his or her "tribal" past: they cut the children's hair; exchanged their traditional clothing for Carlisle's stiff military uniforms; punished children for speaking their native languages; and forced them to abandon their given names for others chosen from an approved list written on a blackboard. Surnames, agents and educators believed, would facilitate the transfer of private property from one generation of newly civilized Indians to the next. Then the children embarked upon a rigorous schedule of academic training, religious indoctrination, and instruction in a "civilized" trade. Some, through the school's "outing program," applied their new skills in the employ of white families in Carlisle and neighboring communities. It is difficult to measure the costs of this type of education, cultural genocide masked as blundering and arrogant goodwill. Some children must have developed a profound feeling of self-loathing as they listened to their teachers denigrate their parents, their people, and their way of life. As the Carlisle faculty taught them that their own culture was worthless, many children became ashamed of who and what they were. Homesickness afflicted many. Some children tried to run away. They could not imagine how far they were from home. Others died from illness and loneliness and disease. The small cemetery at the site of the former Carlisle Indian School still contains the graves of nearly 100 children who died before they could become cooks and laundresses and carpenters and tinsmiths. Children died at all the boarding schools. At the Haskell Institute in Kansas, fifteen children died in 1888 alone, a year in which fewer than 100 students had been enrolled. That many deaths among such a small number of students must have been devastating. Among the dead was an Arapaho, a Cheyenne, a Kaw, an Osage, three Pawnees, a Ponca, a Quapaw, both of the Seminoles enrolled at the school, a Sioux, a Winnebago, and a Wyandot. Two Caddo boys, Willie Gibson and John Guy, both aged eleven, died at Haskell that year as well.

Many of the graduates returned to their communities with outdated skills—the need for wheelwrights declined as rubber-tired cars took to the roadways—but many learned to read and write well. The school did not entirely eradicate native culture, and as time went on, fewer of the Carlisle students came from "savage" tribes. Pratt was, in the end, a propagandist and a self-promoter. He wanted his supporters to appreciate how he transformed savage Indians into civilized students, and his staff produced loads of "before and after" photographs seemingly documenting the children's transformation. In reality, the majority of the young Indians who enrolled at the school came from communities where English was spoken and where many of them had acquired at least some familiarity with the norms and values held by their non-Indian neighbors. Several dozen Caddo, Potawatomi, and California "Mission" Indians attended Carlisle during the years it was open. Over 350 Pueblos attended. So did large numbers of "Iroquois" from New York, including more than 600 Senecas, along with over 500 Christian Oneidas from Wisconsin and hundreds of Cherokees. The largest number of students came from these three groups. These students had extensive exposure to non-Indian culture.

By the time Pratt retired in 1904, federal support for off-reservation boarding schools like Carlisle had begun to dry up. Teddy Roosevelt's Commissioner of Indian Affairs, Francis Leupp, believed that off-reservation boarding schools did more harm than good. "It is a great mistake to try," he wrote in 1905, "to start the little ones on the path to civilization by snapping all the ties of affection between them and their parents, and teaching them to despise the aged and nonprogressive members of their families." Leupp believed that native peoples must change, and that they had the potential to do so. "Our proper work with him," however, "is improvement, not transformation."

There were alternatives to schools like Pratt's. Day schools operated on reservations. Boarding schools were built on reservations, too, or nearby throughout the western states. Native peoples did not approve of the heavy-handed education methods employed in the schools, or an education that equipped children in many cases to do little more than carry out manual labor. At the same time, however, Indians on reservations recognized the value of instruction in reading, writing, and speaking English, in math, and in other academic fields for conducting themselves in the American republic. Vocational training had value to some native peoples whose traditional means of subsistence had been eradicated.

Living Under the New Regime

Schools, missions, and allotment in severalty: federal government support for all three threatened the integrity of native communities. Native peoples, living within a tightening circle, found themselves subject to forces committed to changing the way that they lived.

The Pueblos of the southwest, for instance, had largely been ignored by federal policy-makers who had their hands full with more militant southwestern tribes like the Apaches. The Pueblos began to rely increasingly on herding and farming rather than hunting and gathering for their subsistence. Viewed by white Americans as a peaceful people, settlers apparently felt they could encroach on the lands of the Pueblos along the Rio Grande and at Hopi and Zuni with impunity. In the 1848 Treaty of Guadalupe Hidalgo, which ended the Mexican War, the

Figure 8.2 Acoma Pueblos at the Carlisle Indian Industrial School, 1879. Courtesy of National Anthropological Archives.

United States pledged to recognize the lands guaranteed to the Pueblos by the Mexican government. Whether the Pueblos had the right to sell these lands, however, and citizens of American New Mexico the right to purchase them, was not clearly settled.

Resolution required the intervention of the American court system. In 1869, the federal government filed suit to eject squatters from lands claimed by Cochiti Pueblo. The government sought in this case to protect native lands. The Supreme Court of New Mexico had to determine if the Pueblos came under the protection of the federal Trade and Intercourse Acts, and whether the federal government's intervention was warranted. Certainly the Pueblos suffered from the problems that came when native peoples and newcomers came into contact. In 1862 Kit Carson observed Taos Pueblos in "a daily state of intoxication" owing to the liquor trade. John Watts, a delegate from New Mexico suggested to Congress that he would consider banning the liquor trade in the territory. If alcohol poisoning, however, was "an easy and pleasant way to die," he wondered why Congress should not permit "the poor Indian, for whom our sympathies run out in uninterrupted stream, to enjoy the privilege of dying in that glorious manner?" According to the record, laughter followed Watts' joke, genocide humor on Capitol Hill.

In the case of *United States v. Lucero* (1869), the New Mexico Supreme Court asserted that the Pueblos bore little resemblance to "wild Indians." The Trade and Intercourse Acts, the court believed, Congress intended for savage Indians, and not for people like the Pueblos, who had lived "for three centuries in fenced abodes … cultivating the soil for the maintenance of themselves and families, and giving an example of virtue, honesty, and industry to their civilized neighbors." Because the Pueblos did not conform to the Court's image of what Indians looked and lived like, the theft of their lands fell beyond the power of the federal government to remedy.

The encroachments, as a result, continued. The United States Supreme Court in 1876 upheld the logic of the *Lucero* decision in the case of *U.S. v. Joseph*. Again, a court emphasized the supposed differences between savage Indians and the Pueblos. The Trade and Intercourse Acts, the Court held, applied to the "nomadic Apaches, Comanches, Navajos, and other tribes whose incapacity for self-government required both for themselves and for the citizens of the country this guardian care of the general government." The Pueblos, on the other hand, "had nothing in common with this class." After all, "the degree of civilization which they had attained centuries before, their willing submission to the laws of the Mexican government ... and their adoption into the general mass of the population (except that they held their own lands in common), all forbid the idea that they should be classed with the Indian tribes for whom the intercourse acts were made."

The courts in effect left the Pueblos at the mercy of an encroaching American population. And while the justice system left them defenseless against encroachments upon their lands, they faced these land-hungry settlers in the midst of outbreaks of epidemic disease that took a heavy toll. Between 1889 and 1890, according to one account, 719 Pueblos died, and "all but 8 of these were from smallpox and diphtheria, and all but 86 were of children 5 years of age or less." In one year, then, more than half the children aged five and younger had died. It is difficult to imagine the sorts of trauma this loss of life produced, and the Bureau of Indian Affairs agents who intruded into Pueblo life seemed more interested in outlawing religious practices they saw as offensive and savage than they did in recording the consequences of violent outbreaks of disease. Daniel Dorchester, a Protestant clergyman, described the Pueblos he visited as "dwarfed mentally," living a life of "dark paganism." Dorchester believed that "the Pueblo is no match, in acuteness and breadth of intellect, with the Navajo, the Apache, the Comanche, the Cheyenne, the Nez Perce, or the Sioux." Agents thus compelled Pueblo children to attend day schools to receive a civilized education, and shipped others to boarding schools. Mining operations in the Rio Grande led to erosion and flooding, and a number of non-Pueblo ranching and herding enterprises encroached steadily on their lands. By 1900, virtually half the productive lands worked by the Pueblos had been lost and water supplies had been reduced significantly owing to the diversion of Rio Grande waters farther upstream. The federal government did not help: it appropriated lands to create national forests, including the sacred Blue Lake at Taos. Meanwhile, the Pueblos suffered through the last major smallpox epidemic to afflict native peoples in 1898 and 1899.

The reports written by federal agents played a role in the important Supreme Court case of *U.S. v. Sandoval (1913)*. The defendant, Felipe Sandoval, came under federal prosecution for selling alcohol to the Pueblos. In defense, he asserted that he could not be found guilty because the Pueblos, based on the logic of the earlier cases, were not real Indians. The Supreme Court this time disagreed. The Pueblos were indeed native peoples, and they ought to have been subject to the protection of the federal trade and intercourse laws since 1848, when the lands they lived upon entered the American union. As a consequence, they could not sell or otherwise alienate their lands without federal approval.

The case had enormous consequences. Certainly it validated and invited a large federal presence in Pueblo life. If the Pueblos, like other native peoples, remained wards of the federal government, the Bureau of Indian Affairs would attempt to subject them to missionization, education, and allotment. The *Sandoval* decision also called into question the title to lands held by thousands of non-Indians in New Mexico. In the wake of the decision, the Pueblos would confront once again a renewed assault on their right to exist. Indeed, officials in the Interior Department, the Bureau of Indian Affairs, and Congress attacked Pueblo landholding and culture beginning in the early 1920s.

At the urging of missionary groups, the Board of Indian Commissioners, and the Indian Rights Association, the Interior Department in 1920 appointed a special inspector to gather evidence in the form of affidavits and written statements about the "immorality" of Pueblo dancing. In the 200-page "Secret Dance File," reformers and government agents, who once worried about war-like dances on the Plains, now lamented that Pueblo dancers imitated "animals in the act of sexual intercourse" and engaged in other behaviors that many white reformers viewed as licentious and savage. They wasted a lot of time, too, reformers worried. In response to this shocking behavior, Indian Commissioner Charles Burke in April of 1921 issued Circular 1665, an order banning the Sun Dance and "so-called religious ceremonies" that involved "acts of self-torture, immoral relations between the sexes, the sacrificial destruction of clothing or other useful articles, the reckless giving away of property, the use of injurious drugs or intoxicants, and frequent or prolonged periods of celebration which bring the Indians together from remote points to the neglect of their crops, livestock, and home interest." In a supplement issued in 1923, Burke expressed his hope that the Pueblos and other Indians voluntarily would abandon "these useless and harmful performances" and that if they did not, he would consider "some other course" of action to enforce federal policy.

Not all federal officials in Indian country worried about dancing as much as Burke, but given the disaster at Wounded Knee thirty years before, Pueblos might easily have seen in Burke's order the threat of violent persecution. But they did not quietly acquiesce in this assault on their core spiritual values. Gathered in the All-Pueblo Council, delegates from fifteen pueblos drew up a statement emphasizing their rights as native peoples. The delegates asserted that their ancestors had lived "in a civilized condition" centuries before the first "white man came to America." The All-Pueblo Council called upon non-Indian Americans to join them in a movement to preserve "our lands, our customs," and "our traditions." Many white reformers, writers, and artists, led by Mabel Dodge Lujan and John Collier, who recently had discovered in the Pueblos a "Red Atlantis" that offered a solution to many of the ills that plagued post-World War I America, did rally around the All-Pueblo Council to challenge the federal attempts to suppress Pueblo religious freedom.

Not all Pueblos supported dancing in opposition to the Bureau. The General Council of Progressive Christian Indians, formed in 1924 at Santa Ana Pueblo, expressed their opposition to "pagan customs" that "retarded their economic and social progress. Others criticized white reformers who, they thought, wanted to keep native peoples as museum pieces, locked in time. "What kind of friendship is it," one wrote to Collier, "that would tamper with a race of immortal souls seeking a knowledge of the God who created them, in order to preserve this race as a curious show-case thing for the amusement of a more favored race?" They had no objection to bans on certain dances, and these objections to the reformers' efforts showed that definitions of what constituted Indian identity were becoming increasingly contested.

The Pueblos and the allied white reformers saw assaults on their dancing and attempts to appropriate Pueblo land as part of a coordinated program to dispossess native peoples and eradicate their culture. In 1922, Senator Holm Bursum of New Mexico introduced legislation that promised to resolve the crisis in land titles created by the *Sandoval* decision nine years before. Heavily biased against the Pueblos, the Bursum Bill constructed procedures to grant legitimate title to non-Indians who could demonstrate their continuous occupation of Pueblo land. Recognizing squatter's rights, the bill would have resulted in the loss of 60,000 acres of Pueblo land, as well as control of the water that flowed through these lands.

Led initially by Stella Atwood, a Californian who headed the General Federation of Women's Clubs, reformers began to mobilize against what they saw as a patently prejudicial piece of legislation. Artists and writers living in Taos brought further attention to the Pueblos' attempts to preserve their lands, publishing their "Protest of Artists and Writers against the Bursum Bill." Other reform groups formed in opposition to the Bursum Bill, including the important American Indian Defense Association headed by a reformer named John Collier.

These reformers brought much attention to the Pueblos, but throughout the All Pueblo Council actively fought for Pueblo rights. They saw the Bursum Bill as more than a threat to their lands. Like the bans against dancing, the Bursum Bill threatened Pueblo culture and control over their communities. New Mexico state courts, traditionally responsive to the interests of the state's citizens, received under the Bursum Bill jurisdiction over the "internal affairs and government" of the Pueblos.

And herein may lie part of the significance of the movement to ban dancing. In the nineteenth century, reformers uniformly believed that Christianity was necessary for the wellbeing of native peoples, and that "pagan" practices where possible ought to be suppressed. By the 1920s, that consensus no longer existed. Cultural modernists, men and women who wanted to replace religious with secular authority in American life, increasingly became active in Indian affairs. They were skeptical of assimilation as a policy goal because they could see that it had produced little actual good. They saw much of American Indian policy as directed by the government toward the acquisition of native peoples' land.

The opposition of these reformers succeeded in raising enough questions that the Bursum Bill lost support. In June of 1924, Congress passed instead the Pueblo Lands Act that allowed non-Indians title to Pueblo lands only if they had paid taxes on the lands since 1889. Those Pueblos who lost lands, under the legislation, were entitled to compensation. But even in victory the Pueblos achieved less than they had hoped. The appointees to the Pueblo Lands Board routinely ruled in favor of the settlers, and the federal courts in the state defined the paying of taxes so broadly as to accommodate all but the most irresponsible settler. Attempts to appeal the decision of the Land Board failed to produce results. Still, if the All-Pueblo Council and its non-Indian supporters could not claim victory in their attempts to reclaim lands taken by squatters over many decades, they had shown that native peoples could find support among sympathetic non-Indians and mobilize support to defend their interests. Those who sought to eliminate native cultures and proscribe those religious practices they deemed offensive, irreligious, immoral, and savage, and those who sought to claim the lands and resources of native peoples, could be placed on the defensive by native peoples determined to force the federal government to honor its responsibilities.

The New Life in the Indian Territory

Like the Pueblos, the Cherokees faced challenges to their existence during the era of allotment. Outside forces clamored for their lands, while cultural and demographic changes forced the members of the nation to consider closely what it meant to be Cherokee.

Some of their children attended the Chilocco Boarding School, founded in 1884 and located in northeastern Oklahoma. Others attended the boys and girls seminaries founded and funded by the Cherokee Nation. In these schools, white educators hired by the Nation provided young Cherokees with the skills they needed to compete in American society. Girls learned to become the teachers of Cherokee children; boys, it was hoped, would pursue college after graduating, and return to the nation as leaders in tribal government and business. Certainly some of the graduates enjoyed considerable success, but it is difficult to generalize too much about the children who enrolled in the school. Some students retained more of their traditional culture than others; some students were "full-bloods," while others had blonde hair and blue eyes and came from Christian, English-speaking families. Some were very poor and illiterate in both Cherokee and English, while others came from wealthy, educated, and "mixed-blood" families. In the early twentieth century, the state of Oklahoma took over the administration of the Cherokee schools.

The Cherokees wanted to control the formal education of their children. They also tried to hold back the numerous outsiders who wanted to open their lands to development and exploitation. The Cherokees granted rights of way for railroad companies in the 1866 treaty the government had compelled them to sign after the Civil War. Some Cherokees, without question, welcomed white business interests, and saw through the use of federal and corporate power a means to acquire political advantages within the nation. Support for the railroads, however, quickly dissipated and as early as the 1870s many Cherokees saw the railroad as a mortal enemy.

Large numbers of white intruders entered the Cherokee Nation. A small number, recruited and hired by wealthy Cherokees, came as contract workers, but many more followed the railroad. Construction crews did great damage as they laid the tracks through the nation. They cut timber without paying compensation, and killed Cherokee livestock. In addition to the surveyors, engineers, managers, and work crews were the hordes of others who saw opportunity in the Cherokee Nation. They sold alcohol to work crews and to Indians, and they frequently fought with their native neighbors. Some illegally appropriated Cherokee land, fenced these tracts, and erected the buildings that they hoped might give them some sort of squatter's rights to the land. As Principal Chief S.H. Mayes wrote to President Grover Cleveland in 1895, white intruders entered the nation to "settle down and make farms on the fairest portion of our public domain." Thousands of acres, Mayes continued, "which of right should be in the possession of the poor and homeless of our people, are occupied by these people."

The Nation had tried to control railroad development. Its leaders worried about the influx of white people. The presence of American citizens in Cherokee territory had, after all, justified their removal fifty years before. Nation leaders wanted to control town site development along the railroad lines. Railroad interests challenged the Cherokees on these points. They depicted the Cherokee Nation as lawless and chaotic. Spokesmen for the Missouri–Kansas–Texas Railroad described the Cherokees as "a degraded, shabby, do nothing set, filthy to nausea." Their depraved condition, and the supposed lawlessness of their territory, led to calls to end tribal government, and to bring the Indian Territory under more direct federal control. Western interests sought government assistance to secure control of Cherokee lands.

Railroad lobbyists asserted that the Cherokees' "mixed-blood' leadership skimmed tribal annuities and lived off the fat of the nation while their benighted "full-blood" followers toiled below in poverty and ignorance, unaware entirely of the advantages assimilation into the mainstream of American society would bring them. Arguments of this sort were nothing new. Those who sought access to Indian lands long had argued that assimilation and civilization would benefit native peoples. Taking from Indians always could be justified in the name of giving them assimilation and entry to the broader American society. These corporate spokesmen and their congressional supporters found it convenient, in this context, not to refer to the Cherokees as one of the well-known "Five Civilized Tribes." Cherokee leaders spoke English, to be sure, and many belonged to Christian congregations, had received quality educations, and desired to play a role in public affairs. Even those at the bottom of the Cherokee social structure, who still spoke their native language, practiced customs that predated the arrival of Europeans, and preserved as much as possible traditional gender roles and family structures, farmed a few acres and raised a small amount of livestock, similar in many ways to their non-Indian neighbors. Cherokees could change without becoming any less Cherokee.

The lobbyists ignored this. Through their efforts, Congress debated and voted on a number of "Territorial" or "Oklahoma" bills designed to place the Indian Territory on a plane equal to that of other territories administered by the federal government. Territorialization, as a process, would have required the abolition of tribal governments and, supporters hoped, the opening up of additional land to white development. The Cherokees knew that they could not close off the white world. They knew as well, that they could not rely upon their treaties for support. The Supreme Court, after all, in the "Cherokee Tobacco" case of 1870, had held that "a treaty may supersede a prior act of Congress, and an act of Congress may supersede a prior treaty." Congress thus possessed the power unilaterally to alter that Nation's relationship with the federal government.

The Cherokees thus adopted the same pressure politics that their opponents employed to defeat proposed legislation that they saw as a fundamental threat to the continuance of the Nation. Cherokee delegations to the nation's capital denounced the territorial bills as acts of violence against native peoples, as acts designed to benefit frontiersmen at the expense of an Indian nation that had done everything the United States had asked of it. The Cherokees succeeded into the 1880s in defeating this legislation, but after the end of the Indian wars, the pressures on their lands grew too great.

In April of 1889, Congress opened the so-called "Unassigned Lands" in the Indian Territory to white settlement. These lands, acquired by the government from the Creeks and Seminoles after the Civil War, had not been assigned to other tribes. Squatters already occupied much of this land. With the passage of congressional legislation opening the unassigned lands, 50,000 additional settlers flooded into the region. The next year Congress created the Oklahoma Territory.

With the large numbers of settlers pouring into the lands surrounding the Cherokees and their neighbors, pressure on the federal government to allot the Cherokee Nation's land increased. President Benjamin Harrison appointed the Jerome Commission, headed by David Jerome, to negotiate allotment agreements with the Indian tribes in Oklahoma. In December of 1891, the Cherokees sold the "Cherokee Outlet," a tract of more than 6 million acres that extended their reservation on a narrow line to the west, but the Nation had little interest in allotment.

Two years later, President Cleveland appointed Henry Dawes, now retired from the Senate, to head a commission to negotiate agreements for allotting the lands held by the Cherokees, Creeks, Choctaws, Chickasaws, and Seminoles. Representatives of all five tribes opposed the "Dawes Commission," but none as forcefully as the Cherokees, who argued that allotment would lead to the dispossession and impoverishment, rather than the improvement and civilization, of the Nation. Dawes himself pushed back. He argued that a mixed-blood Cherokee elite dominated the nation, enriching itself as it impoverished tribal "full-bloods." Violent crime, he asserted, occurred frequently in the Indian Territory, while the enormous natural resources of the Cherokee homeland went untapped. Allotting the land belonging to the Five Civilized Tribes, Dawes argued, promised to benefit the Indians themselves, the surrounding white population, and the nation as a whole.

The Cherokees resisted the Dawes Commission, but its leaders clearly recognized the determination of Congress to allot their lands in severalty. The Curtis Act, passed by Congress in the summer of 1898, did by statute what the Dawes Commission had failed to achieve through negotiation. The act opened up Cherokee lands for development, extended the provisions of the Dawes Act to the Indian Territory (the Five Civilized Tribes and the Iroquois of New York had been exempted from the 1887 law), and declared that the "laws of the various tribes or nations of Indians shall not be enforced at law or in equity by the courts of the United States in the Indian Territory." The Curtis Act, as well as a supplemental agreement negotiated by the Cherokees with the Interior Department in 1902, eviscerated Cherokee tribal sovereignty and the control over its lands that the Nation had struggled to preserve for over half a century. Before allotment, the Cherokees had approximately 7 million acres of land in northeast Oklahoma. By 1920, 90% of this land was gone.

In a sense, the Cherokee Nation confronted during these years questions and challenges that other Americans faced. The growing power of corporations in American life, the future for predominantly rural communities in an urbanizing America, all provoked passionate debate and discussion. Immigrants from southern and eastern Europe who arrived in large numbers at the end of the nineteenth- and the beginning of the twentieth century raised questions in the United States about what it meant to be American. Cherokees, similarly, confronted the challenge of defining just what it meant to be a Cherokee.

When Cherokee spokesmen wrote about American Indian policy, they occasionally made reference to an "Indian race." There were characteristics—cultural, legal, spiritual, and historical—they suggested, that all native peoples shared and that distinguished them from other Americans. But defining who was Cherokee—who belonged to the Nation and who did not—proved complicated. First, there were the questions raised by intermarriage. Many more Cherokee women than men took white spouses. The presence of so many white males in the Nation challenged fundamental beliefs that many Cherokees long had held. White fathers, married into a matrilineal society, wanted their children to enjoy citizenship rights in the Cherokee Nation. They called upon the federal government to pressure the Cherokees to allow for the patrilineal descent of property. Intermarriage produced a growing number of "mixed-race" individuals who carried into the Nation assumptions about gender and the social order very different from those held by traditional Cherokees.

Meanwhile, the children of black fathers and Cherokee mothers were not citizens. Under the Cherokees' 1866 reconstruction treaty, the Freedmen received guarantees of citizenship if they returned to the nation by the end of January in 1867. Some returned by the deadline, but others arrived later. Of the 2500 freedmen living in the Cherokee Nation, less than half had received recognition of their rights as citizens. Some Cherokee leaders wanted to admit all the latecomers to citizenship. Most Cherokees, however, seem to have opposed this, hostile toward people of African descent and unwilling to accept the slight diminution inclusion of all the freedmen would produce in the amount of their annuity payments. The Cherokees clearly found their former slaves (and their descendants) unworthy of the rights of citizens, and the tribal government did all it could to deny them equal rights. The Cherokees' experience shows that native nations could engage in the same sorts of discriminatory racism most often associated with the Jim Crow South. African Americans remained at the bottom of the racial hierarchy Cherokees constructed in the decades after the Civil War. The racial thinking of the Cherokees, indeed, was incorporated within the Oklahoma's first constitution when it entered the union in 1907. Words such as "colored" or "negro," the Constitution read, "shall be construed to mean or apply to all persons of African descent. The term 'white race' shall include all other persons," including the state's large Native American population. By this point, the Cherokees were declared to be citizens of the State of Oklahoma, not their nations. They were Americans now.

Some Cherokees resisted this change. Led by Redbird Smith, members of the Keetowah band of Cherokees opposed allotment and called for the creation of a separate Indian state rooted in traditional Cherokee culture. Other communities in the former Indian Territory had called for the erection of an Indian state upon the lands of the Five Civilized Tribes. Smith failed to stop allotment, and the United States government never took seriously calls for Indian statehood, but the movement nonetheless shows that Indians had neither abandoned their identity as native peoples, nor accepted whole-heartedly the policies imposed upon them by the United States.

At the other end of the Indian Territory, the Kiowas attempted to reconcile themselves at last to the reservation. They lived lives, according to James Mooney, of "patient resignation." They faced considerable hardship. Smallpox and measles hit them in 1877, and whooping cough brought death in 1882. Smallpox returned in 1900, and "many Indians died, hundreds and hundreds of them." The bison had disappeared, returned back into the mountains. Hunger was commonplace. Some Kiowas lived in houses built by the agency staff; others tried to make a go of it as farmers.

Like native peoples elsewhere, the Kiowas confronted teachers who wanted their children, missionaries who sought their souls, and settlers who clamored after their lands. In 1892 the Jerome Commission negotiated an agreement for the allotment of Kiowa lands and the sale of the surplus. Most Kiowas opposed the agreement, pointing out what they believed to be forged signatures and other irregularities in the approval process. Congress did not care. In 1900 it approved the plan. A Kiowa delegation, led by Lone Wolf, traveled to Washington to attempt to prevent the implementation of the Jerome Commission agreement. Lone Wolf asserted that the 1867 Medicine Lodge Creek Treaty, which stated that no cession of any part of the reservation "shall be of any validity or force ... unless executed and signed by at least three-fourths of all the adult male Indians" prevented allotment without the Kiowas' assent. Congress, again, did not care. Lone Wolf sued.

These were dark days in the history of Indian tribal sovereignty. With the Major Crimes Act of 1885, Congress declared that federal authorities now had the power to try cases of murder, manslaughter, rape, assault, burglary, and larceny committed on reservations. The Supreme Court, in the 1886 case of *U.S. v Kagama*, affirmed the constitutionality of the law, on the grounds that native peoples remained "wards of the nation," and "communities dependent on the United States." The weakness of native communities, the Court suggested, justified attempts to limit the power of tribal government over an important area of its jurisdiction. The decision in *Lone Wolf v. Hitchcock*, handed down by the Supreme Court in 1903, intensified the assault on native sovereignty. The existence of treaties, by their very nature agreements between sovereigns, was seen by native peoples as a recognition on the part of the United States of the tribes' rights to self-government and the management of their affairs. Not so, said the Court. Congress had *plenary*, or absolute, power over Indian affairs. It could, if it desired, unilaterally abandon a treaty. "The power exists to abrogate the provisions of an Indian treaty," the Court held, "though presumably such power will be exercised only when circumstances arise which will not only justify the government in disregarding the stipulations of the treaty, but may demand, in the interest of the country and the Indians themselves, that it should do so." This strained reading of the Constitution and the place of native peoples in it—legal scholars have denounced what one called "the extra-constitutional plenary power doctrine"—had enormous consequences. The Kiowas lost their lands through an allotment program that they clearly had opposed. By 1906, three years after the *Lone Wolf* decision, only 17% of the original reservation remained.

While the Kiowas fought a losing battle against those who sought to acquire their lands, they also confronted federal officials who wanted to educate their children. The Rainy Mountain Boarding School opened on the Kiowa-Comanche-Apache (KCA) Reservation in the fall of 1893. Like other Indian schools, the staff at Rainy Mountain hoped to transform Kiowa children by teaching them those values that reformers associated with the white middle class: individuality, a respect for discipline and order, and a willingness to engage in hard work. The staff at Rainy Mountain associated the acceptance of these values with one's appearance, so the children, like those who attended other boarding schools, received haircuts and wore military uniforms. Many received new names, often translated from English or anglicized and combined with new American-sounding first names.

Boys and girls attended Rainy Mountain but their caretakers separated them by age and sex. Children faced harsh discipline for violating school rules. Speaking Kiowa, something the administrators never succeeded in eradicating entirely, frequently brought punishment. Running away brought punishment, too. The teachers forced one runaway, upon his return to Rainy Mountain, to eat rotten food and then, after he became ill, to eat his own vomit. Life in the school appears to have been harsh. Illness at times coursed through the school. In 1916, for instance, trachoma afflicted all but five of the students at Rainy Mountain.

Yet despite the harsh discipline and the assault on Kiowa culture that enrollment carried with it, Kiowa parents sent their children to the school. Indeed, Kiowa parents complained about a lack of educational opportunities for their children, not that their children had to attend school. Kiowa parents recognized that their children needed to learn English, that literacy provided them with a vital tool for surviving in the modern world. The crafts Kiowa children learned in the shops and classrooms at Rainy Mountain offered them a chance at a livelihood in a world framed by dispossession, isolation, and the destruction of traditional economies. The transformation of the children's appearance and the prescription that they must wear uniforms and mold their lives to martial discipline could not destroy Kiowa culture. It was tougher than that. Many children emerged from Rainy Mountain bilingual, literate, and with a craft that helped them make their way in American society.

Surveyors and speculators, teachers and agents and school administrators: the Kiowas faced them all. They faced as well an assortment of Christian missionaries who tried to persuade them to walk the "Jesus Road." These missionaries denounced Kiowa cultural practices that they thought of as savage, and in places federal officials helped by banning certain dances. The Kiowas began to listen to the missionaries, despite the disdain in the preacher's tone. Some denominations, like the Baptists and Methodists, trained Kiowas as ministers and preachers, providing certain men both with a means of salvation and a rare opportunity to assume leadership roles in their communities. Missions, moreover, often had been constructed near sites where Kiowas traditionally had camped and gathered; after allotment and the dispersal of the population across the KCA Reservation, churches provided a vital meeting place for Kiowas seeking to preserve a sense of community.

J.J. Methvin established a church at Anadarko with the support of the Board of Missions of the Methodist Episcopal Church South in 1887. He opened a school three years later attended by thirty-four Kiowa, Caddo, and Wichita students. By 1897, the Methodists operated six missions on the reservation, four of these with predominately Kiowa congregations. The Methodists were not alone. In 1891 Father Isidore Ricklin opened a Catholic church in Anadarko for the Kiowas, and in November of the next year, a school attended by thirty-five students and staffed by teachers from the Sisters of St. Francis. Within a year, St. Patrick's became the largest mission school on the reservation, with 106 students. Efficient and clean and well run, few of the children in attendance suffered from the illnesses that children at other schools experienced. A flood of Catholic homesteaders forced Ricklin to divide his time between his white and his Kiowa parishioners, and the influence of the Catholics remained tiny outside of Anadarko. Still, the Kiowas respected Ricklin, and at his death in 1921 every business in Anadarko closed down for the day.

Baptists also operated missions in the Kiowa country. G.W. Hicks, a Cherokee from North Carolina, opened a mission in 1893, where he converted Lone Wolf to Christianity. Isabel Crawford, a Canadian, also arrived that year, and opened a chapel and a day school at Saddle Mountain. Deaf and of fragile health, Crawford worked diligently with her followers, and allowed the deacons she appointed to give communion. Though her willingness to allow Kiowas to play a leadership role in her church caused her to run afoul of some of her coreligionists, she became a revered and respected figure among the Kiowas.

We might dismiss missions and missionary activity as part of a quiet assault on native culture, but that is too simple an explanation. Though many Christian Kiowas spoke out against dancing and against the practices that white missionaries denounced, acceptance of Christianity did not require Kiowas to abandon all aspects of their culture. Still, there was significant resistance to Christianity and Christian missions. The revival of the Kiowa Ghost Dance in 1894 offered a challenge to missionaries and converts who believed that Christianity offered an antidote to the problems that plagued them in the final decades of the nineteenth century.

The death of nearly 400 Kiowa infants between 1890 and 1892 may have provided the spark that reignited the Ghost Dance. When James Mooney arrived at the KCA Reservation in the summer of 1892, he observed that nearly every Kiowa woman had her hair cut short, her face and arms slashed by knives. These were the physical symbols of mourning. Winter counts for that year show a human figure with red spots on his face. Measles struck them hard. The wagons, houses, and other property of the deceased the Kiowas burned; their dogs and horses the Kiowas shot. 221 Indians on the KCA died during the 1892 epidemic. A winter count for the preceding year, 1891, recorded the deaths of three boys who fled from the Rainy Mountain Boarding School after one of them had been whipped. They froze to death in a blizzard. These were tough years indeed, as grieving parents hoped to see once again lost children, innocents slaughtered by measles, whooping cough, and pneumonia. Missionaries denounced the Ghost Dance as an attempt to keep alive old traditions and old beliefs, but the most astute recognized the grief that lay at the broken heart of the movement.

The Ghost Dance drew on elements from a number of religious traditions. Ghost Dancers sought spiritual power, a concern that informed the actions of native seekers long before Europeans arrived, but they also spoke of "the man with long hair" who lived in the clouds, of going to Heaven, and of a day of judgment followed by a time when "the world will shake."

Federal officials maintained bans against the Sun Dance on the KCA reservation, but they did not prevent Kiowas from participating in the Ghost Dance. The Ghost Dance was, after all, non-violent, and avoided what agents and missionaries saw as the needless self-mutilation and torture of the Sun Dance. Only during the administration of Bureau of Indian Affairs

Commissioner Cato Sells did pressure mount on the Kiowas to discontinue the Ghost Dance. Afraid of Bears, the leader of the Kiowa Ghost dancers, appealed the government's action by emphasizing those elements of the ceremony that resembled Christianity. "We hold our meetings on Sundays all the year around," Afraid of Bears wrote, "and I pray on Sundays and on the Fourth of July and the twenty-fifth of December we dance outside of the tabernacle; and the dance I have danced, I called it a religious dance, but the missionaries called it a Ghost Dance." Reservation superintendent C.V. Stinchecum, however, would not be dissuaded. Compiling a long list of Ghost Dancers, Stinchecum declared that any Kiowa found guilty of unauthorized dancing would forfeit their annuity payment and their rations. The Kiowas continued to dance. They held patriotic "Fourth of July" dances. They held "injurious dances," one Agency official complained, "under the guise of Red Cross Meetings." They danced to celebrate Armistice Day, and to honor their returning warriors. Kiowas continued to sing Ghost Dance songs at powwows. Local merchants, eager to draw in tourists, encouraged Kiowa dancing at county fairs. Noting that the Kiowas charged admission to these dances, Stinchecum observed with some frustration that the performance "was quite liberally patronized by both Indians and whites, as has been the case for a number of years." The Kiowas had been changed as a result of the reservation experience, and they actively sought to improve the quality of their lives. Though the context had changed, they still danced and there is no doubt that they managed to preserve against long odds key components of their traditional culture.

Meanwhile, in 1876, one observer noted that the Caddos were "a quiet inoffensive people, most of whom have adopted the habits of civilized life." They were, according to those who watched them, "much interested in the school at the agency." Two years later, however, the Caddos moved to the northern borders of the reservation, hoping to avoid their Kiowa and Comanche neighbors. At first this movement caused federal officials to fear that the Caddos might return to their "savage" ways, but the agents had their hands full with the Kiowas and Comanches. On their remote corner of the reservation, the Caddos farmed, cultivated orchards, and raised cattle, hogs, and chickens. This, along with the limited rations they received, meant that the Caddos met most of their needs and made the adjustment to life on the reservation.

Still, the Caddos faced the same forces that transformed native peoples who settled on other reservations. The Caddos opposed the General Allotment Act. They opposed the efforts of the Jerome Commission, with whom they met in May of 1891. Despite their protests, the Jerome Commission extracted an agreement by June providing for the allotment of the Caddos' land. The Caddos had little choice, Jerome told them, for "one way or the other, either as we propose or under the law," allotment was coming.

Congress approved the agreement in 1895, but the Caddos continued to protest. Thomas Wister, a Caddo spokesman who traveled to Washington in 1899, asked the Commissioner of Indian Affairs "to protect us in the possession of our homes, so that we may keep our land for our wives and children." Wister was adamant. "We cannot be white men," he said, and he hoped that the Commissioner would "take pity" on the Caddos and "let us follow the Indian road" so "we can support ourselves and be happy." Wister and the Caddos knew that the size of the proposed allotments was too small to allow for stock raising, and they knew that allotment had led to the impoverishment of other native communities.

These arguments mattered not a bit to federal authorities. After a number of delays, President William McKinley, on Independence Day in 1901, opened the Caddos' surplus lands to white settlement. A total of 957 Caddo heads-of-household received their 160-acre allotments, amounting to a bit over 150,000 acres in all. White settlers overran the remaining

Figure 8.3 Thomas Wister, Caddo Leader, 1898. Courtesy of National Anthropological Archives.

586,468 acres of the reservation. The Caddos and their Wichita and Delaware neighbors received $1.25 per acre, far below the market value for the sale of their surplus lands.

Allotment resulted in the Caddos losing over 80% of their lands. But land loss was not the only cost of life on the reservation. Missionaries and educators worked to save Caddo children, as they had toiled to save others. Some of the children attended reservation day schools run by Christian missionaries, the first of which was opened by the Society of Friends. Nearly 100 Caddos attended the Chilocco Boarding School in Oklahoma, and an additional number attended the Haskell Institute in Kansas. Many Caddo leaders encouraged their children to attend the schools, and supported the efforts of the educators: they recognized the need for literacy in English if their people were to survive. Caddo children learned to read and write, and they learned crafts and skills intended to prepare them for a future as agriculturalists and husbandmen. They joined Christian congregations—Baptist, Presbyterian, and Catholic. But as they adopted a new life on the reservation, like the Kiowas, they did not completely abandon older ways of understanding the world.

Take, for example, the career of the Caddo leader named George Washington, born in Louisiana in 1816, who farmed, ranched, and lived comfortably in a two-story framed house. Washington lived well on the reservation, and adjusted to the demands of this new world. But he also served as a leader in the Caddos' peyote religion, and he may have seen the world through an ancient lens. Washington, for instance, according to one story went to his father's house and killed him with an axe when he learned that his father had attempted to bewitch him. He then split the old man open, and found that "he was all the colors of the rainbow inside." He tore out the heart, the lungs and the liver, and threw them in the grave with the rest of his father's body. "About four days

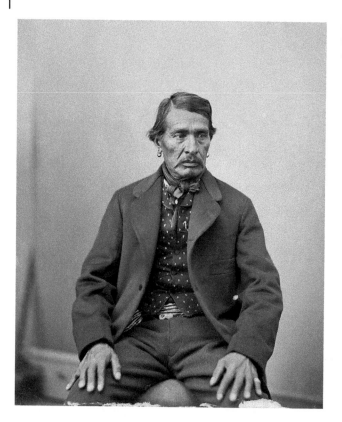

Figure 8.4 George Washington, Caddo Leader. Courtesy of National Anthropological Archives.

later," Washington reported, "they noticed mescal bean shoots coming up out of the grave" and "sometimes people would see a tiger standing in the grave." The witch was a man of great power.

George Washington died in 1883. The peyote religion did not die with him. John Wilson, also known as Nishkunto or Moon Head, taught his followers that peyote allowed its users to learn the difference between good and evil. As with the Ghost Dance, with which he also was involved, Wilson preached a message of peace and harmony. Like other adherents of the peyote religion, including the followers of the Comanche Quanah Parker (who preached a slightly different variant of peyotism) Wilson called upon Indians to avoid alcohol, to abstain from violence, to respect their families. He also lived in a log house, owned twenty horses, forty hogs and fifty head of cattle, and encouraged Caddo children to attend the Catholic mission school at St. Patrick's. The peyote religion was not a rejection of the new world, but a means to make it comprehensible, and to allow native peoples to adapt themselves to it, to make sense of it. Peyotism among the Caddos endured, well after Wilson's death in 1901 and despite opposition from reformers and government officials.

The Crows and the Life on the Northern Plains

Federal officials founded Crow Agency on the Bighorn River in 1883, and planned to resettle the Crows there the next year. One hundred and thirty families made the journey, escorted by federal troops. Others followed Plenty Coups to a location on Pryor Creek, sixty miles from

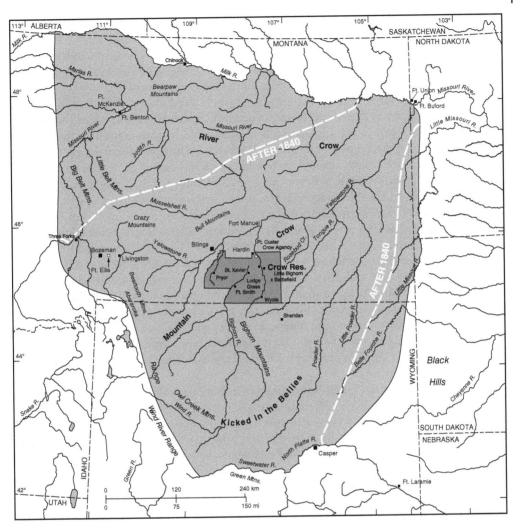

Map 8.1 The Crow Country. Source: *Smithsonian Handbook of North American Indians*, Vol. 13 (2), Plains, pp. 13: 696. Courtesy of Smithsonian Institution.

the new agency. Prior to their resettlement, the Crows faced little interference from outsiders. After 1884, they no longer had to worry about their Sioux enemies, but they did confront land-hungry settlers and ranchers, railroad men and reformers, intent upon appropriating their lands and changing their way of life. Agents banned the Sun Dance and prohibited Crows from leaving the reservation to hunt without a pass. Indian policemen, answerable to the agent, picked up violators and dragged them before the Court of Indian Offenses for trial and punishment that included fines, the withholding of rations, and forced labor. With the destruction of the bison, and the restrictions on their movement, they knew they would have to learn to live with the federal officials who distributed annuities and supplies at the agency.

It was not easy. Evidence from agency records suggests that the Crows suffered a significant decline in population as they adjusted to life on the reservation. In 1887, when agents undertook their first census, they found 2456 Crows living in 630 families. Seven years later, the population had fallen to 2126, and nine years later to 1941. Nearly one-third of the Crows listed on the 1887 census had died during the decade of the 1890s, and three Crows on average died each week on the reservation. Many of them were young, under twenty years old. The Crows lost much of a generation during their first decade at Crow Agency. Infectious diseases, and the changes in diet brought about by resettlement, largely account for the significant loss of life.

In addition to the farmers and ranchers, the Crows learned to live with missionaries and educators determined to save them from extinction by assimilating them into the broader American culture. The Montana Industrial School, founded by Unitarians near the meeting point of the Bighorn and Yellowstone rivers in 1886, was the first protestant establishment on the reservation. Jesuit priests opened their school and mission at St. Xavier in 1887 and another, the St. Charles Mission, at Pryor Creek, in 1893. Crow leaders recognized the importance of education, and saw the independent Catholic schools as an alternative to the disciplinarian education offered at a federal boarding school established at the Agency in 1885.

Some Crows accepted the new religions that agents and missionaries preached, but they did so on their own terms. They held dances on American holidays, and attempted to persuade federal officials that their gatherings were strictly social and did not represent a rejection of Christianity or American authority. Through these means, Crows kept alive expressions of their traditional culture. Though a small and short-lived uprising took place at Crow Agency in 1887 led by a young warrior named Sword Bearer, few Crows joined him, and they attempted to make the best of their lives on the reservation. They visited other native peoples on other reservations, recognizing that they and their old rivals faced similar problems and similar challenges in the new era. They attempted to preserve what they could of their culture in a restrictive environment.

The Crow woman Pretty-Shield, when asked years later about the transformation of Crow lives that the reservation produced, told her white interviewer that "I have never let myself hate the white man, because I knew that this would only make things worse for me, but he changed everything for us," and "did many bad deeds before we got used to him." White ranchers, she said, "shot down our horses on our own lands, because they wanted all the grass for themselves." White ranchers gunned down Crow horses, she recalled bitterly, as though they "were wolves that killed the white men's sheep." Pretty-Shield remembered a time when "white cowboys met a deaf and dumb Crow boy on the plains, and because he could not answer their questions, could not even hear what they said, they roped him and dragged him to his death." Pretty Shield's interviewer changed the subject; he wanted to focus on nostalgic stories of the bison, and not the anger of colonized peoples who frequently confronted the avarice and racism of their white neighbors.

Had he probed more deeply, he might have seen some of the deeper changes occurring at Crow. The creation of the reservation system eliminated many of the sources of tension that had existed between different communities on the northern Plains. Crows, and the residents of other reservations, visited one another, and emerged with a new appreciation of their Indianness, of their shared identity as native peoples who faced similar problems and confronted similar challenges. It was not always easy. With scarce resources on reservations, the Crows could not always accommodate outsiders from other reservations who wanted to work or live there. Crows wrestled with what it meant to be a member of the Crow Tribe, at the same time that they interacted with other native peoples who shared their experiences and their concerns.

And the greatest of these concerns remained encroachment upon their lands. These aggressive farmers and ranchers called for the allotment of the Crow Reservation, the sooner "the better for themselves, and for the nation, particularly for the citizens of Montana." At the beginning of the reservation period, the Crow reservation consisted of more than 3.4 million acres. By 1920, less than 2 million acres remained. Roughly 400,000 acres had been allotted to individual Crows, and white ranchers worked much of what remained under leases approved by the Commissioner of Indian Affairs. An expensive project to irrigate Crow lands brought employment to Crow men, but white ranchers benefited the most. They ended up with most of the irrigated acreage.

Federal officials tried to purchase the Crows' unallotted lands, but each effort generated a determined opposition. To counter these measures, the Crows developed new models of community leadership. Leaders chosen from geographic districts across the reservation represented what the Crows increasingly saw as a nation—their nation—in Washington. Their protests stalled and defeated legislation in 1905, 1910, 1915, and 1917. During the 1917 visit, Plenty Coups, on his seventh mission to the Capital, reminded his fellow delegates that "we are preparing to fight a different kind of fight." In their room at the National Hotel in Washington, the Crows burned buffalo chips (that they had taken from the Washington Zoo) and sweet grass, and told stories of their past martial glories. Now, they would go before congressmen and senators "to protect our women and children" from what the Indian Rights Association declared a legislative "raid" on Crow lands. The Crow delegates in 1917 selected Robert Yellowtail, a graduate of the Riverside Indian School in southern California, to speak for them before the Congress. The delegates succeeded in staving off another attack on the reservation, and the episode marked the emergence of educated young men, born after the buffalo had disappeared and after the Crows had been consigned to the reservation, to positions of preeminence in Crow politics.

Yellowtail and other Crow leaders understood that attempts to open their reservation to white settlement would continue, so in 1919 he led a delegation to Washington once again, this time to negotiate a compromise. Allotment would come, Yellowtail knew; the trick was to control the process, to make it serve the interests of the Crows as a nation as much as possible. The Crow Act of 1920 resulted, which distributed all the remaining reservation lands to members of the Nation. The Crows retained control of the mineral rights on these lands, and oversight of the process of allotting the land. Although the individual Crow allottees might lose their land, reservation lands as a whole would not be opened to white settlement. Indeed, no further wholesale openings of Crow land would occur after Congress approved the legislation. Yellowtail and his fellow leaders, chosen from the several districts of the Crow Reservation, had compromised in important ways with federal officials, who recognized that the Crows would continue to exist in Montana as an Indian nation. Indeed, before the Senate Indian Affairs Committee, Yellowtail announced that in his view "the Crow Indian Reservation is a separate semisovereign nation in itself, not belonging to any state, nor confined within the boundary lines of any State of the Union" and that "no Senator, or anybody else, so far as that is concerned, has any right to claim the right to tear us asunder by the continued introduction of bills here without our consent and simply because of our geographical proximity to his State or his home, or because his constituents prevail upon him so to act." The Crows would remain where they were. Their leadership spoke English, understood American law, and worked to protect their people's interests through the American political system. Some were Christian, but others preserved elements of traditional religion intact. Crow leaders drew upon cultural resources both new and old to protect their lands and their people from the outside forces who sought to dispossess them.

Native Peoples in the Eastern United States

In May of 1872 a small number of Mohegans sent a petition to the Connecticut state legislature. They asked that the lawmakers allot the Mohegans' remaining land, and terminate the guardianship the state had exercised over them. Other Mohegans, led by Anson Cooper and Emma Baker, argued that the petition did not represent the wishes of the community. The Mohegans were, they said, "satisfied with our condition and status," and they feared the consequences of losing the protection of their guardians. The Connecticut lawmakers ignored these protests, and enacted legislation the following July that effectively terminated and individualized the Mohegans, granting them citizenship in the state of Connecticut, annexing their lands to those of the neighboring town of Montville, and placing the Mohegans' school under the control of the Montville School district. The allotted lands became the legal property of the individual Mohegans who received them, and they would be liable to state taxation. The remaining Mohegan lands were sold with the proceeds divided among the members of the community.

This legislation was, in the eyes of many of Connecticut's white leaders, a move in favor of full civic equality for native peoples. If, in the wake of the American Civil War, Americans could include the 4 million former slaves in the reconstructed body politic, why not include native peoples as well? Why should Indians be treated as something less than full citizens, and why should they be denied the same rights, privileges, and responsibilities as their black and white neighbors? That many Mohegans preferred to preserve their separate status seemed beside the point.

Despite Connecticut's legislative termination of their existence, the Mohegans remained a distinct community in eastern Connecticut. Elders drawn from the leading Mohegan families—notably the Bakers and Fieldings—continued to play an important role in the community, and Mohegans continued to maintain the cemetery and church buildings. Emma Baker and Fidelia Fielding kept alive much of the Mohegans' aboriginal culture, including elements of the Mohegan-Pequot language and many stories and tribal traditions. New Englanders, who by the early twentieth century began to take an interest in the region's Indian "antiquities," provided a market for books on the Mohegans and their neighbors. Buffalo Bill Cody, the hero and promoter of the famous Wild West Shows, visited Montville in 1907, in fact, and laid a wreath at the grave of Uncas. With interest in their past growing, and with the growing assertiveness of America Indian reform leaders, the Mohegans began an effort to shape understandings of their people and their culture. Mohegans gathered every summer, for instance, at the Wigwam Festival to celebrate their culture, and in 1931 the Tantaquidgeon family, including Fielding's protégé Gladys Tantaquidgeon, opened the Tantaquidgeon Indian Museum in Montville. The Indians that white New Englanders spoke about were noble savages, romanticized images drawn from the Indian past: the Mohegans, meanwhile, asserted that despite the best efforts of those who sought to dispossess and transform them, their people still endured.

While the Mohegans continued to assert their identity as native peoples in the face of Connecticut's assimilationist policies, many white Virginians would have been surprised to learn that "real" Indians still lived in the Old Dominion. Because Virginia law and custom defined people who were not white as "colored," the state's native peoples faced a difficult dilemma. In order to show that they were native peoples, they had to convince the Commonwealth's white residents that they were not descended from Africans or African Americans, while on the other they tried to convince their white neighbors that they were, in fact, Indians. This was not easy to do, and the strategy could alienate both whites and blacks. Like other native peoples living in the east, they began to assert their Indian identity through clothing, wearing attire that non-Indians recognized as distinctly "Indian." As early as 1880, a group of Pamunkeys restaged for predominately white audiences at the Yorktown Centennial Pocahontas's rescue of Captain John Smith and they sent a representative, William Terrill Bradby, to the Columbian Exposition in Chicago in 1893.

The Powhatans' emerging pride in their history and culture attracted the attention of anthropologists and ethnologists. In 1889, James Mooney began to gather information about Virginia's native peoples. Albert Gatschet and John Garland Pollard followed Mooney to the Pamunkeys' homeland. Mooney found 100 people living in twenty-seven wooden houses on the Pamunkeys' land, while another twenty had left the reservation. A decade later, 152 people lived at Pamunkey. The men hunted, fished, trapped, and served as guides for white sportsmen who came to the Pamunkey reserve to hunt and fish. They still paddled about in canoes carved from a single large log, and each family raised a small crop of corn. Much of the land was still held in common. Gatschet and Pollard learned from the Pamunkeys about the Mattaponis, Chickahominies, Nansemonds, Upper Mattaponis, and Rappahannocks, all once part of the paramount chiefdom that greeted John Smith and the Jamestown colonists in 1607.

Each of these observers noted that the Pamunkeys took pains to avoid association with African Americans. "No one who visits the Pamunkey could fail to notice their race pride," wrote Pollard. "Though they would probably acknowledge the whites as their equals," he

Figure 8.5 William Terrill Bradby, Pamunkey Leader, dressed in traditional attire. Courtesy of National Anthropological Archives.

continued, "they consider the blacks far beneath their social level." Each of these observers agreed, moreover, that the native peoples they encountered in Virginia looked *Indian.* When the commonwealth sent an African American school teacher to instruct pupils at the Pamunkey school, the Pamunkeys sent her home. They hired lawyers to help them combat state segregation laws requiring that colored people ride in separate coaches. In the wake of their protests and threatened litigation, the president of the local railroad accepted the Pamunkeys' argument that they were not "Colored," and that therefore they could board the white coach. The Pamunkeys began to issue identification cards indicating that the bearer was Pamunkey.

In 1919, the anthropologist Frank Speck arrived in Virginia. He came looking for Algonquian remnants with which he could reconstruct the aboriginal culture of coastal peoples. Speck described how the Pamunkeys hunted and fished, and recorded bits of legend and oral culture. He did not stay for long, but his visits had an impact. He encouraged the Pamunkeys, and the Mattaponis and Nansemonds as well, to formally organize themselves into tribes. They had, of course, no treaties with the United States, and lived on the margins of Virginia society. Organization, Speck argued, could provide Virginia's Indian peoples with the institutional structure to preserve their culture and ways of living. The Rappahannock leader George Nelson, acting on this advice, petitioned the president of the United States, seeking recognition for his community as native peoples and redress for past injustices.

And in the first decades of the twentieth century in the Jim Crow south, this remained a difficult thing to do. In March of 1924, the Virginia legislature passed its odious "Racial Integrity Act," which defined white people as having "no trace whatever of any blood other than Caucasian." The act included the so-called "Pocahontas exception," stating that "persons who have one-sixteenth or less of the blood of the American Indian and have no other non-Caucasic blood shall be deemed white persons." Many Virginians, blissfully unaware that some of Pocahontas's descendants had sired children with slaves, attempted to tie themselves firmly to Virginia's romantic past by claiming descent from Pocahontas. Their interests had to be protected. Anyone who was not white, under the provisions of the law, was "colored."

All of this was ridiculous and nonsensical at a fundamental level: race was a construction, an invented category, a myth imbued with fake scientific gravitas. The blood that flowed through one's veins did nothing to affect culture and belief and values and behavior. Still, Virginians enforced the Racial Integrity Act with a vengeance, and the Commonwealth's first registrar of the Bureau of Vital Statistics, Walter Ashby Plecker, was a true believer. "Let us turn a deaf ear," he wrote revealingly in 1925, "to those who would interpret Christian brotherhood as racial equality." Virginia Indians, he believed, were not *real* Indians: they had been mongrelized, mixed with peoples of African descent, and as such he ordered his employees to alter the birth certificates of Indian children. This was erasure, an attempt at extermination carried out with pens and paper. The certificates now would read "colored." Plecker claimed that he had science on his side—the same "eugenics" that later fueled the Nazi holocaust—but he admitted to close friends that he routinely changed racial designations from Indian to colored without any evidence.

Plecker's racist crusade made it difficult for many native peoples in Virginia to prove that they were Indians. The vital records upon which such a designation relied, after all, had been altered. Native peoples in Virginia asserted a third racial identity in a biracial society. They did not attend black schools because they felt no necessity to accept Plecker's logic. Many wanted access to the better facilities available to white Virginians. Some of those who could pass as white did so, but many of Wahunsonacock's descendants struggled in the face of this racist legal code.

The Senecas, meanwhile, struggled against other forces. Many New Yorkers cast a covetous eye toward the remaining Seneca reservations at Allegany and Cattaraugus. Though the General Allotment Act of 1887 did not apply to the New York Indians, a function of the Ogden Company's old claim to their territory, leaders in the New York Assembly looked forward to state legislative action to allot Allegany, Cattaraugus, and other Iroquois lands in New York State. Indeed, in 1889 the New York State Assembly Special Committee to Investigate the Indian Problem, chaired by Representative Henry Whipple, concluded that native peoples in New York "have been kept as 'wards' or children long enough." It was time, Whipple concluded, for the Indians in New York "to be educated as men, not Indians, in order to finally and once and for all solve the 'Indian problem.'"

The "Whipple Report" included hundreds of pages of testimony from white people familiar with the state's native populations and from many Indians themselves. Witnesses testified to the poverty and immorality of the Indians, and indicated that allotment would provide New York's native peoples with an incentive to work. And while Seneca adults learned to work their own plots of land, the state would see to the uplift and enlightenment of their children.

The State of New York, for instance, operated nine schools on the Cattaraugus Reservation and another six at Allegany. Of the 700 children of school age on the reservations, almost 600 were registered but the average daily attendance was 237. Witnesses testified that the Senecas "are indifferent to schools and some people oppose their establishment. Here, as upon most of the reservations, the wages paid are too low to secure the most suitable teachers." The state also operated the Thomas Indian School on the Cattaraugus Reservation, a boarding school that enrolled students from all the Iroquois communities in New York.

It began as an orphanage for Indian children in 1855, after a typhoid epidemic swept across the reservation. Founded by the missionary Asher Wright, and named after a prominent Philadelphia Quaker, the Thomas School opened its doors twenty years before Carlisle, and remained open into the 1950s. It provided a typical boarding school education. Boys learned trades and how to manage a farm, while girls learned housewifery. The Whipple Committee reported that in 1889 110 students attended the school, ranging in age from three to sixteen. The school grounds, the committee continued, "are pleasing and the buildings well adapted to the needs of such a school. All the departments are noticeable for good order and neatness."

Some children spent much of their childhood at the Thomas School. They saw their families only occasionally. Many parents who sent their children to Thomas, it seems, viewed the institution as a refuge from the struggles of reservation life. Disease, poverty, the ravages of alcohol—all took their toll on Seneca and other Iroquois families in the second half of the century. Institutions like Thomas, despite the harsh discipline, the isolation from family, and a lack of love and affection that children who attended the school remember, provided Iroquois children with a place to go when their families could no longer care for them. The school, as such, always remained something of an asylum, even if only a small percentage of the children in attendance were orphans.

The Senecas survived through these years in part through the distribution of annuities on a per capita basis. But the Nation never relied solely on these funds. Men and women at Allegany and Cattaraugus farmed their lands. According to a special census supplement compiled in 1892, the Senecas produced a surplus which they exchanged with local merchants for cash or items that the members of the Nation could not produce themselves. Senecas sold crafts and performed manual labor for wages as well. But the Nation also leased its lands to outsiders, a risky proposition because it forced Senecas to engage in legal arrangements with non-native communities hostile toward native peoples and their culture.

By the middle of the nineteenth century, leasing began at Allegany and Cattaraugus. The largest influx of lessees came later as a result of the interest of railroad companies in cutting a right-of-way through Allegany. Six villages—Salamanca, West Salamanca, Red House, Great Valley, Vandalia, and Carrollton—developed along the railroad line entirely within Seneca territory. According to a report from the Military Affairs Committee of the United States House of Representatives, these leases violated the laws of both the United States and the state of New York. Despite this, Congress eagerly assisted those seeking to profit from Seneca land by approving an act on February 19, 1875 to ratify all existing leases and to allow for their renewal for an additional twelve years. To eliminate obstacles to the future development of the region, Congress in 1892 authorized ninety-nine-year leases to lands contained within the surveyed bounds of the six towns established on the reservation.

The Seneca Nation also derived an income by leasing its lands to oil interests. The non-Indian Seneca Oil Company struck oil on lands it leased at Allegany in 1897. In 1899, it produced over 75,000 barrels of oil, creating oil fever in western New York and growing demands for both allotting the Senecas' lands and opening up their remaining reservations to exploitation by New Yorkers. The Senecas resisted these demands. The Senecas worked their lands. Its leaders collected at least some of the rent owed by those who leased the nation's lands. By distributing these funds to individual members of the tribe, the Seneca Nation managed to look after the interests of its people.

A Movement for Reform

Charles Eastman, the newly appointed doctor at the Pine Ridge Agency in South Dakota, learned of the massacre at Wounded Knee when the wounded started coming in. Most were women and children. "Many," he wrote, "were frightfully torn by pieces of shell, and the suffering was terrible." A blizzard blew in, and it took Eastman a couple of days before he could return to the battlefield. The first physician to arrive at that frozen and bloody ground, the experience affected Eastman deeply. He saw the mangled bodies, and did what he could for the small number who had miraculously survived the federal artillery and gunfire. When he reached the site of Big Foot's camp, he "saw the frozen bodies of men who had been in council and who were almost as helpless as the women and babes when the deadly fire began." Eastman struggled to keep his composure. All about him he heard the "excitement and grief of my Indian companions, nearly every one of whom was crying aloud or singing his death song." He found a few survivors, all babies. All were adopted by white people. "All this was a severe ordeal for one who had so lately put all his faith in the Christian love and lofty ideals of the white man," he concluded, "yet I passed no hasty judgment, and I was thankful that I might be of some service and relieve even a small part of the suffering."

A Santee Sioux, Eastman was born in 1858. His father had participated in the uprising in Minnesota and fled after the Santees' defeat in 1862. Federal troops captured Eastman's father and imprisoned him at Fort Snelling. Nobody told the boy. Eastman believed that his father had been among those hanged in the aftermath of the uprising.

With his grandmother, Eastman joined those who fled from Minnesota out onto the Dakota prairies and from there to southwestern Manitoba. There Eastman lived what he described as a beautiful life. But then his father appeared, a decade after his capture. The father had converted to Christianity during his captivity, taken up farming near Flandreau, South Dakota, and had come to believe firmly in the value of an American-styled education. He determined to prepare his son to live in a nation dominated by white people. He sent the boy to the Santee Normal School, a boarding institution that taught crafts and trades but also instructed its mostly Sioux students to read and write in their own language. From Santee, Eastman moved on to Knox College, Dartmouth, and, finally, the medical school at Boston University.

Eastman, like Yellowtail of the Crows, represented a new generation of well-educated native people, familiar fully with both their own culture and the norms and values of white society. Born after the reservation period had begun, they had lived their entire lives with at least some awareness of federal efforts to dismantle their culture and their traditional ways of living. They wrote and spoke English, and emphasized that native peoples had much to contribute to the United States. They hoped to establish a place for native peoples in modern American society. They saw themselves both as Americans and as representatives of an assertive Indian "race."

The men and women of this generation viewed American society through a critical eye, aware fully of their people's history. Many of them struggled at various points in their lives, and found themselves at times out of place in American society. Eastman, over time, grew increasingly disenchanted with the United States, and its inability to live up to the ideals it professed. He became especially disillusioned with American Christianity and what he viewed as the hypocrisy and corruption of American politics. Wounded Knee would not have happened, he believed, had it not been for the greed of "dishonest politicians."

Many of these Indian reformers, like Eastman, attempted to hold the United States to its principles. The Lakota writer Gertrude Bonin, known also as Zitkala Sa, looked forward to the peace conference following World War I because now, she hoped, the "little peoples are to be granted the right of self-determination." Robert Yellowtail, too, called for self-determination for his people. Yellowtail attempted to apply the logic of Woodrow Wilson's call for self-determination to all native peoples. Levi General, an Iroquois League sachem, traveled to Geneva in 1923 to present the grievances of the Six Nations against Canada before the League of Nations.

Others spoke out generally on matters of concern to native peoples, to the Indian "race." Indian reformers denounced the United States for its sins. Simon Pokagon, for instance, a Catholic Potawatomi from Michigan little respected by his own people but well-received in eastern lecture halls where white audiences willingly paid to hear about the demise, disappearance, and extinction of native peoples, said in 1893 that "we have been driven from the homes of our childhood and from the burial places of our kindred and friends" by white settlers, "and scattered far westward into desert places, where multitudes have died from homesickness, cold and hunger, and are suffering and dying still for want of food and blankets."

Many other Indian reformers wrote in the pages of the journal of the Society of American Indians (SAI). Founded in Columbus, Ohio, in 1911, the Society offered full-membership only to men and women of Indian descent. It was, in a sense, a Native American corollary to the National Association for the Advancement of Colored People (NAACP), which had been founded two years earlier in 1909. The Seneca Arthur Parker, the editor of its journal, wrote in 1914 that the SAI, brought "together in a society all Indians who believe that Indians ought to stand up for their own rights before the whole country." As Parker told a prospective member, "if you believe that all Indians should stick together and be friends and get acquainted with each other and know what each other is interested in, if you love your people well enough to think about what they ought to do and what is going to become of them, then you ought to become a member of this society." The members of the society, Parker continued, "believe that the time has come when the Indian must show his willingness to stand up for himself before the whole world and through a Society prove his ability to carry on a movement for the betterment of his own race."

Parker had been born at Cattaraugus, but moved to the New York City suburbs as a child, where he lived with his white mother and his Seneca father. He graduated from high school there and attended the Dickinson Seminary in Williamsport, Pennsylvania, and began working in 1903 at the New York Museum of Natural History. A powerful writer, Parker was proud of his Seneca heritage but also felt that native peoples must embrace the opportunities white society offered. A native leader must, he wrote, "step upward where he can be seen, and he must speak where he can be heard. He must use a language and a logic that appeals above the tumult and wins attention." Parker did this in the pages of the Society's journal.

The United States, Parker argued, had robbed "a race of men—the American Indian, of their intellectual life," of their "social organization," and their native freedom, economic independence, "moral standards and racial ideals," their "good name among the peoples of the earth," and their "definite civic status." America had ignored its obligations to its native peoples, and owed them justice. Government oppression, in the form of the heavy hand of the Bureau of Indian Affairs; the lack of citizenship for native peoples; and poor opportunities for educational advance, Parker concluded, "is more awful than the robbery of our lands, more hideous than the scalping and burning of Indian women and babies, more harrowing than tortures at the stake." The government's treatment amounted to "the crushing of a noble people's spirit and the usurpation of its right to be responsible, self-supporting and self-governing." Many of the founders of the SAI were veterans of the boarding schools. They opposed the institutions that kept native peoples from enjoying all that the American republic offered. Parker denounced the reservation system, and wrote that "the evils of the reservation system have continued to corrupt the Indian and render a just understanding of citizenship, taxation and social service, things difficult to inculcate or to achieve." Members of the SAI saw themselves as Indians and as Americans.

Native reformers criticized allotment, a policy that had enriched whites and impoverished native peoples. They called for respect for native peoples and their culture. Some criticized the Wild West Shows for celebrating the supposed violence and viciousness of native peoples, and for depicting Indians solely as part of the past, while others defended the use of peyote in religious rituals. Some joined the Native American Church. Founded in Oklahoma in 1918 by Poncas, Otos, Comanches, and Kiowas, the Church fostered and promoted "the religious beliefs of the several tribes of Indians in the State of Oklahoma, in the Christian religion with the practice of the Peyote Sacrament ... and to teach the Christian religion with morality, sobriety, industry, kindly charity, and right living and to cultivate a spirit of self-respect and brotherly union among the members of the Native Race of Indians." Members of the Church and their sympathizers invoked the first amendment to the Constitution to protect the religious freedom of native peoples.

Other reformers, like Parker, called for better educational opportunities for Indians. Native peoples were capable of more than the limited training in trades that they received at many government Indian schools. Native peoples should have access to the professions. These men and women called for, as well, the reform of the Bureau of Indian Affairs, while others, like Carlos Montezuma, called for its abolition. And they demanded full citizenship in the United States, something that some native peoples had acquired through the allotment process or through service in the armed forces during World War I, but which Congress did not formally enact until it passed the Indian Citizenship Act in 1924.

The reformers did not acquire all that they wanted, of course. At times they seemed to have little to say that was relevant to native peoples on reservations: they expressed the concerns of Indians who sought to assimilate into American society. They spoke less about poverty and disease and the oppressions of reservation life than they did about mismanagement in the bureaucracy and the systems that kept educated and articulate native leaders from becoming all that they might become. Still, they expressed pride in being members of an Indian "race." They associated with Indians from a wide range of native communities, and they began to emphasize problems that, in their view, all native peoples shared. They inspired other reformers. The Northern Federation of American Indians, made up of the descendants of those who negotiated with Governor Isaac Stevens in Washington Territory, copied the constitution of the SAI nearly word-for-word in its own charter documents. These native peoples spoke easily and proudly of an Indian identity. They also contributed to an emerging consensus that changes needed to be made in the conduct of the American nation's Indian policy, and encouraged the climate for reform that began to take root in the 1920s.

The Origins of the Indian New Deal

Many non-Indians involved themselves in this movement. John Collier, for instance, who had helped the Pueblos defeat the Bursum Bill, continued to agitate for changes in the nation's Indian policy. As chairman of the newly created American Indian Defense Association, Collier opposed government policies that in his view seemed directed toward the eradication of native culture. The constant criticism of federal Indian policy provoked the government into action. In 1926, Secretary of the Interior Hubert Work authorized Lewis Meriam of the Institute for Government Research in Washington to undertake an investigation of the nation's Indian affairs. Meriam made public his commission's findings in his report, *The Problem of Indian Administration*, released by the Interior Department early in 1928.

The report called upon the government to increase funding for the Bureau of Indian Affairs, an agency which the Meriam Commission believed had not achieved its fundamental objective of helping Indians learn to live in modern America. The Bureau needed the means to hire better personnel, and improve the quality of its educational and other programs. The report criticized the poor health conditions on many reservations, including unacceptably high rates of tuberculosis and trachoma. Too many Indians, the commissioners wrote, "are poor and living below any reasonable standard of health and decency."

The commissioners looked as well at native peoples living away from reservations. There were urban Indians, many of whom felt that the education they had received in boarding schools or on the reservation had not prepared them adequately for life in America's cities. The Meriam Commission described the groups of Pueblos working in railroad repair shops for the Santa Fe, living in company housing in Gallup, New Mexico, and Winslow, Arizona. Their children attended the public schools where they lived, but their parents maintained their ties to their pueblos and frequently returned for visits and for celebrations.

The Meriam Commission made a large number of recommendations in the area of health and in terms of increasing the efficiency of the Bureau of Indian Affairs. It also advocated changes in the way the Bureau of Indian Affairs educated children, changes consistent with the arguments that reformers had made over the preceding decade. The Bureau of Indian Affairs should respect the wishes of native people. "Some Indians proud of their race and devoted to their culture and their mode of life have no desire to be as the white man is," the commissioners reported, and "they wish to remain Indians, to preserve what they have inherited from their fathers, and insofar as possible to escape from the ever increasing contact with and pressure from the white civilization." Meriam and his staff did not believe that Indians could be isolated from white society, and they recognized that the "economic foundation upon which the Indian culture rested" had been destroyed. Indians who wished to assimilate "into the social and economic life of the prevailing civilization of this country should be given all practicable aid and advice in making the necessary adjustments," while those who want "to remain an Indian and live according to his old culture should be aided in doing so" in a way that guarantees they can live "in accordance with a minimum standard of health and decency."

The Hoover Administration did little to implement the recommendations of the Meriam Commission; it could not, really, for the onset of the Great Depression in October of 1929 meant that resources were especially scarce. The Bureau of Indian Affairs called upon the Red Cross for assistance, which supplied flour and crushed wheat for the relief of Indians, and the army contributed emergency supplies as well. There can be no doubt that the Depression affected native peoples. As jobs off the reservation disappeared, many Indians who had left for work returned home. The number of Americans who could afford vacations declined, so the revenue native peoples like the Pueblos derived from tourism dropped substantially. The revenue from timber, coal, and gas leases also declined as the economy ground to a halt.

Franklin Delano Roosevelt, elected in 1932, appointed Harold Ickes to head the Department of the Interior, and Collier to head the Bureau of Indian Affairs. That both men served in the American Indian Defense Association showed that Roosevelt felt sympathy for the reformers' calls for a restructuring of Indian affairs. Quickly, Collier set to work. He and Ickes abolished the Board of Indian Commissioners, which had continued to advocate assimilationist policies. Collier closed twenty boarding schools. He also called upon the president to issue executive orders reducing the influence of missionaries over Indian education and calling upon federal agencies to place native religious traditions on a par with Christian denominations. Roosevelt's executive order, dated January 3, 1934, asserted that "the fullest constitutional liberty, in all matters affecting religion, conscience, and culture exist for all Indians." It was one of the first occasions where the federal government recognized native religions as legitimate and called upon its employees to halt their efforts at suppression. Accordingly, Collier lifted Bureau prohibitions on the Sun Dance and other religious practices that his predecessors had seen as diabolical, savage, and dangerous.

Collier called for the suspension of the Dawes Act. He ordered his employees to sell no more trust lands and to do nothing that could lead to the further alienation of native lands. After nearly half a century, the damage the Dawes Act had done was remarkably clear. As Collier and his staff surveyed the wreckage, they recognized that two-thirds of all Indians were either landless or owned parcels that were not large enough for them to make a living. In 1887, native peoples owned 138 million acres; by 1934, only 52 million acres remained.

In June of 1934, Congress approved the Indian Reorganization Act, the centerpiece of Collier's reform program and the highlight of the "Indian New Deal." The Indian Reorganization Act, or the IRA, formally ended the policy of allotment. All remaining surplus lands were returned to the control of Indian tribes, and the trust period for Indian lands, set at twenty-five years in the original Dawes Act, was extended indefinitely. The federal government would now protect Indian lands. The IRA encouraged Indian tribes to adopt written constitutions and by-laws and to apply for charters of incorporation that would enable them to own and manage property and conduct businesses. The IRA also authorized tribes to establish their own governments with authority placed in the hands of an elected council and a tribal chairman. Congress created a revolving credit fund upon which tribes could draw to fund their enterprises. The IRA attempted to expand educational opportunities for native peoples by providing funding for the improvement of schools in Indian country. The repressive policies of the past were abandoned, and the IRA called for the preferential hiring of native peoples in the Bureau of Indian Affairs.

The Indian Reorganization Act offered the promise of revolutionizing Indian affairs. For the first time, the federal government had embarked on an Indian policy not predicated on the eradication of Indian cultures and the assimilation of native peoples into the American mainstream. Under the IRA, the United States government increased its funding to native peoples, and provided them with the opportunity to govern their own affairs. Collier saw in the legislation the promise of rebirth. As he told students at the Haskell Institute, a Kansas boarding school, in 1934, native peoples need not look to the "shallow and unsophisticated individualism" that characterized so much of the "modern white world." Instead, they needed to look to "the tribe, the nation and the race," and by doing so they would find that "their fulfillment would come by holding to ideas and passions that mattered."

Collier's polices came under attack by conservative politicians and western interests almost immediately. That these groups opposed his policies Collier saw as evidence that he was doing a good job. Much more surprising, however, was the widespread opposition to the IRA in many native communities. Ideas mattered in native communities, but not all Indians shared Collier's views of what was best for native peoples.

9

NEW DEALS AND OLD DEALS

Reforming Indian Policy

John Collier hoped to bring to native peoples renewal and restoration. The Indian Reorganization Act (IRA), the centerpiece of Collier's Indian New Deal, ended the impoverishing policies of the allotment era and allowed tribes to regain control of surplus lands that had not yet been taken up by farmers and ranchers. Should they choose to accept its provisions, the IRA empowered native peoples to write constitutions and govern their own communities, so long as their governing instruments and intentions accorded with the priorities and interests of the commissioner. These "municipal councils," the Blackfeet author and reformer D'Arcy McNickle wrote, ultimately would take "over more and more of the authority which in the past was exercised by the Commissioner of Indian Affairs and his agents." Collier and those agents brought significant change to the conduct of American Indian policy. No more dispossession, and no more disrespect, he suggested. With their cultures valued, deemed worthy of preservation, and celebrated by the commissioner, and with their lands at last secured, Collier intended for the IRA to save native peoples from the misbegotten policies of the past.

The evidence that allotment had damaged native communities was apparent to any who chose to look. Hoping to secure title to their lands as a way to resist white intruders, Lummis, Nisquallys, Squaxin, Skokomish, Suquamish, Tulalips, Muckleshoots, and Puyallups had accepted individual allotments on their Washington reservations. By 1918, only six Puyallup families still lived on the original allotments. Dispossession moved quickly. The allotment of the Sisseton Reservation in North Dakota in 1892, for instance, left the Dakotas with only 300,000 of their original million-acre reserve. After the implementation of the Burke Act, the amount of land in Sisseton hands fell by an additional two-thirds. Only 10% of the original reservation remained. The experience of the Sissetons was not unique. Collier viewed allotment as yet another effort to dispossess American Indians. No more, Collier and his supporters said. Even though some native peoples, like the Kiowas, continued to sell allotments after the passage of the IRA, his administration did not aim at assimilation or the moral uplift of native peoples, nor did he seek directly to transform native culture. His policies, he noted proudly, would not be imposed on native peoples without their consent, a dramatic change from the past.

The Indian New Deal consisted of more than the IRA. The Omnibus Mineral Leasing Act of 1938 provided the secretary of the interior with the power to manage reservation natural resources and to enter into leasing arrangements with corporate interests for the development of those lands. The legislation opened reservations to exploitation by timber and mining operations in exchange for the small royalty payments that went to members of the reservation community. The Indian Arts and Craft Board, established by act of Congress in 1935, attempted to protect the integrity of Native American artwork. The application of the Civilian Conservation Corps to native communities provided some work relief for reservation residents. The Seneca Arts Project, a product of the Works Progress Administration, employed more than 100 people from Tonawanda and from the Seneca Nation of Indians. It produced more than 5000 works of art expressing the cultural values of Seneca people. Preferential hiring for positions at the Bureau of Indian Affairs provided unprecedented opportunities for native peoples to work at the federal level. Gladys Tantaquidgeon, soon to become an important leader in the Mohegan community, found employment working to implement Collier's policies. Still, the IRA rested at the very heart of the Indian New Deal, and native peoples divided deeply over whether or not to resist its application.

The IRA, according to the rules Congress set for its implementation, would "not apply to any reservation wherein a majority of the adult Indians, voting at a special election duly called by the Secretary of the Interior, shall vote against its application." Native peoples who opposed the legislation, as a result, must mobilize their supporters, bring them to the election called by the secretary of the interior, and persuade them to vote against the IRA. Those who did not vote, the legislation assumed, favored the IRA. Collier and his congressional supporters hardwired the legislation for approval. Paternalism died slowly.

Figure 9.1 Kiowas recording traditional songs, 1939. © AP/Photo.

Ultimately 174 tribes, with a total population approaching 130,000, accepted the IRA. Seventy-eight tribes, with a population of approximately 86,000, voted to reject Collier's program. Of those tribes that accepted the IRA, only ninety-two elected to draw up the constitutions. The Dakota Sioux at the Santee Reservation in Nebraska offer an instructive example. They voted 260 to 27 to accept the IRA and, "in order to organize for the common welfare of ourselves and our posterity and to insure domestic tranquility; to conserve and develop our natural resources; to form business and other organizations; to enjoy certain rights of home rule; to provide education in schools of higher learning, including vocational, trade, high schools, and colleges for our people," the tribe wrote a constitution that the secretary of the interior approved in April 1936. Like most IRA-based constitutions, the Santees specified tribal membership requirements, defined the structure and powers of a tribal council consisting of twelve members elected equally from the four districts on the reservation, and enacted rules on how to administer their unallotted lands for the benefit of their community. The Santees also requested a corporate charter to enable the tribe to secure for its members "an assured economic independence" through the careful management of its remaining resources and by borrowing money for economic development.

The constitutions, by-laws, and corporate charters approved by the Interior Department bear a boiler-plate similarity. Felix Cohen, Collier's associate and arguably the father of the modern field of American Indian law, prepared in 1934 a "Basic Memorandum on Drafting of Tribal Constitutions" to provide guidance to the Interior Department. The result was uniformity, with only minor variations that reflected differences in tribal history and that related to the conditions on a given reservation. For instance, in January of 1938, two years after the Oklahoma Indian Welfare Act extended the provisions of the IRA to Indians in that state (they had been exempted from the original law), the secretary of the interior ratified the constitution and by-laws prepared for the "Caddo Indians of the Kiowa Indian Agency Jurisdiction of Oklahoma, in order to promote our common welfare and to secure to ourselves and our descendants the rights, powers and privileges" of self-government. As with the Santee constitution, the Caddos spelled out the requirements for tribal membership, the structure of tribal government under the constitution, and rules for the election and removal of officers. The constitution included a bill of rights, guaranteeing that all tribal members would "enjoy without hindrance freedom of worship, conscience, speech, press, assembly and association." Like the Santees, the Caddos' newly constituted council in November of 1938 asked the interior secretary to issue a charter of incorporation to the tribe intended to "define and safeguard the rights and powers of the Caddo Indian Tribe of Oklahoma and its members" and to "advance the standard of living of the Tribe through the development of tribal resources, the acquisition of new tribal land, preservation of existing land holdings, the better utilization of land, and the development of a credit program for the tribe" to allow it to undertake commercial development.

Tribes who approved of the IRA incorporated, and drew up tribal constitutions; they felt that doing so best served the interests of their people. Other native peoples rejected the new law. Delos Lonewolf, a Kiowa, told Collier in 1935 that reorganization would reverse six decades of Indian progress toward assimilation. Lonewolf, reflecting some of the arguments of Indian reformers from the Progressive era, wanted all that American society offered, and he said he would "rather pay taxes and be a man among men than a useless Indian forever." The Potawatomi leader W.W. Gilbert pointed out that most of the members of his tribe had assimilated, and had little interest in self-government or revitalizing life on the reservation. Though the Potawatomis favored the financial assistance that could come with the IRA because they had "everything to gain and nothing to lose," Gilbert and many others remained suspicious of a program to reform Indian affairs that seemed, to some native peoples, to isolate them from the American mainstream. They had worked hard to learn how to operate in modern America, and feared that isolation would lead to continuing marginalization.

Important tribes opposed the IRA. The Crows had looked forward to Roosevelt's election in 1932, and expected that his presidency would bring much needed change to the administration of Indian affairs. Robert Yellowtail and his associates, in fact, traveled to Washington to lobby on behalf of Crow interests in March of 1933 as they awaited Roosevelt's inauguration. Yellowtail believed that the choice of Collier to head the Bureau of Indian Affairs was a wise one.

The Crows, however, looked with suspicion at the IRA. The tribal council appointed a committee to review the legislation, and sent a delegation to the Plains Indian Congress in Rapid City, South Dakota, in March 1934 to hear from the commissioner about the new plan. Max Big Man and Frank Yarlott, two of the Crow delegates, asked Collier to exempt their tribe from the legislation. The Crows had acquired rights to a substantial amount of land through the passage of the Crow Act in 1920 and their current tribal council and governing institutions were more than adequate to defend their interests. To them the law seemed redundant and unnecessary. Collier assured the Crow delegates that they would not be required to accept the IRA.

Collier, meanwhile, appointed Robert Yellowtail to the position of superintendent at Crow Agency, the first time that a native leader had been appointed to oversee the agency responsible for his reservation. Yellowtail, a man educated at boarding schools, comfortable in white society, but thoroughly dedicated to the independence and autonomy of the Crows, walked a narrow path between his supporters on the reservation and the commissioner. Initially supportive of the IRA, Yellowtail sensed the mood on the reservation. He could see that the Crows deeply distrusted the new program. It originated in Washington, after all, the seat from which sprung so many other disastrous policies. The Crows, Yellowtail recognized, had little faith that Congress approved the new initiative with their best interests in mind. They feared that the new tribal governments approved by the Interior Department would be too subject to manipulation by federal officials.

Yellowtail called meetings to rally support for the IRA, but he did so with little enthusiasm or energy. Collier sensed that Yellowtail's heart was not in the work. He told Yellowtail to explain to the Crows the advantages they stood to receive. Yellowtail did so, but half-heartedly. He favored the IRA because it provided a means for protecting and managing Crow lands. He liked the access to credit offered in the legislation. He said little about the new tribal constitutions. In the end, the Crows' distrust of the United States remained too powerful a force for Yellowtail to overcome. They overwhelmingly rejected the IRA because they felt that Collier's program threatened the tribe's right to home rule.

Yellowtail could not persuade the Crows to support the IRA, but he did bring to the tribe other benefits from the New Deal programs created by the Roosevelt administration. He negotiated an agreement with the National Park Service to relocate excess bison from Yellowstone National Park to the Crow Reservation, a symbolic act of great importance. The Crows continue to maintain their bison herd today. New Deal funds allowed the Crows to acquire an additional 40,000 acres of grazing land and led to the construction of the first hospital on the reservation. Young men on the reservation found work improving roads and trails, repairing homes and ranches, and building reservoirs through a variety of programs funded by the Works Progress Administration and the Indian Emergency Conservation Works.

The Civilian Conservation Corps offered work to young Crows as members of logging, firefighting, and pest control crews. As a result, many Crows moved closer to Crow Agency and the federal jobs there, causing members of the tribe to become more reliant upon federally funded employment than upon agriculture. Crows leased their unused lands to white farmers and ranchers. Regardless of their rejection of the IRA, the Indian New Deal brought great change to the Crow Reservation.

The Iroquois nations in New York also rejected overwhelmingly the IRA. The Six Nations fiercely asserted their sovereignty in the twentieth century. They had asserted their rights to lost lands, demanded recognition of their rights as members of sovereign nations to cross the international boundary between Canada and the United States, and, in Canada, attempted to bring their concerns before the League of Nations in Geneva. They wanted less, not more, interference in their internal affairs and they feared that the IRA would bring complete control by outsiders over Iroquois communities. The Senecas, who had governed themselves under their own written constitution since 1848, saw little need for a new framework of government approved by the Interior Department. The Constitution of the Seneca Nation of Indians worked well. The Senecas at Allegany and Cattaraugus, furthermore, had successfully resisted earlier efforts to allot their lands. The IRA, the first several sections of which dealt with halting allotment, thus had little relevance to them.

Some Senecas feared, furthermore, that the definition of "Indians" in the IRA could undermine the Seneca Nation's government, and its own beliefs about who qualified for membership in the community. The IRA defined as an Indian for the purposes of the act members of recognized tribes and "all other persons of one-half or more Indian blood." Cayugas, Onondagas, Mohawks, and Oneidas lived at Allegany and Cattaraugus, and they had the requisite "blood-quantum." But they were not Senecas. There also were people who resided on the reservation who had white mothers and Indian fathers. These people, the Seneca activist Alice Lee Jemison pointed out, did not have the right "to hold lands and vote at tribal elections." Citizenship came through the mother in matrilineal Seneca communities, and the inclusion of these outsiders in a new Seneca Nation created and supported by the Interior Department raised the prospect that "our Seneca Nation will be entirely destroyed, because the new chartered community that will be set up will not be the Seneca Nation of Indians but will consist of other persons who on June 1, 1934, were living on our reservation."

Iroquois peoples, moreover, deeply distrusted the state and the federal government. They viewed the proposed reorganization as dangerous and unnecessary, and they wondered about Collier's "real" motives. Why, after more than a century of allowing the state of New York's attempts to dispossess and destroy the Six Nations, Iroquois leaders asked, would the federal government offer now to help and protect them? Of the 3000 eligible voters on the six Iroquois reservations in New York State, only 249 voted in favor of the IRA. More than 1500 voted no. Seneca leaders, and leaders of other Iroquois communities, could not see how the legislation helped them to survive as a people.

The Sissetons and Wahpetons at Traverse Lake also rejected the IRA, but for reasons different from those of the Crows and Senecas. Allotment resulted in large numbers of whites taking possession of their reservation lands. The Dakotas thus found themselves living scattered across their reservations, their access to neighbors interrupted by white farmers and ranchers who felt little affection for native peoples. Though Sisseton leaders like Amos Oneroad recognized that a written constitution would allow them more formally to govern their own affairs, the Sissetons and Wahpetons rejected Collier's program. They would write a constitution in 1946 that received the approval of the Interior Department, but in 1934 the Sissetons and

Wahpetons rejected the IRA because, in the words of their agent, they "took pride in their progress toward civilization, and in the fact that they were like white people."

Collier thus confronted two fundamental varieties of opposition in native communities. Native peoples with their own governing institutions, whether traditional or the product of innovations during the reservation era as among the Crows and the Seneca Nation of Indians, did not trust the federal government and felt that their own institutions suited their purposes admirably. If the government would honor its responsibilities as trustee, cease its century-long campaign to dispossess and transform them, and uphold its obligations in treaties, they required little else. Native peoples who sought assimilation, on the other hand, rejected a government reform program that in their eyes seemed to continue their segregation on reservations. Collier cherished a specific image of Indians. Basing his policies to some extent on a romantic understanding of Pueblo life that he had adopted during his time in the southwest, he believed that in these communities there existed a kernel from which non-Indian Americans might learn how to live richer and more meaningful lives. As opposed to a white world that Collier viewed as "psychically, religiously, socially, and aesthetically shattered, dismembered, [and] directionless," Collier saw traditional tribal peoples "of unyielding wills," who are "even today the expressions, even today the harborers, of a great age of integrated, inwardly seeking life and art." Certainly there were native peoples who fit this description. But there were many others who had received education in white institutions, had received training in American professions, and sought to attain for themselves all that the American Nation had to offer. If Collier thought, as the historian Brian Dippie wrote, that inside every Indian stood a communal Pueblo waiting to emerge, many Indians seem to have had little interest in helping Collier resolve his own moral anxieties by conforming to the commissioner's understanding of who native peoples were and what they ought to be. Indeed, many Pueblos were unhappy with Collier's program. Though only Jemez Pueblo rejected the IRA, the majority of them decided against adopting written constitutions. Some Pueblos saw the proposed revisions of tribal government as inconsistent with their traditions.

The rebukes he received from native peoples stung Collier, but he cherished the criticism he received from western land interests. Criticism from missionaries he viewed in similar terms: he had halted the ambitions of those who sought to eradicate native culture. Yet criticism of his policies was widespread, and as his term in office extended into the 1940s, and as World War II consumed the energies and the attention of the American people, Collier found himself increasingly on the defensive. The American Indian Federation (AIF), founded by conservative native leaders in 1934 to oppose the IRA, called for the abolition of the Bureau of Indian Affairs and the freeing of native peoples from government paternalism. This was not a new argument and many native reformers during the Progressive era had called for the elimination of the Bureau. The Bureau of Indian Affairs kept Indians down, AIF leaders said. It stifled their individualism, their ingenuity, and their initiative. Some AIF members saw the IRA as dangerous and subversive, and at times their rhetoric tended toward the hysterical.

The AIF was a small group, with few adherents in Indian country, but its advocates made a lot of noise. The Anti-Semite Elwood A. Towner, a Portland attorney of mixed racial descent who appeared in public in Indian costume as Chief Red Cloud, and who wore a swastika in the center of his white, gold, green, and purple headdress, denounced Collier as a "Jew-loving Pink Red" who fraternized with Communists. Joseph Bruner, a Creek and one of the founders of the AIF, denounced the IRA as an attempt to establish "Russian communistic life in the United States." Alice Lee Jemison, the reformer with deep but ambiguous ties in Seneca society, and who maintained a long career in Indian affairs, willingly accepted the

Figure 9.2 Senecas assert their sovereignty in ceremony commemorating the 1794 Treaty of Canandaigua. © AP/Photo.

financial support of American pro-Nazi groups who saw in the AIF an opportunity to broadcast anti-American propaganda. Jemison's unsavory associations, which Collier pointed out when he described the AIF as a fascist organization, prevented the group from effecting a repeal of the IRA, but they did force Collier nonetheless to spend an inordinate amount of time defending his programs before a hostile Republican leadership in Congress.

Despite its extremist rhetoric, hateful sloganeering, and hysterical use of anti-communist images, it would be risky to dismiss the AIF entirely as a gathering of mean-spirited crackpots, however crazy some of its members seemed. Jemison based her opposition to the IRA, it should be noted, on an understanding of Seneca sovereignty that many Iroquois people shared. The 1794 Treaty of Canandaigua, she argued, allowed the Six Nations "the free use and enjoyment" of their lands without any interference. The IRA, by requiring the approval of the Interior Department for any contemplated action by the tribe, infringed directly upon that sovereignty. Similarly, she based her opposition to the Selective Service Act on the assumption that Senecas retained the power to determine when and where their men would fight. She, and many members of the AIF, however detestable their rhetoric or obscene their associations, saw in the IRA a grave threat to native peoples.

Native Peoples and World War II

Collier's Indian New Deal dramatically transformed the conduct of American Indian policy. He halted the crusade to eradicate native cultures, and tried to bring economic development to impoverished reservation communities. Under the programs he initiated, native peoples found space to begin revitalizing as they reshaped and reformed their communities. That the accomplishments of the Indian New Deal never lived up to its ideals testifies to the depth of the challenges native peoples faced. By 1940 the Indian New Deal had lost much of its momentum. Reservations remained poor. Congressional opponents of Collier began to mount assaults on the Indian New Deal, and the commissioner increasingly found himself on the defensive just as America's entry into World War II brought additional profound change to America's native communities.

Native peoples faced conscription, and by the spring of 1941, over 7000 Indians had registered for the draft. When news of the attack on Pearl Harbor arrived in Indian country, many traveled to the nearest recruitment center and volunteered. The best known of these were the several hundred "Code Talkers," Navajos mostly, who transmitted radio messages the Japanese never succeeded in decoding. But the Code Talkers comprised only a small percentage of the American Indians who participated in the war effort. Over 21,000 Indians served in the United States Army, 1900 in the navy, nearly 900 in the Marines, and approximately 120 in the Coast Guard. Two hundred Native American women served in the various women's auxiliaries of the armed forces or as nurses in military hospitals. Five hundred and fifty Indian servicemen died in combat during the war, and another 700 were wounded.

Native peoples fought in integrated units, making their wartime experience significantly different from that of African American soldiers, who faced discrimination and segregation. In this sense, the war did much to assimilate native peoples, who found themselves fighting, suffering, and dying alongside their white brothers-in-arms. Large numbers of men left reservations to join the service, seeing different parts of the United States and the world. They encountered more white people, and more of white culture, than ever before. They made friends and, as Peter Nabokov learned from the Crow veterans he interviewed, they returned to their reservations as changed men. "They felt worldly, returning with an awareness of lands and people beyond America," Nabokov wrote. "They had been brothers in arms with non-Indians, and had learned more about their own nation in the process." But this participation in the war effort also caused some native people to draw parallels between their people's struggles and those of other peoples around the world fighting colonialism. Fighting for their homelands and for the United States, participation in the war effort fostered nationalism among native peoples that would surface after the war.

Indeed, though soldiers found themselves in closer contact with non-Indians than ever before, the process was not so powerful that it resulted in the eradication of native culture. Frankie Redbone, a Kiowa, for instance, attributed his survival in a German prisoner-of-war camp to the sacred medicine bundle he kept with him. Tribal religious leaders conducted rituals to protect their young men at war. Soldiers aboard a landing craft sailing toward Guadacanal performed a war dance. Close contact with white soldiers, and the inclusion of American Indian communities in the war effort, made many native peoples aware of their shared identity as Indians and the things that set them apart from white society.

Not all native peoples supported the war effort unconditionally. The Senecas, for instance, viewed the Selective Service Act as a threat to their sovereignty. In October of 1940, Seneca President Wilfred Crouse asserted that the United States had no right to conscript Seneca young men for military service. According to the 1794 Canandaigua Treaty, he said, "we are a distinct race, nation and people owning, occupying and governing the lands of our ancestors." Collier pledged to support Iroquois sovereignty, but only to the point that they agreed with him. Already stung over their rejection of the IRA a half decade earlier, Collier did not believe that the Six Nations could legitimately claim freedom from military service. When a federal court in 1942 issued its decision in the case of *Ex Parte Green*, Seneca defiance ended. The court, Collier noted, ruled that "the Selective Service Act is applicable to *all* Indians," regardless of the terms of their treaties. Still, in June 1942 a handful of delegates from the Six Nations gathered to declare war on their own against the Axis powers. "The New World's oldest democracy," an Associated Press reporter wrote in the *New York Times*, gathered to declare "that a state of war exists between our Confederacy on the one part and Germany, Italy, Japan and their allies against whom the United States has declared war on the other part." Widely reported in the media, the Six Nations' declaration was cast as propaganda, a symbol that all Americans supported the war effort. They missed the significant point that the members of the Six Nations still believed strongly in and valued greatly their sovereignty, and that they would send their men to fight and die only in wars that they had declared themselves.

Members of the Six Nations resisted the Selective Service Act as a threat to their sovereignty, but they did fight. Meanwhile, native peoples in Virginia challenged their classification by local draft boards as "colored," a designation that required them to serve in African American units in America's segregated armed forces. Here again, Indians in Virginia confronted the racism of their nemesis, Walter Ashby Plecker, who conducted policy in accord with his belief that "no native-born Virginians claiming to be Indians ... are unmixed with Negro blood."

Collier complained to Plecker that the racial policies he pursued were too strict, but the head of the commonwealth's Bureau of Vital Statistics worried that thousands of "mulattoes" in Virginia "are striving to pass over into the white race by the Indian route." Plecker determined to keep the races pure, and the lines between them distinct. The Selective Service determined in 1941 that local draft boards possessed the power to determine the racial classification of registrants. The boards could use physical characteristics to make their determination. To be considered Indians, the War Department stated, native soldiers must not have "lived in association with negroes" and they must be "considered Indians by their neighbors." Designation of draftees, then, remained dependent upon local draft boards left free to indulge their considerable prejudices.

When a draft board in Richmond ordered three Rappahannock men to report to an induction station for African American soldiers in Maryland, they refused. Authorities in Virginia prosecuted the men and sentenced them to six months in prison. The government allowed Chickahominy soldiers to serve in white units only after the tribe demonstrated its own racism toward African Americans: Chickahominies who married black people faced expulsion from the community; they tried to keep African American farmers away from the reservation, and prohibited black doctors and preachers from visiting their communities. Most of the Virginia Indians who served did so in white units, but not without an enormous struggle.

American Indians served in all branches of the armed forces. Native peoples also supported the war on the home front, and did so with great devotion. The Indian New Deal never solved the problem of poverty on reservations. The Great Depression, which began late in 1929, affected native peoples less directly than other Americans only because Indians had less far to fall. Their poverty remained an intractable problem. The federal government offered relief, but could not solve the deep structural problems affecting reservations. Funding from the federal government allowed tribes to repurchase some of the lands that they had lost during the allotment era—Dakota Sioux at the Santee reservation purchased nearly 3400 acres, but this was less than both the tribe and the government had hoped to acquire. These funds allowed for the purchase of livestock, and investment in reservation infrastructure. But with the war, funding for many of Collier's programs dried up. Still, native peoples purchased war bonds, and offered what they could to the government. The Crows sent $10,000 to President Roosevelt, instructing him to use it to purchase weapons and ammunition. Pueblos from Santa Clara, Jemez, and Santo Domingo, in addition to sending 10% of their population into the military, volunteered to work at the Naval Supply Depot in Clearfield, Utah, so long as they could return home to plant and harvest their crops. A total of 625 Senecas lived on the Tonawanda reservation, and 102 of them served in the military. More than 10% of the population of the Seneca Nation's Allegany reservation fought in the American war effort.

The wartime experience, whether Indians served in the military or took advantage of opportunities offered by wartime employment, did more to integrate native peoples into the mainstream of American society than any governmental policy. During the first half of the twentieth century, the urban Indian population steadily increased, as migrants looked to take advantage of opportunities in nearby cities. They moved to escape stagnant reservation economies, and in so doing they transformed pockets of American cities into Indian Country.

The pace of this migration accelerated dramatically during the war years. Before the attack on Pearl Harbor, less than 5% of native peoples lived in cities; by 1950, nearly one in five did. Thousands of native peoples left their communities to enlist or to work in war-related industries. State officials in New York reported in 1942 that nearly all "employable" Indians were at work as a result of the enormous demand for the labor of native peoples.

Commissioner of Indian Affairs Collier observed that between 1941 and 1943 the number of native peoples living on reservations fell by 15%. Federal agents who worked with the Dakotas at Sisseton, the Pueblos, and the Potawatomis all reported that more than a quarter of the tribal population had relocated to urban areas to take advantage of the employment opportunities there. Between 1940 and 1960, the native population of the Santee reservation in Nebraska fell by 65%. Potawatomis joined members of six other native nations in Wisconsin in migrating to Milwaukee. In the spring of 1937 these newcomers established the Consolidated Tribes of American Indians, an organization that provided support and comradery to new arrivals. Senecas and other Iroquois found employment in New York City, Buffalo, Syracuse, and Rochester, where they worked for Curtis Aircraft, Bethlehem Steel, Alcoa, Kodak, and Bausch and Lomb. Like the Potawatomis, urban Senecas constructed organizations to help with the needs of Native American city people. It was difficult. In Rochester, meetings of the Neighborhood Indian Society occurred irregularly owing to the long hours worked by the migrants. Annual celebrations of National Indian Day at a park in Rochester stopped entirely during the war.

The experience of fighting the war, and relocating to take advantage of the numerous employment opportunities it created in American cities, provided native peoples with exposure to the higher standards of living in white America and provided them with an incentive to organize to demand full respect as citizens. They need not merely react to federal policies. With a national organization, native peoples could more effectively shape and influence the government policies that so dramatically impacted their lives.

Founded at Denver in 1944, the National Congress of American Indians (NCAI) drew its leadership from veterans of the Indian New Deal, men and women who had worked with the Bureau of Indian Affairs under Collier or who had been active in writing and implementing new tribal constitutions and corporate charters under the terms of the IRA. Among the founders—eighty Indians drawn from more than fifty tribes—was the Cherokee Ruth Muskrat Bronson and the Caddo Dan Madrano. They gathered at the Metropolitan Hotel, and drew up a constitution for the NCAI. Its purpose, the delegates declared, was "to secure to ourselves and our descendants the rights and benefits to which we are entitled under the laws of the

United States ... to enlighten the public towards a better understanding of the Indian race; to preserve Indian cultural values; to seek an equitable adjustment of tribal affairs; to secure and preserve rights under Indian treaties with the United States; and otherwise to promote the common welfare of the American Indians."

Native Americans demonstrated enormous patriotism during the war. They fought in the armed forces. They supported the war effort with great determination. They committed their resources to defeating the Axis powers. American industries energetically mined reservations while the American government used native land—more than a million acres—for airfields, gunnery ranges, and camps for the internment of Japanese Americans. Native peoples, in this sense, had proven themselves ready to stand on their own feet as Americans, and many critics of John Collier's Indian New Deal called for the dismantling of his programs. His efforts to reorganize and revitalize native communities had, in the eyes of many of his critics, lost their relevance as so many Indians left their reservations for jobs in urban centers or for military service. Native peoples, the argument went, were ready for full citizenship, no longer needed to be treated as wards of the federal government, and should be freed from the supervision of the Bureau of Indian Affairs. As journalist O.K. Armstrong pointed out in *Readers Digest* in 1945, Indians "live under conditions of racial segregation, and they are subject to special limitations and exemptions *because they are Indians*." Reservations, he continued, invoking a powerful image for World War II-era Americans, are "concentration camps" where Indians "live in poverty" and where "tribal control and governmental regulations constantly remind the Indian of his inferior status." The Indian New Deal, Armstrong said, though well-intentioned, moved Indians in the wrong direction, by forcing "a collectivist system upon the Indians, with bigger doses of paternalism and regimentation." Indians were ready for citizenship, Armstrong believed. As one Winnebago veteran told him, "give our boys and girls training as Americans, and not as Indians, and they'll set themselves free!"

Termination and the Coalminer's Canary

The Indian New Deal could not withstand the attacks it increasingly faced. As early as 1943, the Senate Committee on Indian Affairs had called for the abolition of the Bureau of Indian Affairs. Congressman Karl Mundt of South Dakota one year later denounced the Bureau of Indian Affairs for its inefficiency and policy failures, and asserted that it was time for the Indian "to take his place in the white man's community on the white man's level and with the white man's opportunity and security status." States, especially New York, clamored for more control over the administration of Indian affairs, especially after a 1942 federal court decision called into question the scope of state jurisdiction over Seneca land. Assaulted from all sides, Commissioner Collier accepted the premise in February 1944 that federal protection might be withdrawn from roughly 150,000 Indians who had acculturated sufficiently that they no longer required it. These Indians, Collier suggested, could be "released" from federal oversight.

Collier resigned in 1945. Harry Truman's acting commissioner, William Zimmerman, appeared before Congress in February 1947 and edged the country farther down this road, suggesting that Indian reservations be placed into three categories. Groups like the Senecas and their Iroquois kin in New York, the Kansas Potawatomis, and the Klamaths, Menominees, Osages, and the small California bands, had assimilated so far that they no longer needed federal services. Because they lived a lot like their white neighbors, and had experienced some measure of economic success, Zimmerman believed that they no longer needed to be treated as native peoples. Their nationhood, their sovereignty, were beside the point. The Bureau of Indian Affairs could withdraw all services from them immediately. A second group required more time, ten years, before they could survive without the oversight and protection of the Bureau of Indian Affairs. A final group would require federal services for the foreseeable future.

Zimmerman's plan provided the foundation for the policy of termination, a diffuse program directed toward the withdrawal of federal services for Indians. The government would end its treaty relations with native communities that had shown themselves ready to carry the burden of full citizenship. Congress would repeal laws that applied to these Indians *as Indians*, and transfer services run previously by the Bureau of Indian Affairs either to the tribes themselves or to state and local authorities. Senator Arthur Watkins, a Republican from Utah and champion of the termination policy, noted that "since the first decade of our national life the Indian, as tribesman and individual, was accorded a status apart." There were reasons for this, of course, and Watkins ignored completely the political status of native nations and the place of these polities in the American constitutional order. Indians, Watkins and other advocates of termination argued, had shown their readiness to join the mainstream of American society. Indians could and should be treated like every other American citizen. Now, Watkins said happily, "we think constructively and affirmatively of the Indian as a fellow American," and "seek to assure that in health, education, and welfare, in social, political, economic and cultural opportunity, he or she stands as one with us in the enjoyment and responsibilities of our national citizenship."

Felix Cohen, who understood that the policy shift toward termination reflected broader changes in post-war American society, argued in 1949 that "like the miner's canary, the Indian marks the shift from fresh air to poison gas in our political atmosphere; and our treatment of Indians, even more than our treatment of other minorities, reflects the rise and fall in our democratic faith." Indian reservations, with their communal ownership of the land, seemed subversive to some, and backwards to others, in the midst of a Cold War with the communist Soviet Union. Native peoples must be individualized and detribalized and take their place in American society. The racial segregation of Indian reservations could be eliminated, just as President Harry Truman had desegregated the nation's armed forces by executive order in 1947. Indeed, encouraging native peoples to preserve their culture ran counter to the powerful forces for conformity that coursed through Cold War America. And Republicans, who took control of both houses of Congress in 1952, wanted to cut massive federal budgets and retain the full employment of the war years without sliding back into economic hard times, a legitimate fear for a generation that had lived through the Great Depression. The aggressive exploitation of mineral and other resources in the western United States, much of it found in Indian country, seemed essential for national prosperity.

In August of 1953, Congress approved House Concurrent Resolution 108, setting in motion the policy of termination. Congress intended, the resolution read, "as rapidly as possible, to make the Indians within the territorial limits of the United States subject to the same laws and entitled to the same privileges and responsibilities as are applicable to other citizens of the United States, to end their status as wards of the United States, and to grant them all the rights and prerogatives pertaining to American citizenship." Because native peoples "should assume their full responsibilities as American Citizens," the House of Representatives resolved that "at the earliest possible time, all of the Indian tribes and the individual members thereof located within the states of California, Florida, New York and Texas," including the Chumash, the Senecas, and the Kansas Potawatomis, "should be freed from all Federal supervision and control and from all disabilities and limitations specially applicable to the Indians."

Two weeks after the approval of HCR 108, Congress passed Public Law 280, which transferred jurisdiction "with respect to criminal offenses and civil causes of action committed or arising on Indian reservations within" California, Minnesota, Nebraska, Oregon, and Wisconsin to state authorities. By allowing these states to extend their criminal and civil jurisdiction over the reservations within their bounds, and without the consent of the native tribes involved, PL 280 hacked away at the notion of tribal sovereignty, an outdated and irrelevant concept in the view of termination's proponents. Some members of Congress went so far as to propose a constitutional amendment removing the phrase "and Indian tribes" from the commerce clause of the Constitution. In the following weeks and months, congressmen who favored termination submitted a series of bills ending federal relations with native communities in California, with the Confederated Salish and Kootenai tribes of the Flathead Indian Reservation in Montana, and with the Seminoles in Florida. Another bill scheduled the Iowas, the Sacs and Foxes, the Kickapoos, and Prairie Band of Potawatomis for termination.

How these policies were supposed to help Indians was never clearly spelled out. It was true that despite the Indian New Deal, reservation communities remained mired in poverty. Despite relief and recovery programs, the median income for Indian families was less than a quarter of that for non-Indians. The life expectancy for native peoples in the United States stood at forty-two years, twenty years less than that of other Americans. Twice as many American Indian babies died during their first year of life than among the non-Indian population. Educational attainment remained low, with few children attending schools regularly. Only 5% of the native population had a high school diploma. Many homes lacked electricity and running water.

Indian communities in many cases lacked the resources to compete in an American capitalist system. Pueblo farmers lacked the machinery, education, and financing to succeed as commercial farmers. Some of the men who returned to their communities after the war took advantage of the G.I. Bill to pursue higher education; others left to look for work in cities or in American-owned mines. The Bureau of Indian Affairs continued to live up to its reputation for mind-boggling inefficiency, and its employees exercised an extraordinary amount of control over the lives of reservation residents. Termination would do away with the heavy-handedness of the Bureau of Indian Affairs, but no proponent of the policy offered a coherent explanation for how the ending of federal supervision would solve deeper, more structural, problems.

Answering difficult questions of these sorts, of course, could not have benefited the proponents of termination. Rather than addressing how, specifically, termination would help Indian tribes, Senator Watkins and others placed their reliance upon glittering generalities. "Firm and constant consideration for those of Indian ancestry should lead all of us to work diligently and carefully for the full realization of their national citizenship with all other Americans," Watkins wrote in May of 1957. Who could disagree, he seemed to suggest. "Following in the footsteps of the Emancipation Proclamation," he continued, "I see the following words emblazoned in letters of fire above the heads of the Indians—*THESE PEOPLES SHALL BE FREE!*"

Several years earlier, Watkins contemptuously argued that native peoples really wanted "representation without taxation." He complained that Indians "can tax all the rest of us and vote for people who do tax us; but he doesn't want to pay taxes himself even though he is able to do so." Indians, Watkins thought, were lazy. They received special advantages with which they did little to help themselves, and they possessed a special category of rights not available to other Americans. In this sense termination, like earlier federal Indian policies, responded more to the interests of the white communities who lived in close contact with native peoples, the commercial and corporate interests who sought to exploit the resources on or under their lands, than to the needs of American Indians. White resentment, white frustration, and white avarice certainly contributed to the policies enacted during these years. The Bureau of Indian Affairs routinely rubber-stamped contracts for the exploitation of oil, gas, and mineral wealth on Indian lands, commercial operations for which tribes received poor rates of return and the destruction of reservation environments. Terminating the paltry, haphazard, and inefficient guardianship of the Bureau promised to open even more tribal resources to commercial development. Termination may not have been designed to aid Indians at all.

Between 1954 and the end of the 1960s, Congress terminated over 100 tribes, including forty-one small rancheria and mission communities in California in one piece of legislation in 1958. Only 3% of the nation's native population suffered termination—about 11,000 people living on 1.3 million acres—but the policy devastated those upon whom it fell. To focus only on terminated tribes, however, is to miss the entire significance of this destructive era. Tribes whose relationship with the United States remained unchanged faced significant legislative aggression from the 1940s into the 1960s. Since the late nineteenth century, for instance, the Senecas had fought New York's efforts to claim political and legal jurisdiction over the Nation. The state government was a presence in the lives of New York's Indians. It ran the Thomas Indian School, and other public schools on Iroquois land, claimed oversight of public health on reservations, and maintained the highways and roads that passed through Seneca lands. But the legal basis for this exercise of state authority was murky at best, and on a number of occasions between the late 1880s and 1940, lawmakers sympathetic to the state's interests tried to enact legislation that would clearly have given New York the jurisdiction it sought.

The Senecas could not help but notice that the same men who long had clamored to allot their lands were those who called for the extension of state jurisdiction over their affairs. They thus resisted both movements. Indeed, in the spring of 1939, in an effort to secure their right to control the lands they had leased to outsiders, the Seneca Nation decided to cancel more than 800 delinquent leases, and asked the United States Department of Justice to help them set up the test cases that could secure and confirm that right. In *United States v. Forness*, a federal court recognized in 1942 the right of the Nation to cancel delinquent leases and held that federal law trumped the laws of New York State when it came to Indian affairs. New York legislators retaliated and worked with allies in Congress to secure what the Senecas described later as the "Spite Bills" of 1948 and 1950. The two controversial acts extended New York's criminal and then civil jurisdiction over Indian lands within the state.

Federal authorities did more than aid the state in extending its jurisdiction. At the end of the war, the US Army Corps of Engineers resuscitated a decades' old plan to construct the Kinzua Dam on the Allegheny River in northern Pennsylvania, not far from the Senecas' Allegany Reservation. Earlier attempts to build the dam never progressed beyond the planning stage because federal authorities in the Interior and Justice Department believed that the flooding resulting from the dam would constitute a violation of the 1794 Treaty of Canandaigua. These concerns disappeared during the Termination era, as planners brushed aside these legal arguments as antiquated nonsense. Pennsylvania Senator Edward Martin said that because the Senecas "are now citizens of America and they are subject to eminent domain just the same way as any other American citizen," the treaty no longer restrained the actions of the United States government.

Figure 9.3 George Gillete, chairman of the Fort Berthold Indian Tribal Business Council, weeps in the office of Secretary of the Interior J.A. Krug in Washington, DC after signing agreement allowing for construction of dam on the Missouri River. © AP/Photo.

The Seneca Nation mobilized to fight the proposed dam. It would flood a third of the reservation, including much of its most valuable and culturally significant land. They enlisted support from sympathetic religious and civic groups committed to the treaty rights of native peoples. They looked into alternatives to the dam, including a more cost-effective proposal to divert excess water westward toward Lake Erie. It also fought in the courts. To raise money for the legal fight, the Seneca Nation reluctantly granted highway and pipeline rights of way to the state. Facing the loss of nearly one-third of the reservation, the Seneca Nation granted land concessions in the hope that doing so might provide them with the wherewithal to protect what remained.

Their efforts came up empty. In April of 1958, the federal district court in Washington ruled that the United States had the right to take reservation land through the exercise of eminent domain. Echoing the devastating logic of the *Lone Wolf* decision, the Court found that "a federal Indian treaty" like Canandaigua "could not rise above the power of Congress to legislate." The United States could do what it wanted, regardless of the wishes of native peoples, with dire consequences for the Senecas. Indians could not be allowed to retard the economic progress of the American nation.

Over Seneca protests, the construction of Kinzua Dam began. Between 9000 and 10,000 acres, fertile bottom lands lying beside the river rich in wildplants, ideal for agriculture, and containing the best habitat for bear and deer, sank beneath the floodwaters. Thousands of Seneca graves, including that of their great leader Cornplanter, as well as the site of the Coldspring Longhouse, had to be relocated to avoid the rising waters. Six hundred Senecas from 160 families had to find new homes. In 1964, President Lyndon Johnson signed legislation paying the Senecas a settlement for the damages caused to their homelands, $15 million. Some of this money the tribe distributed to its members. Some it invested to build housing and rehabilitate the reservation. The money helped the Senecas, but it could not offset the loss of a third of their homeland to a federal government that felt itself unbound by the treaties it negotiated and declared the "supreme law of the land." The wounds inflicted by Kinzua in many ways remain open still.

The Crows faced a challenge similar to that of the Senecas. In 1954, federal and state authorities began to pressure the Crows to allow the construction of a dam on the Big Horn River. If the Crows did not sell, government officials suggested, the federal government might seize the land necessary, 5000 acres in the Bighorn Canyon. The Crows, who had written a constitution in 1948 that placed tribal government in the hands of a chairman who governed with the assistance of a general council consisting of all adult members of the tribe, divided bitterly over the proposal. Although the dam would not require the sorts of relocation created by the construction of Kinzua, and although tribal members recognized that the government intended to pay the Crows "a just and equitable settlement for this vital resource," Crows debated the consequences of the construction project and how best to control an important segment of the tribe's homeland. Robert Yellowtail, who served as tribal chairman from 1952 until 1954, led the River Crows while his opponents, William Wall and Edward Posey Whiteman, led the Mountain Crows. Both sides worked to secure what they believed was the best possible deal from federal authorities.

In 1955, Yellowtail and his supporters proposed to lease the lands needed for the dam to the federal government, $1 million per year for fifty years. At the end of the lease period, the land would revert to the Crow Tribe. Yellowtail's opponents proposed to sell the lands to the United States for $5 million. Government officials informed the Crows that if they chose not to sell the lands, the United States intended to begin eminent domain proceedings. Yellowtail denounced these federal tactics as "blackmail, treason to a sacred trust by the guardian, extortion by threats, intriguing, crafty, cunning, deceitful, foxy, and sly action to extort by compulsion, through the power and force of Government, the tribal property and treaty lands of the Crows." The tribal government, deeply divided, voted to sell the lands for $5 million and to retain mineral rights to the canyon. Montana's congressional delegation supported the proposal but President Dwight Eisenhower refused to pay that sum of money merely for the rights to construct a dam and vetoed the legislation. Eisenhower, interested in economy, decided to drive a hard bargain.

While this legislation moved through the Congress and toward the president's desk, the federal government filed suit to claim more than 5600 acres of Crow land. The question before the court involved the power of the federal government over waterways flowing through Indian land, and the power of the Congress to seize lands guaranteed to an Indian tribe by treaty. The *Lone Wolf* decision, it seemed, had effectively eradicated the Crows' position on the latter issue, but the 1908 case of *Winters v. United States*, an important water rights decision in which the Supreme Court held that when the United States established a reservation for a tribe, it implicitly established as well a right to the water that flowed through that reservation, seemed to offer some hope. Indians, the Court argued, had been placed on reservations at least in part to learn how to become agriculturalists. It was absurd to assume that in depriving them of their old way of life, the Court ruled, that Congress did not mean for them to have the water for irrigation that could allow them to change their ways.

The Crows took the *Winters* doctrine a step further, arguing that the government must pay them compensation for the taking of their lands and their water and, as well, that it must pay them compensation for the potential power that the river might generate. The Court, swayed by these arguments, found that the government could condemn the land, but that it must pay to the Crows adequate and just compensation. Before further proceedings to establish a proper value of the lands and the flow of the river, the United States withdrew its suit. It did not want to pay so great a sum for the lands in question. Montana's congressional delegation then submitted legislation paying the Crows $2.5 million, and allowed the tribe to sue the United States for additional damages, so long as the tribe agreed to pay back the $2.5 million from whatever award they received. President Eisenhower, in July of 1958, signed the legislation. Though the courts in 1963 agreed that the Crows were entitled to additional damages, the tribe never received that money.

The construction of the Yellowtail Dam, named after the tribal chairman who had opposed the terms under which it was constructed, constituted part of the enormous Pick-Sloan plan to build twelve large dams in Montana, Wyoming, and in the Dakotas. Tribes throughout the region faced a heavy-handed government that demanded access to their lands. The tribes had little choice but to surrender. Treaties provided little protection, short of ensuring that the government paid to the tribes a sum of money for lands it already had determined to seize. In the postwar era, native nations from New York to California faced a federal government firmly committed to the principle that native nations must not be permitted to stand in the way of progress.

Two months after President Eisenhower signed into law the agreement compensating the Crows in part for the flooding of their lands, his secretary of the interior, Fred Seaton, announced that "no Indian tribe or group should end its relationship with the Federal Government unless such tribe or group has clearly demonstrated—first, that it understands the plan under which such a program would go forward, and second, that the tribe or group affected concurs in and supports the plan proposed." Seaton declared it "absolutely unthinkable … that consideration would be given to forcing upon an Indian tribe a so-called termination plan which did not have the understanding and acceptance of a clear majority of the members affected." Some members of some tribes unquestionably desired an end to the guardianship of federal authorities. According to the Bureau of Indian Affairs in a 1954 report, tribes in Oklahoma including the Eastern Shawnee, Seneca-Cayugas, Wyandots, Ottawas, Quapaws, Miamis, Modocs, and Peorias sought an end to federal protection. A number of native leaders, like the Cherokee Reed Buzzard, called for the elimination of the Bureau and federal oversight of the nation's affairs.

These voices, however, remained part of a small minority. The vast majority of native peoples feared and opposed termination. A group of Iroquois, for instance, traveled to Washington in March of 1959 during the height of the Kinzua dam controversy and attempted to place Commissioner of Indian Affairs Glen Emmons under arrest for his "anti-Indian" attitudes and because he "permitted crimes against Indians." The Six Nations also intended to take their case before the United Nations. Joseph Garry, the head of the National Congress of American Indians, opposed these tactics. Garry struck a conciliatory tone and argued that his organization had "confidence and faith in our congressmen, our Government officials, our attorneys and courts and we shall continue to bring our problems to them and co-operate with them for their solution." His organization, in a quiet and measured fashion, played a significant role in mobilizing opposition to the termination policy. It is owing to this activism, at least in part, that Seaton announced the effective suspension of termination in the fall of 1958.

Indeed, buoyed by the importance of the military service they had performed during the war, many veterans joined the NCAI. Pueblo veterans, for instance, told the members of a congressional committee that they had willingly served in the armed forces "in order to save our country," but now they faced policies "which will mean total destruction of all tribes." The president of Santa Clara Pueblo, Manuel Holcomb, complained that "during the war we were accepted as equals. But now that the war is over we are savages again," ripe for exploitation. Garry denounced HCR 108 as the gravest threat to native peoples since the passage of the General Allotment Act. Reservations, he said, were not the prisons that the advocates of termination claimed, but "ancestral homelands, retained by us for our perpetual use and enjoyment." Termination impoverished its victims and it did nothing for Indians, a claim increasingly borne out by the experience of terminated communities.

Cleaning the Slate

The formal end of relations between native peoples and the federal government by congressional enactment constituted only one part of post-war America's effort to get out of the Indian business. In August of 1946, Congress created the Indian Claims Commission, a tribunal before which native leaders and their attorneys could seek redress for lands taken from them in violation of federal law or Indian treaty, or for unjust compensation. Prior to 1946, the United States Court of Claims could hear suits from Indian tribes against the government only if Congress passed legislation specifically allowing the claim to move forward. The process was expensive and time-consuming and often unjust. Now, a tribe could present a claim before the Indian Claims Commission seeking compensation for loss of lands. President Harry Truman, at the signing ceremony, announced that the creation of the Indian Claims Commission marked "the beginning of a new era," one in which the United States showed to a watching world that it recognized and respected the rights of "little peoples" at home, if not abroad.

To advance a claim against the United States, the petitioners had to move through a three-step process. First, they had to demonstrate their descent from the "tribes, bands and other identifiable groups of American Indians" who had suffered the original injury. This posed a difficulty for some native peoples, as many communities like the Potawatomis had fragmented over the span of time since they originally had lost their lands. Groups not recognized by the federal government, like the Mohegans or the Powhatan communities, found this requirement an insuperable obstacle. Assuming that a native group had standing to bring a claim against the United States, the Commission heard testimony and gathered evidence to determine the value of the land in question at the time it was lost. This required extensive research, and in effect limited the award native peoples might receive. The legislation creating the Indian Claims Commission allowed awards for the value of lands lost at the time of dispossession; nothing could be done about rental value or interest for the unauthorized use of these lands over the span of many decades. Finally, once the Commission arrived at a value for the lands in question, it had to consider the value of all gratuitous "offsets" the tribe had received—the goods and services provided to the tribe since the land had been taken. The sum of the offsets was deducted from the historic value of the land. The Commission awarded the difference to the tribes.

Congress originally intended the Indian Claims Commission to hear cases for ten years. It extended the life of the ICC on a number of occasions. When the Indian Claims Commission finally ended its work in 1978, slightly more than thirty years after its creation, it had paid out more than $818 million in 274 successful claims out of the 852 that were filed. The Cherokees received $14.7 million as compensation for the loss of their lands opened to white settlement in 1893. The Caddos received a relatively small sum of $383,475 for the Brazos River lands Texans forced them to flee in the 1850s. For the loss of their lands at the 1868 Fort Laramie Treaty for much less than their market value, the Indian Claims Commission ruled that the Crows could collect over $10 million in 1961. Acoma Pueblo received more than $6 million for its losses, while the Seneca Nation of Indians received more than $5 million, a ruling based on the historical legacy of the Big Tree Treaty of 1797. By paying damages for the lands it had taken from native peoples unfairly or illegally, supporters of the Indian Claims Commission hoped to eliminate any remaining obligations the government owed to American Indians. Compensation thus walked hand in hand with termination, and was entirely consistent with the desire of the United States to individualize and assimilate natives. We owe you nothing now, the government might have said, and we can cut you loose.

While the Indian Claims Commission ruled on the merits of the claims native nations brought against the United States, the federal courts wrestled with the place of native peoples in post-war America. In 1951, the United States Department of the Interior sold timber on lands claimed by the Tee-Hit-Tons, an Alaskan Tlingit community. The Tee-Hit-Tons filed suit, arguing that the unauthorized sale constituted an unlawful taking of their resources. In 1955, the Supreme Court disagreed. Because neither federal law nor treaty defined the status of these lands, the Court held that the Tee-Hit-Tons possessed nothing more than a right to use the lands in question at the government's will. "No case in Court has ever held that taking of Indian title or use by Congress required compensation," Justice Stanley Reed wrote. The land rights of native peoples, then, he asserted were limited. "The American people have compassion for the descendants of those Indians who were deprived of their homes and hunting grounds by the drive of civilization," but the "generous provision made to allow the tribes to recover for wrongs," like the Indian Claims Commission Act, came "as a matter of grace, not because of legal liability."

Four years later, the Court weighed in again on the question of the rights of native nations under the Constitution, this time considering the relative power of state governments over the native communities existing within their borders. A non-Indian businessman operated a general store on the Navajo Indian Reservation in Arizona. He filed suit in state court against a Navajo husband and wife who owed him money. In *Williams v. Lee*, the Court ruled that allowing state jurisdiction in this instance would violate Navajo rights as defined in an 1868 treaty. The tribal court had the authority to hear and rule on this contract dispute. In *Williams*, the Court held that "the question has always been whether the state action infringed on the right of reservation Indians to make their own laws and be ruled by them."

In the 1832 *Worcester* decision, the Court had asserted that Indian Country was an arena into which the states could never intrude because the Constitution placed under Congress all power to oversee commerce with Indian tribes. Now, states could extend their authority into Indian Country up to the point where it began to *infringe* upon tribal powers of self-government, a standard that the Court did not define precisely. Tribal sovereignty, in this sense the ability of native peoples to protect their laws, lands, and liberties, would come under increasing legal attack in the decades that followed.

A fourth component of the termination era, in addition to the Indian Claims Commission, the passage of termination legislation by the Congress, and the beginning of the Court's assault on American Indian tribal sovereignty, involved a program to move native peoples from reservations to the cities, an idea that seemed to possess much promise to policy-makers who noted that many Indians relocated during World War II to seek employment. During the Indian New Deal, Congress and Commissioner Collier for the first time had enacted policies designed to preserve native lands and transform reservations into homelands. Collier and his supporters envisioned a reservation future for native peoples. This was no longer the case after World War II.

President Harry Truman appointed Dillon Myer in 1950 to head the Bureau of Indian Affairs. Myer's previous experience included overseeing the War Relocation Authority, the federal agency responsible for the internment of Japanese and Japanese Americans in a number of prison camps located in the western United States. Now, instead of isolating one group, he would oversee as head of the Bureau a Voluntary Relocation Program designed to encourage migration to the cities. Though native peoples had been moving to urban centers for decades, Myer's program, which continued under his successor, Glen Emmons, marked a significant change in federal Indian policy. Earlier policies had aimed at transforming the residents of reservations into hardy farmers, working their lands like their white neighbors. They would, policy-makers hoped, accept American rural life as their own. During the Indian New Deal, John Collier removed the emphasis on acculturation and assimilation, but he still looked for ways to develop the agricultural economies of Indian reservations. Myer broke with this past. Life on the reservations had not helped Indians. No future existed for them on the land. They should leave, and move to the cities, and join the nation's burgeoning industrial workforce. American Indian policy had swung back sharply toward assimilation and the absorption of the nation's native peoples into the American body politic.

Thirty thousand American Indians participated in the Voluntary Relocation Program, 10% of the total reservation population. Perhaps another 70,000 Indians, from the end of the war until 1958, moved to the cities without any government assistance. They did so to provide for their families, and to escape poverty at home. Many of them had worked in cities during the war years only to be displaced after the soldiers returned home. These native men and women likely found the promise of high wages immensely attractive. By 1960, 30% of the nation's native population lived in urban centers, and that figure would increase to nearly 45% by 1970. To facilitate this considerable migration, the Bureau of Indian Affairs established offices in Oakland, Oklahoma City, Denver, Minneapolis, Chicago, and in other cities to aid native peoples in finding housing and employment. Pueblos moved to Phoenix, Albuquerque, Los Angeles, and Tucson. Kiowas moved to cities throughout the western United States. A 27-year-old Kiowa named Dale Beck, for instance, lived in Redondo Beach, California, and was one of the 500 native peoples employed by North American Aviation in 1955. Caddos, Cherokees, and others moved to Oklahoma City and urban centers farther from their reservations. Movement was widespread, and people from nearly every native community in the United States moved during the postwar years.

Adjusting to life in the cities was not easy for the new arrivals. Many lacked the education necessary to find those elusive well-paying jobs. They performed the most menial labor, and concentrated in impoverished neighborhoods. Often the last hired and first fired, many of them struggled to get by. Alcoholism and violence affected many, as they dealt with the strains of adjusting to new homes. A Seneca attorney named Fred Gabourdie who practiced in Los Angeles found that for his Indian clients, alcohol was involved in 75% to 80% of the crimes they stood accused of committing, or 95% of the time when his client stood accused of a violent crime. Policemen in Los Angeles looked for opportunities to roll Indians, and a Chumash living there complained of frequent police brutality.

Life could be tough, no question. Native peoples who moved to Seattle found discrimination in housing and employment, the denial of basic services, and unsympathetic police when they became the victims of violent crime. Wilma Mankiller, who later became the principal chief of the Cherokee Nation, described the experience of relocation as yet another "removal," her very own "trail of tears," caused by "the fear and the anguish that occur when you give up your home, your community, and everything you have ever known to move far away to a strange place." A Kiowa woman lamented the difficult conditions. "I have seen divorces," she said, and "I have seen the kids," and "I have seen so many women that go to prostitute, you know they have to have money." N. Scott Momaday, the Kiowa author, captured some of this dislocation in his Pulitzer Prize-winning novel *House Made of Dawn* (1968). Many of the migrants returned home: proponents of the relocation program said that less than a third returned home, but critics said that as many as three-quarters of the migrants gave up and returned to their reservations.

These numbers raise questions, and may be based upon faulty assumptions. Native peoples who moved to Los Angeles, for instance, in many cases established themselves there and entered the middle class. Many others traveled back and forth, preserving their connections both to the new urban setting and life on reservations. Residents of Laguna Pueblo, for example, who traveled to cities around the southwest to work on the railroad and in other industries, established "colonies" in Barstow, California, Winslow, Arizona, and in Gallup and Albuquerque, New Mexico. These colonies helped Laguna Pueblos maintain their language and culture in an urban setting and preserve the bonds that united them at home. Cherokees like Mankiller who left their reservation in Oklahoma also maintained community ties in the cities they moved to. Cherokees in Albuquerque, for instance, met to preserve their culture and to provide support for each other in a new and often unfamiliar setting. Organizations for native peoples living in cities sprang up across the country, and significant and identifiable neighborhoods occupied by American Indians developed in cities across the southwest, and in Denver, Seattle and Tacoma, Oklahoma City, Minneapolis, Chicago, Los Angeles, and New York. Senecas moved to Buffalo, and Crows to Billings, Montana. These urban migrants came to work, but they returned home when the need arose.

Many of these emigrants were poor and struggled with the requirements of city life and urban employment. Their experience, however, was not dissimilar to that of other rural migrants to America's cities. Native peoples who moved to cities, who according to President Richard Nixon lived "lost in the anonymity of the city ... drifting from neighborhood to neighborhood" and who struggled to adjust, were not in reality an exceptionally or unusually unstable group, and the cultural resources they carried with them—language, belief, community ties—did not necessarily leave them any less well-suited to urban living than other immigrant groups. The history of native peoples moving to American cities is not markedly dissimilar to that of other historical immigrant groups, and many of these new arrivals struggled to survive in cities that were often unfriendly to their newest residents.

Indeed, as a gathering of urban Indians pointed out in a report to the Washington state legislature, "the Indian" was not a victim. "He is part of his community, often is not recognized by his physical features as Indian," and "shares with the majority the belief that good education, peace, and justice, health and clean living are important." He would get along, and work with the majority society, but also "remain Indian and preserve the special rights he may still retain." Urban Indians respected the past, but looked to the future and, importantly, pointed out that "he is as likely to succeed on the job as anyone else and no more likely to be absentee." He could be a farmer or a laborer "or the successful graduate student in the urban university." Native peoples succeeded in finding native spaces in American cities, in Seattle as elsewhere.

There was a final component to the termination policy. While Congress attempted to get out of the "Indian Business," erase its obligations to native peoples, and encourage their relocation to the nation's cities, officials in the Bureau of Indian Affairs launched in 1958 the Indian Adoption Project, a horrifying assault upon Native American families and children. When officials in the Bureau of Indian Affairs spoke of Indian families, they too often thought in terms of single mothers. It was the broken structure of Indian families, the logic went, rather than poverty, inequality, and the legacies of conquest and colonialism, that accounted for the troubles afflicting native peoples.

Even though the evidence that unwed motherhood had reached epidemic proportions in Indian Country was largely unsubstantiated, and that the Bureau of Indian Affairs ignored entirely the importance of extended families in child-rearing, and that policies aimed at attacking poverty and economic inequality might have been better suited for remedying the problems native peoples faced, the Bureau of Indian Affairs and the Indian Adoption Project looked to dismantle these families by pressuring mothers to give up their children for adoption. The benefits for the Bureau were substantial. It cost $750 per year, for example, to support a native child at Minnesota's Pipestone Boarding School, but only $470 to support that child in the state's foster care system. Both the Bureau and the states could save even more money if these children were adopted. Thus, according to historian Margaret Jacobs, "the BIA and state agencies looked to the ultimate 'private' sector—in this case, white families—to take over the expense of raising Indian children." Viewing Indian families as drunken and degraded, state officials deceived and coerced Indian mothers, took their children from them against their will, and then denied them due process when they tried to fight back. The BIA Adoption Program was perhaps the most brutal example of the termination policy in action.

New Frontiers

Termination did not end after Secretary of Interior Fred Seaton's announcement in 1958. Public Law 280 remained on the books, and progress on the construction of the Kinzua Dam moved forward. As late as 1966 and 1967, in fact, Congress terminated nine small *rancherias* of California Indians. Still, a consensus emerged that the policy, as enacted by Congress, contained major flaws. Indians opposed it, and saw it as a threat to their way of life. Though advocates asserted that nothing in the policy required native peoples to surrender any aspect of their culture, and that native peoples, like other ethnic Americans, could still express their pride in their culture, native peoples found the prospect of termination terrifying. In attacking American Indian nationhood, their attachment to ancestral homelands, the policy seemed like an American final solution to the Indian problem, one bent toward the eradication of American Indian communities. Native peoples were not simply the members of an ethnic group, but members of "domestic dependent nations," the Supreme Court said, who retained elements of an inherent tribal sovereignty. They saw the policy as an attack, but they also pointed out that after a decade and a half of attempts to reduce the federal government's role in the conduct of American Indian policy, native peoples continued to lag behind their fellow citizens in almost every measure of social well-being: 10% of native children under the age of 14 had never attended school; only 12% of native peoples received a high school education; only 1% of Indians had attended four years of college; and Indians lived shorter and poorer lives than white Americans. Some evidence suggested that Public Law 280 led to increases in crime on reservations and declining income in those communities.

John F. Kennedy's election as President in 1960 signaled only a slight break with the failed policies of the termination era. Kennedy himself no more respected the notion of tribal sovereignty than his predecessors, but his administration did make funds available through the Area Redevelopment Act of 1961 to provide assistance to Indian reservations and other "pockets of poverty." Commissioner of Indian Affairs Phileo T. Nash used funds from the Bureau of Indian Affairs budget and monies from federal agencies such as the Public Housing Administration and the Small Business Administration in an attempt to improve the quality of life on Indian reservations.

The flow of federal funding to Indian reservations increased under Lyndon Baines Johnson's "Great Society." Head Start, Upward Bound, and the Job Corps all included funding for native communities. The most significant source of funding came from the Office of Economic Opportunity (OEO). OEO grants, owing to the lobbying of native peoples in the nation's capital, went directly to Indian governments, securing for them an important independence from the Bureau of Indian Affairs.

The OEO, as a result, which worked through congressionally mandated "Community Action Programs" that mobilized community members in the Johnson Administration's "War on Poverty," in essence became the first federal program based upon the principle of self-determination. Native peoples could best decide where and how to spend federal funds intended to revitalize their communities and eradicate poverty. The OEO funded education programs on reservations, the construction of health centers, housing projects, and a variety of other programs. The OEO provided important on-the-job training to native peoples on how to run a federally funded program. It provided opportunities for ambitious and talented native peoples as well, and the infusion of federal funding, greater than during the Indian New Deal, provided important medical and educational services to reservation residents. By 1967, a third of Native American children attended Head Start programs.

The War on Poverty did not eradicate the grinding conditions on many reservations. Still, the Johnson administration brought significant change to the nation's Indian policy. In March of 1968, Johnson proposed "a new goal for our Indian programs: A goal that ends the old debate about termination of Indian programs and stresses self-determination; a goal that erases old attitudes of paternalism and promotes partnership self-help." Native peoples, he said, in addition to having a standard of living equivalent to that of other Americans, should have the freedom to choose "to remain in their homelands … without surrendering their dignity" or the "opportunity to move to the towns and cities of America, if they choose, equipped with the skills to live in equality and dignity." The choice was theirs. In either case, Johnson said, "Indians must have a voice in making the plans and decisions in programs which are important to their daily life."

The trend toward self-determination continued under President Richard Nixon. In a speech on Indian affairs delivered in July of 1970, Nixon declared that "it is long past time that that the Indian policies of the Federal government began to recognize and build upon the capacities and insights of the Indian people." The time, Nixon said, was right for significant change, and the government must start acting "on the basis of what Indians have been telling us." The time had arrived "to break decisively with the past and to create the conditions for a new era in which the Indian future is determined by Indian acts and Indian decisions."

By the time Nixon made this statement, the return of Blue Lake to Taos Pueblo had moved to the top of his agenda for American Indian affairs. A sacred site and the center of Taos religious life, Blue Lake became part of the Carson National Forest in 1906. The Forest Service opened the area to the American public soon after but also to timber interests. As early as 1350 AD, Pueblos from Taos had farmed lands watered by rivers flowing from Blue Lake. They depended upon Blue Lake, and did not feel that this precious resource could be shared. Taos Pueblo brought a suit before the Indian Claims Commission. New Mexico's congressional delegation and representatives of the United States Forest Service challenged Taos Pueblo every step of the way.

In September of 1965 the Indian Claims Commission found that the United States had taken Blue Lake and the surrounding lands without just compensation. The Commissioners ordered that researchers determine the value of the lands Taos Pueblo had lost. The ruling pleased the Pueblos, but they did not want monetary damages. They sought the return of the land. Editorials appeared in newspapers around the United States supporting Taos Pueblo, and New Mexico Senator Clinton Anderson reluctantly introduced legislation in 1966 to arrange for the return of Blue Lake.

Other native nations sought the return of their lands. Some won their cases before the Indian Claims Commission and, like Taos Pueblo, refused to accept the monetary award because they wanted the land. Acceptance of the award would, under the law establishing the Indian Claims Commission, have quieted all their claims. Unlike other native peoples, however, Taos Pueblo succeeded. The Taos and their numerous supporters argued on religious and moral grounds; the significance of the lands they had lost lay in their religious and spiritual importance. Their leaders pursued a vigorous campaign to inform the public about the importance of Blue Lake in their religious life and made their struggle a symbol of the historic mistreatment of native peoples. In this sense, President Nixon was only too happy to sign the legislation returning Blue Lake to Taos Pueblo when it finally reached his desk late in 1970. It cost him nothing to do so. The president said at the signing ceremony that "this is a bill that represents justice, because in 1906 an injustice was done in which land involved in this bill, 48,000 acres, was taken from the Indians involved." Nixon argued that by signing the legislation, his administration had broken with a troubling past. The United States, he said, had embarked "in a new direction in which we will have the cooperation of both Democrats and Republicans, one in which there will be more of an attitude of cooperation than paternalism, one of self-determination rather than termination, one of mutual respect." The bill returned Blue Lake to Taos Pueblo, a significant act by the man who presided over a government that had done so much historically to dispossess native peoples.

Red Power

Yet native peoples might have pointed out to the president that plenty of injustice remained, and that many of the crimes of the past still occurred in Indian country. The president could choose his battles, addressing symbolic measures that helped specific native communities. The representatives of Taos Pueblo were well-behaved, but growing numbers of young native peoples, on college campuses and in relocated Indian communities, on the reservations and at protests against the Vietnam War, lurked behind them, determined to combat what they considered their continuing marginalization. Had not these young activists organized to protest the existing state of affairs in the government, it is not likely that the president would have felt compelled to act.

The roots of this activism ran deep. Though many historians have paid more attention to the dramatic, attention-grabbing tactics of the American Indian Movement, the modern movement for Indian rights began with struggles against termination in the immediate aftermath of World War II and continue today. Native men who had fought in the war returned assertive and determined to enjoy their full rights as citizens. Many of them took advantage of the G.I. Bill of Rights to attend college, acquiring skills that they carried back to their communities and channeled into activism, or the administration of OEO programs that played so large a role in the War on Poverty. These veterans had fought for freedom and democracy in Europe and the Pacific, for the United States and for their homelands. They expected those things for their people at home.

Many of them were aware of decolonization struggles in Asia and Africa. According to the journalist Edmund Wilson, who visited the Iroquois in the late 1950s, "the leaders of these Indian movements ... have sensed that the white man has been losing his hold, and, like the rest of the non-white races, they are sick of his complacency and arrogance." They believed, Wilson continued, that "in view of our righteous professions in relation to the Germans and Russians, they know that, for the first time in history, they are in a position to blackmail us into keeping our agreements and honoring their claims."

Certainly Wilson overstated his case, but he was fundamentally correct that native peoples were coming together in unprecedented ways to criticize government policies. There were the moderate proposals offered by the Fund for the Republic, which published in January of 1961 "A Blueprint for Indian Citizens," written by a special blue-ribbon commission headed by Cherokee chief and oil executive W.W. Keeler. "An objective which should undergird all Indian policy," the Keeler Commission wrote, "is that the Indian individual, the Indian family, and the Indian community be motivated to participate in solving their own problems." Favoring assimilation, and writing from the position that "only men who have a foot in each way of life and an appreciation of both can effectively" bridge the chasm between native peoples and white Americans, the Commission concluded that tribes should not be terminated, and that "the Indian must be given an opportunity he can utilize."

The summer of 1961 brought the American Indian Chicago Conference. Some 467 delegates from ninety native communities attended the gathering organized by the anthropologists Sol Tax and Nancy Lurie. The conference brought national attention to a host of local problems in Indian country, but also placed the movement for the rights of native nations in an international context. Senecas educated attendees about Kinzua, for example, while the Santa Clara Pueblo delegate Edward Dozier described the struggles of native peoples for freedom as part of a larger moment, "manifested in many parts of the world," and of which "the situation in Africa, in Southeast Asia and elsewhere are examples."

It was a diverse gathering. The delegates wanted different things. They could not agree on everything, but they did produce a startling "Declaration of Indian Purpose," a manifesto that laid out the goals of Indian activists. They argued that the United States had "a positive national obligation to modify or remove the conditions which produce the poverty and lack of social adjustment as these prevail as the outstanding attributes of Indian life today." That meant abandoning the desiccated logic of termination, but also providing native peoples with the assistance they required to solve the problems they faced in their own ways. "What we ask of America," the delegates wrote, "is not charity, not paternalism, even when benevolent." Rather, they asked "that the nature of our situation be recognized and made the basis of policy and action."

But getting the government to act was difficult. Sometimes direct action was needed to prod American officials to do the right thing. The National Indian Youth Council (NIYC), founded in Gallup, New Mexico, in August, in a sense grew out of the Chicago Conference. The founders, drawn from a cross-section of Native America that included Crows, Potawatomis, Mandans, Sioux, and many others, had been active in college Indian clubs and organizations going back to the 1950s. They hoped to effect the repeal of HCR 108, and they wanted to protect the treaty rights of native nations. Under the leadership of the Ponca Robert Warrior, they adopted confrontational rhetoric, denouncing more accommodating Native American leaders as "Uncle Tomahawks" and as "Apples," red on the outside but white within. Warrior and other members of the NIYC spoke of "Red Power," the right of native peoples to protect their rights and their culture on their own terms in modern America.

The NIYC, for instance, involved itself in the effort to defend the fishing rights guaranteed to native communities in Washington State by their federal treaties. Ever since the 1950s, native peoples in the Pacific Northwest caught fewer fish each year, a product of dam construction, competition from non-native fishermen, and environmental destruction of riverine ecosystems by the timber industry.

Washington State fish and game officers harassed native fishermen, beating, tear-gassing, and arresting native peoples. The violence grew to so great an extent that witnesses likened it to the segregated American south. The NIYC and Washington native fishermen demonstrated in defense of the rights guaranteed them in their 1855 treaties, a series of "Fish-Ins" designed to educate the public and capture their attention.

The NIYC received outside assistance—journalists like Hunter S. Thompson and celebrities like Marlon Brando. The protesters issued statements and manifestos, like that of the Nisqually Indians in January of 1965 that called upon "any and all nations, kindred, and tongues" to recognize that "if the policies enacted by the United States government concerning the Indian people were examined under close scrutiny the similarities between them and Hitler's policies concerning the Jewish people would be self-evident." Hyperbole, to be sure, but the "Fish-In" protests slowly bore fruit. By 1974, a circuit court in Washington recognized the Indians' right to their fair share of the fish, a right guaranteed to them in the treaties negotiated 120 years before.

The emergence of the NIYC contributed to the revitalization of the National Congress for American Indians (NCAI), which had stood largely alone as a national, Indian-run organization advocating for the interests of native peoples. The activist and scholar Vine Deloria ran for and was elected executive director of the NCAI. Under his energetic leadership, the organization revived. At the time of his election, nineteen tribes belonged; by the end of his three-year term, 156 native groups had joined. The NCAI raised money, established its solvency, and became an effective lobbying force in Washington, D.C. Deloria believed that the NCAI should work with groups like the NIYC and, later, AIM, the American Indian Movement. It needed to demonstrate its relevance to the struggles waged by a younger generation of Native American activists. Deloria contributed to this effort through his writings. Watching treaties being broken in Washington and western New York and places in between, Deloria wondered in *Custer Died for Your Sins: An Indian Manifesto* if America's word was "good only to support its ventures overseas in Vietnam or does it extend to its own citizens?"

Dennis Banks and Clyde Bellocourt founded AIM in the Twin Cities of Minnesota in 1968, an organization that resulted from the challenges native peoples faced as a result of relocation. AIM protested police brutality in the Twin Cities by monitoring and filming police patrols as they moved through Indian neighborhoods. They soon broadened their agenda, looking to improve housing and educational opportunities in the cities. Membership grew. John Trudell, a Santee Sioux, brought his considerable charisma to the organization. Russell Means joined AIM in 1970, a strident leader who would soon become one of the movement's best-known spokesmen.

While AIM gained strength in the Twin Cities, on the west coast "Indians of all Nations" claimed Alcatraz Island, the home of a former federal penitentiary in the San Francisco Bay. The occupiers brought attention to the conditions under which native peoples lived, and educated the public about the rights of native communities. Dozens of Indian groups across the country lent their support to the Alcatraz occupation and President Nixon received thousands of letters, telegrams, and petitions urging him to give the island to the Indians. He could not do that, but the sympathy the occupation generated pressured Nixon to take action on issues of Indian affairs, and inspired other protests. American Indian activists occupied a number of strategically significant sites. The United Indians of All Tribes in Seattle, for instance, after an occupation lasting two years, negotiated with US Senator Henry "Scoop" Jackson a lease to part of the former Fort Lawton military base, on which they established in 1976 the Daybreak Star Cultural Center. Their protest produced results. AIM activists in Milwaukee seized an abandoned Coast Guard installation on Lake Michigan. Women involved with Milwaukee's alternative Indian Community School began to hold classes at the Coast Guard station while men from AIM ran drug and alcohol treatment programs. The AIM activists would move on by 1972, but the Indian Community School continued to meet there.

Protests, as well, took place outside of Bureau of Indian Affairs offices throughout the western United States. In October of 1972 leaders from AIM and the National Indian Youth Council began planning for a march on Washington dubbed the "Trail of Broken Treaties." They occupied the Bureau of Indian Affairs building, the headquarters of the agency many native peoples most closely associated with their mistreatment and marginalization. Four hundred Indians occupied the building, chaining the doors or barricading them with office furniture. The protestors stayed for a week. They stood on the steps of the building, wearing war paint and carrying weapons fashioned from whatever they could find inside. They readied Molotov cocktails, should police seek to remove them from the headquarters by force. They would die there, if necessary, the occupiers told reporters covering the occupation. And they ransacked the Bureau completely, carrying away tons of incriminating documents that highlighted the agency's historical mismanagement of Indian affairs. But the Trail of Broken Treaties suffered from poor planning and disorganization. The occupiers achieved none of their goals. The Nixon administration dismissed their calls for fundamental change in federal Indian policy as "impractical." When the stolen Bureau of Indian Affairs documents began to appear in newspaper columns written by syndicated columnist Jack Anderson, the Nixon administration began persecuting and prosecuting the occupiers and their sympathizers.

Several months after the occupation of the Bureau of Indian Affairs, the activism of the Nixon years reignited in South Dakota. In January of 1973, a white man killed a Sioux named Wesley Bad Heart Bull outside a bar in Custer County. Local authorities charged the attacker with manslaughter, nothing more, and AIM arrived to protest. Led by Dennis Banks, they asked the prosecutor to consider more serious charges. When he refused, a riot broke out. The protestors set the local Chamber of Commerce building on fire; local police and county sheriffs responded with tear gas and violence. Twenty-two people were arrested, nineteen of them native peoples.

In the aftermath of the Custer riot, elders at the Pine Ridge Reservation invited AIM to aid them in their struggles against tribal chairman Dick Wilson, the head of an IRA-based government notorious for its corruption and strong-arm tactics. Wilson maintained a

Figure 9.4 The occupation of Alcatraz Island. © AP/Photo.

personal police force, the well-armed GOON squad (Guardians of Ogallala Nation) to control and intimidate dissenters. He had defeated efforts by the Reservation's residents to impeach him. His authority challenged, he called upon federal authorities for support: federal marshals with automatic weapons came to Pine Ridge, setting the stage for a showdown.

Led by Russell Means and Dennis Banks, AIM hoped to bring the attention of the world to the Pine Ridge Indian Reservation. If they had little familiarity with tribal traditions—both had spent much of their lives in cities—they knew how to draw the media and generate interest. Late in February of 1973, they and a group of their followers, perhaps 300 in all, occupied the small village of Wounded Knee, the site of the massacre of Sioux Ghost Dancers eighty-three years before. The majority of the occupiers came from the surrounding Lakota reservations, but they received support from their fellow occupiers, among them Kiowas, Pueblos, Potawatomis, Senecas, and many others. Two Rappahannocks who had lived in New Jersey traveled west to join AIM at Wounded Knee. The occupiers had a handful of rifles; one of the occupiers had an AK-47 with an empty banana clip. Some had served in Vietnam, and felt keenly the injustice of the colonial system existing at Pine Ridge, where reservation residents had few rights and no redress. Desperate means called for desperate measures. Wilson's GOONs and federal forces quickly surrounded the occupiers with an impressive array of the latest military technology: armored personnel carriers, high-powered rifles, machine guns, grenade launchers, and armor. The federal authorities fired off more than 130,000 rounds of ammunition during the occupation. In cities like San Francisco and Washington, the Nixon Administration was willing to exercise restraint in its response to Native American protests. Not so on a remote reservation in South Dakota.

On March 11, the occupiers issued a statement declaring the independence of the Oglala Nation. "We are a sovereign nation by the treaty of 1868," the occupiers said, and "we want to abolish the Tribal Government under the Indian Reorganization Act. Wounded Knee will be a corporate state under the Independent Oglala Nation." They rejected the "reorganized" government of the Pine Ridge Reservation, and objected to a corrupt government out of touch with tribal traditions and willing to harass and violently persecute its opponents. Means and Banks were out of touch with these traditions as well, but they held numerous news conferences. They succeeded in attracting a considerable amount of attention but they could not succeed in achieving their fundamental goals, for the federal government would not see to the removal of Wilson, or address the fundamental structural causes of so much misery on Indian reservations. The occupation of Wounded Knee lasted seventy-one days. At its end, two of the occupiers had died, and one federal marshal received a wound that left him paralyzed. Given the number of rounds fired, that so few were killed and injured was something of a miracle.

Figure 9.5 AIM Leader Russell Means and Dennis Banks photographed during Wounded Knee showdown in 1973. © AP/Photo.

The occupiers left Wounded Knee in May of 1973. According to Banks, "Wounded Knee was the greatest event in the history of Native America in the twentieth century. It was," he continued, "our shining hour." Leonard Crow Dog, the spiritual leader and another of the occupiers, agreed that "our seventy-one day stand was the greatest deed done by Native Americans." Still, Crow Dog noted, "we never got our Black Hills back, the Treaty of Fort Laramie was not honored, nor did the government recognize us as an independent nation." In the words of historian Paul Chaat Smith, "there was a clear-eyed, if often unspoken, acknowledgment that frequently our elders are lost or drunk, our traditions nearly forgotten or confused, our community leaders co-opted or narrow," but "they knew only one thing for sure: business as usual was not working, their communities were in pain and crisis, and they had to do something." AIM brought considerable attention to the problem native peoples faced. Thanks to the organization's efforts, many American people became aware for the first time of their nation's long history of injustices toward American Indians. These achievements are significant.

Still, federal authorities relentlessly harassed and prosecuted the leaders of AIM. After the occupation, Dick Wilson resumed his campaign of repression and violence against what he viewed as outside agitators. And the protests did little to remove the fundamental problem: the United States, though willing to embrace self-determination, and to consider piecemeal changes in its policies toward native peoples, never abandoned the notion that Indians remained wards of the nation. It is important to remember this. The federal government favored self-determination and, in specific cases, implemented programs and policies that addressed historic injustice and the poor conditions under which many native peoples lived. But it would only go so far. A tension existed, between self-determination and wardship, between sovereignty and colonialism, that individual native peoples, tribal, local, state and federal governments, and the federal courts would wrestle with over the coming years. Native peoples gained more control over their lives, but the ambiguities created by the conflicting forces of sovereignty and colonialism remained.

The Red Power movement—Alcatraz, the BIA takeover, and Wounded Knee—has received so much attention in a sense that it has diverted attention from the efforts of native peoples to act on the principles of self-determination, as limited as they may have been, to promote the interests of their communities. The Cherokees, for instance, governed after 1907 by a principal chief appointed for them by the Bureau of Indian Affairs, used the award money it received from the Indian Claims Commission to assert itself as a regional economic power. The Cherokee Nation in 1967 built a hotel and restaurant on its land, and employed its own people in the construction and management. A tribal complex followed, which included an arts and craft center and tribal government offices. In 1969, the Cherokee Nation founded Cherokee Nation Industries to provide jobs in manufacturing for Cherokee Nation citizens. The Cherokee Nation won approval from the Interior Department in 1975 on revisions to its tribal constitution that allowed for the popular election of the principal chief.

Landless and urban Indians in Washington, in a powerful 1973 report that charged the state government with carrying out a campaign of "ethnic genocide by assimilation," and supporting the process of "destroying our identity," announced that they would hold on to "the scraps and parcels" of their culture that remained and to work "as earnestly as any small nation or ethnic group was ever determined to survive and retain its identity." They were critical of AIM. The destruction of records at the Bureau of Indian Affairs Headquarters in 1972, they feared, might inadvertently have covered up the incompetence and corruption of federal officials by destroying the evidence of their wrongdoing. Wounded Knee, "as a drawn out affair with many unprioritized demands," in fact "did nothing to help Indian development," they said. Native peoples pursuing self-determination never spoke with one voice.

And in Washington, they spoke of institution-building. Because the Puyallup Reservation was so close to Tacoma, the tribal government had created a number of programs for the urban Indian population: the Indian Education Center, established in 1971, with representation coming from the Puyallup, Nisqually, and Muckleshoot communities; the Tacoma Area Native American Center (TANAC) incorporated in 1972 "with the express purpose of providing community organization for Indians and Alaskan Natives which in turn would promote unity and cooperation among all Indian people"; and groups for Native American students at Tacoma Community College. There were a host of organizations in Seattle: service organizations like the Chief Seattle Club, the Seattle Indian Center, and the United Indians of All Tribes Foundation; education and employment programs, advocacy groups, legal aid, health, and recreation.

Tribal governments confronted dissent, as did other governments, but they began to assert themselves with greater force and determination in the postwar years. They learned to develop the administrative machinery to govern effectively. Like many governments in the United States they failed on occasion. But the important point is that native peoples began to assert themselves in the second half of the twentieth century, to call upon the federal government to acknowledge its past mistreatment of Indians, and to give them an increasingly large share of the power to determine how they would live their lives and govern their communities.

10

Sovereign Nations and Colonized Nations

When Richard Nixon returned Blue Lake to Taos Pueblo, and declared his intention to support self-determination for native peoples, he acted not only on principle, but because of the pressures placed upon him by Indians opposed to the heavy-handed control exercised by the federal government in all areas of Indian life. His desire to work with members of Congress and the leaders of native communities to construct "a new road which leads us to justice in the treatment of those who were the first Americans" resulted in a significant number of accomplishments. Nixon appointed Louis Bruce to head the Bureau of Indian Affairs, the first Native American to head the agency since Ely Parker. Between 1970 and 1980 the percentage of Native American Bureau of Indian Affairs employees increased from 53% to 78% of the agency's work force. The Supreme Court, in the 1974 *Morton v. Mancari* decision, upheld the constitutionality of the preferential hiring of native peoples in the Bureau of Indian Affairs. Nixon, meanwhile, signed legislation establishing an Office of Indian Education, job training programs for native peoples, and rules that guaranteed "freedom of religion and culture" for Native American students in schools operated by the Bureau of Indian Affairs. The Indian Financing Act of 1974 provided "capital on a reimbursable basis to help develop and utilize Indian resources" so that native peoples "will enjoy a standard of living from their own productive efforts comparable to that enjoyed by non-Indians in neighboring communities."

Nixon resigned in August of 1974, but Congress and his successors continued his policies. The Indian Self-Determination and Education Assistance Act of 1975 marked the new federal commitment to decentralizing control over Indian affairs. Congress hoped "to provide maximum Indian participation in the Government and education of Indian people; to provide for the full participation of Indian tribes in programs and services conducted by the Federal Government for Indians and to encourage the development of human resources of the Indian people." It allowed tribes to contract with the government to operate their own health, education, social service and law enforcement programs. Premised on the belief that "true self-determination in any society ... is dependent upon an educational process which will insure the development of qualified people to fulfill meaningful leadership roles," the Indian Self-Determination and Education Assistance Act provided an unprecedented opportunity for native peoples to administer the programs that immediately impacted their lives.

Native America: A History, Second Edition. Michael Leroy Oberg.
© 2018 John Wiley & Sons, Inc. Published 2018 by John Wiley & Sons, Inc.

The Importance of 1978

Self-determination thus remained the nation's Indian policy under Nixon's successors. The year 1978, for instance, witnessed the enactment of a number of significant pieces of legislation intended to redress past wrongs and remedy long-standing problems. Acknowledging that in the past the United States had pursued policies that "resulted in the abridgment of religious freedom for traditional American Indians," Congress in August approved the American Indian Religious Freedom Act, which pledged the United States "to protect and preserve for American Indians their inherent freedom to believe, express, and exercise the traditional religions of the American Indian, Eskimo, Aleut, and Native Hawaiians, including but not limited to the access to sites, use and possession of sacred objects, and the freedom to worship through ceremonies and traditional rites."

Aware of the growing number of native peoples who belonged to communities that had neither signed treaties with the United States nor been the specific objects of federal legislation, Congress in early October established a set of guidelines for the "Federal Acknowledgment of Indian Tribes" that had not been officially recognized by the government in the past as Indian. The "acknowledgment" statute required that an Indian tribe, in order to be formally recognized as such by the Interior Department, must demonstrate that they have "been identified from historical times until the present on a substantially continuous basis as 'American Indian,' or 'aboriginal.'" They must demonstrate as well that the members of the community had inhabited a specific area or that they live "in a community viewed as American Indian and distinct from other populations in the area." The petitioning tribe must also establish that it had "maintained political influence or other authority over its members as an autonomous entity throughout history until the present." Acknowledgment, the statute read, "is a prerequisite to the protection, services, benefits, from the Federal Government available to Indian tribes." Such acknowledgment, the statute continues, "shall also mean that the tribe is entitled to all the immunities and privileges available to other federally acknowledged Indian tribes by virtue of their status as Indian tribes as well as the responsibilities and obligations of such tribes."

Two weeks later, Congress passed the Tribally Controlled Community College Assistance Act, which provided grants for the operation of junior colleges on Indian reservations in order "to insure continued and expanded educational opportunities for Indian students." Native communities long had recognized the importance of higher education, but access had always been a challenge. Cankdeska Cikana Community College, formerly known as Little Hoop College, was founded by the Spirit Lake Dakotas in North Dakota in the early 1970s. The college provides vocational and technical training, but also emphasizes "the teaching and learning of Dakota culture and language toward the preservation of the tribe." Other communities established colleges throughout the west early in the 1970s, beginning with Navajo Community College. In response to the passage of the 1978 statute, a number of western tribes established new institutions of higher learning emphasizing a culturally relevant curriculum. Little Big Horn College, founded at Crow Agency on the Crow Reservation, struggled to survive with scarce resources in its early years but grew into a successful junior college. From thirty-two students during its first semester in 1981, now more than 300 students enroll each term. All take courses in Crow Studies, but also in a variety of skills-based courses and courses designed to prepare them for transfer to four-year colleges.

Congress in 1978 attempted to address the legacies of some of the nation's most destructive policies toward native peoples. Early in November, Congress enacted a series of educational reforms for schools operated by the Bureau of Indian Affairs, designed to provide equal educational opportunity for native children. One week later, Congress passed the Indian Child Welfare Act, an important piece of legislation designed to halt the traumatic removal of native children from their homes through fostering and adoption. The problem was severe. Dakota Sioux at Spirit Lake, for example, asked the Association of American Indian Affairs (AAIA) to conduct an investigation, and the AAIA reported that of the 1100 Dakotas under the age of 21 who lived at Spirit Lake in 1968, 275 had been removed from their families. In states with large Native American populations, the AAIA found that between 25 and 35% of children had been removed from their homes. Native peoples organized to halt this highly destructive practice, and the battle for the passage of the Indian Child Welfare Act, according to its best historian, "represented one of the most fierce and successful battles for Indian self-determination of the 1970s." The legislation committed the United States "to protect the best interests of Indian children and to promote the stability and security of Indian tribes and families by the establishment of minimum standards for the removal of Indian children from their families and the placement of such children in foster or adoptive homes which will reflect the unique values of Indian culture."

While Congress approved and the executive signed some of the most important legislation in recent memory, the United States Supreme Court worked to undermine the power of native nations. Four important cases decided beginning in 1978 help hammer home the important lesson that the United States government is an enormous machine, and that its different parts can work at crossed purposes.

In March of 1978, for example, the Court confronted the question of whether an Indian tribal government could exercise criminal jurisdiction over non-Indians who resided on their lands. Mark Oliphant was charged by the Suquamish Tribe of Washington State with resisting arrest and assaulting a tribal police officer. The Suquamish argued that its tribal government "retained inherent powers of government over the reservation" because no congressional law or federal treaty had explicitly deprived it of that right.

The Court disagreed. Inherent tribal powers, Justice William Rehnquist wrote, could be taken away from a native nation *explicitly* through an act of Congress or a federal treaty, as the Suquamish had argued, but also *implicitly* if the power exercised by the nation was "inconsistent with their status" as a "domestic dependent nation." The Court cited no law to support its reasoning, and made no effort to square its logic with the sparse language of the United States constitution.

Oliphant was a stunning defeat. As one legal scholar wrote, the *Oliphant* case showed that imperialism was alive and well. The legal doctrine of "implicit divestiture," conceived by Justice Rehnquist, replaced military men and agents and missionaries with the Court as the agent of colonialism. While Congress and the president worked to breathe life into the governing institutions in Indian Country, the Court, in retreat from "the position that Indians are sovereigns" as Rehnquist later put it, began to significantly limit those powers.

Two weeks after *Oliphant* the Court held in *United States v. Wheeler* that the prosecution of a Navajo by a tribal court for contributing to the delinquency of a minor and a federal court for the more serious charge of statutory rape did not violate the constitutional prohibition against double jeopardy. Native nations derived their powers to prosecute from their inherent sovereignty, the United States from the American people: separate sources of sovereignty meant no double jeopardy. Citing *Oliphant*, the Court held that "the sovereign power of a tribe to prosecute its members for tribal offenses clearly does not fall within that part of sovereignty which the Indians implicitly lost by virtue of their dependent status." The ruling was a victory for the Navajos on the narrow question of prosecuting a tribal member who also faced federal prosecution, but the Court made clear that it could eliminate a tribal government's powers at will. *Explicit divestiture*, the earlier doctrine, had drawn a bright line that became increasingly hazy under the doctrine of *implicit divestiture.*

Oliphant and *Wheeler* dealt with the powers of tribal government. In *Santa Clara Pueblo v. Martinez*, decided in May of 1978, the Court found that the 1968 Indian Civil Rights Act was intended by Congress to both protect individual native peoples and the powers of tribal governments. But what to do when these two goals conflicted? Julia Martinez, a member of Santa Clara Pueblo, sued the tribe after it denied tribal membership to her daughter. Martinez had married a non-member, and her seriously ill daughter could not as a result obtain medical treatment at the nearby Indian Health Service Hospital. Martinez pointed out that the children of Pueblo men who married outsiders could become members, and she argued that this double standard violated the Indian Civil Rights Act. The Court rejected this argument. Tribes could set their own membership requirements, and to allow Martinez to sue the tribe under the provisions of the Indian Civil Rights Act would thus significantly "unsettle a tribal government's ability to maintain its authority." The Court, in effect, gutted the Indian Civil Rights Act and left Martinez with no legal remedy. Tribes could deny to their own people rights enshrined in the Constitution and the victims had no redress.

Finally, two months after Ronald Reagan took office in 1981, the Court ruled on the legality of a law passed by the Crows that prohibited hunting and fishing by non-members even on reservation lands the non-member owned. Non-members owned nearly 30% of the Crow Reservation, a legacy of the allotment policy. Applying the logic of the *Oliphant* decision, a criminal case, to the regulatory powers a native nation might possess, the Court held that "the inherent sovereign powers of an Indian tribe do not extend to the activities of non-members of the tribe." Tribes could only regulate non-member activities when those activities resulted from a "consensual relationship," or when the non-members' conduct threatened or had a "direct effect on the political integrity, the economic security, or the health and welfare of the tribe." Hunting and fishing by non-members on their own land did neither.

In *Oliphant, Montana*, and its other cases, the Supreme Court significantly limited the authority of native nations over non-Indians who lived within reservation boundaries. As historian Frank Pommersheim pointed out in a blistering critique of the Court, the justices did so "without reference to any constitutional justification ... and ultimately without reference to any coherent doctrinal underpinning." If the *Lone Wolf* decision of 1903 had established the doctrine of congressional plenary authority over Indian affairs, itself a strained reading of the commerce clause of Article I, Section 8 of the Constitution, the Court, beginning in the last quarter of the twentieth century, established a practice of judicial plenary power that eviscerated the rights of native nations over outsiders living or doing business on their lands.

Reagan said nothing about the *Montana* decision. He came into office determined to slash federal spending, in Indian affairs as elsewhere. Republican Senator Barry Goldwater thought the depth of Reagan's cuts "crazy," while Montana Democratic Congressman Pat Williams worried that they could turn "reservations into the worst ghettos in America." Benefiting from a white backlash against civil rights advances during the preceding decades, Reagan stood against attempts to remedy past injustices, like Indian land claims.

But in other areas, the Reagan administration pursued a pragmatic set of policies designed to support self-determination. Seven days after Interior Secretary James Watt in January of 1983 described native peoples as "incompetent wards" of the United States, living on reservations rife with sexual immorality and drug abuse, all of which Watt viewed as "the failures of socialism," Reagan delivered a statement on Indian policy that his administration had been working on since he took office.

Reagan hoped to create workable tribal governments that could stand on their own. He warned tribes that "it is important to the concept of self-government that tribes reduce their dependence on federal funds by providing a greater percentage of the cost of their self-government." He called upon Congress to remove what he described as "the federal impediments to tribal self-government and tribal resource development," and pledged to continue to assist tribes in determining "the best way to meet the needs of their members and to establish and run programs which best meet those needs." Clearly Reagan hoped that in the future, native peoples would stand on their own two feet, free entirely from federal assistance. By cutting federal spending in the realm of Indian affairs, however, the Reagan administration limited the resources and funding available for tribes interested in contracting to run their own programs.

In response to native leaders unsatisfied with the limited nature of the Indian Self-Determination and Education Assistance Act, Reagan lent his support to a trial program administered by the Bureau of Indian Affairs to allow compacting on reservations, the allocation of a lump sum payment to tribes for the entire range of federal programs they chose to administer. Compacting gave tribes more flexibility than they had with the contracting allowed under the Indian Self-Determination and Education Assistance Act, for now tribal governments could move funds around from program to program and more efficiently administer them.

President Bill Clinton, elected in 1992, worked to restore funding cut during the Reagan years, and took dramatic steps during his presidency to encourage Indian self-determination. He signed into law the Tribal Self-Governance Act of 1994, which made permanent the pilot program begun under Reagan. At an unprecedented White House gathering in April of 1994, Clinton assembled 322 tribal leaders and conducted a summit with America's native nations. The president vowed "to honor and respect tribal sovereignty based upon our unique historic relationship," and pledged "to continue my efforts to protect your right to fully exercise your faith as you wish." The federal government, he continued, must respect "your values, your religions, your identity, your sovereignty," and must work to "dramatically improve the Federal Government's relationships with the tribes and become full partners with tribal nations." Through an executive order signed at the summit, Clinton ordered every executive branch agency "to remove all barriers that prevent them from working directly with tribal governments and, second, to make certain that if they take action affecting tribal trust resources, they consult with tribal governments prior to that decision." Wilma Mankiller, the principal chief of the Cherokee Nation, remembered that she accomplished more in this single meeting with President Clinton than she had in all her meetings with his two predecessors.

The State of the Nations

Contracting under the Indian Self-Determination and Education Assistance Act and compacting under the provisions of the 1994 Tribal Self-Governance Act raised the ironic prospect for some critics that tribal government might become little more than a puppet administering federal programs and relieving federal authorities of the responsibility for caring for native peoples. These tribal governments, critics pointed out, did the federal government's dirty work, and might wittingly or unwittingly become instruments of colonial control over native peoples, their lands, and their lives. "We cannot preserve our nations," wrote the Kahnawake Mohawk scholar and activist Taiaiake Alfred, "unless we take action to restore pride in our traditions, achieve economic self-sufficiency, develop independence of mind, and display courage in defense of our lands and rights." Native peoples, Alfred warned, must remain vigilant lest their leaders end up "looking, sounding and behaving just like mainstream politicians."

Without healthy economies and a healthy people, self-determination meant little. Despite some progress over the past few decades, significant inequalities and disparities remain. According to the United States Census Bureau, the total "American Indian and Alaska Native population" increased by more than 25% between 2000 and 2010, from 4.1 million to 5.2 million, figures that include people who identify themselves as Native American "alone or in combination" with another racial category. This population by any standard is poor. Median household income, again according to the Census Bureau, for Native Americans stood at $39,715 in 2012, and $56,746 for all other Americans. The poverty rate for native peoples in 2012 approached 30%, while the national average for all other groups combined is half that. Childhood poverty among native peoples that year was 34%, and 21% for all other races. Their unemployment rates are higher, as is the probability that they live in a home without complete plumbing or a complete kitchen.

Health problems pose a significant challenge to native communities. Though tribes that run their own health programs have enjoyed considerable success in addressing the challenges they face, and have done so in a manner often consistent with their traditions, there remains much work to be done. According to the myriad figures released by the Indian Health Service, the Centers for Disease Control, the National Institutes of Health, and a number of Native American advocacy groups, native peoples are six times more likely to die from alcohol-related causes, almost three times as likely to suffer from diabetes, and nearly 2.5 times as likely to die in a motor vehicle accident. Native peoples are twice as likely to be murdered as other Americans. At sixty-eight years, Native Americans have the lowest life expectancy of any population in the United States. More Native Americans than any other group describe themselves as being in poor or fair health.

Mental health is a problem as well. More than four out of five Native American women experience the trauma of sexual violence during their lifetimes. For Native American youth, 40.9% are overweight or obese, compared to 30% for the population as a whole. Native American children between the ages of ten and nineteen suffer from diabetes at three times the rate for all other races. Rates of drug, cigarette, and alcohol abuse are very high. Suicide is the second leading cause of death among youth aged fifteen to twenty-four, four times the national rate.

To some extent, these problems are the bitter fruits of colonialism, the product of many decades of marginalization and isolation and neglect. But there is cause for cautious optimism. The native population is young and it is growing rapidly. Although native peoples remain behind white people in nearly every measure of economic and social well-being, the poverty rate for native peoples is slowly falling and the inflation-adjusted per capita income of native peoples living on Indian reservations has grown significantly. Culturally specific tribal health programs, when adequately funded and staffed, show the promise of great success. Too much can be made of these figures: the poverty in many communities is deeply rooted, and at the current rate of ascent it will take more than half a century to close the gap. Still, in the self-determination era native peoples have managed to close some of the gaps between them and the rest of the American population.

Progress certainly has been slow, but important signs of change can be seen. As late as 1981, after all, the Bureau of Indian Affairs reported that "the story of Pocahontas somewhat typifies the sad tale of those indigenous peoples along the Eastern Coast who 'met the boat' when it arrived bearing European colonists." Eastern Indians had been "caught up in the settlers' wars, infected with the white man's diseases, and subject to plundering of land and resources," and as a result had been "scattered" or "forcibly removed west" or "totally destroyed." The Powhatans were gone, as were many others. Indeed, the Bureau of Indian Affairs claimed that "the famous novel by James Fenimore Cooper, *The Last of the Mohicans,* had its base in the very real disappearance of a Connecticut tribe."

It did not, and these native peoples had not disappeared. The communities that made up Wahunsonacock's chiefdom still lived on their ancestral lands in Virginia, despite the efforts of Walter Ashby Plecker and others to erase any record of their existence. The Mohegans still lived in eastern Connecticut. The Native American population grew by 72% between 1970 and 1980, 38% between 1980 and 1990, 30% between 1990 and the end of the century, and by 26% between 2000 and 2010. The number of native peoples, based on the number who chose to identify themselves as American Indian to the Census Bureau, has increased much faster than the American population as a whole. A small portion of this increase might be accounted for by improved life expectancy and a lowered infant mortality rate in native communities, but the rate of increase cannot be explained by these factors alone. Many Americans, most experts agree, have begun to identify themselves as native peoples, either out of a craving for an authentically ethnic identity, or because of a renewed pride in being Indian that the era of self-determination, and the activism that preceded it, generated.

With increasing numbers of people identifying themselves as Native American, and growing numbers of native communities seeking federal acknowledgment, a backlash has occurred against these "new Indians." Many argue that the federal acknowledgment process has not worked out the way Congress intended. It is a time-consuming and expensive process, for one thing, with standards that are difficult to meet. Nonetheless, establishing an acknowledgment procedure was an important step by the government, an explicit rejection of the long-cherished notion that native peoples would vanish or blend into the American mainstream. The federal government, despite the law's shortcomings and many difficulties, willingly acknowledged its responsibilities to a growing number of tribal groups, and established procedures for beginning government-to-government relations with previously unrecognized native communities.

The Mohegans, for instance, landless as a community since the nineteenth century and never recognized as native peoples by the federal government, filed for acknowledgment at their first opportunity. They also sued Connecticut, asserting that the state seized the community's lands in violation of the federal Indian Trade and Intercourse Acts, which stated that all land transactions required federal oversight and approval. In 1989, eleven years after they first filed for recognition, the Bureau of Indian Affairs issued a "proposed finding" that rejected the Mohegans' application on the grounds that the community had not provided adequate evidence of political and social activity in the 1940s and 1950s to prove the tribe's continuous existence. The Mohegans submitted additional materials and, in 1994, after sixteen years and 20,000 pages of documentation, the Bureau of Indian Affairs acknowledged the Mohegans as an Indian tribe. Several months later, in October of 1994, President Clinton signed legislation settling the Mohegans' suit for lands in Connecticut in return for the creation of a 240-acre reservation consisting of lands the government agreed to hold in trust for the newly acknowledged native nation.

The Mohegans moved through the slow and burdensome acknowledgment process. Not all tribes have followed that route. The Mohegans' neighbors, the Mashantucket Pequots, received acknowledgment through the enactment of a congressional law specifically for that purpose. So did the Tigua Pueblos. Living in Ysleta del Sur in Texas, the Tiguas maintained and preserved their identity as native peoples. They had descended from Pueblos who left New Mexico with Spaniards who fled from Po'pay's uprising in 1680. They fought no wars with the colonial powers or the United States in the centuries following, and though they received their lands at Ysleta by virtue of a grant from the Spanish crown in 1751, they had never signed a treaty. They spoke Spanish, attended Catholic mass, and lived in an American city, but neither they nor their Mexican American neighbors had any difficulty distinguishing them as Indians. They remained distinctly Indian despite their poverty and significant inter-marriage with non-Indians.

They felt threatened when the city of El Paso annexed Ysleta in 1955. They feared the consequences of paying city taxes that could reach $100 when the average income in the community was only four times that amount. Obtaining federal acknowledgment as an Indian tribe seemed to offer one method for insulating the Tiguas from local taxation. But this was the termination era—no one was quite sure how to proceed. Little that could be considered decisive occurred until 1967, when a delegation of Tiguas at the state capitol in Austin performed traditional songs and dances identical to those performed by Pueblos in New Mexico. With the support of the National Congress of American Indians, whose spokesperson affirmed that the Tiguas were "true Indians," they won critical state support. Pueblos from New Mexico offered additional assistance after the Tiguas convinced them of the validity of their claim to be Indians.

In 1968, President Lyndon Baines Johnson signed legislation acknowledging the Tiguas of Ysleta Del Sur in El Paso as an Indian tribe, but placed them under the jurisdiction of the state of Texas. "Nothing in this act," the law read, made the newly recognized tribe "eligible for any services performed by the United States for Indians because of their status of Indians." Nearly two decades later, President Reagan signed the Ysleta del Sur Pueblo and Alabama and Coushatta Indian Tribes of Texas Restoration Act of 1987, establishing formal federal recognition for the community, making them eligible for federal services, but also placing a requirement that members of the tribe have a "blood-quantum" of one-eighth to be eligible for tribal membership. To be a member of the tribe, in other words, members had to have a "full-blood" great grandparent. Legislation lifting the blood-quantum restriction passed the House of Representatives in 2007, but progressed no further. In the meantime, the Tiguas contracted with federal agencies to carry out programs that benefited the tribe and the broader community, opened a casino, and a number of other enterprises.

The Tigua Pueblo community of Ysleta del Sur achieved recognition, but ran into considerable opposition from the state of Texas over Indian gaming. The state fought to close the casino, despite the fact that it provided significant benefits to the local economy and created a large number of jobs, on the grounds that it violated state gaming laws. The Tiguas lieutenant governor, Carlos Hisa, told an El Paso reporter early in 2009 that the revenue from their gaming enterprise could finance the tribe's other underfunded operations. Their legal battle to gain the right to open a gaming facility has in recent years made slow progress.

Other native communities, with long and well-documented histories, have not been able to move as far as did the Tiguas. The constituent communities of the Powhatan Chiefdom, recognized as Indian tribes by the Commonwealth of Virginia in 1983, have struggled to obtain acknowledgment by the United States. The House of Representatives enacted legislation to acknowledge the Chickahominy, Eastern Chickahominy, Upper Mattaponi, Rappahannock, Nansemond, and Monacan tribes, but the legislation made little progress in the Senate, where opponents remain concerned that the acknowledgment process had been corrupted by illegitimate Indians who wanted federal recognition solely so that they could open gaming operations.

Problems certainly exist with the acknowledgment process, but the proposed legislation to recognize the Virginia Indians prohibited gaming, and community leaders made clear that they had no interest in casinos. They sought recognition to help their people. According to the anthropologist Helen C. Rountree, who testified on behalf of the Virginia tribes, they sought acknowledgment in order to acquire "better access to health programs, which are badly needed by their elders now." Many of their elders, deprived of educational opportunities unless they attended "colored" schools, were quite poor. The communities possessed few resources, and they hoped that the government would help. Native peoples in Virginia, as in many states, continue to meet opposition as they seek acknowledgment. They struggle against racial stereotypes held by the dominant society about what Indians are and what they ought to be. Living in a state that insisted for much of its history that only two races existed, and victimized by Walter Plecker's racist crusade that resulted in their erasure from the sorts of historical documents upon which researchers rely, Virginia's native peoples routinely face skepticism that they are "real" Indians, because they do not conform to the dominant white stereotype of the mounted plains warrior. Thus far only the 200-member Pamunkey Tribe has obtained recognition, something they achieved in a favorable ruling from the Office of Federal Acknowledgment late in 2015, after a struggle that lasted more than thirty years and that cost them more than $25 million in expenses.

The example of the Duwamish, the descendants of Chief Seattle, illustrates some of the capriciousness of the acknowledgment process. On the same day it announced its approval of the Pamunkey's petition, the Office of Federal Acknowledgment rejected the last effort of the Duwamish to win federal recognition. They had struggled for years. Fifteen years earlier, on the last full day of the Clinton presidency, January 19, 2001, the acting assistant secretary of the Interior wrote a hand-written approval of the Duwamish petition for recognition. Eight months later, however, citing procedural problems in the approval document, the administration of George W. Bush reversed the decision. Cecile Hanson, the Duwamish chairwoman, cited the pain that came with having one's claim to identity denied. Recognition would have allowed the Duwamish to assert their fishing rights under the Point Elliott Treaty, as well as the right to acquire lands and have them placed in trust. The Duwamish vowed to fight on. In March 2013, a federal court ordered another review of the record, but in the summer of 2015 the Interior Department rejected the Duwamish petition for acknowledgment on the grounds that they had failed to prove that they had "been identified as an American Indian entity on a substantially continuous basis since 1900," that a "predominant portion of the petitioning group comprises a distinct community and has existed as a community from historical times to the present," and that the Duwamish had "maintained political influence or authority over its members as an autonomous entity from historical times to the present." Despite having a treaty with the United States, a long and well-documented connection to the city of Seattle, and an important place in American myths and memories about native peoples in the well-known story of Chief Seattle's environmental message, the Office of Federal Acknowledgment felt that the landlessness of the Duwamish and their interconnectedness with other signatories to the Point Elliott Treaty meant that the people who claimed to be Duwamish in 2015 could not prove that they met the government's difficult standards for recognition.

Some opponents of the federal acknowledgment process have asserted that tribes with dubious claims to authenticity seek recognition in order to open lucrative gaming operations. The notion that "fake Indians" seek to enrich themselves through gambling is so widespread that it has appeared in satirical television shows like *The Simpsons* and *South Park*. "Rich Indian racism," the resentment expressed by non-Indians toward native peoples with profitable gaming enterprises, has grown significantly. In the last thirty years, few issues have proven as divisive and controversial as Indian gaming, an enormously powerful economic force. In 2014, Indian gaming generated $28.5 billion in revenues nationwide.

The modern controversy over Indian gaming began in California, where the Cabazon and Morongo Bands of Mission Indians operated a pair of highly profitable bingo halls on their reservations, not far from the desert resort of Palm Springs. The state, which had criminal jurisdiction over Indian lands as a result of Public Law 280, asserted that the tribes' bingo games constituted illegal gaming under state law. California ordered that the tribes close their high-stakes bingo halls. The tribes sued, and in 1987 the Supreme Court in *California v. Cabazon Band of Mission Indians* held that states had a right to regulate Indian gaming, but they could not prohibit the tribes from exercising this element of the inherent sovereignty that they retained.

In response to calls from several states to define the limits of these regulatory powers, Congress in 1988 passed the Indian Gaming Regulatory Act. The IGRA, as it is commonly known, did not grant tribes the right to conduct gaming operations; rather, it limited their autonomy by giving states the right to regulate certain aspects of gaming. In order to engage in the most profitable type of gaming—table games and slot machines—commonly associated with casinos, tribes and states must enter into compacts that spell out the terms under which the tribe conducts its business. Though there is no solid requirement that the states engage in good-faith negotiations with the tribes, most compacts contain provisions that benefit both the tribe and the state. The Mohegans, for instance, pay to the state of Connecticut each year a quarter of the revenue from the slot machines in their "Mohegan Sun" casino or $100 million, whichever is greater. Given that the Mohegans made in February of 2016 nearly $50 million on slot machines alone, the compact results in a considerable financial benefit to the state. Since opening, the Mohegans have paid to the state over $1.5 billion.

In early 2016, there were almost 500 American Indian casinos operated by 240 tribes in 28 states. Some of them have been enormously successful, others less so. In 2014, for instance, the wealthiest 5.7% of Indian gaming operations brought in 40% of all gaming revenues. The top 17% brought in more than 70%. The bottom 35% of casinos, on the other hand, accounted for just 2% of all gaming dollars. The thirty casinos operated in the National Indian Gaming Commission's Washington, DC region, which includes Mohegan Sun and the three facilities operated by the Seneca Nation of Indians, brought in revenues totaling $6.8 billion in 2014, nearly a quarter of the total.

These revenues have benefited the gaming communities financially in a variety of ways. Members of the small Dakota Shakopee Mdewakanton community in Minnesota, made up of descendants of those imprisoned at Fort Snelling after Little Crow's uprising, are paid over $80,000 per month as their share of the community's casino revenue. The Dakotas at Shakopee Mdewakanton operate the Little Six and Mystic Lake casinos. The community's gaming and other enterprises bring in enough revenue to pay entirely for the tribe's infrastructure, including road, sanitation, and emergency services. As of late 2012, the Shakopee Mdewakanton Dakotas had made grants of more than $243 million to neighboring native communities, and loaned other tribes more than $400 million to finance the construction of casinos, golf courses, and police departments.

The Shakopee Mdewakantons are among the wealthiest of the gambling tribes. Among the Senecas, tribal per capita income is approximately $12,000 per year. Over the course of the last forty years the Seneca Nation has begun to break out of the cycle of chronic economic deprivation under which it has suffered, and gaming clearly has helped. The Nation currently provides a wide range of services to citizens of the Nation, other residents, and to visitors in the sectors of medical care, housing, law enforcement, and language preservation. The Santa Ynez band of Chumash, the only federally recognized Chumash community, lived in poverty on its small reservation before it opened its casino in 1994. The casino produced a profit of $31 million in its first year and revenues have grown steadily ever since. Casino revenue pays for the community's expenses and for the costs of tribal government and administration. The tribe donates money generously to local municipalities and charities. Revenue from the casino has paid for the paving of streets, the installation of streetlights, and a variety of construction projects, including a much larger casino that opened in 2003 with a large expansion set to open in 2017. Members of the Santa Ynez band receive free medical care at the reservation's health clinic, and reservation profits pay for private schooling and college education for band members. Much of the rest of the profit is distributed to the enrolled members of the community. Each enrolled member in 2004 received monthly checks in excess of $30,000. Gambling has not brought this sort of dizzying wealth to the Seneca country but Seneca Nation Enterprises, primarily but not exclusively focused on gaming, is the fifth largest employer in an economically depressed region of western New York. In addition, a Seneca private sector economy has emerged, focusing on the retail sale of cigarettes and gasoline.

Gaming revenues have in places engineered a complete revolution in Indian communities. Tribes have used the revenue from their gaming operations to diversify, and to invest in alternative operations. Gaming revenue has paid for fire departments, police forces, improved schooling, and college scholarships. Gaming revenue has underwritten efforts, among Mohegans and Cherokees and others, to revitalize elements of an aboriginal culture that had been eradicated by the forces of colonization, to pay for tribal archaeology programs, and language revitalization efforts. Gaming operations give rise to a host of affiliated enterprises. Golf courses, hotels, and restaurants spring up in Indian communities. Tribes have purchased convenience stores, gasoline stations, and smoke shops. The Citizen Potawatomi Nation in Oklahoma has gone into banking, while other native communities have used casino revenues to enter the commercial real estate market. Hundreds of thousands of native peoples and their non-native neighbors find employment in these businesses.

Certainly the white backlash against Indian gaming is real, and in states like New York the government has sought to capitalize on the Senecas' successes by permitting competing non-Indian gaming operations. Gaming compacts, in a sense, give state governments a means to appropriate the resources of native peoples and chip away at their sovereignty by insisting on the right, for example, to police casinos. States can demand, furthermore, that native nations waive their sovereign immunity to lawsuits in order to obtain a gaming compact. There is evidence from some reservations, moreover, that when gaming revenues are distributed on a per capita basis, that poverty and unemployment have increased. Still, in many communities, a "brain drain" of native youth away to search for work has halted. As Kevin Washburn, the assistant secretary of Indian affairs, said in 2008, "Indian gaming is simply the most successful economic venture ever to occur across a wide range of American Indian reservations."

Gaming represents only one part of a larger drive for economic self-sufficiency, a vital foundation for self-determination. The Mohegans have invested in a range of economic enterprises. The Swinomish community on the Salish Sea opened a cannery on its reservation north of Seattle. The Sioux Manufacturing Corporation, owned by the Spirit Lake Dakotas in North Dakota, manufactures Kevlar panels and other sorts of armor for the United States military. Cherokee Nation Industries, founded by the Cherokee Nation in 1969, manufactures office equipment and a variety of products for the telecommunications industry and for use by the military. The Cherokee Nation invests the profits from its enterprises to create additional employment opportunities for its people, and to support educational, health care, social service, and tribal government programs. Some tribes pursue energy development, including environmentally destructive practices like hydro-fracking. The Crows, well aware that some of the richest coal seams in the American west are located on Indian land, have looked to develop their own energy resources. Even though in recent years coal prices have fallen and opposition to coal as a "dirty" fuel has increased, the Crows see coal development as a means to combat poverty. Coal revenue could pay for schools and for roads. Noting that his people have survived warfare, epidemic diseases, and attempts to assimilate them and eradicate their culture, Crow tribal chairman Darren Old Coyote told a journalist late in 2015 that "we're going to continue moving forward to survive, and the only way I know how now is to develop our coal." The Crows, he said, "have the manpower," and "we have the capability of being self-sufficient. There is no reason why we should be this poor."

Exercising Sovereignty

Native Peoples have become increasingly willing to assert their nationhood, define their culture, secure their rights, and guard their autonomy. It was the pressure placed by native peoples that led the federal government to abandon the destructive policies of the termination era and begin the shift toward self-determination. The policies of the self-determination era helped bring significant change to native communities. As tribes grew in economic power, and in the strength of their determination to make the fundamental decisions that affected their lives, however, new challenges arose. No tribal government could afford to ignore the power of the federal government. State and local governments sought to regulate Indian country and to skim the cream off of the increased prosperity that many tribes began to experience. The New York State government, for instance, has threatened for years to begin taxing the sale of cigarettes by Senecas to non-Indian customers, a claim that the courts have supported but tribes like the Senecas have vigorously contested. Competing political powers have constrained the exercise of true self-determination. So, too, does the continuing poverty in many tribal communities, misgovernment and corruption on the part of some tribal political leaders, and a land base that is only a fraction of what it once was.

Self-determination also has generated a backlash among white citizens who resent what they see as the "special rights" enjoyed by native peoples. Opponents of Indian tribes argue that treaty rights confer unfair advantages on tribal communities. Indians have special privileges—freedom from state and local taxes on their reservations, for instance, or "special" fishing rights in a variety of northern and western states—that critics charge are based on ethnicity but not merit. When, for example, a gaming tribe purchases a local gas station, places that land into trust, and then proceeds to sell gasoline for less than their non-Indian competitors who must pay the state taxes, treaty rights do provide native nations with a measure of competitive advantage. Similarly, when native communities reacquire land, that acreage comes off local tax rolls. Schools and roads and libraries and police and fire departments still must be paid for, and the resulting tax burden for non-Indians in the community can increase proportionately. Those who see themselves as disadvantaged appeal to their elected leaders, some of whom take aggressive postures against self-determination. Where native peoples are a relatively small percentage of the population, Indian-bashing can bring political rewards to the bigots, the opportunists, and the demagogues. Detailed discussions of the history of Indian treaties, and the legal status of native nations, do not usually factor in these debates, in which critics saddle prosperous tribes with blame for larger macroeconomic changes in a given state.

Tribes ignore these threats at their peril. The measure of prosperity that native communities enjoy is inherently fragile because Congress, should it choose to do so, can repeal those policies that made self-determination possible. Congress retains "plenary power" over Indian affairs, despite the sparse constitutional backing for this spurious doctrine, and as a result Indian tribes remain subject to congressional oversight and interference.

In addition to these political threats, native peoples face significant challenges to their identity. Many non-Indians have expressed skepticism about the authenticity of many gaming tribes, and they have asserted that because of their appearance, their culture, and their business acumen, the members of these native communities are somehow not "real" Indians. These charges, to some extent, are based on a belief that "real" Indians are "primitive," poor, and in all sorts of ways unable to function in the "modern" world. Native peoples whose gaming operations have prospered, like the Mohegans and their Pequot neighbors in Connecticut, as a result face charges that they are either "too white" or "too black" to be real Indians. Ada Deer, who headed the Bureau of Indian Affairs during the presidency of Bill Clinton in the 1990s, noted that non-Indians in her native Wisconsin still "are surprised to see that Indians don't live in tepees, that they have cars, TV's, houses." The agency Deer headed itself has played an enormous role historically in defining what it takes to be an Indian. The Bureau of Indian Affairs always has privileged certain types of native leaders. To qualify for the variety of services offered by the Bureau of Indian Affairs, for instance, Indians must demonstrate that they possess a certain "blood-quantum," or percentage of Indian "blood." Indian-ness, using this logic, is genetic. It is racial, passed on to children from their mothers and fathers. And Indian identity is a complex thing. Not all native peoples look alike, of course, and the components of "authentic" indigenous culture vary widely across Native America. Mohawks living along the St. Lawrence, and Potawatomis now scattered over several states and 1000 miles, were Christians before half the thirteen American colonies had been founded. Native peoples have been speaking, reading, and writing European languages for hundreds of years. As well, they have engaged with the economies of their colonizers, studied in their educational institutions, lived in their cities, and continued to exist. Yet native peoples who are multi-racial or multi-ethnic commonly face questions about their identity. Indeed, no other racial group in North America is asked so frequently to prove that they are who they say they are.

Approximately two-thirds of all federally recognized native communities themselves accept the flawed logic of blood and blood-quantum to determine tribal membership. Native peoples indeed must have some means for regulating entrance into their communities, however problematic the endeavor. Indians find themselves today confronted by a dazzling array of non-Indians who, for a variety of reasons, want to be Indian. New-agers who have fetishized what they believe to be "Native American spiritual traditions" have in places identified with Indian tribes, or even claimed to have been Indian in past lives. Others have tried to prove that they were Indian "because they thought that securing an Indian-ancestry would bring them some form of material advantage: free health care, per capita payments generated by oil leases or bingo hall profits, or other hoped-for windfalls." The Mohegans have found themselves flooded with applications from non-Indians hoping to reap the substantial economic benefits of tribal membership. Other tribes have established offices to oversee the enrollment of new members. The Caddos, for example, request that prospective members fill out a detailed family tree and document their descent from tribal members over several generations.

Growing numbers of "wannabees" have asserted an Indian identity in order to reap the benefits of Indian gaming. Take, for instance, the story of Sachem Golden Eagle of the Western Mohegan Nation of Indians in New York. Golden Eagle, known to the Bureau of Indian Affairs as Ronald A. Roberts, pleaded guilty to federal fraud charges in the summer of 2004. A failed actor, one-time country and western singer, itinerant preacher, hustler, and slate dealer, Roberts claimed Indian descent, formed a "tribe," and in 1997 attempted to open a bingo hall in a depressed town in the northern reaches of the Catskills. Two years later, he filed suit in order to collect millions of dollars in back rent on nearly a million acres of public land that he claimed the state had taken illegally from his people. Roberts wanted in to the Indian casino business, and steadfastly argued that he descended from Indians. Still, the documents he produced to establish his Indian ancestry included a false genealogy, an altered copy of a state census, and his grandfather's death certificate, on which Roberts crossed out the word "White" and wrote "Indian" with a ball-point pen. More recently, a number of academics and political leaders have confronted accusations that their claims to Indian ancestry were ploys to help them advance their careers.

So tribes like the Mohegans must maintain boundaries to ward off opportunists and charlatans, those who would seek to use Indian identity to benefit themselves. This is, of course, a losing proposition for Indians. As native peoples intermarry with non-natives, their blood presumably becomes thinned. With more than half of all native peoples marrying non-Indians, one scholar has estimated that over the course of this century the percentage of the native population with more than one-half "blood" will fall to 8%. Blood-quantum as a measure of Indian identity dooms native peoples to eventual extinction. Indeed, blood is so tragically flawed a marker of Indian identity, that it excludes many people with legitimate claims to Indian-ness. Blood excludes the millions of urban mixed-bloods who, according to the "urban mixed-blood" writer W.S. Penn, "have grown up influenced by a mixture of Native traditions as a result of their participation in urban Indian centers such as those in Los Angeles or Chicago, where Hopi children learned Apache ways, or Nez Perce children learned Osage dances." The Cherokee Freedmen, the descendants of slaves once owned by members of the Cherokee Nation, have been excluded from tribal membership. When Indians adopt non-Indian notions of race to determine who is Indian and who is not, a large number of people will be left out.

What to do? The case of the Chumash is instructive, and raises some vexing questions. How does one decide who is authentically and traditionally Chumash? Who speaks for a community to which 3000 people trace their descent and that includes people who are, as one anthropologist pointed out, "Catholic, Protestant, pagan, atheist, and others"? To whom shall archaeological artifacts and human remains be repatriated? What practices, in communities that have faced religious conversion, significant levels of intermarriage and, apparently, for some parents, so much shame and fear of persecution and discrimination that they concealed from their children their Indian identity, ought to be considered consistent with Chumash traditionalism? And who gets to decide?

By 1870, according to the surviving records, more than half of all Chumash Indian women married non-Indians. Though traces of the culture survived, it did so with difficulty. Chumash languages declined and then disappeared. Parents told their children that they descended from the region's Mexican and Spanish settlers rather than from its Chumash population. Native identity, in a region where Indians had been a despised minority, was something to be ashamed of, and disappearing became a way to survive.

That began to change in the 1960s. Chumash people began to reassert their identity. They claimed that elements of their culture had been kept alive, in secret and away from the prying eyes of judgmental whites, despite the efforts to eradicate it. Others learned they were Indian for the first time, a product of the Red Power movement and increasing assertions of pride in native identity. One event, more than many others, seems to have brought to the attention of the larger population that Chumash people still existed.

In 1978, developers hoped to build a liquefied natural gas terminal at Point Conception, along the coast in Santa Barbara County. Ranchers and homeowners hoped to prevent the construction of the plant, and they enlisted the aid of a group of people who identified themselves as Chumash who based themselves in nearby Santa Barbara. There did exist some evidence in the ethnographic record that Point Conception possessed some spiritual significance to some Chumash, but that claim was contested by scholars, and those who surfaced to fight the proposed project seemed to have weak claims to Chumash ancestry. They also modified and magnified the significance of the site.

Point Conception, to them, had immense spiritual significance and the Chumash were the site's traditional guardians. They were the "Keepers of the Western Gate." No doubt many of the Chumash who occupied the site and took part in protests there sincerely believed that the site was spiritually significant. But they were involved in a process of reinvention that many native communities have been forced to confront: faced with the loss of their culture, a bitter product of the colonial experience, disease, and dispossession, they have been forced to invent and borrow and imagine to recreate communities whose history had been stolen. Reconstructing elements of a culture that missionaries and landowners and aggressive whites sought to eradicate is not easy, and some of what the Chumash at Point Conception described as "traditional" was, in fact, a relatively recent innovation, an invented tradition. The non-Indian opponents of the liquefied natural gas plant exploited these images for their own purposes, relying on stereotypes of timeless natives, in tune with the earth and an ancient spirituality, in an effort to halt the construction of an energy facility that might have threatened their pristine views of the Pacific.

There can be no doubt that the occupation of the site at Point Conception was a vital moment in the resurgence and reappearance of the Chumash, but it raises important questions nonetheless. Were the Chumash linking their interests, in the words of Lakota scholar Vine Deloria, with the non-Indian "wandering scholar, the excited groupie, and the curious filmmaker and writer"? Were they being used? And, if not, can a resurgent native community be allowed to shut down a development project when anthropologists critical of their claims point out that these native peoples have a weak claim to native identity? A Gabrieleño woman, a defender of the Chumash, asserted that "we don't question the identity of our anthropologists and we don't appreciate having them question our identity," but that really does not address the point. Certainly native peoples, unlike members of other groups in American society, are too often forced to demonstrate their "authenticity" as Indians to the satisfaction of non-Indians with misguided or ignorant or stereotypical understandings of who Indians are and what they ought to be. It is a complicated problem with no easy answer.

To demonstrate that they are in fact native peoples, some of these Indian communities, most but not all of them located in the eastern United States, have felt themselves compelled to assert their culture in ways that non-Indians might recognize as "authentically" Indian. The tribal by-laws of the Mattaponis, for instance, a community once part of Wahunsonacock's chiefdom in today's Virginia, require that chiefs representing the tribe on official business wear ceremonial garb so that an ill-informed non-Indian public can recognize them as Indian. Elsewhere, individuals in native communities replace their given names with "native-sounding" names, often rendered in English, and tribes in Connecticut like the Mohegans decorate their casinos with the intent of educating their patrons about traditional culture that they have had to reconstruct from a variety of eastern ethnohistorical sources. The point is that if individuals make choices about their racial and ethnic identity, it is the broader society that ultimately accepts those assertions as legitimate or dismisses them as inauthentic. Indians all-too-often have had to confront white standards of Indian-ness, standards that too often justify the impoverishment and marginalization of native peoples as inherently connected to nature by powerful spiritual bonds, as primitive, and thus as out of place in modern American society.

Native peoples challenged these assumptions, and in the self-determination era devoted considerable time and energy to the protection and revitalization of traditional cultures that government policies systematically attacked over the span of many decades. Since the passage of the Indian Self-Determination and Education Assistance Act, many tribes have created their own education departments with inventive curricula and culturally attuned pedagogy tailored to the concerns of their young people. These schools provide their students with an education equivalent to what they would receive in off-reservation public schools, but also employ programs designed to encourage the preservation of the community's culture. Dakota students at the Tiospa Zina school on the Sisseton-Wahpeton reservation, for instance, take courses in Dakota language and literature. They learn at an institution that rests solidly and creatively upon Dakota values, and that strives to produce learners who "will retain their own unique culture and be prepared for a technological/multi-cultural society."

Native peoples see schools such as these as vital to the survival of their culture, and employ federal funding, once directed toward the eradication of their systems of belief, their language, and their traditions, toward the preservation and revitalization of their culture. It is an enormous task. According to one study, 196 native languages still exist in North America but 155 of these are in danger of dying out. According to another study, by 2050 only twenty native languages will remain in the United States. The Alaska Native Language Center reported that of the 210 languages spoken by native peoples, only thirty-five of them still were spoken by children. More people in the United States speak Danish than any individual native language. Many of the Pueblos in New Mexico have managed to preserve their languages, and over 50% of Crows still speak their language. To a great extent this is a function of the determination of community members to keep them alive. Still, the relative isolation that characterized so many reservation communities is breaking down. Satellite dishes, cable television, the internet, and an omnipresent media are inundating native children in an American kid culture. Younger Indians are less likely to speak their native language because the schooling they receive and the media they consume are in English.

Schools simply are not enough to preserve tribal languages. The Cherokees manage a language project that is comprehensive, in that it includes a Cherokee-language radio show, online programs, extensive teacher training programs, and both an immersion school and language courses in the regular school. Children enter the program in kindergarten. Potawatomi communities in the United States and Canada have worked together since 1973 to preserve their language. More recently, members of the Prairie Band have purchased translation equipment designed for the United States military to aid them in their effort to preserve their language and teach it to a new generation. Some native peoples have developed native language "apps" for use on smart phones. Other communities, like the Mohegans, have had to reconstruct their language. A diary written in the Mohegan-Pequot language, composed by the Mohegan Fidelia Fielding, exists from the early twentieth century, and that provided a baseline of nearly 1000 Mohegan words. Additional research in archives and libraries produced additions to this vocabulary. With the help of linguistic experts specializing in the reconstruction of lost languages, the Mohegans have begun to fill in the blanks, to move from words to phrases to sentences. The Mohegans hope that their well-supported effort produces in time a new generation of Mohegans capable of speaking what many outsiders had assumed was a lost language.

Higher education is necessary to provide native peoples with leaders capable of mastering the intricacies of day-to-day administration. Tribal colleges do important work here. Many tribes without their own colleges provide financial support for their members who wish to pursue higher education. The Prairie Band of Potawatomis, for example, provides grants of up to $4500 per semester for tribal members enrolled as full-time college students. Grants of up to $5000 per calendar year were available for Prairie Potawatomis enrolled in graduate programs.

Institutions and programs such as these do important work in the effort to preserve indigenous culture, and prepare native students to pursue advanced degrees at other institutions. Still, threats to Native American culture continue to confront native peoples. The 1978 American Indian Religious Freedom Act provided insufficient guidance on the range of religious issues confronting native peoples. Religious sites provided one area of controversy. Indians sought access to sacred sites located on public land. Sometimes compromises can be reached. Sometimes more decisive action is required. Only after President Clinton issued an executive order in 1996 requiring federal agencies "to accommodate access to, and use of, sacred sites by Indian religious practitioners," did the National Park Service limit access by rock climbers to Devil's Tower in Wyoming during June, when native peoples held ceremonies at the site. But when religious sites are located on public lands open to all Americans, or that are ripe for economic development, then finding compromises that respect the rights of Indians to practice their religion with the rights of other Americans to enjoy the nation's public lands can be extremely difficult. In 1998, in *Lyng v. Northwest Indian Cemetery Protective Association*, the Supreme Court held that the United States could make use of its public lands even if doing so might "have devastating effects on traditional Indian religious practices," so long as there was a "rational basis" for doing so. The *Lyng* decision was one of a number of cases in which the Court ruled on the scope of the "free exercise" clause of the First Amendment. Previously, the government could only limit one's right to exercise their religious beliefs if it had some "compelling interest" to do so. *Lyng* helped develop a lesser standard.

And that standard was at work in the 1990 case of *Employment Division, Department of Human Resources of Oregon v. Smith*. Two Native American drug counselors were fired as a result of having used peyote as part of the sacramental practice at a meeting of the Native American Church, a religious organization that found its origins at the beginning of the reservation period on the Plains. As the pair lost their jobs because of a drug offense, the state of Oregon denied them unemployment benefits. The Court argued that Oregon, with an interest in preventing the abuse of controlled substances, even when those substances were a vital part of the religious practice in the Native American Church, acted on a rational basis. The "rational basis" test, then, weakened significantly the constitutional protections enjoyed by members of minority groups in their religious life.

Then there is the matter of archaeological remains. For years, collectors had looted Indian cemeteries and other sacred sites. Museums and universities had amassed large collections that included many thousands of human remains. At times, research on these objects and remains yielded important knowledge about native cultures, but for many native peoples, that their ancestors remain unburied and subjects of study, investigation, and experimentation in publicly funded institutions, seemed a bitter reminder of their colonial status, and of their lack of control over their own lives. Native peoples, rightfully resentful of this treatment and the powerlessness that it represented, pressured the federal government to enact the Native American Graves Protection and Repatriation Act (NAGPRA) in 1990, which required museums and other institutions receiving federal funds to inventory their collections of Native American remains and sacred objects. If the community desired the return of these objects, Congress required the institution to repatriate them. The legislation has generated considerable controversy: archaeologists, for instance, on occasion have challenged tribal claims to ownership of the remains in question, or have argued that the application of NAGPRA has retarded much scientific investigation. That may be so, but the legislation clearly reflected a desire to balance the interests of scientists and native peoples over a subject that has caused enormous pain. Native communities across the country have created museums of their own, funded and overseen additional archaeological research on these remains and on their own terms, and energetically worked to preserve and strengthen their culture. Many communities, including the Senecas, Potawatomis, Caddos, Cherokees, Kiowas, and others, have agencies responsible for implementation of NAGPRA, and with responsibility for interacting with the public and the scientific community on issues relating to the repatriation of religious and funerary objects and remains.

In the self-determination era, native peoples have become increasingly effective in governing their communities. Tribal governments provide a range of services for their members and in most cases have established increasingly efficient and professional bureaucracies. Tribal governments try to preserve law and order. They also have taken steps to oversee economic life on their reservations. For years, outside interests had exploited the natural resources in Indian country, extracting from the Department of the Interior lucrative leasing contracts that opened tribal lands to mining and timbering. Now tribes seek more control. Nearly every reservation government has created agencies to oversee natural resources and economic planning, with responsibility for everything from fish and wildlife, to water quality to the oversight of mineral resources and fossil fuels. Tribal resources should sustain the community, not enrich corporate interests. To control these resources, and to bring sustainable economic development to their communities, tribes must establish efficient and effective governments resting upon a solid foundation of tribal values. They must be legitimate in the eyes of their members, and to outsiders. The planning commission for the Prairie Band of Potawatomis, for instance, in emphasizing the importance of planning, asserted that tribal planners "must understand the responsibility that everything he does will echo through time" and that they must recognize the serious responsibility of maintaining "cultural integrity" as they seek to develop reservation economies. Planners must recognize that any program of economic development "has to build on the tribal culture and identity." Exercising sovereignty in this fashion has provided the foundation for a significant amount of economic development in Indian country.

And as tribes have developed their economies, many of them have kept before them the importance of the land. Western tribes have sought to reacquire lands in their historic homelands. In the east, the Seneca Nation of Indians threatened to evict New Yorkers who had leased their lands in Salamanca for terms of ninety-nine years at unconscionably low rates. Congress intervened, paying the Senecas a settlement of close to $13 million. The Salamanca controversy involved leased lands. As a result of the Supreme Court's 1974 decision in the case of *Passamaquoddy Tribe v. Morton*, tribes filed suit to acquire lands that states had acquired in violation of the federal Indian Trade and Intercourse Acts, which stated that "no sale of lands made by any Indians, or any nation or tribe of Indians within the United States, shall be valid … unless the same shall be made and duly executed at some public treaty, held under the authority of the United States." The six Iroquois tribes in New York State had lost much of their land to the state of New York in transactions that never received federal approval, and so the individual tribes sued. But their efforts to recover those lands have hit a significant snag. The Senecas' suit to recover Grand Island was dismissed, a circuit court ruled, because New York already acquired these lands as a result of the American Revolution. Hence New York in this instance had not violated the Trade and Intercourse Act's prohibition on state purchases of Indian land without federal supervision. Why the state would pay the Senecas for land it already owned, the district court never bothered to adequately explain.

Iroquois land claims in general were dealt a more serious blow in 2005, when the United States Supreme Court ruled in the case of *Sherrill v. the Oneida Nation of Indians.* The Oneidas, flush with cash from their casino in central New York, began to purchase lands in their ancestral territory. The Oneidas refused to pay property taxes to the town of Sherrill because these lands stood within the boundaries of their original reservation. The Court held, however, that Indian tribes could not rekindle "the embers of sovereignty that long ago grew cold." Though the state's purchases may have violated the law, New York and its counties had governed these lands for nearly two centuries the court held, and the Oneidas, despite the fact that no court was open to them, had waited too long to seek relief. Allowing a remedy after the passage of so much time would be too disruptive to the white residents of Sherrill, even though the Court made no effort to demonstrate how purchasing land on the open market from willing sellers caused disruption. It is worth remembering that the Oneidas, and others of the Six Nations who have filed suit against the state of New York, had asked for nothing more than that the laws of the United States be enforced. They asked for justice. They did not mention the thousands of their people, or other native peoples, who had died over centuries of contact from European epidemics. They did not ask for recompense for the wars of conquest launched against them by those who sought their lands. They sought no damages for the assault on their way of life, or the re-education of their children in boarding schools. Dispossession was a crime, the Iroquois argued, a clear and explicit violation of the federal Indian Trade and Intercourse Acts. The Supreme Court, of course, felt no need to address these issues. These questions were not before the Court, and they left the Six Nations without a remedy. More than any other act, perhaps, the Court's decision made clear a fundamental truth: though native peoples had made enormous strides during the self-determination era, exercised unprecedented control over their communities, and for the first time did not have to contend with efforts by religious and political leaders to eradicate their culture, there remained still significant limitations on the rights of native peoples and native communities. Federal, state, and local authorities would support the self-determination of native peoples only to the point that a Native American community's desire to exercise their sovereignty clashed with the interests of non-Indian Americans.

Toward the Future

In May of 2008, Senator Barack Obama, who six months later would be elected the first African American president of the United States, visited the Crow Indian Reservation in Montana. The Crows adopted Obama and gave him a name, "One Who Helps People Throughout the Land." He became Obama Black Eagle, a member of a Crow family. His visit, like so much of his candidacy, was historic: Barack Obama was the first presidential candidate ever to visit Crow country. Crow tribal chairman Carl Venne asked Obama to meet regularly with tribal leaders, to consult with them when formulating policy, to respect past Indian treaties, and back the Declaration of the Rights of Indigenous People, approved by the United Nations in September of 2007.

Obama pledged that he would never forget the Crows. "I am," he said, "a member of the family now." Indeed, in his platform Obama expressed his "commitment to tribal nation building and enforcing the federal government's obligations to Indian people"; upholding the sovereignty of native nations and the "government-to-government relationship with the United States federal government that is recognized expressly in treaties with the United States"; appointing "an American Indian policy advisor on his senior White House staff so that Indian Country has a direct interface with the highest level of the Obama Administration"; and increasing funding for the Indian Health Service, for the support of language immersion and preservation programs, and the construction of new schools for Indian children. Obama pledged to support as well the right of Indian tribes to operate the gaming facilities that "are important tribal resources for funding education, healthcare, law enforcement, and other essential government functions," and to reform the broken system for overseeing monies held in trust, and historically mismanaged, by the Bureau of Indian Affairs for Indian tribes.

Figure 10.1 Barack Obama at Crow Agency, May 2008. © AP/Chris Carlson.

Native peoples voted for Obama in overwhelming numbers, contributing to his landslide victory in 2008 over his Republican rival, John McCain, a candidate with a solid record and thorough knowledge of American Indian policy, and his reelection in 2012. Obama's presidency has been, in many ways, one of consequence for native peoples. Obama worked with Congress to secure significant increases in funding for the Indian Health Service. He fulfilled his promise by appointing a policy advisor to counsel him on Native American issues, and he held an annual White House Tribal Nations Conference in order to "strengthen the government-to-government relationship with Indian Country and to improve the lives of American Indians and Alaska Natives." When Obama signed legislation reauthorizing the Violence Against Women Act, it included a new provision allowing tribes to arrest and prosecute non-Indians who committed acts of domestic violence against Native American women. In 2010, he announced his support for the United Nations Declaration on the Rights of Indigenous Peoples.

Significant challenges remain. Though the UN Declaration states that native peoples have the right to "freely determine their political status and freely pursue their economic, social, and cultural development," it is unlikely the United States is willing to go that far. The federal government is willing to contract with Indian tribes to take over the administration of their own affairs. Government agencies no longer seek to eradicate native cultures, but there are limits. And still native peoples face a Supreme Court that has consistently limited the rights of native peoples over their lands. They face, still, concerted assaults on important pieces of legislation like the Indian Child Welfare Act. Racial violence remains a problem, with a "Red Lives Matter" movement quietly growing in the shadow of the Black Lives Matter movement protesting police brutality. Nationhood and sovereignty remain under assault. And, of course, the slow, burning insult of cultural appropriation and the use of Native American symbols and images as offensive mascots for sports teams continue.

As the legal historian Charles F. Wilkinson pointed out, there are many limitations on the rights of native peoples. Their sovereignty is constrained, always, by the plenary authority of the Congress. Still, he optimistically writes, "for all of its many flaws, the policy of the United States toward its native peoples is one of the most progressive of any nation." Native peoples have used that sovereignty to create and reinvigorate communities, revitalize language and culture, provide for the well-being of their people, engage in sustainable economic development, and lay plans for a future in which they will play an important role in American society. The United States, and state and local governments, today routinely express their willingness to support self-determination. This in itself is a significant break from a not-so-distant past when federal officials anticipated the disappearance of tribal governments and the assimilation of native peoples into the American mainstream. At times, non-Indian Americans speak of justice, of building long-term relationships with their native neighbors. But the recent past has shown as well that despite the significant accomplishments of native peoples in governing their communities and promoting their people's interests, the promising signs of cooperation, and the increasing presence and acceptance of native peoples on the national stage, that in general non-Indian Americans will support freedom and autonomy for native peoples only to the point where the exercise of these rights begins to threaten their own interests. Native peoples can meet this challenge. They have little choice. For nearly half a millennia, Europeans expressed their expectations that native peoples would disappear. For much of the nineteenth century, American policy-makers anticipated Indian extinction. And even within the last half-century, American officials looked towards the "termination" of American tribes. No longer. Sovereign tribes are stronger today in terms of their culture, their economic strength, their governing capacity than they have been for a long time. They are more active in defining and shaping their identities—with all the ambiguities and complexities that accompany that endeavor—than at any time in the past. We close this history, then, with a statement that would have been difficult to express at earlier periods when missionaries spoke of converting and transforming Indians, or when soldiers plotted to burn their fields, or reformers carried off their children to boarding schools, or settlers and bureaucrats swiped their lands: native peoples have a future. There are challenges to be met and obstacles to overcome, but native peoples will remain, paradoxically, vital members of nations that are both colonized and sovereign.

Bibliography

Abler, Thomas S. *Cornplanter: Chief Warrior of the Allegany Senecas* (Syracuse, NY: Syracuse University Press, 2007).

Abler, Thomas S. "Beavers and Muskets: Iroquois Military Fortunes in the Face of European Colonization," in *War in the Tribal Zone*, eds. R. B. Ferguson and N. L. Whitehead (Santa Fe: SAR Press, 1992).

Abler, Thomas S. "European Technology and the Art of War in Iroquoia," in *Cultures in Conflict: Current Archaeological Perspectives*, eds. D. C. Tkaczuk and B. C. Vivian (University of Calgary Archaeological Association, 1989).

Abram, Susan M. "'To Keep Bright the Bonds of Friendship': The Making of a Cherokee-American Alliance During the Creek War," *Tennessee Historical Quarterly*, 71 (September 2012), 228–257.

Ackerman, Lillian. *A Necessary Balance: Gender and Power among Indians on the Columbia Plateau* (Norman: University of Oklahoma Press, 2003).

Ackerman, William V. and Rick L. Bunch. "A Comparative Analysis of Indian Gaming in the United States," *American Indian Quarterly*, 36 (Winter 2012), 49–74.

Ackley, Kristina. "Reviewing Haudenosaunee Ties: Laura Cornelius Kellogg and the Idea of Unity in the Oneida Land Claim, *American Indian Culture and Research Journal*, 32 (2008), 57–81.

Adams, David Wallace. *Education for Extinction: American Indians and the Boarding School Experience, 1875–1928* (Lawrence: University Press of Kansas, 1995).

Adelman, Jeremy and Stephen Aron. "From Borderlands to Borders: Empires, Nation-States and the People in Between in North American History," *American Historical Review*, 104 (1999), 814–41.

Agnew, Brad. "Wilma Mankiller," in *The New Warriors: Native American Leaders since 1900*, ed. R. David Edmunds (Lincoln: University of Nebraska Press, 2001).

Akee, Randal K. Q., Katherine A. Spilde, and Jonathan B. Taylor. "The Indian Gaming Regulatory Act and its Effect on American Indian Economic Development," *Journal of Economic Perspectives*, 29 (Summer 2015), 185–208.

Aker, Donna L. "Removing the Heart of the Choctaw People: Indian Removal from a Native Perspective," *American Indian Culture and Research Journal*, 23 (1999), 63–76.

Alden, John R. *John Stuart and the Southern Colonial Frontier* (Ann Arbor: University of Michigan Press, 1944).

Alfred, Taiaiake. *Peace, Power, Righteousness: An Indigenous Manifesto* (Don Mills, Ontario, Canada: Oxford University Press, 1999).

Allen, Paula Gunn. *Pocahontas: Medicine Woman, Spy, Entrepreneur, Diplomat* (San Francisco: Harper San Francisco, 2003).

Native America: A History, Second Edition. Michael Leroy Oberg.
© 2018 John Wiley & Sons, Inc. Published 2018 by John Wiley & Sons, Inc.

Allen, Robert S. *His Majesty's Indian Allies: British Indian Policy in the Defense of Canada, 1774–1815* (Toronto, Canada: Dundurn Press, 1992).

Anderson, Fred. *Crucible of War: The Seven Years' War and the Fate of Empire in British North America, 1754–1766* (New York: Vintage Books, 2000).

Anderson, Gary Clayton. *The Conquest of Texas: Ethnic Cleansing in the Promised Land* (Norman: University of Oklahoma Press, 2005).

Anderson, Gary Clayton. *The Indian Southwest: Ethnogenesis and Reinvention* (Norman: University of Oklahoma Press, 1999).

Anderson, Gary Clayton. *Kinsmen of Another Kind: Dakota-White Relations in the Upper Mississippi Valley, 1650–1862* (Lincoln: University of Nebraska Press, 1984).

Anderson, Gary Clayton and Allan R. Woodworth, eds. *Through Dakota Eyes: Narrative Accounts of the Minnesota Indian War of 1862* (St. Paul: Minnesota Historical Society Press, 1988).

Anderson, Harry H., ed. "Myths and Legends of Wisconsin Indians, Collected by Jeremiah Curtin," *Milwaukee History*, 15 (1992), 2–36.

Anderson, Lani-Henrik. *The Lakota Ghost Dance of 1890* (Lincoln: University of Nebraska Press, 2008).

Anderson, Virginia DeJohn. "King Philip's Herds: The Problem of Livestock in Early New England," *William and Mary Quarterly*, 51 (1994), 601–624.

Andrew, John A. III. *From Revivals to Removal: Jeremiah Evarts, the Cherokee Nation, and the Search for the Soul of America* (Athens, GA: University of Georgia Press, 1992).

Appelbaum, Robert. "Hunger in Early Virginia: Indians and English Facing Off Over Excess, Want and Need," in *Envisioning an English Empire: Jamestown and the Making of the North Atlantic World*, eds. Robert Appelbaum and John Wood Sweet (Philadelphia: University of Pennsylvania Press, 2005).

Aquila, Richard, *The Iroquois Restoration: Iroquois Diplomacy on the Colonial Frontier, 1701–1754* (Detroit: Wayne State University Press, 1983).

Armstrong, William. *Warrior in Two Camps: Ely S. Parker, Union General and Seneca Chief* (Syracuse: Syracuse University Press, 1978).

Arnn, John Wesley, III. *Land of the Tejas: American Identity and Interaction in Texas, 1300–1700* (Austin: University of Texas Press, 2012).

Arnold, Jeanne, ed. *The Origins of a Pacific Coast Chiefdom: The Chumash of the Channel Islands* (Salt Lake City: University of Utah Press, 2001).

Arnold, Jeanne. "Complex Hunter-Gatherer-Fishers of Prehistoric California: Chiefs, Specialists, and Maritime Adaptations of the Channel Island," *American Antiquity*, 57 (January 1992), 60–84.

Asher, Brad. "A Shaman-Killing Case on Puget Sound, 1873–1874: American Law and Salish Culture," *Pacific Northwest Quarterly*, 86 (Winter 1994/5), 17–24.

Ashley, Jeffrey S. and Secody J. Hubbard. *Negotiated Sovereignty: Working to Improve Tribal-State Relations* (Westport: Praeger, 2004).

Avery, George E. "Archaeological Investigations of the Results of a Geophysical Survey at Los Adaes, 18th Century Capital of the Province of Texas," *Southern Studies*, 20 (Fall/Winter 2013), 13–32.

Axtell, James M. *Natives and Newcomers: The Cultural Origins of North America* (New York: Oxford University Press, 2001).

Axtell, James M. *The Invasion Within: The Contest of Cultures in Colonial North America* (New York: Oxford University Press, 1985).

Axtell, James M. *The European and the Indian: Essays in the Ethnohistory of Colonial North America* (New York: Oxford, 1981).

Babcock, Matthew. "Roots of Independence: Transcultural Trade in the Texas-Louisiana Borderlands," *Ethnohistory*, 60 (Spring 2013), 245–268.

Bahr, Diana Meyers. *The Students of the Sherman Indian School: Education and Native Identity Since 1892* (Norman: University of Oklahoma Press, 2014).

Baird, W. David. "Are There Real Indians in Oklahoma? Historical Perceptions of the Five Civilized Tribes," *Chronicles of Oklahoma*, 68 (no. 1, 1990), 4–23.

Baine, Rodney M. "Indian Slavery in Colonial Georgia," *Georgia Historical Quarterly*, 79 (1995), 418–24.

Baker, Emerson W. and John G. Reid. "Amerindian Power in the Early Modern Northeast: A Reappraisal," *William and Mary Quarterly*, 61 (2004), 77–106.

Banks, Dennis with Richard Erdoes. *Ojibwa Warrior: Dennis Banks and the Rise of the American Indian Movement* (Norman: University of Oklahoma Press, 2004).

Banner, Stuart. *How the Indians Lost Their Land* (Cambridge, MA: Harvard University Press, 2005).

Barbour, Philip. *The Three Worlds of Captain John Smith* (Boston, MA: Houghton Mifflin, 1964).

Barr, Daniel P., ed. *The Boundaries between Us: Natives and Newcomers along the Frontiers of the Old Northwest Territory, 1750–1850* (Kent: Kent State University Press, 2006).

Barr, Juliana. "The Red Continent and the Cant of the Coastline," *William and Mary Quarterly*, 69 (July 2012), 521–26.

Barr, Juliana. "Geographies of Power: Mapping Indian Borders in the 'Borderlands' of the Early Southwest," *William and Mary Quarterly*, 69 (January 2011), 5–46.

Barr, Juliana. "How Do You Get from Jamestown to Santa Fe? A Colonial Sun Belt," *Journal of Southern History*, 73 (August 2007), 553–66.

Barr, Juliana. *Peace Came in the Form of a Woman: Indians and Spaniards in the Texas Borderlands* (Chapel Hill: University of North Carolina Press, 2007).

Barr, Juliana. "A Diplomacy of Gender: Rituals of First Contact in the "Land of the Tejas," *William and Mary Quarterly*, 3d. ser., 61 (2004).

Barsh, Russel Lawrence. "Puget Sound Indian Demography, 1900–1920: Migration and Economic Integration," *Ethnohistory*, 34 (Winter 1996), 65–97.

Basso, Keith H. *Wisdom Sits in Places: Landscape and Language among the Western Apache* (Albuquerque: University of New Mexico Press, 1996).

Basson, Lauren L. *White Enough to be American? Race Mixing, Indigenous People, and the Boundaries of State and Nation* (Chapel Hill: University of North Carolina Press, 2008).

Bauerle, Phenocia, ed. *The Way of the Warrior: Stories of the Crow People* (Lincoln: University of Nebraska Press, 2003).

Baumgardner, Frank H., III. *Killing for Land in California: Indian Blood at Round Valley* (New York: Algora Publishing, 2005).

Beal, Merrill D. *I Will Fight No More Forever: Chief Joseph and the Nez Perce War* (Seattle: University of Washington Press, 1963).

Beck, Magaret E. and Sarah Trabert. "Kansas and the Postrevolt Pubeloan Diaspora: Ceramic Evidence from the Scott County Pueblo," *American Antiquity*, 79 (no. 2, 2014), 314–36.

Beebe, Rose Marie and Robert M. Senkewicz. *Junipero Serra: California, Indians, and the Transformation of a Missionary* (Norman: University of Oklahoma Press, 2015).

Bellorado, Benjamin A. and Kirk C. Anderson. "Early Pueblo Responses to Climate Variability: Farming Traditions, Land Tenure, and Social Power in the Eastern Mesa Verde Region," *Journal of Southwestern Anthropology and History*, 78 (Summer 2013), 377–416.

Bender, Norman J. *"New Hope for the Indians": The Grant Peace Policy and the Navajos in the 1870s* (Albuquerque: University of New Mexico Press, 1989).

Beninato, Stephanie. "Pope, Pose-yemu, and Naranjo: A New Look at Leadership in the Pueblo Revolt of 1680," *New Mexico Historical Review*, 65 (no. 4, 1990), 417–35.

Benn, Carl. *The Iroquois in the War of 1812* (Toronto, Ontario: University of Toronto Press, 1998).

Benson, Larry V., Timothy R. Pauketat, and Edward R. Cook. "Cahokia's Boom and Bust in the Context of Climate Change," *American Antiquity*, 74 (July 2009), 467–83.

Benson, Megan. "The Fight for Crow Water, Part II: Damming the Bighorn," *Montana: The Magazine of Western History*, 58 (Spring 2008), 3–23.

Berg, S. Carol. "Arthur C. Parker and the Society of the American Indian, 1911–1916," *New York History*, 81 (April 2000), 237–46.

Berkhofer, Robert F. *The White Man's Indian: Images of the American Indian from Columbus to the Present* (New York, 1978).

Bernstein, Alison. *American Indians and World War II: Toward a New Era in Indian Affairs* (Norman: University of Oklahoma Press, 1991).

Bieder, Robert E. *Science Encounters the Indian, 1820–1880* (Norman: University of Oklahoma Press, 1986).

Bilharz, Joy A. *The Allegany Senecas and Kinzua Dam: Forced Relocation through Two Generations* (Lincoln: University of Nebraska Press, 1998).

Bilodeau, Christopher J. "Creating an Indian Enemy in the Borderlands: King Philip's War in Maine, 1675–1678," *Maine History*, 47 (January 2013), 10–41.

Biolosi, Thomas. *Deadliest Enemies: Law and the Making of Race Relations on and off the Rosebud Reservation* (Berkeley: University of California Press, 2001).

Biolosi, Thomas. *Organizing the Lakota: The Political Economy of the New Deal on the Pine Ridge and Rosebud Reservations* (Tucson: University of Arizona Press, 1992).

Blackhawk, Ned. *Violence over the Land: Indians and Empires in the Early American West* (Cambridge, MA: Harvard University Press, 2006).

Blackhawk, Ned. "I Can Carry on from Here: The Relocation of American Indians to Los Angeles," *Wicazo Sa Review*, 11 (1995), 16–30.

Bletzer, Michael. "The First Province of that Kingdom: Notes on the Colonial History of the Piro Area," *New Mexico Historical Review*, 88 (October 2013), 437–59.

Blu, Karen I. *The Lumbee Problem: The Making of an American Indian People* (New York: Cambridge, 1980).

Bohaker, Heidi. "'Nindoodemag': The Significance of Algonquian Kinship Networks in Eastern Great Lakes Region, 1600–1701," *William and Mary Quarterly*, 63 (January 2006), 23–52.

Bordewich, Fergus. *Killing the White Man's Indian: Reinventing Native Americans at the End of the Twentieth Century* (New York: Doubleday, 1996).

Bossy, Denise I. "Spiritual Diplomacy, the Yamasees, and the Society for the Propagation of the Gospel: Reinterpreting Prince George's Eighteenth-Century Voyage to England," *Early American Studies*, 12 (Spring 2014), 366–401.

Bottinger, Patrick. "Prophetstown for their Own Purposes: The French, Miamis, and Cultural Identities in the Wabash-Maumee Valley," *Journal of the Early Republic*, 33 (Spring 2013), 29–60.

Boulware, Tyler. *Deconstructing the Cherokee Nation: Town, Region and Nation Among Eighteenth-Century Cherokees* (Gainesville: University Press of Florida, 2011).

Bowden, Henry Warner. *American Indians and Christian Missions: Studies in Cultural Conflict* (Chicago: University of Chicago Press, 1981).

Bowles, John P. *Exiles and Pioneers: Eastern Indians in the Trans-Mississippi West* (Cambridge: Cambridge University Press, 2007).

Boxberger, Daniel. "Ethnicity and Labor in the Puget Sound Fishing Industry, 1880–1935," *Ethnohistory*, 33 (Spring 1994), 179–91.

Boxberger, Daniel. "The Lummi Indians and the Canadian/Ameican Pacific Salmon Treaty," *American Indian Quarterly*, 12 (Autumn 1988), 299–311.

Boxberger, Daniel. "In and Out of the Labor Force: The Lummi Indians and the Development of the Commercial Salmon Fishery of North Puget Sound," *Ethnohistory*, 35 (Spring 1988), 161–90.

Boyd, Maurice, ed. *Kiowa Voices: Myths, Legends and Folktales,* volume II (Fort Worth: Texas Christian University Press, 1983).

Boyd, Robert. *The Coming Spirit of Pestilence: Introduced Infectious Diseases and Population Decline Among Northwest Coast Indians, 1774–1874* (Seattle: University of Washington Press, 1999).

Braccio, Audrey Bryant. "How the Anti-Gaming Backlash is Redefining Tribal Government Functions," *American Indian Law Review*, 34 (no. 1, 2009–2010), 171–201.

Bragdon, Kathleen J. *Native People of Southern New England* (Norman: University of Oklahoma Press, 1996).

Bragdon, Kathleen J. "Gender as a Social Category in Native Southern New England," *Ethnohistory*, 43 (1996), 573–92.

Brand, Johanna. *The Life and Death of Anna Mae Aquash*, 2nd edn (Toronto: Lorimer, 1993).

Brandao, Jose Antonio. *Nation Iroquoise: A Seventeenth-Century Ethnography of the Iroquois* (Lincoln: University of Nebraska Press, 2003).

Brandao, Jose Antonio. "Iroquois Expansion in the Seventeenth Century: A Review of Causes," *European Review of Native American Studies*, 15 (no. 2, 2000), 7–18.

Brandao, Jose Antonio. *Your Fyre Shall Burn No More: Iroquois Policy Toward New France and its Native Allies to 1701* (Lincoln: University of Nebraska Press, 1997).

Brandao, Jose Antonio. "War and the French Alliance," *European Review of Native American Studies*, 5 (1991), 15–20.

Brandao, Jose Antonio and William A. Starna, "The Treaties of 1701: A Triumph of Iroquois Diplomacy," *Ethnohistory*, 43 (1996), 209–44.

Brandao, Jose Antonio and Michael Shakir Nassaney. "Suffering for Jesus: Penitential Practices at Fort. St. Joseph (Niles, Michigan) During the French Regime," *Catholic Historical Review*, 84 (July 2008), 476–99.

Braund, Kathleen A. Holland. *Deerskins and Duffels: The Creek Indian Trade with Anglo-America, 1685–1815* (Lincoln: University of Nebraska Press, 1993).

Braund, Kathleen A. Holland, "Guardians of Tradition and Handmaidens to Change: Women's Roles in Creek Economic and Social Life During the Eighteenth Century," *American Indian Quarterly*, 14 (Summer 1990), 239–58.

Brenner, Elise M. "Sociopolitical Implications of Mortuary Remains in 17th Century Southern New England," in *The Recovery of Meaning: Historical Archaeology in the Eastern United States*, Eds. Mark P. Leone and Parker B. Potter (Washington, DC: Eliot Werner Publications, 1988).

Brenner, Elise M. "To Pray or Be Prey, That is the Question: Strategies for Cultural Autonomy of Massachusetts Praying Town Indians," *Ethnohistory*, 27 (1980), 135–52.

Britten, Thomas. *American Indians in World War I: At War and at Home* (Albuquerque: University of New Mexico Press, 1997).

Brooks, James. *Mesa of Sorrows: A History of the Awat'ovi Massacre* (New York: Norton, 2016).

Brooks, James. "Women, Men, and Cycles of Evangelism in the Southwest Borderlands, AD 750–1750." *American Historical Review*, 118 (2013), 738–64.

Brooks, James, ed. *Confounding the Color Line: The Indian-Black Experience in North America* (Lincoln: University of Nebraska Press, 2002).

Brooks, James. *Captives and Cousins: Slavery, Kinship and Community in the Southwest Borderlands* (Chapel Hill: University of North Carolina Press, 2002).

Brooks, Joanna. "Samson Occom at the Mohegan Sun," *Common-Place*, 4 (July 2004) (common-place.org).

Brooks, Lisa. *The Common Pot: The Recovery of Native Space in the Northeast.* (Minneapolis: University of Minnesota Press, 2008).

Brooks, Michael. "The Potawatomi, Europeans, and the Great Black Swamp: An Examination of *Nishnabek*-Newcomer Interactions in Northwest Ohio," *Northwest Ohio History*, 81 (Fall 2013), 24–39.

Bross, Kristina. *Dry Bones and Indian Sermons: Praying Indians in Colonial America* (Ithaca: Cornell University Press, 2004).

Brown, Dee. *Bury My Heart at Wounded Knee: An Indian History of the American West* (New York: Holt, 1995).

Brown, Jennifer S. H. *Strangers in Blood: Fur Trade Company Families in Indian Country* (Vancouver: University of British Columbia Press, 1980).

Brown, Michael F. *Who Owns Native Culture?* (Cambridge, MA: Harvard University Press, 2003).

Brown, Tracy L. "Stratified or Egalitarian? The Sociopolitical Dynamics of Eighteenth-Century Pueblo Communities," *Kiva*, 69 (no. 3, 2004), 283–304.

Buchholtz, Debra. "Telling Stories, Making History: Place and Identity on the Little Bighorn," *Journal of Anthropological Research*, 67 (2011), 421–45.

Buckley, Thomas. "The Shaker Church and the Indian Way in Native Northwestern California," *American Indian Quarterly*, 21 (Winter 1997), 1–14.

Burich, Keith. "'No Place to Go': The Thomas Indian School and the 'Forgotten Indian Children of New York.'" *Wicazo Sa Review*, 22 (Fall 2007), 93–110.

Burke, Joseph C. "The Cherokee Cases: A Study in Law, Politics, and Morality," *Stanford Law Review*, 21(February 1969), 500–31.

Burt, Larry W. *Tribalism in Crisis: Federal Indian Policy, 1953–1961* (Albuquerque: University of New Mexico Press, 1982).

Calloway, Colin. *White People, Indians and Highlanders: Tribal Peoples and Colonial Encounters in Scotland and America* (New York: Oxford, 2010).

Calloway, Colin. *The Shawnees and the War for America* (New York: Penguin, 2007).

Calloway, Colin. *One Vast Winter Count: The Native American West Before Lewis and Clark* (Lincoln: University of Nebraska Press, 2003).

Calloway, Colin. ed. *After King Philip's War: Presence and Persistence in Indian New England* (Hanover, NH: Dartmouth, 1997).

Calloway, Colin. *New Worlds for All: Indians, Europeans and the Remaking of Early America* (Baltimore: Johns Hopkins University Press, 1997).

Calloway, Colin. *The American Revolution in Indian Country: Crisis and Diversity in Native American Communities* (London: Cambridge University Press, 1995).

Calloway, Colin. *Crown and Calumet: British-Indian Relations, 1783–1815* (Norman: University of Oklahoma Press, 1987).

Camenzind, Krista. "Violence, Race and the Paxton Boys," in *Friends and Enemies in Penn's Woods: Indians, Colonists, and the Racial Construction of Pennsylvania*, eds. William A. Pencak and Daniel K. Richter (University Park: Pennsylvania State University Press, 2004).

Campion, Thomas J. "Indian Removal and the Transformation of Northern Indians," *Indiana Magazine of History*, 107 (March 2011), 32–62.

Campisi, Jack and William A. Starna. "The Road to Canandaigua: The Treaty of 1794" *American Indian Quarterly*, 19 (Fall 1995), 471–90.

Canny, Nicholas. "The Permissive Frontier: The Problem of Social Control in English Settlements in Ireland and Virginia, 1550–1650. *The Westward Enterprise: English Activities in Ireland, the Atlantic, and America, 1480–1650*, ed. Nicholas Canny, K. E. Andrews, and P. E. H. Hair (Detroit: Wayne State University Press, 1979).

Canny, Nicholas. "The Ideology of English Colonization: From Ireland to America," *William and Mary Quarterly*, 30 (1973), 575–98.

Carpenter, Roger M. *The Renewed, the Destroyed, and the Remade: The Three Thought Worlds of the Iroquois and the Huron, 1609–1650* (East Lansing: Michigan State University Press, 2004).

Carpio, Myla Vicenti. "Countering Colonization: Albuquerque Laguna Colony," *Wicazo Sa Review*, 19 (Fall 2004), 61–78.

Carroll, Al. *Medicine Bags and Dog Tags: American Indian Veterans from Colonial Times to the Second Iraq War* (Lincoln: University of Nebraska Press, 2008).

Carroll, Clint. "Shaping New Homelands: Environmental Production, Natural Resource Management, and the Dynamics of Indigenous State Practice in the Cherokee Nation," *Ethnohistory*, 61 (Winter 2014), 123–47.

Carson, James Taylor. *Searching for the Bright Path: The Mississippi Choctaws from Prehistory to Removal* (Lincoln: University of Nebraska Press, 1999).

Carson, James Taylor. "Horses and the Economy and Culture of the Choctaw Indians, 1690–1840," *Ethnohistory*, 42 (Summer 1995), 495–513.

Carter, Cecile Elkins. *Caddo Indians: Where We Come From* (Norman: University of Oklahoma Press, 1995).

Carter, William. "Bison, Corn and Power: Plains-New Mexico Exchange in the Sixteenth and Early Seventeenth Centuries," *Heritage of the Great Plains*, 30 (no. 1, 1997), 20–32.

Cassady, Joslyn. "'Strange Things Happen to Non-Christian People': Human-Animal Transformation Among the Iñupiat of Arctic Alaska," *American Indian Culture and Research Journal*, 32 (2008), 83–101.

Castile, George Pierre, ed. *The Indians of Puget Sound: The Notebooks of Myron Eells*. (Seattle: University of Washington Press, 1985).

Cave, Alfred F. "The Shawnee Prophet, Tecumseh, and Tippecanoe: A Case Study of Historical Myth-Making." *Journal of the Early Republic*, 22 (Winter 2002), 637–73.

Cave, Alfred F. "The Delaware Prophet Neolin: A Reappraisal," *Ethnohistory*, 46 (Spring 1999), 254–78.

Cave, Alfred F. *The Pequot War* (Amherst: University of Massachusetts Press, 1996).

Cave, Alfred F. "Who Killed John Stone? A Note on the Origins of the Pequot War," *William and Mary Quarterly*, 49 (July 1992), 509–23.

Cave, Alfred F. "The Pequot Invasion of Southern New England: A Reassessment of the Evidence." *New England Quarterly*, 62 (1989), 27–44.

Cayton, Andrew. "Not the Fragments but the Whole." *William and Mary Quarterly*, 69 (July 2012), 513–516.

Chamberlain, Ava. "The Execution of Moses Paul: A Story of Crime and Contact in Eighteenth Century Connecticut," *New England Quarterly*, 77 (September 2004), 414–50.

Child, Brenda. *Boarding School Seasons: American Indian Families, 1900–1940)* (Lincoln: University of Nebraska Press, 1998).

Childs, H. Terry and Charles H. McNutt. "Hernando De Soto's Route from Chicaça throughout Northeast Arkansas: A Suggestion," *Southeastern Archaeology*, 28 (Winter 2009), 165–83.

Chipman, Donald. *Spanish Texas, 1519–1821* (Austin: University of Texas Press, 1992).

Clark, Ella. *Indian Legends of the Pacific Northwest* (Los Angeles: University of California Press, 1953).

Clark, Mary Whatley. *Chief Bowles and the Texas Cherokees* (Norman: University of Oklahoma Press, 1971).

Clarkin, Thomas. *Federal Indian Policy in the Kennedy and Johnson Administrations* (Albuquerque: University of New Mexico Press, 2000).

Clifton, James A. *The Prairie People: Continuity and Change in Potawatomi Indian Culture, 1665–1965* (Iowa City: University of Iowa Press, 1998).

Clifton, James A., ed. *Being and Becoming Indian: Biographical Studies of North American Frontiers* (Chicago: Dorsey Press, 1989).

Clifton, James A. "Simon Pokagon's Sandbar," *Michigan History*, 71 (September/October 1987), 12–19.

Cobb, Amanda J. *Listening to our Grandmothers' Stories: The Bloomfield Academy for Chickasaw Females, 1852–1949* (Lincoln: University of Nebraska Press, 2007).

Cobb, Daniel M. *Say We are Nations: Documents of Politics and Protest in Indigenous America Since 1887* (Chapel Hill: University of North Carolina Press, 2015).

Cobb, Daniel M. *Native Activism in Cold War America: The Struggle for Sovereignty* (Lawrence: University of Kansas Press, 2008).

Cobb, Daniel M. "'Us Indians Understand the Basics': Oklahoma Indians and the Politics of Community Action, 1964–1970," *Western Historical Quarterly*, 33 (Spring 2002), 41–66.

Cobb, Daniel M. "Philosophy of an Indian War: Indian Community Action in the Johnson Administration's War on Indian Poverty, 1964–1968," *American Indian Culture and Research Journal*, 22 (no. 2, 1998), 71–102.

Cobb, Daniel M. and Loretta Fowler, eds. *Beyond Red Power: American Indian Politics and Activism Since 1900* (Santa Fe: School of America Research Press, 2007).

Cochran, Mary E. *Dakota Cross-Bearer: The Life and World of a Native American Bishop* (Lincoln: University of Nebraska Press, 2004).

Cohen, Fay G. *Treaties on Trial: The Continuing Controversy over Northwest Indian Fishing Rights* (Seattle: University of Washington Press, 1986).

Cohen, Felix S. *On the Drafting of Tribal Constitutions* (Norman: University of Oklahoma Press, 2007).

Cohen, Matt. *The Networked Wilderness: Communicating in Early New England* (Minneapolis: University of Minnesota Press, 2010).

Coleman, Michael C. *American Indian Children at School, 1850–1930* (Jackson: University Press of Mississippi, 1993).

Conable, Mary H. "A Steady Enemy: The Ogden Land Company and the Seneca Indians," PhD Diss., University of Rochester, 1994.

Conner, Thaddeus W. and William A. C. Taggart. "Assessing the Impact of Indian Gaming on American Indian Nations: Is the House Winning?" *Social Science Quarterly*, 94 (2013), 1016–44.

Conrad, Maia. "Disorderly Drinking: Reconsidering Seventeenth-Century Iroquois Alcohol Abuse," *American Indian Quarterly*, 23 (1999), 1–12.

Conroy, David W. "The Defense of Indian Land Rights: William Bollan and the Mohegan Case in 1743," *Proceedings of the American Antiquarian Society*, 103 (1993), 395–424.

Cook, Noble David. *Born to Die: Disease and New World Conquest* (Cambridge: Cambridge University Press, 2005).

Cook, Peter. "'Onontio Gives Birth': How the French in Canada Became Fathers to their Indigenous Allies, 1645–1673," *Canadian Historical Review*, 96 (June 2015), 165–93.

Cook, Sherburne F. *The Conflict between the California Indians and White Civilization* (Berkeley: University of California Press, 1976).

Corbett, Steve and Jeanne Drisko. "Health Conditions among the Potawatomi Indians of Kansas in 1928," *Plains Anthropologist*, 56 (August 2011), 215–42.

Cordell, Linda S. *Ancient Pueblo Peoples* (Washington, DC: Smithsonian Institution Books, 1994).

Corkran, David. *The Cherokee Frontier: Conflict and Survival, 1740–1762* (Norman: University of Oklahoma Press, 1962).

Cornell, Stephen. *The Return of the Native: American Indian Political Resurgence* (New York: Oxford University Press, 1988).

Cothran, Boyd. *Remembering the Modoc War: Redemptive Violence and the Making of American Innocence.* (Chapel Hill: University of North Carolina Press, 2014).

Cotterill, R. S. *The Southern Indians: The Story of the Five Civilized Tribes Before Removal* (Norman: University of Oklahoma Press, 1954).

Countryman, Edward. "Indians, the Colonial Order, and the Social Significance of the American Revolution," *William and Mary Quarterly*, 3d ser., 53 (April 1996), 342–62.

Cowger, Thomas W. *The National Congress of American Indians: The Founding Years* (Lincoln: University of Nebraska Press, 1999).

Cramer, Renee Ann. *Cash, Color and Colonialism: The Politics of Tribal Acknowledgment* (Norman: University of Oklahoma Press, 2005).

Crane, Verner W. *The Southern Frontier, 1670–1732* (Ann Arbor: University of Michigan Press, 1929).

Creamer, Winifred. "Re-examining the Black Legend: Contact Period Demography in the Rio Grande Valley of New Mexico," *New Mexico Historical Review*, 69 (July 1994), 263–280.

Cronon, William. *Changes in the Land: Indians, Colonists and the Ecology of New England* (New York: Hill and Wang, 1983).

Crosby, Alfred. *Ecological Imperialism: The Biological Expansion of Europe, 900–1900* (New York: Cambridge University Press, 1986).

Crosby, Alfred. "Virgin Soil Epidemics as a Factor in Aboriginal Depopulation in America," *William and Mary Quarterly*, 30 (1976), 176–207.

Crosby, Constance. "The Algonkian Spiritual Landscape," in *Algonkians of New England: Past and Present*, ed. Peter Benes (Boston, MA: Boston University, 1993), 35–41.

Crosby, Constance. "From Myth to History, or Why King Philip's Ghost Walks Abroad," *The Recovery of Meaning Historical Archaeology in the Eastern United States* (Washington, DC: Smithsonian Institution Press, 1988).

Crow Dog, Leonard and Richard Erdoes. *Crow Dog: Four Generations of Sioux Medicine Men* (New York: Harper, 1995).

Cumfer, Cynthia. *Separate Peoples, One Land: The Minds of Cherokees, Blacks and Whites on the Tennessee Frontier* (Chapel Hill: University of North Carolina Press, 2007).

Cumfer, Cynthia. "Local Origins of National Indian Policy: Cherokee and Tennessean Ideas about Sovereignty and Nationhood, 1790–1811," *Journal of the Early Republic*, 23 (Spring 2003), 21–46.

Daily, David W. *Battle for the BIA: G.E.E. Lindquist and the Missionary Crusade Against John Collier* (Tucson: University of Arizona Press, 2004).

Daly, Heather Ponchetti. "Fractured Relations at Home: The 1953 Termination Act's Effect on Tribal Relations Throughout Southern California Indian Country," *American Indian Quarterly*, 33 (September 2009), 427–39.

Dando-Collins, Steven. *Standing Bear is a Person: A True Story of a Native American's Quest for Justice* (New York: DeCapo, 2004).

Daniels, John D. "The Indian Population of North America in 1492," *William and Mary Quarterly*, 49 (1992), 298–320.

Danziger, Edmund Jefferson. *Indians and Bureaucrats: Administering the Reservation Policy during the Civil War* (Urbana: University of Illinois Press, 1974).

Dartt-Newton, Deana and Jon M. Erlandson, "Little Choice for the Chumash: Colonialism, Cattle, and Coercion in Mission Period California," *American Indian Quarterly*, 30 (2006), 416–30.

Delage, Denys. *Bitter Feast: Amerindians and Europeans in Northeast North America, 1600–1664* (Vancouver: University of British Columbia Press, 1993).

DeLay, Brian. *War of a Thousand Deserts: Indian Raids and the US-Mexican War* (New Haven: Yale University Press, 2008).

Deloria, Philip. *Indians in Unexpected Places* (Lawrence: University Press of Kansas, 2004).

Deloria, Philip. *Playing Indian* (New Haven: Yale University Press, 1998).

Deloria, Vine. *Custer Died for Your Sins: An Indian Manifesto* (Norman: University of Oklahoma Press, 1969).

Deloria, Vine and Clifford M. Lytle. *The Nations Within: The Past and Future of American Indian Sovereignty* (New York: Pantheon, 1984).

DeLucia, Christine. "The Memory Frontier: Uncommon Pursuits of Past and Place in the Northeast after King Philip's War," *Journal of American History*, 98 (March 2012), 975–97.

Demos, John. *The Unredeemed Captive: A Family Story from Early America* (New York, 1994).

Den Ouden, Amy. *Beyond Conquest: Native Peoples and the Struggle for History in New England* (Lincoln: University of Nebraska Press, 1999).

Den Ouden, Amy E. and Jean M. O'Brien, eds. *Recognition, Sovereignty Struggles, and Indigenous Rights in the United States: A Sourcebook* (Chapel Hill: University of North Carolina Press, 2013).

Denevan, William M., ed. *The Native Population of the Americas in 1492* (Madison: University of Wisconsin Press, 1976).

Dennis, Matthew. *Seneca Possessed: Indians, Witchcraft, and Power in the Early American Republic* (Philadelphia: University of Pennsylvania Press, 2010).

Dennis, Matthew. *Cultivating a Landscape of Peace: Iroquois-European Encounters in Seventeenth Century America* (Ithaca: Cornell University Press, 1993).

Dennis, Matthew. "Sorcery and Sovereignty: Senecas, Citizens, and the Contest for Power and Authority on the Frontiers of the Early American Republic," in *New World Orders: Violence, Sanction, and Authority in the Colonial Americas*, eds. John Smolenski and Thomas J. Humphrey (Philadelphia: University of Pennsylvania Press, 2005).

Densmore, Christopher. *Red Jacket: Iroquois Diplomat and Orator* (Syracuse: Syracuse University Press, 1999).

Denson, Andrew. "Native Americans in Cold War Public Diplomacy: Indian Politics, American History, and the US Information Agency," *American Indian Culture and Research Journal*, 36 (2012), 3–27.

Denson, Andrew. *Demanding the Cherokee Nation: Indian Autonomy and American Culture, 1830–1900* (Lincoln: University of Nebraska Press, 2004).

Denson, Andrew. "'Unite with us to Rescue the Kiowas': The Five Civilized Tribes and Warfare on the Southern Plains," *Chronicles of Oklahoma*, 81 (no. 4, 2003), 458–79.

Devens, Carol. *Countering Colonization: Native American Women and Great Lakes Missions, 1630–1900* (Berkeley: University of California Press, 1992).

De Vorsey, Louis. *The Indian Boundary in the Southern Colonies, 1763–1775* (Chapel Hill: University of North Carolina Press, 1961).

Dickason, Olive Patricia. *The Myth of the Savage and the Beginnings of French Colonialism in the Americas* (Edmonton: University of Alberta Press, 1984).

Dilworth, Leah. *Imagining Indians in the Southwest: Persistent Visions of a Primitive Past* (Washington, DC: Smithsonian Institution Press, 1996).

Dimitrova-Grajzl, Valentina, Peter Grajzl, and A. Joseph Guse. "Jurisdiction, Crime, and Development: The Impact of Public Law 280 in Indian Country," *Law and Society Review*, 48 (no. 1, 2014), 127–60.

Din, Gilbert C. "Empires Too Far: The Demographic Limitations of Three Imperial Powers in the Eighteenth Century Mississippi Valley," *Louisiana History*, 50 (Summer 2009), 262–92.

Dinwoodie, David H. "Indians, Hispanos, and Land Reform: A New Deal Struggle in New Mexico," *Western Historical Quarterly*, 17 (no. 3, 1986), 291–323.

Dippie, Brian W. *The Vanishing American: White Attitudes and U.S. Indian Policy* (Middletown: Wesleyan University Press, 1982).

Dobyns, Henry F. *Their Number Became Thinned: Native American Population Dynamics in Eastern North America* (Knoxville: University of Tennessee Press, 1983).

Dorris, Michael. "Indians on the Shelf," in *The American Indian and the Problem of History*, ed. Calvin Luther Martin (New York: Oxford University Press, 1987).

Dorsey, George A. *Traditions of the Caddo*, reprint edn (Lincoln: University of Nebraska Press, 1997).

Dowd, Gregory Evans. *War under Heaven: Pontiac, the Indian Nations, and the British Empire* (Baltimore: Johns Hopkins University Press, 2002).

Dowd, Gregory Evans. *A Spirited Resistance: The Indians Great Awakening, 1745-1815* (Baltimore: Johns Hopkins University Press, 1992).

Drake, James D. *King Philip's War: Civil War in New England, 1675–1676* (Amherst: University of Massachusetts Press, 1999).

Drake, James D. "Symbol of a Failed Strategy: The Sassamon Trial, Political Culture, and the Outbreak of King Philip's War," *American Indian Culture and Research Journal*, 19 (1995), 111–41.

Drooker, Penelope. "The Ohio Valley, 1550–1750: Patterns of Sociocultural Coalescence and Dispersal," in *The Transformation of the Southeastern Indians, 1540–1760*, eds., Robbie Ethridge and Charles Hudson (Jackson: University Press of Mississippi, 2002).

Dudas, Jeffrey R. *Treaty Rights and the New Right* (Stanford: Stanford University Press, 2008).

Dumont, Clayton W., Jr. "Contesting Scientists' Narrations of NAGPRA's Legislative History: Rule 10.11 and the Recovery of 'Cultural Identifiable' Ancestors," *Wicazo Sa Review*, 26 (Spring 2011), 5–41.

Dussias, Allison, M. "Protecting Pocahontas's World: The Mattaponi Tribe's Struggle against Virginia's King William Reservoir Project," *American Indian Law Review*, 36 (no. 1, 2011-2012), 1–123.

Duthu, N. Bruce. *American Indians and the Law* (New York: Viking, 2008).

Du Val, Kathleen. *The Native Ground: Indians and Colonists in the Heart of the Continent* (Philadelphia: University of Pennsylvania Press, 2006).

Eastman, Charles M. *From the Deep Woods to Civilization*. reprint edn (Lincoln: University of Nebraska Press, 1977).

Eastman, Charles M. *The Soul of the Indian*, reprint edn (New York: Johnson Reprint Corporation, 1971).

Ebright, Malcolm. "Advocates for the Oppressed: Indians, Genizaros, and their Spanish Advocates in New Mexico, 1700–1786," *New Mexico Historical Review* (October 1996), 305–39.

Edmunds, R. David. *The Shawnee Prophet* (Lincoln: University of Nebraska Press, 1983).

Edmunds, R. David. *The Potawatomis: Keepers of the Fire* (Norman: University of Oklahoma Press, 1978).

Eells, Myron. *Ten Years of Missionary Work among the Indians at Skokomish, Washington Territory, 1874–1884* (Boston, MA: Congregational House, 1886).

Eid, Leroy V. "The Ojibwa-Iroquois War: The War the Five Nations Did Not Win." *Ethnohistory*, 26 (Autumn 1979), 297–324.

Ellis, Clyde. "'We Had a Lot of Fun, But of Course, That Wasn't the School Part': Life at the Rainy Mountain Boarding School, 1893–1920," in *Boarding School Blues: Revisiting American Indian Educational Experiences*, eds. Clifford E. Trafzer, Jean A. Keller, and Lorene Sisquoc (Lincoln: University of Nebraska Press, 2006).

Ellis, Clyde. *A Dancing People: Powwow Culture on the Southern Plains* (Lawrence: University Press of Kansas, 2003).

Ellis, Clyde. *To Change Them Forever: Indian Education at the Rainy Mountain Boarding School* (Norman: University of Oklahoma Press, 1996).

Emerson, Thomas E. *Cahokia and the Archaeology of Power* (Tuscaloosa: University of Alabama Press, 1997).

Engelbrecht, William. *Iroquoia: The Development of a Native World* (Syracuse: Syracuse University Press, 2003).

Engelbrecht, William. "The Case of the Disappearing Iroquoians: Early Contact Period Superpower Politics," *Northeast Anthropology*, 50 (1995), 35–9.

Erlandson, Jon M. and Kevin Bartoy, "Cabrillo, the Chumash, and Old World Diseases," *Journal of California and Great Basin Anthropology*, 17 (1995), 153–73.

Erlandson, Jon M, et al. *A Canyon through Time: Archaeology, History, and Ecology of the Tecolote Canyon Area* (Salt Lake City: University of Utah Press, 2008).

Erlandson, Jon M, et al. "Forum on Anthropology in Public: The Making of Chumash Tradition: Replies to Haley and Wilcoxen," *Current Anthropology*, 38 (December 1998), 477–510.

Ethridge, Robbie and Sheri M. Shuck-Hall, eds. *Mapping the Mississippian Shatter Zone: The Colonial Indian Slave Trade and Regional Instability in the American South* (Lincoln: University of Nebraska Press, 2009).

Etheridge, Robbie. *Creek Country: The Creek Indians and Their World* (Chapel Hill: University of North Carolina Press, 2003).

Everett, Dianna. *The Texas Cherokees: A People between Two Fires* (Norman: University of Oklahoma Press, 1990).

Fagan, Brian M. *Chaco Canyon: Archaeologists Explore the Lives of an Ancient Society* (New York: Oxford University Press, 2005).

Fagan, Brian M. *The Great Journey: The Peopling of Ancient America* (Gainesville: University Press of Florida, 2004).

Fagan, Brian M. *Ancient North America: The Archaeology of a Continent* (New York: Thames and Hudson, 1995).

Fahey, John. *The Kalispel Indians* (Norman: University of Oklahoma Press, 1986).

Faulk, Odie. *The Geronimo Campaign* (New York: Oxford University Press, 1969).

Fausz, J. Frederick. "'An Abundance of Blood Shed on Both Sides': England's First Indian War, 1609–1614," *Virginia Magazine of History and Biography*, 98 (1990), 3–56.

Fausz, J. Frederick. "Middlemen in Peace and War: Virginia's Earliest Indian Interpreters, 1608–1632," *Virginia Magazine of History and Biography*, 95 (1987), 41–64.

Fausz, J. Frederick. "Patterns of Anglo-Indian Aggression and Accommodation along the Mid-Atlantic Coast, 1584–1634," *Cultures in Contact: The Impact of European Contacts on Native American Cultural Institutions, 100–1800*, ed. William W. Fitzhugh (Washington, DC: Smithsonian Institution Press, 1985).

Fausz, J. Frederick. "Opechancanough: Indian Resistance Leader," in *Struggle and Survival in Colonial America*, eds. David G. Sweet and Gary B. Nash (Berkeley: University of California Press, 1981).

Fausz, J. Frederick. "Fighting 'Fire' with Firearms: The Anglo-Powhatan Arms Race in Early Virginia," *American Indian Culture and Research Journal*, 3 (1979), 33–50.

Fausz, J. Frederick. "The Powhatan Uprising of 1622: A Historical Study of Ethnocentrism and Cultural Conflict," PhD diss., College of William and Mary, 1977.

Fausz, J. Frederick and Jon Kukla, eds. "A Letter of Advice to the Governor of Virginia, 1624," *William and Mary Quarterly*, 34 (1977), 104–129.

Fauvelle, Mikael. "Evaluating Cross-Channel Exchange in the Santa Barbara Region: Experimental Data on Acorn Processing and Transport." *American Antiquity*, 78 (no. 4, 2013), 790–8.

Fawcett, Melissa Jane. *Medicine Trail: The Life and Lessons of Gladys Tantaquidgeon* (Tucson: University of Arizona Press, 2000).

Fawcett, Melissa Jane. *The Lasting of the Mohegans, Part I: The Story of the Wolf People* (Ledyard: Pequot Printing, 1996).

Fear-Segal, Jacqueline. *White Man's Clubs: Schools, Race and the Struggle of Indian Acculturation* (Lincoln: University of Nebraska Press, 2007).

Fenn, Elizabeth A. "Biological Warfare in Eighteenth-Century North America: Beyond Jeffery Amherst," *Journal of American History*, 86 (no. 4, 2000), 1552–80.

Fenton, William N. *The Great Law and the Longhouse: A Political history of the Iroquois Confederacy* (Norman: University of Oklahoma Press, 1998).

Fickes, Michael F. "'They Could Not Endure That Yoke': The Captivity of Pequot Women and Children After the War of 1637," *New England Quarterly*, 73 (2000), 58–81.

Field, Les, et al. "California Forum on Anthropology in Public: Complicities and Collaborations: Anthropologists and 'Unacknowledged Tribes' of California," *Current Anthropology*, 40 (1999), 193–209.

Finger, John R. *The Eastern Band of Cherokees, 1819–1900* (Knoxville: University of Tennessee Press, 1984).

Fischer, Joseph R. *A Well-Executed Failure: The Sullivan Campaign Against the Iroquois, July–September 1779* (Columbia: University of South Carolina Press, 1997).

Fisher, Linford D. "'Dangerous Designes': The 1676 Barbados Act to Prohibit New England Slave Importation," *William and Mary Quarterly*, 71 (January 2014), 99–124.

Fisher, Linford D. "'It Prov'd But Temporary, & Short Lived': Pequot Affiliation in the First Great Awakening," *Ethnohistory*, 59 (Summer 2012), 465–88.

Fisher, Linford D. *The Indian Great Awakening: Religion and the Shaping of Native Cultures in Early America* (New York: Oxford University Press, 2012).

Fisher, Linford D. "'I Believe They Are Papists!' Natives, Moravians and the Politics of Conversion in Eighteenth Century Connecticut," *New England Quarterly*, 81 (September 2008), 410–37.

Fixico, Donald L. *The Urban Indian Experience in America* (Albuquerque: University of New Mexico Press, 2000).

Fixico, Donald L. *The Invasion of Indian Country in the Twentieth Century: American Capitalism and Tribal Natural Resources* (Boulder: University Press of Colorado, 1998).

Fixico, Donald L. "The Alliance of Three Fires in Trade and War, 1630–1812," *Michigan Historical Review*, 20 (no. 2, 1994), 1–23.

Fixico, Donald L. *Termination and Relocation: Federal Indian Policy, 1945–1960* (Albuquerque: University of New Mexico Press, 1986).

Flaherty, Anne F. Boxberger. "American Indian Land Rights, Rich Indian Racism, and Newspaper Coverage in New York State, 1988–2008," *American Indian Culture and Research Journal*, 37 (no. 4, 2013), 53–84.

Fletcher, Matthew L. M. "Tribal Membership and Nationhood," *American Indian Law Review*, 37 (no. 1, 2012–2013), 1–17.

Flint, Richard. "Laguna Pueblo History Revisited," *New Mexico Historical Review*, 90 (Winter 2015), 7–30.

Flint, Richard. "The Flipside of Discovery," *New Mexico Historical Review*, 88 (Winter 2013), 1–14.

Flint, Richard. "Without Them, Nothing Was Possible: The Coronado Expedition's Indian Allies," *New Mexico Historical Review*, 84 (Winter 2009), 65–118.

Flint, Richard. "What They Never Told You About the Coronado Expedition," *Kiva*, 71 (Winter 2005), 203–17.

Flint, Richard and Shirley Cushing Flint. "Parts of the Whole: The Diverse Makeup of the Coronado Expedition," *Journal of the West*, 47 (Summer 2008), 23–31.

Flint, Richard and Shirley Cushing Flint. "A Death in Tiguex, 1542," *New Mexico Historical Review*, 74 (July 1999), 247–70.

Flores, Dan. "Bison Ecology and Bison Diplomacy: The Southern Plains from 1800 to 1850," *Journal of American History*, 78 (September 1991), 465–85.

Fogelson, Raymond D. "The Ethnohistory of Events and Non-Events," *Ethnohistory*, 36 (1989), 133–47.

Foley, Michael F. *The United States and the Santee Sioux: The Treaties of 1858* (Washington, DC: Court of Claims, Sioux Docket no. 363, 1982).

Foster, Morris. *Being Comanche: A Social History of an American Indian Community* (Tucson: University of Arizona Press, 1991).

Fowler, Loretta. *Shared Symbols, Contested Meanings: Gros Ventre Culture and History, 1778–1984* (Ithaca: Cornell University Press, 1987).

Franco, Jere' Bishop. *Crossing the Pond: The Native American Effort in World War II* (Denton: University of North Texas Press, 1999).

Frank, Andrew K. *Creeks and Southerners: Biculturalism on the Early American Frontier* (Lincoln: University of Nebraska Press, 2005).

Franklin, Catherine R. "'If Government Will Only … Fulfill Its Obligations': Colonel Benjamin Grierson, Rations Policy, and the Kiowa Indians, 1868–1872," *Southwestern Historical Quarterly*, 118 (October 2014), 178–199.

Franz, William. "'To Live by Depredations': Main Poc's Strategic Use of Violence." *Journal of the Illinois Historical Society*, 102 (Fall–Winter 2009), 238–47.

Frazier, Patrick M. *The Mohicans of Stockbridge* (Lincoln: University of Nebraska Press, 1992).

Frost, Richard H. "The Pueblo Indian Smallpox Epidemic in New Mexico, 1898–1899," *Bulletin of the History of Medicine*, 64 (no. 3, 1990), 417–45.

Gaines, W. Craig. *The Confederate Cherokees: John Drew's Regiment of Mounted Rifles* (Baton Rouge: Louisiana State University Press, 1989).

Gallay, Alan. *The Indian Slave Trade: The Rise of the English Empire in the American South, 1670–1717* (New Haven: Yale University Press, 2002).

Gallivan, Martin D. "The Archaeology of Native Societies in the Chesapeake: New Investigations and Interpretations," *Journal of Archaeological Research*, 19 (2011), 281–325.

Gallivan, Martin D. "Powhatan's Werowocomoco: Constructing Place, Polity, and Personhood," *American Anthropologist*, 109 (March 2007), 85–100.

Gallivan, Martin D. *James River Chiefdoms: The Rise of Social Inequality in the Chesapeake* (Lincoln: University of Nebraska Press, 2003).

Galloway, Patricia. *Choctaw Genesis, 1500–1700* (Lincoln: University of Nebraska Press, 1995).

Galloway, Patricia, ed. *The Southeastern Ceremonial Complex: Artifacts and Analysis* (Lincoln: University of Nebraska Press, 1989).

Gamble, Lynn H. *The Chumash World at European Contact: Power, Trade and Feasting among Complex Hunter-Gatherers* (Berkeley: University of California Press, 2008).

Garrison, Tim Alan. *The Legal Ideology of Removal: The Southern Judiciary and the Sovereignty of Native American Nations* (Athens, GA: University of Georgia Press, 2002).

Garroutte, Eva Marie. *Real Indians: Identity and the Survival of Native America* (Berkeley: University of California Press, 2003).

Genetin-Pilewa, C. Joseph. *Crooked Paths to Allotment: The Fight over Federal Indian Policy after the Civil War* (Chapel Hill: University of North Carolina Press, 2012).

Genetin-Pilewa, C. Joseph. "Ely Parker and the Contentious Peace Policy," *Western Historical Quarterly*, 41 (Summer 2010), 196–217.

Gidley, M. *With One Sky above Us: Life on an Indian Reservation at the Turn of the Century* (New York: G. P. Putnam's Sons, 1979).

Glatthaar, Joseph and James Kirby Martin, *Forgotten Allies: The Oneida Indians and the American Revolution* (New York: Hill and Wang, 2007).

Gleach, Frederic Wright. "Pocahontas at the Fair: Crafting Identities at the 1907 Jamestown Exposition," *Ethnohistory*, 50 (Summer 2003), 419–45.

Glover, Jeffrey. *Paper Sovereigns: Anglo-Native Treaties and the Law of Nations, 1604–1664* (Philadelphia: University of Pennsylvania Press, 2014).

Goldberg, Mark Allan. "Negotiating Nacogdoches: Hasinai Caddo-Spanish Relations, Trade Space, and the Formation of the Texas-Louisiana Border, 1779–1819," *American Indian Culture and Research Journal*, 33 (no. 1, 2009), 65–87.

Graber, Jennifer. "Religion in Kiowa Ledgers: Expanding the Canon of American Religious Literature." *American Literary History*, 26 (no. 1, 2013), 42–60.

Grandjean, Katherine A. "New World Tempests: Environment, Scarcity, and the Coming of the Pequot War," *William and Mary Quarterly*, 68 (January 2011), 75–100.

Grandjean, Katherine A. "The Long Wake of the Pequot War," *Early American Studies*, 9 (Spring 2011), 379–411.

Graybill, Andrew. *The Red and the White: A Family Saga of the American West* (New York: Norton, 2013).

Graybill, Andrew. "'Strong on the Merits and Powerfully Symbolic': The Return of Blue Lake to Taos Pueblo," *New Mexico Historical Review*, 76 (no. 2, 2001), 125–60.

Graymont, Barbara. *The Iroquois and the American Revolution* (Syracuse: Syracuse University Press, 1972).

Green, Michael D. *The Politics of Indian Removal: Creek Government and Society in Crisis* (Lincoln: University of Nebraska Press, 1982).

Greene, Jerome. *Washita: The U.S. Army and the Southern Cheyennes, 1867–1869* (Norman: University of Oklahoma Press, 2004).

Greer, Allan. *Mohawk Saint: Catherine Tekakwitha and the Jesuits* (New York: Oxford University Press, 2006).

Gregg, Matthew T. and David M. Wishart. "The Price of Cherokee Removal," *Explorations in Economic History* 49 (2012), 423–42.

Gross, Ariela J. *What Blood Won't Tell: A History of Race on Trial in America* (Cambridge: Harvard University Press, 2008).

Grumet, Robert Steven. *Historic Contact: Indian People and Colonists in Today's Northeastern United States in the Sixteenth through the Eighteenth Centuries* (Norman: University of Oklahoma Press, 1995).

Grumet, Robert Steven. "Sunksquaws, Shamans, and Tradeswomen: Middle Atlantic Coastal Algonkian Women during the 17th and 18th Centuries." *Women and Colonization: Anthropological Perspectives*, eds. Mona Etienne and Eleanor Burke Leacock (New York: Praeger, 1980).

Guilmet, George M. and David Lloyd Whited. "American Indian and Non-Indian Philosophies of Technology and their Differential Impact on the Environment of the Southern Puget Sound," *American Indian Culture and Research Journal*, 26 (no. 1, 2002), 33–66.

Gutierrez, Ramon. *When Jesus Came, the Corn Mothers Went Away: Marriage, Sexuality and Power in New Mexico, 1500–1846* (Palo Alto: Stanford University Press, 1991).

Haake, Claudia B. "'In the Same Predicament as Heretofore': Proremoval Arguments in Seneca Letters from the Buffalo Creek Reservation in the 1830s and 1840s," *Ethnohistory*, 61 (Winter 2014), 57–76.

Haan, Richard. "The Problem of Iroquois Neutrality: Suggestions for Revision." *Ethnohistory*, 27 (1980), 317–30.

Haas, Jonathan and Winifred Creamer, "Warfare among the Pueblos: Myth, History, and Ethnography," *Ethnohistory*, 44 (Spring 1997), 235–61.

Hackel, Steven W. *Junipero Serra: California's Founding Father* (New York: Hill and Wang, 2013).

Hackel, Steven W. *Children of Coyote, Missionaries of St. Francis: Indian-Spanish Relations in Colonial California, 1769–1850* (Chapel Hill: University of North Carolina Press, 2005).

Hackel, Steven W. "The Staff of Leadership: Indian Authority in the Missions of Alta California," *William and Mary Quarterly*, 54 (1997), 347–76.

Haeberlin, Hermann and Erna Gunther. *The Indians of Puget Sound* (Seattle: University of Washington Press, 1930).

Haefili, Evan and Kevin Sweeney. *Captors and Captives: The 1704 French and Indian Raid on Deerfield* (Amherst: University of Massachusetts Press, 2003).

Haefili, Evan and Kevin Sweeney. "Revisiting *The Redeemed Captive*: New Perspectives on the 1704 Attack on Deerfield," *William and Mary Quarterly*, 52 (1995), 3–46.

Hagan, William T. *Taking Indian Lands: The Cherokee (Jerome) Commission, 1889–1893* (Norman: University of Oklahoma Press, 2003).

Hagan, William T. "Kiowas, Comanches and Cattlemen, 1867–1906: A Case Study of the Failure of U.S. Reservation Policy," *Pacific Historical Review*, 40 (August 1971), 333–56.

Hagedorn, Nancy L. "Brokers of Understanding: Interpreters as Agents of Cultural Exchange in Colonial New York," *New York History*, 76 (October 1995), 379–408.

Hahn, Steven C. *The Invention of the Creek Nation, 1670–1763* (Lincoln: University of Nebraska Press, 2003).

Haley, Brian D. and Larry R. Wilcoxen. "How Spaniards Became Chumash and Other Tales of Ethnogenesis," *American Anthropologist*, 107 (September 2005), 432–45.

Haley, Brian D. and Larry R. Wilcoxen. "Anthropology and the Making of Chumash Tradition [and Comments and Reply]," *Current Anthropology*, 38 (December 1997), 761–94.

Hall, John W. *Uncommon Defense: Indian Allies in the Black Hawk War* (Cambridge: Harvard University Press, 2009).

Hall, Joseph M., Jr. *Zamuno's Gifts: Indian-European Exchange in the Colonial Southeast* (Philadelphia: University of Pennsylvania Press, 2009).

Hämäläinen, Pekka. "The Politics of Grass: European Expansion, Ecological Change, and Indigenous Power in the Southwest Borderlands," *William and Mary Quarterly*, 67 (April 2010), 173–208.

Hämäläinen, Pekka. *The Comanche Empire* (New Haven: Yale University Press, 2009).

Hämäläinen, Pekka. "The Rise and Fall of Plains Indian Horse Cultures," *Journal of American History*, 81 (December 2003), 833–62.

Hämäläinen, Pekka and Samuel Truett. "On Borderlands," *Journal of American History*, 98 (September 2011), 338–61.

Hamilton, Milton W. *Sir William Johnson: Colonial American, 1715–1763* (Port Washington: Kennikat Press, 1976).

Hammell, George R. "The Iroquois and the World's Rim: Speculations on Color, Culture, and Contact." *American Indian Quarterly*, 16 (Fall 1992), 451–69.

Hammell, George R. "Strawberries, Floating Islands, and Rabbit Captains: Mythical Realities and European Contact in the Northeast during the Sixteenth and Seventeenth Centuries," *Journal of Canadian Studies*, 21 (1987), 72–94.

Hammerstedt, Scott W., Amanda L. Regnier and Patrick C. Livingood. "Geophysical and Archaeological Investigations at the Clement Site, a Caddo Mound Complex in Southeastern Oklahoma," *Southeastern Archaeology*, 29 (Winter 2010), 279–91.

Hansen, Karen V. and Grey Osterud. "Landowning, Dispossession, and the Significance of Land among Dakota and Scandinavian Women at Spirit Lake, 1900–1929," *Gender and History*, 26 (April 2014), 105–27.

Harmon, Alexandra. *Rich Indians: Native People and the Problem of Wealth in American History* (Chapel Hill: University of North Carolina Press, 2010).

Harmon, Alexandra. "American Indians and Land Monopolies in the Gilded Age," *Journal of American History*, 90 (June 2003), 106–33.

Harmon, Alexandra. *Indians in the Making: Ethnic Relations and Indian Identities Around Puget Sound* (Berkeley: University of California Press, 1998).

Harvard Project on American Indian Economic Development. *The State of Native Nations* (New York: Oxford University Press, 2008).

Harvey, Sean P. *Native Tongues: Colonialism and Race from Encounter to Reservation* (Cambridge: Harvard University Press, 2015).

Hatfield, April Lee. *Atlantic Virginia: Intercolonial Relations in the Seventeenth Century* (Philadelphia: University of Pennsylvania Press, 2004).

Hatfield, April Lee. "Spanish Colonization Literature, Powhatan Geographies, and English Perceptions of Tsenacommacah/Virginia." *Journal of Southern History*, 69 (May 2003), 245–82.

Hatley, Tom. *The Dividing Paths: Cherokees and South Carolinians through the Era of Revolution* (New York: Oxford University Press, 1995).

Hatley, Tom. "Cherokee Women Farmers Hold Their Ground," in *Appalachian Frontiers: Settlement, Society and Development in the Preindustrial Era*, ed. Robert D. Mitchell (Lexington: University Press of Kentucky, 1991), 37–51.

Hatley, Tom. "The Three Lives of Keowee: Loss and Recovery in Eighteenth Century Cherokee Villages," in *Powhatan's Mantle: Indians in the Colonial Southeast*, eds., Peter H. Wood, Gregory A. Waselkov, and M. Thomas Hatley (Lincoln: University of Nebraska Press, 1989).

Hauptman, Laurence M. "On and Off State Time: William N. Fenton and the Seneca Nation of Indians in Crisis, 1954–1968," *New York History*, 93 (no. 2, 2012), 183–232.

Hauptman, Laurence M. "On Our Terms: The Tonawanda Seneca Indians, Lewis Henry Morgan, and Henry Rowe Schoolcraft," *New York History*, 91 (Fall 2010), 314–35.

Hauptman, Laurence M. *Conspiracy of Interests: Iroquois Dispossession and the Rise of New York State* (Syracuse: Syracuse University Press, 1999).

Hauptman, Laurence M. "Governor Blacksnake and the Seneca Indian Struggle to Save Oil Spring Reservation," *Mid-America*, 81 (1999), 51–73.

Hauptman, Laurence M. "The State's Men, the Salvation Seekers and the Seneca: The Supplemental Treaty of Buffalo Creek, 1842," *New York History*, 78 (January 1997), 51–82.

Hauptman, Laurence M. *Between Two Fires: American Indians in the Civil War* (New York: Simon and Schuster, 1996).

Hauptman, Laurence M. *The Iroquois and the Civil War: From Battlefield to Reservation* (Syracuse: Syracuse University Press, 1993).

Hauptman, Laurence M. and James D. Wherry, *The Pequots in Southern New England: The Fall and Rise Of an American Indian Nation* (Norman: University of Oklahoma Press, 1990).

Hauptman, Laurence M. "Alice Lee Jemison: A Modern 'Mother of the Nation,'" in *Sifters: Native American Women's Lives*, ed. Theda Perdue (New York: Oxford University Press, 2001).

Hauptman, Laurence M. *Formulating American Indian Policy in New York State, 1970–1986* (Albany: State University of New York Press, 1986).

Hauptman, Laurence M. *The Iroquois Struggle for Survival: World War II to Red Power* (Syracuse: Syracuse University Press, 1986).

Hauptman, Laurence M. *The Iroquois and the New Deal* (Syracuse: Syracuse University Press, 1981).

Hauptman, Laurence M. "Refugee Havens: The Iroquois Villages of the Eighteenth Century," *American Indian Environments: Ecological Issues in Native American History*, eds. Christopher Vecsey and Robert W. Venables (Syracuse: Syracuse University Press, 1980).

Hauser, Raymond, "The Berdache and the Illinois Indians Tribe during the Last Half of the Seventeenth Century," *Ethnohistory*, 37 (Winter 1990), 45–65.

Hedren, Paul. "Map of the Great Sioux War of 1876," *Nebraska History*, 95 (Spring 2014), 40–51.

Hedren, Paul. "Fort Robinson, Custer, and the Legacy of the Great Sioux War," *Nebraska History*, 95 (Spring 2014), 4–13.

Heizer, Robert F. *The Natural World of the California Indians* (Berkeley: University of California Press, 1980).

Heizer, Robert F. *The Destruction of the California Indians* (Santa Barbara: Peregrine Smith, 1974).

Heizer, Robert F. "A California Messianic Movement of 1801 among the Chumash," *American Anthropologist*, 43 (1941), 128–29.

Hendricks, Steve. *The Unquiet Grave: The FBI and the Struggle for the Soul of Indian Country* (New York: Thunder's Mouth Press, 2006).

Heninge, David P. "Recent Work and Prospects in American Indian Contact Population," *History Compass*, 6 (2008), 183–206.

Heninge, David P. *Numbers from Nowhere: The American Indian Contact Population Debate* (Norman: University of Oklahoma Press, 1998).

Hennepin, Louis. *A New Discovery of a Vast Country in America*, ed. Reuben Gold Thwaites (Chicago: A. C. McClurg, 1903).

Hermes, Katherine. "'As A Snow Before a Summer Sun': The Imagined Demise of Connecticut's Native Peoples," *Connecticut History*, 49 (Summer 2010), 157–65.

Herndon, Ruth Wallis and Ella Wilcox Sekatau, "The Right to a Name: The Narragansett People and Rhode Island Officials in the Revolutionary Era," *Ethnohistory*, 44 (Fall 1997), 433–62.

Herzberg, Hazel. *The Search for American Indian Identity: Modern Pan-Indian Movements* (Syracuse: Syracuse University Press, 1971).

Herzog, Tamar. *Frontiers of Possession: Spain and Portugal in Europe and the Americas* (Cambridge: Harvard University Press, 2015).

Hickerson, Daniel A. "Historical Processes, Epidemic Disease, and the Formation of the Hasinai Confederacy," *Ethnohistory*, 44 (Winter 1997). 31–52.

Hilbert, Vi. *Haboo: Native American Stories from Puget Sound* (Seattle: University of Washington Press, 1985).

Hill, Christina Gish. "'General Miles Put Us Here': Northern Cheyenne Military Alliance and Sovereign Territorial Rights," *American Indian Quarterly*, 37 (Fall 2013), 340–69.

Himmel, Kelly F. *The Conquest of the Karankawas and Tonkawas, 1821–1859* (College Station: Texas A&M University Press, 1999).

Hinderaker, Eric. *The Two Hendricks: Unraveling a Mohawk Mystery* (Cambridge: Harvard University Press, 2010.

Hinderaker, Eric. *Elusive Empires: Constructing Colonialism in the Ohio Valley, 1673–1800* (New York: Cambridge University Press, 1997).

Hinderaker, Eric and Peter C. Mancall, *At the Edge of Empire: The Backcountry in British North America* (Baltimore: Johns Hopkins University Press, 2003).

Hirsch, Adam J. "The Collision of Military Cultures in Seventeenth-Century New England," *Journal of American History*, 74 (1988), 1187–212.

Hoig, Stan. *The Sand Creek Massacre* (Norman: University of Oklahoma Press, 1961).

Holton, Woody. "The Ohio Indians and the Coming of the American Revolution in Virginia," *Journal of Southern History*, 60 (August 1994), 453–78.

Horn, James. *A Land as God Made It* (New York: Vintage, 2005).

Horsman, Reginald. *Race and Manifest Destiny: The Origins of American Racial Anglo-Saxonism* (Cambridge, MA: Harvard University Press, 1981).

Horsman, Reginald. *The Frontier in the Formative Years, 1783–1815* (Albuquerque: University of New Mexico Press, 1975).

Houghton, Frederick. "The History of the Buffalo Creek Reservation," *Publications of the Buffalo Historical Society*, 24 (Buffalo: BHS, 1920).

Houser, Theresa. "Native American Sovereignty and Coal Mining in the Powder River Basin," *Mining History Association 2013 Journal* (2013), 53–67.

Howey, Meghan C. L. "Colonial Encounters, European Kettles and the Magic of Mimesis in the Late Sixteenth and Early Seventeenth Century Indigenous Northeast and Great Lakes," *International Journal of Historical Archaeology*, 15 (September 2011), 329–57.

Hoxie, Frederick E. *This Indian Country: American Indian Political Activists and the Place They Made* (New York: Penguin, 2012).

Hoxie, Frederick E. *Parading Through History: The Making of the Crow Nation in America, 1805–1935* (Cambridge: Cambridge University Press, 1995).

Hoxie, Frederick E. *The Final Promise: The Campaign to Assimilate the Indians, 1880–1920* (Lincoln: University of Nebraska Press, 1984).

Hoxie, Frederic and Tim Bernardis. "Robert Yellowtail, Crow," in *The New Warriors: Native American Leaders since 1900*, ed. R. David Edmunds (Lincoln: University of Nebraska Press, 2001).

Hudson, Charles S. *Conversations with the High Priest of Coosa* (Chapel Hill: University of North Carolina Press, 2003).

Hudson, Charles S. *Knights of Spain, Warriors of the Sun: Hernando de Soto and the South's Ancient Chiefdoms* (Athens: University of Georgia Press, 1997).

Hudson, Charles S. *The Southeastern Indians* (Knoxville: University of Tennessee Press, 1976).

Huebner, Karin L. "Clubwomen, John Collier, and the Indians of the Southwest, 1917–1934," *Pacific Historical Review*, 78 (no. 3, 2009), 337–66.

Huhndorf, Shari M. *Going Native: Indians in the American Cultural Imagination* (Ithaca: Cornell University Press, 2001).

Hunt, George T. *The Wars of the Iroquois: A Study in Intertribal Trade Relations*, reprint edn (Madison: University Press of Wisconsin, 1967).

Hurtado, Albert. *Indian Survival on the California Frontier* (New Haven: Yale University Press, 1988).

Hyman, Colette A. *Dakota Women's Work: Creativity, Culture and Exile* (St. Paul: Minnesota Historical Society Press, 2012).

Hyman, Colette A. "Survival at Crow Creek, 1863–1866," *Minnesota History*, 61 (Winter 2008/2009), 148–61.

Ishii, Izumi. *Bad Fruits of the Civilized Tree: Alcohol and the Sovereignty of the Cherokee Nation* (Lincoln: University of Nebraska Press, 2008).

Isenberg, Andrew. *The Destruction of the Bison: Social and Environmental Changes in the Great Plains, 1750–1820* (New York: Cambridge University Press, 1999).

Iverson, Peter. *Carlos Montezuma and the Changing World of American Indians* (Albuquerque: University of New Mexico Press, 1982).

Jackson, Helen Hunt. *A Century of Dishonor: The Early Crusade for Indian Reform*, ed. Andrew F. Rolle (New York: Harper and Row, 1965).

Jackson, Robert H. "The Population of the Santa Barbara Channel Missions (Alta California), 1813–1832," *Journal of California and Great Basis Anthropology*, 10 (1990), 268–74.

Jackson, Robert H. "Patterns of Demographic Change in the Alta California Missions: The Case of Santa Ines," *California History*, 71 (Fall 1992), 362–9.

Jacobs, Margaret. "Remembering the 'Forgotten Child': The American Indian Child Welfare Crisis of the 1960s and 1970s," *American Indian Quarterly*, 37 (Winter/Spring 2013), 136–59.

Jacobs, Margaret. *Engendered Encounters: Feminism and Pueblo Culture, 1879–1934* (Lincoln: University of Nebraska Press, 1999).

Jacobs, Margaret. "Making Savages of Us All: White Women, Pueblo Indians, and the Controversy over Indian Dances in the 1920s," *Frontiers*, 17 (1996), 178–209.

Jacobs, Wilbur R. *Wilderness Politics and Indian Gifts: The Northern Colonial Frontier 1748–1763* (Palo Alto: Stanford University Press, 1950).

Jacoby, Karl. *Shadows at Dawn: An Apache Massacre and the Violence of History* (New York: Penguin Books, 2008).

Jaenen, Cornelius J. *Friend and Foe: Aspects of French-Amerindian Cultural Contact in the Sixteenth and Seventeenth Centuries* (New York: Oxford University Press, 1976).

Jaenen, Cornelius J. "Amerindian Views of French Culture in the Seventeenth Century," *Canadian Historical Review*, 55 (1974), 261–91.

Jennings, Francis. *Empire of Fortune: Crowns, Colonies and Tribes in the Seven Years War in America* (New York: Norton, 1988).

Jennings, Francis. *The Ambiguous Iroquois Empire: The Covenant Chain Confederation of Indian Tribes with the English Colonies* (New York: Norton, 1984).

Jennings, Francis. *The Invasion of America: Indians, Colonists and the Cant of Conquest* (Chapel Hill: University of North Carolina Press, 1975).

Jevec, Adam. "Semper Fidelis, Code Talkers." *Prologue*, 33 (Winter 2001).

John, Elizabeth A. H. *Storms Brewed in Other Men's Worlds: The Confrontation of Indians, Spanish and French in the Southwest, 1540–1795*, 2nd edn (Norman: University of Oklahoma Press, 1996).

Johnson, Greg. *Sacred Claims: Repatriation and Living Tradition* (Charlottesville: University of Virginia Press, 2007).

Johnson, John R. *The Chumash Indians after Secularization* (Santa Barbara: California Mission Studies Association, 1995).

Johnson, Richard R. "The Search for a Usable Indian: An Aspect of the Defense of Colonial New England," *Journal of American History*, 64 (1977), 623–51.

Johnson, Troy R. *The Occupation of Alcatraz Island: Indian Self-Determination and the Rise of Indian Activism* (Champaign-Urbana: University of Illinois Press, 1996).

Johnson, Troy R., Joane Nagel, and Duane Champagne, eds. *American Indian Activism: Alcatraz to the Longest Walk* (Champaign-Urbana: University of Illinois Press, 1997).

Jones, David S. "Virgin Soils Revisited." *William and Mary Quarterly*, 60 (October 2003), 703–42.

Jones, Dorothy. *License for Empire: Colonialism by Treaty in Early America* (Chicago: University of Chicago Press, 1982).

Jones, Douglas C. *The Treaty of Medicine Lodge: The Story of the Great Treaty Council as Told by Eyewitnesses* (Norman: University of Oklahoma Press, 1966).

Jones, W. R. "England against the Celtic Fringe: A Study in Cultural Stereotypes," *Journal of World History*, 13 (1971), 155–71.

Jordan, Kurt A. "Enacting Gender and Kinship around a Large Outdoor Fire Pit at the Seneca Iroquois Townley-Read Site, 1715–1754," *Historical Archaeology*, 48 (no. 2, 2014), 61–90.

Jordan, Kurt A. *The Seneca Restoration, 1715–1754: An Iroquois Local Political Economy* (Gainesville: University Press of Florida, 2008).

Josephy, Alvin M., Joane Nagel and Troy R. Johnson, eds., *Red Power: The American Indians' Fight for Freedom* (Lincoln: University of Nebraska Press, 1999).

Kane, Maeve. "'Covered with Such A Cappe': The Archaeology of Seneca Clothing, 1615–1820," *Ethnohistory*, 61 (Winter 2014), 1–25.

Karr, Ronald Dale. "'Why Should You Be So Furious': The Violence of the Pequot War," *Journal of American History*, 85 (1998), 876–909.

Kavanaugh, Thomas. *The Comanches: A History, 1706–1875* (Lincoln: University of Nebraska Press, 1999).

Kawashima, Yasuhide. *Igniting King Philip's War: The John Sassamon Murder Trial* (Lawrence: University Press of Kansas, 2001).

Kawashima, Yasuhide. "Forest Diplomats: The Role of Interpreters in Indian-White Relations on the Early American Frontier," *American Indian Quarterly*, 13 (1989), 1–14.

Kawashima, Yasuhide. *Puritan Justice and the Indian: White Man's Law in Massachusetts, 1630–1763* (Middletown, CT: Wesleyan University Press, 1986).

Kellaway, William. *The New England Company, 1649–1776: Missionary Society to the American Indians* (New York: Greenwood Press, 1962).

Keller, Robert H, Jr. *American Protestantism and United States Indian Policy, 1869–1882* (Lincoln: University of Nebraska Press, 1983).

Kellogg, Louise Phelps, ed. *Early Narratives of the Northwest, 1634–1699* (New York: Charles Scribner's Sons, 1917).

Kelley, Lawrence C. "The Indian Reorganization Act: The Dream and the Reality," in *Constitutionalism and Native Americans, 1903–1968*, ed. John R. Wunder (New York: Taylor and Francis, 1996).

Kelley, Lawrence C. *The Assault on Assimilation: John Collier and the Origins of Indian Policy Reform* (Albuquerque: University of New Mexico Press, 1983).

Kelley, Lawrence C. "John Collier and the Pueblo Land Board Act," *New Mexico Historical Review*, 58 (no. 1, 1983), 5–34.

Kelton, Paul. "The British and Indian War: Cherokee Power and the Fate of Empire in North America." *William and Mary Quarterly*, 69 (October 2012), 763–92.

Kelton, Paul. *Epidemics and Enslavement: Biological Catastrophe in the Native Southeast, 1492–1715* (Lincoln: University of Nebraska Press, 2007).

Kelton, Paul. "Avoiding the Smallpox Spirits: Colonial Epidemics and Southeastern Indian Survival." *Ethnohistory*, 50 (Fall 2003), 45–71.

Kelton, Paul. "'At the Head of the Aboriginal Remnant': Cherokee Construction of a 'Civilized' Identity during the Lakota Crisis of 1876," *Great Plains Quarterly*, 23 (Winter 2003), 3–17.

Kenagy, Suzanne, G. "Stepped Cloud and Cross: The Intersection of Pueblo and European Visual Symbolic Systems," *New Mexico Historical Review*, 64 (no. 3, 1989), 325–40.

Kenny, Kevin. *Peaceable Kingdom Lost: The Paxton Boys and the Destruction of William Penn's Holy Experiment* (New York: Oxford University Press, 2009).

Kersey, Harry A. *The Florida Seminoles and the New Deal* (Boca Raton: Florida Atlantic University Press, 1989.

Kessell, John L. "A Long Time Coming: The Seventeenth-Century Pueblo-Spanish War," *New Mexico Historical Review*, 86 (April 2011), 141–56.

Kessell, John L. *Kiva, Cross and Crown: The Pecos Indians and New Mexico, 1540–1840*, 2nd edn (Albuquerque: Western National Parks Association, 1987).

Kidwell, Clara Sue. *The Choctaws in Oklahoma: From Tribe to Nation, 1855–1970* (Norman: University of Oklahoma Press, 2007).

Kidwell, Clara Sue. "Native American Systems of Knowledge," in *A Companion to American Indian History*, ed. Philip Deloria and Neal Salisbury (Malden, MA: Blackwell, 2002).

Kidwell, Clara Sue. "Native American Women's Response to Christianity," *Ethnohistory*, 43 (1996), 721–6.

Kidwell, Clara Sue. *Choctaws and Missionaries in Mississippi, 1818–1918* (Norman: University of Oklahoma Press, 1995).

King, C. Richard and Charles Fruehling Springwood, eds. *Team Spirits: The Native American Mascot Controversy* (Lincoln: University of Nebraska Press, 2001).

Klein, Laura F. and Lilian Ackerman, eds. *Women and Power in Native North America* (Norman: University of Oklahoma Press, 1995).

Knaut, Andrew L. *The Pueblo Revolt: Conquest and Resistance in Seventeenth-Century New Mexico* (Norman: University of Oklahoma Press, 1995).

Kopelson, Heather Miyano. *Faithful Bodies: Performing Religion and Race in the Puritan Atlantic* (New York: New York University Press, 2014).

Kotlowski, Dean J. "From Backlash to Bingo: Ronald Reagan and Federal Indian Policy," *Pacific Historical Review*, 77 (November 2008), 617–52.

Kracht, Benjamin R. "'It Would Break Our Hearts Not To Have Our Kiowas': War Dancing, Tourism, and the Rise of Powwows in the Early Twentieth Century," *Chronicles of Oklahoma*, 90 (September 2012), 286–309.

Kracht, Benjamin R. "Kiowa Powwow: Tribal Identity through the Continuity of the Gourd Dance," *Great Plains Research*, 4 (August 1994), 257–69.

Kracht, Benjamin R. "The Kiowa Ghost Dance, 1894–1916: An Unheralded Revitalization Movement," *Ethnohistory*, 29 (Autumn 1992), 452–77.

Kraft, Lisa. "Thrice Purchased: Acquisition and Allotment of the Citizen Potawatomi Reservation," *Chronicles of Oklahoma*, 86 (Spring 2008), 64–87.

Krech, Shepard III. *The Ecological Indian: Myth and History* (New York: Norton, 1999).

Krouse, Susan Applegate. *North American Indians in the Great War* (Lincoln: University of Nebraska Press, 2007).

Kuhn, Robert D. and Martha L. Sempowski. "A New Approach to Dating the League of the Iroquois," *American Antiquity*, 66 (2001), 301–14.

Kulisheck, Jeremy. "Pueblo Population Movements: Abandonment and Settlement Change in Sixteenth and Seventeenth Century New Mexico," *Kiva*, 69 (September 2003), 30–54.

Kunitz, Stephen J. and Bill G. Douglas. "European Contact and the Contemporary Household Demography of the Pueblo Indians of New Mexico and Arizona," *Journal of Anthropological Research*, 66 (Fall 2010), 329–50.

Kupperman, Karen Ordahl. *The Jamestown Project* (New York: Norton, 2007).

Kupperman, Karen Ordahl. *Indians and English: Facing Off in Early America* (Ithaca: Cornell University Press, 2000).

Kupperman, Karen Ordahl, ed. *America in European Consciousness, 1493–1750* (Chapel Hill: University of North Carolina Press, 1995).

Kupperman, Karen Ordahl. *Roanoke: The Abandoned Colony* (Savage, MD: Rowman and Littlefield, 1984).

Kupperman, Karen Ordahl. *Settling with the Indians: The Meeting of English and Indian Cultures in America, 1580–1640* (Totowa, NJ: Rowman and Littlefield, 1981).

Kvasnicka, Robert M. and Herman J. Viola, eds. *The Commissioners of Indian Affairs, 1824–1977* (Lincoln: University of Nebraska Press, 1979).

Lange, Charles H. "A Report on Data Pertaining to the Caddo Treaty of July 1, 1835: The Historical and Anthropological Background and Aftermath (1954)," in *Caddoan Indians II*, David Agee Horr, comp. (New York: Garland Publishing, 1974).

Larson, Daniel O., et al. "Missionization among Coastal Chumash of Central California: A Study of Risk Minimization Strategies," *American Anthropologist*, 96 (1994), 263–99.

Larson, Robert W. *Red Cloud: Warrior Statesman of the Lakota Sioux* (Norman: University of Oklahoma Press, 1997).

Lassiter, Luke E., Clyde Ellis, and Ralph Kotay. *The Jesus Road: Kiowas, Christianity and Indian Hymns* (Lincoln: University of Nebraska Press, 2002).

LaVere, David. *Contrary Neighbors: Southern Plains and Removed Indians in the Indian Territory* (Norman: University of Oklahoma Press, 2000).

Lawson, Michael L. *Damned Indians: The Pick-Sloan Plan and the Missouri River Sioux* (Norman: University of Oklahoma Press, 1982).

Leach, Douglas Edward. *Flintlock and Tomahawk: New England in King Philip's War* (New York: Norton, 1958).

Leader, Jeanne P. "The Potawatomis and Alcohol," *Kansas History*, 2 (1979), 157–65.

Leavelle, Tracy Neal. *The Catholic Calumet: Colonial Conversions in French and Indian America* (Philadelphia: University of Pennsylvania Press, 2012).

Lee, Dayna Bowker. "A Social History of Caddoan Peoples: Cultural Adaptation and Persistence in a Native American Community," PhD diss., University of Oklahoma, 1998.

Lekson, Stephen H. *A History of the Ancient Southwest* (Santa Fe: School for Advanced Research, 2008).

Lengel, James H. "The Role of International Law in the Development of Constitutional Jurisprudence in the Supreme Court: The Marshall Court and American Indians." *American Journal of Legal History*, 43 (1999), 117–32.

Lepore, Jill. *The Name of War: King Philip's War and the Origins of American Identity* (New York: Knopf, 1998).

Levine, Frances and Anna LaBauve, "Examining the Complexity of Historic Population Decline: A Case Study of Pecos Pueblo, New Mexico," *Ethnohistory*, 44 (Winter 1997), 75–112.

Lewis, Clifford M. and Albert J. Loomie. *The Spanish Jesuit Mission in Virginia, 1570–1572* (Chapel Hill: University of North Carolina Press, 1953).

Lewis, David Rich. *Neither Wolf nor Dog: American Indians, Environment, and Agrarian Change* (New York: Oxford University Press, 1994).

Liebler, Carolyn A. and Meghan Zacher. "American Indians without Tribes in the Twenty-First Century," *Ethnic and Racial Studies*, 36 (2013), 1910–34.

Lightfoot, Kent G. *Indians, Missionaries and Merchants: The Legacy of Colonial Encounters on the California Frontiers* (Berkeley: University of California Press, 2005).

Lightfood, Kent G. and Otis Parrish. *California Indians and their Environment: An Inroduction* (Berkeley: University of California Press, 2009).

Lightfoot, Kent G., et al. "The Study of Indigenous Political Economies and Colonialism in Native California: Implications for Contemporary Tribal Groups and Federal Recognition," *American Antiquity*, 78 (no. 1, 2013), 89–104.

Linderman, Frank Bird. *Pretty-Shield: Medicine Woman of the Crows*, reprint edn (Lincoln: University of Nebraska Press, 1972).

Linderman, Frank Bird. *Plenty-Coups: Chief of the Crows*, reprint edn (Lincoln: University of Nebraska Press, 1962).

Lindsay, Brendan C. *Murder State: California's Native American Genocide, 1846–1873* (Lincoln: University of Nebraska Press, 2012).

Lindsey, Donal F. *Indians at Hampton Institute, 1877–1923* (Urbana: University of Illinois Press, 1995).

Little, Ann M. *Abraham in Arms* (Philadelphia: University of Pennsylvania Press, 2006).

Little, Ann M. "'Shoot that Rogue, For He Hath an Englishman's Coat On!': Cultural Cross-Dressing on the New England Frontier, 1620–1760," *New England Quarterly*, 74 (2001), 238–73.

Littlefield, Daniel F. *Africans and Seminoles: From Removal to Emancipation* (Jackson: University Of Mississippi Press, 2001).

Lomawaima, K. Tsianina. *They Called it Prairie Light: The Story of the Chilocco Indian School* (Lincoln: University of Nebraska Press, 1994).

Lookingbill, Brad D. *War Dance at Fort Marion: Plains Indian War Prisoners* (Norman: University of Oklahoma Press, 2006).

Love, W. DeLoss. *Samson Occom and the Christian Indians of New England* (Syracuse: Syracuse University Press, 2000).

Lowe, Marjorie J. "Let's Make it Happen: W. W. Keeler and the Cherokee Renewal," *Chronicles of Oklahoma*, 74 (no. 2, 1996), 116–29.

Lurie, Nancy Oestreich. "Indian Cultural Adjustment to European Colonization: The Case of Powhatan's Confederacy." In *Interpreting Colonial America: Selected Readings*, ed. James Kirby Martin (New York: Dodd, Mead, and Company, 1978).

Luthin, Herbert. *Surviving Through the Days: A California Indian Reader* (Berkeley: University of California Press, 2002).

Lyman, Stanley David. *Wounded Knee, 1973: A Personal Account* (Lincoln: University of Nebraska Press, 1991).

McBride, Bunny. *Molly Spotted Elk: A Penobscot in Paris* (Norman: University of Oklahoma Press, 1995).

McCartney, Martha W. "Cockacoeske, Queen of Pamunkey: Diplomat and Suzeraine," in *Powhatan's Mantle: Indians in the Colonial Southeast*, eds. Peter H. Wood and M. Thomas Hatley (Lincoln: University of Nebraska Press, 1989).

McCleskey, Turk. *The Road to Black Ned's Forge: A Story of Race, Sex, and Trade on the Colonial American Frontier* (Charlottesville: University Press of Virginia, 2014).

McConnell, Michael N. "Peoples 'In Between': The Iroquois and the Ohio Indians, 1720–1768," in *Beyond the Covenant Chain: The Iroquois and Their Neighbors in Indian North America, 1600–1800* (Syracuse: Syracuse University Press, 1987).

McDonnell, Janet A. *The Dispossession of the American Indian, 1887–1934* (Bloomington: Indiana University Press, 1991).

McDonnell, Michael A. *Masters of Empire: Great Lakes Indians and the Making of America* (New York: Hill and Wang, 2016).

McGuire, Thomas R., William B. Lord, and Mary G. Wallace, eds. *Indian Water in the New West* (Tucson: University of Arizona Press, 1993).

McKee, Irving. "The Trail of Death: Letters of Benjamin Marie Petit," *Indiana Historical Society Publications*, 14, no. 1 (Indianapolis: Indiana Historical Society, 1941).

McKenzie-Jones, Paul R. *Clyde Warrior: Tradition, Community, and Red Power* (Norman: University of Oklahoma Press, 2015).

MacLeod, D. Peter. "Microbes and Muskets: Smallpox and the Participation of the Amerindian Allies of New France in the Seven Years War," *Ethnohistory*, 39 (Winter 1992), 42–64.

McLoughlin, William G. *After the Trail of Tears: The Cherokees' Struggle for Sovereignty, 1839–1900* (Chapel Hill: University of North Carolina Press, 1993).

McLoughlin, William G. *Cherokee Renascence in the New Republic* (New Haven: Yale University Press, 1986).

McLoughlin, William G. *Cherokees and Missionaries, 1789–1839* (New Haven: Yale University Press, 1984).

McLoughlin, William G. "Experiment in Cherokee Citizenship, 1817–1829," *American Indian Quarterly*, 33 (Spring 1981), 3–25.

McMillan, Christian W. "Rain, Ritual and Reclamation: The Failure of Irrigation on the Zuni and Navajo Reservations, 1883–1914," *Western Historical Quarterly*, 31 (Winter 2000), 435–56.

McNickle, D'Arcy. *Native American Tribalism: Indian Survivals and Renewals* (New York: Oxford University Press, 1993).

Maddox, Lucy. *Citizen Indians: Native American Intellectuals, Race, and Reform* (Ithaca: Cornell University Press, 2005).

Maddra, Sam A. *Hostiles? The Lakota Ghost Dance and Buffalo Bill's Wild West* (Norman: University of Oklahoma Press, 2006).

Madley, Benjamin. "Unholy Traffic in Human Blood and Souls: System of California Indian Servitude under U. S. Rule," *Pacific Historical Review*, 83 (November 2014), 626–67.

Madley, Benjamin. *An American Genocide: The United States and the California Indian Catastrophe, 1846–1873* (New Haven: Yale University Press, 2013).

Magliari, Michael F. "Free Soil, Unfree Labor: Cave Johnson Couts and the Binding of Indian Workers in California, 1850–1867," *Pacific Historical Review*, 73 (August 2004): 349–89.

Malone, Patrick M. *The Skulking Way of War: Technology and Tactics among the New England Indians* (Baltimore: Johns Hopkins University Press, 1993).

Mancall, Peter C. *Deadly Medicine: Indians and Alcohol in Early America* (Ithaca: Cornell University Press, 1995).

Mancall, Peter C. *Valley of Opportunity: Economic Culture along the Upper Susquehanna, 1700–1800* (Ithaca: Cornell University Press, 1991).

Mandell, Daniel R. *Tribe, Race, History: Native Americans in Southern New England, 1780–1880* (Baltimore: Johns Hopkins University Press, 2008).

Mandell, Daniel R. "Shifting Boundaries of Race and Ethnicity: Indian-Black Intermarriage in Southern New England, 1760–1880," *Journal of American History*, 85 (September 1998), 466–501.

Mandell, Daniel R. *Behind the Frontier: Indians in Eighteenth Century Eastern Massachusetts* (Lincoln: University of Nebraska Press, 1996).

Mann, Charles. *1491: New Revelations of the Americas Before Columbus* (New York, 2006).

Mapp, Paul W. *The Elusive West and the Contest for Empire, 1713–1763* (Chapel Hill: University of North Carolina Press, 2011).

Markowitz, Harvey. "The Reformer, the Monsignor, and the Pueblos of New Mexico: Catholic Missionary Responses to New Directions in Early Twentieth-Century Indian Policy," *New Mexico Historical Review*, 88 (Fall 2013), 414–26.

Marriott, Alice. *The Ten Grandmothers* (Norman: University of Oklahoma Press, 1945).

Marriott, Alice. *Saynday's People: The Kiowa Indians and the Stories They Told* (Lincoln: University of Nebraska Press, 1963).

Martin, Calvin Luther. *Keepers of the Game: Indian-Animal Relationships and the Fur Trade* (Berkeley: University of California Press, 1978).

Martin, Joel. *The Land Looks After Us: A History of Native American Religion* (New York: Oxford University Press, 1999).

Martin, Joel. *Sacred Revolt: The Muskogees Struggle for a New World* (Boston, 1991).

Martinez, David. "Remembering the Thirty-Eight: Abraham Lincoln, the Dakota, and the U. S. War on Barbarism," *Wicazo Sa Review*, 28 (Fall 2013), 5–29.

Martinez, David. "Carlos Montezuma's Fight against 'Bureauism': An Unexpected Pima Hero," *American Indian Quarterly*, 37 (Summer 2013), 311–30.

Matthews, Becky. "Changing Lives: Baptist Women, Benevolence and Community on the Crow Reservation, 1904–1960," *Montana: The Magazine of Western History* 61 (Summer 2011), 2–29, 86–89.

Mayhall, Mildred. *The Kiowas*. 2nd edn (Norman: University of Oklahoma Press, 1971).

Meadows, William C. "Honoring Native American Code Talkers: The Road to the Code Talkers Recognition Act of 2008 (Public Law 110–420)," *American Indian Culture and Research Journal*, 35 (no. 3, 2011), 3–36.

Medicine Crow, Joseph. *From the Heart of Crow Country: The Crow Indians' Own Stories* (New York: Orion Books, 1992).

Meek, Ronald L. *Social Science and the Ignoble Savage* (Cambridge: Cambridge University Press, 1976).

Meredith, Howard. "Cultural Conservativsm and Revival: The Caddo and Hasinai Post-Removal Era, 1860–1902," *Chronicles of Oklahoma*, 79 (no. 3, 2001), 278–287.

Meredith, Howard. *Dancing on Common Ground: Tribal Cultures and Alliances on the Southern Plains* (Lawrence: University Press of Kansas, 1995).

Meredith, Howard and Vynola Newkumet. "Melford Williams: Caddo Leadership Patterns in the Twentieth Century," *Chronicles of Oklahoma*, 22 (no. 3, 1984), 64–9.

Merrell, James H. "Forum: Second Thoughts on Colonial Historians and American Indians," *William and Mary Quarterly*, 69 (July 2012), 451–512.

Merrell, James H. "Coming to Terms with Early America," *William and Mary Quarterly*, 69 (July 2012), 535–40.

Merrell, James H. *Into the American Woods: Negotiators on the Pennsylvania Frontier* (New York: Norton, 1999).

Merrell, James H. "'The Customes of Our Countrey': Indians and Colonists in Early America," in *Strangers Within the Realm: Cultural Margins Of the First British Empire*, eds. Bernard Bailyn and Philip D. Morgan (Chapel Hill: University of North Carolina Press, 1991).

Merrell, James H. *The Indians' New World: Catawbas and Their Neighbors from European Contact through the Era of Removal* (Chapel Hill: University of North Carolina Press, 1989).

Merrell, James H. "The Indians' New World: The Catawba Experience," *William and Mary Quarterly*, 3d. ser., 41 (1984), 537–65.

Merritt, Jane. *At the Crossroads: Indians and Empires on a Mid-Atlantic Frontier, 1700–1763* (Chapel Hill: University of North Carolina Press, 2003).

Merwick, Donna. *The Shame and the Sorrow: Dutch-Amerindian Encounters in New Netherland* (Philadelphia: Pennsylvania, 2006).

Metcalf, P. Richard. "Who Should Rule at Home? Native American Politics and Indian-White Relations," *Journal of American History*, 61 (1974), 651–65.

Meyer, Melissa. *White Earth Tragedy: Ethnicity and Dispossession at a Minnesota Anishinaabe Reservation, 1889–1920* (Lincoln: University of Nebraska Press, 1994).

Meyer, Roy W. *History of the Santee Sioux: United States Indian Policy on Trial*, revised edn (Lincoln: University of Nebraska Press, 1993).

Mihesuah, Devon. "Sustenance and Health among the Five Tribes in Indian Territory, Postremoval to Statehood," *Ethnohistory*, 62 (April 2015), 263–84.

Mihesuah, Devon. *Choctaw Crime and Punishment, 1884–1907* (Norman: University of Oklahoma Press, 2009).

Mihesuah, Devon. *Cultivating the Rosebuds: The Education of Women at the Cherokee Female Seminary, 1851–1909* (Urbana: University of Illinois Press, 1993).

Mihesuah, Devon. "Out of the 'Graves of the Polluted Debauches': The Boys of the Cherokee Male Seminary," *American Indian Quarterly*, 15 (1991), 503–21.

Miles, Tiya. *Ties that Bind: The Story of an Afro-Cherokee Family in Slavery and Freedom* (Berkeley: University of California Press, 2006).

Miller, Bruce G. "Life on the Hardened Border," *American Indian Culture and Research Journal*, 36 (no. 2, 2012), 23–45.

Miller, Bruce G. *The Problem of Justice: Tradition and Law in the Coast Salish World* (Lincoln: University of Nebraska Press, 2001).

Miller, Bruce G. "Centrality and Measures of Regional Structure in Aboriginal Western Washington," *Ethnology*, 28 (June 1989), 265–76.

Miller, Bruce G. and Daniel L. Boxberger. "Creating Chiefdoms: The Puget Sound Case," *Ethnohistory*, 41 (Spring 1994), 267–93.

Miller, Christopher L. and George R. Hamell, "A New Perspective on Indian-White Contact: Cultural Symbols and Colonial Trade," *Journal of American History*, 73 (1986), 311–28.

Miller, Douglas K. "Willing Workers: Urban Relocation and American Indian Initiative, 1940s–1960s," *Ethnohistory*, 60 (Winter 2013), 51–76.

Miller, Jay. "Changing Moons: A History of Caddo Religion." *Plains Anthropologist*, 41 (no. 157, 1986), 243–59.

Miller, Mark Edwin. *Forgotten Tribes: Unrecognized Indians and the Federal Acknowledgment Process* (Lincoln: University of Nebraska Press, 2004).

Milner, George R. and George Chaplin. "Eastern North American Population at ca. AD 1500," *American Antiquity*, 75 (October 2010), 707–26.

Miner, H. Craig. "Cherokee Sovereignty in the Gilded Age," *Chronicles of Oklahoma*, 71 (no. 2, 1993), 118–37.

Miner, H. Craig. *The Corporation and the Indian: Tribal Sovereignty and Industrial Civilization in Indian Territory, 1865–1907* (Norman: University of Oklahoma Press, 1976).

Mooney, James. "Myths of the Cherokee," *Journal of American Folklore*, 1 (July–September 1888).

Mooney, James. *Calendar History of the Kiowa Indians*, introduced by John C. Ewers, *Classics of Smithsonian Anthropology* (Washington, DC: Smithsonian Institution Press, 1979).

Mooney, James. *Myths of the Cherokee*, Nineteenth Annual Report of the US Bureau of American Ethnology to the Secretary of the Smithsonian Institution, 1897–98.

Morgan, Edmund S. *American Slavery, American Freedom: The Ordeal of Colonial Virginia* (New York: Norton, 1975).

Morgan, Lewis Henry. *League of the Iroquois*, reprint edn (New York: Citadel, 1962).

Morrison, Kenneth M. "Native Americans and the American Revolution: Historic Stories and Shifting Frontier Conflict," in *Indians in American History: An Introduction*, ed. Frederick E. Hoxie (Arlington Heights: Wiley, 1988).

Morrison, Kenneth M. *The Embattled Northeast: The Elusive Ideal of Alliance in Abenaki-Euramerican Relations* (Berkeley: University of California Press, 1984).

Morrison, Kenneth M. "Baptism and Alliance: The Symbolic Meditations of Religious Syncretism," *Ethnohistory*, 37 (Autumn 1990), 416–37.

Moulton, Gary E. *John Ross: Cherokee Chief* (Athens, GA: University of Georgia Press, 1978).

Murphy, Lucy Eldersveld. *Great Lakes Creoles: A French-Indian Community on the Northern Borderlands, Prairie du Chien, 1750–1860* (New York: Cambridge University Press, 2014).

Murray, David. "Spreading the Word: Missionaries, Conversion and Circulation in the Northeast," in *Spiritual Encounters: Interactions Between Christianity and Native Religions in Colonial America*, eds. N. Griffiths and F. Cervantes (Lincoln:University of Nebraska Press, 1999).

Murray, Laura J., ed. *To Do Good to My Indian Brethren: The Writings of Joseph Johnson, 1751–1776* (Amherst: University of Massachusetts Press, 1998).

Nabokov, Peter. *Where Lightning Strikes: The Lives of American Indian Sacred Places* (New York: Viking, 2006).

Naeher, Robert James. "Dialogue in the Wilderness: John Eliot and the Indian Exploration of Puritanism as a Source of Meaning, Comfort and Ethnic Survival," *New England Quarterly*, 62 (1989), 346–68.

Nagel, Joane. *American Indian Ethnic Renewal: Red Power and the Resurgence of Identity and Culture* (New York: Oxford University Press, 1986).

Nammack, Georgiana C. *Fraud, Politics and the Dispossession of the Indians: The Iroquois Land Frontier in the Colonial Period* (Norman: University of Oklahoma Press, 1969).

Naumec, David J. "Connecticut Indians in the War of Independence," *Connecticut History*, 47 (Fall 2008), 181–218.

Naumec, David J. "From Mashantucket to Appomattox: The Native American Veterans of Connecticut's Volunteer Regiments and the Union Navy," *New England Quarterly*, 81 (December 2008), 596–635.

Nelson, Douglas and Jeremy Johnston. "Janine Pease Pretty-on-Top," in *The New Warriors: Native American Leaders since 1900*, ed. R. David Edmunds (Lincoln, NE: University of Nebraska Press, 2001).

Neylan, Susan. "Shaking up Christianity: The Indian Shaker Church in the Canada-U.S Pacific Northwest." *Journal of Religion*, 91 (April 2011), 188–222.

Nichols, David Andrew. *Red Gentlemen and White Savages: Indians, Federalists and the Search for Order on the American Frontier* (Charlottesville: University of Virginia Press, 2008).

Nichols, David Andrew. "Land, Republicanism and Indians: Power and Policy in Early National Georgia, 1780–1825," *Georgia Historical Quarterly*, 85 (Summer 2001), 199–226.

Novak, Steven J. "The Real Takeover of the BIA: The Preferential Hiring of Indians," *Journal of Economic History*, 50 (September 1990), 639–54.

Nye, William Sturtevant. *Bad Medicine and Good: Tales of the Kiowas* (Norman: University of Oklahoma Press, 1962).

Oberg, Michael Leroy. *Peacemakers: The Iroquois, the United States, and the Treaty of Canandaigua, 1794* (New York: Oxford University Press, 2015).

Oberg, Michael Leroy. *Professional Indian: Eleazer Williams's American Odyssey* (Philadelphia: University of Pennsylvania Press, 2015).

Oberg, Michael Leroy. *The Head in Edward Nugent's Hand: Roanoke's Forgotten Indians* (Philadelphia: University of Pennsylvania Press, 2007).

Oberg, Michael Leroy, ed. *Samuel Wiseman's Book of Record: The Official Account of Bacon's Rebellion in Virginia, 1676–1677* (Lanham: Lexington Books, 2005).

Oberg, Michael Leroy. *Uncas: First of the Mohegans* (Ithaca: Cornell University Press, 2003).

Oberg, Michael Leroy. *Dominion and Civility: English Imperialism and Native America, 1585–1685* (Ithaca: Cornell University Press, 1999).

O'Brien, Greg. *The Choctaws in a Revolutionary Age, 1750–1830* (Lincoln: University of Nebraska Press, 2001).

O'Brien, Jean M. *Firsting and Lasting: Writing Indians out of Existence in New England* (Minneapolis: University of Minnesota Press, 2010).

O'Brien, Jean M. *Dispossession by Degrees: Indian Land and Identity in Natick, Massachusetts, 1650–1790* (Cambridge: Cambridge University Press, 1997).

O'Brien, Sharon. *American Indian Tribal Governments* (Norman: University of Oklahoma Press, 1989).

Odell, Marcia Larson. *Divide and Conquer: Allotment among the Cherokee* (New York: Arno Press, 1979).

O'Donnell, James H. *Southern Indians in the American Revolution* (Knoxville: University of Tennessee Press, 1973).

Oliphant, John. *Peace and War on the Anglo-Cherokee Frontier, 1756–1763* (Baton Rouge: Louisiana State University Press, 2001).

Olson, James C. *Red Cloud and the Sioux Problem* (Lincoln: University of Nebraska Press, 1965).

Oneroad, Amos and Alanson B. Skinner. *Being Dakota: Tales and Traditions of the Sisseton and Wahpeton*, ed. Laura L. Anderson (St. Paul: Minnesota Historical Society Press, 2003).

Onuf, Peter. "'We Shall All Be Americans': Thomas Jefferson and the Indians." *Indiana Magazine of History*, 95 (1999), 103–41.

Ortiz, Alfredo. *The Tewa World: Space, Time, Being and Becoming in a Pueblo Society* (Chicago: University of Chicago Press, 1969).

Ortman, Scott G. *Winds from the North: Tewa Origins and Historical Anthropology* (Salt Lake City: University of Utah Press, 2012).

Ostler, Jeffrey. "'To Extirpate the Indians': An Indigenous Consciousness of Genocide in the Ohio Valley and Lower Great Lakes, 1750s–1810," *William and Mary Quarterly*, 72 (October 2015), 587–622.

Ostler, Jeffrey. *The Lakota and the Black Hills: The Struggle for Sacred Ground* (New York: Penguin, 2010).

Otis, D. S. *The Dawes Act and the Allotment of Indian Lands* (Norman: University of Oklahoma Press, 1973).

Owen, Narcissa. *A Cherokee Woman's America: Memoirs of Narcissa Owen, 1831–1907*, ed. Karen L. Kilcup (Gainesville: University Press of Florida, 2005).

Owsley, Frank L., Jr. *Struggle for the Gulf Borderlands: The Creek War and the Battle of New Orleans* (Gainesville: University Press of Florida, 1981).

Pagden, Anthony. *Lords of All the World: Ideologies of Empire in Spain, Britain, and France, c. 1500–c.1800* (New Haven: Yale University Press, 1995).

Palmer, Mark H. "Sold! The Loss of Kiowa Allotments in the Post-Indian Reorganization Era," *American Indian Culture and Research Journal*, 35 (no. 3, 2011), 37–57.

Parman, Donald L. *Indians and the American West in the Twentieth Century* (Bloomington: Indiana University Press, 1994).

Parmenter, Jon. *The Edge of the Woods: Iroquoia, 1534–1701* (Lansing: Michigan State University Press, 2012).

Parmenter, Jon. "After the Mourning Wars: The Iroquois as Allies in Colonial North American Campaigns, 1676–1760," *William and Mary Quarterly*, 64 (January 2007), 39–82.

Parmenter, Jon. "Pontiac's War: Forging New Links in the Anglo-Iroquois Covenant Chain, 1758–1766," *Ethnohistory*, 44 (1997), 617–54.

Pauketat, Timothy R. *Cahokia: Ancient America's Great City on the Mississippi* (New York: Penguin, 2009).

Pearce, Roy Harvey. *Savagism and Civilization: A Study of the Indian and the American Mind*, rev. edn (Baltimore: Johns Hopkins University Press, 1965).

Pearcy, Thomas L. "The Smallpox Outbreak of 1779–1782: A Brief Comparative Look at Twelve Borderland Communities," *Journal of the West*, 36 (January 1997), 26–37.

Peckham, Howard. *The Colonial Wars, 1689–1762* (Chicago: University of Chicago Press, 1964).

Peckham, Howard. *Pontic and the Indian Uprising* (Chicago: University of Chicago Press, 1947).

Perdue, Theda. "The Legacy of Indian Removal," *Journal of Southern History*, 78 (February 2012), 3–36.

Perdue, Theda. "Race and Culture: Writing the Ethnohistory of the Early South." *Ethnohistory*, 51 (Fall 2004), 701–723.

Perdue, Theda. *"Mixed Blood" Indians: Racial Construction in the Early South* (Athens: University of Georgia Press, 2002).

Perdue, Theda. "'Clan and Court' Another Look at the Early Cherokee Republic," *American Indian Quarterly*, 24 (Fall 2000), 562–9.

Perdue, Theda. *Cherokee Women: Gender and Culture Change, 1700–1835* (Lincoln: University of Nebraska Press, 1998).

Perdue, Theda. "The Conflict Within: The Cherokee Power Structure and Removal," *Georgia Historical Quarterly*, 73 (1989), 467–91.

Peroff, Nicholas C. *Menominee Drums: Tribal Termination and Restoration, 1954–1974* (Norman: University of Oklahoma Press, 1982).

Perry, Jennifer E. "Chumash Ritual and Sacred Geography on Santa Cruz Island, California," *Journal of California and Great Basin Anthropology*, 27 (no. 2, 2007), 103–24.

Perry, Jennifer E. and Christopher S. Jazwa. "Spatial and Temporal Variability in Chert Exploitation on Santa Cruz Island, California." *American Antiquity*, 75 (January 2010), 177–98.

Perttula, Timothy K. "How Texas Historians Write About Pre-AD 1685 Caddo Peoples of Texas," *Southwestern Historical Quarterly*, 115 (April 2012), 364–76.

Perttula, Timothy K., Mary Beth Trubitt, and Jeffrey S. Girard. "The Use of Shell-Tempered Pottery in the Caddo Area of the Southeastern United States," *Southeastern Archaeology*, 30 (Winter 2011), 242–67.

Pertusati, Linda. *In Defense of Mohawk Land: Ethnopolitical Conflict in Native North America* (Albany: SUNY Press, 1997).

Pesantubbee, Michelene. "Nancy Ward: American Patriot or Cherokee Nationalist?" *American Indian Quarterly*, 38 (Spring 2014), 177–206.

Pesantubbee, Michelene. *Native Americans and the Christian Right: The Gendered Politics of Unlikely Alliances* (Durham: Duke University Press, 2008).

Peterson, Jacqueline. "Ethnogenesis: The Settlement and Growth of a `New People' in the Great Lakes Region, 1702–1815," *American Indian Culture and Research Journal*, 6 (1982), 23–64.

Phillips, George Harwood. "Indians in Los Angeles, 1781–1875: Economic Integration, Social Disintegration," *Pacific Historical Review*, 49 (August 1980), 427–51.

Philp, Kenneth R. *Termination Revisited: American Indians on the Trail to Self-Determination, 1933–1953* (Lincoln: University of Nebraska Press, 1999).

Philp, Kenneth R. *John Collier's Crusade for Indian Reform, 1920–1954* (Tucson: University of Arizona Press, 1977).

Piker, Joshua A. *The Four Deaths of Acorn Whistler: Telling Stories in Colonial America* (Cambridge: Harvard University Press, 2013).

Piker, Joshua A. *Okfuskee: A Creek Indian Town in Colonial America* (Cambridge, MA: Harvard University Press, 2004).

Piker, Joshua A. "Colonists and Creeks: Rethinking the Pre-Revolutionary Southern Backcountry," *Journal of Southern History*, 70 (August 2004), 503–40.

Piker, Joshua A. "'White & Clean' and Contested: Creek Towns and Trading Paths in the Aftermath, of the Seven Years War." *Ethnohistory*, 50 (Spring 2003), 315–48.

Plane, Ann Marie. *Dreams and the Invisible World in Colonial New England: Indians, Colonists, and the Seventeenth Century* (Philadelphia: University of Pennsylvania Press, 2014).

Plane, Ann Marie. *Colonial Intimacies: Indian Marriage in Early New England* (Ithaca: Cornell University Press, 2000).

Pommersheim, Frank. *Broken Landscape: Indians, Indian Tribes, and the Constitution* (New York: Oxford University Press, 2009).

Pommersheim, Frank. *Braid of Feathers: American Indian Law and Contemporary Tribal Life* (Berkeley: University of California Press, 1995).

Potter, Stephen R. *Commoners, Tribute and Chiefs: The Development of Algonquian Culture in the Potomac Valley* (Charlottesville: University Press of Virginia, 1993).

Powell, William S. "Aftermath of the Massacre: The First Indian War, 1622–1632," *Virginia Magazine of History and Biography*, 66 (1958), 44–75.

Preston, David L. *The Texture of Contact: European and Indian Settler Communities on the Frontiers of Iroquoia, 1667–1763* (Lincoln: University of Nebraska Press, 2009).

Pulsipher, Jenny Hale. "'Dark Cloud Rising from the East': Indian Sovereignty and the Coming of King William's War in New England," *New England Quarterly*, 80 (December 2007), 588–613.

Pulsipher, Jenny Hale. *Subjects unto the Same King: Indians, English and the Contest for Authority in Early New England* (Philadelphia: University of Pennsylvania Press, 2005).

Prucha, Francis Paul. *The Great Father*, 2 vols. (Lincoln: University of Nebraska Press, 1984).

Prucha, Francis Paul. *The Churches and the Indian Schools, 1888–1912* (Lincoln: University of Nebraska Press, 1979).

Prucha, Francis Paul. *American Indian Policy in the Formative Years: The Indian Trade and Intercourse Acts, 1790–1834* (Cambridge: Harvard University Press, 1962).

Quimby, George I. "Culture Contact on the Northwest Coast, 1785–1795," *American Anthropologist* 50 (April–June 1948), 247–55.

Quintana, Frances Leon. "Land, Water, and Pueblo-Hispanic Relations in Northern New Mexico," *Journal of the Southwest*, 32 (no. 3, 1990), 288–99.

Quitt, Martin H. "Trade and Acculturation at Jamestown, 1607–1609: The Limits of Understanding," *William and Mary Quarterly*, 52 (April 1995), 227–58.

Ramenofsky, Ann. *Vectors of Death: The Archaeology of European Contact* (Albuquerque: University of New Mexico Press, 1987).

Ramsey, William L. *The Yamasee War* (Lincoln: University of Nebraska Press, 2008).

Ramsey, William L. "A Coat for 'Indian Cuffy': Mapping the Boundary Between Freedom and Slavery In Colonial South Carolina," *South Carolina Historical Magazine*, 103 (2002), 48–66.

Reed, Julie L. "Family and Nation: Cherokee Orphan Care, 1835–1903." *American Indian Quarterly*, 34 (Summer 2010), 312–43.

Reff, Daniel T. "The 'Predicament of Culture' and Spanish Missionary Accounts of the Tepehuan and Pueblo Revolts," *Ethnohistory*, 42 (Winter 1995), 63–90.

Reff, Daniel T. "The Introduction of Smallpox in the Greater Southwest," *American Anthropologist*, 89 (1987), 704–8.

Rein, Christopher. "'Our First Duty was to God and our Next to our Country': Religion, Violence and the Sand Creek Massacre," *Great Plains Quarterly*, 34 (Summer 2012), 217–238.

Resendez, Andres. *The Other Slavery: The Uncovered Story of Indian Enslavement in America* (New York: Houghton-Mifflin, 2016).

Reyes, Lawney L. *Bernie Whitebear: An Urban Indian's Quest for Justice* (Tucson: University of Arizona Press, 2006).

Rice, Alanna. "'To Save Their Substance that they May Live Together': Rethinking Schooling and Literacy in Eighteenth-Century Algonquian Communities in Southern New England," *American Indian Culture and Research Journal*, 34 (no. 3, 2010), 47–70.

Rice, James D. "Beyond 'The Ecological Indian' and 'Virgin Soil Epidemics': New Perspectives on Native Americans and the Environment," *History Compass*, 12/9 (2014), 745–57.

Rice, James D. *Tales from a Revolution: Bacon's Rebellion and the Transformation of Early America* (New York: Oxford University Press, 2014).

Rice, James D. *Nature and History in the Potomac Country: From Hunter-Gatherers to the Age of Jefferson* (Baltimore: Johns Hopkins University Press, 2009).

Richards, Kent D. *Isaac I. Stevens: Young Man in a Hurry* (Pullman: Washington State University Press, 1993).

Richardson, Heather Cox. *Wounded Knee: Party Politics and the Road to an American Massacre* (New York: Basic Books, 2010).

Richter, Daniel K. *Facing East from Indian Country: A Native History of Early America* (Cambridge: Harvard University Press, 2001).

Richter, Daniel K. "Onas, the Long Knife: Pennsylvanians and Indians, 1783–1794," in *Native Americans and the Early Republic*, eds. Frederick Hoxie, Ronald Hoffman, and Peter J. Albert (Charlottesville: University Press of Virginia, 1999), 125–61.

Richter, Daniel K. "'Believing that Many of the Red People Suffer Much for the Want of Food': Hunting, Agriculture, and a Quaker Construction of Indianness in the Early Republic," *Journal of the Early Republic*, 19 (Winter 1999), 601–28.

Richter, Daniel K. *The Ordeal of the Longhouse: The Peoples of the Iroquois League in the Era of European Colonization* (Chapel Hill: University of North Carolina Press, 1992).

Richter, Daniel K. "Iroquois Versus Iroquois: Jesuit Missions and Christianity in Village Politics, 1642–1686," *Ethnohistory*, 32 (Winter 1985), 1–16.

Richter, Daniel K. "Crossing the Cultural Divide: Indians and New Englanders, 1605–1763," *Proceedings of the American Antiquarian Society*, 90 (April 1980), 23–99.

Rindfleisch, Bryan. "'Our Lands are Our Life and Breath': Coweta, Cusseta, and the Struggle for Creek Territory and Sovereignty during the American Revolution," *Ethnohistory*, 60 (Fall 2013), 581–603.

Rivaya-Martinez, Joaquin. "A Different Look at Native American Population: Comanche Raiding, Captive Taking, and Population Decline," *Ethnohistory*, 61 (Summer 2014), 391–418.

Rockwell, Stephen J. *Indian Affairs and the Administrative State in the Nineteenth Century* (Cambridge: Cambridge University Press, 2010).

Rollings, Willard. "The Pueblos of New Mexico and the Protection of Their Land and Water Rights," in *Working the Range: Essays on the History of Western Land Management and the Environment*, ed. John R. Wunder (Westport:Greenwood Press, 1985), 3–24.

Ronda, James P. *Lewis and Clark among the Indians* (Lincoln: University of Nebraska Press, 1984).

Ronda, James P. "Generations of Faith: The Christian Indians of Martha's Vineyard," *William and Mary Quarterly*, 3d ser., 38 (1981), 369–94.

Ronda, James P. and Jeanne Ronda. "The Death of John Sassamon: An Exploration in Writing New England Indian History," *American Indian Quarterly*, 1 (Summer 1974) 91–102.

Rosen, Deborah A. *American Indians and State Law* (Lincoln: University of Nebraska Press, 2007).

Rosen, Deborah A. "Pueblo Indians and Citizenship in Territorial New Mexico," *New Mexico Historical Review*, 78 (no. 1, 2003), 1–28.

Rosenthal, Harvey D. *Their Day in Court: A History of the Indian Claims Commission* (New York: Garland, 1990).

Rosenthal, Nicolas G. *Reimagining Indian Country: Native American Migration and Identity in Twentieth-Century Los Angeles* (Chapel Hill: University of North Carolina Press, 2012).

Rosier, Paul C. *Serving Their Country: American Indian Patriotism in the Twentieth Century* (Cambridge: Harvard University Press, 2009).

Rosier, Paul C. "'They Are Ancestral Homelands': Race, Place and Politics in Cold War Native America, 1945–1961," *Journal of American History*, 92 (2006), 1300–1326.

Rosier, Paul C. "Dam-Building and Treaty-Breaking: The Kinzua Dam Controversy, 1935–1958," *Pennsylvania Magazine of History and Biography*, 119 (October 1995), 345–68.

Rountree, Helen C. *Pocahontas, Powhatan, Opechancanough: Three Indian Lives Changed by Jamestown* (Charlottesville: University Press of Virginia, 2005).

Rountree, Helen C. *Pocahontas's People: The Powhatan Indians of Virginia Through Four Centuries* (Norman: University of Oklahoma Press, 1990).

Rountree, Helen C. and E. Randolph Turner, III. *Before and After Jamestown: Virginia's Powhatans and their Predecessors* (Gainesville: University of Florida Press, 2002).

Rubertone, Patricia E. *Grave Undertakings: An Archaeology of Roger Williams and the Narragansett Indians* (Washington, DC: Smithsonian Institution Press, 2001).

Rusco, Elmer R. *A Fateful Time: The Background and Legislative History of the Indian Reorganization Act* (Reno: University of Nevada Press, 2000).

Rushforth, Brett. *Bonds of Alliance: Indigenous and Atlantic Slaveries in New France* (Chapel Hill: University of North Carolina Press, 2012).

Rushforth, Brett. "Slavery, the Fox Wars, and the Limits of Alliance," *William and Mary Quarterly*, 63 (January 2006), 53–81.

Rushforth, Brett. "'A Little Flesh We Offer You': The Origins of Indian Slavery in New France," *William and Mary Quarterly*, 60 (October 2003), 777–808.

Rzeczkowski, Frank. *Uniting the Tribes: The Rise and Fall of Pan-Indian Community on the Crow Reservation* (Lawrence: University Press of Kansas, 2012).

Sabo, George III. "Dancing Into the Past: Colonial Legacies in Modern Caddo Indian Ceremony," *Arkansas Historical Quarterly*, 62 (Winter 2003), 423–45.

Sabo, George III. "Encounters and Images: European Contact and the Caddo Indians," *Historical Reflections*, 21 (no. 2, 1995), 217–42.

Sadosky, Leonard J. *Revolutionary Negotiations: Indians, Empires and Diplomats in the Founding of America* (Charlottesville: University Press of Virginia, 2010).

St. Jean, Wendy B. "Inventing Guardianship: The Mohegan Indians and their 'Protectors,'" *New England Quarterly*, 72 (1999), 362–87.

Saler, Bethel. *The Settlers' Empire: Colonialism and State Formation in America's Old Northwest* (Philadelphia: University of Pennsylvania Press, 2015).

Salisbury, Neal. "Embracing Ambiguity: Native Peoples and Christianity in Seventeenth-Century North America," *Ethnohistory*, 50 (Spring 2003), 247–60.

Salisbury, Neal. "The Indians Old World: Native Americans and the Coming of Europeans," *William and Mary Quarterly*, 3d ser., 53 (1996), 435–58.

Salisbury, Neal. "Religious Encounters in a Colonial Context: New England and New France in the Seventeenth Century," *American Indian Quarterly*, 16 (1992), 501–9.

Salisbury, Neal. *Manitou and Providence: Indians, Europeans and the Making of New England, 1500–1643* (New York: Oxford University Press, 1982).

Samuels, David. *Massacre at Camp Grant: Forgetting and Remembering Apache History* (Tucson: University of Arizona Press, 2007).

Sandos, James A. *Converting California: Indians and Franciscans in the Missions* (New Haven: Yale University Press, 2004).

Sandos, James A. "'Levantamiento!' The 1824 Chumash Uprising," *The Californians*, 5 (1987), 8–20.

Sandos, James A. and Larry E. Burgess. *The Hunt for Willie Boy: Indian-Hating and Popular Culture* (Norman: University of Oklahoma Press, 2004).

Satterlee, Marion P. *Outbreak and Massacre by the Dakota Indians*, ed. Don Heinrich Tolzmann (Bowie: Heritage Books, 2001).

Satz, Ronald N. *American Indian Policy in the Jacksonian Era* (Lincoln, NE: University of Nebraska Press, 1975).

Saunt, Claudio. "'My Medicine is my Punishment': A Case of Torture in Early California, 1775–1776," *Ethnohistory*, 57 (Fall 2010), 679–708.

Saunt, Claudio. "Telling Stories: The Political Uses of Myth and History in the Cheroke and Creek Nations," *Journal of American History*, 93 (December 2006), 673–97.

Saunt, Claudio. "Taking Account of Property: Stratification among the Creek Indians in the Early Nineteenth Century," *William and Mary Quarterly*, 57 (2000), 733–60.

Saunt, Claudio. *A New Order of Things: Property, Power and the Transformation of the Creek Indians, 1733–1816* (Cambridge: Cambridge University Press, 1999).

Saunt, Claudio. "'The English Has Now a Mind to Make Slaves of them All': Creeks, Seminoles and the Problem of Slavery," *American Indian Quarterly*, 22 (1998), 157–81.

Sayer, John William. *Ghost Dancing the Law: The Wounded Knee Trials* (Cambridge: Harvard University Press, 1997).

Schaap, James I. "The Growth of the Native American Gaming Industry: What Has the Past Provided, and What does the Future Hold?" *American Indian Quarterly*, 34 (Summer 2010), 365–89.

Schambach, Frank F. "The End of the Trail: The Route of Hernando De Soto's Army through Southwest Arkansas and East Texas," *The Arkansas Archaeologist*, 27/28 (1989), 9–33.

Schneider, Tammy. "'This Once Savage Heart of Mine': Joseph Johnson, Wheelock's Indians, and the Construction of a Christian/Indian Identity, 1764, 1776," in *Reinterpreting New England Indians and the Colonial Experience*, eds. Colin G. Calloway and Neal Salisbury (Boston, MA: Colonial Society of Massachusetts, 2003).

Schnell, Steven M. "The Kiowa Homeland in Oklahoma," *Geographical Review*, 90 (April 2000), 155–76.

Schoolcraft, Henry R. *Notes on the Iroquois: Or, Contributions to the Statistics, Aboriginal History, Antiquities, and General Ethnology of Western New York* (New York: Bartlett and Welford, 1846).

Schroedel, Jean and Ryan Hart. "Vote Dilution and Suppression in Indian Country," *Studies in American Political Development*, 29 (April 2015), 40–67.

Schulze, Jeffrey M. "The Rediscovery of the Tiguas: Federal Recognition and Indianness in the Twentieth Century," *Southwestern Historical Quarterly*, 105 (July 2001), 15–39.

Secunda, Ben. "The Road to Ruin? 'Civilization and the Origins of a 'Michigan Road Band' of Potawatomi," *Michigan Historical Review*, 34 (Spring 2008), 118–49.

Seed, Patricia. *Ceremonies of Possession in Europe's Conquest of the New World* (Cambridge: Cambridge University Press, 1995).

Seymour, Deni J. "Mobile Visitors to the Eastern Frontier Pueblos: An Archaeological Example from Tabira," *Plains Anthropologist*, 66 (February 2015), 4–39.

Shannon, Timothy J. *Iroquois Diplomacy on the Early American Frontier* (New York, 2008).

Shannon, Timothy J. *Indians and Colonists at the Crossroads of Empire: The Albany Congress of 1754* (Ithaca: Cornell University Press, 2000).

Shannon, Timothy J. "Dressing for Success on the Mohawk Frontier: Hendrick, William Johnson and the Indian Fashion," *William and Mary Quarterly*, 3d ser., 53 (1996), 13–42.

Sheehan, Bernard W. *Savagism and Civility: Indians and Englishmen in Colonial Virginia* (Cambridge: Cambridge University Press, 1980).

Sheehan, Bernard W. *Seeds of Extinction: Jeffersonian Philanthropy and the American Indian* (Chapel Hill: University of North Carolina Press, 1973).

Shoemaker, Nancy. "Mr. Tashtego: Native American Whalemen in Antebellum New England," *Journal of the Early Republic*, 33 (Spring 2013), 109–32.

Shoemaker, Nancy. *A Strange Likeness: Becoming Red and White in Eighteenth-Century America* (New York: Oxford University Press, 2004).

Shoemaker, Nancy. "How Indians Got to Be Red," *American Historical Review*, 102 (June 1997), 625–44.

Shoemaker, Nancy, ed. *Negotiators of Change: Historical Perspectives on Native American Women* (New York: Routledge, 1995).

Shoemaker, Nancy. "The Rise and Fall of Iroquois Women." *Journal of Women's History*, 2 (1991), 39–57.

Sider, Gerald M. *Lumbee Indian Histories: Race, Ethnicity and Indian Identity in the Southeastern United States* (New York: Cambridge University Press, 1993).

Silliman, Stephen W. "Change and Continuity, Practice and Memory: Native American Persistence in Colonial New England." *American Antiquity*, 74 (April 2009), 211–30.

Silliman, Stephen W. "Culture Contact or Colonialism? Challenges in the Archaeology of Native North America." *American Antiquity*, 70 (January 2005), 55–74.

Silliman, Stephen and Thomas A. Witt. "The Complexities of Consumption: Eastern Pequot Cultural Economics in the Eighteenth-Century New England," *Historical Archaeology*, 44 (no. 4, 2010), 46–68.

Silverman, David J. *Red Brethren: The Brothertown and Stockbridge Indians and the Problem of Race in Early America* (Ithaca: Cornell University Press, 2010).

Silverman, David J. "The Curse of God: An Idea and Its Origins among the Indians of NewYork's Revolutionary Frontier," *William and Mary Quarterly*, 66 (July 2009), 495–534.

Silverman, David J. *Faith and Boundaries: Colonists, Christianity and Community Among the Wampanoag Indians of Martha's Vineyard, 1600–1871* (Cambridge: Cambridge University Press, 2005)

Silverman, David J. "Indians, Missionaries and Religious Translation: Creating Wampanoag Christianity in Seventeenth-Century Martha's Vineyard, *William and Mary Quarterly*, 62 (April 2005), 141–74.

Silverman, David J. "'We Chuse to Be Bounded': Native American Animal Husbandry in Colonial New England," *William and Mary Quarterly*, 60 (July 2003), 511–48.

Silverman, David J. "Deposing the Sachem to Defend the Sachemship: Indian Land Sales and Native Political Structure on Martha's Vineyard," *Explorations in Early American Culture*, 5 (2001), 9–44.

Silverman, David J. "The Impact of Indentured Servitude on the Society and Culture of Southern New England Indians, 1680–1810," *New England Quarterly*, 74 (December 2001), 622–66.

Simmons, Marc. "New Mexico's Smallpox Epidemic of 1780–1781," *New Mexico Historical Review*, 41 (October 1966) 319–26.

Simmons, William S. *Spirit of the New England Tribes: Indian History and Folklore, 1620–1984* (Hanover: University Press of America,1986).

Simmons, William S. "Red Yankees: The Narragansetts in the First Great Awakening," *American Ethnologist*, 40 (1983), 253–71.

Simonson, Jane E. *Making Home Work: Domesticity and Native American Assimilation in the American West, 1860–1919* (Chapel Hill: University of North Carolina Press, 2006).

Simpson, Audra. *Mohawk Interruptus: Political Life across the Borders of Settler States* (Durham, NC: Duke University Press, 2014).

Sleeper-Smith, Susan, *Indian Women and French Men: Rethinking Cultural Encounter in the Western Great Lakes* (Amherst: Massachusetts, 2001).

Smith, F. Todd. *The Caddos, the Wichitas, and the United States, 1846–1901* (College Station: Texas A&M University Press, 1996).

Smith, F. Todd. "A Native Response to the Transfer of Louisiana: The Red River Caddos and Spain," *Louisiana History*, 37 (no. 2, 1996), 163–85.

Smith, F. Todd. *The Caddo Indians: Tribes at the Convergence of Empire, 1542–1854* (College Station: Texas A&M University Press, 1995).

Smith, Katy Simpson. "'I look on You ... as My Children': Persistence and Change in Cherokee Motherhood, 1750–1835," *North Carolina Historical Review*, 87 (October 2010), 403–30.

Smith, Paul Chaat and Robert Allen Warrior, *Like a Hurricane: The Indian Movement from Alcatraz to Wounded Knee* (New York: The New Press, 1996).

Smith, Sherry. *Hippies, Indians and the Fight for Red Power* (New York: Oxford University Press, 2012).

Smith, Sherry. *Reimagining Indians: Native Americans Through Anglo Eyes, 1880–1940* (New York: Oxford University Press, 2000).

Smith, Troy. "Nations Colliding: The Civil War Comes to Indian Territory," *Civil War History*, 59 (September 2013), 279–319.

Smithers, Gregory D. *The Cherokee Diaspora: An Indigenous History of Migration, Resettlement, and Identity* (New Haven: Yale University Press, 2015).

Smits, David D. "The Frontier Army and the Destruction of the Buffalo, 1865–1883," *Western Historical Quarterly*, 25 (Autumn 1994), 312–38.

Smoak, Gregory E. *Ghost Dances and Identity: Prophetic Religion and American Indian Ethnogenesis in the Nineteenth Century* (Berkeley: University of California Press, 2006).

Smyth, Willie and Esme Ryan. *Spirit of the First People: Native American Music Traditions of Washington State* (Seattle: University of Washington Press, 1999).

Snapp, J. Russell. *John Stuart and the Struggle for Empire on the Southern Colonial Frontier* (Baton Rouge: Louisiana State University Press, 1996).

Snell, Alma Hogan. *Grandmother's Grandchild: My Crow Indian Life*, ed. Becky Matthews (Lincoln: University of Nebraska Press, 2003).

Snyder, Charles M., ed. *Red and White on the New York Frontier: A Struggle for Survival* (Harrison: Harbor Hill Books, 1978).

Snyder, Christine. *Slavery in Indian Country: The Changing Face of Captivity in Early America* (Cambridge: Harvard University Press, 2010).

Soderlund, Jean R. *Lenape Country: Delaware Valley Society before William Penn* (Philadelphia: University of Pennsylvania Press, 2015).

Southwell, Kristina L and John R. Lovett. *Life at the Kiowa, Comanche, and Wichita Agency: The Photographs of Annette Ross Hume* (Norman: University of Oklahoma Press, 2010).

Spielmann, Katherine A. "Late Prehistoric Exchange Between the Southwest and the Southern Plains," *Plains Anthropologist*, 28 (November 1983), 257–72.

Stahle, David W. "The Lost Colony and Jamestown Droughts," *Science*, 280 (1998), 564–7.

Stanciu, Cristina. "An Indian Woman Has Many Hats: Laura Cornelius Kellogg's Embattled Search for an Indigenous Voice," *American Indian Quarterly*, 37 (Summer 2013), 87–115.

Starkey, Armstrong. *European and Native American Warfare, 1675–1815* (Norman: University of Oklahoma Press, 1998).

Starna, William A. "The Diplomatic Career of Canasatego," in *Friends and Enemies in Penn's Woods: Indians, Colonists, and Racial Construction of Pennsylvania*, eds. William A. Pencak and Daniel K. Richter (University Park: Penn State University Press, 2004), 144–63.

Steele, Ian K. *Warpaths: Invasions of North America* (New York: Oxford University Press, 1994).

Steele, Ian K. *Betrayals: Fort William Henry and the "Massacre."* (New York: Oxford University Press, 1990).

Stevens, Laura. *The Poor Indians: British Missionaries, Native Americans, and Colonial Sensibility* (Philadelphia: University of Pennsylvania Press, 2004).

Stremlau, Rose. *Sustaining the Cherokee Family: Kinship and Allotment of an Indigenous Nation* (Chapel Hill: University of North Carolina Press, 2011).

Sturm, Circe. "Race, Sovereignty, and Civil Rights: Understanding the Cherokee Freedmen Controversy." *Cultural Anthropology*, 29 (no. 3, 2014), 575–98.

Sturm, Circe. *Blood Politics: Race, Culture and Identity in the Cherokee Nation of Oklahoma* (Berkeley: University of California Press, 2002).

Sturm, Circe. "Blood Politics, Racial Classification, and Cherokee National Identity: The Trials and Tribulations of the Cherokee Freedmen," *American Indian Quarterly*, 22 (1998), 230–58.

Sundstrom, Linda. "Smallpox Used Them Up: References to Epidemic Disease in Northern Plains Winter Counts, 1714–1920," *Ethnohistory*, 44 (1997), 305–43.

Sundstrom, Linda. "Blood Politics, Racial Classification, and Cherokee National Identity: The Trials and Tribulations of the Cherokee Freedmen," *American Indian Quarterly*, 22 (1998), 230–58.

Swanton, John. *Source Material on the History and Ethnology of the Caddo Indians*, reprint edn (Norman: University of Oklahoma Press, 1996).

Szasz, Margaret Connell. *Education and the American Indian: The Road to Self-Determination Since1928* (Albuquerque: University of New Mexico Press, 1999).

Szasz, Margaret Connell, ed. *Between Indian and White Worlds: The Cultural Broker* (Norman: University of Oklahoma Press, 1994).

Szasz, Margaret Connell. *Indian Education in the American Colonies, 1607–1783* (Albuquerque: University of New Mexico Press, 1988).

Tanner, Helen Hornbeck. "The Glaize in 1792: A Composite Indian Community." *Ethnohistory*, 25 (1978), 15–39.

Tanner, Helen Hornbeck. "The Territory of the Caddo Tribe of Oklahoma (1972)." In *Caddoan Indians IV*, David Agee Horr, comp. (New York: Garland Publishing, 1974).

Tate, Michael L. *Indians and Emigrants: Encounters on the Overland Trails* (Norman: University of Oklahoma Press, 2006).

Taylor, Alan. *The Divided Ground: Indians, Settlers and the Northern Borderland of the American Revolution* (New York: Knopf, 2006).

Taylor, Alan. "Captain Hendrick Aupaumut: The Dilemmas of an Intercultural Broker," *Ethnohistory*, 43 (no. 3, 1996), 431–57.

Taylor, Graham D. *The New Deal and American Indian Tribalism: The Administration of the Indian Reorganization Act, 1934–1945* (Lincoln: University of Nebraska Press, 1980).

Taylor, Jonathan B. and Joseph P. Kalt, *American Indians on Reservations: Databook of Socioeconomic Change between the 1990 and 2000 Censuses* (Cambridge, MA: Harvard Projecct on American Indian Economic Development, 2005).

Textor, Lucy Elizabeth. *Official Relations between the United States and the Sioux Indians* (Palo Alto: Stanford University Press, 1896).

Thomas, David Hurst. *Skull Wars: Kennewick Man, Archaeology, and the Battle for Native American Identity* (New York: Basic Books, 2000).

Thomas, Peter A. "The Fur Trade, Indian Land, and the Need to Define Adequate Environmental Parameters," *Ethnohistory*, 28 (Autumn 1981), 359–79.

Thomas, Peter A. *In the Maelstrom of Change: The Indian Trade in the Middle Connecticut River Valley* (New York: Garland, 1980).

Thomas, Peter A. "Contrastive Subsistence Strategies and Land Use as Factors for Understanding Indian-White Relations in New England," *Ethnohistory*, 23 (1976), 1–18.

Thornton, Russell. "Boundary Dissolution and Revitalization Movements: The Case of the 19th-Century Cherokees," *Ethnohistory*, 40 (Summer 1993), 359–83.

Thornton, Russell. *American Indian Holocaust and Survival: A Population History since 1492* (Norman: University of Oklahoma Press, 1987).

Thornton, Russell. "Cherokee Population Losses during the Trail of Tears: A New Perspective and a New Estimate," *Ethnohistory*, 31 (Autumn 1984), 289–300.

Thrush, Coll. *Native Seattle: Histories from the Crossing-Over Place* (Seattle: University of Washington Press, 2007).

Thrush, Coll. "City of Changers: Indigenous People and the Transformation of Seattle's Watersheds," *Pacific Historical Review*, 75 (February 2006), 89–117.

Tiro, Karim. *The People of the Standing Stone: The Oneida Nation from the Revolution through the Era of Removal* (Amherst: University of Massachusetts Press, 2011).

Tiro, Karim. "A 'Civil' War? Rethinking Iroquois Participation in the American Revolution," *Perspectives in Early American Culture*, 4 (2000), 148–65.

Townsend, Kenneth William. *World War II and the American Indian* (Albuquerque: University of New Mexico Press, 2000).

Townshend, Camilla. *Pocahontas and the Powhatan Dilemma* (New York: Hill and Wang, 2004).

Trachtenberg, Alan. *Shades of Hiawatha: Staging Indians, Making Americans* (New York: Hill And Wang, 2004).

Trafzer, Clifford E. and Joel R. Hyer, eds. *Exterminate Them! Written Accounts of the Murder, Rape and Slavery of Native Americans during the California Gold Rush, 1848–1868* (Lansing: Michigan State University Press, 1999).

Trask, David S. "Episcopal Missionaries on the Santee and Yankton Reservations: Cross-Cultural Collaboration and President Grant's Peace Policy," *Great Plains Quarterly*, 33 (Spring 2013), 87–101.

Treglia, Gabriella. "The Consistency and Inconsistency of Cultural Oppression: American Indian Dance Bans, 1900–1933." *Western Historical Quarterly*, 44 (Summer 2013), 145–66.

Trelease, Allen W. *Indian Affairs in Colonial New York: The Seventeenth Century* (Ithaca: Cornell University Press, 1960).

Trennert, Robert A. Jr. *The Phoenix Indian School: Forced Assimilation in Arizona, 1891–1935* (Norman: University of Oklahoma Press, 1988).

Trigger, Bruce G. "Early Native North American Responses to European Contact: Romantic versus Rationalistic Interpretations," *Journal of American History*, 77 (March 1991), 1195–215.

Turner, Frederick Jackson, "The Significance of the Frontier in American History," in *The Frontier in American History*, ed. Wilbur R. Jacobs (Tucson: University of Arizona Press, 1986).

Ulrich, Roberta. *Empty Nets: Indians, Dams, and the Columbia River* (Corvallis: Oregon State University Press, 1999).

Unrau, William E. *White Man's Wicked Water: The Alcohol Trade and Prohibition in Indian Country* (Lawrence: University of Kansas Press, 1996).

Usner, Daniel H., Jr. "'A Savage Feast They Made of It': John Adams and the Paradoxical Origins of Federal Indian Policy," *Journal of the Early Republic*, 33 (Winter 2013), 607–41.

Usner, Daniel H., Jr. *Indian Work: Language and Livelihood in Native American History* (Cambridge: Harvard University Press, 2009).

Usner, Daniel H., Jr. *American Indians in the Lower Mississippi Valley: Social and Economic Histories* (Lincoln: University of Nebraska Press, 1998).

Usner, Daniel H., Jr. *Indians, Settlers and Slaves in a Frontier Exchange Economy: The Lower Mississippi Valley Before 1783* (Chapel Hill: University of North Carolina Press, 1992).

Utley, Robert M. *The Lance and the Shield: The Life and Times of Sitting Bull* (New York: Holt, 1993).

Utley, Robert M. *The Indian Frontier of the American West, 1846–1890* (Albuquerque: University of New Mexico Press, 1984).

Van Kirk, Sylvia. *Many Tender Ties: Women in Fur Trade Society, 1670–1870* (Norman: University of Oklahoma Press, 1983).

Van Kirk, Sylvia. "Toward a Feminist Perspective in Native History," *Papers of the Eighteenth Algonquian Conference*, ed. William Cowan (Ottawa: Carleton University Press, 1987), 377–89.

Van Lonkhuyzen, Harold W. "A Reappraisal of the Praying Indians: Acculturation, Conversion and Identity in Natick, Massachusetts, 1646–1730," *New England Quarterly*, 63 (1990), 396–428.

Vaughan, Alden T. *Transatlantic Encounters: American Indians in Britain, 1500–1776* (Cambridge: Cambridge University Press, 2006).

Vaughan, Alden T. "Frontier Banditti and the Indians: The Paxton Boys' Legacy, 1763–1775," *Pennsylvania History*, 51 (1984), 1–29.

Vaughan, Alden T. "From White Man to Red Skin: Changing Anglo-American Perceptions of the American Indian," *American Historical Review*, 86 (1982), 917–53.

Vick, R. Alfred. "Cherokee Adaptation to the Landscape of the West and Overcoming the Loss of Culturally Significant Plants," *American Indian Quarterly*, 35 (Summer 2011), 394–417.

Vickers, Daniel. "The First Whalemen of Nantucket," *William and Mary Quarterly*, 40 (1983), 560–583.

Voget, Fred W. *They Call Me Agnes: A Crow Narrative Based on the Life of Agnes Yellowtail Deernose* (Norman: University of Oklahoma Press, 1995).

Vlasich, James A. *Pueblo Indian Agriculture* (Albuquerque: University of New Mexico Press, 2005).

Wade, Maria F. *Missions, Missionaries and Native Americans: Long-Term Processes and Daily Practices* (Gainesville: University Press of Florida, 2008).

Wadewitz, Lissa K. *The Nature of Borders: Salmon, Boundaries, and Bandits on the Salish Sea* (Seattle: University of Washington Press, 2012).

Wallace, Anthony F. C. *Jefferson and the Indians: The Tragic Fate of the First Americans* (Cambridge: Harvard University Press, 1999).

Wallace, Anthony F. C. *The Long Bitter Trail: Andrew Jackson and the Indians* (New York: Hill and Wang, 1993).

Wallace, Anthony F. C. *The Death and Rebirth of the Seneca* (New York: Knopf, 1970).

Wallace, Pamela S. "Indian Claims Commission: Political Complexity and Contrasting Concepts of Identity," *Ethnohistory*, 39 (Fall 2002), 743–67.

Wallace, Paul A. W. *Conrad Weiser (1696–1760): Friend of Colonist and Mohawk* (Philadelphia: University of Pennsylvania Press, 1945).

Walker, Chester P. and Timothy K. Perttula. "Archaeological Investigations at an Eighteenth-Century Caddo Site in Nacogdoches County, East Texas," *Southeastern Archaeology*, 29 (Winter 2010), 310–22.

Wandres, Patrick W. "Indian Land Claims: Sherrill and the Impending Legacy of the Doctrine of Laches," *American Indian Law Review*, 31 (2006/2007), 131–42.

Warren, Louis S. "Buffalo Bill Meets Dracula: William F. Cody, Bram Stoker, and the Frontiers of Racial Decay," *American Historical Review*, 107 (October 2002), 1124–57.

Warren, Stephen. *The World the Shawnees Made: Migration and Violence in Early America* (Chapel Hill: University of North Carolina Press, 2014).

Warren, Stephen. *The Shawnees and Their Neighbors, 1795–1870* (Champaign: University of Illinois Press, 2005).

Waselkov, Gregory A. "The Eighteenth Century Anglo-Indian Trade in Southeastern North America," in *New Faces of the Fur Trade: Selected Papers of the Seventh North American Fur*

Trade Conference, ed. Jo-Ann Fiske, Susan Sleeper Smith, and William Wicken (East Lansing: Michigan State University Press, 1998).

Washburn, Wilcomb E. *The Assault on Indian Tribalism: The General Allotment Law (Dawes Act) of 1887* (Philadelphia: Lippincott, 1975).

Washburn, Wilcomb E. *The Governor and the Rebel: A History of Bacon's Rebellion* (Chapel Hill: University of North Carolina Press, 1957).

Watson, Blake A. *Buying America from the Indians:* Johnson v. McIntosh *and the History of Native Land Rights* (Norman: University of Oklahoma Press, 2012).

Webb, Stephen Saunders. *1676: The End of American Independence* (New York: Knopf, 1984).

Weber, David J. *Barbaros: Spaniards and Their Savages in the Age of Enlightenment* (New Haven: Yale University Press, 2005).

Weber, David J. *The Spanish Frontier in North America* (New Haven: Yale University Press, 1992).

Weibel-Orlando, Joan. *Indian Country, LA: Maintaining Ethnic Community in a Complex Society* (Urbana: University of Illinois Press, 1999).

Wenger, Tisa. *We Have a Religion: The 1920s Pueblo Indian Dance Controversy and American Religious Freedom* (Chapel Hill: University of North Carolina Press, 2009).

West, Elliott. *The Last Indian War: The Nez Perce Story* (New York: Oxford University Press, 2009).

West, Elliott. *The Contested Plains: Indians, Goldseekers, and the Rush to Colorado* (Lawrence: University of Kansas Press, 1998).

Wetzel, Christopher. *Gathering the Potawatomi Nation: Revitalization and Identity* (Norman: University of Oklahoma Press, 2015).

Wetzel, Christopher. "Neshnabemwen Renaissance: Local and National Potawatomi Language Revitalization Efforts," *American Indian Quarterly*, 30 (2006), 61–86.

Wheeler, Rachel. *To Live Upon Hope: Mohicans and Missionaries in the Eighteenth Century Northeast* (Ithaca: Cornell University Press, 2007).

Whelan, Mary K. "Dakota Indian Economies and the Nineteenth Century Fur Trade," *Ethnohistory*, 40 (Spring 1993), 246–76.

White, Bruce M. "Encounters with Spirits: Ojibwa and Dakota Theories about the French and their Merchandise," *Ethnohistory*, 41 (1994), 369–405.

White, Louellyn. *Free to be Mohawk: Indigenous Education at the Akwesasne Freedom School* (Norman: University of Oklahoma Press, 2015).

White, Richard. *The Middle Ground: Indians, Empires and Republics in the Great Lakes Region* (Cambridge: Cambridge University Press, 1991).

White, Richard. *The Roots of Dependency: Subsistence, Environment, and Social Change Among the Choctaws, Pawnees, and Navajos* (Lincoln: University of Nebraska Press, 1983).

White, Richard. "The Winning of the West: The Expansion of the Western Sioux in the Eighteenth and Nineteenth Centuries," *Journal of American History*, 65 (September 1978), 319–43.

Wilkins, David E. *American Indian Sovereignty and the U.S. Supreme Court* (Austin: University of Texas Press, 1997).

Wilkins, David E. and K. Tsianina Lomawaima, *Uneven Ground: American Indian Sovereignty and Federal Law* (Norman: University of Oklahoma Press, 2001).

Wilkinson, Charles. *Blood Struggle: The Rise of Modern Indian Nations* (New York: Norton, 2005).

Wilkinson, Charles. *American Indians, Time, and the Law: Native Societies in a Modern Constitutional Democracy* (New Haven: Yale University Press, 1987).

Williams, Robert, A. Jr. *Linking Arms Together: American Indian Treaty Visions of Law and Peace, 1600–1800* (New York: Oxford University Press, 1997).

Williams, Walter. *The Spirit and the Flesh: Sexual Diversity in American Indian Culture* (Boston, MA: Beacon Press, 1986).

Williamson, Margaret Holmes. *Powhatan Lords of Life and Death: Command and Consent in Seventeenth Century Virginia* (Lincoln: University of Nebraska Press, 2003).

Wilson, Diane and Timothy K. Perttula. "Reconstructing the Paleodiet of the Caddo through Stable Isotopes," *American Antiquity*, 78 (no. 4, 2013), 702–23.

Wilson, Edmund. *Apologies to the Iroquois* (New York: Vintage Books, 1959).

Witgen, Michael. "The Native New World and Western North America." *Western Historical Quarterly*, 43 (Summer 2012), 292–9.

Witgen, Michael. *An Infinity of Nations: How the Native New World Shaped Early North America* (Philadelphia: University of Pennsylvania Press, 2012).

Wonderley, Anthony. "'Good Peter's Narrative of Several Transactions Respecting Indian Lands': An Oneida View of Dispossession, 1785–1788," *New York History* 84 (Summer 2003), 237–76.

Wood, Peter H., Gregory A. Waselkov, and M. Thomas Hatley, eds. *Powhatan's Mantle: Indians in the Colonial Southeast* (Lincoln: University of Nebraska Press, 1989).

Woolworth, Alan R., comp. *Santee Dakota Indian Legends* (Agency Village: Prairie Smoke Press, 2003).

Wray, Jacilee, ed. *Native Peoples of the Olympic Peninsula: Who We Are* (Norman: University of Oklahoma Press, 2002).

Wright, J. Leitch. *The Only Land They Knew: The Tragic Story of the American Indians of the Old South* (New York: Basic Books, 1981).

Wright, Robin K. *A Time of Gathering: Native Heritage in Washington State.* (Seattle: University of Washington Press, 1991).

Yarbrough, Fay A. *Race and the Cherokee Nation: Sovereignty in the Nineteenth-Century* (Philadelphia: University of Pennsylvania Press, 2008).

Yirush, Craig Bryan. "Claiming the New World: Empire, Law and Indigenous Rights in the Mohegan Case, 1704–1743," *Law and History Review*, 29 (May 2011), 333–73.

Young, Mary. "The Exercise of Sovereignty in Cherokee Georgia," *Journal of the Early Republic*, 10 (1990), 43–63.

Young, Mary. "The Cherokee Nation: Mirror of the Republic," *American Quarterly*, 33 (Winter 1981), 502–24.

Zappia, Natale. *Traders and Raiders: The Indigenous World of the Colorado Basin, 1540–1859* (Chapel Hill: University of North Carolina Press, 2014).

Zissu, Erik M. *Blood Matters: The Five Civilized Tribes and the Search for Unity in the 20th Century* (New York: Routledge, 2001).

Zontek, Ken. *Buffalo Nation: American Indian Efforts to Restore the Bison* (Lincoln: University of Nebraska Press, 2007)

Index

Native America: A History, Second Edition. Michael Leroy Oberg.
© 2018 John Wiley & Sons, Inc. Published 2018 by John Wiley & Sons, Inc.

CPSIA information can be obtained
at www.ICGtesting.com
Printed in the USA
FSHW021121271120
76245FS

9 781118 937112